DATE DUE

			PRINTED IN U.S.A.

MAGILL'S
SURVEY
OF
CINEMA

MAGILL'S SURVEY OF CINEMA

English Language Films

SECOND SERIES
VOLUME 2
COB-HAL

Edited by

FRANK N. MAGILL

Associate Editors

STEPHEN L. HANSON

PATRICIA KING HANSON

SALEM PRESS
Englewood Cliffs, N.J.

LIBRARY OF CONGRESS CATALOG CARD NUMBER: 81-84330

Complete Set: ISBN 0-89356-230-0
Volume 2:   ISBN-0-89356-232-7

PRINTED IN THE UNITED STATES OF AMERICA

LIST OF TITLES IN VOLUME TWO

LIST OF TITLES IN VOLUME TWO

MAGILL'S
SURVEY
OF
CINEMA

COBRA WOMAN

Released: 1944
Production: George Waggner for Universal
Direction: Robert Siodmak
Screenplay: Gene Lewis and Richard Brooks; based on an original story of the same name by W. Scott Darling
Cinematography: George Robinson
Editing: Charles Maynard
Running time: 70 minutes

Principal characters:
Toilea/Nadja	Maria Montez
Ramon	Jon Hall
Kado	Sabu
Hava	Lon Chaney, Jr.
Martok	Edgar Barrier
Queen	Mary Nash
Father Paul	Samuel S. Hinds
MacDonald	Moroni Olsen

Cobra Woman will probably never make any reputable critic's Ten Best list. The film is an unabashed "B"-movie, hurriedly made on a low budget by director Robert Siodmak, a German filmmaker recently arrived in Hollywood and looking for opportunities to prove himself to the American studios. Nevertheless, *Cobra Woman* merits inclusion in any comprehensive survey of cinema. It is a good example of the enormously popular "Arabian Nights"-oriented fantasy films of the 1940's, and is also an example of the cinematic contributions of three actors—Maria Montez, Sabu, and Jon Hall—whose careers rose and fell with the popularity of this kind of fantasy.

The plot of *Cobra Woman* is pure Saturday matinee hokum. Somewhere in the Tropics, a young man of uncertain nationality—his name, Ramon (Jon Hall), suggests Latin blood, but his appearance and accent are very American—is about to marry a local girl named Toilea (Maria Montez), when the girl is kidnaped by Hava (Lon Chaney, Jr.), a strange cultist, and taken to the mysterious and much-feared Cobra Island (where, it develops, she was born). Ramon and his young native sidekick Kado (Sabu) attempt to rescue Toilea, but fall into the clutches of the Cobra Islanders.

Toilea, as it happens, is the twin sister of Nadja (also played by Maria Montez), Princess of the island, and consort of Martok (Edgar Barrier), the high priest. Nadja and Martok terrorize their subjects by their manipulation of the local religion: the residents revere the King Cobra, as well as the island's active volcano (the connection between the two is never quite clarified). Predictably, Ramon at first confuses Najda with Toilea, and this gives rise to several subplots. Nadja falls in love with Ramon and tries to drop

Martok, who wants to kill Ramon. Kado's only concern is to save Ramon. Ramon, meanwhile, only wants to rescue Toilea, who has been given asylum in the palace by her elderly grandmother the Queen (Mary Nash). The Queen cares little about Ramon and Kado; her plan is for Toilea to take Nadja's place and rule the island with liberty and justice for all.

In the end, a knock-down, drag-out fight settles the affair in favor of the good guys. Nadja and Martok are killed; the god of the volcano is appeased; and Ramon and Kado head for home, accompanied by Toilea. Everyone, we may assume, lives happily ever after. Fortunately, *Cobra Woman* is even funnier than it sounds in synopsis. The costumes and sets, the casting and acting, and the direction all come together in *Cobra Woman* to produce the kind of film that made the concept "camp" necessary.

Although Cobra Island is supposed to be somewhere in the mysterious East (perplexing might be a more appropriate adjective than mysterious), the cast is polyglot: some of them speak pidgin English, while others are perfectly articulate. Among the principals in the cast, Toilea/Nadja, the native twins, speak with a slight but distinct Hispanic accent; Ramon, despite his Latin name, speaks pure Hollywood American; and Kado speaks Sabu-ese. The costumes and sets are as diverse as the accents. An Egyptian/Aztec motif predominates, but some of the costumes appear to have been salvaged from the set where the Flash Gordon serials were shot a few years earlier.

The dialogue, provided by Gene Lewis and Richard Brooks, juxtaposes the exotic with the mundane in a way that must have been as obviously funny to audiences in the 1940's as it is today. An incident early in the film is typical. Father Paul (Samuel S. Hinds), the man who was to have married Ramon and Toilea, delivers a long disquisition on the terrors of Cobra Island, culminating in the exclamation "I was *tortured*, lad!" Ramon replies "Oh, I see," as mildly as he might have had the padre been telling him how to operate a can opener. When the Queen of Cobra Island tells Kado that Ramon is to be executed, Kado remarks innocuously "Ramon will not like that." Neither line is delivered sarcastically, the way Humphrey Bogart as Sam Spade or Philip Marlowe might have done them; nor were they intended to have been delivered that way. The dialogue, like the characters, is perfectly neutral; it is utterly innocent and reflects the absolute naïveté of the characters who speak it.

Films of this sort run all kinds of risks, of course—primarily the risk of being merely bad, instead of sublimely ridiculous. That *Cobra Woman* escaped this fate was due to its director, Siodmak, and to its cast, particularly the peripatetic trio of Montez, Hall, and Sabu.

Siodmak was an up-and-coming Jewish filmmaker in Germany in the 1930's who arrived in the United States in 1940 looking for work. He found it directing "B"-movies for a variety of studios, including Universal, for whom he made *Cobra Woman*. His craftsmanship was rewarded later in the 1940's, as he directed a series of outstanding thrillers for Universal, among them *Phantom Lady* (1944), *The Killers* (1946), and *The Spiral Staircase* (1946). His gift in earlier years, however, was the ability to make an honest "B"-movie, and to direct material below his talents without mocking it. Siodmak knew that *Cobra Woman* was low art, but he also knew that it was not trash.

Siodmak was aided and abetted by Montez, Hall, and Sabu, a trio of veteran fantasy actors. Between 1942 and 1946, they appeared together in three such films: *Arabian Nights* (1942), *White Savage* (1943), and *Cobra Woman*, as well as in four others in various pairings: Montez and Sabu in *Tangier* (1946); Montez and Hall in *Ali Baba and the Forty Thieves* (1944), *Gypsy Wildcat* (1944), and *Sudan* (1945).

Hall is perhaps the least likely member of the trio. Handsome enough, but thoroughly middle American in appearance, he made his film debut in John Ford's *The Hurricane* in 1937. Thereafter he was cast in a variety of implausibly exotic roles, including a television stint as Ramar of the Jungle, but his career faded and he did little acting in the last years before his death in 1980.

Sabu (born Sabu Dastigar in India) built his career on playing exotic Eastern versions of Tom Sawyer, the eternal kid. Prior to *Cobra Woman*, he had starred in *Elephant Boy* (1937) and *The Thief of Bagdad* (1940). As the American appetite for his films waned in the 1950's, Sabu moved on to Europe and continued his career there. He resurfaced briefly in 1958 with *Sabu and the Magic Ring*, but by his death in 1963, at the age of thirty-nine, it was clear that his time had past.

Th career of Montez, although far more prolific, paralleled that of Sabu in many ways. Born Maria Africa Vidal de Santos Silas in the Dominican Republic, she appeared in thirty-one films during her ten-year career in cinema. Naturally enough, she specialized in playing mysterious foreigners; and while her acting skills were rudimentary, her screen appearances were not without their charm. Her Cobra Dance—meant, no doubt, to reek of sensuality—merely reeks; it is a guaranteed showstopper. She was so associated with this type of film that often films of this type have been so-called "Maria Montez Movies" even if she did not star in them. As Montez began to put on weight, her career as a screen siren began to wane. Like Sabu, she sought to resuscitate her career in Europe; like Sabu, she was unsuccessful; she died in her early thirties in 1951.

It remains to account for the film's popularity when it was first released; for *Cobra Woman* and similar films were well received by audiences and critics in the 1940's. This popularity probably owed a great deal to the films' complete lack of pretension; they were fluff—fantasy, pure and simple. If they were no more than "B"-movies, however, they were certainly no less, either. Children could enjoy them on a literal level, and adults could laugh along at the silliness on the screen. Indeed, *Cobra Woman* provides a welcome counterpoint to the multimillion-dollar special-effects films of the present day. We may never recapture the innocence of the 1940's, but films such as *Cobra Woman* offer us a glimpse of it, and an enjoyable glimpse, at that.

Robert Mitchell

COLONEL BLIMP
(THE LIFE AND DEATH OF COLONEL BLIMP)

Released: 1943
Production: Michael Powell and Emeric Pressburger for United Artists
Direction: Michael Powell and Emeric Pressburger
Screenplay: Michael Powell and Emeric Pressburger
Cinematography: George Perinal and Jack Cardiff
Editing: John Seabourne
Running time: 146 minutes

Principal characters:
Clive Candy .... Roger Livesey
Edith Hunter/Barbara Wynne/
Johnny Cannon .... Deborah Kerr
Theo Kretschmar-Schuldorff .... Anton Walbrook
Colonel Betteridge .... Roland Culver
Lady Margaret .... Muriel Aked

The Life and Death of Colonel Blimp was, in its time, one of the most expensive and ambitious films ever made in England. It cost one million dollars to produce and runs, as edited for American distribution, two hours and twenty-six minutes—a leisurely length. The result is an uncommonly rich and pleasant study in character, both human and national. The film marks the screen introduction of one of the greatest English characters since Pickwick—the famous Colonel Blimp, cartoonist David Low's bloated, walruswhiskered symbol of unenlightened self-centeredness. When one hears someone referred to as a "Colonel Blimp," one conjures up an image of a pompous, old-fashioned British officer, someone who recalls war as a game with rules to be played by gentlemen. In Low's popular cartoons, the Blimp character acts out, in black-and-white simplicity, the whole sad yet somehow comical history of a special type of uniquely British stupidity.

Michael Powell and Emeric Pressburger trace the development of a Blimplike military man from the beginning of his career as a hero in the Boer War, in which he won the Victoria Cross, to his anachronistic efforts to help the British forces during World War II. Warfare has changed, and the general's ideas of how to fight a war are outmoded. The code of honor by which he has lived has vanished from the real world, but has survived intact within himself.

The screen version of Colonel Blimp is not treated as a despicable old anachronism. The film presents a chronology of Blimp's life and career depicting with gentle sympathy the way he grew fat for the honor and glory of Britain. In fact, watching the old man's life unfold in the theater, one would never suspect that the Colonel and his kind had anything to do with bringing on many of the conditions that led England into World War II. In the cartoons, Blimp and others of his class are depicted waddling into the insular comforts of their clubs, fortifying themselves with good sherry and claret, and reclining in deep leather chairs clutching in their hands the reassuring words of *The Times*. In the cartoon, Blimp frequently expressed his disapproval, in gouty terms, of anything that might change the way things had always been done, and "by God Sir," ought always to be done. He, like many of his kind in the British prewar government (at least in the minds of many Englishmen), paid only reluctant attention to the earth-shaking events occurring in Europe in the 1930's.

Blimp first appears in the film as a gallant and quite naïve young officer named Clive Candy (Roger Livesey) just back from the Boer War. Impulsive and quick to anger, he takes offense when he learns of the spread of some anti-British propaganda in Berlin. He hurdles Home Office diplomatic red tape and travels without diplomatic portfolio to Berlin to refute the popular German misconceptions about British treatment of Boer prisoners. "Lies!" he calls the German stories. A quarrel in a café leads to a remark insulting the German army, and Candy is challenged to a duel; in fact, the entire German officer corps would love to take on the brash British officer. Theo Kretschmar-Schuldorff (Anton Walbrook) is the lucky officer who receives the chance to defend the honor of Germany, but the duel ends in a draw with both combatants receiving wounds. The duel accomplishes several things that will affect young Candy's later life. First, it gives him the saber wound on the cheek that causes him to grow his Blimpish mustache; second, it makes a lifelong friend of his opponent; and third, it loses to this Prussian officer a charming English girl, Edith Hunter (Deborah Kerr), whom Candy has shyly begun to love.

Theo becomes impressed with Candy when he finds out that the Englishman was a hero in the Boer War and won the Victoria Cross. Although the two wounded officers cannot directly communicate verbally, they show their mutual respect by having a drink together and playing cards. Later, when Candy is recovered enough to leave for England, Theo comes to see him again. His English has improved enough for him to confess to Candy that he loves Edith and that she also loves him. Theo expects another duel based on this revelation, but to his surprise, the Englishman is delighted. He tells Theo that Edith never was his fiancée. In fact, he drinks a toast to the happiness of the pair, says good-bye, and hopes they will meet again.

Candy is next found in England, passing the time with hunting trips to Africa. When in London, he stays alternately at his club and with his aunt, Lady Margaret (Muriel Aked). The camera indicates the passage of years in Candy's life by showing increasing numbers of animal heads on the walls of Lady Margaret's home, which are souvenirs of his time in South Africa; then it comes to rest prophetically on a German helmet.

Candy serves creditably and quietly through World War I. At a convent in Flanders, he catches sight of a nurse, Barbara Wynne (Deborah Kerr again), who is the image of the young lady he lost in Berlin. After the war, he marries her, and then begins the process of searching for Candy's old friend, the Prussian officer. Finally Candy receives a letter from the Prisoner of War Committee. They have located Theo Kretschmar-Schuldorff in an internment camp in England. Candy and Barbara visit the camp, where a concert is in progress. Theo is handed a message announcing Candy's arrival, to which he replies "No answer," refusing to see his old friend. Candy decides to go personally and find out why Theo rejected him, but he is snubbed. The German is suffering from wounded pride, and an attendant at the camp tells Candy that all the Germans stopped taking English lessons on Armistice Day. Soon, however, Candy, who has been promoted to General, gets a call from Theo, who says that he is going back to Germany, and apologizes to his old friend for the way he behaved at the prisoner-of-war camp. Candy goes immediately to the railroad station to see Theo, who shows the Englishman photos of Edith and their children.

Time passes, Candy's young wife dies, and the flow of time is cleverly depicted via newspaper articles, memorabilia, scrap books, and hunting trophies. The audience sees a 1926 newspaper obituary notice announcing the death of Barbara, and subsequently the walls of Candy's home grow ever more thickly studded with the big game victims of his loneliness. Finally, it is 1939, and Theo is applying for British citizenship.

Theo tells the immigration officer that he left Germany in 1934 because he is anti-Hitler, and arrived in England in 1935. He recaps his life by saying he quit the army in 1920 and became a military chemist. His wife, like Candy's, is dead; his two children have become Nazis and he has lost contact with them. He depicts himself as a tired old man who came to England because he got "homesick." The government official is hesitant about accepting a German as a British subject, until he asks Theo if he has someone he knows who can be a character witness. Although the two men have not seen each other in twenty years, Candy appears on behalf of Theo. The Englishman is now bald, fat, and mustached, much like the cartoon character "Colonel Blimp." The immigration officer says Candy can take Theo with him for the present.

Later, Johnny Cannon (Deborah Kerr), Candy's military driver, takes Theo home. While she is physically like Edith and Barbara, she is nothing like either in personality. She has none of their old world charm or gentility. Rather, she is a product of the new generation, outspoken and a little rough around the edges. She tells Theo she had been a photographer's model before the war, and the audience learns that the general chose her out of seven hundred girls to be his driver.

By the time World War II begins, Candy has become completely the stately old lobster depicted in the Colonel Blimp cartoon. He is angry and bewildered to find his age and his military experience in low esteem with the new army. Additionally, Theo's application for permanent residence is denied. The German realizes, however, that this is a new war—not the gentlemen's wars of earlier times. They are fighting against a horrible evil, and every German is suspect. Candy cannot give up his own ideas as easily as his friend, but Johnny, who is still his driver, tells him that he must change. She suggests the Home Guard as the place in which he could form a new army, and Candy reluctantly takes the advice.

During training maneuvers with the Home Guard an incident occurs that serves as the crowning blow to Candy's way of life. In a simulated military action, the sharp young men of the new army jump the gun and capture him, surprised and enraged, in a Turkish bath hours before the sham battle was scheduled to begin. Heartsick, Candy begins at last to understand the one thing that the film is trying to teach its Colonel Blimp: that the code which has ruled his life is a suicidal anachronism in a world threatened by global gangsters. Candy is last seen saluting. He has become a grand old man but will never completely accept the new order.

At the film's opening in London in the summer of 1943, there were shouts of protest from both government officials and film reviewers who felt that this dramatization of Low's famous cartoon character should not be viewed by foreign eyes. Although Blimp emerges as a likable human being described by the *London News Chronicle* as "a witty and quite sensible soldier, who would lose a war with dignity and might win it with a little luck," he was not considered by all comers to be a boon to England's world prestige. Another London newspaper, *The Daily Mail*, was, in fact, highly outraged and devoted an entire column to the portrayal of Blimp's life. The paper felt that during the war, when the respect and confidence of other nations was of vital importance to the British Isles, "To depict British officers as stupid, complacent, self-satisfied and ridiculous, may be legitimate comedy in peacetime, but it is disastrously bad propaganda in times of war."

The film itself is alternately illuminating and touching. The detailed protocol of preparation for the duel in the opening moments of the film and the duel itself between the brave but reluctant opponents is one of the most devastating satires on diplomacy, war, and national character ever achieved by a film. Candy's relationships with the women in his life, reticent and almost childishly idealistic, are deeply felt and are a poignant exposition of the kind of love that is rarely depicted on film. The interweaving stories of the subtle German and the quick-to-anger Englishman constitute a beautiful study of two sides of the aging process. One man is seasoned through suffering, the other remains invincibly innocent. Although the film is long, *Colonel Blimp* seems short because it is constructed with a constant feeling for lightness and for style.

Colonel Blimp is also marvelously well acted. Kerr plays contrasting roles, first as the governess, later as the middle-aged Candy's wife, and finally as his World War II chauffeur, with a charm and versatility that would normally be sufficient to win the film a wide international audience. Yet Walbrook is almost equally fine as Candy's German friend. His performance in their duel, set in a Berlin gymnasium and heavily laden with Prussian detail, is one of the film's deftest satires. The success of the film, however, rests upon the characterization of Colonel Blimp, whether he is the personable young Candy or the paunchy, lobster-red old has-been. Livesey is virtually perfect in his depiction of the character at all stages of his career. Excellent makeup jobs transform a dashing young officer into an amazing facsimile of the famous cartoon figure.

Colonel Blimp was a major product of the writer-director team known as "the Archers"—a collective pseudonym for the collaboration of British director Michael Powell and Hungarian director Emeric Pressburger. Their collaboration began in 1942 with *One of Our Aircraft Is Missing* and continued until 1957. A notable characteristic of many of their joint efforts was a sympathetic portrayal of foreign characters, no doubt symbolizing in some respects the working relationship of the two directors; in the case of *Colonel Blimp*, their relationship was symbolized in the friendship between Clive Candy and Theo Kretschmar-Schuldorff. The sympathetic portrayal of Theo was no mean feat in a British wartime film, and it worked extremely well.

Fern L. Gagné

THE COLLECTOR

Released: 1965
Production: Jud Kinberg and John Kohn for Columbia
Direction: William Wyler
Screenplay: Stanley Mann and John Kohn; based on the novel of the same
  name by John Fowles
Cinematography: Robert Surtees
Editing: Robert Swink
Music: Maurice Jarre
Running time: 120 minutes

> *Principal characters:*
> Freddie Clegg .... Terence Stamp
> Miranda Grey .... Samantha Eggar
> Aunt Annie .... Mona Washbourne
> The Neighbor .... Maurice Dallimore
> Crutchley ....William Beckley

The Collector is essentially a two-character film. One character is a man
with an obsession and the other is a woman, the unwilling object of that
obsession. Freddie Clegg (Terence Stamp), a London bank clerk in his mid-
twenties, wins seventy-one thousand pounds on the sports betting pools and
retires from his job. He buys a large home in the Sussex countryside and
devotes himself to his extensive hobby of butterfly collecting. He also increasingly admires an art student, Miranda Grey (Samantha Eggar), and often
spends time following her. Freddie is painfully shy, however, and she fails to
take any notice of him. Freddie daydreams that Miranda would return his
love if she only got to know him well, so he makes elaborate plans to kidnap
her. The basement of his home is remodeled in order to accommodate her,
and Freddie supplies it with records, numerous art books, and clothes that
are the colors he has seen her wear. On the sound track, we hear Freddie say
that he does not intend to carry out his scheme, but on the screen we see him
stalking Miranda in a nondescript van. Finally, he effectively uses his vehicle
to block her passage through an alley and is able to seize her. Miranda has
only a brief moment in which to register surprise before she is overcome by
chloroform and loses consciousness. Freddie is very gentle with her, and when
they arrive at his house, he places her carefully onto the bed in her prison
room and pulls her skirt down so that it will cover her knees.

This shy gesture underlines Freddie's approach to sexuality. He is childishly
modest and uses an awkwardly formal style of speech to circumvent direct
discussion of the subject. The morning following the kidnaping, he explains
his reasons for bringing Miranda to be his "guest" and emphasizes that it is
not for "the other thing." He insists that he will show "all the proper respect."

Freddie is obviously naïve and inexperienced, believing that he can generate love by giving a woman material comfort and benevolently forcing her to spend time with him; this childish conception of love is based on the relationship between a pet and its master. In a flashback, the film re-creates Freddie's experience as a clerk. He is taunted by his coworkers with a mobile made of butterflies, which make grotesque shadows across his face and the office walls as they jiggle over his head. This is essentially the only information the film gives about Freddie's youth, and hence it is important. The viewer infers that Freddie has had few friends and has suffered for his only love, that of collecting beautiful butterflies. When Miranda is disgusted by the display of his hobby, Freddie is terribly hurt. It is the beginning of his disillusionment with her, as he begins to realize that he has selected an imperfect specimen.

Freddie is obviously dangerous because his power over Miranda is absolute. His motives for kidnaping her indicate that his moral development is similar to that of a young child who has not yet been taught to differentiate between fantasies and goals. His overly polite behavior is that of a repressed child who has been disciplined but not educated. He is as innocent as a child because he suffers no guilt. What seems to have been instilled in Freddie is a rigourous code of etiquette in place of ethics.

There are several scenes in the middle of the film in which his most consistent expression is one of petulance. In one scene, he squats on the top step of Miranda's room like a small child who has been denied a favorite toy, and in another he draws his knees close to his body, places his elbows on them, and rests his chin in the palms of his hands. His huge eyes look solemnly at Miranda while she paints. She completes many pictures, including portraits of him. He claims not to understand them, but he is quite pleased when she gives him a portrait of herself. She angrily signs it "prisoner" when he asks her to autograph it, but this does not diminish the pleasure the painting gives him.

The day-to-day childishness of Freddie lulls Miranda into treating him like one and also into expecting him to be childishly weak. Stamp's performance in the role is exceptional, for although his usual appearance could be called virile and handsome, in *The Collector* he is a chameleon, changing back and forth from a forlorn waif to a powerful demon. The change from child to man often takes place in close-up, and Stamp expresses Freddie's schizophrenic changes subtly but powerfully. The audience gradually can anticipate these changes although Miranda ignores the warning signs. *The Collector* relies somewhat upon Miranda's lack of perception in order to create suspense. Since she is an intelligent, well-educated, and self-sufficient person we might expect her to be more perceptive, but because Freddie's background is so different from her own she is unable to judge him accurately, and ultimately her failure to recognize that Freddie is dangerous leads to her doom.

Miranda assumes Freddie is stupid because he is not articulate about his emotions and beliefs; and she takes his ignorance about certain cultural items to be additional evidence of this stupidity. Freddie wants to share some of Miranda's experience and reads *Catcher in the Rye* on her recommendation. He tries to discuss it with her but begins by criticizing it as "dirty." When she dismisses his criticism with patronizing statements that he is just judging it as dirty because he "can't grasp it right away," he begs her, "How do I grasp it?" Her refusal to take the time to explain it further indicates her contempt for his intelligence and also, perhaps, her own lack of a full understanding of the book. Her pride in her supposedly superior cultural aptitude is unfounded; she does not realize that most of her knowledge is the result of cultural conditioning. Freddie, however, sees her attitudes as mere affectations.

Miranda's underestimation of Freddie's intelligence makes her incapable of coping with him successfully. She continually fails in her attempts to escape or to get him to release her because she cannot understand him. At one point, it vaguely occurs to her that her kidnaping required imaginative intelligence and complex resourcefulness, but she accepts Freddie's own humble estimation of the deed when he says, "There'd be a lot more of this if people had the time and money." Freddie realizes that it is money which has given him power, but Miranda is under the delusion that her education has given her power. She attempts to reason with Freddie by using the platitude that "We all want things we can't have" as evidence that he should realize the impossibility of having her. Freddie does have her, however, and he answers, "We take what we can get."

Miranda deludes herself into believing that Freddie is trustworthy, and condemns him for breaking his promise when he does not keep his bargain of releasing her after four weeks. Freddie simply shrugs, however, and says, "I can do what I want." He is not bound by the social conventions which inhibit Miranda. Finally, Miranda does break her moral code in order to save herself, by attempting to seduce Freddie. Once again, however, she has misinterpreted him. She should have realized from all of his sexual subterfuge that such an action was taboo. She ceases to be important to Freddie the moment she offers her body to him. His sense of etiquette, the only moral code he knows, is completely outraged. She falls from her pedestal of mysterious beauty and perfection and thus is not a worthy "specimen" for Freddie to "collect." At the end of the film, Miranda tries to escape from Freddie, but is caught by him again after she has contracted pneumonia in a heavy rainstorm that prevents her from reaching freedom. She eventually dies, and Freddie decides to drive around in his van again, this time hoping that he will encounter a better specimen.

William Wyler is generally considered an "actor's director" because the actors and actresses he has directed have consistently won Oscars and other accolades for their performances in his films. In *The Collector*, Wyler gets a *tour-de-force* performance from Stamp, and Eggar gives a creditable performance in a less demanding role. Wyler's direction concentrates on the interplay between the characters and leads to the chilling final scene in which it becomes obvious that "The Collector" will continue unapprehended.

Elizabeth Ward

COMMAND DECISION

Released: 1948
Production: Sidney Franklin for Metro-Goldwyn-Mayer
Direction: Sam Wood
Screenplay: William R. Laidlaw and George Froeschel; based on the play of
   the same name by William Wister Haines
Cinematography: Harold Rosson
Editing: Harold F. Kress
Running time: 112 minutes

> *Principal characters:*
> General K. C. "Casey" Dennis .... Clark Gable
> General Roland Goodlow Kane .... Walter Pidgeon
> General Clifton Garnet .... Brian Donlevy
> Sergeant Immanuel T. Evans .... Van Johnson
> Colonel Edward Rayton Martin .... John Hodiak
> Elmer Brockhurst .... Charles Bickford
> Congressman Arthur Malcolm .... Edward Arnold
> Captain George Washington
> Bellpepper Lee .... Marshall Thompson
> Captain Incius Malcolm Jenks .... Michael Steele

   World War II and the period shortly afterwards saw a number of films that
extolled bravery and heroism in combat while presenting war itself to be, if
not attractive, at least an exciting, patriotic activity. *Command Decision* belongs with a different group of war films, however—one including William
Wellman's *Battleground* (1949) and Henry King's *Twelve O'Clock High*
(1949)—that deglamorizes war in favor of an appraisal of the effects it has
on the human spirit. *Command Decision* had been a novel, then a successful
play (still running on Broadway while the movie was in production), with
Paul Kelly as General Dennis. The screenplay follows the stage play closely,
adding only a few outdoor scenes. Sam Wood directed mainly routine films
in his long career; but now and then he proved himself with creditable projects
such as two of the Marx Brothers comedies, *A Night at the Opera* (1935) and
At Day at the Races (1937), *Goodbye, Mr. Chips* (1939), parts of *Gone with
the Wind* (1939), and *For Whom the Bell Tolls* (1943). In *Command Decision*
he handles his materials competently and unobtrusively, but because his direction rarely adds to the immediacy of the drama, the film's strength rests
in an intelligent script and some first-rate performances.
   The "command decision" is the decision to destroy, with daylight, precision
bombing, German production of a new jet fighter. The first and second missions, deep into Germany, result in the loss of some hundred planes and a
thousand men dead or missing. The division commander General K. C.

"Casey" Dennis (Clark Gable), fights hard to defend his action against his superior, General Roland Kane (Walter Pidgeon), who knows that such prohibitive losses could cause the Air Force to abandon daylight bombing. Then the mission leader, Colonel Edward Martin (John Hodiak), reveals that the second mission has missed the target, Schweinhafen, and destroyed instead a town which looks almost identical to it from the air. Although a Congressional committee appears at the base, Dennis convinces Kane to let the bombers return to Schweinhafen, with the consequent loss of another fifty planes and their crews. Dennis' determination to order the final mission, along with pressure from one of the Congressmen, forces Kane to replace him with General Clifton Garnet (Brian Donlevy). Garnet, however, appreciating the importance of that final mission, orders it himself.

Command Decision explores the responsibilities of a man battling, in addition to the Germans, a formidable amount of obstruction from both above and outside. Dennis has set into action a well-planned maneuver, Operation Stitch (for "stitch in time"), against the three centers manufacturing parts for the jet fighter. Dennis' heavy losses have already drawn pointed criticism from the war correspondent Elmer Brockhurst (Charles Bickford), who arrives at the base with Kane and Garnet. Although Kane completely approves of Stitch, he is distressed that Dennis has chosen to implement it now, because of a four-day break in the weather. Kane must contend with the reactions of the Combined Chiefs of Staff and also the Appropriations Committee in Congress, soon to be allocating monies to the various services. Stitch entails the continued heavy losses of men and planes at a time when the importance of precision bombing, or of air supremacy, for that matter, generally has not been recognized. Then, too, Kane has a group of influential Congressmen under foot. In his commitment to Stitch, Dennis shows himself indifferent, almost insensitive, to the problems of public relations. With the Congressmen at the base and the news of the group's bombing the wrong target only a few hours old, Dennis unabashedly uses blackmail to get the division back to Schweinhafen. Captain Incius Malcolm Jenks (Michael Steele), a much-publicized flying ace and the nephew of one of the Congressmen, Representative Arthur Malcolm (Edward Arnold), is to receive yet another decoration; but Dennis threatens to charge Jenks with desertion in the face of the enemy for refusing to fly the morning's mission, adding that the young man's problem results from too much publicity. Kane, after much haggling with Dennis, finally capitulates.

Dennis' major antagonist becomes Congressman Malcolm. A blustering, meddling politico, Malcolm openly criticizes Dennis' tactics, making slight effort to comprehend why Dennis has had to sacrifice so many men and planes. Malcolm's ill-informed tirades embarrass even his colleagues; nevertheless, he is an important member of Congress and must be mollified. With considerable effort Dennis manages to keep his temper (largely) in bounds when Malcolm incredulously asks if he ordered the bombers into Germany, beyond fighter protection, on his own initiative. Then Kane, who has backed Dennis, can no longer do so after Dennis' blunt exchange with Malcolm shortly afterwards. While the division proceeds back to Schweinhafen, word comes of a new son for Colonel Martin, a close friend of Dennis and leader of the attack. Dennis, however, receives the message that Martin's plane has gone down in flames; Malcolm begins a noisy, tasteless commentary on Martin's death, and Dennis angrily tells him to shut up several times, then stalks out of the room to plan the last phase of Stitch. Kane believing Dennis now beyond reach, orders him back to the United States.

Dennis often seems a hardened man concerned almost exclusively with the results of his tactics, and thus little with their costs. Normally taciturn, he delivers to Kane and some others a spirited, carefully reasoned dissertation on air supremacy, citing the example of the Luftwaffe as the shaping force in the German war machine. Another dimension of Dennis appears, however, as he gently nurtures a scared but nevertheless resolute bombardier at the controls of a damaged Flying Fortress whose pilot is dead and copilot gravely wounded. While Dennis barks at him to stay off the brakes, the plane crashes and explodes; Dennis stands silently with the dead microphone, visibly dismayed and frustrated. He appears not as a warmonger but a leader with a strong sense of exigency. His determination to complete Stitch remains unqualified throughout, for if Stitch requires many lives, it will save many more lives as the war goes on. When Dennis tells Garnet, now in command of the division, that the men's faces in time become a blur, that he must try to make each man count before he has to kill him, Dennis admits that he has abhorred the burden of ordering men on perilous missions, daily pushing aside his own feelings to carry out his duty. The way Dennis understands that duty furnishes a precedent for Garnet to order the completion of Stitch, that in the end brings Dennis a prestigious B-29 command in the Pacific and a new set of responsibilities, rather than the training command in the United States he wants.

Command Decision, a film about the air war over Germany, is set entirely on the ground and therefore lacks the kind of variation in pace that combat sequences afford. Although the photoplay often betrays its origins in a stage play, with one exception, the memorable scenes in the film still have the quality of the stage about them. Kane delivers a masterful reminiscence of his and others' struggles to get air power for America, diluting his bitterness with fond musings. During his seven-minute monologue no one moves or speaks, as he ranges from the dilapidated planes he flew without a parachute twenty years before to the strike photos he falsifies and the statistics he juggles even now. Later, Garnet, pondering whether to implement the third phase of Stitch, encounters an artless young captain from the Deep South appropriately named George Washington Bellpepper Lee (Marshall Thompson).

The lightness of the context aside, Lee's remarks become extremely touching: he apologizes for having caused a ruckus outside Garnet's window on "Easter Sunday," that is, what he calls his own day of resurrection, for later that day he will fly his twenty-fifth (last) mission, the easy mission or "milk run" the men expect from a new commander, then return home forever. On the other hand, the best outdoor scene, and arguably the best scene in the film, is the one in which Dennis on the command tower talks down the bombardier trying to land the pilotless B-24. Wood's direction picks up markedly as he cuts in long shots of the plane with medium and close shots of Dennis, giving the audience only the voice of the young man in the plane.

Gable had always shone in breezy, cocky roles that let him display his special kind of self assurance, but here he plays cautiously and deliberately in a part ill-suited to his abilities. His Dennis too frequently seems a brusque and compulsive megalomaniac rather than an introspective leader afflicted with the moral agony that results from ordering near suicidal missions. Other performances however, compensate. As Dennis' orderly, Sergeant Immanuel Evans (Van Johnson), skillfully balances irreverence with low-key humor. At one point, while the generals debate with much vigor the return to Schwein-hafen—and thus the fate of many men—he matter-of-factly inquires of Dennis, "Shall I put the chicken back in the oven, Sir?" Arnold, the strident Representative Malcolm, maintains his usual excellence in this role that a lesser actor would surely have turned into a hopeless caricature. Pidgeon's General Kane is outstanding in one of his best performances in a long career. Although not the star, Pidgeon nevertheless becomes the focus of every scene in which he appears. His Kane strides through the film with uncompromised dignity, always in command but exercising his authority infrequently, prefer-ring to rely on his charm and considerable facility for *rapprochement*.

Command Decision recognizes the necessity of war while affirming it as uncivilized activity that, to be carried on effectively, requires a huge expen-diture in human life. Dennis and Kane represent sharply distinct attitudes toward the same immediate goal, the establishment of daylight precision bombing in concert with America's air supremacy in Europe. To Kane falls the responsibility of soothing the Congress and the press as well as the policy-makers in the military hierarchy; no matter what he believes about the right conduct of the air war, he moves circumspectly with his plans, anticipating the kind of backlash that excessive casualties bring. He flourishes in high-level chicanery. Dealing with the Congressmen is "my kind of war," he tells Dennis, who counters with, "You're welcome to it." War for Kane means glib appeasements and outright deceptions, a number of behind-the-scenes strategies that finally can be reduced to supplying peanuts to a deserving member of the local aristocracy. Dennis' war is a dirty one whose grim statistics call up the faces of men personally known. Because he hates war and its trappings, Dennis insulates himself with a conscientious adherence to his duty, a tactic that finds a parallel in Sergeant Evans' flippancies and in the dogged optimism of Captain George Washington Bellpepper Lee. The last frames show the plane taking Dennis (and the loyal Evans) to the Pacific, to an assignment, coming directly from Washington, that will be more important than the one he leaves. He emerges the obvious although unwilling hero: learning of this new command, he asserts quietly, with real dismay, "They can't do this to me." "They" can, however, and do, for Dennis has shown himself always capable of the task in spite of his own spiritual and emotional depletions.

William H. Brown, Jr.

THE CONCRETE JUNGLE
(THE CRIMINAL)

Released: 1960
Production: Jack Greenwood; released by Anglo Amalgamated
Direction: Joseph Losey
Screenplay: Alun Owen; based on the original screenplay *The Criminal* by
  Jimmy Sangster
Cinematography: Robert Krasker
Editing: Reginald Mills and Geoffrey Muller
Art direction: Scott MacGregor
Production design: Richard MacDonald
Music: John Dankworth
Running time: 97 minutes

> *Principal characters:*
> Johnny Bannion .... Stanley Baker
> Mike Carter .... Sam Wanamaker
> Frank Saffron .... Gregoire Aslan
> Suzanne .... Margit Saad
> Maggie .... Jill Bennett
> Barrows .... Patrick Magee
> Kelly .... Kenneth Cope

At the end of *The Concrete Jungle* there is an overhead shot of the murdered Johnny Bannion (Stanley Baker) lying in a snow-covered field while his killers search vainly for a hidden cache of money. The camera moves further away, and the shot dissolves into one of the inmates methodically circling a prison yard. It recalls the opening image of the film—a circle of prisoners frantically gambling for what turns out to be cigarettes. Indeed, *The Concrete Jungle* shares with other Joseph Losey films, most notably *Time Without Pity* (1957), *The Damned* (1961), and the underrated *Modesty Blaise* (1966), not only the circular image but also the view of society as a hostile environment in which free will becomes an act of heroic resistance. In *The Concrete Jungle* the prison is a microcosm of society in which Johnny Bannion unsuccessfully attempts to assert his own self-determination.

Like several other Losey protagonists, Johnny Bannion is an independent outsider. Most obviously opposed to him is Barrows (Patrick Magee) the Chief Warden of the prison, whose attempts at crushing Bannion into conformity are met with equal resistance. Although alone, Bannion is obviously also a leader and looked upon by many of the inmates as a hero. Ironically, it is when Bannion comes to love Suzanne (Margit Saad), which is a positive act, that he finally makes himself vulnerable.

The first part of the film takes place entirely within the prison. During the credit sequence, the camera follows a prisoner named Kelly (Kenneth Cope) as he is being processed into the prison. We learn that Kelly has earned the enmity of the other prisoners for some violation of their own rigid, although unofficial, set of rules. There are two codes of conduct which rule the prison— the one set down by Barrows and the one that the prisoners have made for themselves. The complicity of Barrows in the prisoners' code is made explicit during the sequence in which Kelly is being punished by other prisoners. A chorus of rattling plates and cups to drown out Kelly's screams is further echoed by Barrows' keys, which he taps rhythmically against a rail. Later, Barrows also tries to punish Bannion through the actions of a couple of prisoners.

After Bannion is released, a fellow criminal, Mike Carter (Sam Wanamaker), organizes a party to celebrate his release. In contrast to the easy camaraderie which Bannion is able to inspire in prison, there is an uneasiness and lack of occasion to the party. The party breaks down when Maggie (Jill Bennett), Bannion's old girl friend, becomes hysterical. The circular image recurs when she is first introduced, seen refracted through a kaleidoscope by Carter. During her outburst it is implied what she had a sexual relationship with Carter while Bannion was in prison.

Part of Bannion's eventual downfall is tied to his inability to estimate properly Carter's power, or at least that of the people he represents. Bannion does not realize that his style of independence is no longer relevant in a world ruled by the sort of corporate crime to which Carter belongs. Although Bannion's fate seems equally bleak both inside the prison and out, the one positive note grows out of his relationship with Suzanne. In sharp contrast to the rest of the film's oppressiveness, the scenes between Bannion and Suzanne are characterized by a joyous spontaneity. Unfortunately, as the film finally makes clear, it is already too late for Bannion. Betrayed by Carter after a robbery, he is implicated further by an expensive bracelet which he had bought for Suzanne with part of the stolen money. Bannion is sent back to prison, but his old gang uses Suzanne as bait to induce him to escape.

Bannion gets Frank Saffron (Gregoire Aslan) to engineer his escape. Ironically, in order to succeed, Bannion has to become a traitor in the eyes of his fellow prisoners. Now, except for Suzanne, he is truly alone, wanted by the law and without friends in the underworld. He is taken to a boat where Suzanne is being held prisoner, but although they are able to escape, he is fatally wounded during the struggle. In the end, he dies in the field where he had buried the money, babbling prayers that had long since lost any meaning for him. Before he dies he sends Suzanne away in order to save her.

As in any Losey film, *The Concrete Jungle* is filled with a number of visual and behavioral details which create a complex and interwoven mosaic on the screen. Of particular note is the manner in which Losey uses setting and composition for dramatic comment. The racetrack robbery is shot plainly with one simple camera set-up, but the scene in which it is planned subtly presents the conflicts that will later lead to disruption and betrayal. The setting for this scene, a park, is startling in itself for its incongruity. Significantly, the men are seated on benches at off-angles to one another. In fact, all the outdoor scenes, not only the final one of Bannion's death, contain an aura of desolation.

In Losey's English films he usually employed Richard MacDonald as production designer, and in the interiors of these films great emphasis is placed upon the relationship of the decor to the action. Very often the effect is ironic, as is the case when the poster of a nude woman is contrasted with the real nudity of Suzanne in the bathtub. Overall, there is also a certain air of artificiality and incompleteness to Bannion's apartment which comments upon his character. In the boat, the narrowing of Bannion's hopes is mirrored by the narrowness of the space. Most strikingly of all, the prison interiors are shot from low angles, emphasizing the prison's repressiveness.

Aside from the visual wealth found in Losey's work, there is also a precision to each gesture found in the film. A good example occurs after the party when Bannion undresses and neatly folds his clothes prison-style and then, realizing what he has done, knocks the pile over. Bannion's fear of death in the final scene gains its irony from an earlier scene of a mass held in the prison. Uninvolved in the ceremony, Bannion discusses his plans unemotionally with Saffron. In contrast, Barrows seems to be almost sexually involved in the ceremony. Losey had incidentally intended to end the film with Barrows, but it can be inferred from the finished product that Barrows is as much a prisoner as the men that he guards.

Three performances in this film stand out—Baker as Bannion, Wanamaker as Carter, and Magee as Barrows. Welsh-born and from the working-class, Baker's rough aggressiveness never received the appreciation that it deserved in a British cinema dominated by more gentlemanly and genteel types. He was knighted, however, in 1976. Only one month before his death of lung cancer at the age of forty-nine. His work for Losey, in this film as well as in *Eva* (1962), was by far his best. As for Wanamaker and Magee, they are both striking in their respective portrayals of men inclined toward opportunism and sadism. If there is a jarring note in the film, it is the character of Suzanne (rather than Saad's acting), which was forced upon Losey because of the plot.

The Concrete Jungle marked an important point in the evolution of Losey's art. Never before had Losey made a film with such an unrelentingly bleak outcome. From the relative optimism of *The Boy with Green Hair* (1948) and *The Lawless* (1950), through several other films before *The Concrete Jungle*, a growing pessimism can be detected in the director's outlook. It was certainly

no momentary lapse into cynicism, for if anything the films which followed—
Eva, *The Damned*, *The Servant* (1963), and *King and Country* (1964)—projected an even darker view.

Mike Vanderlan

CONFIDENTIAL AGENT

Released: 1945
Production: Robert Buckner for Warner Bros.
Direction: Herman Shumlin
Screenplay: Robert Buckner; based on the novel of the same name by Graham Greene
Cinematography: James Wong Howe
Editing: George Amy
Music: Franz Waxman
Running time: 118 minutes

Principal characters:
Denard	Charles Boyer
Rose Cullen	Lauren Bacall
Contreras	Peter Lorre
Mrs. Melandez	Katina Paxinou
Elsie	Wanda Hendrix
Licata	Victor Francen

In 1942 Warner Bros. had had a surprise smash hit with *Casablanca*. From then on they were on the alert for a similar success, an adventure intrigue with good portions of love and espionage, preferably in a foreign locale with suitably vague World War II references. In 1944 they converted Ernest Hemingway's novel *To Have and Have Not* into just such a film and created a new star, Lauren Bacall, at the same time. In 1945 they tried again with one of Graham Greene's novels, *Confidential Agent*. At first sight it must have had all of the right elements, although the book was seven years old and dealt with prewar England. Perhaps that is why so few changes were made. A strong conflict centered on a sufficiently remote subject (the Spanish Civil War) with an intriguing romance, a fair amount of action, and especially vivid, almost grotesque, supporting roles, the very sort of thing at which Warner Bros. was quite good. The package looked strong enough for the studio to go into production disregarding any potential problems.

There were problems, however; for one thing, Greene was no Hollywood hack—he was not even a conventional espionage author along the lines of Eric Ambler or E. Phillips Oppenheim. He constructed his "entertainments," as he called them, as much as examples of harsh atmosphere and Depression realism as amusing thrillers. His hero, the agent of the title, is a middle-aged, incredibly weary Spanish musician forced by events to become a cloak-and-dagger representative of the Loyalists on a desperate mission to industrial England to buy much-needed coal. Greene's heroine is a bitter, rootless coal manufacturer's daughter deeply resentful of the upper-class aims her father has foisted on her but unable to get along without them. Worst of all, from a conventional thriller's point of view, there is no happy ending. The hero is unable to buy his coal, and appeal to the miners' conscience falls on deaf ears, and it is only through the sort of irony seldom seen at Warner Bros. that the villains are also kept from the coal.

The problem the studio faced was that the tale, in its tone, in its unfolding, and in its resolution, was intriguingly, amusingly, but thoroughly depressing. Their only answer to this was to cast it in the manner of a lush romance. For the thoroughly unromantic Denard, the hero of the novel, they cast one of the few authentic screen lovers, Charles Boyer. As the confused English heroine, Rose Cullen, they assigned Bacall, whose come-hither eyes and gruff voice had just added a new look to American sexuality in *To Have and Have Not*. Bacall, for one, was not amused. "To cast me as an aristocratic English girl was more than a stretch," she recalls in her autobiography, "It was dementia. . . . The British broad was totally straight and dreary. No way, no way possible to deal with her."

Another problem for Bacall was director Herman Shumlin. Shumlin had a most distinguished record on stage—he had directed most of Lillian Hellman's works among others—but he had only one previous film to his credit, Hellman's *Watch on the Rhine* (1943). For Bacall that was not enough. "Herman Shumlin would take no advice from anyone," she recalls ". . . and gave me none of the help which I desperately needed." It may have been merely studio politics on Shumlin's part, for, looking at the film, it is obvious that Warners did not want anything particularly new or different; they wanted the growly sex kitten Bacall had established, no matter how inappropriate. It is indeed inappropriate, even though Greene himself had kind words for Bacall after seeing the film. The studio wanted Boyer to be the romantic lover doing his best for the country as well as the woman he loves in the approved Humphrey Bogart-Gary Cooper manner. It was chance that the actor's chronic insomnia was then particularly severe, giving him a proper haggard and wan look. Warners was the maker of formula films *par excellence*—James Cagney gangster films and Busby Berkeley musicals for example—and they did not like to tamper with anything that had once been financially successful.

Greene, perhaps predating the present-day tradition of John Le Carre, Len Deighton, and his own later works, saw nothing romantic in the spy business; Warner Bros. did, and thus the film tends to pull in two directions at once. The elements are there, but they do not mesh. It has a nicely romanticized look at times—racy touring cars rushing through the English fog and dingy backwater hotel rooms with just the right air of seedy menace—but the dialogue and plot situations keep suggesting a very different kind of film. Boyer, the epitome of Continental romance, tells Bacall that he cannot make love to her because "I have no such emotions left." The lady, covered in luxurious furs and hanging bangs that rival Veronica Lake's, is required to voice such unhappy disdain as "What you want and what you settle for are not often the same." To which Boyer replies, "And often what you want is no good either." It is a good, taut Greene line, and Bacall's part is better than she has remembered it, but it does not work in the traditional Warners' context. Director Shumlin is not able to resolve the problem. Because *Confidential Agent* was not a big success at the box office, he was never to direct another film.

The film was not a great success critically either. The stage was set for conventional heroics, but instead viewers got interesting but largely unwanted glimpses of trade unionism in England, a hazy view of the war in Spain, exchanges between hero and villain that harkened back to the "nothing personal" attitudes of World War I authors such as John Buchan, and a hero who starts out looking defeated and keeps on getting defeated by everyone until he finally sails back to Spain with one thing only—Cullen. It is therefore not surprising that much of the audiences' attention turned to a subplot involving Boyer with two veteran scene stealers, the slyly insinuating Peter Lorre and Katina Paxinou, a volcanic Greek actress in the Irene Pappas mold who had won an Oscar for *For Whom the Bell Tolls*. They play compadres of Boyer who soon turn out to be anything but friends. Directed to find a way to get him in serious trouble with the police, the pair contrive to implicate him in the death of a little servant girl (winningly played by newcomer Wanda Hendrix, who was soon cast in a similar role in *Ride the Pink Horse*, 1947). Frustrated and vengeful, Boyer eludes the police and sets out to track the pair down. In the end however (with a nod perhaps toward Production Code requirements), Boyer does not really have to do anything. His presence is enough to terrify Contreras (Peter Lorre) into a heart attack, and Mrs. Melandez (Katina Paxinou), discovering that evidence has been found which implicates her, takes poison. Both performers get bravura moments in a very rich theatrical vein, and, needless to say, they make the most of them. Their performances easily cast the rest of the film and its much subtler plot into the background in 1945.

Ironically, time has somewhat reversed the film's virtues. The pessimism and weary viewpoint that fell limply on a World War II propaganda-oriented audience now seems more realistic and up-to-date. Those excellent supporting performances now look like fustian although extremely good fustian. Free from his romantic image, Boyer, who died in 1978, can now be appreciated for the really good and convincing performer that he was. Warner's influence on the film now seems less, and Greene's more. For *Confidential Agent* remains a rather chameleon motion picture, one that by trying to be a bit different while staying within the confines of a well-known formula ended up really pleasing no one. That was the film's disadvantage, but as the years go by its greater advantage shows up. This film adapts with the times, with new things surfacing, new interests appearing, and the old clichés receding. As many another "classic" retreats with its time and place, something about films like *Confidential Agent* manages to stay always fresh and useful.

Lewis Archibald

THE CONSTANT NYMPH

Released: 1943
Production: Henry Blanke for Warner Bros.
Direction: Edmund Goulding
Screenplay: Kathryn Scola; based on the novel of the same name by Margaret
    Kennedy and the play of the same name by Margaret Kennedy and Basil
    Dean
Cinematography: Tony Gaudio
Editing: David Weisbart
Music: Erich Wolfgang Korngold
Running time: 112 minutes

> *Principal characters:*
> Lewis Dodd .... Charles Boyer
> Tessa Sanger .... Joan Fontaine
> Toni Sanger .... Brenda Marshall
> Florence Churchill .... Alexis Smith
> Charles Churchill .... Charles Coburn
> Lady Longborough .... Dame May Whitty
> Fritz Bercovi .... Peter Lorre
> Kate Sanger .... Jean Muir
> Paula Sanger .... Joyce Reynolds
> Albert Sanger .... Montagu Love

The Constant Nymph was derived from a very popular 1925 novel of the
same name written by Margaret Kennedy. Following the book's great success,
Kennedy collaborated with British producer/director Basil Dean to adapt her
sentimental novel into an equally successful stage play, and subsequently
Dean directed two English film versions of the novel. The first was the 1929
silent picture starring Mabel Poulton as Tessa and Ivor Novello as Lewis
Dodd. It was regarded as "appealing" but did not realize the full dramatic
potential of the plot. The second screen version came in 1934, this time in
sound, and starred Dean's then-wife Victoria Hopper as Tessa and Brian
Aherne as Dodd. This was the more popular of the two versions, not only
because of the all-important musical score, but also because it captured the
livable gaiety of the bohemian Sanger family who are at the center of the
plot. Certainly the best and most popular screen adaptation of all, however,
was the 1943 Warner Bros. production starring Joan Fontaine and Charles
Boyer.

The Constant Nymph can be described as both a romantic tearjerker and
a woman's picture, but it is more than that. On the surface it is a poignant
story of unrequited love, which in itself is enough to qualify it as a romantic
favorite, but Kennedy's story is more involved. Her real message is the ageless
conflict between spiritual and material worlds and the resultant heartache in

man's effort to bridge the gap between those two worlds.

The Warner Bros. screen version succeeds admirably in presenting both of these elements in a film full of good humor, heart, and sadness. It contains excellent acting by all its cast members and by Fontaine in particular. Its production values are top-notch. It contains a lush and romantic musical score by Erich Wolfgang Korngold, and it is ably directed by Edmund Goulding. In other words, the film is a good example of the Hollywood studio system at its best, bringing together as it does the various elements that go to make a good motion picture.

Goulding was a natural as director of this project. During his nearly thirty-five years as a Hollywood director he had successfully handled a great many actresses, such as Greta Garbo in *Grand Hotel* (1932), Dorothy Maguire in *Claudia* (1943), Gene Tierney in *The Razor's Edge* (1946), and Bette Davis in four popular films: *That Certain Woman* (1937), *Dark Victory* (1939), *The Old Maid* (1939), and *The Great Lie* (1941). He understood the subtle blend necessary in bringing romantic and sentimental stories to the screen with some sense of maturity and realism.

The Constant Nymph is the story of a Belgian composer named Lewis Dodd (Charles Boyer) who is a musician of considerable talent but who is unable to discover and harness that within himself which will transform his music into greatness. He leaves his native Brussels to pay a visit to his old friend and musical mentor, Albert Sanger (Montagu Love), an elderly, broken-down musician who drinks too much brandy and lives in a chalet in the Swiss Alps with his four daughters. The Sanger "Circus," as this unconventional house-hold is called, consists of Toni (Brenda Marshall), Kate (Jean Muir), fifteen-year-old Tessa (Joan Fontaine), and Paula (Joyce Reynolds). The girls are impish, elfin children full of good humor, madcap mischievousness, and a love for music. Their quaint, eccentric life style, while unorthodox, is encour-aged and nurtured by their loving father, who, as an artist, believes they should be reared to enjoy and appreciate the essence of life rather than be restricted by the constraints of society. The only thing marring their happiness is Tessa's weak heart.

The opening of the film is highlighted by the "fire and abandon" of a Liszt Rhapsody emphasizing the intensity with which the Sangers and Dodd regard music. Dodd's arrival at the Sangers' chalet increases the already free-spirited mayhem of the happy household. At once we see that Tessa, a radiant child-woman in gingham and pigtails, is in love with Dodd, but Dodd's response is one of simple friendly affection. He refers to all four girls as "the children."

Dodd discusses with Albert Sanger his inability to write the kind of music of which he knows he is capable. The elder Sanger plays some of Dodd's work-in-progress—a symphonic poem called "Tomorrow"—and tells the com-poser that he will never be great until he has loved. Dodd's response is "My music is sophisticated and doesn't need heart."

The Sanger sisters enlist Dodd's help in planning a birthday party for their father, and Dodd composes a special song for the occasion. All seems ideal with the Sanger household when suddenly Albert Sanger dies on his birthday. The tragedy brings an end to the idyllic life of the Sanger children. An English uncle, Charles Churchill (Charles Coburn), and his daughter Florence (Alexis Smith) arrive at the chalet to decide the family's future, and a romance between Dodd and Florence blossoms, to the chagrin of the young Tessa. It is decided that the two older girls will marry their respective beaux and that Tessa and Paula will be sent to boarding school in England. One afternoon Tessa returns from a swim to learn that Dodd and Florence are engaged to be married. She collapses, but quickly recovers and assures Dodd and her family that it was just a fainting spell brought on by too much excitement.

The members of the family tearfully go their separate ways, Tessa and Paula off to school and Dodd and Florence to their London wedding. In London, Dodd is passed off to his wife's friends as an "artiste," a genius—just one more ornament in her stuffy circle of friends. Troubled by the useless lives of his wife's aristocratic friends, inspiration continues to elude Dodd and he broods. Tessa and Paula rebel at the regimentation of boarding school and run away to Dodd in London. Florence is visibly annoyed by the girls' presence, and it is finally agreed that Paula will go to live in Paris with Kate, and that Tessa will stay on in the Dodd house in London despite Florence's reluctance to accept her as anything but an intruder.

Tessa's infatuation with Dodd soon creates a triangle of jealousy and innuendo. Dodd, at last realizing that, regardless of her youth, Tessa does love him with all her heart and that he likewise loves her, is inspired to finish work on "Tomorrow." Tessa makes him see that they are kindred souls who must be free of the conventions of society.

On the evening that Dodd is to conduct his symphony in public, he proclaims his love to Tessa and asks her to go away with him. Tessa declines but knows that she herself must go away alone. She packs her belongings and plans to leave after listening to the broadcast on the radio. At the concert hall Florence admits to Dodd that their marriage is over and that he is free to go to Tessa. The concert is a personal triumph for Dodd, and as soon as it is over he rushes home to try once more to convince Tessa to go away with him. He finds her lying dead on a sofa, her heart unable to withstand the excitement of hearing the music that she has inspired. Goulding's direction never panders to the melodramatic elements of the plot, and he maintains throughout the tenderness of the love story, which is further enhanced by the Korngold score.

Legal complications over the copyright to this film prevent it from being shown commercially, which is unfortunate, since its star, Fontaine, considers it the favorite of all her films, and many viewers feel it contains her finest performance, although she received an Oscar for *Rebecca* two years before. Fontaine was nominated for an Academy Award for *The Constant Nymph* but lost to newcomer Jennifer Jones for *The Song of Bernadette*, another role which required an adult actress to play the part of a child for most of the film. None of the other actors were nominated for Oscars, although Coburn did win the Best Supporting Actor award for *The More the Merrier* the same year.

Ronald Bowers

THE CONVERSATION

Released: 1974
Production: Francis Ford Coppola for Paramount
Direction: Francis Ford Coppola
Screenplay: Francis Ford Coppola
Cinematography: Bill Butler
Editing: Richard Chew
Sound: Walter Murch
Running time: 113 minutes

> *Principal characters:*
> Harry Caul .... Gene Hackman
> Stan .... John Cazale
> Bernie Moran .... Allen Garfield
> Mark .... Frederic Forrest
> Ann .... Cindy Williams
> Paul .... Michael Higgins
> Meredith .... Elizabeth MacRae
> Amy .... Teri Garr
> Martin Stett .... Harrison Ford
> The Mime .... Robert Sheilds
> The Director .... Robert Duvall

Francis Ford Coppola commenced work on his screenplay for *The Conversation* in 1966, but it was to be eight long years before the finished film would reach the screen. During that period, from 1966 to 1974, American society underwent profound and cathartic changes, alterations wrought by the Vietnam War, a revolution in style and attitude, and the shattering revelations of, among other things, the Pentagon Papers and Watergate scandals. These tumultuous events only served to make the themes outlined in *The Conversation* all the more relevant and ominous, for the film clearly and devastatingly makes the statement that our value systems and civil liberties have eroded considerably, and that if left untended, our new technologies will certainly destroy our democratic heritage.

The film opens with a long shot of San Francisco's famed Union Square, viewed from above. The camera gradually zooms inward to focus on a young couple (Cindy Williams and Frederic Forrest) moving through the lunchtime crowd. The sound level, barely audible at first, rises slowly. Music, muffled voices, and strange mechanical noises merge together, move apart, and merge again. These innocuous sounds will become frighteningly familiar as the film unwinds, but for the present, all seems to be simply a jumble of noise.

It quickly becomes evident that the couple, Ann and Mark, are under surveillance for some reason. On a roof high above, a man aims a combination camera/directional microphone at the moving couple. Another antenna is seen in a window overlooking the square. A third microphone is hidden in a shopping bag carried by a man who discreetly follows close to the pair. A van parked across the street serves as the command center for the undercover team, a group headed by Harry Caul (Gene Hackman), a nondescript man who, we soon learn, is the "best bugger on the West Coast," a genius at surveillance and sound recording. Harry's assistant, Stan (John Cazale), is seen monitoring the incoming sounds, pieces of the couple's conversation mingled in with the noise of a festive Union Square crowd. When Stan asks his employer for the reasons behind their assignment, Harry flatly answers, "I don't know what they're talking about. All I want is a nice, fat recording." Harry never questions, for to question would bring both danger and the responsibilities of knowledge. Just do the job, he reasons. Do it right, and keep your eyes and mouth closed.

The day's work completed, Harry arrives at his apartment, its front door bolted securely by an impressive array of locks and alarms that inform us that Harry is indeed a very private man who tries with all his might to let no one inside his life or his mind. The apartment is sparsely and cheaply furnished. As Harry moves around, the camera remains still, focusing on the bare interior, emphasizing Harry's isolation. His only release comes from playing his saxophone in accompaniment to a jazz album—a live recording which ends with a cheering crowd. Harry bows his head as if to acknowledge the applause that he knows was not meant for him.

The next morning, Harry goes to his workshop, a large warehouse floor with his work area isolated and caged into a far corner. He begins to work on the tapes which were recorded the previous day, and slowly the voices and sounds merge into a coherent whole. The young couple's words gradually jell into sentences, phrases which always seem to mirror Harry's own mental state. We flashback to Union Square as the couple stares at a drunk asleep on a park bench. The girl, whose name we have learned is Ann, says that whenever she sees a man like that, she imagines that once he was someone's baby boy. As she says this, we are brought forward in time to Harry sitting at his work bench and listening to her words. The equation is complete. Later in the day, Harry places a call (from a pay phone, naturally) and asks to speak to the "Director." A male assistant tells him to bring the tapes the next afternoon, and he will be paid off.

That night, Harry visits his girl friend's apartment. Amy (Teri Garr) seems to do nothing in life except wait for Harry. Her life is, like Harry's, empty, but she has the capacity to love and care for someone, a quality that Harry seems to lack. She begins to question Harry about his job, background, and interests. Obviously, he has told her nothing about himself, and he becomes upset at her prying. "I don't have any secrets," he tells her, as he leaves her room after putting her rent money on the kitchen counter. Amy can no longer stand the strain of waiting, however, and tells him that she will not wait anymore.

The next day, Harry keeps his appointment at the "Director's" office. It is situated atop a cold, concrete high-rise, an ultramodern, sterile edifice. The Director's assistant Martin Stett (Harrison Ford) takes the tapes and hands Harry his money. Harry is unwilling to part with the tapes, however, for they were to be placed in the Director's hands personally. The assistant allows Harry to leave with the tapes but warns him that they are dangerous and that someone may get hurt; he is advised not to get involved. As Harry departs he spots the young man and woman, and it spooks him.

Harry returns to his workshop and listens to the tapes again. Now they reveal that something sinister and deadly is to happen later in the week—specifically, on Sunday at three o'clock in room 773 of the Jack Tarr Hotel. After much dial-twisting and tape noise, Harry deciphers a crucial line in which the young man flatly asserts, "He'd kill us if he got the chance."

The next reel is filled with scenes of the annual surveillance convention, a national gathering of the nation's top buggers, wiretappers, and security men, among whom Harry's name is legendary. Later that night, Harry sleeps with a woman he met at the convention, who, after he falls asleep, steals the tapes. Discovering the theft, Harry runs to the Director's office. The tapes are there, and the Director (Robert Duvall in a cameo) is listening to them. Harry asks what will become of the young couple, but is answered only by the words on the tape: "He'd kill us if he got the chance."

After a long and involved series of events, it becomes apparent that the couple (for reasons that will never be certain) have killed the Director and have disguised his death so that it looks as if he died in an auto crash. Since Harry is the only man outside of the company who seems to have any knowledge of the circumstances, his own insulated life is threatened. He returns home to discover that somehow his apartment has been bugged. The film ends with Harry Caul ripping his belongings, furnishings, and his entire apartment to shreds, but he is unable to discover how the bugging was done. The final shot shows Harry sitting amid the rubble of his possessions playing his saxophone, absently playing away as his world crumbles down around his ears.

The plot description in no way does justice to the complexity and eloquence of Coppola's film, which by anyone's standards is one of the cinematic landmarks of the 1970's. It must be viewed many times to be appreciated and understood fully.

Thematically, *The Conversation* touches upon a great number of late twentieth century concerns and problems: among them, modern society's devotion to media and technology over the needs of people, modern man's alienation from himself and from others, the question of individual responsibility and morality, voyeurism and the lack of privacy, the oppression of city existence and runaway corporate power, and above all, the feeling of what it is like to live through a period of intense disillusionment and extensive social disintegration.

On the level of style, *The Conversation* rates as one of the most mature works ever filmed. Its combination of long-lens cinematography and marvelously effective sound mixing (in which background ambience, intimate verbal exchanges, and featherlike, Satie-influenced piano accompaniment blend to form an astonishingly cohesive whole) is stunningly effective. Coppola here exhibits an intelligence and sensitivity far more complex than his previous films had suggested, and indeed, *The Conversation* remains today his most satisfying screen effort, with the possible exception of *Apocalypse Now* (1979).

Hackman gives a letter-perfect, beautifully controlled performance as Harry Caul. The actor's own unattractive (in the traditional sense) face and unassuming style works frighteningly well to create a man whose only contact with the world comes through his ears. His is a devastating portrayal of a man literally unable to communicate with anyone, and to whom sound is a universe in itself, utterly personal and terrifyingly lonely.

The Conversation was clearly influenced by Italian director Michelangelo Antonioni's 1960 film *Blow-Up*, both in its overwhelming sense of alienation and in the fact that it, too, demonstrates that technological prowess can only detect and cannot comprehend. *The Conversation* offers no hope. It is a bleak film which, if taken correctly, should inform us that unless something is done immediately to rectify the mess in which the post-World War II world has mired itself, things will only get much, much worse.

Daniel Einstein

COPS AND ROBBERS

Released: 1973
Production: Elliott Kastner for United Artists
Direction: Aram Avakian
Screenplay: Donald E. Westlake
Cinematography: David L. Quaid
Editing: Barry Malkin
Music: Michel Legrand
Running time: 89 minutes

Principal characters:
> Tom .... Cliff Gorman
> Joe .... Joseph Bologna
> Patsy O'Neill (Pasquale Aniello) .... John P. Ryan
> Eastpoole .... Shepperd Strudwick
> Secretary .... Ellen Holly
> Mr. Joe .... Nino Ruggeri

Cops and Robbers did not win any awards nor did it ripple many people's consciousness as *Serpico* (1973) did earlier with its story about police corruption, yet this film is a well-crafted work in which director Aram Avakian produces an interesting type of comedy. His source of humor stems from the shooting and editing of satirical sequences rather than from witty dialogue, providing a lasting but subtle type of comedy. This film's humor is most appreciated through multiple viewings in order to note fully the visual subtleties of ironic sequences contrasting with one another through clever editing.

Tom (Cliff Gorman), a detective, and Joe (Joseph Bologna), a patrolman, both working for the New York City police force, are average family men who tire of their jobs and of their mundane lives and decide to execute a robbery. As the title indicates, they become both "cops" and "robbers," playing a game in which they fluctuate between roles and stumble through comic events. The ambiguity of roles between police and criminals is established in the first sequence when a patrolman, presumably walking his beat, strolls into a liquor store and almost casually robs it. He calmly steps out onto the street again, followed by the clerk, who tries to convince other pedestrians that the man was a robber, not a cop. The sequence is puzzling until we find out during a conversation between Tom and Joe that Joe was the robber and not a street punk disguised in a police uniform. Joe brags about his stunt, claiming that he came away with more than two hundred dollars—enough to buy four pairs of shoes for his children. In this sequence lies the first hint of the materialism that grasps these men's lives. They are paid to protect other people's property, but are frustrated because they themselves are unable to accumulate property on the salaries they earn. Surrounded by wealth and by the thousands of products which that wealth can buy, Joe states that only a policeman who controls himself can remain honest. The most revealing aspect of Joe's crime is that he discovers how easy it was for him because, as a policeman, he was the last person anyone would suspect of committing a crime. Tom slowly becomes convinced that stealing is the only to "make up the difference between what we are paid and what we are worth."

In the first half of the film we are shown the motivation behind their intent to steal through the depiction of their life styles, families, mortgaged homes, and lack of money to buy the goods they want, contrasted with their dangerous work. Joe, especially, is constantly exposed to murderers, robbers, and surly street people. In one sequence, Joe and his partner are embroiled in a gunfight in which Joe's partner is wounded. As Joe stops to help his partner, the storekeeper denounces him for letting the robber get away with his money. Tom investigates one robbery case in which he finds that one art object in the wealthy woman's home is worth more than all of the items that were stolen. Preoccupied with money, Tom asks Joe as they shop in a supermarket what he would do with a million dollars. As they fantasize about committing a large-scale robbery, Tom suddenly suggests that they actually commit the crime. They discuss their plans for the robbery in their backyards, in the car to and from work, and when they shop, as if they were discussing a legitimate business agreement. Since they need a buyer for whatever they steal, Tom decides they must contact the Mafia.

They ineffectively disguise themselves with mustaches and wigs, and as Joe pretends to walk his dog, Tom meets with Pasquale Aniello, alias Patsy O'Neill (John P. Ryan), a man with Mafia connections. O'Neill shrewdly sees through the disguise and asks if Tom is a cop. Tom is taken aback but asks anyway what the Mafia would buy for two million dollars. O'Neill informs him that he will pay twenty cents on the dollar for "Bearer bonds," treasury bonds which say "pay to the bearer," (no matter whom), and an agreement is made that Tom and Joe will steal ten million dollars worth of bonds and that the exchange will be arranged when O'Neill reads about the robbery in the newspapers. This scene is especially good in that it contrasts O'Neill's cool efficiency and businesslike attitude with Tom's bumbling attitude toward crime. The wealthy atmosphere of Pasquale's house resembles more the wealthy robbery victim's home than it does Tom's and Joe's suburban houses. The gentility and opulence is further underscored by the baroque music playing in the background during their conversation about the heist.

One of the most satirical sequences in the film is Tom's reconnoiter of Wall Street and of the American Stock Exchange. It is also a good example of director Avakian's subtle humor. The area is portrayed reverently as if Tom has tread upon holy ground and features a shot looking up into the interior of the Stock Exchange as if it were a cathedral dome. We almost expect to see stained glass windows and an altar. The background music again emphasizes the humorous intent with hushed voices singing hymns combined with a businesslike voice chanting the stock-market news. Tom wanders through the building noting the security guards and television monitors and becomes stymied as to how to pull off the caper. As he rides home from work with Joe, he reads in the newspaper that a parade is being planned to honor the astronauts who landed on the moon, and he decides that they should rob the exchange during the parade. The two men sign up for extra patrol on the parade route and disguise themselves with mustaches in preparation for the heist.

They pretend to investigate a complaint about employees throwing objects from the windows of the exchange and are escorted into the interior offices by an executive named Eastpoole (Shepperd Strudwick). When Tom announces their intent to rob the exchange, Eastpoole and his secretary are surprisingly cooperative, and the robbery runs smoothly until another group of police suddenly arrive in the lobby to investigate a murder-robbery which occurred in the building's elevator. Tom succeeds in bringing the securities from the vault to Eastpoole's office without being detected, but he realizes that he and Joe will also be searched when they leave. He locks Eastpoole and his secretary in the bathroom, handcuffing them to the sink, and then to Joe's amazement, feeds the securities into the paper shredder and throws the resulting confetti out the window. Tom reveals his plan to Joe: they will escape from the building but the securities will still be reported stolen and they will "steal a headline" and pretend to make an exchange with the Mafia.

The newspapers report the next day that two men disguised as New York City policemen stole twelve million dollars worth of bonds. Tom and Joe are puzzled at the twelve million figure until Tom realizes that Eastpoole must have reported the extra two million in order for him and his secretary to steal a million apiece. This turn of events illustrates the invasion of corruption into all economic levels of society and shows us the framework in which Tom and Joe's actions are to be viewed.

Tom instructs the Mafia to meet them in Central Park on bicycle day, when cars are banned from the park's interior, and to bring a picnic basket filled with money. Tom and Joe bring a stolen patrol car into the park and quickly succeed in driving away with the picnic basket, but O'Neill is tipped off and blocks all the exits. Joe races around the park, searching futilely for an unguarded exit, while Mafia men, on foot and bicycles, try to capture them. This is the ultimate irony: a chase scene in which the criminals pursue the police. Joe finally rams through a fence and lands in a precinct yard, the same one, in fact, from which they stole the patrol car. They leave the damaged car before the police discover them. The Mafia, of course, is unable to follow them into the precinct. In a final twist to this successful caper, Tom and Joe have no transportation, so they ride the city bus free because they are policemen. They keep with them the picnic basket filled with millions.

Several days later, Tom and Joe are driving to work as if nothing has changed. Joe, however, feels guilty now for robbing the liquor store and he vents his frustration with shouts at other drivers on the expressway until Tom advises him to return the money. As they inch past a cemetery, we notice a funeral in progress and discover that it is for O'Neill. All of his Mafia cohorts are assembled to mourn his untimely passing, including Mr. Joe (Nino Ruggeri), his boss, who mourns not for O'Neill whom he probably had killed but for his stolen two million. The film ends as Mr. Joe is seen bowing his head in mock sorrow over his former employee's grave.

Tom and Joe become robbers, but they never shed their identities as cops. Joe refuses a bribe from a speeding motorist, telling him, "buy your kid a pair of shoes." He also defends the police against accusations of corruption and feels guilty about his liquor store robbery. Tom and Joe are much more competent at police work than are their counterparts at the exchange. The security guards there claim that the two robbers were not real policemen and assess themselves as alert and observant when the opposite is shown to be true. After the caper, Tom and Joe are going to work as usual acting as if they had never deviated from their law enforcement role. Only when we see the funeral is there any indication that their situation is indeed different.

The vivid locations and street language and the depiction of the dangerous situations in police work are realistic and well-executed. The dialogue, although subordinate to the action, is snappy and sprinkled with police slang which conveys a picture of hard-edged cynicism. An enjoyable aspect of the film is Michel Legrand's music, which enhances the facetious treatment of certain scenes and provides a disquieting undercurrent to others. The use of radio and television in the background adds to the cacophony of materialism and of corrupt city life while the theme song, "Cops and Robbers," is light and catchy in keeping with the general tone of the film.

One limitation of the film is writer Donald Westlake's choice of plot: the limited caper story with the required robbery and chase sequences. Although both sequences are well done, we still come away with the feeling of having seen it all before. Westlake attempts to push the limitations of this genre with his digging into the protagonists' motivations for the robbery, but this does not alleviate the overused quality of the story and only confuses the farcical tone until the comedy becomes ambivalent at times. One advantage of this plot, however, is that Avakian's comedy springs from action, location, and an ironic view of situations.

Bologna and Gorman portray well ordinary men caught up in a situation in which they succeed only through native intelligence and fortuitous circumstances against more experienced criminals. They successfully balance the realistic portrayals of police life with comic aspects of the caper without letting the characters get lost in the farcical plot. Tom and Joe are portrayed as sympathetic characters who naïvely earn their living at the beginning of the film but by the end have "grown up" and been initiated into a morally ambiguous society in which everyone steals and only hustlers strike it rich.

Ruth L. Hirayama

COQUETTE

Released: 1929
Production: United Artists
Direction: Sam Taylor
Screenplay: John Grey and Allen McNeil; based on the play of the same name by George Abbott and Ann Preston Bridgers, with additional dialogue by Sam Taylor
Cinematography: Karl Struss
Editing: Barbara McLean
Running time: 75 minutes

Principal characters:
Norma Besant	Mary Pickford (AA)
Michael Jeffery	Johnny Mack Brown
Stanley Wentworth	Matt Moore
Dr. John Besant	John Sainpolis
Jimmy Besant	William Janney
Julia	Louise Beavers

Just one year after the premiere of Warner Bros'. *The Jazz Singer* (1927), it was conceded that the day of the silent film was gone forever. An epidemic of hybrids, part-talkies, had ensued, only bringing closer that time when all feature films would be "all-talking, all-singing, all-dancing." There was considerable speculation as to what would be done by the Big Four who had created United Artists—Mary Pickford, Douglas Fairbanks, Charles Chaplin, and director D. W. Griffith. All of them had come from the theater, adapting what they had learned there to the pantomimal technique of the silent screen. It was obvious that the three who were players could talk as well as mime, and everybody knew that Griffith, as a director, still used rehearsals in order to set his scenes before the actual photography began. It would seem, therefore, that the four had little to fear from the microphone and new sound picture technique; yet, only one of them continued for any amount of time as a sound artist.

Chaplin stayed away entirely as long as he could, finally using a patter song but no dialogue in *Modern Times* (1936), but he did not make an all-talking film until *The Great Dictator* (1940), of which the best parts were still mimed. His last films only became more old-fashioned. Griffith directed only two talking features—*Abraham Lincoln* (1930) and *The Struggle* (1940). Neither made money, and Griffith withdrew from filmmaking. Fairbanks had no luck with the few talking films he made, and he had only personal pleasure in two of the semitravelogue features he made—*Around the World in 80 Minutes* (1931) and *Mr. Robinson Crusoe* (1932). His last picture was *The Private Life of Don Juan* (1934). Pickford was the only one who had any faith in the talking medium, although she did maintain that in her opinion talking pictures should have come first and from them silent films, for the silents were a far more difficult and artistic medium. She would have preferred going on as a silent screen star, but the talking picture had come to stay, representing an intimidating challenge, and one that she was determined to meet successfully.

Pickford knew that for her first talking feature a good story and workable screenplay were vital. She was determined not to do a talkie remake of any of her silent successes because she wanted a new image; she did not want a vehicle that would merely further the adventures of "Our Mary," "Little Mary," or "America's Sweetheart," as she had been called for years, endearing herself to the cinema world. She did not want to play a little girl any more; in 1929 she was a twice-married actress who had learned her trade in the theater under Belasco and in films under Griffith. In an effort to change her image, she determined that although she was then thirty-five years old, she would bob her hair. Because her figure was still girlish and her face unwrinkled, a chic, close-fitting, shingled hair style was designed for her; and she could easily have passed for a heroine half her age.

Throughout the years, Pickford had acquired the film rights to a number of story properties, but most of them were literary, and she wanted something modern. The search began for an up-to-date story, preferably a best-selling novel or a new play. It was a good friend, silent screen star Lillian Gish, who suggested that she consider a new hit play that starred Helen Hayes on Broadway: *Coquette*, written by George Abbott and Ann Preston Bridgers. It was a moving romantic tragedy with a heroine far removed from the popular, well-beloved image of "America's Sweetheart." It even had some highly censorable scenes, which were treated in such a way that they were allowed to remain in the final product although they were daring and dramatic. John Grey and Allen McNeil, two new screenwriters, turned out a new adaptation with additional dialogue by Sam Taylor, who was also directing. Karl Struss, one of the best cinematographers in Hollywood, was chosen to photograph the film; he was known for his ability to make middle-aged stars look at least ten years younger and very seductive. Sound for the film was by the Western Electric system on discs, and later, when sound was being recorded on an accompanying track, the dialogue was transferred to the film track. *Coquette*, released in April of 1929, was an instant hit everywhere, and the Motion Picture Academy, in its second year of awarding Oscars, chose Pickford as Best Actress for her performance in the film.

The story takes place in the deep South, and all the characters speak with a Southern accent; Pickford's accent sounds as natural and as beguiling as English actress Vivien Leigh's as Scarlett O'Hara in *Gone with the Wind* (1939). Pickford has charm and vivacity; she flirts without being coy, while she handles her dramatic scenes with real power. *Coquette* is the story of Norma Besant (Mary Pickford), who lives with her doctor father (John Sainpolis) and young brother (William Janney) in a typical small town in the South. Norma is the town's most popular young girl. Certainly, every young man wants to be her beau, and when there is a dance, the line of those wanting to escort her is long. A kindly family friend, Stanley Wentworth (Matt Moore), loves Norma in silence, but she only uses him to further her own conquests. Supposedly, Norma does not favor any of the young men, flirting with all of them, writing names on her program card as if it were a public petition.

Actually, however, Norma has more than a crush on young Michael Jeffery (Johnny Mack Brown). He is considered a roughneck, unsuitable, because of his quarrelsome nature and his drinking and gambling, for a young lady with all of Norma's refinements. Norma nevertheless cajoles Stanley into putting in a good word for Michael with her father, and she makes a date with Michael to escort her to the country club dance. On the afternoon of the dance Michael has a street fight outside the florist's when a suitor who has been disdained calls Norma nothing but a silly coquette. Michael thrashes him soundly. Word of the fight spreads, and Dr. Besant, after a word with Stanley, forbids his daughter to be escorted by Michael.

Norma prefers not to go to the dance, and when Michael calls on her to explain why he cannot escort her, she asks him into the parlor to talk. They confess that they have long been attracted to each other. Dr. Besant comes in and coldly tells Michael that he will have to ask him to discontinue seeing his daughter. Dr. Besant has also learned that in the street fight that afternoon, Michael had had the presumption to boast that he would marry Norma. This only promotes further ill feeling between Michael and Dr. Besant.

Later, when Norma and Michael meet, they reaffirm their love, and when he asks her to marry him, she is secretly frightened, but agrees to do so. They agree to part for a time, however, in order to let the scandal die down. Some months later, Michael returns and seeks out Norma, and she drives off with him in his old Ford, staying out with him until dawn. When Dr. Besant, who carries his old revolver with him, learns that Michael not only spent most of the night with his daughter, but that they are also now planning to run away and be married, he faces Michael and shoots him. Michael dies in Norma's arms.

Dr. Besant goes to give himself up to the law. Norma refuses to lie and claim that her father killed Michael while defending her good name. A trial is held and Besant is accused of murder. Norma has been on the point of staging a scene on the stand out of revenge for Michael's murder, accusing her father of premeditation, but she realizes she cannot do it. At the time Dr. Besant realizes that his daughter has not been seduced by Michael, who had respected her as the girl he loved and wanted to marry. When there is a brief recess, Besant secretly takes the revolver and kills himself in the courtroom. Weeping and inconsolable, Norma leaves the courthouse and goes down the road, where she is met by the understanding Stanley Wentworth. At the end, Stanley puts an arm around Norma, and they go back together to the Besant house.

Those who read the play or saw Hayes in the leading role on the stage can immediately spot the changes censors demanded. In the play, Norma and Michael not only spend the night together, but he also seduces her, and she becomes pregnant. In the courtroom scene, Norma makes her peace with her father in a very effective and touching scene, and then goes to the adjoining room, where she kills herself.

Both endings play well, but the stage finale is admittedly the more shocking and realistic. It was only because of the supreme artistry of Pickford that the screen resolution made by Norma gives her sympathy and dignity. The ending satisfied the censors and at the same time pleased Pickford's fans. Pickford went on to make only four more feature films, but none was very successful, and she retired from the screen in 1933.

DeWitt Bodeen

COTTON COMES TO HARLEM

Released: 1970
Production: Samuel Goldwyn, Jr., for United Artists
Direction: Ossie Davis
Screenplay: Ossie Davis and Arnold Perl; based on the novel of the same name by Chester Himes
Cinematography: Gerald Hirschfeld
Editing: Robert Q. Lovett and John Carter
Running time: 97 minutes

Principal characters:
Gravedigger Jones	Godfrey Cambridge
Coffin Ed Johnson	Raymond St. Jacques
Rev. Deke O'Malley	Calvin Lockhart
Iris	Judy Pace
Uncle Bud	Redd Foxx
Bryce	John Anderson
Mabel	Emily Yancy
Calhoun	J. D. Cannon

Cotton Comes to Harlem is not the greatest American film ever made: others have been more suspenseful; others have been funnier; and still others have had better performances and direction. In 1970, however, the year in which the film was released, no other major Hollywood motion picture had ever successfully utilized the creative input of so many Black Americans. The stars, Raymond St. Jacques and Godfrey Cambridge, and major supporting cast members were mostly black. The director and coauthor of the screenplay, Ossie Davis, and Chester Himes, the author of the original material, were also black. The film thus was made by blacks, for blacks.

Cotton Comes to Harlem is an entertaining comedy/drama, starring St. Jacques and Cambridge as Gravedigger Jones and Coffin Ed Johnson, respectively, New York City police detectives who were the main characters in a series of novels by Himes. In the film, the Reverend Deke O'Malley (Calvin Lockhart), a preacher and con man, has organized a Back-to-Africa crusade and swindled $87,000 from poor people in Harlem. The money is seized by O'Malley's white partner, Calhoun (J. D. Cannon), who escapes in a meat truck and hides the money in a bale of cotton. During a chase sequence in which Calhoun is followed by O'Malley and both are pursued by Gravedigger Jones and Coffin Ed Johnson, the bale bounces from the truck and is found by Uncle Bud (Redd Foxx), a junkman, who sells it as a prop to a stripper named Mabel (Emily Yancy). While she is undressing onstage, Calhoun and O'Malley appear, search for the money, and are arrested by Gravedigger and Coffin Ed. The $87,000, however, cannot be found. Eventually, the detectives coerce a Mafia leader into compensating O'Malley's congregation for the missing money, and at the finale, they receive a postcard from Uncle Bud, who had found the loot and is now living the high life in Africa.

The whites in *Cotton Comes to Harlem* are depicted as hoodlums and morons. In one sequence, for example, a sexy black woman lures a white police officer into taking off his clothes. He ends up in the corridor of a building with his gun in his hand but without his uniform—and wearing a paper bag over his head. Yet all the blacks are not saintly, by any means. The Reverend O'Malley has indeed defrauded his people. Other black characters—with the glaring exception of Gravedigger and Coffin Ed—are greedy and amoral. Uncle Bud does not return the $87,000, but treks off to Africa; and, of course, a key character is Mabel, the sexy stripper. Jones and Johnson, the heroes, however, are honest and do not accept graft. They are not janitors or Pullman porters, and they do not jump out of their skins at the first sign of trouble. They are tough, aggressive cops concerned with doing their job.

In most respects, other than presenting blacks as heroes, *Cotton Comes to Harlem* is not a message film; its main purpose is to entertain its audience. There is plenty of action and suspense, but none of the gratuitous violence and bloodletting which was to become a staple of black-oriented crime dramas released during the early and middle 1970's. The film is crammed with inside jokes about Harlem life. There are comedy bits which effectively and good-naturedly satirize life in the ghetto and the stereotypical ghetto dweller. After chasing O'Malley and Calhoun, for example, Gravedigger Jones drives into a cart of watermelons. *Cotton Comes to Harlem* unabashedly pokes fun at its audience.

The film is directed and coauthored (with Arnold Perl) by Ossie Davis, the stage and screen actor and playwright. It was shot on location in Harlem and Davis makes excellent use of Harlem landmarks, notably 125th Street and the famed Apollo Theater, as well as the bars, pool halls, and rib joints lining the side streets. Although a contemporary of Sidney Poitier, Davis never became a major star in films, nor was he as influential a personality as Poitier. His film career nevertheless goes back to 1950's *No Way Out* (which starred Poitier), and his screen appearances include *The Cardinal* (1963), *The Hill* (1965), and *The Scalphunters* (1968). His play *Purlie Victorious* was made into the 1963 film *Gone Are the Days*, a low-budget effort about a self-appointed black preacher who plans to outwit a despotic plantation owner. The film (directed by a white, Nicholas Webster) is notable mainly as the screen debut of Alan Alda.

St. Jacques and Cambridge are perfectly cast as Gravedigger Jones and Coffin Ed Johnson. Both were very active in films from the mid-1960's to mid-1970's. St. Jacques' best roles were in *The Pawnbroker* (1965), *The Comedians* (1967), *If He Hollers, Let Him Go* (1968), and Jules Dassin's *Up Tight* (1968), a remake of John Ford's classic, *The Informer* (1935), with black revolutionaries replacing Irish rebels. St. Jacques has virtually disappeared from films in the past few years, however, appearing occasionally on television. Cambridge, known mainly as a comedian, appeared in Davis' *Gone Are the Days* and *The President's Analyst* (1967), *Bye Bye Braverman* (1968), and Melvin Van Peebles' *Watermelon Man* (1970). In the latter, he portrayed a white insurance man (in whiteface) who wakes up one morning to find that his skin has turned black. Cambridge died of a heart attack in 1978 during the filming of the television movie *Victory at Entebbe* in which he was to have played Idi Amin. Lockhart gives a fine performance as O'Malley. The talented and strikingly handsome actor had star potential and appeared in such films as *Joanna* (1968), *Halls of Anger* (1970), and *Leo the Last* (1970). He, too, never reached stardom, however; in fact, the only performer in the film to sustain a career throughout the 1970's is Redd Foxx, star of television's *Sanford and Son*, and later *Sanford*.

Cotton Comes to Harlem, which cost $1.2 million to make, earned $4,458,401 in the first year of its release and was ranked eleventh on *Variety's* list of top-grossing films. It was estimated that between seventy and eighty percent of the film's audience was black. A sequel, *Come Back, Charleston Blue* (1972), in which Gravedigger and Coffin Ed become involved with black and white rival gangs fighting to control the Harlem heroin trade, lacked the humor of the original. Directed by black television director Mark Warren, the film was not a box-office success.

Cotton Comes to Harlem was a major force in establishing the fact that big money could be made from films featuring blacks as heroes, that blacks were capable of directing major motion pictures, and that a market was thirsting for films specifically fashioned for black audiences. Yet during the 1980's black films have disappeared, replaced by the more successful "integrated" films of black comedian Richard Pryor. 1980's *Stir Crazy* featuring the comic actor was one of the highest-grossing films in motion picture history. It was directed by Sidney Poitier.

Rob Edelman

THE COUNT OF MONTE CRISTO

Released: 1934
Production: Edward Small for United Artists/Reliance
Direction: Rowland V. Lee
Screenplay: Philip Dunne, Dan Totheroh, and Rowland V. Lee; based on the
   novel of the same name by Alexandre Dumas, *père*
Cinematography: Peverell Marley
Editing: Grant Whytock
Running time: 113 minutes

Principal characters:
Edmond Dantes	Robert Donat
Mercedes de Rosas	Elissa Landi
Raymond de Villefort, Jr.	Louis Calhern
Mondego	Sidney Blackmer
Danglars	Raymond Walburn
Abbe Faria	O. P. Heggie
Captain Leclerc	William Farnum
Jacopo	Luis Alberni
Albert, son of Mercedes	Douglas Watson
Valentine de Villefort	Irene Hervey

In all the world's literature which is popularly called "classic" there is possibly no tale of revenge that so grips the imagination of its readers as Alexandre Dumas' *The Count of Monte Cristo*. The filmed versions of the story have not lessened its impact. Its fans revel in each of the three revenges wrought upon the trio of archvillains. When Danglars is driven in terror to suicide, applause is in order; when Mondego goes hopelessly mad, the audience is delighted; and when Edmond Dantes achieves his final and greatest moment of revenge in exposing the villain, de Villefort, Jr., in a stirring court trial, the audience is ecstatic. Three more merciless villains never existed, and it is satisfying to the audience to know that each has received his comeuppance.

The 1934 version of the story is a handsome production which was brought to the screen by producer Edward Small, and enhanced by the American debut of the splendid English romantic actor, Robert Donat. In *The Count of Monte Cristo*, the romantic spirit of Donat literally imbues the essence of the role he plays. This is bravura acting at its best and most believable. When he escapes from prison and exults over the boundless riches he has gained, crying, "The world is mine!," it is a chilling moment of victory. Not even the eminent dramatic actor James O'Neill, who created the role and played it countless times with unbridled exaltation, could have so gloried in that triumph. There are no subtleties in this story. It must be played with catastrophe piled upon catastrophe—and yet it works. Melodrama was always Dumas' strength, and the more outrageous it was, the more effectively it played.

The story is simplified on film: there are three rather than four betrayals. The three antagonists all meet bad ends, but they die differently from the way they do in the book. The story's action opens on a day in 1815 when the *Pharaon* sails proudly into Marseilles Harbor. Mondego (Sidney Blackmer) covets the hand of the lovely Mercedes (Elissa Landi), who is engaged to seaman Edmond Dantes (Robert Donat). Mondego and his two conspirators, Danglars (Raymond Walburn) and Raymond de Villefort, Jr. (Louis Calhern), plot to apprehend Dantes just as he is about to take his marriage vows. Lies are invented, conspiracies hatched, and Dantes is torn from the arms of his impending bride, brought in secret to the desolate dungeon of the Chateau d'If, and placed there in solitary confinement. He is declared dead and will most assuredly be forgotten.

Dantes loses all track of time; his clothes become filthy and ragged and he becomes increasingly bitter. He is a young man, but he has become so heavily bearded and pale that he appears to be old. Time has passed from the days of Napoleon Bonaparte and his abortive *coup d'etat* to the luxurious period of the monarch Louis Napoleon. Then, one day when he hears a tapping sound, Dantes becomes aware that somebody is digging in the dungeon cell beyond his. He aids his unknown friend in tunneling through from his own cell, and rejoices in looking again upon a human face. The man, who is the Abbe Faria (O. P. Heggie), has also be unjustly imprisoned, living on the fragments of food set wordlessly in a small trapdoor. Now that the two men are able to be companions the good Abbe spends part of each day in educating Dantes, and telling him finally of the fabulous treasures hidden on the island of Monte Cristo.

As the old Abbe labors, he tires, sickens, and dies. Sewing himself into his old friend's death sack, Dantes is cast into the sea, struggles free, and is picked up by roving smugglers. He pretends to be ill, and is left on the island of Monte Cristo, to be picked up later. He searches for and finds the cave with its untold treasures and then feels that the world is his at last.

The mysterious "Count" of Monte Cristo makes his appearance upon the Parisian social scene accompanied by his faithful servant Jacopo (Luis Alberni). He seems to be middle-aged, handsome, with greying hair, and rich with untold wealth. He uses his enormous wealth to avenge his suffering upon those who caused it. First, the wretched Danglars is destroyed, driven to suicide after he learns of Monte Cristo's true identity. It is Mondego who next feels the relentlessness of the mysterious Count's persecution, and he is driven mad. Mercedes, as it turns out, married Mondego and now is the mother of a handsome young son by him. The son, Albert (Douglas Watson), challenges Monte Cristo to a duel, but Mercedes appeals to the Count, and out of love for her he refuses to kill the boy in the duel. Albert then becomes his ally.

When the Count is arrested as Edmond Dantes, escaped prisoner, he exposes and ruins de Villefort, and his revenge is complete. There remains only forgiveness now, the admission of a love great enough to reunite the lovers torn so cruelly apart many years ago. There still can be happiness in years to come, and Mercedes and Dantes resume their love, finally able to obliterate the past. Their happiness extends also to Albert, who marries his love, Valentine (Irene Hervey), de Villefort's daughter.

Naturally, success of *The Count of Monte Cristo* rises or falls with the actor playing the Count. It rose to the heights with Donat; the Count was the kind of role that might have been written for him. It had everything. He played only a few roles in British films until he took on the role of Thomas Culpeper in *The Private Life of Henry VIII* (1933). His extraordinary good looks, his talent, and the beautiful richness of his voice were immediately arresting. Soon after this, Small enticed him to Hollywood, where he made *The Count of Monte Cristo*. Donat disliked Hollywood, however, because he was allergic to the weather, which brought on severe asthma attacks, and he soon returned to London. He subsequently refused to return to Hollywood for the roles of Peter Ibbetson, Chopin, Lawrence of Arabia, Romeo, Mr. Darcy, and Dr. Jekyll/Mr. Hyde because of his health. Donat went on to a highly successful career in British films which included *The Thirty-Nine Steps* (1935), *The Ghost Goes West* (1936), *Knight Without Armour* (1937), *The Citadel* (1938), and *Goodbye, Mr. Chips* (1939), which won him an Oscar at a time when everybody else was winning the Academy Award for *Gone with the Wind* (1939). He even outclassed Clark Gable and Laurence Olivier for Best Actor with his flawless and touching performance. Donat was dying when he made his last film, *The Inn of the Sixth Happiness* (1958); he died at the age of fifty-three.

The Count of Monte Cristo was filmed as early as 1913 in a version starring James O'Neill, and again in 1922 in a Fox production starring John Gilbert. There was also a *Son of Monte Cristo* (1940) produced by Edward Small with Louis Hayward starring, but this film was more of a sequel than a remake. More recently, *The Count of Monte Cristo* has been produced on British and American television, including a 1975 version with Richard Chamberlain in the title role.

DeWitt Bodeen

THE COUNTERFEIT TRAITOR

Released: 1962
Production: William Perlberg for Paramount
Direction: George Seaton
Screenplay: George Seaton; based on the book of the same name by Alexander Klein
Cinematography: Jean Bourgoin
Editing: Alma Macrorie
Running time: 140 minutes

Principal characters:
Eric Erickson	William Holden
Marianne Mollendorf	Lilli Palmer
Collins	Hugh Griffith
Baron von Oldenbourg	Ernst Schoder
Hans Holtz	Helo Gutschwager
Klara Holtz	Erica Beer
Ingrid Erickson	Eva Dahlbeck
Hulda Windler	Ingrid Van Bergen
Colonel Nordoff	Wolfgang Preiss
Otto Holtz	Carl Raddatz
Max Gumpel	Ulf Palme

When *The Counterfeit Traitor* was made, sex and violence in American films was still fairly mild, strong language was almost nonexistent, and spies were still being portrayed as crusaders for moral causes. 1961 was the year when John F. Kennedy began his presidency, and the time was still a few years away from the violence and cynicism which would permeate society and be reflected in a large percentage of American films. The filmed exploits, both whimsical and serious, of James Bond and all of the other movie spies were just about to burst onto the scene. *The Counterfeit Traitor* was perhaps the last of the traditional spy/adventure dramas. It was an adventure story with definite black-and-white moral values, using a World War II setting which offered little in the way of moral dilemmas to its audience.

Based on the actual story of Eric Erickson, a Brooklyn-born Swedish citizen, the film begins in Stockholm in 1942. Erickson (William Holden) is a prominent oil importer who has recently been "blacklisted" by the Allies for doing business with the Germans. In order to be taken off the list, Erickson is coerced by British agent Collins (Hugh Griffith) into posing as a Nazi sympathizer. The British want Erickson to become more involved with the Germans, find out about their oil refineries, and then pass the information back to the Allies. Erickson is reluctant, but finally agrees to become a "Counterfeit traitor." As part of his new image, he publicly insults his best friend Max Gumpel (Ulf Palme), a Jew, and makes many anti-Allied statements to business associates. He also visits the German embassy and makes an after-dinner speech praising Hitler. His new stance makes him unpopular with his old pro-Allied friends and so alienates his wife Ingrid (Eva Dahlbeck) that she leaves him. Ironically, only Max stands by him; he sends Erickson a note "temporarily suspending" their friendship until they can openly be friends again.

Erickson visits Germany often in his new status by pretending that he plans to build an oil refinery system between Germany and Sweden. He is thus allowed to tour various German oil plants and pass on valuable information to Collins. While in Germany he enlists the aid of two old friends, Baron von Oldenbourg (Ernst Schoder) and Otto Holtz (Carl Raddatz), and passes back information from agent Marianne Mollendorf (Lilli Palmer). Marianne is the socially prominent wife of a German colonel who has been an Allied spy for some time. She and Erickson at first pretend to be lovers, and then actually do fall in love. All of these people and various events in Germany eventually convince Erickson to work willingly for the British.

Otto Holtz is eager to work for Erickson as long as he can have a letter from the British officially acknowledging his assistance during the war, as a help to him when Germany loses. Baron von Oldenbourg, although not a Nazi, helps Erickson only because his son is in an Allied prisoner-of-war camp and Erickson "suggests" that it would be to his son's advantage to do so. Later, when Oldenbourg and Erickson see a striking Polish worker hanged before his coworkers, they both agree that their assistance to the Allies is necessary to rid Germany of the Nazis.

The recruitment of the spies is one of the two moral questions of the film. The other concerns Marianne. She is a Catholic and feels great guilt that some of the information she has passed on has inadvertently caused a school to be bombed, thus killing many children. She attends confession but realizes too late that instead of a priest, her confessor is a Gestapo agent who had been following her. She and Erickson are imprisoned and Erickson watches helplessly from his cell as she is executed. Brokenhearted yet still resourceful, he claims that they were only lovers and that he knew nothing of her spying activities, thus corroborating her own story. He is released from prison, although his room is bugged and he is followed.

He returns to Holtz's home after Holtz dies suddenly, as a friend consoling the bereaved family, and as an agent knowing that his letter to Holtz must be retrieved. He is not fast enough, however, as Holtz's son Hans (Helo Gutschwager), a twelve-year-old member of the Hitler Youth, catches him in the act of hiding the incriminating letter his father had asked for. Hans betrays Erickson to a Gestapo man, and Eric has no alternative but to kill the agent and run.

What follows is a shattering series of adventures as Erickson embarks on his escape to freedom through the underground movement. Various Allied agents in Germany and Denmark assist him in a hazardous route back to Sweden where he is met by Collins and his faithful friend Max. At the end, Erickson is confident that his activities helped to shorten the war, even if the personal price for him has been high. After the war, the real-life Erickson was exonerated and honored for his activities.

Producer William Perlberg and director George Seaton make authenticity paramount. They realize that art directors, with all the research available, could not match actual experience and environment, and also understand that competition for entertainment demanded that stories be set in "foreign-locales." Thus, the film was shot where it happened, on the streets, in the houses, and inside the trains and places where the real Eric Erickson went during his exploits. This film became one of the first to cater to the international market.

The film became complex as cast and crew moved from country to country, picking up vital scenes in the story against the real backgrounds. A key sequence, for example, was done inside the grim Moabit prison in the heart of Berlin. It actually was here that Erickson was taken by the Gestapo and forced to watch the shooting of Marianne. Other scenes used studios in Hamburg, Berlin, Copenhagen, and Stockholm. A selection of great European players, such as England's Griffith, Germany's Klaus Kinsky and Werner Peters, and Sweden's Dahlbeck and Palme, helps to internationalize the film. The distinguished French cinematographer Jean Bourgoin (who had just finished Jacque Tati's *Mon Oncle*) provides the excellent cinematography.

In spite of the demand of making a good return on the costly shooting ($4,500,000), *The Counterfeit Traitor* creates certain moments which are quite artistically and emotionally moving. The first moment is the sequence where Marianne is tricked at the confessional by a Gestapo agent. The audience watches the deception, seeing a phony priest hear her sins. She innocently talks, divulging her role as an Allied spy, until the priest asks "who else is involved?" She stops, thinks, then leans forward, realizing who she has been talking to, and lets out a deafening scream. Also well-done is the later sequence in which Erickson's cover is unmasked by Holtz's twelve-year-old son Hans. Erickson frightens the boy into believing that as the son of a traitor, he will be disgraced, his youth group uniform will be taken away, and his mother will suffer. His victory is short-lived, however, when the agent convinces the boy to inform on Erickson during an air raid with promises of a medal rather than disgrace.

Overall, Erickson's real-life exploits remind us of another era. At that time evil seemed to be more easily understood, men discerned right and wrong, opting for one or the other and finding the just reward as a consequence. Erickson was a reluctant spy who converted to the true moral side when no doubts were left.

Unlike so many patriotic wartime films, *The Counterfeit Traitor* captures a mood of excitement. Holden and Palmer are especially convincing in their roles. Location shots are also major factors in the film's success. Although 140 minutes is usually too long for any film, the script is tautly written, as excitement builds up here and there, explodes, and builds up again. If clichés intrude in the story at times, the plotting and scenery easily distract the viewer.

Lawrence Fargo

THE COUNTY CHAIRMAN

Released: 1935
Production: Edward W. Butcher for Twentieth Century-Fox
Direction: John Blystone
Screenplay: Sam Hellman and Gladys Lehman; based on an original story by
  George Ade
Cinematography: Hal Mohr
Editing: no listing
Running time: 85 minutes

Principal characters:
Jim Hackler .... Will Rogers
Ben Harvey .... Kent Taylor
Lucy Rigby .... Evelyn Venable
Elias Rigby .... Berton Churchill
Mrs. Rigby .... Louise Dresser
Sassafras Livingston .... Stepin' Fetchit
Hy Cleaver .... Frank Melton
Abigail .... Jan Duggan
Riley Cleaver .... Charles B. Middleton
Wilson Prewitt .... Erville Alderson
Uncle Eck .... William V. Mong
Freckles .... Mickey Rooney

To describe Will Rogers as merely a movie star is tantamount to calling Jesus of Nazareth only a carpenter—and to many people just as sacrilegious. For a generation of Americans, Will Rogers was almost a saint. His radio broadcasts were listened to religiously each week. His sayings—the most famous of which is, of course, "I never met a man I didn't like"—have become part of American folklore. He was a homespun American philosopher who dabbled in many crafts, including vaudeville, revue, journalism, and film acting.

Between 1918 and 1935, the year in which he died in a plane crash, Rogers starred in more than sixty features and shorts. The silent films did little to add to his success, but in the twenty-one sound features that he made for Fox, and later Twentieth Century-Fox, he created a screen persona which was peculiarly his own, and along the way he became the cinema's number-one box-office star. All of Rogers' films were natural subjects for him; he played a basic screen character, that of a simple small-town or rural man righting minor wrongs which mirror the major wrongs in American society in a simple fashion. He ad-libbed much in his films, using them as propaganda machines for his Democratic philosophies, a number of which, unfortunately, seem a little racist by today's standards.

In *They Had to See Paris* (1929 and Rogers' first talkie), Rogers plays a small-town fellow from Claremore, Oklahoma (his actual birthplace), who strikes oil and is taken by his family to Paris, where he shows the French that there is more honest sophistication in Claremore than in their capital city. In *So This Is London* (1930), he cements Anglo-American relations by pointing out that "God Save the King" and "My Country 'Tis of Thee" both have the same tune. In *A Connecticut Yankee* (1931), Rogers brings his affable simplicity to the Court of King Arthur in the film based on Mark Twain's story. In *Ambassador Bill* (1931), he is a most undiplomatic ambassador; in *State Fair* (1933), he is a farmer whose one interest in life, outside of his family, is a prize pig; and in *Doubting Thomas* (1935), he demonstrates the phoniness of small-town sophisticates. Only the three films that Rogers made for director John Ford—*Dr. Bull* (1933), *Judge Priest* (1934), and *Steamboat 'round the Bend* (1935)—are in any way removed from the usual Rogers style, probably because Ford proved more strong-willed than his star, and as such these films should not be considered typical Rogers vehicles.

The County Chairman, released in the last year of Rogers' life, is a perfect example of a typical Rogers production, containing all the classic elements that appeared in most of the star's films. It is not particularly well-known, despite its excellent direction by John Blystone (a man usually and unfortunately associated with the films of Laurel and Hardy). Were his name not on the credits, one could well surmise that *The County Chairman*'s director was John Ford. The film has the look of a Ford production, which is quite simply explained by its being made by Ford's studio. If ever an example could be used to disprove the *auteur* theory it is *The County Chairman*, which, viewed with any of Ford's Fox productions, proves that the *auteur* of a film is not the director but the studio.

The film is based on a classic story by George Ade about small-town politics in Wyoming of the 1890's. Rogers plays a local attorney named Jim Hackler who has adopted and brought up Ben Harvey (Kent Taylor), his candidate for public prosecutor; Harvey is fighting a political battle with Elias Rigby (Berton Churchill), an obvious blustering phoney who can only corrupt politics. To complicate matters, Harvey is in love with Rigby's daughter, Lucy (Evelyn Venable). Her mother (Louise Dresser) meanwhile, is an old girl friend of Jim Hackler. In the end, of course, Harvey wins both the girl and the election. Unlike reality, the best man always succeeds in a Rogers film; romance always triumphs and the American political machinery—sometimes with a spot of finagling by Rogers—always elects the honest man. It is life as Rogers the philosopher would wish it to be, and as his millions of devoted admirers hoped it would be under President Franklin D. Roosevelt. As *Variety* (January 22, 1935) wrote, "Story is simple, but the production, direction and histrionisms surmount everything to impress *County Chairman* for box-office satisfaction."

The County Chairman boasts a host of members of the Will Rogers company of character players. Venable and Taylor are perfectly solid, dull, and attractive in a small-town way as the young lovers. Dresser is the bosomy screen mother, understanding and tolerant of everything. Churchill is the blustering villain—although villain is too strong a word—whose eloquence cannot hide his basic fraudulent nature. He continually denies he is running for office, in the true American political tradition, leading Rogers to comment, "That's just the kind of men we want in politics in this country—men who are not candidates." Other Rogers film regulars include Ford's brother Francis, Frank Melton, Charles B. Middleton, William V. Mong, and Russell Simpson.

The quintessential Rogers' black and the cinema's most famous stereotyped black, Stepin' Fetchit, is also in *The County Chairman*. Generally, he does not have anything to do with the plot, but in this case he does add a touch of suspense to the ending by announcing the wrong winner in the race for state prosecutor. As Sassafras Livingston, Fetchit's chief function is to amble slowly around the film, muttering almost indecipherable comments. He is slow in speech, movement, and in thought. To some he is a racist slur, but to many others he is the character he is portraying. In *The County Chairman*, Fetchit uses the pretense of the continuing births of new children to gain dollars from white people for the honor of having the new offspring named after them. Only Rogers sees through the fraud, but he is too kind to expose Fetchit, particularly when his own political rivals are ever willing to pay out dollars to the black. Fetchit's lethargic actions somehow seem an integral part of Rogers' small-town America.

The films of Rogers reflect the man's beliefs, tolerance, and moral stance. As such they succeed. Behind Rogers' humor there is a seriousness of purpose which the philosopher never sets aside. His films may appear dated—even quaint—but they stand as living testaments to his philosophies and ideals. Few filmmakers can make such a claim.

Anthony Slide

CRIME WITHOUT PASSION

Released: 1934
Production: Ben Hecht and Charles MacArthur; released by Paramount
Direction: Ben Hecht and Charles MacArthur
Screenplay: Ben Hecht and Charles MacArthur; based on the story *The Caballero of the Law* by Ben Hecht and Charles MacArthur
Cinematography: Lee Garmes
Editing: no listing
Running time: 70 minutes

> *Principal characters:*
> Lee Gentry .... Claude Rains
> Carmen Brown .... Margo
> Katy Costello .... Whitney Bourne
> Eddie White .... Stanley Ridges
> Buster Malloy .... Paula Trueman
> O'Brien .... Leslie Adams
> Della .... Greta Granstedt
> Miss Keeley .... Esther Dale
> Lieutenant Norton .... Charles Kennedy
> Judge .... Fuller Mellish

Ben Hecht and Charles MacArthur were two of this century's leading playwrights and screenplay writers, responsible for *The Front Page* (1931) and *Twentieth Century* (1934) among many others, who had the happy knack of writing works which appealed both to the masses and to the intelligentsia. Like most writers, they found Hollywood's manner of film production distasteful, but unlike most writers, they decided to do something about it. In 1934, they created their own company, which would combine the best techniques of Broadway and Hollywood. Hecht and MacArthur gathered around them a small staff and made their headquarters not in Hollywood but at the former Paramount Astoria Studios on New York's Long Island. They jointly directed their own productions, with noted cameraman Lee Garmes joining them as associate director; it was an astonishing move to have the cameraman as director, but one certainly not without merit, since a cameraman could best understand lighting set-ups, camera angles, and the basic look of each scene. In all, Garmes photographed eleven films scripted by Ben Hecht, who once wrote, "Nothing I ever encountered in the movies was as uniquely talented as the eyes of Lee Garmes." The production team of Hecht and MacArthur turned out only four features: *Crime Without Passion* (1934), *The Scoundrel* (1935), *Soak the Rich* (1935), and *Once in a Blue Moon* (1936). Although only the first two were moderately successful, the team's effort was a noble experiment in independent production belonging more to the present than to the 1930's.

In their first production, *Crime Without Passion*, Hecht and MacArthur give strong indication of what type of filmmaking they planned. The sets are stark and simple, reminiscent of the stage rather than the screen. For their leading man, they chose Claude Rains, who had just made a big hit in *The Invisible Man* (1933), but who in that film had hardly given the impression he was capable of playing the complex hero of *Crime Without Passion*. The two leading ladies were both unknown. Margo was a dancer, chosen because she photographed well and because the character she was portraying was a dancer. Whitney Bourne was a New York socialite with no previous film experience. As *Photoplay* (October, 1934) explained, "For Hollywood's star system, they have supreme contempt. In choosing a cast for their pictures they use Broadway technique. In other words, they search for players who will fit parts, not for people who are known as favorites."

Crime Without Passion probably has one of the most stunning openings ever conceived, an impressive pseudo-Freudian montage of an eye, the vague image of a man firing a gun, a drop of blood, and then three women, in white, soaring from the blood up through the skyscrapers of New York. With maniacal laughter, they smash windows behind which lustful men and women make love, until the falling, broken glass spells out *Crime Without Passion*. As the first title explains, the three women are the Furies, the three sisters of evil who lurk behind men's dreams. The antihero of *Crime Without Passion* senses their presence as the plot unfolds and comments that they are looking in through the windows at his crime. The opening montage sequence, plus a shorter, less impressive one later in the film, was the work of Slavko Vorkapich, a Yugoslav immigrant who came to Hollywood in the 1920's and soon became recognized as the screen's expert at montage.

The film's leading figure—he is not a hero since he is a damnable character without ethics and totally egotistical, rather like the Noel Coward character in *The Scoundrel*—is a lawyer named Lee Gentry (Claude Rains). He is called "The Champion of the Damned" because his eloquent speeches in the courtroom have helped acquit many a guilty murderer. He is seen in action in the opening scenes, ridiculing the district attorney and the police officer investigating the murder. Later, after a not-guilty verdict is returned by the jury, he will admit unconcernedly that a miscarriage of justice has taken place. When the press—and one of the reporters here bears more than a coincidental resemblance to Hecht—question him about a Grand Jury investigation of his courtroom behavior and his tampering with evidence, Gentry makes a statement that "the only crime punishable by death is stupidity." It is a statement which he himself will prove to be true later. Of all Gentry's friends and colleagues, the only one that seems to have a genuine affection for him is his middle-aged secretary, Miss Keeley (Esther Dale).

Lee Gentry has fallen in love with wealthy and elegant Katy Costello (Whitney Bourne), but rather than simply admit to his former girl friend, nightclub dancer Carmen Brown (Margo), that he no longer loves her Gentry must devise a complex scheme to end the affair. When Carmen's former boyfriend Eddie White (Stanley Ridges) visits her, Gentry contrives to arrive immediately afterwards and feign jealousy in order to end the affair. All appears to have worked out as he planned, except that a fellow nightclub performer reveals to Carmen that Gentry knew more than he pretended.

Carmen sends a telegram to Gentry indicating that she will take her own life and, in a telephone call, hysterically says she cannot live without him. Gentry goes over to Carmen's apartment and, in a struggle, accidentally shoots her. Good—if not particularly honest—criminal lawyer that he is, Gentry quickly moves to cover up his crime. He fakes an alibi, pretending to have been at the movies all afternoon. He even tells Katy of his crime, knowing that by revealing the truth to her she will not give him away. Here his plan backfires, however, for although Katy will not expose him, neither will she have anything more to do with him. When the police officer and the district attorney come to escort him to a Grand Jury hearing, Gentry even tricks them into going via Carmen's apartment building so that he may retrieve an incriminating telegram that he had accidentally dropped there.

The Grand Jury, of course, exonerates the wiley Gentry, and that evening he goes to Carmen's nightclub—all part of his elaborate cover-up scheme— only to meet a female acquaintance who had accidentally seen him that afternoon and reveals she knows he was not at the movies at the time he claims. Gentry gets hysterical with her, just as her companion, Eddie White, returns to her table. The two men get into a ridiculous, unnecessary fight, and Gentry kills White. Turning from the body to the dance floor, Gentry is horrified to see Carmen appear—he had not killed her at all; the bullet had merely grazed her head. As Gentry has so succinctly put it at the beginning of the film, "the only crime punishable by death is stupidity."

Press and public alike are delighted to see Lee Gentry a broken man about to face trial for murder. He is being tried for murder in the first degree because in his elaborate plan to rid himself of Carmen Brown, he had threatened Eddie White, thus explaining the motive for the shooting in the nightclub. Gentry's alter ego, which appears frequently in double exposure during the second half of the film, helping him to cover up the supposed murder of Carmen Brown, now urges Gentry to take the murder weapon and shoot himself. Gentry cannot, and his alter-ego calls him a coward while the three furies laugh hysterically. In perhaps an unprecedented move for a film from this era, the technical credits appear on screen after the film is over, something which did not become commonplace until the 1960's.

Crime Without Passion was received with considerable enthusiasm by the critics. Mordaunt Hall in *The New York Times* (September 1, 1934) wrote, "It is a drama blessed with marked originality and photographed with consummate artistry." *Photoplay* (November, 1934) described it as "A picture you can never forget." *Variety* (September 4, 1934) considered it "An exciting seventy minutes of entertainment." The public, unfortunately, was less enthusiastic, and *Crime Without Passion* basically played only at art houses, such as the Filmarte in Los Angeles. Viewed today, it is a taut, tightly constructed, psychological melodrama, well photographed and conceived. The dialogue sounds stilted, however, not perhaps because of the writing but rather because of the delivery of inexperienced players.

Anthony Slide

THE CRIMSON PIRATE

Released: 1952
Production: Harold Hecht for Warner Bros.
Direction: Robert Siodmak
Screenplay: Roland Kibbee
Cinematography: Otto Heller
Editing: Jack Harris
Running time: 104 minutes

> *Principal characters:*
> Captain Vallo, The Crimson Pirate ... Burt Lancaster
> Ojo .... Nick Cravat
> Consuelo .... Eva Bartok
> Baron Gruda .... Leslie Bradley
> Humble Bellows .... Torin Thatcher
> Professor Prudence .... James Hayter
> Sebastian, El Libre .... Frederick Leister

There is a joy found in *The Crimson Pirate* that exists in few other films. Whether it is through Burt Lancaster's smiling asides to the audience or through the near-slapstick distortions of scientific principle and historical facts that this feeling of impish amusement is conveyed is of little significance. What is crucial is that everyone from director Robert Siodmak on down was able to appreciate the limitations of a project of this nature, shot on location without the facilities of a modern Hollywood studio, and abandon themselves to the fun inherent in the script. If it did nothing else, *The Crimson Pirate* can certainly be remembered as one film which focused almost entirely on thrills and the exhilaration of exciting action.

As the film opens the Crimson Pirate (Burt Lancaster) overtakes a king's ship bound for the isle of Cobra. It is discovered that the cargo of the captured ship is a large cache of munitions and the sole passenger is Baron Gruda (Leslie Bradley), an emissary from the king sent to crush an impending rebellion on the island headed by a lover of democracy called "el Libre." In true pirate fashion the captain of this band of cutthroats plans to sell this booty of captured munitions to the rebels while at the same time informing the king's men where the rebels are based. In order to do this he must first rescue el Libre from prison where he awaits execution. This beautiful double-cross is complicated when the captain falls in love with Consuelo (Eva Bartok), el Libre's daughter.

Realizing that the Crimson Pirate's new plan to turn the guns over to the rebels without payment violates the "pirate code," the crew decides to mutiny. The newly elected skipper, Humble Bellows (Torin Thatcher), cannot kill his captain so he sets the Crimson Pirate, his first mate Ojo (Nick Cravat), and

Professor Prudence (James Hayter), an associate of el Libre, adrift shackled to a small dingy without food or water. By a clever bit of deductive reasoning Professor Prudence manages to capsize their dingy and eventually walk to shore using air trapped in the overturned boat to breathe. It soon becomes apparent that the Crimson Pirate must join the rebels if he is to rescue his crew, who have themselves been double-crossed by the treacherous Baron Gruda, save el Libre, whose real name is Sebastian (Frederick Leister), from his planned execution, and snatch Consuelo from the greedy hands of the governor of Cobra, who intends to marry her in the hopes of stopping the rebellion. At the back of his mind, however, is the overriding desire to destroy Gruda.

A wild battle takes place on the day of the governor's planned wedding with all sorts of crazy, anachronistic weapons, high-explosives, hot-air balloons, and flame throwers designed by Professor Prudence. With this exotic arsenal and the element of surprise it is hoped that the rebels can overcome the king's troops. The inevitable final showdown takes place onboard the Baron's ship. The Crimson Pirate and his repatriated crew engage the king's marines in savagely funny hand-to-hand combat. The outcome of this free-for-all puts Consuelo in the arms of the Crimson Pirate and the mute Ojo into a comic mime forecasting the perils of wedlock.

"Remember, in a pirate ship, in pirate waters, in a pirate world ask *no* questions; believe only what you see. . . . No! believe half of what you see!" From these few well-chosen words from Lancaster before the credits of the film, Siodmak manages to create the perfect aesthetic climate for one of Hollywood's purest examples of high-camp entertainment. Shot on location in Europe, this remarkable swashbuckler features Lancaster and his former circus partner Cravat as a pair of devil-may-care pirates. The film is nonstop action from start to finish. Throughout the twisting plot, Lancaster as the Crimson Pirate, seems to embody the reincarnated spirit of Douglas Fairbanks. There are sequences in which Lancaster and Cravat elude two squads of guards through acrobatic feats that can only be described as sheer escapism.

A review of Siodmak's career as a director reveals some interesting facts. One is his association with Lancaster from his debut in the stunning *film noir The Killers* (1946) and the equally celebrated *Criss Cross* (1948). Another fact is his peripheral treatment of escapist genre films such as *The Son of Dracula* (1943) and *The Cobra Woman* (1944). In *The Crimson Pirate* Siodmak is able to combine both of these strengths to create one of Hollywood's most popular swashbucklers. Although this film does not have the element of studio-based control which is so apparent in the films Siodmak made at Universal and for David O. Selznick during the mid-1940's, there is a certain charm in the exploits of the Crimson Pirate that allows it to transcend its modest budget. The stunts performed by Lancaster and Cravat are nothing less than incredible, as they bounce from building to building, run toward a three-story-tall grain silo that is splitting at the seams, and hang from ropes attached to a hot-air balloon in order to transfer onto the rigging of a ship anchored in a secluded harbor.

Warner Bros. had a great tradition of swashbucklers with films such as *Captain Blood* (1935), *The Sea Hawk* (1943), and *The Adventures of Robin Hood* (1938), starring Errol Flynn. With *The Crimson Pirate* and *The Flame and the Arrow* (1950) Lancaster almost singlehandedly rejuvenated Warner Bros.' role as the prime producer of swashbuckling films. By the early 1950's, however, audiences were not as eager to suspend disbelief and give in to a dashing hero, and the genre soon died.

There is a certain panache that Flynn possessed that was able to permit him to transcend the banality of the scripts of the later swashbucklers such as *The Master of Ballantrae* (1953) and *The Adventures of Captain Fabian* (1951). Lancaster, on the other hand, was more at home in the broad lampoon of the swashbuckling tradition found in *The Crimson Pirate* than in the earlier, more serious *The Flame and the Arrow*. This comic sense has rarely been displayed by Lancaster on screen, however; his acrobatics were displayed well in *Trapeze* (1956), but few of his later films deviated from the serious, almost melodramatic roles with which he has become associated. While *The Rainmaker* (1956) and *Elmer Gantry* (1962), the latter for which he won an Oscar, contain many light, playful moments, it is the Lancaster of *The Sweet Smell of Success* (1957) and *Seven Days in May* (1964) that most filmgoers remember. It is unfortunate that in recent years he has confined himself (or has been confined) to brooding characterizations.

Carl F. Macek

CROSSFIRE

Released: 1947
Production: Adrian Scott for RKO/Radio
Direction: Edward Dmytryk
Screenplay: John Paxton; based on the novel *The Brick Foxhole* by Richard Brooks
Cinematography: J. Roy Hunt
Editing: Harry Gerstad
Running time: 86 minutes

Principal characters:
Captain Finlay .... Robert Young
Sergeant Peter Keeley .... Robert Mitchum
Montgomery .... Robert Ryan
Ginny Tremaine .... Gloria Grahame
The Man ....Paul Kelly
Joseph Samuels .... Sam Levene
Mary Mitchell .... Jacqueline White
Floyd Bowers .... Steve Brodie
Mitchell ....George Cooper
Leroy .... William Phipps

Post-World War II film releases from Hollywood often turned to less appealing aspects of American life such as racial bigotry, religious animosity, and crime for thematic story lines. In the case of the 1947 film *Crossfire*, racial hatred manifested by the vicious anti-Semitic soldier, Montgomery (Robert Ryan), leads to a tragic conclusion: the murder of a Jew in a senseless and brutal fashion. Although 1947 would also witness the release of another major American film dealing with the existence of anti-Semitism in America, the Oscar-winning *Gentleman's Agreement*, *Crossfire* had the added distinction of treating a sociological problem within the context of a suspenseful narrative, carefully designed by director Edward Dmytryk to draw the audience into the inner world of a bigot.

In the story, Montgomery harbors an irrational hatred for foreigners and Jews. He is a soldier on active duty who conveys his seething hatreds to anyone who will listen. He is obsessed and fearful of the "contamination" he believes will be the natural result of contact with Jews. As the character is artfully developed by Ryan, we see a man with the mind and temperament of a bully, often caught up in the midst of a racial diatribe. In a bar one night with two of his soldier friends, Montgomery finds himself seated next to a mild-mannered man named Joseph Samuels (Sam Levene) whom Montgomery discovers is a Jew. As he becomes drunker, Montgomery's rage increases toward the Jew; he sees himself confronted with his absolute enemy and, in a spasm of brutality passively watched by his army friends, Montgomery pursues the man outside and beats him to death. The murder scene stuns the audience, for the crime itself is so wrapped up in the taunting, irrational anti-Semitism of Montgomery. There is a motive for the crime: a man is dead because of what he is pictured to be within the paranoid mind of a disturbed human being.

Now that the narrative has been firmly established and a motive for a crime, however senseless, planted in the audience's mind, it remains for the director to shift the focus of the film to the major theme: the discovery by men of good will—in this case the civilian police inspector Captain Finlay (Robert Young)—that hatred can inspire murder. Finley begins to understand the crime. Through careful reconstruction of the facts of the crime itself based on the recollections of one of the soldiers who has known Montgomery and who watched him murder Samuels, Finlay sees a motive. Through careful crosscutting, director Dmytryk shows how Finlay makes a case against Montgomery, slowly, with great care for details. Montgomery himself knows that he must cover up and protect himself. Realizing that he will soon be directly accused by the soldier, Montgomery kills him. The investigation, continues, however, and, aided by army Sergeant Peter Keeley (Robert Mitchum), a trap is constructed.

Together with the police, Keeley has amassed evidence directly implicating Montgomery in Samuels' murder. Through careful cross-examinations in Finlay's office, Keeley confronts those who knew Montgomery well, and, as the camera focuses tightly on the faces of Montgomery's acquaintances, the depth of the man's racial sickness is made plain: each person who knew Montgomery was aware of the incredible hatred the soldier felt. Once Montgomery himself is brought to face his accusers, his shifting glances and strained voice articulate what Finlay and Keeley have long since discovered. Montgomery is placed under arrest, attempts to escape from jail, and is shot and killed.

It is the suspense involved in the investigation of the personality and life of Montgomery that carries the entire film. Although it is not easy to understand the basis of Montgomery's attitudes (his blind hatred of anything he considers to be different is never actually explained; the actual causes are, one is led to believe, part of an aura of religious and racial animosity that simply exists within society), it does become clear that tragedy will result from such feelings. Dmytryk's direction carefully pulls together the subtle nuances of the very real personality changes occurring within the minds of the major characters. Finlay is appalled by what he sees in Montgomery's life; the camera closes in on his face as he begins to unravel for himself the motive for the crime. In a startling moment of brilliant cinematography, the audience can note the disgust Finlay feels as he stares at the accused soldier. Here is a man of good will who, for the first time in his life, discovers hatred in the face of another man.

Crossfire avoids a simplistic presentation of a highly charged theme. The nature of the story—a man obsessed by a furious bigotry causing him to respond and act—might have been, in the hands of less skilled filmmakers, turned into a moralistic and didactic work. Instead, one is introduced, through the superb acting of Ryan, to a character whose feelings and reactions are imbued with a realistic fervor; Montgomery hates openly, and all of his overt mannerisms are carefully crafted. There are, for example, several scenes in which Montgomery, confronted by his accusers, dramatically changes—his face begins to reveal the psychopathic nature of his illness. Dmytryk has established a tempo for the film—sharply defined crosscuts illustrating the reactions of Finlay to the emotional diatribes of Montgomery—that manage to convey a sense of the depth of the man that the policeman has encountered. The same is also true of the scenes involving Montgomery and Keeley, a man who, like Finlay, discovers a hatred he has never experienced before. *Crossfire* deserves attention as a psychological portrait that focuses on men under great pressure of discovery, and also as a social message film.

At the same time that one becomes involved with the discovery and changes taking place in the minds of the major characters, there is always a sense of the tragedy inherent in the film's theme: an innocent man has been murdered. The gentleness of the victim's expressions are in marked contrast with those of his murderer. Once again, the camera captures the sense of discovery felt by the victim who, although he is unaware of his ultimate fate, still feels through the malicious tension conveyed by Montgomery that the man he has met, through accident, is evil.

By juxtaposing several simply photographed scenes (much of the film's action occurs within the confines of simply staged sets), Dmytryk and his players have accomplished a great deal. The viewer is presented with a case study of a perverted crime. Despite the occasional lengthy dialogue between the central characters, *Crossfire* succeeds as a dramatic rendering of what was, in the postwar world of American society, a seriously neglected problem. Film critics were quick to notice that the film was setting a pattern for an improved, although uncomfortable, thematic emphasis; the darker side of human motives had, it seemed, finally arrived in Hollywood.

The film, which was shot entirely at night, has held its dramatic impact over the years. Although *Gentlemen's Agreement* won an Oscar that same year as Best Picture, contemporary critics feel that *Crossfire* is by far a better film.

Larry S. Rudner

THE CRUEL SEA

Released: 1953
Production: Leslie Norman for J. Arthur Rank; released by Universal
Direction: Charles Frend
Screenplay: Eric Ambler; based on the novel of the same name by Nicholas Monsarrat
Cinematography: Gordon Dines
Editing: Jerome Thoms
Running time: 121 minutes

Lieutenant Commander Ericson	Jack Hawkins
Sub-Lieutenant Lockhart	Donald Sinden
Sub-Lieutenant Ferraby	John Stratton
Sub-Lieutenant Morell	Denholm Elliott
Julie Hallam	Virginia McKenna
Mrs. Morell	Moira Lister
Chief Petty Officer Watts	Liam Redmond

The cruel sea is the bleak and cold North Atlantic, where, during the grimmest hours of World War II, British convoys ran an unseen gauntlet of German submarines to maintain England's lifelines with the outside world. Ealing Studios' 1953 production of *The Cruel Sea*, however, opens with the ocean at peace while a calm voice narrates the film's prologue: "This is the story of an ocean, of two ships and a handful of men." Accordingly, the heroes of the story are the men, the heroines are the ships, and the villain, of course, is the sea—"the sea that man has made more cruel."

Eric Ambler, a master of suspense fiction, performed the difficult task of adapting Nicholas Monsarrat's long and somewhat cliché-ridden novel to the screen. The screenplay, in fact, improves upon the novel by eliminating the author's emphasis upon various sailors' lives ashore and instead focusing with an almost documentary fidelity upon the war at sea. Concentrating on a handful of seamen in a small ship, the film tells only enough of their personal histories to make their struggle with the sea more human.

The sea in the film is perhaps more capricious than cruel. In the novel, Monsarrat had been primarily concerned with the unpredictable cruelties of the sea, wh ile Ambler and the film's director, Charles Frend, are more interested in the overwhelming demands made by war upon men trained only for peacetime existence. Thus, the film concentrates upon vital trials and tortures, often of the body but more frequently of the mind. Of the ship's officers, only Captain Ericson (Jack Hawkins) is a professional seaman. Much of the plot's interest arises from the transition of the young lieutenants from journalists, bankers, and lawyers into seasoned sailors.

Ericson is captain of *H.M.S. Compass Rose*, a corvette, a British vessel somewhat smaller, slower, and uglier than an American destroyer but an important early World War II weapon against U-boats. The ship's other major officers are Sub-Lieutenant Lockhart (Donald Sinden), a former freelance journalist; Sub-Lieutenant Ferraby (John Stratton), an ex-bank clerk; and Sub-Lieutenant Morell (Denholm Elliott), formerly a lawyer. These men are depicted in their early nervousness as the film opens and the *Compass Rose* attends to its grim, relentless, and exhausting business. There is convoy after convoy interrupted by fiery encounters with submarines, desperate rescues, and gut-wrenching jobs of first aid. Through these episodic experiences emerges the growing capability and confidence of the young officers and crew. Particularly significant is the growth of Lieutenant Lockhart, who becomes first officer after a bullying, Queeg-like older lieutenant is removed. He sees plenty of action, becoming increasingly war-hardened.

Between voyages Lockhart falls in love with a pretty WREN, Julie Hallam (Virginia McKenna), and has a relationship that omits the novel's explicit sex and tragic ending. On approximately the same schedule, the other officers also make alterations in their lives. Morell comes gradually to the realization that his wife, an actress (Moira Lister), is, in fact, a tramp, and the middle-aged courtship of the chief engineer, Chief Petty Officer Watts (Liam Redmond), reaches a sudden termination through his fiancée's death in a London bomb blast.

The brutality of warfare rises to a gruesome height when Ericson is forced to decide whether, in order to depth charge a U-boat thought to be nearby, he should drop his explosives into a sea already filled with swimming merchant sailors escaping one of the convoy's sinking ships. Regulations say that he must, and the scene is rendered with brutal clarity. Finally the *Compass Rose* herself is torpedoed, and most of the crew sink with her. In a scene rendered with the most meticulous realism of any such scene in film history, the process of abandoning ship is tragically effected. The small band of survivors endure a nightlong ordeal on two life rafts upon a rolling, freezing sea. After a period on shore during which all of the officers' individual stories reach fruition, Ericson goes aboard a new command, *H.M.S. Saltash Castle*, and returns to sea. The film ends undramatically with Ericson on the bridge of his new charge announcing through his speaking tube, "Finished with main engine."

Despite its episodic construction, the film is held together through its skillful evocation of the extraordinary heroism of ordinary men. Some of the vignettes, well acted by a cast of relatively unknown performers, are a little too slickly contrived, but several powerful sequences stand out. Notable are the stunned reaction of two petty officers to the tragic bombing that has killed an only relative; the captain's awful although necessary decision to run down the swimming, helpless survivors of a torpedoed vessel in order to attack a hidden submarine; and the graphic but humorous description of antisubmarine detection recounted by a serious and self-possessed instructor.

These ordinary men in extraordinary circumstances are portrayed by an extremely worthy and competent, although hardly star-filled cast. Hawkins, for example, as the harried captain projects a polished portrait of a man ready to accept the staggering burden of command. Yet he is also a man with human frailties who almost cracks under the strain but who finally turns out to be made of stern enough stuff to finish the job. It is doubtful whether any actor will ever equal the realistic suffering, fatigue, and nervous strain of Hawkins in the film's most significant role—a captain who molds a green crew of lawyers, reporters, and bank clerks into first-class seamen. Sinden as the first lieutenant is also worthy of note. Although his character does not possess the captain's self-assurance, he exhibits a grim determination. As interpreted by Sinden, the officer believably grows and adapts under his taxing wartime assignment.

Perhaps the greatest strength of *The Cruel Sea* is that it provides a graphic record of a crucial chapter in English history. The stature of its drama is, in fact, surpassed by its journalistic, documentary realism. Director Frend mirrors the sea in all its moods and fills in vast seascapes with brush-stroke detail. The screen reflects watchful, intent faces behind binoculars, scanning the ocean in violent activity and treacherous calm; the radar antenna circling an invisible horizon; the sea churning with depth charges; and blinding flashes of gunfire at night. Neither the sea nor the desperate turmoil of abandoning ship has ever before or since been rendered with such meticulous camera realism. There are the harsh shots of shells bursting on deck armor, the shattering explosions of ammunition, and the groaning, shuddering image of a small ship floundering in a monstrous sea. Although many war films will surpass *The Cruel Sea*, as drama, the film will long be studied for its nonglamorous rendering of the transition of ordinary men into warriors. As a documentary, it may well rank with *Victory at Sea* (1944) in its realistic depiction of the war on water.

Stephen L. Hanson

CRY THE BELOVED COUNTRY

Released: 1951
Production: Zoltan Korda for Lopert Films
Direction: Zoltan Korda
Screenplay: Alan Paton; based on his novel of the same name
Cinematography: Robert Krasker
Editing: David Eady
Running time: 105 minutes

Principal characters:
Stephen Kumalo	Canada Lee
James Jarvis	Charles Carson
Reverend Msimangu	Sidney Poitier
Father Vincent	Geoffrey Keen
Margaret Jarvis	Joyce Carey
Martens	Michael Goodlife
Absalom	Lionel Ngakane
John Kumalo	Edric Connor
Gertrude	Ribbon Dhlamini
Mary	Vivien Clinton
Mrs. Kumalo	Albertina Temba

Cry the Beloved Country is the sort of film generally praised for its good intentions and noble characters rather than for the successful dramatic realization of its themes. It is a bit too plodding to be particularly revelatory and too self-conscious to be electric. It is well-meaning, however, and it does get its anti-apartheid message across.

The film opens in the country with parallel stories of two men who have left their village to go to Johannesburg: black Absalom Kumalo (Lionel Ngakane), the son of Stephen Kumalo (Canada Lee), the local umfundisi, or priest; and white Arthur Jarvis (who is not seen on screen), the son of a wealthy farmer, James Jarvis (Charles Carson), who has devoted his life to bettering relations between black and white men. Absalom murders Arthur while robbing his home. Hearing that his son is in trouble, the umfundisi journeys to Johannesburg, where, with the help of priests from a poor mission, especially Father Msimangu (Sidney Poitier), Kumalo begins to search for Absalom and for his daughter, Gertrude (Ribbon Dhlamini), who has become a prostitute. He discovers that Absalom had been in a reformatory, and then had left to marry a girl whom he had made pregnant, and then, turning to robbery, had shot Arthur. Kumalo finds his son, but it is too late; the boy stands trial and is found guilty and sentenced to hang. Kumalo returns to his church believing that his son's shame dictates that he must leave it. Margaret Jarvis (Joyce Carey), Arthur's mother, dies, Kumalo sends flowers, and James tells him that it was her last wish that he build a new church for the village and that Kumalo must stay to be its umfundisi. If Kumalo leaves the countryside, it will mean that their suffering will have taught them nothing.

Cry the Beloved Country is a well-rounded film, carefully worked out so that each event has its parallel, each beginning its end; every negative act has its positive counterpart. It opens with a narrator praising the rich South African soil and saying that although some is fertile and well irrigated, nearby there is other land that cannot support its people. The young men have left their villages to seek work elsewhere. The film closes with Kumalo striding across the hills, looking at the glory of his "beloved country" and kneeling to pray. The film tells the stories of two men who go to Johannesburg and die there, one covering himself with honor and praise, the other becoming a criminal and dying a murderer's death. In both cases their fathers come after them and, in the city, learn to understand why their sons behaved as they did. James Jarvis does not approve of Arthur's mixing with blacks; he feels that even shaking hands with a black man is shameful. At Arthur's funeral, however, a black who worked with him offers to shake his hand and Jarvis takes it. He has been reading Arthur's thoughts on apartheid and prejudice and has begun to see how meaningful his son's life was. Kumalo, frustrated at every turn by the poverty and meanness of his people's lives and unable to find Absalom, becomes bitter and nearly loses his faith, but is restored by the kindness of Father Vincent (Geoffrey Keen), the head of the mission, and Reverend Msimangu. Even this sequence has its double. Martens (Michael Goodlife), the kind-hearted warden at the reformatory, temporarily loses his conviction that he can help people like Absalom who have been entrusted to him. Absalom's reversion to criminal behavior shakes his faith. In the last scene, Jarvis and Kumalo meet and shake hands. Both have turned away from resentment toward comprehension and peace.

The film has a tendency to become preachy, as in the rather static sequences in which Jarvis reads Arthur's ideas. The action simply stops, and director Zoltan Korda plasters Arthur's notes, full of compassion and do-goodism, up on the screen. Kumalo trudges around Johannesburg confronted by waste and destitution. In his somber way he tries to instill those he meets with some notion of "the right thing." He is like a black saint (and the film has a white one in the memory of Arthur) who has taken vows of poverty to move among the poor bringing the light. He is more human and believable at the beginning when, arriving in the city, he is taken in by a black sharpie who steals his bus fare, or when he confesses his dismay at everything that has happened and begins to feel sorry for himself.

The most meaningful statement *Cry the Beloved Country* makes is about the disruption of men's lives. The white man's greed has pushed ugly hills up out of the earth on the outskirts of Johannesburg. The black man's need for work has caused a social dislocation in his home village and in the city. There is not enough labor to work the farms; the towns are inhabited by the very old and the very young; and in the cities there is a lack of adequate housing for the people who flock there looking for work.

Over and over the film stresses the damage apartheid causes and the importance of the efforts men like Arthur are making to mend the wounds caused by separatism. When Kumalo rides through the suburbs of the city in a wooden third-class train compartment, he sees the luxurious apartments the whites inhabit. Then he finds his daughter living in Sophiatown, a collection of shacks slanting together on unpaved streets. For further contrast there is Arthur's home, a large airy house on a residential street. There is the difference in opportunities for white and black. Arthur has received an education and uses it to better the lives of men less fortunate than himself; Absalom Kumalo has none and is forced into a life of petty crime.

In spite of being filmed on location, *Cry the Beloved Country* has almost no visual style. The sharp black and white of the sun against the shanty towns and the gloomy interiors lit by naked light bulbs are presented without refinement. The white hills formed by the gold digging, the industrial area around Johannesburg, make a nighttime hell out of Kumalo's first look at the city. There is no stress on any of these aspects, however; the emphasis is entirely verbal, as the characters explain, sometimes repetitively, how they feel.

The acting is generally first-rate. Lee, grizzled and sorrowful, is a bit ponderous, but he is also moving and dignified. Not yet a star, Poitier has third billing in this, his second film; he is dynamic and brings energy to his role. The individuals in the film are, after all, spokesmen for a point of view; they are emblems as much as they are human beings, and as a result the film has an overall air of piety that becomes annoying at times.

Still, *Cry the Beloved Country* is a commendable effort, a film that actually has something worthwhile to say and delivers its message in a straightforward manner without bothering to make it more palatable by cloaking it in Hollywood prettiness. *Lost in the Stars*, the Kurt Weill/Maxwell Anderson musical based on Alan Paton's novel, opened on Broadway in 1949. The lyrics of "Train to Johannesburg" contain the theme of the film reduced to its most essential terms: "White man go to Johannesburg. He come back. Black man go to Johannesburg. Never come back." It is this dichotomy, indicative of inequality and injustice, which is the heart of the film.

Judith M. Kass

CUL-DE-SAC

Released: 1966
Production: Gene Gutowski for Filmways
Direction: Roman Polanski
Screenplay: Roman Polanski and Gerard Brach
Cinematography: Gilbert Taylor
Editing: Alastair McIntyre
Running time: 107 minutes

Principal characters:
George ....Donald Pleasence
Teresa .... Françoise Dorleac
Richard ....Lionel Stander
Albert .... Jack MacGowran

Roman Polanski's *Cul-de-Sac* was not well received when it had its premiere in New York in the winter of 1966. As the years have passed, however, its reputation has grown until it has become a regular fixture in revival houses. It is now considered one of Polanski's classic flms and is generally acknowledged as brilliant. *Cul-de-Sac's* early dismissal can most likely be attributed to the fact that it was only Polanski's third feature film, following *Knife in the Water* (1961) and *Repulsion* (1965), and audiences did not yet appreciate his style or orientation in filmmaking. Even those who did often found his subject matter distasteful. Because critics were put off by the unorthodox subjects and grotesque characterizations, they allowed themselves to become blind to Polanski's frequently marvelous directing technique.

Once their bizarre framework is accepted, however, Polanski's films provide a good deal of enjoyment, as well as offer some telling comments about the relationship of an individual to his environment, to his society, and to his fellow man. Polanski delights in keeping his audience on a string, a ploy used by many directors (especially Alfred Hitchcock), but seldom as effectively as in this film. The first indication of this technique is the choice of the deliberately enigmatic title, *Cul-de-Sac*. Since the entire film takes place on a lonely beach in Northumbria, England, with only one dwelling, a crumbling eleventh century castle, the conventional meaning of "cul-de-sac" as a dead-end street is useless. As the film develops, however, the audience gradually comes to realize that the characters are indeed on a dead-end street, but it is one of their own making. By choosing to live in such an isolated area, they have deluded themselves into thinking that they have bought their freedom from all the problems and responsibilities of the modern world. Polanski, however, does not let them off the hook so easily. Through a series of outlandishly unlucky and surrealistic coincidences, their problems compound and multiply until everyone is finally overwhelmed.

The film opens strikingly, with a hulking, sweating man in a rumpled suit pushing a small foreign car along a tide-slicked causeway on the coast. Ranting inside the car is his evidently seriously injured partner. Although the landscape looks thoroughly unfamiliar, more like a different planet than a foreign country, both men speak English, another twist from Polanski, whose previous films had been in Polish and French. What are these men doing here? How did they get to such an isolated location? Why does the injured one speak with a Cockney accent and the one pushing the car talk like an American gangster of the 1930's? Our curiosity is aroused, and Polanski keeps the game going by refusing to answer these and other questions that continue to accumulate as the film proceeds.

It eventually becomes clear, however, that there are no answers because there need be no questions. The men are there because it is absurd for them to be there; the occupants of the castle are likewise simply there, with a minimum of explanation. The point the film makes has nothing to do with motivations of the characters, their backgrounds, or any sort of conventional story logic. The theme of the film is the inability to run away from responsibility, and Polanski and his cowriter Gerard Brach devised the story to depict the theme in an odd, sometimes upsetting, but thoroughly entertaining way. Their vision has the improbability and vividness of a nightmare.

As the story continues, the character pushing the car, Richard (Lionel Stander), decides to follow the mysterious telephone poles by the road, reasoning that they will lead to a telephone. Reassuring his injured friend Albert (Jack MacGowran) that he will return with help, he sets off. Arriving at the castle, Richard is unable to rouse anyone. Dawn is breaking, and the occupants, if there are any, are still asleep, so he does the logical thing for a gangster: he breaks in. The castle itself is as absurd as its surroundings; the things most in evidence are squawking chickens and their byproducts, contributing to a refrigerator already full of rotten eggs. Famished, Richard disgustedly settles down to make an omelette and waits for somebody to appear.

The occupants of the house are a weak, ineffectual man, George (Donald Pleasence), and his incongruously beautiful wife Teresa (Françoise Dorleac). When they are first introduced, they are engaged in a sex game, with Teresa playfully tossing a woman's nightgown on George then dabbing makeup and lipstick on him. Too passive and foolish to do more than protest limply, George submits, and his humiliation is complete when he comes upon Richard, the very image of primal virility, while still dressed in this improvised costume.

Richard immediately takes charge of the situation, since George almost begs to be preempted whenever there is a decision to be made or an action to be taken. Richard's first priority is to get Albert out of the car and then to contact the mysterious Mr. Kattelbach, who employs these two mobsters, so that they can be rescued. The plans soon go awry: the tide has come in, almost swamping the car and drowning Albert; Kattelbach cannot send any-one right away to pick them up; and then, just after they get to the house, Albert dies from his gunshot wounds, evidently received on the unspecified "job" from which he and Richard have just fled.

Although the steps the characters take flow logically from one to the next, the original surreal premise allows everything to slide quickly and smoothly from mere disorientation to outright fantasy. In order to ensure that the weird couple will not call the police, Richard severs the telephone lines. Since it was a line of telephone poles that led to the castle in the first place, Richard's act of cutting the lines symbolically cuts him and the couple off from the outside world and any vestiges of reality. The entire context of the story is now exclusively the nightmare world of the castle.

There are intruders, but by the time they arrive, George, Teresa, and Richard are so bound up in their own situation, that the guests, who are old friends of George, are driven away. In a hilarious sequence, Richard is forced to masquerade as a butler, serving a disastrous luncheon to the unwanted visitors. Since the film is also about the destruction of carefully erected façades, we see that by disrupting their routine, Richard has indirectly done George and Teresa a favor—the guests are exposed as pompous, impolite bores, with a particularly nasty little child, as well as a pretty companion played by a very young Jacqueline Bisset, and the audience is delighted when George finally musters the wherewithal to kick them out.

By the film's end, everyone has been thoroughly demolished. George's wife stands revealed as an unfaithful tart, the castle and the only car are destroyed in a fire, Richard is killed in a shoot-out, and only George himself, master of his own private castle at last, is left. The conclusion is not so much downbeat as bitterly ironic; the story is, after all, not a tragedy but a black-humor lesson in the perils of worldly noninvolvement.

Joel Bellman

D.O.A.

Released: 1949
Production: Leo C. Popkin for United Artists/Cardinal
Direction: Rudolph Maté
Screenplay: Russell Rouse and Clarence Green
Cinematography: Ernest Laszlo
Editing: Arthur H. Nadel
Music: Dmitri Tiomkin
Running time: 83 minutes

> *Principal characters:*
> Frank Bigelow .... Edmond O'Brien
> Paula Gibson .... Pamela Britton
> Majak ....Luther Adler
> Miss Foster .... Beverly Campbell
> Mrs. Phillips .... Lynn Baggett
> Halliday .... William Ching
> Chester .... Neville Brand
> Marla Rakubian .... Laurette Luez
> Bell Hop .... Jerry Paris

An elementary thematic concern of literally every *film noir* involves the intrusion of a nightmarish criminal underworld into the orderly stream of everyday life, provoking an irreversible transition from a stable existence toward one filled with painful insecurity, rampant cynicism, and violent, unforeseen death. The heart of Rudolph Maté's *D.O.A.* lies well within this basic premise, and while it is by no means the perfect example of *film noir*, it does contain a great many specific elements normally associated with the classics of the genre. Both its underlying cinematic structure and its moral tone fall well within the confines of *film noir* sensibility, and its demonstration of the tendency for ordinary people to become enmeshed in a chain of events beyond their control places *D.O.A.* firmly inside the *film noir* tradition.

The primary inspiration for *D.O.A.* was a little-known German film entitled, *Der Mann, Der Seinen Morder Sucht* (1931, The Man Who Seeks His Murderer). Directed by Robert Siodmak, the film dealt with a dying man's frantic attempts to uncover the cause of his impending unnatural demise. *D.O.A.* maintains this basic plot premise in which a murder victim functions as his own detective, and by doing so, brings to the film a refreshingly unique point of view.

As the opening credits roll, we follow a man walking unsteadily along a dark street into a police station and through its winding corridors which inevitably lead to a door marked "Homicide Division." He is Frank Bigelow (Edmond O'Brien), an accountant who lives "in a little town called Banning out in the desert on the way to Palm Springs," a sedate little community lying just beyond the bright lights, wealth, and corruption of a more glittering metropolis. Bigelow informs a group of detectives that he wishes to report a murder, and when questioned as to just who has been killed, he blankly replies, "I was." Thus the stage has been set for a lengthy flashback in which Bigelow relates the unfortunate circumstances surrounding his "death." A superimposed whirlpool effect draws both viewer and participant into Bigelow's tormented brain as the story unfolds through his own narration.

We enter Bigelow's life just prior to his immersion into the dark world of vice, uncertainty, and death that is the realm of *film noir*. He is depicted here as a modestly successful accountant with a small yet comfortable office and practice. He has an attractive secretary named Paula Gibson (Pamela Britton) who happens also to be his fiancée, and a vague, undefined troubling of the spirit. As Bigelow prepares to leave for a short vacation in San Francisco, Paula outlines his dilemma as she sees it. "You're just like any other man only a little more so," she explains. "You have a feeling of being trapped, hemmed in, and you don't know whether or not you like it." Bigelow, then, is the archtypal *film noir* hero: an ordinary man leading an ordinary life, who has a stable income, the respect of his peers, and a woman's love, but who still yearns for the excitement and passion that the American dream has forever promised, but rarely delivers.

These initial scenes are shot in what has become known as the "American style," utilizing flat, straight-on medium shots and unadventurous, regularized lighting strategies, all of which are beacons to Bigelow's normal, stable lifestyle and environment. As Bigelow descends deeper and deeper into the horrors of the underworld, however, this style disappears and the more common *film noir* elements of odd angles, darkness illuminated by blazing spots of light, and irregular cutting begin to dominate.

On his first night in San Francisco, Bigelow goes to a nightclub with a group of people he met at his hotel. A jumping black jazz band pours hot music into the room. Musicians and patrons alike become caught up and swept away with the ecstasy of the crazy jive. Sexual tension and unbridled sensuality fill the club as Bigelow, also captivated by the atmosphere, approaches a beautiful blond seated at the bar. As he arranges a liaison for later in the evening, a sinister-looking man, seen only from the rear, switches drinks on Bigelow, who, concentrating on the woman , notices nothing. When he finally returns to his drink, he senses that it tastes peculiar, and promptly orders a replacement.

Returning to his hotel room, Bigelow is clearly caught between his feelings for the simple, loving Paula and the excitement generated by the big city and its sensual pleasures. He decides in favor of his stable relationship when he tears up the phone number given him by the blond at the bar, but his momentary deviation from the straight and narrow will not go unpunished.

Later in the evening he wakes up feeling quite ill, a condition he naturally attributes to too much alcohol and the nightclub atmosphere. When he still feels poorly in the morning, however, he undergoes a medical examination in a local hospital. The doctors inform him that he has suffered "luminous" (radiation) poisoning and will die within just a few days. To demonstrate, a doctor brings out a vial of radioactive liquid, turns out the lights, and shows Bigelow the fluid's luminosity. When he utters the words, "and then death!," he turns the lights back on. Clearly Bigelow has been murdered, but his lights have not yet gone out.

While preparations are being made to admit him to the hospital, Bigelow escapes in a panic. He races through the city streets, and everywhere he turns, he is reminded that as he is dying and that life continues all around him. He rests by a newsstand where displayed copies of *Life* magazine form a solid line around his head. He sees a lovely little girl playing ball and a beautiful young couple in love. People everywhere are enjoying life, but Bigelow is already "dead."

Determined to unmask his killers (the thought of going to the police or of spending his last hours with Paula never enter his mind), Bigelow begins a frantic and initially fruitless search. Finally, Paula tells him that a man named Phillips, for whom Bigelow had notarized a bill of sale for a shipment of iridium, has been desperately trying to locate him. Bigelow flies down to Phillips' Los Angeles-based firm and discovers to his horror that the man committed suicide just the day before. The iridium, he learns, was stolen and Phillips had been arrested for selling it. Bigelow reasons that Phillips had wanted to find him, as the notarized bill of sale would clear Phillips with the law. He also concludes that Phillips has been murdered and that his killers are also responsible for his own impending death. Both conclusions turn out to be true as Bigelow discovers that Phillips' wife (Lynn Baggett) and her lover Halliday (William Ching), who is now the company's new president, killed Phillips. After this first murder, they had poisoned Bigelow, fearing he knew everything. After a lengthy chase through the streets of Los Angeles, Bigelow kills Halliday and explains his story to the police. "All I did was notarize one little paper, one little paper out of hundreds," he tells the police. Those prove to be his last words, and he dies as the police silently look on.

D.O.A. is filled with *film noir* elements that lie firmly within its convoluted narrative. It is a film caught between the documentary and the surreal, for its plot content is entirely factual (a technical adviser is credited at the end) while its visual style constantly and ironically undercuts these facts. Darkness, crazy shadows, eerie music, odd camera placements, interior voices, flashbacks, wipes, dissolves, and ironic juxtapositions abound. Criminal types range from seemingly respectable businessmen to effete, cultured foreigners to childish, psychotic killers. The fact that Bigelow becomes an obsessed, revenge-motivated killer himself reveals the *film noir* assumption that any man can be as tough as the most vicious murderer when pushed far enough.

Above all, *D.O.A.* demonstrates that the criminal world always lurks just under the surface of, and often poses as, middle-class normality, pointing to a rather radical dichotomy between the seamy and safe sides of life, never letting go of the implication that the former will someday usurp the latter. All of these factors show the world as being a state of nature rather than an aberration, as it was in the gangster films of the 1930's. Chaos and confusion have become the new social norms. No one is safe; no one can control his life to any great degree; and no one can escape once the wheels begin to turn. Along with every other *flm noir* from 1945 to the present day, *D.O.A.* reveals that while American society may appear calm on the surface, dark currents run just beneath our rain-slicked city streets.

Daniel Einstein

DANGEROUS

Released: 1935
Production: Harry Joe Brown for Warner Bros.
Direction: Alfred E. Green
Screenplay: Laird Doyle; based on his original screen story
Cinematography: Ernest Haller
Editing: Thomas Richards
Running time: 80 minutes

> *Principal characters:*
> Joyce Heath .... Bette Davis (AA)
> Don Bellows .... Franchot Tone
> Gail Armitage .... Margaret Lindsay
> Mrs. Williams .... Alison Skipworth
> Gordon Heath .... John Eldredge

If Bette Davis had not won the Best Actress Academy Award in 1935, *Dangerous* might long ago have been forgotten. She gives a stunning performance as Joyce Heath, an alcoholic stage star with a self-destructive complex, although she herself described her condition as "punch drunk" by the time she started filming the story, because she had made four features in a row during 1934 and four more in 1935 when she was assigned to *Dangerous*. In 1934 Davis had played opposite Leslie Howard in *Of Human Bondage*, as the selfish, cruel waitress who persecutes the crippled hero who is hopelessly in love with her, and finally dies a wretched, lonely death. Despite the critical praise given to Davis for that film, she failed to win even an Academy Award nomination for her role. This caused considerable notoriety at the time, even creating a faction of Academy of Motion Picture Arts and Sciences members who wanted to start an unprecedented "write-in" campaign for the final voting. This did not happen, however, and Claudette Colbert won the Oscar for Best Actress for her role in Frank Capra's multi-Oscar-winning comedy, *It Happened One Night*.

When nominations for Best Actress were made the following year, Davis was among the women so honored, perhaps in response to her snub of the previous year. Although Davis has said that she thought that Katharine Hepburn in *Alice Adams* gave the best performance of 1935, Davis won the award, her first of two. Many people today agree with Davis' estimation of the film that it was "maudlin and mawkish, with a pretense at quality," but reviewers at the time praised it for its "colorful, punchy dialogue." They also applauded director Alfred E. Greene's treatment of the story as well as Ernest Haller's cinematography.

In the film, Joyce Heath (Bette Davis), a "vitally tempestuous creature," has ruined her reputation as an actress and has come to be regarded in her profession as something of a jinx. She not only has calamities happen to her, but also seems to invite them to happen with her outrageous, willfully unprofessional conduct, which includes excessive drinking. Joyce, however, not only has a record for self-destruction; she has also destroyed the men in her life, ruining or bankrupting anyone who has shown her the slightest affection or loyalty.

At the time when the story begins, no producer will hire her. Theatrically blacklisted, she has become an alcoholic in the depths of her own self-destruction. One night while she is in this state, a talented and wealthy architect named Don Bellows (Franchot Tone) recognizes her in a seedy bar. She is alone, downing straight gin at ten cents a glass (cheap even in 1935). She has been Bellows' idol ever since his adolescence when he saw her give a classic performance as the young Juliet in William Shakespeare's *Romeo and Juliet*. Fascinated again in spite of her bedraggled alcoholic condition, he takes her home with him. He lives in the country in the kind of perfect house that one would associate with a rich architect, but his housekeeper, Mrs. Williams (Alison Skipworth), is not very happy at the prospect of having a drunken woman in her house.

Joyce does not reform immediately while staying with Bellows. She delights in warning him to have nothing to do with her, and is alternately vicious, coy, hysterical, and full of self-pity. He is attentive and kind to her, however, and she eventually falls as much in love with him as he is with her. He breaks his engagement to wed Gail Armitage (Margaret Lindsay), a society girl, and puts up money for a play to star Joyce. He hopes that this will reestablish her as Broadway's leading actress. He also asks Joyce to marry him, but as it turns out, she is trapped in a secret marriage that she made long ago to Gordon Heath (John Eldredge), a failure whose worst crime was that he loved her to excess. She asks Heath for a divorce, but he, still in love with Joyce, refuses. Frustrated and furious, Joyce plans to destroy both Heath and herself in an accident. As she drives her car at top speed, she hits a tree, causing serious injury to herself and permanent damage to Gordon. By this time, Bellows, disillusioned and finally completely aware of Joyce's innate destructive nature, backs out of his association with her and goes back to Gail. Joyce finally recognizes the fact that she is her own worst enemy and by hard work reestablishes herself triumphantly on Broadway. She also devotes her private life to the disabled Gordon, the loving husband she almost totally destroyed.

The character of Joyce Heath gave Davis an opportunity to convey all of the most intense emotions of which she was capable, from anxiety to zealousness, including liberal amounts of her famous screen "bitchiness." The character of Mildred in *Of Human Bondage* had prepared her well for such a characterization. The happiness that Joyce finds at the finale of *Dangerous* is made believable only by the actress' convincing switch to selflessness. Davis is surrounded by professionals in *Dangerous* who were not as fortunate as she, however; Tone, Lindsay, Skipworth, and Eldridge are unable to do much with their one-dimensional supporting roles. The weak script creates pasteboard characters, and only the hardest work by the actors gives their characters even the slightest believability. The film is almost totally carried by the character of Joyce Heath, and Davis uses all of her well-known acting tricks to make the role credible.

Dangerous was successful at the box office, particularly as a "woman's picture," although men also responded to it. It turned out to be one of Warner Bros.' biggest financial successes of 1935. It might seem that after Davis won the Oscar for *Dangerous*, her home studio would have given her a succession of brilliant starring roles, but that was not the case. In the following year, Davis had only one role (with Howard and Humphrey Bogart in *The Petrified Forest*) that had any quality. After a subsequent film, *Satan Met a Lady* (1936), a zany version of *The Maltese Falcon* by Dashiell Hammett, she refused her next assignment and was suspended by Warner Bros. She promptly went to England to make a film, but was sued by her studio, who won the suit, forcing her to return to her contract work. Ironically, however, Warner Bros. treated her much better after that, gave her many roles well-suited to her screen *persona*, and even paid her legal costs for the lawsuit. Three years after *Dangerous* she earned her second Oscar for *Jezebel*, a film thought by many critics to be her best effort.

Davis was nominated for Oscars eight more times: for *Dark Victory* (1939), *The Letter* (1940), *The Little Foxes* (1941), *Now, Voyager* (1942), *Mr. Skeffington* (1944), *All About Eve* (1950), and *What Ever Happened to Baby Jane?* (1962). She is also the only woman ever to win the Life Achievement Award given by the American Film Institute.

Davis has stated that "Everything in my career dates B. B. (Before *Bondage*) and A. B. (After *Bondage*)." Actually it was *Dangerous* that officially turned the tide in her favor, although she still had to fight after that to get good starring roles at her studio. *Dangerous* is better than its script because Davis gives it "class"; she makes it an important film through her multidimensional, realistic, and flamboyant portrayal of Joyce Heath. *Dangerous* proved that Davis was a star in her own right and eased the way for her to demand and get star treatment from her studio. Grudgingly they came around, and somehow, even today, one thinks of Davis as a Warner Bros. star. She gave that studio prestige, and she was the only female star that they had who was a lasting box-office draw as well as a critic's delight.

Larry Lee Holland

THE DARK MIRROR

Released: 1946
Production: Nunnally Johnson for Universal-International
Direction: Robert Siodmak
Screenplay: Nunnally Johnson; based on an original story by Vladimir Pozner
Cinematography: Milton Krasner
Editing: Ernest Nims
Special effects: J. Devereaux Jennings and Paul Lerpae
Running time: 85 minutes

> *Principal characters:*
> Terry Collins/Ruth Collins .... Olivia de Havilland
> Dr. Scott Elliott .... Lew Ayres
> Lieutenant Stevenson .... Thomas Mitchell
> District Attorney .... Charles Evans
> Dr. Peralta's secretary .... Marta Mitrovich

The Dark Mirror is an intriguing murder mystery in which most of the detective work is done by a psychologist because the police lieutenant is baffled and seems to be blocked by a legal loophole. Identical twins are involved in the crime and become the focus of the film, but the carefully crafted script by Nunnally Johnson makes the device more than a clever gimmick. The audience remains just as perplexed as is the lieutenant because of an intricate series of events that lead bit by bit to a conclusion that seems consistent with what has gone before rather than being a surprise ending in which the least likely person is found to be the murderer.

Robert Siodmak was an ideal choice to direct the film, having directed *The Spiral Staircase* (1946), a quite successful thriller that also combined psychology and atmosphere. His opening is characteristic of the *film noir* works that were so prominent in the 1940's. We see a dark, shadowy room lighted only by a knocked-over lamp, then we see a broken mirror, and finally a man's body with a knife in it.

The film then shifts to the police detective investigating the crime, Lieutenant Stevenson (Thomas Mitchell). He finds that the murdered man was a Dr. Frank Peralta, and in interviews with people who knew him or lived near his apartment he finds that two people saw a young woman leave the apartment house at about the time the murder probably occurred. Based on information from Dr. Peralta's secretary (Marta Mitrovich), they suspect Terry Collins (Olivia de Havilland), who works at a newsstand in the medical building where the doctor had his office. When both witnesses positively identify her as the woman who left the scene of the murder, Lieutenant Stevenson is sure he has a strong suspect, but the young woman has a perfect alibi for the whole evening and three people support that alibi. In exasperation

Stevenson exclaims that the whole situation makes no more sense to him "than Chinese music."

When the lieutenant visits Miss Collins at her apartment he finds the solution to the puzzle, but he also finds himself in an even more difficult and frustrating predicament. Terry Collins has a twin sister, Ruth (also played by de Havilland), although no one at the medical building knows it, and the two alternate in the job at the magazine stand. Stevenson is now certain that he has in front of him one woman who may very well have killed Dr. Peralta and one who was four miles away at the time. His only problem is which is which. The sisters refuse to tell, and the law will not allow him to arrest both. They are taken to the office of the District Attorney (Charles Evans), but all he can do is lecture them on the immorality of what they are doing and set them free.

Lieutenant Stevenson is, however, unwilling to drop the case. He has learned that another doctor in the building, Scott Elliott (Lew Ayres), is a psychologist who has studied twins for much of his professional career. He asks Dr. Elliott if he can find out which sister is the guilty one, but Elliott balks at the idea because he believes that as a scientist he should not be doing undercover work for the police. He does, however, decide to study the two if they will agree, simply as a research project. The sisters, surprisingly, agree to be studied, partly because they need the money, and thus begins a long series of sessions at Elliott's office in which he examines each individually, using such devices as ink blots, word association tests, and a lie detector.

Meanwhile we have seen the sisters alone together and have found out that it was Terry who was in Dr. Peralta's apartment that night, but she does not admit killing him. In fact, she bitterly accuses Ruth of unfairly suspecting her.

After Elliott has studied them for a while, he tells the lieutenant that "one of the young ladies is insane," and two elements of the plot begin to interact. Dr. Elliott is falling in love with Ruth, and Terry—whom Elliott has described as "a paranoiac, capable of doing anything"—has begun to threaten Ruth and to try to drive her insane. Terry is motivated partly by fear of being found out and partly by jealousy, since she wants Elliott's romantic attention. "If you ever suspected me," Terry says to Ruth, "I don't know what I'd do." Later she tells Ruth that she (Ruth) has been waking in the night and sobbing, and she acts surprised that Ruth does not remember this; when she says to Ruth, "Just remember, I'll always be with you," it is chilling rather than comforting to the audience and to Ruth.

After Lieutenant Stevenson convinces Dr. Elliott that he must warn Ruth that her sister is dangerously mentally ill, Elliott calls Ruth and makes an appointment to see her that night at eleven o'clock. It is Terry, however, pretending to be Ruth, who talks to him on the telephone, setting up what could be a dangerous situation for both Ruth and Elliott. Ruth, however, happens to stop by to see the doctor earlier in the evening; so when Terry arrives at eleven we are fairly sure that the doctor recognizes her even though she continues the pretense that she is Ruth and Elliott talks to her as if she were Ruth. He tells her that her sister Terry is sick and abnormal and should receive professional treatment. He attributes Terry's illness to the agonies of jealousy she has felt because men have always preferred Ruth to her. When "Ruth" resists the idea of treatment for Terry, Elliott turns to her and says, "If *you* refuse, *Terry*, I'm afraid I'll have to tell who killed Frank Peralta and why." Elliott has deduced that Terry had come to realize that Peralta, who was dating Terry but frequently saw Ruth at the magazine stand (without knowing she was a different person), was actually in love with Ruth and that Terry killed Peralta in a jealous rage.

Then Lieutenant Stevenson calls with the news that Ruth has killed herself, and Terry and Elliott rush to the apartment, although Terry is unmoved by the news. At the apartment however, Terry becomes upset, claims to be Ruth, and "confesses" that it was her dead sister Terry who murdered Peralta. Then Ruth comes into the room alive and all the pretense and mystery are over. The film ends with Elliott asking Ruth, "Why are you so much more beautiful than your sister?"

Thus the case has been solved by a combination of the police detective's expertise and the psychologist's intellectual approach, with each gaining a new appreciation of the other's work. Indeed, even before the final events, the lieutenant has remarked to one of his associates that Elliott is "a very smart guy for a college man."

Although he gets only third billing, Mitchell as Lieutenant Stevenson gives what is in many ways the most engaging and convincing performance in the film. He conveys a common-sense professionalism as well as a conviction that no one should "beat a square rap." His performance is quite different from those of the usual "Irish drunk" parts which characterized much of his career. The excellent low-key portrayal of the psychologist by Ayres avoids the common Hollywood stereotype of the intellectual as too stuffy to know anything about real life.

It is, of course, de Havilland playing twin sisters (with some help from the special effects department) who is at the center of *The Dark Mirror*. She accomplishes the difficult task of constructing two separate characterizations that must many times overcome the confusion of the audience. The fact that she does so with subtle distinctions rather than exaggerated effect is a great credit to her talent and that of the director, Robert Siodmak. Ironically, de Havilland won the Oscar in 1946 for another film, *To Each His Own*; it was the first of her two Academy Awards for Best Actress. It is a tribute to her abilities as an actress that she gave her brilliant performance in *The Dark Mirror* in the same year as an Oscar-winning one.

Marilynn Wilson

DAVID AND LISA

Released: 1962
Production: Paul M. Heller for Continental
Direction: Frank Perry
Screenplay: Eleanor Perry; based on the book of the same name by Theodore Isaac Rubin
Cinematography: Leonard Hirschfield
Editing: Irving Oshman
Running time: 94 minutes

Principal characters:
David Clemens	Keir Dullea
Lisa	Janet Margolin
Doctor Alan Swinford	Howard da Silva
Mrs. Clemens	Neva Patterson
John	Clifton James
Mr. Clemens	Richard McMurray
Simon	Matthew Arden
Carlos	Jaime Sanchez

David and Lisa, based on an actual case history written by Dr. Theodore Isaac Rubin, is a brilliant, sensitive film which explores the need that human beings have for one another; the strength and healing power of love; and the discomfort that the outside world experiences in confronting the fact of mental illness.

David (Keir Dullea) is a seventeen-year-old boy who has a high I.Q. and suffers from an obsessive neurosis. He lives in morbid fear of dirt and has an insane desire to stop time in order to cheat death. He avoids being touched because "a touch can kill." He hates his mother, distrusts his father, and is antagonistic toward the head of the school for the mentally disturbed which he attends. He avoids the other patients except for a girl named Lisa (Janet Margolin), a fifteen-year-old girl with brown eyes who suffers from schizophrenia. In the guise of Lisa, she is a silly little four-year-old who talks constantly in gibberish seasoned with rhyme; as Muriel, she is a demure, reticent adolescent who communicates in writing because she cannot talk. Unwittingly, David and Lisa help each other by caring; Lisa's trouble (the film never explains its roots) is somewhat ameliorated by David's feelings for her. Since the characters' psychological states are not very clearly defined, the audience must accept the situation primarily at face value; but the visual and verbal aspects of mental illness are strongly conveyed by Dullea and Margolin. They poignantly present their characters' increasing curiosity and ultimate attachment to each other in the environment of a cheerless institution; their performances are the core of the film. The change in the two patients as they become more friendly and as David learns to accept the psychiatrist fully is recounted in good cinematic style and with sound psychology.

As the film opens, David Clemens is brought to the school for the mentally disturbed by his mother (Neva Patterson). As he waits in the hall, he is silently observed by another patient, Lisa (Janet Margolin), who is hiding behind the balustrade. When another student, Simon (Matthew Arden) comes downstairs to welcome David and accidentally touches him, David's reaction verges on hysteria; he says that touch can kill. Later, after David is shown to his room, Dr. Swinford (Howard da Silva) talks with his mother, who is defensive and contends that David's phobia about being touched did not result from anything that she or her husband did.

The next day, David explores the school, and in a day room, he sees Lisa with her teacher, John (Clifton James). He is fascinated as he watches Lisa stomping around and speaking in rhymes. In subsequent scenes, David's antisocial attitude is established. He arrives late for dinner and does not respond to his tablemates. He ignores their suggestions concerning activities and refuses to join any clubs, because he despises clubs, bowling, and exercise, claiming that they are for idiots. At other times, he walks out of his classroom, keeps to himself, and refuses to let Dr. Swinford in to see him.

The only one that David seems drawn to is Lisa. Oddly enough, he is interested in psychiatry, and he first views Lisa only as a fascinating case. He watches her as she leaps up and down saying "I'm a lump and I like to jump." When John says, "You're a girl, Lisa," she abruptly stops jumping and begins to draw. Later, as David is seated alone at a table, Lisa sits down and watches him and then shows him something she wrote. He corrects her spelling and then asks her why she does not comb her hair. He tells her that he will play with her, but she feels rejected by his criticism and walks away.

Another time, David observes Lisa drawing. Her hand goes off the pad of paper, however, and she begins to write on the walls. When John immediately takes the crayon away from her, she shouts angry rhymes at him. Later, a concerned David asks John if he might speak with him about Lisa's case. He says that he has been studying Lisa and thinks that she has adolescent schizophrenia and has a difficult time with authority figures. He suggests that John must be permissive with her. When John tells him that he appreciates his ideas and touches him on the shoulder as he speaks, David responds with fury. After he calms down, he has another confrontation with Lisa and asks her why she rhymes. She expresses her anger with him, however, by advancing toward him with her finger pointed at his chest. He begins to panic and warns her not to touch him. Although she stops short of actual physical contact and walks away, the audience realizes that now she is capable of exercising some control in her relationship with David despite her lack of elaborate verbalization.

At a subsequent meeting between David and his own doctor, the boy brings up one of the themes of the film—love between people. David talks to Dr. Swinford about clocks and time pieces, expressing disgust that most of them are inaccurate. He advances a plan to construct an electronic clock which would always keep the exact time. David believes that time is important and cannot be stopped. He tells Dr. Swinford that he (the doctor) is going to die and asks him if he is afraid. He says that if they could stop time, they would be safe. The psychiatrist tells David that they cannot add to the time allotted them; they can only be alive. He adds that one takes a chance whenever he or she loves another person. In another brief scene which is equally important to the beginning of Lisa's recovery, David meets her outdoors. She asks him: "David, David, look at me. Who do you see? Who do you see?" He responds: "I see a girl who looks like a pearl." She smiles broadly and runs to tell John that she is a pearl of a girl. Later, in bed, Lisa strokes her own face and body; she is becoming aware of herself as a young woman in a positive sense.

In the following sequence, David's mother comes to visit and becomes upset by one of the students, Carlos (Jaime Sanchez), who starts to flirt with her and speaks of his own mother, who, he claims, is a prostitute. This unfortunate visit causes David's parents to remove him from the school against his will. He becomes angry with Dr. Swinford since he believes the doctor does not care for him, although the psychiatrist assures him that he tried to fight the parents' decision. At home, Mrs. Clemens deludes herself that there is nothing wrong with her son and expresses her wish that David go to an Ivy League school. David's responses are icy; his cold fury very obvious. He runs away from home and returns to the school, asking Dr. Swinford to take him in since he has no place else to go. Later, he tells Dr. Swinford that when he left home he saw a black woman at the train station. She had her arm around her little boy, and David pretended he was her son because she really liked her child. When the doctor informs David that he talked with his parents and they consented to his remaining at the school, David says that he hates his parents.

On a subsequent student outing to an art museum, Lisa begins to act strangely when she, David, and Simon look at a sculpture of a family group. After the boys leave, Lisa climbs onto the work and embraces the figure of the mother and child. It takes David and one of the teachers to persuade her finally to come down, which she does reluctantly. Although Lisa's background is neither discussed nor depicted in the film, this scene serves to give the viewer a tiny clue as to Lisa's needs and offers a small piece in the puzzle of what may have caused her illness.

One evening as she is drawing, Lisa makes an important breakthrough. When she signs her name, she writes "Muriel X Lisa," circles the two names, and then adds "Me." John says that that is right, that she is Lisa, not Muriel. She dashes off happily to find David, who is listening to Simon play the piano.

Simon resents her intrusion and becomes upset when she turns on the metronome and begins to move her head in rhythm with its ticking. David sides with Simon and tells the girl to get out. She hollers back in rhyme and runs away from school, taking a train to the city.

The film then cuts back and forth between the school and Lisa's bewildered wanderings in the city. Her adventure frightens her, and she returns to the art museum seeking comfort from the statue she remembers embracing. She peers through the locked door, but cannot get to the sculpture. Back at the school, David expresses to Dr. Swinford the thought that one does not run away from something, but goes to something just as he did the night he returned to the school. David's intuition leads him to believe that Lisa may have gone back to the museum to find solace from the mother figure she liked.

David and the psychiatrist drive to the museum. In the early morning light, David rushes up the steps of the building and finds Lisa asleep in the doorway. He calls to her and she answers him, but not in rhyme. She complains that he was nice to Simon but mean to her. David apologizes. He points out to her that she did not talk in rhyme, therefore she is Muriel. She responds: "Lisa-Muriel, the same. I am me." David begins to weep. The film ends with the young people walking down the museum steps hand in hand. The conclusion does not leave the viewer with the feeling that David and Lisa are completely cured, yet one does perceive that their journey toward recovery has begun.

David and Lisa was the first feature film made by Frank and Eleanor Perry; he directed it, and she wrote the script. Since it was a low-budget film, they used location shots in Philadelphia, which enhances the realistic feeling of the production. Also, since they could not afford to employ well-known stars, two unknowns were cast in the principal roles. Both Dullea and Margolin turn in impeccable, sensitive performances as disturbed adolescents who find the road to recovery via their love for each other. In fact, they received Best Actor and Best Actress awards at the 1962 San Francisco Film Festival for their parts in this film. Dullea in particular works with a subtlety, accuracy, and intensity of feeling that indicates significant talent. Silva is believable and low-keyed in his part as the psychiatrist. The entire cast gives fine performances and provides good backup for the principals.

Director Perry, previously an associate producer of Broadway plays, apparently found his forte in cinema; his first film won the Best Picture by a New Director award at the 1962 Venice Film Festival. In his use of the camera and in the pace of his cutting, he displays a rare film sense. Yet in his inspiration and direction of his performers, he reveals a more profound gift: a psychological sensitivity toward the humanity in his characters and an appreciation for the strength of the human heart.

Fern L. Gagné

DAVID COPPERFIELD

Released: 1935
Production: David O. Selznick for Metro-Goldwyn-Mayer
Direction: George Cukor
Screenplay: Howard Estabrook; based on Hugh Walpole's adaptation of the novel of the same name by Charles Dickens
Cinematography: Oliver T. Marsh
Editing: Robert J. Kern
Running time: 133 minutes

Principal characters:

Micawber	W. C. Fields
David Copperfield (younger)	Freddie Bartholomew
David Copperfield (older)	Frank Lawton
Mrs. Copperfield	Elizabeth Allan
Nurse Peggoty	Jessie Ralph
Dan Peggoty	Lionel Barrymore
Mr. Murdstone	Basil Rathbone
Betsey Trotwood	Edna May Oliver
Mr. Dick	Lennox Pawle
Dora	Maureen O'Sullivan
Agnes (younger)	Marilyn Knowlden
Agnes (older)	Madge Evans
Little Em'ly (younger)	Fay Chaldecott
Little Em'ly (older)	Florine McKinney
Ham	John Buckler
Steerforth	Hugh Williams
Uriah Heep	Roland Young
Mr. Wickfield	Lewis Stone

In *David Copperfield*, director George Cukor brought to the screen one of the most beloved works in English literature. Cukor's film is a fairly literal adaptation of Dickens' novel, and like the original, the film has its flaws. Both are episodic and overly sentimental; however, also like Dickens' novel, Cukor's *David Copperfield* has strengths that far outweigh its weaknesses. Dickens had no peer when it came to creating and bringing to life a gallery of marvelously engaging (or in the case of his villains, repulsive) characters; and it is on this aspect of the novel that Cukor has chosen to concentrate. Cukor and producer David O. Selznick gathered a star-studded cast, and, given the large number of important roles in the film (some of which had to be filled twice, as the characters moved from childhood to adulthood), the two men managed to match the actors and the parts remarkably well.

The ups and downs of young Master David Copperfield are, of course, familiar to all. His story, and thus the film, divides fairly neatly into two parts: that of David the boy (Freddie Bartholomew) and David the young man

(Frank Lawton). David's father dies six months before he is born. David and his mother (Elizabeth Allan) are inseparable until, when David is about six, Mrs. Copperfield is courted by, and eventually marries, Mr. Murdstone (Basil Rathbone), a cold, self-righteous man who comes to dominate his young wife and her son. David's principal ally through this strife is his nurse, Peggoty (Jessie Ralph), a large, cheerful woman who is eventually dismissed by Murdstone. Before that happens, however, David spends a few idyllic weeks with Peggoty at the home of her brother Dan (Lionel Barrymore), a sailor. At Dan's home in Yarmouth, David meets two children who will play important roles in his adult life: Peggoty's niece, Little Em'ly (Fay Chaldecott), and his nephew, Ham (John Buckler).

When David's mother dies in childbirth, Murdstone abandons all pretense of caring for David, and the young lad is packed off to London "to work, to work, to work." Thus begins David's involvement with one of the novel's and the film's most memorable characters, Wilkins Micawber (W. C. Fields), with whom Murdstone has chosen to board David. Micawber is a fraud, but he is such a genial fraud that David, as well as the audience, loves him from the start. He makes his initial entrance climbing gingerly over the rooftops of London in an effort to elude the creditors that perpetually dog his trail. As he drops through the skylight into the midst of his startled family and their new lodger, he announces grandly "I have thwarted the malevolent machinations of our enemies. In short, I have arrived." Although he admits to being temporarily short of funds (a chronic condition, as David soon discovers), Micawber is always "confidently expecting something to turn up." David is separated from his new friend when Micawber and his family are arrested and sent to debtors' prison. "Copperfield," says the dejected Micawber, "you perceive before you the shattered fragment of a temple once called man."

David's last stop in his boyhood is Dover, where he seeks shelter from his father's sister, Betsey Trotwood (Edna May Oliver), who lives with her eccentric cousin, Mr. Dick (Lennox Pawle). One of the most engaging characters in the film, Mr. Dick is quite mad, but friendly and entirely harmless. He and David take to each other immediately, and once again David is happy. In Dover, he is sent to live with the Wickfield family, which includes old Mr. Wickfield (Lewis Stone), a prosperous but alcoholic businessman; his daughter Agnes (Marilyn Knowlden), who is David's age; and Wickfield's clerk, Uriah Heep (Roland Young), an obsequious toady who is forever proclaiming what an "'umble person" he is, all the while worming his way into his employer's confidence.

Several years pass. By the time David graduates from school, many important things have transpired. It is clear to the audience (although not to David) that Agnes (Madge Evans) is in love with young Copperfield; Mr. Wickfield has fallen completely under Uriah Heep's influence; and Heep has employed Mr. Micawber. David, meanwhile, returns to London to seek his fortune as a writer. In London, David meets Steerforth (Hugh Williams), an old school chum, and the two become inseparable. They attend an opera, where David meets the beautiful but childlike Dora (Maureen O'Sullivan), whom he will soon marry.

In a fateful turn of events, he takes Steerforth to meet the Peggotys. This meeting, although cordial, turns out to be disastrous for everyone concerned. Although Em'ly (Florine McKinney), by now grown up, is engaged to marry Ham, she falls in love with Steerforth, who takes her away and later abandons her in Italy. In a bit of overly neat irony, Steerforth and Ham die together shortly thereafter, as Steerforth's yacht capsizes in a storm near Yarmouth, and Ham, not knowing its owner, dies in an attempt to save the ship.

Meanwhile, David marries Dora, hurting loyal Agnes deeply. The Copperfields' happiness is shortlived, however, when David's child-bride withers and dies of a mysterious ailment soon after their marriage. Agnes is threatened by Uriah Heep, who has by now taken over Wickfield's business and is demanding the hand of his former employer's daughter. Heep's chicanery is unmasked by his trusted clerk, Micawber, who, surrounded by David, the Wickfields, Betsey Trotwood, and Mr. Dick, calls Heep "the most consummate villain that ever existed. Heep of infamy, I defy you," he declaims. Confronted by evidence of forgery and other duplicity, Heep reverts to his 'umble self, and the day is saved. Beaming, Micawber asserts that "What I have done, I have done for England, home, and beauty."

After all this melodrama, everything ends on a happy note. As Betsey Trotwood and Mr. Dick look on, David confesses his love to Agnes. " High time, too, eh, Mr. Dick?" asks Aunt Betsey. Mr. Dick replies with a broad wink, which ends the film.

The successful cinematic adaptation of *David Copperfield* hinged on two points—the audience's familiarity with and love for Dickens' novel, and the cast of characters assembled by Cukor and Selznick that bring it to life. Clearly, far too much goes on in Dickens' sprawling novel to bring it all to the screen in a film of manageable length. Instead, Cukor and his writers, Howard Estabrook and Hugh Walpole, have selected the most important episodes from the novel and have woven them together in a coherent series of vignettes which (thanks to the English novelist Walpole's marvelous ear for language) convey a genuine sense of the novel's unique joys.

The casting was, in many instances, genuinely felicitous. The challenge here, as Cukor himself has noted, was to find actors who could preserve the eccentricities of the Dickens characters without turning them into caricatures. Indeed, the only character with no quirks or peculiarities is David Copperfield himself, which tends to render him, as many critics of the novel have pointed out, the least interesting character in his own story. Young David, as played by Bartholomew, gives an all-out assault on the tear ducts of the audience which would have been disastrous in a less sentimental story; here, his performance is just right. Lawton is agreeably earnest as David Copperfield the man, although somewhat bland in comparison to the rich assembly of Hollywood's finest character actors.

Rathbone and Young make suitably loathsome villains. Rathbone's Murdstone is cold and soulless, showing no emotion except hostility. Young's Uriah Heep, on the other hand, fairly oozes with sleazy, sycophantic greed. Oliver is wonderful as the horsey but loving Aunt Betsey Trotwood, and Pawle is even better as the mad Mr. Dick. Pawle's sweet gentleness lights up the screen during his brief appearances in the film. Fields, who got top billing in the film for his portrayal of Mr. Micawber, inevitably brought much of himself to Micawber; his penchant for placing his hat on his upturned cane is only the most obvious example. There is a good deal of Dickens in the larcenous but good hearted screen *persona* that Fields created for himself. Wilkins Micawber was Fields's only straight dramatic part (if Micawber can be said to be a straight dramatic part), and he performed beautifully.

Cukor's *David Copperfield* rates high marks for an honest and satisfying effort at what must be conceded was an impossible task. The film ranks with David Lean's *Great Expectations* (1947) and *Oliver Twist* (1948) and with Carol Reed's 1968 musical *Oliver!* as the most successful of the numerous cinematic adaptations of Dickens' novels.

Robert Mitchell

THE DAWN PATROL

Released: 1930
Production: Robert North for First National/Warner Bros.
Direction: Howard Hawks
Screenplay: Howard Hawks, Dan Totheroh, and Seton I. Miller; based on the short story "The Flight Commander" by John Monk Saunders (AA)
Cinematography: Ernest Haller
Editing: Ray Curtiss
Running time: 95 minutes

> *Principal characters:*
> Courtney .... Richard Barthelmess
> Scott .... Douglas Fairbanks, Jr.
> Major Brand .... Neil Hamilton
> Gordon Scott (younger brother) .... William Janney
> Hollister .... Gardner James

This classic saga of British flyers in World War I is one of a group of films spanning the transition from silents to sound which skillfully reenacted that war. Although a late example of its type, *The Dawn Patrol* was well-received and won an Academy Award in the original story category. Its success ultimately prompted a remake in 1938 which cleverly incorporated the stunning aerial sequences of the original. Formally, its story would be adaptable to any wartime setting. Rather than an episode, it relates a pattern of action and reaction, perceived by the film to be so unchanging and unresolvable that it becomes a cycle which can only be endlessly repeated. War never ends in *The Dawn Patrol.*

At the center of the drama is the friendship between Courtney (Richard Barthelmess) and Scott (Douglas Fairbanks, Jr.), two young men whose relationship precedes their service as flyers. At the outset of the story, "Court" and "Scotto" (as they call each other) are veterans, flying each mission together and coming through alive as younger and greener men die. It is the job of the flight commander, Major Brand (Neil Hamilton), to send into the air the unseasoned replacements as needed and to expect death to be a routine part of each mission. The job has taken a toll on his nerves; he drinks too much and sleeps little. Sustained by camaraderie, Courtney, Scott, and the other men know only that they must follow orders and be prepared to die. The psychological pressures of command are beyond their understanding, and Brand must remain aloof from their circle. A leader among the flyers, Courtney is openly scornful of Brand, but ironically, it is he who must take Brand's place when the major is promoted. Like his predecessor, he begins to go without sleep and to drink compulsively. His relationship with Scott is strained as his friend assumes his own former role as leader among the group of flyers. Finally, a rupture occurs. Scott's younger brother Gordon (William Janney) arrives with a group of replacements, and Scott unreasonably implores Courtney not to send him on a mission the next day. Courtney's duty is clear. All the flyers are needed, and he cannot make an exception for the sake of friendship. The young man dies on his first mission, and Scott blames Courtney. When a single flyer is needed for a daring suicide mission over Germany, Scott volunteers; but Courtney, remembering the other's low tolerance for alcohol, cleverly gets him drunk and takes his place. Succeeding in bombing his targets, Courtney is then shot down by ace German flyer von Richter. He dies knowing that Scott's feelings toward him have never really changed. The grief-stricken Scott takes command; in the final scene, he emerges calmly from his office to give orders to the group from which he is himself now isolated.

The behavior of the characters in *The Dawn Patrol* has been described as stoical and existential. They never appear to be motivated by patriotism or even a keen sense of duty, and they demonstrate professional respect rather than hatred for their enemy counterparts. Their willingness to keep flying missions until they die is understood to be the manifestation of an acceptance that this defines their existence and that it is a situation which must be honored out of self-respect. As a result, while they complain that the war is rotten and tragically absurd, they invariably respond to orders with the words "Right" and "It'll be done." The narrative is a bleak one, but the values it unsentimentally celebrates stand against its chilling background with a steadfast warmth. The film finds a place for individual feeling and action, even if they must ultimately be absorbed into the cycle. For example, at the outset of the story, one of the flyers, Hollister (Gardner James), returns from a mission on which his best friend has died. Overwhelmed by the loss, he appears to suffer a breakdown, alienating himself from his comrades and bitterly resenting the surface gaiety with which they carry on. Later in the film, we learn that Hollister has himself died, and that he has perished bravely, helping save another flyer. Expressions of extreme emotion are constantly permitted in the film, but they never rupture the fundamental sense of professionalism which prohibits the flyers from abandoning their roles.

The most telling instance of an individual altering an event without betraying the nature of his world is Courtney's decision to fly in Scott's place. Easily understood as a gesture of friendship, the action is even more meaningful if it is perceived as a gesture of the will. Knowing that either he or Scott will die, Courtney makes a choice; and this choice exists independently of his position as flight commander, affirming his individuality without being an act of rebellion. It is not incidental that on an earlier mission, Scott's plane had been shot down and he had been presumed dead. Courtney's response to the apparent fact of Scott's death has already registered, and it is something which he does not wish to suffer twice. The tone of the reunion between the two men when Scott turns up alive and that of Courtney's tender farewell later as Scott passes out after having apologized are very similar. Scott has also shown that he knows how to die, but Courtney's decision is more thoughtful. He knows that Scott has volunteered in the aftermath of his brother's death, for which Scott was not responsible. Replacing him, Courtney is able to restore the sense of things as they were, not as his command dictates they will be.

As war and flying tended to connote masculinity in this period, *The Dawn Patrol* is presented with an opportunity which it daringly engages. The characters of Courtney and Scott possess a softness and vulnerability which could be described as feminine. Classically gallant in manner and bearing in responding to orders and doing their jobs, the two male protagonists are soft-spoken and gentle in their more personal moments, especially with each other. Scott wears a loud polka-dot shirt, and the song he listens to endlessly on a worn record during the evenings is the bittersweet "Poor Butterfly." He relies on Courtney to put him to bed when he has had too much to drink, and the other always obliges with a smile. Both men weep openly and unashamedly during the course of the film, and as Courtney leaves Scott for the last time, he tenderly caresses the other's hair. Clearly, the two men openly love each other, but in a way that no one could find objectionable or questionable. Necessarily lacking the company of women, they do not suppress the emotions which are part of male-female relationships, even if the sexual fulfillment that normally accompanies such emotions is not available and not desired with another male. Secure in their masculinity, they are finding a way to express themselves as integrated human beings. These two characters and the presentation of their relationship make recent attempts in the cinema to break down "macho" stereotypes seem timid.

The adventurous treatment of characterization and narrative structure in the film extends to other aspects of its presentation. This was the first sound film of director Howard Hawks, and although his silent films (most notably, *A Girl in Every Port* in 1928) are not negligible works, it was with *The Dawn Patrol* that he hit his stride. One of the unfortunate myths of cinema is that the first years of sound were aesthetically dull—that the sound was primitive and that the camera never moved. In fact, while there have been technological advances in sound recording, aesthetic approaches to it were most interesting in this early period, as demonstrated in films directed by Josef von Sternberg, Jean Renoir, Alfred Hitchcock, and others. At the same time, these films possess considerable fluidity of camera movement often enhanced by image-sound tensions. *The Dawn Patrol* addresses the challenges posed by sound with resourcefulness and subtlety. The aerial sequences were photographed in the same manner as in a silent film, with the accompanying sound imaginatively invented afterward. The interior dialogue scenes were generally recorded directly, and Hawks's predilection for direct and concise (but not static) images registers the terse dialogue exchanges effectively. At other times, a sophisticated sound mix softens the effect of these unadorned readings.

Sequences such as those in the recreation room where the men drink, listen to records, and join in communal song combine dialogue, music, and sounds of offscreen action, providing a rich complexity of direct and indirect sound which does not inhibit the camera. In the middle of one of these sequences, the camera might abruptly track in to a close-up of Hollister's anguished face or concentrate on a doorway while the men continue their conversations offscreen.

It is sometimes claimed that actors trained in the silent cinema were unsure of themselves when asked to deliver dialogue. This is unfortunately true in the case of Hamilton, who is a bit stiff and theatrical as Brand. On the other hand, the performances of both Barthelmess and Fairbanks are carefully judged and very moving. In the more intimate scenes, they lower their voices and register a disarming genuineness, seemingly oblivious of camera and microphones.

The thoughtfulness with which Hawks was approaching formal problems as he defined his artistic personality is as exciting in this film as in the superficially more dazzling *Scarface* (1932). He was moving toward a deceivingly informal style, defined by a camera which would feign unobtrusiveness and by playing which would seem spontaneous and free of self-consciousness. These stylistic qualities are present but not pronounced in *The Dawn Patrol*. The intermittent melodramatic titles, describing stages of the action like those of a silent film, underline the artificial presentation of the story in the same way as the film's technically ostentatious and visually expressionistic moments. At the same time, artifice consistently yields to understatement in the most dramatic moments. The subject of *The Dawn Patrol* was clearly one for which Hawks had great feeling—a fact confirmed by the recurrence of similar situations, characters, and narrative structures in such later films as *The Road to Glory* and *Ceiling Zero* (both 1936) and *Only Angels Have Wings* (1939). Compatible material and the challenge of sound combined to hasten his maturity as an artist. Both the screenplay, which he adapted with two others from John Monk Saunders' admirably spare story, and the direction reveal his distinctive artistic voice at this relatively early stage.

The 1938 remake of *The Dawn Patrol*, a respectable work in its own right, compares intriguingly with the original. Although it follows the screenplay of the Hawks film with considerable fidelity, it has a different tone, the causes of which are several. The remake seeks a conventional dramatic vividness in the most emotional moments. For example, when Scott returns after being thought dead, the writing is unaltered. Director Edmund Goulding, however, displays large close-ups of both Courtney and Scott and has them welcome each other heartily, while Hawks keeps the two men in two-shot and affect-ingly underplays their evident responses to each other. The 1930 version is essentially a pacifist work, consistent in this respect with other war films of its time. The 1938 version was made at a time when America's involvement in World War II was becoming imminent, and while it superficially retains the feeling of tragic waste embedded in the narrative, it views the flyers' actions less abstractly. Courtney's speech to Scott's brother is one scene that is subtly transformed. In the original, Courtney simply tells the other that although death is virtually inevitable for each of the flyers, the important thing is for each man to die knowing that he has done his best. The Courtney of the remake (played by a well-cast Errol Flynn) again delivers the speech quietly but says more, seeking through his words to find a larger purpose for the required deaths.

Interestingly, Hawks himself subsequently made a film, *Air Force* (1943), in which patriotic sentiment was not only desirable but also required. A very typical Hawks film in its emphasis on devotion among the members of a group, it makes no effort to undermine the attitudes which understandably prevailed in almost every film made during World War II. Free of such attitudes, his version of *The Dawn Patrol* possesses a perspective on men in war which remains comprehensible and stimulating to the contemporary mind. Both aesthetically and philosophically, it is a film which has aged exceptionally well.

Blake Lucas

A DAY AT THE RACES

Released: 1937
Production: Max Siegal for Metro-Goldwyn-Mayer
Direction: Sam Wood
Screenplay: Robert Pirosh, George Seaton, and George Oppenheimer; based
on a story by Robert Pirosh and George Seaton
Cinematography: Joseph Ruttenberg
Editing: Frank E. Hull
Running time: 109 minutes

Principal characters:
Doctor Hugo Z. Hackenbush .... Groucho Marx
Tony .... Chico Marx
Stuffy .... Harpo Marx
Gil Stewart .... Allan Jones
Judy Standish .... Maureen O'Sullivan
Emily Upjohn .... Margaret Dumont
Flo Marlowe .... Esther Muir

Nothing about a Marx Brothers film is either off-the-wall or spontaneous,
although many people believe this to be the case; and everything about a
Marx Brothers film is zany, inspired, and riotous. The true aficionado of the
Marx Brothers catalogue could probably discuss at length the reason why *A
Day at the Races* (1937) is not as good as (or is better than) *A Night at the
Opera* (1935), which is not as good as (or is better than) *Duck Soup* (1933)
or *Horse Feathers* (1932). The average viewer and relisher of comedic anarchy,
however, would be hard put to say anything about any one of those films until
he was able to stop laughing. No Marx Brothers film is capable of garnering
awards for plots rife with probing, sensitive dialogue, but no one seems to
care. The wonderful thing about their films is that they make us laugh, and
A Day at the Races is no exception.

In this film, Groucho is Dr. Hugo Z. Hackenbush, a horse doctor who
takes charge of a sanatorium owned by Judy Standish (Maureen O'Sullivan).
The sanatorium is in trouble. A deep-eyed villain named Morgan (Douglas
Dumbrille), is going to foreclose on the sanatorium's mortgage unless Judy
can come up with the funds to save it. One of her rich patients, Emily Upjohn,
played by the unbeatable and underrated Margaret Dumont, will make up
the deficit only if her "dear Dr. Hackenbush" is put in charge. She is an
admirer of the doctor because he has told her that she has double-blood
pressure, which confirms her worst suspicions. Hackenbush's true professional
status is doubted by Stuffy (Harpo Marx), a jockey, and Tony (Chico Marx),
a racing tipster, who are friends of Judy. He is also under suspicion by the
villainous bankers who are scheming to get control of the sanatorium. Only

when Stuffy and Tony have proof that Hackenbash is indeed a fraud do they have confidence in him. In a wonderful salute to loyalty they both follow suit when, Hackenbush, with his leg shot full of novocaine, exits with that leg wrapped around his other one, and his two new supporters walk out the door the same way.

Gil Stewart (Allan Jones) is a struggling singer who owns a race horse (hence the connection with the title) and, because of his beautiful singing voice, good looks, and winning ways, is Judy's suitor. Their road to true love is not without mishap, however, which the Marx Brothers try to ease for them. There is a subplot involving Flo Marlowe (Esther Muir), a slinky seductress hoping to catch Hackenbush, but she gets caught by Stuffy and Tony, who in order to save their friend, wallpaper her to the wall. It is one of the funniest scenes in the film, but even it is topped by a gem of a scene in which Stuffy tries to pantomine for Tony that Hackenbush is in trouble. Harpo's mime as Stuffy is perfect, but outmatched by Chico as Tony's misinterpretation. First, Harpo outlines a large mustache to indicate who the message is about. Chico understands—it is about Buffalo Bill. Harpo tries again, now adding the famous Groucho crouching walk. Buffalo Bill ice skating? In frustration Harpo leaps into a furious attack on a nearby hedge. "Oh," Chico says with immediate recognition, "Hack-a-bush."

Of course, in the end, all is well. Stewart's horse wins the race, which saves the day, the sanatorium, and his love, Judy. Before the predictable conclusion, however, comes much madness and a spectacular production sequence at a water carnival with bathing beauties smiling, although water is running into their eyes and an audience precariously seated on floating rafts. Another similarly zany scene is an embarrassing number (at least by today's standards) in which Stuffy leads a cavalcade of stereotypical blacks in a silly pied-piper number to "All God's Children Got Rhythm." Neither sequence has anything to do with the progression of the fragile plot, which is of almost no consequence in this, or any, Marx Brothers film.

Two classic routines are placed, seemingly regardless of the sequence of events, between the main titles and the end credits. First, there is a code-book bit. As a tipster, Tony sells Hackenbush a tip on a horse; then, in order to interpret the tip, he sells him a code book, and finally a Breeder's Guide. The scene is fast, short, and furiously funny. The other hilarious routine is the examining-room sequence. In order to appreciate the scene's precise choreography, one should see it repeatedly, however, so much happens so fast. Dumont as Emily Upjohn is strapped into the examining chair, and the medical profession's most infamous examination gets under way. The patient is given a shave by Tony, has her shoes shined by Hackenbush, and is manicured by Stuffy. Back to business, Groucho calls for "X-ray! X-ray!," and in comes Stuffy with an armload of evening newspapers. A nurse's uniform is whisked off her, the fire sprinklers are turned on, and a horse gallops in, then out, with the Marx Brothers on its back. If this makes no sense, it does not matter at all, because it is not supposed to.

What went into the making of *A Day at the Races*, however, was not as funny or madcap or spontaneous as one would like to believe. It may seem like fun to imagine a trip to the set where "Minny's boys" (a well-known nickname given to the brothers because their mother's name was Minny) frolicked on the set and threw the crew into convulsions of laughter as they clowned their way into box-office successes. Such was not the case, however; from its inception, *A Day at the Races* took two years and eighteen scripts before it received final approval. When that approval was given, it then went on the stage before live audiences across the country as *Scenes from a Day at the Races*. Farmers, car salesmen, housewives, and insurance salesman all were given the opportunity, by means of preview cards, to voice their likes and dislikes; and each voice was listened to and seriously considered.

Irving Thalberg, a true "Hollywood mogul" in every sense of the word, was in command of the film as head of production at M-G-M, and it was at his insistence that story-line after story-line be revised. Because the writers and the Marx Brothers so respected him, they complied. Unfortunately during the writing phase, at the age of thirty-seven and with a serious heart condition, Thalberg died of pneumonia. Eventually Thalberg's brother-in-law, Laurence Weingarten, was placed in charge, and a completely new regime began, which meant more story conferences, more production meetings, and more revisions. Once the script got final approval, the incredible saga of the screenplay credit hassles began with Al Boasberg, the dissident writer, eventually coming away with no credit at all.

The reception of *A Day at the Races* was varied. It won many new fans, but lost many others. Many thought the movie was a film of stolen gags, as the joke went, because someone must have stolen the gags since they were not in the film. In the Republic of Latvia the film even was banned on the grounds that it was "worthless."

The relationship between the stars and the director was at best testy. There is a popular story that one day in a fit of frustration, the director, Sam Wood, noted more for such films as *King's Row* (1942), directed the following tirade at his stars: "You can't make an actor out of clay," to which, Groucho responded, "And you can't make a director out of Wood." The anecdote may not be true, but, as with a vast majority of *bona fide* and specious Marxisms, nobody seems to mind. As in all of the Marx Brothers films, the gags in *A Day at the Races* are the most important things, not the believability of the plot.

Juliette Friedgen

THE DAY OF THE LOCUST

Released: 1975
Production: Jerome Hellman for Paramount
Direction: John Schlesinger
Screenplay: Waldo Salt; based on the novel of the same name by Nathanael
   West
Cinematography: Conrad Hall
Editing: Jim Clark
Music: John Barry
Running time: 144 minutes

> *Principal characters:*
> Homer Simpson .... Donald Sutherland
> Faye Greener .... Karen Black
> Harry .... Burgess Meredith
> Tod Hackett .... William Atherton

Nathanael West, more a prophet than a monitor of contemporary issues, wrote about many timely themes during his short life. In *The Day of the Locust*, he gave a thorough treatment of an insidious but familiar process in American life: how the dreams we are taught to nurture die, and what can become of human nature as it helplessly watches the slow death. British director John Schlesinger's film of this short novel came at an especially poignant time. Americans, no longer involved in war or other burning social issues, began to turn back upon themselves and their history as a source of entertainment. This phenomenon resembled in many ways the vanity of the 1930's that prompted so many to drop everything and head for Southern California in search of the "big break" into motion pictures, hoping it would bring them the security and happiness they could not find elsewhere. Accordingly, both the subject matter and the sheer appearance of Schlesinger's film of West's story are significant in contemporary American cultural history.

In the film, Tod Hackett (William Atherton), a set designer, has come to Hollywood in an attempt to make a name for himself. He lives in a court where Faye Greener (Karen Black) also rents a bungalow as she, too, waits for her opportunity to achieve fame as an actress. Tod becomes quite taken by Faye, and although she is able to mete out occasional evidence of affection and caring for those who demand it of her, her life is clearly governed by her own egoistic search for stardom. Tod becomes wrapped up first in his shared enthusiasm for the progress Faye sees taking place in her career, then by his helpless and pitying interest in how she strives to reach her goals. The woman displays her true self to Tod long before she admits to herself what she is doing. She decides to live with an older man, Homer Simpson (Donald Sutherland), who is willing to give her all his money, thereby providing her with the accoutrements she feels she needs to make herself more available for "discovery." All he asks in return is that she stay with him. His intention is that he will likewise be more available for her affection, should she grow to love him.

As this film progresses, however, it becomes obvious that the essence of life in this success-crazed industry lies in the striving and longing for goals, rather than in attainment of the desired end. In the film, no one ever reaches those goals. The film luminaries are treated as superhuman, if not inhuman, individuals. On the other hand, individuals who still strive to attain one status or another show various ways of molding themselves to the contorted values and standards of a culture lying in wait for instantaneous stardom, wealth, and happiness.

Faye attempts to achieve her desired status by manipulating her outward appearance to coincide with what she wants to become, hoping that her goal will be realized all in good time. Black's interpretation of this character makes it clear that Faye has been able to last as long as she has through sheer persistence and a willingness to see herself as nothing more than her character on the screen. In this she is similar to those who only know her from her brief moments on film. She has a definite underlying penchant toward violence and mercilessness, and this is a necessary and pivotal quality in both West's novella and screenwriter Waldo Salt's script. In both the film and the novella from which the screenplay was derived, the traits of mercilessness and violence pervade a large segment of this culture that allows itself to be duped into thriving on brief glimpses of fictitious characters and holding those images up as models for the rest of life. In Faye's case, these traits are not only necessary for the development of her career, but they also allow her to take advantage of Homer and his offers with very little, if any, regret at all.

Homer, on the other hand, appears to be the direct opposite of Faye. Willing to relinquish all his money for Faye's happiness, he houses her, feeds her, clothes her, and allows himself to be abused by her to the point that Faye eventually despises him for his very spinelessness. In actuality, however, both he and Faye are leeches. Each of them is convinced that what he needs and wants exists in his distorted version of society, and each is convinced that all he needs to do to accomplish his goals is to wait and persist.

Although Tod does not come any closer to true success than either Faye or Homer, he has one capacity that neither of the others possesses, the ability to evaluate and reject. Whereas both Faye and Homer are consumed by their goals, Tod is able to recognize that his efforts have led him to circumstances incompatible with human life. Although his ambition is strong, his desire to survive is even stronger.

In addition to this primary plot, *The Day of the Locust* contains episodic events for the major and minor characters that afford Schlesinger the opportunity for many spectacular sets. Each is increasingly larger than life. The first such set is an actual one, the huge Hollywood sign which symbolizes for many the grand-scale fame and success they crave. It is at this site that Faye first tells Tod, in a provocative and coquettish manner usually reserved only for the screen, of her aspirations and minor successes so far. Yet in the background of this scene, there is a group of tourists who have just disembarked from their tour bus and are listening to their guide. By listening with them to this scenario in the background, we learn a bit of the sign's history, including the fact that a Broadway actress who had hoped to find stardom in motion pictures, but did not, hanged herself in desperation from one of the letters of the sign. As Faye and Tod talk, the wind blows, and we see that the sign, too, is fragile and blows in the wind.

Schlesinger's scenes help to underscore the increasing violence found in West's novella and Salt's screenplay. One of the first explicitly violent scenes concerns a bloody cockfight to which Tod and Faye go in search of diversion. The building in which the cockfight is held is large and airy, yet the men attending are crowded together in the center hovering over the bloody, fighting cocks, talking and laughing loudly, waving their money for bets above their heads and encouraging still more bloodshed.

The final scene of *The Day of the Locust* is a chaotic synthesis of all the dehumanizing and violent themes inherent in the body of the film. A major event, a Hollywood movie premiere, is scheduled, and many of the characters are drawn into the crowd to worship the filmstars in a bizarre rendition of what appears to be some ancient and sacred tribal ritual. For no ascertainable reason, the event turns into a riot, and fighting and bloodshed are rampant, not merely within the ranks of the spectators, but also against the film luminaries they have come to worship. In this scene, a major theme of West's work comes to the fore. The crowd not only wants to adore its gods and goddesses, but, parallel to ancient legends of many cultures, it also wants virtually to consume them, and this is a succinct example of the film's view of the whole of American society. The people are hungry for violence; they need it to survive. As they hover on the brink of World War II (Schlesinger inserts newspaper headlines forboding this fact throughout the film), if they cannot find a suitable target for their aggressions and bloodthirstiness, they will turn on themselves, even on their heroes. For in order to survive they must destroy, and their will to survive is strong.

Although not particularly successful at the box office, the film did well critically and in retrospect is a fine example of Schlesinger's work. Like West's original work, it is not enjoyable, but it has something to show society, and particularly the film industry, about itself.

Bonnie Fraser

THE DAY THE EARTH STOOD STILL

Released: 1951
Production: Julian C. Blaustein for Twentieth Century-Fox
Direction: Robert Wise
Screenplay: Edmond H. North; based on the novel *Farewell to the Master* by
   Harry Bates
Cinematography: Leo Tover
Editing: William Reynolds
Music: Bernard Herrmann
Running time: 93 minutes

Principal characters:
Klaatu .... Michael Rennie
Helen Benson .... Patricia Neal
Tom Stevens .... Hugh Marlowe
Dr. Barnhardt .... Sam Jaffe
Bobby Benson .... Billy Gray

The anxieties felt at the dawning of the atomic age, combined with the rise of UFO sightings in the late 1940's, set the stage for this literate science-fiction thriller concerning a flying saucer which lands in Washington, D.C. As the film opens, Klaatu (Michael Rennie), an envoy from a highly advanced galactic federation, emerges from his star ship accompanied by a nine-foot-tall robot. His initial reception is misread as hostile by a complement of troops who have surrounded the flying saucer. After an interrogation in which Klaatu's warnings are not conveyed to the authorities, the alien escapes from his detention and becomes a fugitive while hoping to find someone willing to listen to his crucial message. Disguised as a human, Klaatu eventually turns to the scientific community, represented by Dr. Barnhardt (Sam Jaffe), with his warning. He explains that the earth has been monitored for years by a federation of advanced beings dedicated to universal peace. Klaatu goes on to explain that the aggressive nature of humanity, enhanced by the potential for destruction inherent in nuclear weapons, endangers not only the earth but also in many ways the entire universe. His mission is to convince the major world powers to rechannel their aggressive tendencies and concentrate on humanitarian goals or face total annihilation.

   To illustrate that what he is saying is not merely an idle threat, Klaatu completely shuts down all forms of man-made power (except in essential areas such as hospitals) for a period of twenty-four hours. Realizing that he might not be able to convince the world leaders to react in time and also anticipating that he could be killed before he has completed his mission, Klaatu entrusts to a sympathetic widow, Helen Benson (Patricia Neal), with whom he lives in a boarding house and who is aware of his secret, a particular phrase which must be repeated to Gort, his cybernetic bodyguard, in the event of his death. The alien's suspicions are borne out when he is discovered and killed. Later, making her way through a security area, the widow reaches the robot and repeats the phrase, "Gort, Klaatu berrada nikto." At these words, the once immobile guardian stalks the streets of the nation's capital in search of the corpse of his companion.

After returning the lifeless body of Klaatu to the star ship, Gort proceeds to resurrect him for a brief period of time. It is at this point that Klaatu reminds the assembly of scientists of the threat of nuclear destruction. Before he leaves, Klaatu entrusts Gort with the task of remaining behind to make sure that the new course of peace and human rights is rigidly adhered to by the people of the earth.

The Day the Earth Stood Still is an unusually effective science-fiction film. One reason for this is the semidocumentary style in which director Robert Wise chose to present his film. There is a sense of immediacy inherent in this particular style of filmmaking which gives the fantastic subject matter a more convincing environment. Wise's direction is crisp and straightforward. His earlier work as editor of Orson Welles's *Citizen Kane* (1941) and his directorial assignments of *film noir* subjects such as *Born To Kill* (1947) and *The Set-Up* (1949) contribute to make *The Day the Earth Stood Still* a film of powerful, uncomplicated images.

The period of the Cold War and the UFO hysteria in which *The Day the Earth Stood Still* was produced also added to the effectiveness of the film. There were a great many anxieties about atomic secrets and the possibility of a third world war, so when a film dealing with a powerful liberal philosophy was presented, it was received with mixed emotions. There is an overriding social allegory which is woven into the very fabric of this thriller, and which allows the film to transcend its fantastic premise and concentrate on a fundamental faith in the goodness of humanity. It is easy to construe Klaatu as a Christ figure who sacrifices his life in order to preserve civilization. Simple situations such as his resurrection or his choice of "Carpenter" as his surname when he passes for human underline the overt Christian philosophy of this so-called federation of advanced beings. It was a refreshing point of view which gave an optimistic energy to *The Day the Earth Stood Still*, a point of view which relieved some of the tensions of the world condition. Additionally, the importance of a faithful child, Helen's son Bobby (Billy Gray), as Klaatu's ally and helper was a look toward a future of hope.

Beyond this philosophical prediliction *The Day the Earth Stood Still* is a masterful piece of entertainment. Rennie as Klaatu is perfectly restrained and noble. Neal as the widow is believable, and the supporting cast is excellent. The implications of atomic abuses also must have struck a cord with many filmmakers at the time, since this film heralded a series of science-fiction thrillers overflowing with monsters formed out of the ashes of atomic bombs and nuclear waste. Few were as restrained as *The Day the Earth Stood Still*. Yet Rennie remained the model of the benevolent visitor from the stars for years to come.

The music by Bernard Herrmann is also an important factor in the success of *The Day the Earth Stood Still*. There is a feeling of otherworldliness that is uncanny in Herrmann's music; he creates a proper atmosphere of tension and fear through electronic manipulation and eerie tonal effects. It is not often that the music can serve as a correlative for the action of a film, and yet in this particular assignment Herrmann was able to instill into his music an alien beauty and force which completely complements the film.

Although *The Day the Earth Stood Still* has its roots in a short story by Harry Bates published in a science-fiction magazine more than a decade earlier, this film was able to capture the fear and anxieties of both the UFO craze and the fears of an impending nuclear holocaust. There was very little in the way of exotic special effects (as in later science-fiction films such as *Close Encounters of the Third Kind*, 1977). The film concentrated on the implications of dealing with a race of beings more powerful and technologically advanced than humans, rather than becoming overwhelmed at the fact that "we are not alone."

It is not inconceivable to draw a comparison between this film and Steven Speilberg's *Close Encounters of the Third Kind*. In a sense, both films deal with the discovery that life exists outside this planet. While *Close Encounters of the Third Kind* deals introspectively with the problems of an average man trying to come to grips with the fact of his close encounter, *The Day the Earth Stood Still* eliminates the sense of wonder, replacing it with anxiety and mistrust. The conclusion of both films is optimistic, although *The Day the Earth Stood Still* betrays the cynicism of the cultural climate during the 1950's.

The message found in *The Day the Earth Stood Still* might seem banal by contemporary standards. In a period of ultraconservatism, however, this altruistic ambience was a very different and perhaps even courageous statement.

Carl Macek

DEAD END

Released: 1937
Production: Samuel Goldwyn for Goldwyn Studios
Direction: William Wyler
Screenplay: Lillian Hellman; based on the play of the same name by Sidney
    Kingsley
Cinematography: Gregg Toland
Editing: Daniel Mandell
Art direction: Richard Day
Running time: 93 minutes

> *Principal characters:*
> Baby Face Martin .... Humphrey Bogart
> Drina .... Sylvia Sidney
> Dave .... Joel McCrea
> Kay .... Wendy Barrie
> Francie .... Claire Trevor
> Tommy .... Billy Halop
> Dippy .... Huntz Hall
> Angel .... Bobby Jordan
> Spit .... Leo Gorcey
> T. B. .... Gabriel Dell
> Philip .... Charles Peck
> Mrs. Martin .... Marjorie Main

In 1937, Warner Bros. seemed to have a monopoly on films dealing with
social problems and injustice in America. *Dead End*, adapted from Sidney
Kingsley's long-running Broadway hit play of the same name, was Samuel
Goldwyn's version of this type of Warner Bros. film, for its theme was poverty
and corruption in New York's lower East Side. The play was about slum
children who lived in close proximity to both the rich penthouse dwellers and
the criminals spawned in the city streets. Still feeling the effects of the depression, Americans could easily identify with this subject. In spite of its many
overtheatrical moments, there is enough of a documentary flavor in *Dead
End* to have convinced audiences of the 1930's that what they were seeing on
the screen was the genuine human condition.

Goldwyn wisely chose William Wyler to direct the film. Although they had
developed a rapport while working together on *Dodsworth* (1936) and *These
Three* (1936) for Goldwyn Pictures, Goldwyn still did not trust Wyler completely and vetoed the director's request to shoot the film on location on the
East side of Manhattan. Goldwyn thought he could retain more control by
building sets and keeping the production tied to his back lot. The set that
was finally built was the talk of Hollywood. Designer Richard Day, who had
just won an Oscar for *Dodsworth*, created a magnificent complex of seedy

apartment buildings, shops, a luxury hotel complete with penthouse, and a model of the filthy East River in which the Dead End Kids could swim. Goldwyn hired Lillian Hellman, whose hit play *The Children's Hour* had been the basis for *These Three*, to write the screenplay. As for casting, Humphrey Bogart was borrowed from Warner Bros. to play Baby Face Martin, the criminal antihero who is one of the role models for the youthful slum dwellers. Bogart was still relatively new to films, and in *Dead End* he was able to build his first complete character since his role as the psychopath Duke Mantee in *The Petrified Forest* (1936) at Warner Bros.

As the film opens, cinematographer Gregg Toland beautifully swings his camera around to show a group of adolescent boys, obviously very poor, swimming in the East River, while around them life of all sorts is teeming. In the penthouse of the hotel apartment off the river, an expensively dressed young boy is having breakfast with his father. Women from the tenements are hanging out clothes and men are loitering on street corners. Tommy (Billy Halop), the leader of the gang of boys, has been reared by his sister Drina (Sylvia Sidney), a sensitive girl waging a losing battle to get herself and her brother away from their pitiful surroundings. Drina is in love with Dave (Joel McCrea), an unemployed architect who is also anxious to escape the neighborhood. In melodramatic fashion, however, Dave is infatuated with Kay (Wendy Barrie), a woman kept very luxuriously by a New York businessman in an apartment on the river.

As the horseplay between the gang of boys goes on, including beating up Philip (Charles Peck), the "rich kid," into the neighborhood comes Baby Face Martin (Humphrey Bogart), a known killer who has returned to his childhood home to see his mother and his ex-sweetheart. Martin has a price on his head and has had his face changed by plastic surgery. His confrontations with the neighborhood form the rest of the story. For the boys he is a hero who enjoys an easy life of crime, full of excitement and money; for Dave, Martin represents what he could have become if he had given in to the despair he so often felt. Martin's mother (Marjorie Main) completely rejects her son. In one of the most memorable scenes in the film, the work-weathered old woman tells her son that he has never brought her anything but trouble, then slaps him and slams the door in his face. Francie (Claire Trevor), Martin's girl, did not wait for him and is now out on the streets.

Events culminate when Martin, in an effort to "get back" at the neighborhood, decides to kidnap Philip. When Dave tries to interfere, he is superficially stabbed by Martin, but he still manages to overpower one of Martin's henchmen, take his gun, and kill Martin. The police come, and Dave learns that he will receive a reward for turning in Martin. He sees this as his chance to go away with Kay, but decides she is really not for him. The police look for Tommy, who has stolen Philip's watch and who nearly kills Spit (Leo Gorcey), the gang member who reported him to the police. Drina and Dave find Tommy in time to save Spit and talk Tommy into giving himself up to the police. The officers take Tommy away as Drina finds comfort in Dave's arms. The film ends on a hopeful note with Dave planning to use his reward money to hire a lawyer who will save Tommy from reform school and enable them to leave the dead end street forever.

Dead End seems a bit dated now, especially since its protagonists are portrayed as such glaring examples of good and evil; it contains so many outstanding moments, however, that it is still fascinating. When Sidney pushes back her hair to show the bruise on her forehead that resulted from a blow received on the picket line, she represents the working girl of the 1930's fighting with her union to give her a break. Just as moving are the Dead End Kids—Billy Halop, Huntz Hall, Bobby Jordan, Leo Gorcey, and Gabriel Dell. They were also in the stage production and seemed to come from the very tenements in which the story took place. When they are on screen, the forced histrionics of the film fade away and *Dead End* becomes a social document. The film launched the careers of the Dead End Kids, who were to appear together in numerous other films of a similar, although less socially significant, vein.

Dead End pleased both critics and audiences, and *The New York Post* devoted an editorial to it stating that the best thing that could have been done at the last session of Congress would have been to show the film to the committee that crippled the Wagner Housing Act. The film received four Oscar nominations, for Best Picture, Best Supporting Actress, Best Direction, and Best Art Direction, but lost in a year which boasted *Lost Horizon, The Life of Émile Zola, The Good Earth*, and the original *A Star Is Born*. The combination of Goldwyn, Wyler, and Hellman was to surface again, however, four year's later when they collaborated on another unforgettable film, *The Little Foxes* (1941).

Joan Cohen

DEAD OF NIGHT

Released: 1945

Production: Michael Balcon for Ealing Studios; released by Universal

Direction: Basil Dearden ("The Linking Story" and "The Hearse Driver"), Alberto Cavalcanti ("The Christmas Story" and "The Ventriloquist's Dummy"), Robert Hamer ("The Haunted Mirror"), and Charles Crichton ("The Golfing Story")

Screenplay: John Baines, Angus MacPhail, and T. E. B. Clarke; based on the stories "The Linking Story" and "The Hearse Driver" by E. F. Benson and "The Golfing Story" by H. G. Wells

Cinematography: Jack Parker and H. Julius

Editing: Charles Hasse

Music: Georges Auric

Running time: 104 minutes

Principal characters:

The Linking Story

Walter Craig	Mervyn Johns
Eliot Foley	Roland Culver
Mrs. Foley	Mary Merrall
Dr. Van Straaten	Frederick Valk
Mrs. Craig	Renee Gadd

The Hearse Driver

Hugh Grainger	Antony Baird
Joyce Grainger	Judy Kelly
Hearse Driver	Miles Malleson

The Christmas Story

Sally O'Hara	Sally Ann Howes
Jimmy Watson	Michael Allan
Dr. Albury	Robert Wyndham

The Haunted Mirror

Joan Courtland	Googie Withers
Peter Courtland	Ralph Michael
Dealer	Esme Percy

The Ventriloquist's Dummy

Maxwell Frere	Michael Redgrave
Sylvester Kee	Hartley Power
Beulah	Elisabeth Welch
Mitzi	Magda Kun
Harry Parker	Garry Marsh

The Golfing Story

George Parratt .... Basil Radford
Larry Potter .... Naunton Wayne
Mary Lee .... Peggy Bryan

Dead of Night comprises a group of five horror stories loosely linked together. In many ways, the stories are rather cozy ones, which is not to say that they are not spine-chilling, but that they have an admirable lack of blood and violence. There is something terribly proper and terribly English about the tales, even down to the setting of the linking story, a charming English farmhouse which emits not the tiniest hint of evil or horror. The film is beautifully made and conceived, and it is not surprising that it had no problem in gaining an original American release through Universal.

To a farmhouse in rural England, to join a group of very English individuals and to discuss remodeling the place, comes an architect named Walter Craig (Mervyn Johns). He is perturbed by the feeling that he has been there before in his dreams and that he has met all the characters gathered there before. "I've seen you in my dreams—it sounds like a sentimental song, doesn't it?" he says to Dr. Van Straaten (Frederick Valk), a psychiatrist who is the only member of the group unwilling to accept the existence of the supernatural. The only problem is that Craig does not remember how his dream ends, only that it ends in horror and that within minutes of awakening he has forgotten all about it. The group, while accepting Craig's dream, do not fail to find humor in the situation. When the architect tells teenaged Sally O'Hara (Sally Ann Howes) that she cannot leave because in his dream he must hit her, the girl's mother tells him reassuringly, "I'm sure you'll find somebody else you can hit."

Each member of the group, aside from Mrs. Foley (Mary Merrall), the wife of the owner of the farmhouse Eliot Foley (Roland Culver), proceeds to tell of a strange occurrence in his or her life. The first to speak is Hugh Grainger (Anthony Baird), a racing driver, who recounts—as the camera pictures the events—how he was injured in a racing accident and sent to a hospital where he met a nurse named Joyce (Judy Kelly) who was to become his wife. While in the hospital he is troubled by dreams, and shortly before his release he is sitting up in bed one evening reading. Slowly the sounds in the room, the radio and the ticking clock, stop. He looks at the clock, which reads 4:15, and goes to the window, across which the drapes are drawn. When he pulls the drapes back, he is amazed to discover that it is daylight outside and horrified to see a hearse standing in the driveway. The driver of the hearse (Miles Malleson) looks up at him and says, "Just room for one more inside, sir." Grainger returns to his bed, the sounds of the room return, and it is once more late evening. What Grainger had experienced, however, was not a dream but a premonition. Recovered, he leaves the hospital and stands in line at a bus stop, where he is asked the time: 4:15. When the bus comes along, the conductor is the same man that Grainger saw as the hearse driver, and, again, he says, "Just room for one more inside, sir." Horrified, Grainger refuses to board the bus and watches as it crashes through an embankment, presumably killing all its passengers.

Back at the farmhouse, Grainger's wife arrives, whom Craig had also seen in his dream as "the penniless brunette," and Sally O'Hara says she must leave, but not before she recounts her story. She is on a Christmas vacation in Somerset, in a house full of happy children playing a game called "Sardines," similar to Hide-and-Seek. One of the other children tells Sally of a murder committed in the house in the 1800's, when the daughter murdered her younger brother, and shortly thereafter Sally wanders into a bedroom she had not seen before and finds a sobbing boy who tells of his unhappiness and how hateful his sister is to him. After she has tucked the child up in bed, Sally returns to the other children, tells them of the child she came across, and, of course, learns that the boy, who identified himself to her as Francis Kent, was the child murdered years earlier in the house.

Each of these stories is easily explained away by Dr. Van Straaten, as is the next one, told by Joan Courtland (Googie Withers). She had purchased an antique mirror as a birthday present for her fiancé and each time he looked in it he could see another room from an earlier age with a four-poster bed and a fire burning in the grate. Only when she held his hand tightly did the image disappear and he see the room in which he was standing. Behind the mirror lurked something evil, and, as her fiancé explained, "I feel that room in the mirror is trying to claim me." Finally the evil image disappears and the two are married, but when the wife goes on a visit to her mother, the image reappears, strengthening its grip on the husband. While visiting her mother, Joan Courtland spies in the same antique shop in which she had purchased the mirror a four-poster bed identical to the one her husband had seen in the mirror's image. Questioning the owner (Esme Percy), the wife discovers that both came from the same estate, that of an arrogant and violent-tempered man who was confined to his bed after a riding accident, and who spent his days staring in the mirror and imagining his wife's infidelity. Eventually, in a jealous rage, he had strangled his wife in front of the mirror and then cut his own throat.

Nervous, Joan Courtland returns home to find her husband sitting in front of the mirror, having assumed many of the personality traits of the dead man. He accuses her of spending the weekend with another man and attempts to strangle her in front of the mirror. As he tightens the scarf around her neck, Joan Courtland for the first time sees the mirror image her husband has been seeing. Desperately she breaks free and smashes the mirror, thus smashing its grip on her husband, who is totally unaware of what has occurred.

Craig has become more agitated, and despite his appearing less and less like a particularly acceptable house guest, he is persuaded to stay and listen to another story, a humorous tale of two golfing buddies. Basil Radford and Naunton Wayne are the two pals, expertly playing together as they had done in countless British films from Alfred Hitchcock's *The Lady Vanishes* (1938) onward. They have both fallen in love with the same girl, and, naturally, the only way to decide which one gets the girl is to play golf for her. At the eighteenth hole, the two are neck-and-neck, but Parratt (Naunton Wayne) cheats, and, being a gentleman of honor, Potter (Basil Radford) walks into a nearby pond and drowns himself. When Parratt is next at the eighteenth hole he is confronted by Potter's ghost who has discovered the trick Parratt played, and proceeds to ruin his former friend's game. Unfortunately, Potter, who has been able to make himself visible only to Parratt, forgets how to make himself invisible. He accompanies his friend to the wedding, and on the wedding night, when the desperate Parratt, trying to find the signals that Potter needs to make himself invisible, becomes invisible himself, it is Potter who gleefully enters the bride's room. This is the weakest story in *Dead of Night*. Mrs. Foley declares it "totally incredible and decidedly improper," but it is also very English and not very funny.

The final story is told by Van Straaten and is the best known and the best directed—by Alberto Cavalcanti—sequence in the film. It concerns a ventriloquist, splendidly played by Michael Redgrave, who is taken over by his dummy. When he suspects that his dummy plans to leave him for another ventriloquist, he shoots the man. In his prison cell, Van Straaten has the dummy brought to the ventriloquist who, in fury, suffocates it in a pillow. When Van Straaten and the other ventriloquist, who was only wounded, visit Redgrave in an asylum they find him speaking with the dummy's voice. It is a classic story, directed in a style of which Ingmar Bergman would have been proud, and has rightly been classified as one of the greatest Gothic horror stories of all time. In some scenes, according to *The New York Times* (June 30, 1946), the dummy was actually played by a real person, one Johnny Maguire, dubbed Charlie Macabre for obvious reasons, and whose voice is used for the dummy. Aside from a *tour-de-force* performance by Redgrave, the ventriloquist sequence also offers a song by one of the great black singers of the 1920's and 1930's, Elisabeth Welch.

The stories ended, the house guests disappear on one errand or another, leaving only Craig and Dr. Van Straaten—unable to see without his accidentally broken glasses—in the darkened room. The four stories merge in Craig's mind, with his participating in each, as he proceeds to strangle Van Straaten for reasons which are unclear. Suddenly, the scene changes and Craig is back at home in his bedroom: it was all a dream. Then he receives a telephone call to attend a weekend house party and discuss remodeling a farmhouse. The film ends, as it began, with Craig's car driving down the lane towards the house in his dreams.

Dead of Night was well received in the United States on its initial release. *Time* (July 15, 1946) described it as "smoothly acted, cleverly directed, well off the beaten Hollywood path." *The New Yorker* (July 13, 1946) thought "The cast of *Dead of Night* runs through its odd paces with utter assurance." *Variety* (July 5, 1946) described the film as "one of the better offerings from British film industry." On its initial American release, two episodes, "The Haunted Mirror" and "The Golfing Story," were cut from the film, giving it a running time of seventy-seven minutes, but *Dead of Night* has always been screened in its entirety on television in this country.

Anthony Slide

DEATH WISH

Released: 1974
Production: Hal Landers, Bobby Roberts, and Michael Winner for Dino de
  Laurentiis; released by Paramount
Direction: Michael Winner
Screenplay: Wendell Mayes; based on the novel of the same name by Brian
  Garfield
Cinematography: Arthur J. Ornitz
Editing: Bernard Gribble
Running time: 93 minutes

Principal characters:
Paul Kersey .... Charles Bronson
Joanna Kersey .... Hope Lange
Inspector Frank Ochoa .... Vincent Gardenia
Carol Kersey Toby .... Kathleen Tolan
Jack Toby .... Steven Keats

1974 saw the release of what normally would have been just another routine
if slickly directed and photographed action film. *Death Wish*'s theme, however,
that an ordinary citizen seeking revenge and becoming a violent, one-man
vigilante squad, hit a raw spot with the American public at a time when crime
in the streets was steadily intensifying while police efforts to quell it seemed
largely ineffectual.

In the film, Paul Kersey (Charles Bronson) is a successful Manhattan
architect who espouses all the "accepted" liberal views. We first see him
beneath the credits frolicking with his wife Joanna (Hope Lange) on an idyllic
sunny vacation in Hawaii. Back in New York, three young thugs posing as
delivery boys assault and kill his wife and rape his married daughter Carol
(Kathleen Tolan), which leaves her in a state of catatonia. Attempting to live
and cope with the horrendous deed, Kersey's liberal beliefs of leniency toward
delinquents and street crime disintegrate. When the police are unable to solve
the crime, Kersey feels a slowly overriding need for revenge. Soon after, on
business and recuperating in Arizona, Kersey is taken by a client to a pistol
range where he demonstrates his long unpracticed but expert skill with a gun.
As a parting gift, the client gives him a pearl-handled .32 caliber revolver.

Returning to New York, and further upset when his son-in-law Jack (Steven
Keats) tells him that Carol is no better, Kersey begins to haunt dark parks,
alleys, and subways, inviting attack, then killing his assailants. He soon
becomes a media hero (although his identity is unknown) called the "N.Y.
Vigilante." The police, with the investigation led by Inspector Frank Ochoa
(Vincent Gardenia), slowly begin to track him down. Meanwhile, with
Kersey's continuing activities, muggings in the city are cut nearly in half, and

city authorities, who do not want Kersey to become a martyr, order Ochoa to act discreetly. Kersey is wounded on one of his forays and captured by the police, although Ochoa denies to the press that he has Kersey in custody. Instead of booking him for his killings, he suggests to Kersey that he seek a business transfer to another city and leave town quietly. The final scene of the film, suggesting the sequel that was eventually made in 1981, has Kersey arriving in Chicago. While at the airport, suitcase in hand, he notices some deadbeat youths disturbing a woman. Silently, he raises his thumb and forefinger like a gun, takes aim, and "fires." (In the sequel, Kersey lives in Los Angeles, where his Mexican maid and teenaged daughter are both raped and killed.)

While restricted to adult attendance by its MPAA rating of R, *Death Wish* set off controversy among all factions of citizenry, no matter what age, race, sex, economic level, or profession, who lined up in droves to see it. It also aroused much ire from the leaders in society, politics, law enforcement, and medicine. Concerning the latter, press inquiries to doctors found only one psychiatrist who felt the film was dangerous, capable of causing imitative behavior, with the rest believing that it functioned as healthy fantasy release for its audience. Characteristic of the establishment "nay"-saying was the United States Catholic Conference, which slapped the picture with its "C" (Condemned) rating as a "pernicious appeal to the dark side of the American character."

Because of such furor, the film was an immediate hit and came to the forefront of a group of other films, beginning in 1971 with *Dirty Harry* and continuing with its sequel *Magnum Force* (1973) and *Walking Tall* and *The Longest Yard* (both 1974), that were denounced for their neo-Fascist philosophy. By 1979, *Variety* showed a distributor rental figure of $8.8 million for the film. It had the quick effect of spawning many imitative, often cheaply made versions of the same revenge/vigilante story, their production not limited to America but worldwide.

Death Wish was popular with audiences for another reason: it was a simple, extremely well-paced and violent melodrama featuring a strong, sympathetic central figure. (The plot is nearly that of a Western.) The film is quite canny in its emotional manipulation of the audience; the opening murder and rape scenes are protracted and ugly, so that viewers immediately side with Kersey in his anger and frustration. The film is also cleverly made to avoid the charge of racism; despite the crime statistics, *Death Wish*'s muggers are a fully integrated lot, and the three responsible for the initial violence are out-and-out inhuman crazies.

Critically, among the professional reviewers, the motion picture had more defenders than attackers. Naturally, in a film as seemingly volatile as *Death Wish*, there was little middle ground of opinion. Several writers did feel that the film presented an unrealistically harsh view of New York, with the film, of course, being made by out-of-towners (director Michael Winner was from London, and screenwriter Wendell Mayes from Los Angeles.) The film originated when Winner took the novel to Dino de Laurentiis, who saw its commercial possibilities. The producer claims that Bronson shared their enthusiasm and signed immediately. Mayes, who had previously written the screenplays for *The Poseidon Adventure* (1972), *Advise and Consent* (1962), and *Anatomy of a Murder* (1957), wrote the script. Production began in Hawaii on January 17, 1974, and continued in Tucson before moving to New York. Principal photography ended in March, and the film was released later that year.

Much of the credit for the film's effectiveness goes to Winner, an ebullient, fast-working English director (snidely described in a film source as "his own best publicist") who took University degrees in law and economics while working as a reporter. He began making short films in the mid-1950's. His early English features, made in the mid-1960's, most notably *I'll Never Forget Whatshisname* (1967), were lively, efficient, intelligent films. Since then, he has prolifically specialized in internationally casted action films in all genres, shot entirely on location with steadily increasing budgets, with varying degrees of success and excess. Several were made with Bronson: *Chato's Land* (1971), *The Mechanic* (1972), and *The Stone Killer* (1973), with the latter uniting the pair with Laurentiis.

By the time of the production of *Death Wish*, Laurentiis had been involved in some six hundred films, and a year earlier had moved his production headquarters to New York (*Death Wish* was his fourth film there) from Rome, where he had built Cinecittà, a huge studio complex. His early films (*Bitter Rice*, 1950; *La Strada*, 1956; and *Cabiria*, 1957) closely associated him with the Italian Neo-Realist movement. From that point on, however, he turned increasingly to more commercial enterprises, from epics such as *The Bible* (1966) and *Waterloo* (1969), to genre items such as *Barbarella* (1968), *Mafioso* (1964), *Anzio* (1968), and the lamentable *King Kong* (1976) remake. On occasion, one of his films, such as *Serpico* (1972), proves distinguished.

Bronson's career has paralleled that of Clint Eastwood to a certain extent. He appeared in routine 1950's films in the United States before going to Europe, where he became a huge star largely with *The Magnificent Seven* (1960), *The Great Escape* (1963), and *The Dirty Dozen* (1967). At one point, Bronson was the world's most "bankable" star, at a time when only buffs with good memories knew who he was. Finally, with *Death Wish*, he became a box-office superstar and has continued to be a much sought-after actor. Many critics found his work in *Death Wish* admirable, forging a convincing portrait of a man slowly and fearfully turning to violence, which he previously abhorred, and ultimately becoming trapped by it.

Almost the only participant unhappy with the film was Brian Garfield, author of the source novel, who felt that the filmmakers unconscionably converted his evil, psychotic killer into a film knight in shining armor. When

CBS, in 1976, announced their intention to telecast the picture, albeit in a heavily edited version, Garfield went to the press to complain, calling the film "dangerous" and sure to "incite kooks." The film, however, was aired without incident. Interestingly, Garfield, partly to atone for the film's sins, wrote a follow-up novel to *Death Wish* called *Death Sentence*, in which he offered alternative solutions to crime other than the vigilantism which the film seemed to advocate. Thus far, it has never been optioned for filming, with Laurentiis one of the first to pass it up.

David Bartholomew

THE DEFIANT ONES

Released: 1958
Production: Stanley Kramer for United Artists
Direction: Stanley Kramer
Screenplay: Nathan E. Douglas and Harold Jacob Smith
Cinematography: Sam Leavitt (AA)
Editing: Frederic Knudtson
Running time: 97 minutes

> *Principal characters:*
> Joker Jackson .... Tony Curtis
> Noah Cullen .... Sidney Poitier
> Sheriff Max Muller .... Theodore Bikel
> Big Sam .... Lon Chaney, Jr.
> The Woman .... Cara Williams
> Billy .... Kevin Coughlin

Throughout his career as a producer and director, Stanley Kramer has stood in diametric opposition to an old Hollywood adage often attributed to Sam Goldwyn, that "if you want to send a message, use Western Union." Many of Kramer's films are overtly concerned with social issues, and his position is always that of a political liberal. If, with the passage of time, some of his theses—in the case of *The Defiant Ones*, the idea of the brotherhood of man and the desirability of racial harmony—have come to seem self-evident, they were by no means self-evident when the films were originally released.

When *The Defiant Ones* was released in 1958, the nation had only tentatively begun to commit itself to the goal of racial equality. The Supreme Court outlawed segregated schools, but the process of integration was resulting in massive resistance in the South, and the passage of the landmark Civil Rights Act of 1964 was still in the future. If, in 1958, it seemed to some observers that many whites would never willingly associate with blacks, Kramer had an answer. He produced *The Defiant Ones*, a film showing how two men filled with violent racial antipathy came to respect each other as human beings when forced by circumstances to do so. Kramer's protagonists are literally chained together. This chain symbolizes the inextricable connection between blacks and whites in American society; the experience of living and working together—even if this cooperation is imposed by law and is initially involuntary—should ultimately produce a greater understanding and harmony between the races. This is the implicit message in *The Defiant Ones*.

As the film opens, a group of convicts on a chain gang is being transported by truck back to prison. One of them, a black man named Noah Cullen (Sidney Poitier), is defiantly singing and chanting a song called "Long Gone from Bowling Green." Joker Jackson (Tony Curtis), the white prisoner to whom he is chained, tells him to shut up and calls him a nigger when he refuses. Racial epithets fill the air, and the two men come to blows. The conflict becomes so violent that the truck driver loses control of his vehicle and it plunges off the road. In the ensuing confusion, Noah and Joker escape, still chained together.

The two men are pursued by Sheriff Max Muller (Theodore Bikel) and a motley crew of white townspeople that Muller is forced to deputize for assistance. This group includes the owner of the bloodhounds and dobermans being used to track the escapees, as well as a dim-witted young man who carries a portable radio that blares rock-and-roll music at top volume, much to the disgust of the rest of the posse. Kramer uses this radio as the only comic relief from the intensity of the rest of the film. In addition, he uses the radio in two other ways. The meaninglessness of the music it plays is contrasted with the poignant and deeply felt blues that Noah Cullen sings at the beginning and end of the film. Almost every time the scene shifts from Joker and Noah to the Sheriff and his posse, the transition is heralded by the appearance of music from this radio on the soundtrack.

The efforts of Noah and Joker to break the chain joining them together are unsuccessful. Kramer uses a series of short scenes alternating between the escapees and the posse to establish the basic predicament of each group. The convicts' problem is how to elude the posse while bound together at the wrist by three feet of chain. The physical problems imposed by the chain are considerable, but these problems are insignificant compared to the problems caused by the fact that the two men hate each other.

Sheriff Muller has problems of his own. He is a humane man and wants to recapture the two escapees without harming them. His posse, however, has no such compunctions; they would gladly see Noah and Joker dead. Kramer thus underlines his point with irony: just as Noah and Joker are slowed by mutual antipathy in their attempt to escape, so is the Sheriff's efforts to apprehend the two men hindered by dissension in his ranks.

With the film's basic themes thus foreshadowed, Kramer begins to concentrate on the subtly changing relationship between Noah and Joker. Of the two men, Joker Jackson, the white, is the more bigoted. His racisim is cultural, something, as Noah says, that he breathed in when he was born and that he has been spitting back out ever since. Noah, on the other hand, has been given a better reason to resent whites: a lifetime of racist oppression which culminated in the eviction of his family from their farm by a white man. When Noah resisted this eviction, he was sent to prison for assault.

The hostility between the two men flares constantly, usually as a result of one of Joker's racist insults. Gradually, however, these incidents grow less frequent. Midway through the film, Noah and Joker have their first real conversation (all previous dialogue between the two having been argument or insult). They have stumbled upon a small village which contains a general store where they hope to find tools to break the chain that binds them together. While they await the cover of darkness, they discuss their personal histories— their childhoods, their families, their hopes and fears. They do not become fast friends as a result, but the fact that they converse at all without fighting is significant.

Up to this point, the two fugitives had kept away from people; then, in two long sequences, they interact with other men and women. The first encounter comes as a result of the two men's abortive raid on the general store. Attempting to enter the store through a skylight, Joker slips and injures his wrist, pulling Noah down on top of him and crashing into loaded shelves in the process. The noise rouses the villagers, and the two men are captured.

The mob of townspeople are eager to lynch the convicts. Protesting that no one ever lynched a white man in the South, Joker is stunned to discover that the chain that links him to Noah physically has also linked the two of them spiritually, at least in the minds of the villagers. Only the intervention of Big Sam (Lon Chaney, Jr.), who later reveals to Noah and Joker that he is an ex-convict himself, saves them from the mob. Sam first dissuades the mob from lynching the escapees, and later that night he sneaks into the barn in which they are being held and sets them free.

After making good their escape, Noah and Joker quarrel once more. Their recent brush with death has pushed both men past the breaking point, and this time words cannot settle the argument. In an impressively staged scene, the two men begin to fight savagely. Kramer enhances the effect by placing the camera close to the ground and shooting up at an angle, thus outlining the action against the sky. With no background to provide a distraction, the ferocity of the battle is enhanced.

Just as it appears that the only way the fight will end is with the death of one of the participants, the two men are stopped by a young boy (Kevin Coughlin) with a rifle. Joker knocks the boy down, and he strikes his head on a rock, rendering him momentarily unconscious. Joker wants to run, but Noah insists that they stay and help the boy. When the boy regains consciousness, he is terrified by the sight of a black man and instinctively runs to Joker for shelter. Kramer here underlines Noah's earlier statement that prejudice is something that is breathed in at birth.

The two men learn the boy's name—Billy—and that he and his mother (Cara Williams) live alone in an isolated farmhouse. Assuming that Noah is Joker's prisoner, Billy leads the men to his home, where they force his mother to fix them a meal. Oddly enough, she is more intrigued than frightened by the situation, although she offers Noah food only after Joker insists. This is the first indication that Joker's attitude toward Noah has changed, and as soon as this psychological link is revealed, their physical link is finally broken. With a hammer and chisel, they sever the chain that has bound them together.

Thus Kramer sets the stage for a genuine test of their new relationship.

The question that must be answered is whether or not the two men respect each other enough to stay together now that cooperation is no longer mandatory. Noah is tested first, and he proves loyal to Joker. No sooner are the two men freed from their chain than Joker collapses; his injured wrist has become badly infected. Noah, who might have taken this opportunity to flee, chooses to stay until his partner recovers.

That night, Billy's mother—never given a name in the film—comes to Joker's bedside. When he awakens, they talk and discover that they have much in common—including a deep sense of loneliness. They sleep together that night. Convinced that Joker is her ticket out of her lonely life and that Noah is a threat to her plans, Billy's mother schemes to separate the two men. She asks Joker to leave with her and suggests that Noah could escape easily on his own by hopping one of the trains that passes on the nearby tracks. Joker is uneasy about splitting up with Noah, but is ultimately persuaded to do so.

After Noah has left, however, the woman reveals that the path between her house and the railroad tracks is an impenatrable swamp, and that Noah has virtually no chance of surviving his run for freedom. Joker is furious; what he thought was only a separation from Noah has become a betrayal. He strikes the woman, and Billy shoots him in the shoulder. Finally, he staggers off in pursuit of Noah. As it turns out, he leaves just ahead of the Sheriff, who has tracked the men down. There is one last confrontation between the Sheriff and his posse over whether to use the vicious dogs to hunt the convicts down. The Sheriff wins the argument, but it is clear that if his humanitarian methods fail, he will lose his job.

Joker catches up with Noah, and the two men race through the swamp pursued by the Sheriff and his posse. They reach the train, and Noah jumps aboard, but Joker, weakened by the loss of blood from his wound, cannot make it. Noah extends his hand and Joker grabs for it, but by now he is dead weight, and Noah is pulled from the train. As they sit, exhausted, Noah cradles the wounded Joker in his arms. "We gave 'em a hell of a run for it, didn't we?," Joker asks. As the Sheriff approaches, Noah begins to sing "Long Gone from Bowling Green;" while the screen fades to black, he chuckles.

Thus Kramer resolves the film's two conflicts in a positive way. The conflict between Sheriff Muller and his posse indicates that the issue of race is not the sole source of disharmony in the world; and the fact that the Sheriff's humane tactics resulted in the recapture of the escapees shows that the humanitarian approach need not be ineffectual. The more important conflict, of course, is the racial antagonism between Joker Jackson and Noah Cullen. The hardwon resolution of this conflict reflects Kramer's basic optimism about the prospect for racial harmony in society at large.

At the time of its release, *The Defiant Ones* was controversial, at least among the general populace. Critics were less divided. The film received eight Academy Award nominations, including Best Picture and Best Director. Bikel as the stolid, oddly pacifistic Sherrif Muller and Williams as the lonely, conniving woman who tries to separate Joker and Noah turn in solid performances that won them justified nominations for Best Supporting Actor and Actress. Chaney is memorable in the smaller role of Big Sam, the ex-convict who helped Noah and Joker escape from the lynch mob. Poitier and Curtis turn in truly memorable performances in extremely demanding roles. Poitier's performance is perhaps the superior of the two, since Noah Cullen's character is a good deal more complex than that of Joker Jackson, and thus requires more subtlety to put across. Joker is all rage and desperation. Noah is angry and desperate too, but he has an instinctive compassion as well, which is something that Joker is only beginning to learn as the film ends. Both men received Academy Award nominations as Best Actor for their performances.

As good as the acting is, however, the primary focus of *The Defiant Ones* is its message, an affirmation of the brotherhood of man. Ironically, the original strength of the film has been diluted somewhat by the passage of time; the sentiments are less radical, more commonplace. If the message of brotherhood seems a bit obvious now, however, it is surely no less valid. *The Defiant Ones* is not merely a social document; it is an important and powerful cinematic landmark.

Robert Mitchell

DESIGN FOR LIVING

Released: 1933
Production: Ernst Lubitsch for Paramount
Direction: Ernst Lubitsch
Screenplay: Ben Hecht; based on the play of the same name by Noel Coward
Cinematography: Victor Milner
Editing: Francis Marsh
Interior decoration: Hans Dreier
Running time: 90 minutes

Principal characters:
Tom	Fredric March
George	Gary Cooper
Gilda	Miriam Hopkins
Max Plunkett	Edward Everett Horton

Although *Design for Living* is adapted from a play by Noel Coward which featured Alfred Lunt, Lynn Fontanne, and Coward himself, the film is a free adaptation owing not much more to the play than the basic premise of a *menage-a-trois*. In place of three sophisticated theater types, the film has down-to-earth Gary Cooper, Fredric March, and Miriam Hopkins; and Ben Hecht, who wrote the screenplay, has boasted of keeping only one line of dialogue originally written by Coward. Ernst Lubitsch could be counted on to invest this material with his own personality, as he invariably did in all of his films, and the result is an affecting comedy that is one of his finest works. Although Lubitsch is sometimes accused of squandering his talent on frivolous trifles, it is to his credit that there is no false solemnity in his films, that he could keep them light and sparkling while unfailingly revealing touching depths of emotion in his characters in the midst of so much laughter.

Lubitsch's heroine is Gilda (Miriam Hopkins), who combines the best qualities of mother, lover, partner, and good luck charm in encouraging the artistic endeavors of Tom (Fredric March) and George (Gary Cooper), two friends who both fall in love with her at the same time. Believing themselves capable of an unconventional arrangement to solve their romantic problems, the three guileless Americans agree that they will live together without sex and that Gilda will be the inspiration for the two unsuccessful men to become famous as playwright and painter, respectively. When Tom's play becomes a hit, however, he must travel to London alone, leaving George and Gilda together on the Continent. The arrangement fails, and Tom returns to find George, now a successful painter, living happily with Gilda. As Gilda still loves Tom as well as George, she becomes Tom's lover in George's absence, and soon the threesome is back where it began, with the result that Gilda resolves to marry the prissy Max Plunkett (Edward Everett Horton). The two buddies manage to steal her away before the wedding, and Gilda, Tom, and George find themselves together in the back of a taxi vowing, perhaps more knowingly, to return to the terms of the original agreement.

The most startling aspect of this situation, which is at once comic and morally challenging, is that the heroine never conceals the fact that she is in love with both men and is unwilling to lose either one. This places Tom and George in a position of having to be liberated men long before such a concept even existed. Gilda may be embraced as a glorious role model who personifies much that is meaningful in an emerging feminist spirit, but Tom and George, although sometimes bewildered and melancholy on her account, deserve our affection for much the same reason. Throughout the film, they strive with Gilda to find a new world, free of jealousy and inappropriate values, without ever failing to be humanly vulnerable. Although the film does not explicitly endorse a life-style which would permit Gilda to be the lover of both men, its images affirm that this is the true solution to the problem, and there is a subtle implication that the threesome is ready to accept this solution after the fadeout.

The film's inherited title cleverly offers a clue to a conflict between reason and instinct. The characters *design* a relationship which excludes physical love, but *living* is not possible within such a design. Whenever Gilda, George, and Tom are shown together in a single image, a feeling of balance and harmony is achieved. The separation of one of these characters from the group creates tension. The two men complement each other in every way, and their friendship is completed by their adoration of Gilda. It makes perfect sense that she is never able to choose between them. The complexity of affection shared by all three of these people makes the situation entrancingly romantic.

Lubitsch has a great deal of fun with this romanticism. In a lovingly designed garret shared by the two starving artists, Gilda shows up for a date and attractively falls back on a couch which immediately reveals that it is covered with dust. The dust rises, causing the *femme fatale* to cough at the exact moment she is most determined to show her composure. Later in the story, when she has put the room into a more orderly fashion, Gilda is left alone with George. They speak of their gentleman's agreement with Tom, and Gilda, unable to resist the temptation of pleasure, once more relaxes on the couch, seductively admitting, "I'm no gentleman."

While all of the scenes involving the threesome are captivating, as are those involving any two of the three characters, the best moment is reserved for Tom alone. Estranged from George and Gilda, Tom is leading the life of a successful playwright without pleasure. He goes to the theater where his inane comedy, *Goodnight, Bassington*, is playing. As he solemnly walks down the aisle with an irresistibly melancholy expression, the audience which fills the theater laughs unreservedly at every ridiculous line of dialogue coming from the stage. The climax of the scene is reached when the curtain line—which finds the hapless Bassington admonished with insipid words of wisdom once spoken by Max Plunkett and remembered by the discerning Tom—is greeted with the loudest laughter yet and thunderous applause. Tom reacts with all the emotional expressiveness of a zombie.

Without forgetting that the 1930's abounded in memorable comedies, it is appropriate to single out *Design for Living* as one of the most sophisticated, provocative, and funny films of that decade. Hecht, a writer supremely adaptable to the differing personalities of an impressive number of great directors, provides a Lubitsch script which rivals those of Samson Raphaelson in romantic richness and sparkling wit. The offbeat casting of March and Cooper is extremely effective, the touch of naïveté which these two actors possess making the characters of Tom and George endearingly sweet and lovable. It must be admitted, however, that March is considerably more convincing than Cooper in a drunk scene. Hopkins had previously appeared in several Lubitsch films, but even her beguiling performance opposite the supremely elegant Herbert Marshall in *Trouble in Paradise* (1932) is less lustrous than her incarnation of the bewitching Gilda, a woman in whom boldness and innocence coexist so appealingly that it is absolutely credible that the two men do not seek relationships with less complex women. The film is also enhanced by the lovely visual design and lighting expected in Lubitsch's work and, above all, by the limpidity and discretion of the director's style, which, at its most assured, is one of the most graceful to be found in cinema.

Blake Lucas

DESIGNING WOMAN

Released: 1957
Production: Dore Schary for Metro-Goldwyn-Mayer
Direction: Vincente Minnelli
Screenplay: George Wells (AA); based on a suggestion by Helen Rose
Cinematography: John Alton
Editing: Adrienne Fazan
Art direction: William A. Horning and Preston Ames; set decoration, Edwin
  B. Willis and Henry Grace
Costume design: Helen Rose
Choreography: Jack Cole and Barrie Chase
Running time: 118 minutes

Principal characters:
Mike Hagen	Gregory Peck
Marilla Hagen	Lauren Bacall
Lori Shannon	Dolores Gray
Ned Hammerstein	Sam Levene
Zachary Wilde	Tom Helmore
Maxie Stultz	Mickey Shaughnessy
Randy Owens	Jack Cole

Designing Woman is reminiscent of films starring the much-loved team of Katharine Hepburn and Spencer Tracy, especially *Woman of the Year* (1942), which had united that couple on screen for the first time. The film grew out of a suggestion, for which costume designer Helen Rose was credited, to have a sports writer and a fashion designer marry. This was a clever and imaginative idea, and it is easy to imagine Tracy and Hepburn in the respective roles, even as late as 1957, with their superb comic timing and the special romantic chemistry between them undiminished by time. Moreover, both had worked very effectively under the direction of Vincente Minnelli, Hepburn in *Undercurrent* (1946) and Tracy in *Father of the Bride* (1950) and *Father's Little Dividend* (1951). For whatever reason, however, it appears they were never involved in the project. James Stewart and Grace Kelly were tentatively set to star in the film, having already demonstrated a pleasing rapport in *Rear Window* (1954), a dissimilar work but one in which the two characters, a rugged journalist and a sophisticated model, are roughly equivalent. According to Stewart, he did not want to do the film without Kelly, who unexpectedly retired as the result of her marriage to Prince Ranier of Monaco.

Warm thoughts of Stewart and Kelly, let alone Tracy and Hepburn, should not obscure the fact that Gregory Peck and Lauren Bacall are more than acceptable in the film. In one sense, their unfamiliarity with each other is an advantage, as the story concerns a man and woman who know almost nothing about each other before their marriage and the adjustments each must make to bring stability and permanence to the relationship. The rare opportunity to play comedy was one which greatly pleased Peck, and both he and Bacall are surprisingly amusing. Inevitable comparisons with Tracy and Hepburn are mildly ungracious, and they do not serve to illuminate the particular charm of *Designing Woman*. For all its affinities with earlier romantic and screwball comedies, the film has a distinctive character of its own. Imagination, wit, and a pleasing unpredictability easily lift it to the level of the best Tracy-Hepburn films.

Marilla (Lauren Bacall) and Mike Hagen (Gregory Peck) are both from New York, but they meet in Southern California; and their brief romantic courtship is not intruded upon by the disparate realities of their respective worlds at home. Once they arrive back in New York as man and wife, however, she is dismayed by his prosaic apartment and he is intimidated by the elegance and spaciousness of hers. Bowing to practicality, Mike moves in with Marilla. The two are then introduced to each other's friends and milieus. Marilla is sickened by the sight of blood at a prize fight, and Mike is contemptuous of the ceremonious gentility of a fashion show. Complicating matters further, both Mike and Marilla must resolve their past romantic involvements. Mike is unreasonably resentful of Broadway producer Zachary Wilde (Tom Helmore), although Marilla had refused Wilde's proposals of marriage. At the same time, frightened by Marilla's potential jealousy, Mike unwisely attempts to conceal his former relationship with musical star Lori Shannon (Dolores Gray). Conflict between the couple accelerates when Mike attempts to hold his weekly poker game at their apartment on the same night that Marilla is hosting a production meeting for a Broadway show on which she is working. Both Mike and Marilla single out one of the other's associates for scorn. Marilla is appalled by punchdrunk ex-fighter Maxie Stultz (Mickey Shaughnessy), while Mike is embarrassed by the effusive choreographer Randy Owens (Jack Cole). Neither is being fair. Maxie, both humorously and pitiably uncomprehending of the realities of life, was once a champion. Randy, although ridiculously posturing, is an artist. Overhearing Mike's brutal and thoughtless insinuation that he is a homosexual, Randy confronts the other with dignity, brandishing photos of his wife and children and expressing his willingness to defend his honor physically.

Resolution of the differences between Mike and Marilla is made more difficult by ensuing events. Both Wilde and Lori are involved in the same Broadway show as Marilla. Mike is sent into hiding by his editor Ned Hammerstein (Sam Levene) in order to complete an exposé of the involvement of mobsters in the fight game. With Maxie assigned as a bodyguard, Mike holes up in a hotel but fools Marilla into believing he is traveling around the country to report on the New York Yankees baseball team. Ultimately, Mike jeopardizes his safety to reconcile with Marilla, and surprisingly, it is the agile

Owens who subdues the gangsters with his balletic kicks and jumps. In the end, Wilde and Lori become romantic partners, Mike and Marilla are reunited, accepting each other with a new maturity, and Maxie continues to train, confident that a comeback awaits him.

Two related motifs, one serious and one fanciful, provide the fabric which serves the work's design. The serious motif is the difficulty of adjustment in marriage. Differing attitudes, experiences, and ways of life must somehow be accepted by even the most ardent lovers if marriage is to succeed. Mike and Marilla both look at life subjectively. Confronted by the other's world, each regards it as bizarre and threatening. The jealousy and petulance evinced in the responses of Mike and Marilla to Zachary Wilde and Lori Shannon may seem childish and quaint, but as a symptom of the mutual insecurity with which they confront their differences, this emotional immaturity is very meaningful.

The second and more fanciful motif is the convergence of four separate worlds: fashion, news reporting, the theater, and the underworld. It is this convergence which aggravates the problems of the central couple and makes the situations presented so funny. A highlight is the sharing of the apartment by the two groups respectively associated with Mike and Marilla. Initially, a dividing screen separates the groups, but as the sequence progresses, people from each group begin to wander throughout the space of the apartment. The screen is opened and the ritual poker players must observe the creative enthusiasm of Randy, who begins to dance about the apartment with abandon. Director Minnelli, enamored of the visual humor and disarming mood implicit in the juxtaposition of milieus, composes much of the sequence so that the groups share the space within a shot. This disharmony between foreground and background is engagingly reckless. It also visually provokes an unsought complicity between the groups which amusingly undermines the accepted patterns of behavior particular to each milieu. The sequence is at once magical and credible, and as a consequence, the individual perceptions of reality to which Mike and Marilla cling are accorded a strange respect at the same time that they are revealed to be tenuous.

These motifs are not at all surprising in a work by Minnelli, and their latent presence in the premise of *Designing Woman* explains his attraction to the project. From *Father of the Bride* to *The Courtship of Eddie's Father* (1963), all of his comedies have involved courtship and marriage. These subjects are not unusual in American comedy, but Minnelli's predilection for finding a whimsical or nightmarish weirdness in character and situation and the humor he derives from this predilection are idiosyncrasies of his art. Minnelli was generally brought into projects at an early stage, and *Designing Woman* was no exception, so it is natural that the director's personality is evident in George Wells's Academy Award-winning screenplay as well as in the realized film.

Both men deserve credit for the delightful character touches and incidental inventiveness which enliven the work. The moment in which Lori, informed by Mike of his sudden marriage, calmly pushes a plate of ravioli onto his lap is a high point, well-placed in the script and hilariously underplayed by Peck and Gray. The use of a multiple point of view to tell the story contributes immeasurably to the playful mood so well-sustained throughout the film. The device of a narrated flashback had been favored by Minnelli in two earlier comedies, *Father of the Bride* and *The Long, Long Trailer* (1954), but in those instances there was only one narrator. In *Designing Woman*, five voices—those of Mike, Marilla, Lori Shannon, Zachary Wilde, and Maxie Stultz—alternate. The resulting contradictory accounts of the events presented in the narrative enriches the audience's perspective as well as enhances the film's comic intentions.

The attention to decor and color characteristic of Minnelli's films is wonderfully manifested in the varying visual moods of *Designing Woman*'s contrasting worlds. Tasteful and lovely, Marilla's apartment is the opposite of the sleazy hotel room in which Mike is isolated with Maxie. The theater, the boxing arena, the fashion salon—each has a distinctive look, sometimes pretty, sometimes gaudy, always evocative. John Alton's lighting also contributes expressively to the film's fanciful nature. One example of this is the distorting glow on Maxie's face whenever his mind is most unhinged. This touch of artificiality is appropriate to Maxie, next to Randy Owens the film's most surprising character. Minnelli's characters often seem to be dreaming while awake, and Maxie provides a nice twist to this predisposition. He sleeps with his eyes open.

Blake Lucas

DESK SET

Released: 1957
Production: Henry Ephron for Twentieth Century-Fox
Direction: Walter Lang
Screenplay: Henry Ephron and Phoebe Ephron; based on the play of the same name by William Marchant
Cinematography: Daniel L. Fapp
Editing: Robert Simpson
Running time: 103 minutes

Principal characters:
Richard Sumner	Spencer Tracy
Barbara "Bunny" Watson	Katharine Hepburn
Mike Cutler	Gig Young
Peg Costello	Joan Blondell
Sylvia	Dina Merrill
Ruthie	Sue Randall
Miss Warriner	Neva Patterson
Smithers	Harry Ellerbe
Mr. Azae	Nicholas Joy

Motion pictures about career women usually focus on an assumed conflict between a woman's career and her femininity. Some of these films, such as *His Girl Friday* (1940), *Woman of the Year* (1942), and *Adam's Rib* (1949), use comedy to illustrate this conflict. *Desk Set* differs from these films because the problem of its career-woman protagonist, Bunny Watson (Katharine Hepburn), is not preserving her womanliness but preserving her job. Bunny's job is one which has been long dominated by women—the reference librarian— but an executive decision has been made to replace her with a machine. Ironically, the machine itself is "female." It has been titled "Miss Emmy," a nickname composed by humanizing its official title of "Emmarac," but it is actually an inside joke against the television media. ("Emmy," of course, refers to the yearly awards presented by the National Academy of Television Arts and Sciences.) "Miss Emmy" is a machine designed to replace "the girls" of the Federal Broadcasting Company's research department. The girls must prove that their job skills cannot be usurped by a machine.

No one questions their femininity. In fact, in Bunny's first scene she waltzes into her office and shows her staff the new dress she has purchased to dazzle Mike Cutler (Gig Young) in hopes that he will ask her to the company's yearly dinner dance. The staff responds with appropriate girlishness. Only Peg Costello (Joan Blondell) throws a bit of cold water onto the gay plans by indicating that Bunny's seven-year romance with Mike Cutler has all the charm of an "old coat."

After the character of Bunny and the office staff is established, Richard Sumner (Spencer Tracy) walks quietly in to visit the department prior to installing the Emmarac computer that he designed. Sumner meets Bunny, and the two wage mental warfare over lunch. This scene takes full advantage of the famous Tracy-Hepburn tradition. She is once again the quick-witted, incisive feminist while he is a seemingly conventional and complacent male with a curious mind but stubborn attitudes. The Tracy-Hepburn tradition informs the audience immediately that these two will fall in love with each other albeit against their wills. Bunny is determined not to allow her staff to be replaced with a machine, and Sumner is determined that his machine shall be installed.

Love emerging out of competition with a man is a familiar theme in films about career women. In the films previously mentioned, *Woman of the Year*, *Adam's Rib*, and others, the woman relinquishes ideals of independence to receive love. The woman is usually pictured as insolently aggressive while the man is tolerantly confident of his point-of-view. This basic premise is especially true in the Tracy-Hepburn films. Tracy's characters usually give Hepburn's just enough rope with which to hang themselves. When Hepburn sneaks into her estranged husband's apartment in George Stevens's *Woman of the Year*, she attempts to prepare a complete breakfast even though she does not even know how to use a toaster successfully. Her cooking is an attempt to win acclaim from him by being more womanly. The idea is offensive to feminists, but the scene is uproariously funny.

Competition in *Desk Set* is of a different sort. Here, the inventor of the computer is not perceived as the competition. Instead, the machine itself is the threat. In fact, Bunny must ultimately compete with "Miss Emmy" in order to win Richard Sumner's love. She orders Richard to prove his love by allowing "Miss Emmy" to go full tilt and break down. When the inevitable destruction has ocurred, Bunny provides the hairpin with which Richard is allowed to repair the machine. Ultimately Bunny and Richard establish a trade-off in which Bunny proves that a human brain is needed in the research department while Richard shows that Emmarac can liberate the research staff from repetitive routine. Thus, this motion picture has at least one fully realized modern idea of the computer age as well as presenting a career woman who does not have to give up her job for love.

Besides the unusual triangle of Bunny, Sumner, and "Miss Emmy," there is also the triangle of Bunny, Sumner, and Mike Cutler, the promising network executive who has courted Bunny for seven years. It is obvious from the beginning that Cutler will be the loser in this contest for Bunny's affections, principally because of our expectations of a Tracy-Hepburn film. Beyond that, however, Cutler's eager-beaver "man in the gray-flannel suit" personality is ill-suited to Hepburn's frizzy hair and independent demeanor. Hepburn looks just as jubilantly nonconformist in *Desk Set* as she did as Jo in *Little Women* some twenty-four years earlier. Cutler, played with banal aplomb by Young, frets constantly about feasibility studies and his imminent promotion. He drops everything, including a marriage proposal, in midsentence if the boss rings for him.

The film's fast-paced narrative and the capable performances of all the actors make *Desk Set* enjoyable entertainment. The dialogue is witty, and Hepburn's barbed jibes are answered with appropriately dry humor by Tracy. Blondell plays Peg, a wise-cracking contrast to the otherwise sophomoric reference staff. Also, her cynicism counters Young's perennial zealousness. The milieu of the television network is not emphasized, and the film could take place within any corporate structure. The film thus misses an opportunity to comment upon the cultural phenomenon of the still-infant electronic media during its first decade of national preeminence.

The original Broadway play was produced by Robert Fryer and Lawrence Carr from the play by William Marchant and starred Shirley Booth. Henry and Phoebe Ephron, who adapted the play for the screen, change the ending considerably: it was their idea for the computer expert and Bunny to fall in love. Indeed, the Ephrons built their careers upon translating Broadway plays to the Technicolor screen. Among their often shared credits are *Carousel* (1956), *Daddy Long Legs* (1955), and *The Best Things in Life are Free* (1956). Director Walter Lang also specialized in transforming plays into motion pictures; his credits include *The King and I* (1956), and *Can-Can* (1960).

Elizabeth Ward

THE DESPERATE HOURS

Released: 1955
Production: William Wyler for Paramount
Direction: William Wyler
Screenplay: Joseph Hayes; based on his novel and play of the same name
Cinematography: Lee Garmes
Editing: Robert Swink
Running time: 112 minutes

Principal characters:

Glenn Griffin	Humphrey Bogart
Dan Hilliard	Fredric March
Jesse Bard	Arthur Kennedy
Eleanor Hilliard	Martha Scott
Hal Griffin	Dewey Martin
Chuck (Cindy's boyfriend)	Gig Young
Cindy Hilliard	Mary Murphy
Ralphie Hilliard	Richard Eyer
Kobish	Robert Middleton

When *The Desperate Hours* opened in October, 1955, the reviews were good, although not ecstatic. Although director William Wyler received critical praise for his fine craftsmanship, and the stars, Humphrey Bogart and Fredric March, were mentioned as having given their usual excellent performances, the film did not receive well-deserved plaudits—perhaps because all of the elements were predictable.

Wyler had, by this point in his career, directed some fifty feature films, received eleven Academy Award nominations and two Academy Awards, plus two New York Film Critics Awards and numerous foreign honors. One of his most successful and best-loved films, *Roman Holiday* (1953), was still fresh in the mind of the public. In short, no one expected him to do less than a fine job.

The same is true of Bogart's performance. In his role as Glenn Griffin, he is the leader of three escaped convicts who take over a typical house in an average American city and hold the family hostage. Outlaws, ex-cons, gangsters, social deviates: Bogart had played them all at one time or another, and he played them to perfection. This was a role he could walk through with his eyes closed; yet a close study of his performance reveals that he gave the part much more than just a walk-through.

His squint-eyed, dry-mouthed portrait of a criminal awaiting his chance for revenge is blood-chilling. There is a ferocity about his being that is just below the surface, always on the verge of exploding, and this is what creates the tension between him and the March character, Dan Hilliard. As Hilliard tells his wife Eleanor (Martha Scott) at one point, "Griffin hates me. He hated

me before he even saw me. I can't explain it. Every hour some new black
hole appears in him. . . . God knows what a mind like that will turn to. . . ."
Bogart makes us believe the truth of that statement in every scene.

As Dan Hilliard, March was also re-creating a familiar role. He had played
solid, upright, perfectly average citizens most of his career. In *The Desperate
Hours*, if Bogart is believably unstable, March is believably average. He is
the unheroic hero, forced into the role and not sure of his ability to change
anything. As the "desperate hours" pass (the Hilliard home is occupied by
the Griffin gang for about thirty-six hours in all), March counsels and comforts
his wife, his ten-year-old son Ralphie (Richard Eyer), and his teenage daughter Cindy (Mary Murphy), but he derives his strength as much from them as
they do from him. When he does act, it is because his family, little by little,
has made him aware of his options and his choices. March's performance
creates as complete a characterization as does Bogart's. Quiet despair coun-
terpointing tense courage is present in his eyes, in the set of his jaw and of
his shoulders. It is a thoroughly believable portrait of an average family man
under siege.

Dan Hilliard works in a department store. We see him going to work one
morning, kissing his wife good-bye. We see his daughter Cindy leave for work
and his son Ralphie leave for school. When the doorbell rings, Mrs. Hilliard
opens the door unsuspectingly and admits the three hoodlums who take over
her home. Glenn Griffin, his younger brother Hal (Dewey Martin), and the
big, hulking Sam Kobish (Robert Middleton) have just escaped from the state
penitentiary. Glenn Griffin has a score to settle with Jesse Bard (Arthur
Kennedy), a cop who not only sent him to prison, but also broke his jaw so
it had to be wired in place for months. Griffin spent those months in the
penitentiary plotting his revenge.

The Griffin gang holes up in the Hilliard home to wait for Glenn's girl
friend to deliver some money; then they intend to hire a killer to go after
Bard. The plan is simple, but problems start to crop up. Glenn receives word
that his girl friend has been arrested for running a red light; she will not be
able to arrive by midnight as they had planned. He instructs her to put the
money in the mail special delivery to Dan Hilliard's office; the gang will have
to remain in the Hilliard home for at least another day.

On day number two, Mr. Patterson, the man who collects the trash, becomes
inquisitive. He spots the gang's getaway car hidden in the garage and makes
the connection between it, some coffee cups and cigarettes on the Hilliard
kitchen table, and a stack of newspapers with headlines telling of the Griffin
gang's escape from prison. He makes a note of the car's license number but
it is the last note he ever writes. Kobish takes him for a ride in his own trash
truck and kills him.

This is the gang's first mistake. Jesse Bard has been at the stationhouse
directing the search for the twenty-four hours since the breakout occurred.

Bard has a hunch that Griffin and his gang will show up locally to settle their old score. When Patterson's body is found and the license number on a scrap in his pocket links him to the Griffin gang, Bard has all he needs. Also in the pocket are the checks he had collected on his morning rounds, and it becomes a simple exercise for Bard to find the neighborhood Patterson had been working. Before he can set to work combing the neighborhood, however, he receives an anonymous note (sent by Dan Hilliard) advising him that innocent people's lives are at stake. Reluctantly, Bard calls off a door-to-door search of the area.

Up until now, the basic point of tension has been the duel of nerves between Dan Hilliard and Glenn Griffin. Now the pace quickens. The duel is amplified; conflicts erupt on all levels. There is one between Bard and a hard-line cop who believes the law should close in, without regard to the anonymous citizen's plea. There is one between Glenn Griffin and his younger brother Hal, who, angered by the long, senseless wait, takes off into the night and is shot and killed by police. There is one between Hilliard and his wife, and another between Cindy and her boyfriend Chuck (Gig Young).

Each conflict, besides demonstrating heightened tension, advances the plot by leading inevitably to the climax. When Cindy and her boyfriend quarrel, he finds himself with her house keys after she slams the door in his face. He is later able to sneak inside the house to make his own inept attempt at heroics. When Hal is shot down, a gun registered to Daniel Hilliard is found in his possession: now Bard knows not only the neighborhood but also the house that is his target. Hal's death also serves to advance Glenn's breakdown and to shift the relationship between Glenn and Hilliard. Instead of the swaggering brute who calls all the shots, Glenn is diminished to an emotional, irrational man with a gun.

The last few minutes of the film are tense and masterfully plotted. Wyler has drawn some criticism for shooting the film using his usual deep focus technique rather than relying on rapid cutting to build suspense. In these last few minutes, that criticism may be justified, yet Wyler's deep focus technique has its advantages. The technique, developed by Wyler and the famous cinematographer Gregg Toland many years before, allowed Wyler to show both action and reaction in one shot, and it eliminated numerous cuts from one character's face to another's. One of Wyler's most famous scenes was one of the earliest he shot in deep focus. In *The Little Foxes* (1941), Bette Davis stands in the foreground in close focus while in deep focus, her invalid husband (Herbert Marshall) struggles to climb the stairs. Davis has been abusing her husband to the point that he becomes short of breath, and he begs her to fetch his medication. Then, out of desperation, he tries to make it upstairs on his own. Wyler holds the focus on Davis' face as we watch Marshall die of a coronary in the background. The effect could not have been more chilling.

Thrillers and melodramas, in particular, generally employ rapid cutting to build suspense. Wyler's technique is less manipulative. It allows the viewer to take in several factors at once and to make his own judgments. In this sense, the technique is an excellent match for cinematographer Lee Garmes' stark, documentary style. Garmes was a veteran cameraman who had worked with Wyler only once before, on *Detective Story* (1951). During that collaboration, he had introduced Wyler to a new invention: with his camera mounted on a crab dolly, it could be moved anywhere without tracks. In both *Detective Story* and *The Desperate Hours*, this technique combines beautifully with the material.

In *The Desperate Hours*, shot in stark black-and-white, the camera seems to stalk through the house and focus on the muzzle of a gun or the menacing snarl of a thug. It picks out the threatening elements, then broadens its view to give us a sense of the hopelessly closed-in setting. The conflict emerges as clearly from the blocking of scenes, the lighting, and the camera angles as it does from the script and plotting. We feel the Hilliards' suffocation, their sense of helplessness, isolated as they are from the outside world, living with the constant threat that if one makes a foolish move, the others will die; and with the equally present threat that one of the hoodlums—or for that matter the police—may become trigger-happy and they will die anyway.

When a film "works," it is because the combination of elements is greater than the sum of the parts. Each of its elements—the casting, the acting, the plotting, the writing, the directing, the lighting, the camera angles and techniques—combines with the others to heighten the effects of the individual components. Wyler, as many critics have noted, is a difficult director to characterize. There is no Wyler "touch"; no signature element. He moves easily from light comedy to searing drama, from Westerns to war movies. He is responsible both for *Funny Girl* (1968) and for *The Collector* (1965). What Wyler does do almost unerringly is to match his material with the right actors and the right technicians to create films that "work."

Julie Barker

DESTINATION MOON

Released: 1950
Production: George Pal for Universal
Direction: Irving Pichel
Screenplay: Rip Van Ronkel, Robert Heinlein, and James O'Hanlon; based
   on the novel *Rocket Ship Galileo* by Robert Heinlein
Cinematography: Lionel Lindon
Editing: Duke Goldstone
Art direction: Ernest Fegte
Set decoration: George Sawley
Special effects: George Pal and Eagle-Lion Classics (AA)
Running time: 90 minutes

> *Principal characters:*
> Barnes .... John Archer
> Cargreaves .... Warner Anderson
> General Thayer .... Tom Powers
> Sweeney .... Dick Wesson

In an era of pseudodocumentary melodramas fostered by postwar neo-
realism, George Pal managed to create, independently, the ultimate fictional
"documentary" in *Destination Moon*. The race for space is the focus of this
serious attempt to show how man could go where he had never gone before.
Destination Moon follows a group of scientists as they convince the government to undergo a project that would send a manned rocket to the moon.
The scientists detail, in very specific terms, the various stresses and hazards
that may be encountered on a voyage through space. There are endless tests:
determinations to be made in regard to the number of crew members, how
to deal with weightlessness, how to walk on the surface of the moon, and
others which are based on actual considerations of space scientists. Every
detail is given a great deal of scrutiny prior to the rocket launching. The
schedule proceeds according to plan, and the four select scientists go into
space like intrepid Cub Scouts out for their first taste of camping in the wilds.

There are minor crises which are encountered on the way to the moon,
none of which prove to be too much for the able-bodied crew. Once on the
moon, however, the scientists realize that they have insufficient fuel to make
the trip back to earth. After serious soul-searching and heroic attempts at
volunteering to stay behind, an ingenious method of discarding empty space
suits and canisters is proposed. They blast back into space and prove that
man is indeed able to conquer the stars.

Destination Moon was praised for its realistic approach to an extremely
fantastic plot. The special effects by George Pal Productions are simple and
effective. The producer, Pal himself, is quite comfortable with the concept

of the fantastic; he produced and directed a large number of stop-motion animated short subjects, called *Puppetoons*, during the early 1940's. He was drawn to this area again and again in such films as *When Worlds Collide* (1951), *War of the Worlds* (1953), *The Conquest of Space* (1955), and the brilliant fantasy film *The Time Machine* (1960). Pal's work has been consistently praised for its elaborate detail and effectiveness, and *Destination Moon* itself received a special citation from the Academy of Motion Picture Arts and Sciences for its "realism." *When Worlds Collide* won an Academy Award the next year for special photographic effects. Other Pal films have become standards of the science-fiction genre, gaining a large cult as well as critical following.

If there is a factor which tends to isolate Pal's films from contemporary science-fiction films, it is their overt piousness. There is a religious presence felt in so many aspects of Pal's films that the introduction of divine providence becomes cloying and at times embarrassing. The most preposterous situation occurs in *Conquest in Space*, which characterizes religious fanaticism to the extreme. *War of the Worlds'* use of the church as sanctuary against the invading Martians and the sermonizing done by the minister also point strongly to this bias. This simplistic view of the universe seen in Pal's films may have been overlooked during the time of their initial release, but on repeated viewings, the message comes through far too loudly.

Of all of Pal's films, *Destination Moon* suffers the least from this piety. The script, adapted by famed science-fiction author Robert Heinlein from his own novel, is rooted in fact. The drama deals with man's conquest of the unknown, and there is a sense of joy laced throughout the technological sophistication of *Destination Moon* that is unmistakable. The actors express this joy on an emotional level that is rather unusual, and their freedom in communicating their triumphs and anxieties is the real pleasure of *Destination Moon*. In an era in which man has actually walked on the moon, the implications of this scientific novel have long since worn off. What remains is the pioneering spirit of Pal and Heinlein as conveyed through the film. Both the physical beauty of a trip through outer space and the emotional response by the actors as they voyage through space contribute to the success of the film.

Pal's later films have generated mixed reactions. His 1975 film *Doc Savage*, which was his last, was received with limited success. What is surprising, however, is that the naïve quality criticized in *Doc Savage* is consistent with Pal's other films. He was an uncomplicated filmmaker who focused on the fantastic element inherent in the medium. From *Destination Moon* through *Doc Savage*, Pal managed to produce a series of imaginative films which bear the stamp of honest innocence and everlasting wonder.

Carl F. Macek

DESTINATION TOKYO

Released: 1943
Production: Jerry Wald for Warner Bros.
Direction: Delmer Daves
Screenplay: Delmer Daves and Albert Maltz; based on an original story by Steve Fisher
Cinematography: Bert Glennon
Editing: Christian Nyby
Running time: 135 minutes

Principal characters:
Captain Cassidy	Cary Grant
Wolf	John Garfield
Cookie	Alan Hale
Raymond	John Ridgely
Tin Can	Dane Clark
Pills	William Prince
Tommy Adams	Robert Hutton
Mike	Tom Tully
Sparks	John Forsythe

When *Destination Tokyo* was released at the end of 1943, the United States was in the midst of World War II. Hollywood joined the rest of the country in promoting the war effort. This film, which deals with the *U. S. S. Copperfin*, a submarine on a secret mission to get into Tokyo Bay and send back meteorological information necessary for the first American bombing of the Japanese capital, was part of Hollywood's patriotic contribution. It is also an excellent example of the type of war propaganda film which was popular at the time.

The film portrays the enemy as accepting values alien to American culture. Tin Can (Dane Clark), a Greek-American crewman aboard the *Copperfin*, articulates all the crew's perception of a vast "difference between them and us." The submarine's skipper, Captain Cassidy (Cary Grant), depicts the Japanese way of life as "a system that puts daggers in the hands of five-year-old children." He hopes that American military might will allow those children to have roller skates instead of weapons of war. Japanese life is also criticized for its economic imbalance; there are no labor unions, and the average worker's salary is only seven dollars per week. Moreoever, the Japanese have no conception of love for women and children as Americans do. Their language, in fact, has no terminology for familial love, according to the film. Despite these criticisms of Japan, however, the submariners realize that it is the despotic government of the country that is the real enemy, not the Japanese people.

Not only is the cultural chasm between Japan and the United States apparent in the negative comments about the enemy's way of life, but the film also affords a positive albeit idealized portrayal of American values as represented by the *Copperfin*'s crew. Special emphasis is placed on family values. Captain Cassidy is a good family man who reminisces about taking his son for his first haircut. Mike (Tom Tully), an Irish-American crewman, also loves his family and frequently retires into the ship's recreation office to listen to a recording of his wife's voice on the phonograph. Another seaman, Tommy Adams (Robert Hutton), is a youth away from home for the first time, who preserves family contact by displaying a picture of his sister while other men do the same for their wives and sweethearts. Tin Can's ties extend beyond the nuclear family to include an honored uncle, executed in his native Greece by the Nazis. Tin Can perceives his role in the war as avenger for his kinsman's death.

While the crew members are devoted to their families back home, they also create a family atmosphere aboard the submarine. Despite their diversity in personality, they cooperate effectively both to accomplish their military objective and to accommodate the personal needs of one another. The first stop on the way to Tokyo is the Aleutian Islands, where they pick up Raymond (John Ridgely), the meteorologist whose analysis of conditions in Japan is required for the success of the bombing of Tokyo. He immediately becomes part of the crew. Two of them, the inveterate ladies' man Wolf (John Garfield) and communications specialist Sparks (John Forsythe), readily agree to join Raymond on his dangerous assignment. This involves their being landed on the shore of Tokyo Bay and remaining there to gather weather data. These men willingly risk their lives for their country as, in fact, do all members of the *Copperfin*'s crew in the perilous mission into mine-infested Tokyo Bay.

The cooperative spirit manifest in the way the crew handles their mission is also evident in their treatment of one another. They are especially concerned with the welfare of young Tommy Adams. For example, when Tommy first assumes his watch, he thinks he sees an enemy plane. The submarine dives and anxiously awaits the explosions of bombs, but a careful search of the sky through the periscope reveals the plane to be an albatross. The captain exhibits a paternal understanding of the inexperienced crewman's error, saying that he would rather dive for innumerable false alarms than to ignore a real danger. Tommy also experiences his first battle death when Mike, who has befriended the young man and has reaffirmed his religious convictions, dies. The pilot of a downed Japanese fighter plane, whom Mike is trying to pull aboard the *Copperfin*, stabs the sailor in the back. The crew share the sense of loss of their beloved compatriot. Tommy proves himself a worthy member of the submarine's family when he defuses a bomb that has lodged in the ship's bulkheads.

Perhaps the most important personal crisis during the film occurs when Tommy contracts an appendicitis while the ship is hiding on the floor of Tokyo

Bay. Since no doctor is available, Pills (William Prince), the pharmacist's mate, must perform surgery. Assisted by Captain Cassidy who administers ether, by the encouraging philosophy of Cookie (Alan Hale), and by Tin Can's reading of the instructions from a medical textbook, Pills successfully removes the inflamed appendix. Not only does Tommy Adams recover, but also Pills, who had not believed in God, finds faith.

As if a dangerous spying mission and a serious operation under difficult conditions were not enough action, *Destination Tokyo* also depicts the *Copperfin* in battle with a Japanese warship. As the submarine leaves Tokyo Bay, having successfully completed its mission, the captain and crew cannot resist sinking an enemy aircraft carrier. This action, while satisfying the bellicose tendencies of the men, reveals the submarine's whereabouts to the Japanese navy. A destroyer bombards them with depth charges until the *Copperfin* turns on its adversary, sending well-aimed torpedoes into its hull.

Destination Tokyo suffers the limitations of any topical film in that it lacks sufficient perspective on its subject, in this case the Pacific theater during World War II. For example, the sentiments of the crew, which represent the film's own point of view, reflect patriotic posturing more than a clear appreciation of the issues being contested in the war. The film is also overly long and contains too many characters who are little more than stock figures even though the acting is well done. Furthermore, as most contemporary critics pointed out, the plot lacks credibility. The film is filled with action, however, and several of the performances are capable. The film's chief interest, however, lies in the attitudes it reveals. A period piece, *Destination Tokyo* both captures and projects the spirit of wartime America.

Frances M. Malpezzi
William M. Clements

DETECTIVE STORY

Released: 1951
Production: William Wyler for Paramount
Direction: William Wyler
Screenplay: Philip Yordon; based on the play of the same name by Sidney Kingsley
Cinematography: Lee Garmes
Editing: Robert Swink
Running time: 103 minutes

Principal characters:
Detective James McLeod .... Kirk Douglas
Mary McLeod .... Eleanor Parker
Detective Lou Brody .... William Bendix
Shoplifter .... Lee Grant
Arthur Kindred .... Craig Hill
Susan Carmichael .... Cathy O'Donnell
Lieutenant Monahan .... Horace McMahon
Endicott Sims .... Warner Anderson
Karl Schneider .... George Macready
Charley Gennini, first burglar .... Joseph Wiseman
Lewis Abbott, second burglar .... Michael Strong

Detective Story tells of one eventful day in a New York City Police Precinct Station. In a change of theme, however, the villain of the piece is *not* one of the criminals brought into the station, although they all are unsavory enough. Giving an outstanding performance, Kirk Douglas plays Detective James McLeod, a man with his own personal code of justice. So certain is McLeod of the difference between right and wrong that he will resort to anything, even violence, to get a judgment that he thinks is deserved. Under the capable hands of director William Wyler, *Detective Story* became a modern morality play acted out in one room. What emerges is an exciting, taut film with unforgettable performances from all involved.

Detective Story was first a long-running Broadway play written by Sidney Kingsley, starring Ralph Bellamy. When Wyler decided to adapt it for the screen, he cast five members of the original Broadway cast—Horace McMahon, Lee Grant, Joseph Wiseman, Michael Strong, and James Maloney. Of these actors, only McMahon had had previous screen experience. Wyler also chose to reproduce almost exactly the Broadway stage set and confine the action to the Police Station—a wise choice that gives the film great strength as the tension builds to an almost unbearable level. Within the contained walls of the Precinct Station, all kinds of characters wander in and out, some giving the film comic relief. There is the wisecracking but scared shoplifter, beautifully executed by Grant; Wiseman's maniacal burglar; and the inquisitive police reporter. It is Detective McLeod, however, who is the film's pivot. Because of his criminal father, who drove his mother insane, McLeod developed a vicious hatred for all law-breakers and lost the distinction between revenge and justice. As Douglas plays him, McLeod sees all men as guilty until proven innocent, and even then there is doubt.

The cast rehearsed with Wyler for two weeks on the set before shooting began, and the resulting film has the poise and the polish of a Broadway repertory company working together. There are no false notes either in the structure of the film or in the performances. Everything is timed perfectly, and the events are presented with vivid honesty; *Detective Story* pulls no punches. In the quiescent 1950's when words such as abortion could not be mentioned on film, the motion picture gets its message across without having to resort to rough language or unnecessary brutality. It is all there, however; McLeod is a man on strings, and when at last he begins to show signs of cracking by beating up a suspect, the scene is highly effective. Yet McLeod is not entirely an unsympathetic character. Although he is warped in judgment, sufficient reason is given for his behavior for the audience to understand, if not to condone his actions. Also, another side of McLeod is shown by his genuine affection for his wife, Mary (Eleanor Parker). When this relationship begins to turn sour on him, it is more than he can bear.

Detective Story was well researched by both Wyler and Douglas. Prior to production, both men saw the New York play and also spent many hours at the 16th precinct on West 47th Street talking with the detectives there. Douglas even helped the policemen interrogate and fingerprint prisoners. He then played the part of McLeod on stage at the Sombrero Theater in Phoenix, Arizona. All of this scrupulous background work, plus the extensive rehearsal time, made the cast and creators of *Detective Story* unusually well prepared. Cinematographer Lee Garmes worked the cameras and light movements simultaneously with the actors' rehearsals, so that by the time the film was ready to be shot, it was a simple matter. This was Wyler's second adaptation of a Kingsley play; he had directed *Dead End* for Samuel Goldwyn in 1937, using a similar one-set approach. Since *Detective Story*, in contrast to *Dead End*, is all interior, its action is more claustrophobic and intense. Furthermore, the film somehow seems less dated than *Dead End* because it is primarily a look into the mind of a disturbed man rather than a probe into social conditions in a particular time period.

The film starts on a busier than usual afternoon at the 21st Police Station in Manhattan. A frightened little shoplifter (Lee Grant) is brought in by one of the detectives, but since the last van leaves before her fingerprints are taken, she must remain at the police station until she is taken to court. Detective Jim McLeod arrives with a young man, Arthur Kindred (Craig Hill), accused of embezzling some of his employer's money. Kindred tries to call his girl friend, Joy Carmichael, but she is not at home, and her sister Susan (Cathy O'Donnell) comes down to the station. McLeod is told by Lieutenant Monahan (Horace McMahon), head of the precinct, that Dr. Schneider (George Macready), the suspected abortionist for whom McLeod has a warrant out, will surrender himself if his lawyer can guarantee that McLeod will not assault him. McLeod reluctantly agrees—he has a reputation for toughness and loathes the disbarred doctor. Out in the squad room, two burglars are brought in who give their names as Charley Gennini (Joseph Wiseman) and Lewis Abbott (Michael Strong). They were caught in the act of stealing, but Charley hysterically denies everything. McLeod has promised his wife Mary that he will be home in an hour, so he quickly tries to get rid of all the business at hand. Mary is the only person about whom he cares.

When Arthur Kindred's employer comes and offers to drop charges if Arthur will replace the money, McLeod refuses to show any leniency, even though it is the boy's first offense. Arthur had stolen money to satisfy the greed of his girl friend Joy, but he is truly repentant. McLeod, however, will not budge, and his partner Detective Brody (William Bendix) feels that he is not human. Dr. Schneider comes into the station with his lawyer Sims (Warner Anderson), but McLeod's case against him fades when it is learned that his star witness has died. In frustrated rage, McLeod beats up Schneider, who has to be taken away in an ambulance. Sims, furious at McLeod, hints at a personal reason for McLeod's hatred of Schneider, and Monahan investigates immediately.

That evening the Lieutenant uncovers something hidden in Mary McLeod's past. Before she met her husband, she had made a youthful mistake with a married man and had gone to Schneider to seek his help in finding someone to adopt her baby. The child died, however, and Mary was unable to have any more children. When McLeod learns of this, he is stunned and overcome with grief. His wife comes to the station, where they have a bitter quarrel. Brody talks to McLeod and convinces him to try to forget what Mary did and to ask her forgiveness. The two have a brief reconciliation, but McLeod cannot stop bitterly referring to Mary's past. Mary realizes that her husband will never let her forget her one big mistake, and she decides to leave him. McLeod is defeated: he has lost the one person who means something to him and is more like his father than he can ever admit.

Out in the squad room, Charley the burglar suddenly overpowers his guards and draws a gun on the assembled detectives. McLeod tries to disarm him, but is mortally wounded. Dying, he makes his first compromise and gasps out to Brody to drop the charge against Arthur Kindred and to free him. As McLeod's colleagues do what they can for him, Susan and Arthur, having fallen in love at the station, walk out into the night hand in hand.

Detective Story was hailed by the critics, with Douglas especially praised. One critic said that "by shifting violence on to the side of the law, Hollywood has neatly sidestepped the censor without sacrificing the box office." This is what so many reviewers found interesting about the film. The quiet men were usually the criminals and the angry, harsh ones the detectives. *Detective Story* was also part of a revival of a genre that had gone out of fashion in the 1950's. Partly in the tradition of Warner Bros.' cops-and-robbers movies such as *Little Caesar* (1931) or *Scarface* (1932), it also resembled *film noir* with such antecedents as *Double Indemnity* (1944) and *Call Northside 777* (1948). It proved that Hollywood could still turn out the tense, exciting crime films for which it was famous. *Detective Story* is certainly at the top of that class of filmmaking. Wyler's adroit handling of his actors and Garmes's expert cinematography help to make it a memorable film. As one writer put it: "*Detective Story* turned melodrama into poetry."

Joan Cohen

THE DEVIL AND DANIEL WEBSTER
(ALL THAT MONEY CAN BUY)

Released: 1941
Production: William Dieterle for William Dieterle and RKO/Radio
Direction: William Dieterle
Screenplay: Dan Totheroh and Stephen Vincent Benét; based on the story
   "The Devil and Daniel Webster" by Stephen Vincent Benét
Cinematography: Joseph H. August
Editing: Robert Wise
Music: Bernard Herrmann (AA)
Running time: 109 minutes

Principal characters:

Daniel Webster	Edward Arnold
Mr. Scratch	Walter Huston
Ma Stone	Jane Darwell
Belle	Simone Simon
Mary Stone	Anne Shirley
Jabez Stone	James Craig
Squire Slossum	Gene Lockhart
Miser Stevens	John Qualen

Stephen Vincent Benét's short story "The Devil and Daniel Webster" was published in the *Saturday Evening Post* in 1937. A reworking of the Faust legend in the guise of an American folktale, it tells the story of a New England farmer, Jabez Stone, who in 1840 agrees to sell his soul to the devil in return for seven years of prosperity. When the devil (who, in deference to local custom, calls himself Mr. Scratch) comes to collect, however, Jabez claims his right as an American citizen to a trial before a judge and jury—an *American* judge and an *American* jury, he emphasizes. Mr. Scratch chuckles and agrees; but he insists that the trial, which will take place in Jabez's barn, has to be conducted before a judge and jury of his choosing. So up they come, out of the floor of Jabez's barn, the ghosts of Judge Hawthorne of the Salem Witch Trials, and of Captain Kidd, Simon Girty, Benedict Arnold, and nine other cutthroats, knaves, and traitors: American all. Jabez would have been lost at this point, except that he has for his lawyer the greatest American of his time: Daniel Webster, United States Senator from Massachusetts, statesman, patriot, and outspoken champion of "Liberty *and* Union, now and forever, one and inseparable!" Webster looks over Scratch's jury and realizes that what these poor damned souls had in common with Jabez was that they, too, had once had an opportunity to participate in the building of a free, new land. He develops this theme with all the eloquence that has made him the foremost speaker in a Senate renowned for its oratory; and when he is done, Jabez is acquitted. Scratch accepts the jury's verdict; but he also promises

Webster that he will see that he never becomes President—which, of course, Webster never did.

Scratch's court sitting in Jabez's barn was a picture to tempt any dramatist, and within a year Benét's story had become the basis for an opera, with music by Douglas Moore, and a play. The fantastic element in the story also made it ideal for presentation as a motion picture, except for one thing: the Hollywood studios of the day were not interested in stories, however "cinematic," that did not provide opportunities for glamour and spectacle and that lacked good parts for star actors. (Daniel and the devil were both good parts; but they could only be played by experienced character actors, not handsome leading men.) Had it not been for director William Dieterle, who had formed his own production company under the aegis of RKO, *The Devil and Daniel Webster* might never have reached the screen. Fortunately, because he was his own producer, Dieterle was allowed to complete the film without any of the usual Hollywood compromises. Benét himself was hired to write the script, in collaboration with Dan Totheroh. To play Daniel and Mr. Scratch, Dieterle was able to hire two of Hollywood's best character actors, who turned in ideal performances in roles for which they were ideally suited. As Daniel Webster, Edward Arnold was the same genial, shrewd political boss he had played for director Frank Capra in *Mr. Smith Goes to Washington* (1939) and *Meet John Doe* (1941), but this time his guile was squarely on the side of right. Walter Huston, in his first good screen role since his stage success in *Knickerbocker Holiday* (1938), played Mr. Scratch as a typical Yankee peddlar, shrewd as Webster, humorous, a ready flatterer, always willing to listen to a proposition but inflexible once a bargain has been struck. The film's most memorable image is of Huston at the end of the picture, after he has stolen and finished eating the pie that Ma Stone (Jane Darwell) baked for Daniel's breakfast. He wipes off his mouth and begins looking around for his next victim. He spies the audience sitting in the theater, and moves closer to the camera. After looking left and right around the auditorium, he suddenly catches sight of the ideal prospect and, with a broad grin on his face, points his finger unmistakably at Y-O-U. This scene does not appear in the text of the screenplay that John Gassner and Dudley Nichols published in *Twenty Best Film Plays* in 1943; and it is possible that it was worked out between Huston and Dieterle on the set during shooting. For his performance, Huston was nominated for the Academy Award for Best Actor of 1941, but lost to Gary Cooper for *Sergeant York*.

In keeping with the story's quality as a folktale, all of the characters were conceived as types rather than as individuals—with the important exceptions of Jabez Stone (James Craig) and his wife, who thus became the audience's "link" with the fantastic happenings on screen. Craig gave what was probably the best performance of his undistinguished career. He had not yet grown the mustache that made him look like a second-string Clark Gable (which seemed to be his function during his later years at M-G-M); and he projected to the full Jabez's boyishness, warm-heartedness, and impetuosity. As Mary, Jabez's wife, Anne Shirley was given little to do for most of the picture except to fret over her husband's growing hardness and estrangement from her once he has made his pact with the devil. Mary is the one who finally goes to Daniel Webster when the seven years are up; but, until then, it is easy to sympathize with Jabez and his impatience at her continual "But Jabez, you said we'd *never* change!" The strange, childlike French actress Simone Simon found in the part of Belle, Scratch's friend from "over the mountain" who comes to tempt Jabez, one of her few good American roles. Her only other effective performance in an American movie was as the obsessed heroine of Val Lewton and Jacques Tourneur's *Cat People* (1942). Gene Lockhart's Squire Slossum was an ordinary small-town hypocrite of the type he played so well; but John Qualen's Miser Stevens, another of Scratch's victims whose soul, when the devil claims it, is no larger than a moth, may just be, after Daniel and Scratch, the best-realized character in the film. Qualen will probably always be identified with his role as the stubborn tenant farmer who refuses to leave his land in *The Grapes of Wrath* (1940); but as Miser Stevens he created an unforgettable portrait of a man whose soul has shrunk to the dimensions of his pocket-book. The presence of Darwell in the cast also calls up memories of *The Grapes of Wrath*, but only because her performance as Ma Stone is indistinguishable from her performance as Ma Joad. This was not Darwell's fault; she had just won the Academy Award for Ma Joad, and, reading the published screenplay for *The Devil and Daniel Webster*, it is impossible to believe that the part of Jabez's mother was written with anyone but Darwell again playing Ma Joad in mind. Ma Stone is supposed to be a type, of course, just as Squire Slossum, Miser Stevens, Mr. Scratch, and even Daniel Webster are types; but one wishes that in this instance Dieterle had selected an actress whose performance might have been a little less predictable, such as Marjorie Main.

In the 1920's when he was a screen actor in Germany, Dieterle had played Valentin in F. W. Murnau's monumental silent production of *Faust* (1926). Not surprisingly, when he came to direct his gentler American version of the story, Dieterle tried to give it a little of the same visual style. With his cinematographer, the great Joseph August, he worked out a lighting scheme that emphasized the supernatural elements in the script (in sequences shot on stylized studio sets) by contrasting them with scenes of everyday life shot as naturalistically as possible (on location, or at least out of doors, in full sunlight). Somehow the mixture works; and even Scratch (who is in his glory, moving through the shadows of Jabez's barn) is no less believable when he suddenly turns up banging a drum among a crowd of townspeople who have assembled to hear Daniel give a speech in the open air.

As a film, *The Devil and Daniel Webster* was just one product of the self-conscious mythologizing of the American past that was a characteristic activity of many artists and writers in the period before and during World War II. When Daniel pleads with Scratch's jury to "give Jabez Stone another chance to walk upon the earth among the trees, the growing corn, the smell of grass in spring," he was speaking for men who had every reason to fear that the "common, small, good" things in life might soon be taken away from them. Bernard Herrmann's Academy Award-winning score, which was based on folk motifs expressed in a sophisticated symphonic idiom, represented a musical affirmation of traditional American values. Along with this affirmation often went a Depression-bred commitment to social activism: the political message of *The Devil and Daniel Webster* seems to be that Jabez Stone should not have sold his soul to the devil when he found himself unable to pay his debts, but should have accepted his neighbors' invitation to join the Grange instead.

It is unhappily still true of Hollywood studios like RKO that, while they are sometimes willing to finance an unconventional production such as *The Devil and Daniel Webster*, they often become frightened and begin tinkering with the completed film before it can find an audience in the form its maker intended. In the case of Dieterle's film, it was pointed out in the first trade reviews that the logical, "pre-sold" title was *The Devil and Daniel Webster*, the title of Benét's well-known original story. There was an old Hollywood superstition, however, that pictures with *Devil* in the title never did well. The example *The Devil Is a Woman* (1935). The film version of "The Devil and Daniel Webster" was therefore previewed as *Here Is a Man* before someone thought of calling it *All That Money Can Buy* (from Scratch's offer of "money—and all that money can buy" in return for Jabez's soul). When the film did poorly in its first engagements, it was withdrawn and reissued at intervals in different parts of the country as *Daniel and the Devil* and, finally, *The Devil and Daniel Webster*, the title under which it is usually shown today. The film is indexed in the 1941 issues of the *Reader's Guide to Periodical Literature* as *All That Money Can Buy*; however, references in publications are evenly divided between *All That Money Can Buy* and *The Devil and Daniel Webster*. To complicate matters further, RKO kept re-editing the film, so that what was trade-shown as *Here Is a Man* at 106 minutes may have run as long as 112 minutes when it opened as *All That Money Can Buy* in New York. At one point in the 1940's, the film may actually have been distributed in versions running less than ninety minutes; but the version of *The Devil and Daniel Webster* that is distributed most widely today, on the nontheatrical circuit and to television, runs 109 minutes.

Charles Hopkins

THE DEVIL AND MISS JONES

Released: 1941
Production: Frank Ross and Norman Krasna for RKO/Radio
Direction: Sam Wood
Screenplay: Norman Krasna
Cinematography: Harry Stradling
Editing: Sheman Todd
Production design: William Cameron Menzies
Running time: 92 minutes

Principal characters:
Mary Jones .... Jean Arthur
J. P. Merrick .... Charles Coburn
Joe O'Brien .... Robert Cummings
Hooper .... Edmond Gwenn
Elizabeth Ellis .... Spring Byington

The Devil and Miss Jones is an unusual comedy—unusual both in its social-minded message, which forms the backbone of the plot, and also in its outlandish production design. The story involves the struggle of workers in Neeley's department store in New York to form a union and negotiate for wages and benefits. J. P. Merrick (Charles Coburn), the richest man in the world (who also happens to own Neeley's), decides to impersonate a humble clerk and uncover the people responsible for the unrest in his store. While working undercover as a slipper salesman, Merrick is befriended by Mary Jones (Jean Arthur), a likable fellow clerk whose altruistic nature begins to affect the snobbish old fogey. He double-dates with Mary and Joe O'Brien (Robert Cummings), one of the union organizers who has been fired. That afternoon at the beach is the turning point in Merrick's life. He is literally surrounded by flesh. Hundreds of people squirm and fight for a small patch of sand and a place in the sun on Coney Island. He discusses economics with Joe and flirts with his date, a delightful middle-aged woman named Elizabeth (Spring Byington).

Eventually, Merrick is separated from his group. Feeling uncomfortable in his rented swimming suit, he tries to find his clothes. He is quite a novice at dealing with people firsthand, and after wandering around tired and hungry for hours, he decides to take matters in his own hands. He tries to swap his expensive gold watch for a dime for the telephone at the drugstore and is arrested. Later at the police station, Mary, Joe, and Elizabeth find him arguing with the desk sergeant. Joe intervenes, and after mouthing all sorts of political rhetoric, he manages to get Merrick out of the grip of the police. This minor triumph is quickly changed when Mary discovers a card which has fallen out of Merrick's wallet stating that he is a private investigator (his cover to the store executives). She panics and during the next working day plans to knock him out to retrieve a list of names given to him by Joe which details all of the workers sympathetic to the unionization of the store.

She never gets a chance to hit him, although a pair of shoes falls on his head. They are hauled into the manager's office, and a minor riot ensues when Mary gets on the loud-speaker and asks the workers to stage a walkout. Everything comes to a head when the leaders of the workers are asked to bring their grievances to Mr. Merrick himself at his mansion. The shock makes Mary scream when she realizes that this humble slipper salesman-cum-private-detective is in reality the richest man in the world; Joe merely faints. Everything ends for the best when Mary and Joe and Merrick and Elizabeth have a double wedding and take the entire work force of the department store with them on an ocean voyage honeymoon to Hawaii.

Throughout this interwoven plot the basic relationship between labor and management is emphasized. The ivory tower environment of Merrick is contrasted vividly with the stark life-style of the middle-class workers. Joe cannot wed Mary because he has no job, and he has no job because of his activities as a union organizer. Merrick, as a lowly shoe salesman, enjoys a brown-bag lunch of tuna puffs prepared by Elizabeth in the park rather than the crumbled graham crackers in milk which he is served day after tedious day in the sanctity of his dark and brooding mansion. The contrasts are strong and basic. Real people enjoy life to the fullest; as Merrick becomes a real person, his carefully constructed world begins to dissolve around him, and he is happier for it. Coburn is excellent in showing the gradual yet inevitable change that takes place in J. P. Merrick. He suits the role of a plutocrat to perfection, yet he has the ability to transform himself into a warm and lovable character. His sympathetic nature is reinforced by Mary's enthusiasm; Arthur plays her character to the fullest. She typifies the free spirit of American woman, and her screen presence is unmistakable.

Sam Wood's direction is perfect during the transitional beach scene. He packs people into the frame of the scene as if they were sardines. His use of low-angle set-ups enhances the sense of alienation felt by Merrick. The true genius of the strong visual quality found in *The Devil and Miss Jones*, however, is the production design provided by William Cameron Menzies.

The attention to detail is quite remarkable. Menzies, who is credited with the beauty of *Gone with the Wind* (1939), is able to give depth and definition to the sets. He suggests personality through different architectural styles. At times this attention to detail seems out of place for a screwball comedy, yet the effect of this highly visual backdrop manages to convey the desired attitudes without wasting time with dialogue.

The Devil and Miss Jones is a comedy that presents a serious economic dilemma. It is quite different from Frank Capra's similar comedies, such as *Mr. Deeds Goes to Town* (1936) or *You Can't Take It with You* (1938), which revolve around the "little man." The difference in *The Devil and Miss Jones*, written by Norman Krasna, is that the major area of concentration is the transition of the plutocrat rather than the confirmation of the average man.

Carl F. Macek

DIARY OF A MAD HOUSEWIFE

Released: 1970
Production: Frank Perry for Universal
Direction: Frank Perry
Screenplay: Eleanor Perry; based on the novel of the same name by Sue Kaufman
Cinematography: Ellis W. Carter
Editing: Grant Whytock
Running time: 100 minutes

Principal characters:
Jonathan Balser	Richard Benjamin
George Prager	Frank Langella
Tina Balser	Carrie Snodgress
Sylvie Balser	Lorraine Cullen
Liz Balser	Frannie Michel
Man in Group Therapy Session	Peter Boyle

In the mid-1960's, increasing numbers of women were becoming aware of the limitations of their role as females. Society dictated that a young girl stayed home and helped her mother wash dishes while her brothers climbed trees and scraped their knees. While "boys would be boys," the thought of girls gashing their elbows was most unladylike. Generally, as a girl got older, she passively waited for Mr. Right to sweep her into heaven. If he did not appear with an engagement ring by the time she was twenty-one, she was sure to be an old maid. Once married, she tended house and managed the babies while her husband earned the money and made the decisions. She had no choices. Later, young women who had been weaned on television, civil rights marches, and Vietnam War protests began to ponder their lives and question the premise that their existences must be based on a traditional dependence on men. *Diary of a Mad Housewife*, released in 1970, is one of the earliest films to chronicle the emerging conflict between the old order and the new woman who must learn to accept responsibility for her own life.

Tina Balser (Carrie Snodgress), has, outwardly, an ideal life for a woman. She is married to Jonathan (Richard Benjamin), a successful lawyer, and has two young daughters. She is not content with her existence, however; her status-seeking husband oppressively nags her, and her children are spoiled and constantly complain. She is propositioned by George Prager (Frank Langella), an egotistical writer, at an art gallery opening. Fed up with her mundane life, she accepts and becomes his mistress, but Prager is no less tyrannical than her husband, and the affair deteriorates. A party Jonathan has been planning fizzles, and he admits to his wife that he has not been a "good" husband—he has had an affair, he has mismanaged their money, and his job with his law firm is in jeopardy. Tina soon ends her relationship with Prager and joins a therapy group in an attempt to sort out her life.

Tina is no robust, dynamic wonder woman, and certainly no icon for feminists. She is awkward and defensive as she ponders her existence and takes action against her negative condition. Her attempt at group therapy is no radical solution. Tina is a pampered housewife who is bored by her drab surroundings and stifled by the unreasonable demands of her husband and children, yet she realizes that she, and she alone, is the only person who can take charge of herself. The act of attending group therapy is a courageous decision for a woman who has been molded and shaped into a set, narrow life-style since birth and who has no peer support for her actions. Tina is a realistic character with conflicts and contradictions who is searching for a life-style in which she can thrive.

As Tina is a fully defined character attempting to gain insights into her life, both her husband and her lover are presented as one-dimensional, chauvinistic villains. Jonathan Balser is a neurotic, bullying lout who is interested only in materialism. He has no mind of his own, his tastes and opinions being dictated by what is acceptable and fashionable to the society of chic, Upper East Side New York. He is obsessed with upward mobility: he spews off brand names of products and high-class clothing as if he were a walking advertisement for posh Fifth Avenue specialty shops. He cheats on his wife—a macho endeavor—but is ultimately depicted as not worthy of manhood. He is unable to manage money and endangers his position in his law firm. George Prager is no less one-dimensional: he is deluded in the belief that he is perfect, that the lady of his choice will be enslaved by his masculinity, and that he can ridicule his women at will. He, too, is less than the man he pretends to be— Tina accuses him of being latently homosexual, and the impression is that he is indeed hiding something. Tina is the only sane person of the three, and screenwriter Eleanor Perry would have done well to humanize Jonathan and George. Both are narrow creations, stereotyped visions of men who, despite their delusions, are not really men and are less human than women.

Nevertheless, the late Perry and her husband Frank, the director of *Diary of a Mad Housewife*, shrewdly capture the essence of a certain New York life-style—plush, chic, upper-middle-class, and "in," but ultimately predatory and phony. Most of the film is shot in interior, enclosed settings, such as art galleries laden with paintings and cluttered apartments, which help to convey Tina's inward confusion. The film is most relevant, however, for its portrayal of a woman who realizes she must take action. Some of the Perrys' other films deal with characters in crisis who also must undergo change or question the values imposed on them by others. In *David and Lisa* (1963), for example, two mentally retarded teenagers realize that they are capable of happiness. In *The Swimmer* (1968), a middle-aged suburban man must come to terms with the affluent existence he despises.

Diary of a Mad Housewife is the forerunner of a genre of films which portray women rebelling against a stultifying life style and environment and searching for their own identities. Among them are *Alice Doesn't Live Here Anymore* (1974), *A Woman Under the Influence* (1974), *Coming Home* (1978), and *An Unmarried Woman* (1978). Snodgress, in her first starring role, received glowing notices for her work. She is appropriately vulnerable as she awkwardly takes action and attempts to resolve the uncertainties in her mind. One critic even suggested that she "evokes . . . the talent of the late Margaret Sullivan." The film did moderately well, taking in $6,100,000 at the box office.

Snodgress was nominated for an Academy Award, losing out (with Jane Alexander in *The Great White Hope*, Ali MacGraw for *Love Story*, and Sarah Miles for *Ryan's Daughter*) to Glenda Jackson in *Women in Love*, but she was a double Golden Globe winner, for Best Actress and Most Promising Newcomer. The actress temporarily chose not to pursue a film career, and left acting to live with rock star Neil Young. She later returned to her profession, and has been cast in uninspired roles in such average-to-mediocre entertainments as Brian de Palma's *The Fury* (1980) and the television movies *Love's Dark Ride* and *Fast Friends*.

Benjamin is appropriately snide and condescending as Jonathan, but Langella is a revelation as Prager. He is menacingly sensual and authoritarian, and was named Best Supporting Actor by the National Board of Review for his performance here and in Mel Brooks's *The Twelve Chairs* (1970). Some of the qualities of George Prager are in his stage and screen portrayal of *Dracula* (1979). In a bit at the end of *Diary of a Mad Housewife*, a pre-*Joe* (1970) Peter Boyle appears as a harassed participant in Tina's therapy session.

Diary of a Mad Housewife is dated when one compares Tina Balser's manner of dealing with her problems and relating to men and to herself with that of the heroines played by Ellen Burstyn, Jane Fonda, Jill Clayburgh, and Gena Rowlands, yet the character of Tina is a definite cinematic step in the direction of the depiction of women as other than happy housewives and hookers.

Rob Edelman

THE DIARY OF ANNE FRANK

Released: 1959
Production: George Stevens for Twentieth Century-Fox
Direction: George Stevens
Screenplay: Frances Goodrich and Albert Hackett; based on their play of the same name and adapted from the novel *Anne Frank: The Diary of a Young Girl*
Cinematography: William C. Mellor (AA)
Editing: David Bretherton, Robert Swink, and William Mace
Art direction: Lyle R. Wheeler and George W. Davis (AA); set decoration, Walter M. Scott and Stuart A. Reiss (AA)
Running time: 170 minutes

> *Principal characters:*
> Anne Frank .... Millie Perkins
> Otto Frank .... Joseph Schildkraut
> Mrs. Van Daan .... Shelley Winters (AA)
> Mr. Dussell .... Ed Wynn
> Peter Van Daan .... Richard Beymer
> Mrs. Frank .... Gusti Huber
> Mr. Van Daan .... Lou Jacobi
> Margot Frank .... Diane Baker

When *Anne Frank: The Diary of a Young Girl* was published in English in 1952, it almost immediately became a best-seller. Its immense appeal was based partly on the personality of the real Anne Frank as revealed in her diary and partly on the specific and personal view it presented of a horror nearly too large to comprehend—the killing of millions of Jews by the Nazis. The smallest personal details in the narrative are set against a huge and impersonal evil. The book has remained in print since 1952 and is still a moving story, especially considering the tender age of its authoress. Frances Goodrich and Albert Hackett transformed the book into a play, *The Diary of Anne Frank*, that began a successful run on Broadway in 1955 and won three major awards, including a Pulitzer Prize. Thus it was a moving, significant, and already popular work that director George Stevens presented on the screen in 1959.

The story is, in essence, a simple one. In order to escape from the Nazis in Amsterdam during World War II, two Jewish families and one other Jewish man hide for more than two years in a loft above a spice factory where their only contact with the outside world is through the two people who hide them and a radio. They never leave the loft until very near the end of the war, when they are discovered and sent to concentration camps. The story is told by Anne Frank, who is thirteen when they enter the hiding place and whose diary is found three years later by her father, the only member of the entire group to survive the camps.

The film interweaves three dominant themes: the fear of discovery by the Nazis, which is ever-present, the frictions caused by a group of people having to live in such close quarters for so long, and a young girl's normal adolescent development taking place in such abnormal surroundings.

The film begins with an old man getting out of a truck and going into a building. It is Otto Frank (Joseph Schildkraut), the sole survivor, who is returning for the first time to the loft where the eight had stayed in hiding for so long. He finds little but his daughter's diary. At the end of this long, nearly wordless sequence he begins reading the diary as a dissolve takes us back to three years before.

The two Jewish families, the Franks and the Van Daans, have just arrived in their attic hiding place, and Mr. Frank is explaining the restrictions under which they must live for as long as they stay. Since they are above a factory, they must be absolutely silent during the day so that the workers below will never suspect anyone is there. Because their protectors have only three forged ration cards with which to buy them food, they will have a very limited supply. Frank's explanation is interrupted by the siren of the "green police," a sound which will be a continual reminder throughout the film of the menace from which they all are hiding.

The Frank family consists of the father, mother (Gusti Huber), and two daughters, Margot (Diane Baker) and her younger sister Anne (Millie Perkins). The Van Daans (Lou Jacobi and Shelley Winters) have a son, Peter (Richard Beymer). After some time they accept one more person into their hiding place, Dussell (Ed Wynn), a dentist who had always considered himself just a Dutch citizen until the authorities discovered his Jewish heritage. He brings with him grim news of the persecution of the Jews in the city, including many that the two families knew personally. The somewhat sour dentist is frequently an irritation to the others, even though he is often correct in his concerns and worries, such as his belief that allowing Peter to keep a cat is an unnecessary risk.

One of Van Daan's chief concerns is food. Before, he was used to indulging his appetite, and in the hiding place he is never able to get used to the sparse rations. Near the end he is caught stealing food from the common supply and breaks down in shame for what he has done. His wife, on the other hand, is inordinately fond of her fur coat, which is her only reminder of her previous style of living. When Anne spills some milk on the coat, Mrs. Van Daan treats the accident as a major catastrophe, and later her husband's desire to have the coat sold precipitates a bitter fight between the two.

Anne has many of an adolescent's usual problems with adults, but they are magnified by the unusual situation. She must share a room with Dussell, and their incompatibility produces a good deal of bickering. Anne gets along quite well with her father, but she is convinced that her mother can never understand her. When she realizes how much she has hurt her mother, she tries to make amends by giving her a gift of a piece of paper saying that she (Anne) will do whatever she is told for ten hours. Dussell's immediate response is, "You wouldn't want to sell that?"

Anne's chief concern, besides the ones they all share, becomes her romance with Peter Van Daan. It is not approved by Mrs. Van Daan and is, of course, quite circumscribed by the confined circumstances. A curious ritual develops in which Anne goes to her own room to get ready to see Peter (while the ousted Dussell fumes outside the door); then she walks through the main room full of adults to Peter's room where they have a prescribed time of privacy. Their first kiss is presented in a dramatic—perhaps too dramatic—fashion. The two figures are seen in silhouette to a silent sound track; then they kiss and the music begins and swells.

There is naturally much tension in the film, particularly in a few scenes in which the group is in danger of being discovered. In one scene a Nazi patrol searches the building below the attic while we watch Peter's cat almost knock a metal funnel off a shelf. In another scene a burglar breaks into the building below but is scared away by noise caused by the animal. There are also moments of comedy. When the group gets the news over the radio that the Allies have landed in Europe, Van Daan is moaning about his shame for stealing the food. Dussell interrupts him: "Stop it. You're spoiling the whole invasion."

The comedy and the tension and the boredom end, however, when finally they are discovered by the "green police." Anne has written in her diary, "I still believe—in spite of everything—that people are really good at heart." After a kiss between Anne and Peter and shots of the anxious group listening to the sound below them there is a freeze frame as Frank says, "We have lived in fear; now we can live in hope."

To capture the confined setting of the film, director George Stevens had an exact replica of the loft, which is still in existence, constructed with only one side removed. Ordinary film sets have movable walls and no ceilings so that the lighting and camera equipment may be put wherever the director desires, but Stevens thought the self-imposed limitation would force him and cinematographer William C. Mellor to keep the audience aware of the claustrophobic quality of the living quarters. The technique is largely successful, although Stevens sometimes defeats his purpose by showing us shots of things going on outside that the group in the loft could never see. He also dissipates some of the force of the film by the length of individual scenes and the length of the whole film (three hours including an intermission); a shorter, more tightly paced film might have better sustained the audience's emotion. Mellor received a well-deserved Oscar for his camerawork, as did four others—Lyle R. Wheeler, George W. Davis, Walter M. Scott, and Stuart A. Reiss—for the art direction and set decoration.

Although only Winters won an Oscar for the acting in *The Diary of Anne Frank*, the three actors who re-created their Broadway roles are also excellent. Schildkraut, who makes the almost too saintly figure of Otto Frank believable, Huger as Mrs. Frank, and Jacobi as Van Daan all expose the human foibles of their characters. Wynn's performance as Dussell is good although he was still a relative novice as a serious actor, having given his first noncomic performance in the 1956 *Playhouse 90* production of *Requiem for a Heavyweight* on television. To play the central role of Anne, Perkins, a young model, was chosen. She looks right for the role and does a good job overall, although her inexperience as an actress occasionally shows.

One of the chief virtues of *The Diary of Anne Frank* is the audience's knowledge that the film presents a true story about one of the greatest evils of our century. Stevens only needed to do justice to his subject, and he has done so.

Timothy W. Johnson

DOCTOR IN THE HOUSE

Released: 1954
Production: Betty Box for General Film Distributors
Direction: Ralph Thomas
Screenplay: Nicholas Phipps; based on the novel of the same name by Richard Gordon
Cinematography: Ernest Steward
Editing: Gerald Thomas
Running time: 92 minutes

Principal characters:
Simon Sparrow .... Dirk Bogarde
Joy .... Muriel Pavlow
Grimsdyke .... Kenneth More
Benskin .... Donald Sinden
Isobel .... Kay Kendall
Lancelot Spratt .... James Robertson Justice
Taffy .... Donald Houston
Stella .... Suzanne Cloutier
Dean .... Geoffrey Keen
Sister Virtue .... Jean Taylor-Smith

Doctor in the House is a lighthearted comedy with a medical background. Based on a novel by a London doctor writing under the pseudonym of Richard Gordon, the screenplay fashioned by Nicholas Phipps is episodic, presenting a series of adventures of a group of medical students as they progress (or fail to progress) through five years of medical school.

When we meet Simon Sparrow (Dirk Bogarde), we see that despite his seriousness and innocence he cannot avoid trouble. Arriving at St. Swithin's for the beginning of his medical education, he is first mistaken for a patient and ordered to take off his clothes, then after a mishap with his suitcase, he finally arrives at the lecture hall just in time to interrupt the professor's discourse on punctuality. Before long he meets three other students who will be his compatriots for the rest of the film. Grimsdyke (Kenneth More), who has already spent some time at the school, frequently offers his assistance and advice to Simon. Grimsdyke's knowledge is limited to extracurricular matters, however, because he purposely does not learn medicine. The reason for this strange behavior, Simon finds, is that Grimsdyke's grandmother left him one thousand pounds per year (a small but adequate income for 1954) for as long as he is in medical school, and he would much rather continue to be a student than finish his studies and have to go to work. Grimsdyke's two friends, Benskin (Donald Sinden) and Taffy (Donald Houston), have less advice to offer. Benskin's main interest is women and Taffy's is rugby. All three think

Simon is too serious and too preoccupied with his medical studies.

Determined to avoid distractions, Simon takes a room in a quiet boarding house for students, but he soon discovers that he cannot avoid the amorous attentions of the landlady's daughter, who keeps coming to his room for medical advice even though he explains that he has barely begun his studies. Before long he tires of this and moves out. He then accepts the offer of Grimsdyke to share the lodgings where he, Benskin, and Taffy reside. The flat, Simon finds when he first arrives, is chaotic and has one more inhabitant than he expected. A young woman preparing for a bath introduces herself as Stella (Suzanne Cloutier), Grimsdyke's fiancée, explaining that she lives in the flat below and is just borrowing the bathroom because hers is not working. Simon is disconcerted by her presence, especially when she asks him to bring her a cup of tea while she is in the bathtub.

At that moment Grimsdyke arrives and soon discovers that he has a problem. Stella announces that she is no longer his fiancée because she wants to be married to a "proper doctor," not a continual student. Therefore, Grimsdyke has to begin studying seriously—or at least more seriously than before—and Stella throughout the film apparently spends most of her time in the students' flat.

Besides following the medical studies of the four, especially Simon, the film also focuses on the amorous adventures of Simon. The others think him too studious and in need of female companionship, but his unwilling acceptance of their advice results in fiascoes. One time, for example, he makes a date with Isobel (Kay Kendall), a rich woman who thinks he is already a practicing physician. When they arrive at the restaurant she has chosen, he finds that it is very expensive and many of the diners are wealthy people who know her; he is out of his depth both socially and financially. He escapes only by having himself called by one of his friends who says he is needed immediately for an emergency. Even after that misadventure Simon agrees—still reluctantly—to take out one of the nurses, Joy (Muriel Pavlow). On their date, however, he makes his reluctance so obvious that she becomes upset and wants to go home. He apologizes and tries to explain, and from this most unpromising of beginnings a true romance begins to develop.

Meanwhile, we are kept abreast of the trials and tribulations of being a medical student at St. Swithin's. We hear bits of abstruse lectures, see the students' anxiety at examination time, and meet some of their most feared professors, particularly Lancelot Spratt (James Robertson Justice). Sir Lancelot, as he is known to all, is a burly, bearded man with a gruff manner and a gleam in his eye. Simon's progression as medical student parallels his romantic one. Despite numerous misadventures, he is ultimately successful. The misadventures include dropping a skeleton in a bus full of passengers who are reading newspapers about a murderer, and fainting the first time he is supposed to assist in an operation.

Simon triumphs, however, the first time he is truly tested. He is at the hospital and is called to go to a woman's house to assist a midwife in delivering a baby. He sets off on a bicycle on a cold, snowy night, but soon has to abandon the bicycle and summon a passing motorist. Then, when he arrives at the woman's house, he finds that the midwife has not arrived and there is no telephone on which he can call for advice or assistance. He is on his own, and he does so well that the woman, who already has given birth to six children, names the new infant after him. "It must be wonderful to be a doctor," she says.

Simon's medical career, however, is threatened by two escapades during his final year of studies. First, after a big rugby match, Simon and the others are arrested after a fight with another group of students over the St. Swithin's mascot, a huge stuffed gorilla. They are fined and put on probation by the school. Later, Joy is helping Simon study for his finals one night when they notice that it is too late for her to get into the nurses' quarters before curfew. They try to sneak her in through a roof entrance, but Simon falls through a skylight into the room of the supervisor of the nurses, Sister Virtue (Jean Taylor-Smith). It looks as if he will be expelled from the school and lose all that he has worked for, but help comes from a surprising source. Sir Lancelot, who had already amazed them by paying their fines, now intercedes with the Dean (Geoffrey Keen). Lancelot brings up the fact that in his own student days the Dean had brought a horse into the school so that a young woman could impersonate Lady Godiva. Lancelot remarks that the students now in the school would find that story quite interesting. This argument soon convinces the Dean to let Simon stay in school, and once we find that the young woman was Sister Virtue, we understand why Joy is not punished.

Simon goes on to pass his final examinations and become a doctor, as does Taffy. Benskin and Grimsdyke fail, but they eagerly look forward to the next year at the school when they will be joined by Stella, who has decided to take up the study of medicine herself. The film ends with an affectionate but ambiguous farewell between Joy and Simon.

The preceding plot description may make *Doctor in the House* sound less episodic and more organized than it actually is. Actually, however, the film moves from episode to episode with little attempt to make connections with earlier ones and little attempt to prepare for later ones. The humor and charm of the individual parts, however, are enough to make the film an entertaining experience. Indeed, audiences responded so well to *Doctor in the House* that a series of sequels were made, but as is usual in such cases, none of the later films was as good as the first. In fact, more successful than any of the sequels was a television series, also called *Doctor in the House*, that began in 1968.

Although Bogarde as Simon has the largest role in the film, it is More as Grimsdyke who steals the picture, as Bogarde in his autobiography freely admits. This is mainly due to the fact that Bogarde has to play the foil to

More's comic *persona*; Bogarde is the serious straight man to More's jokester. In fact, Bogarde initially had some doubts about whether he wanted the part of Simon because "every other character had funnier things to say and do." In later years, however, he realized that *Doctor in the House* was the turning point of his career. It was his first significant role in a successful film, and after establishing himself in several doctor films, he went on to display his talent and range in such distinguished and complex films as *The Servant* (1963) and *Death in Venice* (1971). Also notable in *Doctor in the House* is Justice, whose portrayal of Lancelot Spratt has the subtlety as well as bluster and bravado which he has displayed in dozens of British films.

Sharon Wiseman

DR. KILDARE'S STRANGE CASE

Released: 1940
Production: Metro-Goldwyn-Mayer
Direction: Harold S. Bucquet
Screenplay: Harry Ruskin and Willis Goldbeck; based on the characters created by Max Brand
Cinematography: John F. Seitz
Editing: Gene Ruggiero
Running time: 76 minutes

> *Principal characters:*
> Dr. James Kildare .... Lew Ayres
> Dr. Leonard Gillespie .... Lionel Barrymore
> Mary Lamont .... Laraine Day
> Dr. Stephen Kildare .... Samuel S. Hinds
> Joe Wayman .... Nat Pendleton
> Dr. Carewe .... Walter Kingsford
> Sally .... Marie Blake
> Dr. Gregory Lane .... Shepperd Strudwick
> Nurse Molly Byrd .... Alma Kruger

Throughout the history of cinema, a wide variety of characters have proven popular enough in a single to spawn a series of sequels. From singing cowboys to talking mules, if the first film was a hit, successors very often followed. By the late 1930's, studios began to look for properties that would yield not one but several hits. M-G-M was tremendously successful in 1938 with the first of its Andy Hardy series, and later that same year, the studio came back with a pair of characters that were equally as popular—Dr. James Kildare, a brilliant young diagnostician, and his crusty mentor, Dr. Leonard Gillespie. The characters were taken from a group of popular stories by Max Brand, who was better known as a writer of Western novels. Together, through various actors and directors, Kildare and Gillespie worked their homespun medical miracles for more than ten years.

The first of these films, *Internes Can't Take Money* (1937), was directed by Alfred Santell and featured Joel McCrea as Kildare. Later, when Metro matched director Harold S. Bucquet with actors Lew Ayres and Lionel Barrymore (the best of the Kildares and the only Gillespie, respectively), they hit upon a chemistry that was truly memorable. The first of the Bucquet-Ayres-Barrymore Kildares was *Young Doctor Kildare*, released in 1938. Metro had come out with a jaundiced look at the medical profession in King Vidor's *The Citadel* earlier that year, but *Young Doctor Kildare* took an entirely different approach. The physicians in Kildare's world had the same reverence for medicine that Judge Hardy had for the law in the Andy Hardy series.

This dedication to their calling, along with the affection and mutual respect among the series' principal characters, was the key to the Kildare films' enduring popularity.

The series, which has a definite sequence, begins when Dr. James Kildare (Lew Ayres) returns to his parents' home, having just completed medical school in the footsteps of his father. The younger Kildare has decided to forgo a career as a country doctor; he wants, instead, to broaden his horizons in New York City. Although his father, Dr. Stephen Kildare (Samuel S. Hinds), is disappointed, he accedes to his son's wishes and offers him some homespun advice: "Whenever you are in doubt as to what ails a patient, give him bicarbonate of soda and see how he looks in the morning." Thus armed, Kildare sets off for New York, winding up at Blair General Hospital, under the tutelage of Dr. Leonard Gillespie (Lionel Barrymore), a delightful old curmudgeon who is the wisecracking urban equivalent of the elder Kildare. With the introduction of these two main characters, the film, and, indeed, the whole series begins.

The two men complement each other perfectly. Kildare is every mother's ideal son. He is earnest without being sanctimonious, confident without being brash—in short, a Boy Scout with a medical degree. Gillespie is roguish and rambunctious, despite being confined to a wheelchair (in the Kildare films, the wheelchair is somehow linked to the fact that Gillespie is dying slowly of cancer; in fact, it was a plot device concocted to accommodate Barrymnore's arthritis and hip joint problems). The fact that the whole effect gave Gillespie the appearance of then-President Franklin D. Roosevelt probably did not hurt either. A brilliant diagnostician, Gillespie drives both himself and Kildare mercilessly; nevertheless, his affection for the younger man is evident. He sees Kildare as a worthy successor, and continues, throughout the series, to groom him for that position.

That the two men clicked onscreen was evident to Metro even before the film was released. Thus the studio shot an unusual closing scene for *Young Doctor Kildare*. In what amounted to an epilogue, Ayres and Barrymore appeared on a stage and announced that they would be returning in a series of Kildare sequels. In addition to Ayres and Barrymore, a number of other actors also appeared regularly as characters in the series. Head Nurse Molly Byrd (Alma Kruger) is Gillespie's personal assistant, and fully his match in their verbal jousts. She is as intent on keeping him alive and healthy as he seems to be at working himself to death. Joe Wayman (Nat Pendleton) is the rough but good-natured ambulance driver who figures in many moments of comic relief; Sally (Marie Blake), the hospital switchboard operator, is his girl friend. Dr. Carewe (Walter Kingsford), as the head of Blair General Hospital, is often Kildare's and Gillespie's nemesis, with his insistence on following the rules to the letter. Kildare's romantic interest is most often nurse

Mary Lamont (Laraine Day), to whom he becomes engaged, but who dies in one of the last films of the Ayres/Kildare series, *Dr. Kildare's Wedding Day* (1941). Kildare's impoverished status as an intern—and his highminded reluctance to ask any woman to play second fiddle to his career—keeps his pursuit of Mary low-key, but she always winds up with him rather than any rival suitor by the last reel.

Dr. Kildare's Strange Case, perhaps the best of the Kildare films, contains all of the elements that made the series so successful. There were numerous plots, all going on at once, and many intertwined with the others. Typically, Kildare risks disgrace to follow his conscience, encountering opposition from everyone—even, temporarily, from Dr. Gillespie. By the end of the film, however, Kildare's insight and courage triumph over conventional wisdom, and he is vindicated. As the film opens, the overworked and penurious Kildare is in danger of losing Mary Lamont to a successful brain surgeon at Blair General Hospital. The surgeon, Dr. Gregory Lane (Shepperd Strudwick), however, is having a run of bad luck: all of his recent patients have died. Kildare and Gillespie believe in Lane's surgical skills, and Kildare is put in the awkward position of defending his romantic rival. He handles the situation with dignity and aplomb, as usual, professing sincerely to want only what is best for Mary.

When one of Lane's patients lapses into insanity after a particularly delicate operation, it is the last straw for Dr. Carewe, who is on the verge of suspending Lane. Kildare risks his career to help save Lane's reputation—and his patient's life. With Mary Lamont's help, he administers a hazardous and controversial treatment known as the "insulin shock cure." In the face of the disapproval of both Carewe and Gillespie, Kildare's therapy is nevertheless successful. The patient's sanity is restored, and when he reveals that he has had a history of mental troubles predating the operation, Dr. Lane is vindicated as well.

Meanwhile, Kildare mulls over a lucrative job offer from the prestigious Messinger Institute. He would command five hundred dollars a month (versus his twenty dollars a month salary at Blair General Hospital) and the free use of a house. Gillespie urges him to accept the offer, noting that this would enable him to compete with Gregory Lane financially for Mary Lamont's affections. Kildare is tempted, but ultimately decides to stay an intern, much to Gillespie's—and the audience's—relief. To do otherwise would be to abandon his dream of succeeding Gillespie as Blair's chief diagnostician. Fortunately, all of this prompts Kildare to be honest with Mary about his feelings for her. He asks her to wait for him—five years is the time they agree upon—and she gladly accepts. The film ends with Kildare sneaking away from a lecture by Gillespie to have dinner with Mary.

Dr. Kildare's Strange Case has all of the qualities that made the Kildare series popular—tension, romance, camaraderie, humor, nobility, and dedication. Ayres continued in the series until 1942. At that time, during the early part of World War II, he declared himself a conscientious objector, and M-G-M dropped him from the series because of the unpopularity of his position. After Ayres's departure, the emphasis of the stories switched to Gillespie and a series of young Metro stars, notably Van Johnson, took the role of the young assistant, now under different names in each film. When the series ended in 1947, after no less than fifteen films, the Kildare character was dormant for awhile. The films were resurrected on television late shows around the country in the 1950's, however; and in 1961, a television series called *Dr. Kildare*, starring Richard Chamberlain as Kildare and Raymond Massey as Gillespie, started up the Kildare vogue anew. The television series lasted for seven years. Metro's instincts in 1938 were sound. Dr. Kildare is truly one of the most enduring characters in the history of popular entertainment, and is still seen frequently on late-night television.

Robert Mitchell

DR. NO

Released: 1962
Production: Harry Saltzman and Albert R. Broccoli for United Artists
Direction: Terence Young
Screenplay: Richard Maibaum, Johanna Harwood, and Berkley Mather; based on the novel of the same name by Ian Fleming
Cinematography: Ted Moore
Editing: Peter Hunt
Running time: 111 minutes

> *Principal characters:*
> James Bond (007) ....Sean Connery
> Dr. No ....Joseph Wiseman
> Felix Leiter ....Jack Lord
> Honey Ryder ....Ursula Andress
> "M" .... Bernard Lee
> Miss Taro .... Zena Marshall

It is safe to say that the cinematic exploits of James Bond, Agent 007, have become firmly rooted in popular American culture. Between 1963 and 1981, no less than twelve films have been released detailing the international crises prevented by this super secret agent, and in another film, *Casino Royale* (1967), the Bond character was featured in a satirical fashion. Each new Bond film seems to be more spectacular than the last, filled with all sorts of gimmicks and sexy women. Looking back to the first Bond film, *Dr. No*, however, it is fascinating to see the evolution of both Agent 007 and the spectacular quality of high entertainment that has been squeezed out of the literature of Ian Fleming.

Dr. No is a thriller in the classic British tradition. The unusual exoticism of the scientific power plant on Dr. No's island fortress and the charisma of Sean Connery as James Bond tend to elevate the film from typical espionage dramas. The plot is simple. Someone in the Caribbean is diverting American missile tests. A British agent investigating the activities of an organization in the general vicinity is murdered by three "blind" street-singers. James Bond is called in to take over where the murdered agent left off.

Once on the scene, Bond becomes the target of numerous assassins. He is nearly run off the road in a mad car chase. Later, after meeting with his island contacts, he discovers a huge tropical scorpion placed in his bedroom. Trying to get information on the activities of the sinister Dr. No (Joseph Wiseman), he comes in contact with the predictable femme fatale, Miss Taro (Zena Marshall), who sets him up to be killed as she cooly paints her nails. He handles each situation with a calculating efficiency that is uncanny. Eventually he makes his way to Dr. No's well-guarded island fortress, where he stumbles onto Honey Ryder (Ursula Andress), an innocent diver whose quest for seashells has led her into a web of intrigue created by the notorious Dr. No. Honey was the first of the gorgeous "Bond Women," and her first appearance in a brief bikini is a memorable scene.

There is only one obstacle that Bond is unable to overcome in his search for Dr. No: a camouflaged tank equipped with a flame-thrower which hunts him down spewing fire and death in its path. The bruised and burned Bond is brought to Dr. No for the inevitable confrontation, as is Honey.

The confrontation between Bond and Dr. No is classic. His code name of Agent 007 denotes that he has a license to kill, and the skill employed by Bond in dispatching many of Dr. No's top operatives interests the master criminal. The proposal of working for the "other side" and the expected refusal are made in an atmosphere of building tension. The scene is concluded with both principals realizing that the next meeting will result in death for one.

Bond is returned to his lush prison cell where he eventually makes good his escape through the super-heated air-conditioning ducts. He has only a few minutes in which to stop Dr. No from changing the course of a guided missile which will cause major damage to the Eastern seaboard of the United States. He engages in mortal hand-to-hand combat with Dr. No over a reactor pool, and the death of the archvillain is followed by the destruction of his entire island complex. Democracy is saved once again by 007.

There is an attitude presented in *Dr. No* which is found in only the earliest Bond films. The intensity of dramatic confrontation and the seriousness of the tone make these films function as thrillers. In the later Bond films, the element of self-parody begins to become evident. In *Dr. No* there is none of the flamboyant weaponry associated with the more recent Bond extravaganzas. Rather, Bond's potency arises from his physical strength and intelligence. Connery captures the animalistic flavor of the novels flawlessly in the early Bond films. Both in *Dr. No* and *From Russia with Love* (1964) the final test is one of strength and endurance. In later Bond films such as *Thunderball* (1965), and more recently in Roger Moore's version of 007 in *The Spy Who Loved Me* (1977) and *Moonraker* (1979), the emphasis has been shifted to gadgets and tongue-in-cheek heroics. Much of this *deus ex machina* stems from the sophistication of audiences and the need for the Bond films to become spectacular entertainment rather than the simple, more formalized thrillers.

Unlike most espionage films, which can become bogged down in convoluted twists in the plot, double agents, diplomatic intrigue, and confusing morals, the Bond films are extremely simple. They have refined the confrontation to its most basic: good versus evil. Bond becomes a contemporary hero of mythic proportions. He is unbeatable, and his ability to "save the world" again and again is accepted without question.

The James Bond films inspired a great many imitators in the 1960's. After the success of *Dr. No*, *From Russia with Love*, and *Goldfinger* (1964), there was a renaissance of espionage films in which several other secret agents found themselves adapted to the screen. Donald Hamilton's Matt Helm was brought to the screen in a series of adventure comedies which took the Bondish formula of action and humor and distilled it to a crass level. *In Like Flint* (1967) started another series of spy films; this time James Coburn played a supersophisticated spy whose exploits bordered on burlesque. Copycat films most often evolve into a pattern which stresses form over content; as a result, they are much less appealing and successful.

Dr. No, and the James Bond films in general, are able to transcend their generic handicaps and function on a number of levels. Escapism and entertainment form the key to the Bond series. From the seriousness of *Dr. No* to the shenanigans of *Moonraker*, the plots may change, the cast of characters may shift, and the actors who portray 007 may differ, but the end result is the same: entertaining, well-made films.

Carl F. Macek

A DOLL'S HOUSE

Released: 1973
Production: Joseph Losey for World Film Services
Direction: Joseph Losey
Screenplay: David Mercer; based on the play of the same name by Henrik Ibsen and translated by Michael Meyer
Cinematography: Jerry Fisher
Editing: Reginald Beck
Running time: 106 minutes

> *Principal characters:*
> Nora .... Jane Fonda
> Torvald ....David Warner
> Dr. Rank .... Trevor Howard
> Kristine Linde .... Delphine Seyrig
> Nils Krogstad .... Edward Fox

Between 1879 and 1884 Norwegian playwright Henrik Ibsen wrote a number of plays the radical themes of which shocked and outraged his contemporaries. Approximately a century later some of these plays are being rediscovered by filmmakers because their themes are still relevant if no longer revolutionary. In 1979, Steve McQueen produced and starred in a production of *An Enemy of the People*, in which the theme is the attempt of a town's authorities to suppress an unpleasant truth that could damage the town's livelihood. (The same theme, incidentally, is also seen in *Jaws*, the hugely successful 1975 film.) Six years earlier, in 1973, two films were released of Ibsen's *A Doll's House*, the story of a woman who leaves her husband and children in search of self-development. Neither production of *A Doll's House* is all one might have hoped. The production directed by Patrick Garland starring Claire Bloom is too austere and marred by unnecessary cuts. It is the version directed by Joseph Losey with Jane Fonda in the lead role that is—despite its faults—the more interesting.

The film opens with a number of scenes added by screenwriter David Mercer. These establish some of the background to the main action of the drama, all of which occurs in less than three days. First we see Nora (Jane Fonda) with her friend Kristine (Delphine Seyrig) and then Kristine with Nils Krogstad (Edward Fox). We learn that Nora is looking forward to her marriage to Torvald Helmer (David Warner) but that Kristine is rejecting the man she loves, Krogstad, for a man she does not love but who can provide for her, her helpless mother, and her two young brothers. Then in a few scenes from later times we learn that Torvald is so ill that only a year away from Norway's frigid climate can cure him. Without ever letting him know how serious his illness is, Nora persuades Torvald to spend a year in Italy on money left her by her father, who has just died. The treatment is a success, and Torvald returns completely cured. Thus is set the scene for the principal action of the film, which begins on Christmas Eve, eight years after Nora's marriage to Torvald, and just after Torvald has been appointed manager of a bank (at which Krogstad now works as a menial clerk).

Nora comes into the house with the tree and presents she has bought, but Torvald does not enter into her holiday high-spiritedness; instead, he patronizingly scolds her for being a spendthrift and for eating macaroons, which he has forbidden her to eat. Soon Dr. Rank (Trevor Howard), an old family friend as well as the family physician, joins Torvald in his study, and then Kristine, who is now a widow and has not heard from Nora in a long time, arrives to see her.

This scene, which is the first one in Ibsen's play, establishes Torvald's attitude toward Nora, and the arrival of Kristine triggers most of the events that lead to the film's climax. As the film progresses, we find that the money to finance Torvald's lifesaving year in Italy did not come from Nora's father's will as she told Torvald. Her father left her no money; so she borrowed the money from Krogstad and gave him a bond upon which she had forged her father's signature. She did not tell Torvald the situation at the time because the doctor did not want him to know how ill he was, and later she cannot tell him because, as she tells Kristine, it would be "painful and humiliating" for him to know he owed anything to her. Most of these details come out in Nora's first talk with Kristine, when she wants to prove to her friend that she is not merely a frivolous woman with no cares and unable to do anything on her own. She tells Kristine of doing copying work without Torvald's knowledge in order to pay back part of the loan.

With Torvald's new position at the bank Nora expects to have enough money to pay off the debt and forget it, but an ironic turn of events prevents this solution. Nora asks Torvald to give Kristine a job at the bank and he agrees, but it turns out that he has decided to fire Krogstad and give that job to Kristine. When Krogstad learns this and finds out that the signature on the bond he holds is forged, he resolves to use the bond as a weapon. He goes to Nora and explains to her that she will be in serious legal trouble if he reveals the forged bond and that he will do so if she does not convince her husband to give him back his job. He also tells her that his own career as a lawyer was ruined when he did much the same thing, which makes it doubly important that he not lose his job. "I will fight for my job, Mrs. Helmer," he says, "as I would fight for my life."

Another theme introduced in the scene in which Torvald scolds Nora about being a spendthrift now becomes important. Torvald has told her that she has received this trait from her father and that in his practice of the law he has noticed that criminals usually have bad parents. Nora also learns that Dr. Rank is dying of spinal syphilis that was caused by his father's sexual profligacy. The theme of the sins of the parents being passed on to or destroying their children is a common one in the works of Ibsen. All this talk begins to cause Nora to fear that she may be a bad influence on her children because of her sinfulness in forging the name and lying about the source of the money.

Nora seeks a way out of her predicament when she briefly considers asking Dr. Rank for the money to pay off Krogstad. When, however, she begins to ask the doctor if he will do something for her to protect Torvald because he loves her so much, Dr. Rank replies in a calm but sincere voice, "I too have loved you as deeply as anyone else ever has." Nora is upset by his declaration and decides that it makes it impossible for her to ask him for anything.

Meanwhile, Krogstad has sent Torvald a letter explaining the whole affair, but Kristine offers to go to Krogstad and persuade him to ask for the letter back unread while Nora desperately tries to prevent Torvald from reading his mail. Kristine and Nora are both successful, but then Kristine decides— even though Krogstad has accepted her plea that the two of them should again be together and that Krogstad should retrieve his letter to Torvald— that "Nora's unhappy secret must be revealed." This too is a frequent occurrence in the plays of Ibsen—a character becomes convinced of the importance of telling the truth.

Another day passes, and Torvald and Nora leave a fancy dress ball at which Nora has performed the Tarantella, a dance she learned in Italy. Torvald is overcome with his feeling for Nora and tells her he wishes he could make a great sacrifice—even his life—for her. When he reads Krogstad's letter a few minutes later, however, he is enraged at her for putting him in Krogstad's power and shows no compassion or understanding. Krogstad then delivers another letter saying that a new happiness has come into his life and that he is enclosing the forged bond. Torvald's response is immediate: "I'm saved." He tells Nora that he will forgive her and regard the whole thing as a dream, but Nora has finally seen that Torvald is not the man she thought he was and that continuing to be his "most treasured possession," as he has called her, is not the life she wants. She tells him she is leaving him and responds to his appeals to her duty as wife and mother by saying, "I have another duty equally sacred . . . my duty to myself." The film ends with a shot of the door she has just closed as she leaves.

Certainly the greatest weakness of this film is its script. Many scenes are added to Ibsen's play, usually to furnish the background of the characters or as an excuse for exterior shots, since the entire film was shot on location in Norway. Changes are often necessary for the translation of a stage play into a film, but in this case screenwriter Mercer has taken a tightly written play and merely added unnecessary or interrupting material. Virtually everything spelled out in the early (non-Ibsen) scenes is repeated later, such as the reason Kristine did not marry Krogstad. The script is strongest where it strays least from the original play. The direction by Losey, which features a great many moving camera shots, mirrors, and scenic snow scenes, unfortunately lacks a clear focus for the first part of the film, and the pace is much too leisurely.

It is the acting and the quality of the original material that redeem the film. Howard is fine as the kindly Dr. Rank, and Warner's curiously distant performance owes more to the script and the direction than to a deficiency of the actor. Fox as Krogstad, the most emotional character in the film, has more to do and does it well. Except for the climactic ending, the most moving scene in the film is the one in which he and Kristine agree to reunite their lives. It is, however, Fonda as Nora who is the key of the success of the film. She brings an understanding to the part that conveys all the facets of the character: her willing submission to Torvald, her pride in what she has done for him, her frantic fear of being found out, and her resolution to fulfill her duty to herself.

Julia Johnson

DON'T LOOK NOW

Released: 1973
Production: Peter Katz for Paramount
Direction: Nicholas Roeg
Screenplay: Allan Scott and Chris Bryant; based on the novel of the same name by Daphne du Maurier
Cinematography: Anthony Richmond
Editing: Graeme Clifford
Running time: 110 minutes

Principal characters:
John Baxter .... Donald Sutherland
Laura Baxter .... Julie Christie
Mystic .... Hilary Mason
Wendy .... Clelia Mantana
Bishop Barbarrigo .... Massimo Serato
Christine ....Sharon Williams

Don't Look Now is a Gothic mystery, and like that sort of "irrational" mystery, the film is full of lessons in suspicion. What can one do when every danger is unpredictable and imminent in countless hidden forewarnings? In *Don't Look Now* one must watch for little signs, clues to the scheme of the supernatural. What this sort of story teaches its audience above all is to watch out. Look for the danger which is unseen, which is not rational, and which common sense will not show you. In the world of supernatural mystery, commonplace events carry the promise of unexplained and probably inexplicable death scenes. This brings up the problem inherent in the ironic title of *Don't Look Now*. The film does not trust in sight as a means to explanation or understanding. The question is, how much of the world does sight "see?" A secretly important object, a shadow which seems to carry a threat, a stranger who bears the mark of the supernatural—all are details in a hidden pattern, determining the shape of everyday events. Seeing may be a means of discovering what cannot be understood, and in *Don't Look Now*, characters become convinced that almost any image can present a danger.

The threats to their safety that the Baxter family encounter gradually bring them to a constant alertness for clues. The Baxters have a heightened fear of missing the significance of a piece of tile, or a red raincoat, or a pair of white rats struggling to get out of the water. Anything may be a clue to happenstance, to accident, or to unforeseeable death. Nicholas Roeg, the director, loads the world with these images and leads the audience on a confusing and misleading hunt for clues. John Baxter (Donald Sutherland) is in a line of work which looks for bits which fit a pattern. He is an archaeologist whose specialty is church restoration work. Rebuilding and reading signs from the past is his daily business, a very rational work with a definite pattern of attack. John and his wife Laura (Julie Christie) have two children and enjoy a quiet, middle-class life in the English countryside. One afternoon as John Baxter is examining slides for his work, a drop of red ink is spilled on one of the tiny images. The slide shows a red hooded figure sitting in a pew. For some reason, John thinks of his daughter, out playing by the pond in a red raincoat. Director Roeg crosscuts to the pond, showing the little girl falling into the water and going under. John startles his wife Laura by jumping up and running outside to the pond, but he gets to his daughter too late; she has drowned, wearing her red raincoat.

With her death, the peaceful life of the Baxter family is overturned and shattered. They move from the well-ordered English countryside to Italy for a stay in Venice, where John has an art restoration job. Venice, a damp city of gray canals and medieval buildings in decay, seems in winter full of supernatural signs and possible death scenes. Strangers follow the Baxters without logical reason. A blind mystic (Hilary Mason), tells Laura that she has a message from her dead daughter. "Don't be sad," the stranger says. "I've seen your daughter sitting between you and your husband . . . and she's laughing, she's very happy, you know."

The message from the beyond is not reassuring; the dowdy spinster's unseeing face is a sinister reminder of what cannot be seen. Baxter comes to doubt his ability to make sense of very much of what he sees. Later, after he and his wife have stopped communicating with the unseen world forming a barrier between them, Baxter sees his wife. Laura is on a boat in the canal, in the company of the blind spinster. Her presence on the boat with the blind mystic makes no sense to him, and he shouts at her. She does not answer or seem to hear him. Soon afterward, Baxter will make his own crossing to the "other world." He is about to be killed, without explanation, in a dark passageway in Venice; his daughter Christine's red raincoat is on the back of his murderer.

The plot of the film is very slim, with complications and delays set up by the incidental images which multiply around the Baxters. "Don't expect too much, Mr. Baxter," the police inspector in Venice warns him about the city's maze, but the Baxters expect that anything may result from a small event. Their daughter's death has colored their world with grim possibilities, erected like lenses before everything they see. A tiny mosaic tile smashed beneath a bishop's shoe fascinates John with its sinister possibilities, as does the appearance of a flock of ducks in a dark canal. In another meeting with Bishop Barbarrigo (Massimo Serato), who employs him, Baxter's eye focuses on the handkerchief in the bishop's pocket. An extreme close-up shot of the handkerchief makes it important, but the commonplace conversation reveals nothing to make the handkerchief threatening, and nothing in the plot will refer to it again. The handkerchief is simply another possible sign for which Baxter is searching, a clue which does not pay off.

Roeg's camera mimics the action of an archaeologist, hunting bits and pieces of portents from which to construct the threat Baxter feels in Venice. Like the archaeologist, the camera makes false guesses, hunts for clues, and isolates images which may not be signs of anything. The audience cannot trust the camera to know more than its characters, unlike some mysteries in which the camera reveals what will come. The editing also throws the visual world up in the air, letting it fall back out of kilter. Disjunctive shots, with extreme changes in point of view, depth, or angle, carry the scene around and about as well as forward. Odd time sequences throw the world of perception off balance. Probably the most discussed example of disjunctive time editing is the scene in which the Baxters make love, intercut with very unemotional shots of the two dressing for dinner.

There are larger threats to the Baxters' world than bits and pieces images. A murderer is at large in Venice, and throughout the film, the canals are dredged for bodies. A rickety scaffolding gives way under Baxter as he works on the church exterior, and he is almost killed. Their other child, a boy, is sent back to boarding school in England, where he is injured in an accident. Laura, who is convinced that Venice is a dangerous place, leaves to be with her son, but she cannot convince her husband to join her. Later, when she tries to find John in Venice, they are separated and she fails. Baxter is killed by a figure in red, a dwarf wearing a red raincoat and reflected in a pool of water similar to Christine's.

Roeg had been a cinematographer before codirecting his first film in 1968 with Donald Cammel, *Performance*, for which he also supplied the camerawork. Among his credits as a cinematographer are Roger Corman's *Masque of the Red Death* (1964), François Truffant's *Fahrenheit 451* (1966), and Richard Lester's *Petulia* (1968). His distinctive editing and beautiful saturated images mark all of Roeg's movies with an idiosyncratic, easily recognizable visual style. *Performance*, *Walkabout* (1971), *The Man Who Fell to Earth* (1976), and *Don't Look Now* all share a fascination with ways of seeing as a means of disrupting the commonplace, or social norm. In Roeg's films images present a danger to those who take the visual world for granted, who do not look and look again. The meaning of a detail, lodged in a sequence of details, cannot be announced too readily. To those who decipher images too easily, Roeg has supplied an appropriately titled *Don't Look Now*.

Leslie Donaldson

A DOUBLE LIFE

Released: 1947
Production: Michael Kanin for Universal
Direction: George Cukor
Screenplay: Ruth Gordon and Garson Kanin
Cinematography: Milton Krasner
Editing: Robert Parrish
Music: Miklos Rozsa (AA)
Running time: 103 minutes

Principal characters:
Anthony John .... Ronald Colman (AA)
Brita .... Signe Hasso
Bill Friend .... Edmond O'Brien
Pat Kroll .... Shelley Winters
Max Lasker .... Philip Loeb
Victor Donlan .... Ray Collins

The story of *A Double Life* concerns an actor who becomes so immersed in his roles that his identification with the characters he plays overwhelms his private life. While the situation in this compelling film is so extreme that it leads Anthony John (Ronald Colman) to unreasoning jealousy and murder, the essential problem of an artist's need for detachment from his creative power is moving even without the melodrama of the plot. The character reflects on his difficulties very early in the film, demonstrating a consciousness of his mysterious impulse to live his roles and winning considerable audience sympathy by virtue of his earnestness. Tony is from the beginning a lonely and endearing figure, perhaps too idealistic about himself and too fragile in his emotions. He is estranged from his wife, Brita (Signe Hasso), although they still love each other and still work together. He yearns for a stability which seems remote.

The actor's loss of balance occurs when he takes on the role of Othello in a production of the Shakespearean drama. Before this, we see him playing in a light and witty comedy, *A Gentleman's Gentleman.* The play has been successful and Tony has been playing his role for a long time. As a result, he is as charming and sophisticated offstage as he is on. A reconciliation with Brita seems possible, but Tony yields to the temptation of playing the tragic role which he knows may consume him. Gloomily, he wanders at night through the city, perhaps believing that this noctural solitude will unlock the key to the demanding characterization. He meets a waitress, Pat Kroll (Shelley Winters). Vulgar and unrefined, she is the opposite of Brita, but her openness attracts Tony. He sleeps with her, then forgets her.

Later, when *Othello* has become a smash hit and Tony's brilliant performance as the jealous Moor is starting to take its toll as a result of nightly performances, he seeks out Pat once more. He has already made Othello's jealousy a part of himself, suspecting his wife and an innocent press agent, Bill Friend (Edmond O'Brien), of an affair. As in the case of Shakespeare's protagonist, his suspicions are unwarranted. The difference is that his actor's imagination is the villain, poisoning his thoughts as the character Iago poisoned those of Othello in the play. In a demented state, he projects his jealousy onto Pat, who, with amusing guilelessness, asks if she should "put out the light." The Shakespearean phrase and the visually striking darkness which follows as Tony, repeating the line, does turn out the light, results in the death of the poor waitress. Ultimately, it is Friend who has the insight to suspect that Tony is the murderer, although there is nothing to link him to Pat other than the *Othello* style of the killing. Mortally wounding himself on stage after almost strangling Brita, he dies finishing his role.

In realizing this material, director George Cukor and writers Ruth Gordon and Garson Kanin demonstrate not only a sympathetic understanding of the character but also their love of theater. The rehearsal sequences which precede the major part of the narrative are no less fascinating than the melodrama which follows, although they are completely devoid of melodrama. What we see are actors tirelessly practicing and the details of work on the play's physical presentation, but these moments perfectly capture the process of creating an individual production from a text which exists only in words. The imagination of Cukor's own staging and Milton Krasner's lighting conveys the excitement of theater in a positive way, in contrast to the negative effect this same excitement has on the film's protagonist.

Further, there are lengthy excerpts from the play itself. Fortunately, Colman is a superb actor, and he is a credible Othello, as convincing playing Anthony John acting the role as he is playing Tony as a tragically disturbed individual. The climactic scenes of Shakespeare's tragedy are presented twice. In the second rendition, which is also the climax of the film, Tony gives a more deeply felt reading of his lines, and it is appropriate to call attention to Cukor's discernment and Colman's ability in making the earlier reading not unworthy of comparison to the second. That first reading is dramatically persuasive, convincing as the performance of a celebrated actor, and lacking only the touching self-knowledge of the dying Tony which makes the second reading singularly poignant.

Colman is well-cast as an actor but no less impressive as an individual struggling to make his life as successful as his career. Tony's beautiful voice and gentlemanly bearing do not desert him offstage, but he never appears to be an affected man. On the contrary, he comes across as a man of deep feeling and sensitivity, and he is unfailingly sympathetic, even after he has murdered Pat. Colman's past performances in such films as *Lost Horizon* (1937) and *A Tale Of Two Cities* (1935) were undoubtedly a factor in the Academy Award he won for *A Double Life*, but that does not change the fact that the award is well-deserved. His performance confirms Cukor's richly merited reputation as an actor's director, as do the less central performances. The only other striking role is that of Pat, and Winters perfectly expresses Pat's sexual sophistication and her lack of psychological awareness, but the director commendably balances the playing of Colman and Winters by making the other characterizations restrained but not dull. Hasso's Brita and O'Brien's Friend register as human beings of considerable dimension, whose feelings toward Tony have a rich complexity. Similarly, Ray Collins' insightful director Donlon and Philip Loeb's cultured producer Lasker are not the expected theatrical types.

This was the first of seven films on which Kanin and Gordon collaborated with Cukor. Most of the others are comedies, in some cases featuring the celebrated team of Katharine Hepburn and Spencer Tracy and in others the irrepressible Judy Holliday, although *The Actress* (1953), starring Jean Simmons, is an affectionate reminiscence of Gordon's early years. *A Double Life*, the only straight drama by the Cukor-Kanin-Gordon team, is less highly regarded than the other films, in spite of the awards won by Colman and Miklos Rozsa, who composed a typically evocative score. The film deserves a better reputation. It is generally agreed that the performances are excellent and the theater sequences brilliantly realized, but the story has been spoken of as excessively melodramatic. It is this melodrama, however, which brings out the best in Cukor. The material forces him into a more dazzling visual realization than called for by his previous films. The *film noir* atmosphere and the hallucinations of the possessed Anthony John, as well as the visual commentary on Tony's emotional state which the story requires even when he is performing, are brought off by the director with remarkable flair. It would be unjust to criticize the less visually assertive films which Cukor has made, notably in the 1930's, as many of those films are superb and perhaps more subtle than *A Double Life*. It is impossible not to notice, however, that in most of the films that follow this one, the director shows a greater consciousness with regard to stylistic interpretation. The captivating visual boldness of *A Star Is Born* (1954) and *Bhowani Junction* (1956) can be directly traced to *A Double Life*. If for no other reason, it is a key film.

Blake Lucas

DOWN TO EARTH

Released: 1947
Production: Don Hartman for Columbia
Direction: Alexander Hall
Screenplay: Edwin Blum and Don Hartman
Cinematography: Rudolph Matè
Editing: Viola Lawrence
Running time: 101 minutes

> *Principal characters:*
> Terpsichore .... Rita Hayworth
> Danny Miller .... Larry Parks
> Eddie .... Marc Platt
> Mr. Jordan .... Roland Culver
> Max Corkle .... James Gleason
> Messenger 7013 .... Edward Everett Horton

In the early and middle 1940's Rita Hayworth became Hollywood's "Love Goddess" with such films as *Blood and Sand* (1941) and photographs in *Life* magazine that made her one of the most desired pinups during World War II. *Gilda* (1946) confirmed her status with its famous "Put the Blame on Mame" number. In devising the next vehicle for Hayworth, Columbia went back to its successful 1941 film *Here Comes Mr. Jordan* for three of the characters and the basic plot device, adding Hayworth playing an actual goddess, Terpsichore, the muse of dance in Greek mythology. Playing opposite her is Larry Parks, who had a popular success with his impersonation of Al Jolson in *The Jolson Story* (1946). The combination of these elements produced *Down to Earth*, a mixture of fantasy and the familiar story of the trials and tribulations of putting on a Broadway musical.

The film opens with the police questioning Max Corkle (James Gleason) about some mysterious occurrences. Max is the same Max Corkle who was a fight manager in *Here Comes Mr. Jordan*, but now he has become a theatrical agent. His confusing account of the events leads to a long flashback that comprises virtually the entire film. The flashback begins with the rehearsal of "The Nine Muses," a musical number from a new show being prepared by producer-director-writer Danny Miller (Larry Parks). The show, called *Swinging the Muses*, is Danny's attempt to make a musical about Greek goddesses that relies on uninhibited dancing and catchy songs to make the show popular rather than high-brow. The number being rehearsed conveys that flavor perfectly, with the muses singing about themselves in a distinctly colloquial way. Terpsichore, the muse of dance and the leading character in the show sings, "I put the ants in the dancers' pants."

The approach, we soon find, does not at all please the real Greek muses, whom we see living in a land of clouds and Greek columns. Terpsichore (Rita Hayworth) has found out about the show and is exceedingly angry about being portrayed "in a low and vulgar manner on the public stage." In order to correct the situation, she goes to 7013 (Edward Everett Horton), a heavenly messenger, and then to his boss, Mr. Jordan (Roland Culver), who is in charge of transporting souls to heaven, to persuade him to let her go to earth to do something about the show. (Max Corkle, 7013, and Mr. Jordan are all characters from *Here Comes Mr. Jordan*; the first two are played by the same actors, but Claude Rains played Mr. Jordan in the original film.) The continually dubious 7013 does not even believe that Terpsichore exists, but she charms Mr. Jordan into listening to her, and he agrees to send her to New York. 7013 is sent with her, although he anticipates "nothing but catastrophe." Throughout the rest of the adventure both 7013 and Mr. Jordan occasionally appear, but only Terpsichore can see and hear them.

At the theater Terpsichore quickly wins the leading role in the show (portraying herself) by joining the dancers and dancing so well that Danny exclaims, "I need a goddess, and a goddess comes down from nowhere." She tells him that Max is her agent—which is a great surprise to Max, but he is glad suddenly to have ten percent of a star. She and Max tell Danny that her name is Kitty Pendleton (the boxer Max managed in *Here Comes Mr. Jordan* was named Joe Pendleton), and all goes well until she tells Danny that the show is "cheap and vulgar" and not factually accurate. Danny, although he is falling in love with her, refuses to give in to her and insists that the show be done his way—as a fast-paced musical "that will pack them in."

Seeing that open opposition will not work, Terpsichore decides to act submissive and participates whole-heartedly in a number she does not like, "This Can't Be Legal," about Terpsichore wanting to marry two men, played by Danny and Eddie (Marc Platt). As the show moves to Philadelphia, however, she begins a new tactic: with kisses rather than with arguments she convinces Danny to make the musical more "artistic." By the time it is ready for its first try-out performance, *Swinging the Muses* has become a pretentious pseudo-balletic show with ethereal voices singing to the accompaniment of harp music. Some of the audience goes to sleep, and no one likes the show except some members of a "Pure Art" group. A stagehand remarks to Danny, "Brother, if these long-hairs go for it, you're dead."

He is right; all the reviews are bad. Danny decides to abandon the "phony art" approach and remake the show into one for "people who like jive and baseball and hot dogs." Terpsichore refuses to accept this decision and quits the show until Mr. Jordan lets her see that Danny will be killed by a gangster if the show is not a hit. Then she agrees to do everything Danny's way, and the revised show soon opens in New York. We see bits of the first act and the colorful finale called "People Have More Fun," sung and danced on a large playground set. The show is now a hit, and Terpsichore has fallen in love with Danny, but Mr. Jordan says she has served her purpose by saving Danny's life; now she must return to her Olympian home. The film ends with Mr. Jordan easing her mind by giving her a glimpse into the future to see that Danny will go on to have a very successful career in the theater ("They say he was kissed by a muse"), and after death be reunited with Terpsichore.

The chief weakness of *Down to Earth* is its extremely slow-paced exposition of all the fantasy elements. Each time Mr. Jordan appears we are subjected to long explanations and demonstrations. The chief virtue of the film, of course, is Hayworth's dancing in Technicolor production numbers. At times, unfortunately, the dancing and the music seem to be forgotten for long stretches as unnecessary plot details are explained. Also a weakness is the fact that Parks does not have the screen presence to hold his own in his scenes with Hayworth. Why he thinks her a goddess seems obvious, but why she wants to be a mortal to stay with him is mysterious.

The theme of vulgar popularity versus highbrow art is treated as it usually is in a popular medium such as film. "Serious" art is presented as pretentious and boring while popular art is entertaining and delightful, which is exactly what the audience for a Hayworth musical would want to hear. The film-makers, in fact, were quite worried that the sample of the highbrow version of the show would bore the film audience, so they used color and close-ups to counteract that possibility. One only wishes that they had emphasized the vital popular art of Hayworth's dancing over the duller exposition of the fantasy plot.

Mr. Jordan appeared on the screen again in 1978 in *Heaven Can Wait*, the remake of *Here Comes Mr. Jordan* that starred Warren Beatty. The story of *Down to Earth* was also used again as the basic premise for the 1980 musical *Xanadu*, but Olivia Newton-John could not carry the part of Terpsichore, and the film was a box-office flop, despite the presence of Gene Kelley as a variation of the Parks character.

Although *Down to Earth* is not a great film, it is enjoyable as a Hayworth vehicle, as an outing for always delightful veteran character actors Gleason and Horton, and as an example of the type of fantasy film popular in the late 1940's. This genre was noteworthy for a number of successful films, such as *Here Comes Mr. Jordan*, the 1943 *Heaven Can Wait* (not the same story as the 1978 movie of the same name), *The Ghost and Mrs. Muir* (1947), and *One Touch of Venus* (1948), which combined elements of the usual love story with heavenly intervention.

Marilynn Wilson

DOWNHILL RACER

Released: 1969
Production: Richard Gregson for Wildwood; released by Paramount
Direction: Michael Ritchie
Screenplay: James Salter
Cinematography: Brian Probyn
Editing: Richard Harris
Running time: 101 minutes

Principal characters:
David Chappellet .... Robert Redford
Eugene Claire .... Gene Hackman
Carole Stahl .... Camilla Sparv
D. K. Bryan .... Kenneth Kirk
Johnny Creech .... Jim McMullan
Mr. Chappellet .... Walter Stroud
Lena .... Carole Carle
Machet .... Michael Vogler

Downhill Racer grew out of Robert Redford's desire to make a different kind of sports film. He regarded the typical portrayal of athletes by Hollywood as too idealized and reportedly wished to present an athlete who was a "creep." The problem, of course, in presenting the idea that athletics does not necessarily build character and that a person can be a winner in sports and still be a shallow and limited human being is that the audience may not be interested in such a character. *Downhill Racer* effectively solves this creative problem by portraying not only the personality of the protagonist but also his relations with his coach and team members, the physical excitement of the sport, and its coverage by the media. Although Redford's name appears in the film's credits only for his acting, it was produced by his own production company, Wildwood, and Redford exercised a good deal of creative control over the project, including selecting Michael Ritchie as director even though Ritchie's experience at the time was only in television and he had never before directed a feature film.

Downhill Racer has a definite plot, but that plot is developed in a series of nearly self-contained episodes, essentially long vignettes. Each episode presents another facet of the character of the protagonist or his world of competitive sports. *Downhill Racer* is the story of David Chappellet (Robert Redford), a skier from Idaho Springs, Colorado. We do not, however, see him in the film's first episode. Instead, a montage of shots of ski competition with frequent freeze-frames under the credits builds up to the downhill run of an unidentified American skier who is injured and has to be taken to the hospital. It is not until a few minutes later that we realize that this event has made it necessary for the American ski coach, Eugene Claire (Gene Hackman), to send for Chappellet and D. K. Bryan (Kenneth Kirk) as replacements for the remainder of his team's European skiing season.

When we do see Chappellet, we immediately notice that he is very provincial, unfamiliar with and unsympathetic to foreign lands and foreign customs. We also soon find that he is not inclined to be cooperative with his teammates or his coach. When he is assigned the eighty-eighth position for the first race, he refuses to ski because he believes that he deserves a better position. He does ski, however, in the next race, and almost the entire run is seen from his viewpoint in a sequence which visually stresses the excitement, danger, and beauty of the sport of downhill skiing. He does quite well in the competition, finishing ahead of the star of the American team, Johnny Creech (Jim McMullan). "Maybe next time I'll get to start in the top fifty," Chappellet remarks sarcastically.

Even though he remains essentially callous, boorish, self-centered, and inarticulate, Chappellet's success makes him a focus of attention for the media covering the events as well as for an important ski manufacturer, Machet (Michael Vogler), who wants the winner of the Olympics to use his skis. Chappellet begins an affair with Machet's assistant, Carole Stahl (Camilla Sparv), which continues over two seasons, but he is unable to give her much real attention. In one of the two scenes in which he is most happy with her he listens delightedly as she translates his press notices for him. On the other hand, when they are sitting in her car and she is talking to him about her Christmas vacation, he blows the car horn to stop her.

Between the two seasons we get a glimpse of Chappellet's home life when he returns to Idaho Falls, where he fits in little better than he did in the foreign cities. His father (Walter Stroud) greets him perfunctorily: "Hello. I got your postcard. Your cousin said to thank you for the stamps." He neither gets nor gives much more from his hometown girl friend, Lena (Carole Carle).

The essential thread of the film is David as athlete, although we see that the rest of his life is shaped by the fact that he is an athlete. Rather than teaching him anything, the athletic life of David Chappellet has isolated him so much from "ordinary" life that he seems unable to handle either success or failure. Much of this theme is brought out in the scenes between Chappellet and Claire, his coach. It is Claire's opinion that Chappellet has a certain ability, skill, and dedication to the sport, but that his dedication is only enough to cut him off from the rest of life, not enough to make him a really first-rate skier. The coach tells Chappellet at one point that he has neither consistency nor desire to learn.

Another of Chappellet's deficiencies seen by both the coach and the other members of the team is his lack of consideration for the team. Even though one skier does remark that skiing is "not exactly a team sport," Chappellet ignores his responsibility to the others by challenging Creech to an informal race at the end of a workout. This endangers both skiers and causes Creech to take a spill. Chappellet's only response to criticism of this action is that Creech did not have to race him. In what is obviously (perhaps too obviously) meant to be the statement of the film's theme, Claire says to Chappellet, "You never had any real education did you? All you ever had was your skis, and that's not enough."

Later, Creech breaks his leg and Chappellet is left as the only hope of the American team in the Olympics. He proves equal to the occasion athletically, winning the gold medal in the downhill event, but we see that emotionally and mentally he has still not found his way. Before the event a sportscaster asks him about his plans for after the Olympics and Chappellet can only respond, "This is it." After his victory he is again asked about his plans and he replies, "I don't know" three times. This ending, incidentally, prefigures the ending of a later Redford film, *The Candidate* (1972), in which the Redford character wins the election and then asks what he should do next.

In addition to the episodic nature of the narrative, the most notable element of the style of the film is its semidocumentary photography. A portion of the film is footage of actual skiing events, and much of the scripted portions are photographed as if they were simply being caught by a documentary cinematographer on the scene. this technique both integrates the two types of footage and also adds verisimilitude to the story, especially since modern audiences are familiar with documentaries on sports and sports figures. The keys to the success of *Downhill Racer* are the excellent performances of Redford as the skier and Hackman as the coach. Redford performs the difficult feat of keeping us interested in a character who is neither sympathetic nor expressive, and Hackman nicely keeps his character from being excessively platitudinous or excessively sentimental.

Critical response to *Downhill Racer* was quite favorable, but the box-office response was not as good, perhaps because too many people thought of it as just another sports film.

Timothy W. Johnson

DUCK SOUP

Released: 1933
Production: Paramount
Direction: Leo McCarey
Screenplay: Bert Kalmar and Harry Ruby, with additional dialogue by Arthur Sheekman and Nat Perrin
Cinematography: Henry Sharp
Editing: Leroy Stone
Music: Bert Kalmar and Harry Ruby
Running time: 70 minutes

Principal characters:
Rufus T. Firefly	Groucho Marx
Chicolini	Chico Marx
Brownie	Harpo Marx
Bob Rolland	Zeppo Marx
Mrs. Teasdale	Margaret Dumont
Ambassador Trentino	Louis Calhern
Vera Marcal	Raquel Torres
Lemonade Dealer	Edgar Kennedy

The zany, surreal humor of the Marx Brothers is at once irrational, irreverent, and irrepressible. Each of the four is an individual. Groucho is the consummate phony, with his greasepaint moustache, oversized clothes, and doubletalk. Harpo, the silent one, is touchingly human in his elemental responses to his siblings and to everyone and everything else. Chico is as thick in his Italian accent as he is in intelligence, yet he always manages to outsmart the obtuse Groucho. Zeppo, the least interesting of the quartet, is something of a nice-looking straight man, similar in *Duck Soup* to actor/singer Alan Jones in *A Night at the Opera* (1935), and is easily the closest of the four to approach rationality. Yet as the Marx Brothers collectively assault the pomposity and hypocrisy of a "sane" world in the thick of the Depression and on the brink of a World War, these differences blend into a unified, hilarious whole.

It is hopeless to cite the funniest Marx Brothers film; *A Night at the Opera*, *A Day at the Races* (1937), *Horsefeathers* (1932), *The Cocoanuts* (1929), *Animal Crackers* (1930), and *Monkey Business* (1952) all have their ardent supporters, but *Duck Soup* is undeniably their most striking and most bitingly satiric film. Released during the nadir of the Depression, *Duck Soup* is a lampoon of war and Fascism. Groucho is Rufus T. Firefly, the dictator of a mythical kingdom called Freedonia. Firefly is no mature head of state: even though he is ostensibly the most powerful man in Freedonia, his irresponsibility and pride in his own stupidity continuously mock the concept of authority. Chico is Chicolini, a peanut vender who becomes Freedonia's Minister

of War, and Harpo is Brownie, Firefly's chauffeur; the pair are spies for
Trentino (Louis Calhern), the Ambassador of neighboring Sylvania, and they
comically stand up to both their employers. Zeppo, in his last Marx Brothers
film, appears as Firefly's secretary.

Trentino desires to take control of Freedonia by a *coup d'etat*. Armed
conflict between the countries is inevitable, however, when Firefly slaps Trentino's face once too often—a trivial reason for a declaration of war. The actual
combat is pointless, a slapstick struggle, with no attempt made by Firefly to
defeat the enemy. Margaret Dumont, a veteran of several Marx Brothers
films, is also in the cast as Mrs. Teasdale, the richest widow in Freedonia and
Firefly's most ardent supporter.

Duck Soup is packed with an ample quota of Marx Brothers mayhem. Most
of the bits are in the same comic vein as their earlier films, and *Duck Soup*
is certainly no departure in style for the team. Yet the film is funny whether
or not one is cognizant of their brand of humor. The outbreak of war is
celebrated, as the quartet leads the production number "The Country's Going
to War" replete with barn dance and opera, hillbilly and blues songs, including
"All God's Chillun Got Guns" (although throughout the film, Harpo and
Chico do not play their characteristic instruments, harp and piano). Harpo
hands various personages his leg, which promptly goes limp. He produces a
blow torch from his trousers and cuts cigars, ties, coattails and sausages with
a pair of scissors. Calhern asks Harpo to inquire about Groucho's record as
president; Harpo immediately produces a gramophone record; when Calhern
throws it in the air, Harpo shoots it with a rifle and Chico rings a bell on
Calhern's desk, hands Harpo a cigar as a prize, and slams a cigar box on
Calhern's fingers. Harpo and Chico harass a lemonade dealer (Edgar Kennedy) with a rapid-fire series of physical assaults. Harpo impersonates Paul
Revere and seduces a beautiful blonde whom he sees undressing in her bedroom; her husband, the lemonade seller, returns and eventually settles down
in his bath—on top of a submerged Harpo.

Groucho's initial appearance is heralded by trumpets blasting, guards rais-
ing their swords, and girls tossing flowers; he fails to materialize, and the
singing of the Freedonia National Anthem is repeated; he finally arrives by
sliding down a firepole from his upstairs bedroom, lining up with his own
honor guard and asking, "Who are we waiting for?" Groucho is transported
about in a motorcycle and sidecar driven by Harpo; first, the cycle alone is
operable, then only the car. Groucho keeps his cabinet waiting while he plays
a game of jacks. He and Chico continuously spar in bizarre bits of conversation, with Groucho usually the foil for his brother. For example, questioner
Groucho is convinced by Chico that he must respond to the ridiculous query
he has put to Groucho: "What is it that has four pairs of pants, lives in
Philadelphia and it never rains but pours?" Groucho informs Chico that the
latter will not be commissioned to the position of Minister of War as originally

planned; when Groucho tells Chico what the job is, Chico responds: "Good, I'll take it"; Groucho replies: "Sold."

Shells zoom through a window during the climactic battle sequence, until Groucho pulls down the blinds. Groucho asks assistance from the world: the response is a menagerie of athletes (a runner, rowers, swimmers) and animals (elephants, gorillas, giraffes). Groucho, dressed in a white nightgown and cap, peers into a false mirror; the reflection is first one, then two Grouchos, impersonated by a similarly garbed Harpo and Chico. Last, of course, Dumont is constantly and mercilessly chided and insulted by Groucho: Groucho asks her for a lock of her hair, but quickly amends the request by adding: "I'm letting you off lightly—I was going to ask for the whole wig." At the film's conclusion, when Dumont patriotically sings the Freedonia National Anthem at the victory over Sylvania, she is pelted with cooking apples by the Marx Brothers.

Duck Soup is short, only 70 minutes, and it has been crisply directed by Leo McCarey. McCarey is the only top comedy director ever to helm a Marx Brothers opus: among his other early films are *The Kid from Spain* (1932), with Eddie Cantor, Busby Berkeley musical numbers, and Betty Grable and Paulette Goddard in the chorus; *Six of a Kind* (1934), with Burns and Allen, W. C. Fields, Mary Boland, Charles Ruggles, and Alison Skipworth; *Belle of the Nineties* (1934), with Mae West; *Ruggles of Red Gap* (1935), with Charles Laughton, Zazu Pitts, Charles Ruggles, and Mary Boland; and the classic screwball comedy, *The Awful Truth* (1937), with Cary Grant and Irene Dunne.

Curiously, the critical reception to *Duck Soup* was mixed. Some reviewers heralded it for its humor, but just as many felt that it was not amusing in comparison to the Marx Brothers' previous films. The nonparticipation of S. J. Perelman, George S. Kaufman, and Morris Ryskind in the writing of the screenplay and music was cited as the major culprit. More recently, however, *Duck Soup* has come to be regarded as a spirited, timeless burlesque of the pomposity of politicians and the absurdity of war.

Rob Edelman

DUEL IN THE SUN

Released: 1946
Production: David O. Selznick for Selznick Studios
Direction: King Vidor
Screenplay: David O. Selznick and Oliver H. P. Garrett; based on the novel of the same name by Niven Busch
Cinematography: Lee Garmes
Editing: William Ziegler and John Saure
Running time: 138 minutes

> *Principal characters:*
> Pearl Chavez .... Jennifer Jones
> Lewt McCanles .... Gregory Peck
> Jesse McCanles .... Joseph Cotton
> McCanles .... Lionel Barrymore
> Laura Belle McCanles .... Lillian Gish
> Preacher .... Walter Huston
> Chavez .... Herbert Marshall
> Sam Pierce .... Charles Bickford
> Chavez's wife .... Tilly Losch

Duel in the Sun is one of the most expensive, controversial, and financially profitable Westerns ever made. At a cost of more than five million dollars, it was an attempt by producer David O. Selznick to duplicate the success of his own *Gone with the Wind* (1939) in a new setting. The history of the production of *Duel in the Sun* parallels that of *Gone with the Wind*, with Selznick's ever-changing vision and compulsive perfectionism leading to an almost constant flux in personnel (there were no less than six directors and three cinematographers involved in the project) as well as a ballooning budget. As screenwriter, Selznick revised the script weekly; as producer, he agonized over rushes daily, eventually causing King Vidor, the director credited on the film and who contributed most to the finished product, to throw up his hands in despair and walk off the set. The story of *Duel in the Sun*'s making can be traced in a seemingly unending series of memos from Selznick to the director, the cinematographer, and the stars. No detail was too petty for Selznick's supervision, from lighting to the sweat on Jennifer Jones's face. This extremism did not cease with the film's completion. An advertising blitz, costing more than three million dollars alone, was initiated for the film in major cities throughout the United States, resulting in saturation booking.

The reception of *Duel in the Sun* by the press and the industry was disappointing. Hoping for a repeat of the critical acclaim which greeted *Gone with the Wind*, Selznick was confronted instead with vilification and hostility from all quarters, particularly from the religious community. Over a period of months Selznick became embroiled in negotiations with the Catholic

Church's censorship arm, the Legion of Decency. Each line and each shot of the movie was examined by the Legion, and those considered too explicit were marked for deletion. Ultimately Selznick had no choice but to bow to their wishes, since the Legion's power over American Catholics was, at that time, something to be reckoned with. The film was pulled for editing, and an approved version was released.

What so frightened the Legion of Decency and its coguardians of morality in the religious community was the blatant eroticism of the film. *Duel in the Sun* is a film *par excellence* about what the French call *amour fou*, or mad love. It is the kind of love in which the lovers disregard all conventions of society and morality to pursue their often self-destructive passion for each other, self-destructive because their love is inextricably intermeshed with hate. In the opening scene of the film the heroine's parents are introduced, initiating the cycle of mad love which characterizes the rest of the film. Chavez (Herbert Marshall), a dignified aristocrat who in marrying an unfaithful Indian woman (Tilly Losch) has descended to the depths of border-town life, finds his wife with another man and murders them. The child of this stormy union, Pearl, is sent by her father, before his execution, to live with his ex-fiancée Laura Belle (Lillian Gish), now married to a cattle baron named McCanles (Lionel Barrymore). The marriage between this delicate woman and her greedy, cantankerous husband is a cold and unhappy one with none of the passion which we are led to believe marked Laura Belle's affair with Chavez. The only hint of what might have been a former tenderness in this marriage is revealed during Laura Belle's deathbed scene, when a distraught McCanles collapses in his wheelchair.

The center of the film and the peak of the cycle is Pearl (Jennifer Jones). *Duel in the Sun* is her story, the story of a battle between convention and savagery, respectability and lasciviousness, between a dignity inherited from her father and a sensuality passed on by her mother. As Chavez and his wife symbolize this contradiction in Pearl, so do the McCanles sons, Lewt (Gregory Peck) and Jesse (Joseph Cotton). Jesse is the quiet, genteel, conventional Abel while Lewt is the vicious, sensual, passionate Cain. For Pearl they represent the paths she may choose to follow, and in true schizophrenic fashion she chooses both. Jesse supplies her with stability and educates and protects her, but this is not enough; she needs the intensity of Lewt's passion as well. It is a passion caught up in violence. They make love against the backdrop of a storm after threatening each other with physical harm. While Jesse is associated with warm interiors, docile cattle, and benevolent, progressive builders of railroads, Lewt is tied to guns (he tries to kill his own brother, extending the Cain-Abel analogy even further), dynamite (he blows up a railroad train), stallions, and the barren outdoors. Pearl and Lewt's affair is of highly destructive proportions. Recognizing this, she retreats back into respectability periodically, first with Jesse, but when rejected by him, with an older man, Sam Pierce (Charles Bickford), whom Lewt challenges and kills, forcing Pearl back into his arms.

The final scene takes place in the mountains. Pearl now acts as defender of convention and propriety by stopping Lewt from harming the offspring of Jesse and the genteel Easterner who has taken Pearl's place. Her shoot-out with Lewt is the apotheosis of *amour fou*. In defending convention Pearl commits an act of outrageous savagery as the lovers fatally wound each other and then crawl across rock and sand to rest in each other's arms.

Duel in the Sun has been called a "horse opera" and is one of the few Westerns which deserves that epithet. It takes most of the conventions of the Western and expands them, weighs them down, and elaborates on them in a manner which combines elements of grand opera and Baroque art. A gunfight in a saloon is composed like a Caravaggio painting with a single light cutting the darkness, two figures at opposite sides of the frame in focus, and a blast of gunfire. A dance and barbecue opens up with an incredibly complex tracking shot over the entire crowd. Characters are exaggerated as well. The down-and-out gambler Chavez becomes a tragic Shakespearean figure (especially as played by Marshall); a traveling minister (Walter Huston) becomes a hypocritical, lecherous Bible-thumper who has designs on Pearl. Emotions are also on a grand scale. Love, hate, revenge, and greed rock each character, creating trauma after trauma. Even the plot is overblown, with a simple battle between the railroad (protecting the homesteaders) and the cattle barons over territory (something that often occurred during the opening of the West) becoming, in typical Selznick fashion, an epic allegory of the small individual versus big business, progress versus the old order, and liberty versus authoritarianism. In short, the film is a highly dramatic rendering of American myths.

The eroticism of *Duel in the Sun* is created by a manipulation of the elements of setting, cinematography, acting, and costuming. Pearl is darkened through makeup to give her an earthy look. She wears scoop-necked, tight-fitting blouses which outline her breasts, Indian blankets which reveal soft shoulders, and full, loose skirts which expose shapely legs. Jones breathes a real passion into the role of Pearl, and it is ultimately her sensual savvy which brings the character to life.

The financial success of *Duel in the Sun* was not immediate; it took several re-releases for the film to realize a profit. The lesson Selznick learned from this experience was a bitter one. It taught him that the genre he had worked so hard to perfect—the dramatic epic—would have to be abandoned, at least on his part. A producer with tastes like his would have to learn to control his flamboyance or get out of the business. The day of the creative independent producer striving to mold films in his own grand style was virtually to disappear. Epics would be produced again, but never with a personal touch like Selznick's. After this disappointment, Selznick produced a few more pictures, but none with the scope of *Duel in the Sun* or *Gone with the Wind*. In 1958, after *A Farewell to Arms* (1957), he ceased production activities altogether, and he died in 1965.

James Ursini

DUMBO

Released: 1941
Production: Walt Disney
Supervising direction: Ben Sharpsteen
Story direction: Otto Englander
Screenplay: Joe Grant and Dick Huemler; based on the novel of the same name by Helen Aberson and Harold Perl
Character design: John P. Miller, Martin Provenson, John Walbridge, James Boorero, Elmer Plummer, and Maurice Noble
Animation direction: Vladimer Tytla, Fred Moore, Ward Kimball, John Lounsbery, Art Babbitt, and Woolie Reitherman
Music: Oliver Wallace and Frank Churchill(AA)
Song: Frank Churchill, Oliver Wallace, and Ned Washington
Running time: 64 minutes

> *Voices of principal characters:*
> Mr. Stork .... Sterling Holloway
> Timothy ....Ed Brophy
> Jim Crow .... Cliff Edwards
> Female Elephants .... Verna Felton
> Ringmaster .... Herman Bing

The continuing popularity and critical standing of Walt Disney rests centrally on his first five animated features, a collective achievement unsurpassed and unparalleled in its field. One indication of the richness of this group of films is that each has strongly individual qualities. *Snow White and the Seven Dwarfs* (1937) demonstrated that animation could sustain a fully developed dramatic narrative and inspire terror as well as laughter. Although its heroine is a vacuous figure and the prince is a cipher, these flaws are more than compensated for by the ceaseless invention with which the dwarfs are portrayed, the artfulness with which the songs are integrated into the story, and above all, the power of imagination felt in every frame of the evil queen's transformation into the old witch. The unprecedented depth of field and care in detail in *Pinocchio* (1940), combined with a story of genuine moral authority, make that film Disney's most substantial. Its matchless sequences of Gepetto's shop, the puppet theater, the inside of Monstro the whale, and supremely, Pleasure Island, demonstrate the artistry of the Disney team at its height. *Fantasia* (1940), a financial failure in its time, is the most popular Disney film today, and although it is arguably pretentious and lacking in humor—only the "Dance of the Hours" sequence is unassailably amusing—it could with equal justice be described as a bold and daring experiment. *Bambi* (1942), the most visually serene of the films, presents the most profound story, a moving and gracefully expressed vision of recurring cycles of life and death.

Dumbo is the most modest of the five films, but it is also the most offbeat and charming. Little more than an hour in length, it engages no weighty moral, nor is the virtuosity of its animation insistently stressed. It is simply the story of an elephant with big ears growing up in a circus setting; but the traumas and triumph of the character make a direct appeal to the heart, and along the way, there are a number of unexpected and dazzling sequences which display the creativity of Disney's artists at their most prodigious.

The opening of the film is very relaxed, and considerable time elapses before the premise has been established. We are introduced to Mr. Stork, lost in a storm as he tries to deliver a last bundle to Mrs. Jumbo, a warm-hearted elephant still yearning for motherhood while the other animals contentedly nurture their young. The life of the circus is presented as it leaves one town and moves on to the next, carried by an enchanting little train, Casey Junior. Finally, Mr. Stork delivers the baby elephant. Mrs. Jumbo is bursting with pride as her baby charms the other female elephants, but suddenly he sneezes, and his ears unfold, provoking derision and laughter from the group. They name him Dumbo, and Mrs. Jumbo is ostracized. Constantly taunted by the haughty and small-minded elephants, Dumbo attempts to be a good sport as the ringmaster dreams up new acts which will include him. Mrs. Jumbo, protective of her innocent baby, is less inclined to demonstrate forbearance. Pushed too far, she goes berserk, is declared a mad elephant, and locked up.

Left alone, Dumbo is consoled only by his friend Timothy, a mouse seemingly attached to the circus by virtue of his entertainer's red hat and coat. Timothy takes Dumbo to visit his mother, who sings a lullaby to her unhappy child. The baby elephant then becomes even more unconsolable when the ringmaster degrades him further by putting him into a clown act, in which he is hideously made up as a baby requiring rescue from a burning set. This prompts Dumbo and Timothy to get drunk together. The resulting hallucinations of "Pink Elephants on Parade" provide a *tour de force* for the animators.

Dumbo and Timothy awaken the next morning to find themselves in a tree, not knowing how they have come to be there. They are in the company of a group of "no-account crows" who respond to them with considerable humor. Timothy and Dumbo somehow manage to reach the ground, but Timothy then suggests that Dumbo must have flown up into the tree. The bemused crows treat this idea with the skepticism it seems to deserve and are even inspired to perform a little song about the subject, but knowing what it is to be outcasts, they ultimately find themselves on Dumbo's side and give him a magic feather to encourage him to fly. Dumbo finds that he can indeed fly, and the next night in the clown act, he surprises both the crowd and the circus people and takes some harmless revenge on his tormentors. His confidence is complete when he loses the magic feather and discovers he can fly without it. He goes on to become a star attraction, is reunited with his mother, and shares fame and fortune with his manager Timothy.

An unusual richness of mood exists in *Dumbo*. Gentle comedy and a straightforward depiction of circus life dominate the early scenes. The forcible separation of Dumbo and his mother finds the animators utilizing intense, unsettling imagery. The lovely nocturnal scene that follows, in which Mrs. Jumbo sings to Dumbo, is simple and quietly touching. The bizarre clown act reintroduces bizarre camera angles and vivid colors. Preceding sequences immediately seem restrained, however, when the hallucinations of the "Pink Elephants" sequence begin. This sequence, the most visually outstanding in the film, is so weird and gaudy, both in concept and realization, that it makes the abstractions of *Fantasia* seem tame by comparison. Finally, the crows sequence, with its elating humor and its relaxed atmosphere of a jam session, provides still another pleasing contrast. Many of the varying possibilities of animations are explored in *Dumbo*, and they are all approached with an unpretentious spirit.

Dumbo himself is a mute character throughout the story, but this has the interesting effect of making him very physically expressive and permitting other characters to speculate on his state of mind. Timothy, provided with a voice which reflects a suitably unschooled worldliness by character actor Ed Brophy, is introduced well into the story as he gives a little monologue on Dumbo's predicament. Timothy contrasts interestingly with Jiminy Cricket in *Pinocchio*, as both are small but able companions to the heroes. Jiminy, the selfless conscience of Pinocchio, is a more pure creation, asking no reward for his valiant efforts on behalf of his wooden and easily-misguided friend. Timothy, less of a do-gooder, seems to be motivated by a genuine liking for the hapless pachyderm he befriends, and it is a source of satisfaction that the ending reveals him to be a beneficiary of his insightful encouragement of Dumbo. Other characters are well-drawn and solidly played by the offscreen cast. Verna Felton, whose voice was used in a number of Disney films, turns in a bravura performance, tackling the voices of all of the female elephants, each a distinctive comic characterization. The most memorable characters, however, are undeniably the crows, the brilliantly witty creations of Ward Kimball, animated with a captivating verve and energy. Existing with no other purpose than to laugh and sing, the irreverent crows are provided with street-wise black dialects, which makes it surprising that their voices are provided entirely by white actors.

As with other Disney features, music plays an important role and is always integrated with the mood of the action. The film is scored with skill and versatility, and although none of the half-dozen songs is in a class with "When You Wish Upon a Star" from *Pinocchio* or "Someday My Prince Will Come" from *Snow White and the Seven Dwarfs*, they all serve well. "Baby Mine" effortlessly elicits sympathetic tears for Dumbo and his mother as she poignantly comforts him from inside the prison of a barred circus wagon. "When I See an Elephant Fly" lightens the mood as the insouciant crows neatly restore the balance between sentiment and comedy so precisely judged in the film's overall structure. Interestingly, it is these two sequences which are used in the ambitious comedy *1941* (1979). The responses of General Stillwell, played by Robert Stack, who cries during the first sequence and both chuckles and sings along during the second as he watches the film, provide the most sincere and unstrained moments of humor in that film.

The *1941* tribute, conceived by the young director Steven Spielberg, who was not even born at the time *Dumbo* was made, confirms the enduring appeal of the Disney film. The favor it invariably finds with audiences is gratifying, for it was not based on a classic children's story like *Snow White and the Seven Dwarfs*, *Pinocchio*, and *Bambi*, nor was it the result of cultural ambition like *Fantasia*. The central character is not caught in a struggle between good and evil nor does he carry on a deer's slender back the central truths of existence. Dumbo's problem is his individuality, which he ultimately recognizes as a virtue and an asset. As the thrust of other Disney films is to encourage conformity to certain ideals, this embrace of individuality is very refreshing and curiously inspiring. Children and adults alike respond to the character's situation, delighted to hope and believe that if a flying elephant can make a place for himself in the world, so can they. *Dumbo* inspires this emotional response with admirable ease, while being at once enviably artful and supremely entertaining. Few cherished classics can claim so unsurprising a reputation.

Blake Lucas

DYNAMITE

Released: 1929
Production: Cecil B. De Mille for Metro-Goldwyn-Mayer
Direction: Cecil B. De Mille
Screenplay: Jeanie Macpherson, with additional dialogue by John Howard Lawson and Gladys Unger
Cinematography: Peverell Marley
Editing: Anne Bauchens
Running time: 129 minutes

> *Principal characters:*
> Cynthia Crothers .... Kay Johnson
> Hagon Derk .... Charles Bickford
> Roger Towne .... Conrad Nagel
> Marcia Towne .... Julia Faye
> Katie Derk .... Muriel McCormack
> Marco, the "Sheik" .... Joel McCrea

The addition of dialogue and sound to a motion picture was a device that was certain to intrigue Cecil B. De Mille. He had come from the theater originally, where he had acted in and written plays, and subsequently turned to the silent picture medium, where as a director and producer he presented fifty-two features between 1914 and 1929, most of them big moneymakers for Paramount. During the silent era, he and D. W. Griffith were the only directors whose names were the principal box-office attraction of their films. De Mille could not wait to try dialogue in a feature. In that 1928-1929 season many filmmakers experimented with talking sequences, giving birth to the part-talkie, which was nothing more than a bastard form doomed to fade into oblivion.

After his big religious film, the story of Christ called *The King of Kings* (1927), De Mille wanted something modern and completely different. A wave of atheism was sweeping the country, and De Mille decided to try his luck with a story about those who defy God, called *The Godless Girl* (1929). By the time the picture was made and he had previewed it, he was disappointed. There was little shock value in the film; it had become nothing more than an old-fashioned pictorial sermon. The talking film was what was drawing in the dollars, and De Mille decided to jump on the bandwagon. He held up release on *The Godless Girl*, reshot the last two scenes in dialogue written by Beulah Marie Dix and Jeanie Macpherson, and added sound, which built up the fight scenes and added drama to the burning reformatory sequence. The picture was released as a part-talkie by Pathé, but by that time there were so many of those around that *The Godless Girl* scarcely made a ripple in the current.

De Mille and his wife took a trip abroad, where he reevaluated his career. He made a new releasing deal with M-G-M, and decided that his first full-length talking feature would be the kind of fashionable melodrama that had made him surefire at Paramount. The new picture would have an original story by Jeanie Macpherson, and while she would write some of the dialogue, most of it was designed by two up-to-date playwrights, John Howard Lawson and Gladys Unger. It would have its full quota of sex and sin, and it would be climaxed by the kind of smashing denouement that had made him famous. It would be a lavish society picture about life as it was never lived among the millionaires, and it would build to a wild, melodramatic finale in which the three principals are caught in a mine cave-in deep in the bowels of the earth. It would become the noisiest talkie to date, and, fittingly, it would be called *Dynamite*.

The gimmick that starts the plot was not new; in fact, it went back several centuries to a time in England when, if a bachelor were awaiting the executioner's axe, he might very well be visited by a heavily veiled lady with a priest in attendance. If the man who was to die would agree to marry the heavily veiled lady, those he left behind would be blessed with secret riches, while he would take on the heavy debts his lady had accrued, and his subsequent execution would automatically cancel those debts, freeing her from possibly going to debtor's prison. This device had been used to good effect in an early all-color (Prizma) feature by J. Stuart Blackton, *The Glorious Adventure*, in which Lady Diana Manners became the bride of a criminal (Victor McLaglen) just before the great London fire swept through the city.

De Mille's story tells about Cynthia Crothers (Kay Johnson), rich and very social, who is in love with Roger Towne (Conrad Nagel), a playboy who loves her but unfortunately has a wife, Marcia (Julia Faye) whose every hour is taken up with a handsome gigolo called Marco, the "Sheik" (Joel McCrea). By the terms of her grandfather's will, Cynthia must be married by a certain date or forfeit the extravagant fortune left in waiting for her. Cynthia, however, wants only to marry Roger, who is not available, although his wife Marcia hints that were Cynthia to give her enough money, she might consider a quick divorce from Roger, which would leave her able to afford Marco.

Meanwhile, in the jail of a nearby mining town, Hagon Derk (Charles Bickford) is incarcerated, having been found guilty of murder, although he maintains his innocence. Hagon will be executed at midnight of a certain day, unable to leave his young sister, Katie (Muriel McCormack), anything but tears and a grim future as ward of the court. An attorney makes the deal with Hagon, who consents to marry Cynthia Crothers, and she, in turn, being his widow, will see to it that his sister is well educated and provided for. Cynthia weds Hagon in his cell and returns to her mansion to await word that she is now a widow soon to inherit her grandfather's sizable fortune. On the very eve of Hagon's exection, however, the real murderer is apprehended and confesses to the crime. Hagon finds himself a free man and goes to see the wife he now claims.

Cynthia is appalled by the turn of events, and when Hagon comes to her, she is repelled by him. Likewise, Hagon is disgusted by her and her sybaritic way of life. He returns to the mining town and the job he had once held there. Meanwhile, Cynthia finds that in order to inherit her grandfather's fortune, she must be able to prove that she is lawfully Mrs. Hagon Derk living with her husband in his newly found freedom.

She returns to the mining town with Roger, and they go down inside the mine to seek out Hagon, hoping to finalize a new deal with him. Now comes the big scene, De Mille's long-awaited climax. As the three meet deep in the earth, the ground trembles with an explosion that shakes and wrecks the mine. The three—Cynthia, Hagon, and Roger—are trapped, and in the hours that intervene while their lives are at stake, Cynthia finds that Hagon is a husband worth having and he changes his mind about her being wanton. Roger realizes that only he can open a way of life for the two of them. With a stick of dynamite he clears the shaft so they can escape, although in so doing, he traps himself and is killed. Hagon then leads his wife back to the light and freedom.

Audiences were well aware that the plot was corny, even in 1929, but they relished it just the same. With *Dynamite* De Mille once more proved that he had the public firmly in hand. He knew what they wanted, and he gave it to them. The scenes of high life, with adultery, champagne, and sin, were something in which to revel, and the dramatic disaster in the mine climaxing the action was horrifying, strikingly realistic, and certainly boasted the loudest series of explosions yet recorded on film. *Dynamite* played in Los Angeles at the Carthay Circle Theater, and every night at the same hour for blocks around, residents in the Circle area knew that the cacophony shattering the peaceful quiet of their neighborhood was Mr. De Mille's nightly mineshattering finale.

As players in *Dynamite*, De Mille used in the principal roles three actors who had had vast stage experience and could handle their dialogue like professionals. He chose red-headed Charles Bickford, an actor from Broadway who had made ruffians his specialty, to play Hagon Derk. It was Bickford's first film for De Mille, his first indeed before any camera, and one of the few heroic romantic roles he ever got to play. Cynthia Crothers, the social butterfly who finds that there is more to life than a vast amount of money, is played by Kay Johnson. New to films, she had enjoyed a rich career on the stage as the heroine of such plays as *Beggar on Horseback* (1924), *Crime* (1927), and *A Free Soul* (1928). She was also the wife of the noted director/actor, John Cromwell. Conrad Nagel as Roger Towne was a popular hero in De Mille's silent films who, before he entered pictures, had enjoyed a genuinely successful career onstage as a William A. Brady star. Julia Faye, whose name appears in almost every De Mille cast since 1918, played her first speaking role for De Mille as Marcia Towne. There is also a very distinguished debut in the film: playing Marco, the "Sheik," is Joel McCrea, who was to become a film star for decades and would play the hero for De Mille years later in *Union Pacific* (1939).

Dynamite broke the ice in talking pictures for De Mille and made a great deal of money at the box office. His two subsequent features at M-G-M were hardly of the same caliber. He then signed again at the newly reorganized Paramount Studios, and beginning in 1932 with *The Sign of the Cross* made a long series of extravagant specials that did nothing but make money; there were fifteen extraordinary extravaganzas, ending in 1956 with his extravagant production of *The Ten Commandments*.

DeWitt Bodeen

EASY LIVING

Released: 1937
Production: Arthur Hornblow, Jr., for Paramount
Direction: Mitchell Leisen
Screenplay: Preston Sturges; based on the novel of the same name by Vera
  Caspary
Cinematography: Ted Tetzlaff
Editing: Doane Harrison
Running time: 87 minutes

> *Principal characters:*
> Mary Smith .... Jean Arthur
> J. B. Ball .... Edward Arnold
> John Ball, Jr. .... Ray Milland
> Mrs. J. B. Ball .... Mary Nash
> Mr. Louis Louis .... Luis Alberni
> Van Buren .... Franklin Pangborn

During the 1930's, the "screwball" comedy thrived in Hollywood to an almost manic degree. In a sense, this era of the slapstick comedy was only natural, for it came during the Depression, and by the end of the decade one did not have to be a sage to know that another world war was just over the horizon. The only antidote for the troubled times was laughter, and as the threat of disaster deepened, the comedies turned more hysterical. Most depression comedies were about the very rich, for it is easier to laugh when one knows that even those with money do not have it easy. *Easy Living* was made by a group of experts: novelist Vera Caspary was an expert in the light romantic story; nobody wrote funnier screenplays than Preston Sturges; and there was no director who was so much a master of the elegant soufflé as Mitchell Leisen. With a cast headed by one of the outstanding comediennes in show business, Jean Arthur, *Easy Living* is constructed with one laugh topping the other, the most pleasant hour and twenty-seven minutes then to be seen.

It all begins with J. B. Ball (Edward Arnold), a steel magnate, living in a handsome penthouse on Fifth Avenue, New York. He starts his day quarreling with his extravagant wife (Mary Nash), who has just bought a very expensive fur coat. In a fit of rage, he seizes the coat, marches onto the terrace, and throws the coat out over Fifth Avenue. It plummets downward, landing on the head of a working girl named Mary Smith (Jean Arthur), who is riding to work atop a double-decker bus. She gets off the bus and tries to return the coat, but J. B. Ball not only insists on her keeping it, but also takes her to a milliner's shop, where he buys her a fur hat to match. Then, because she is already late for work, he insists that he drive her in his cab to her office.

Complications immediately snarl the normal life of Mary Smith. She is not only late for work, but she is also boldly wearing a coat and hat she could never afford on her salary as a stenographer for a magazine called *Boy's Constant Companion*. She is fired from her job.

Meanwhile, because she has been seen in the company of J. B. Ball, and he has been billed for the coat and hat, word gets around that he is keeping a mistress named Mary Smith. She, in fact, is counting her change, wondering how she is going to afford lunch. The manager of the Louis Hotel, Mr. Louis Louis (Luis Alberni), thinks it would be very good for business if she were a resident there. Almost before she realizes it, Mary is living in the fanciest suite in the Louis, with unlimited credit and a limousine at her disposal. She finds that she can have anything her heart desires. The one thing she wants most at that moment is a good hot cup of coffee, so she goes to a nearby Automat for it.

At the Automat she meets Johnny Ball (Ray Milland), J. B.'s independent son, who has had an argument with his father and is working behind the counter at the Automat. One of the most hilarious sequences ever staged in a comedy feature follows. Accidentally, the little windows over the commodities offered for sale go out of commission, one row after another flipping open, shooting plates of food out among the startled customers. Word gets onto the street, and in a moment the Automat is jammed with hungry customers snatching at the free food being spewed forth. Through it all, Mary Smith sits calmly by herself at an end table, delicately eating her chicken pie as she sips her coffee. She naturally gets together with Johnny Ball.

Buyers of stock, believing Mary to be the mistress of J. B. and therefore privy to inside information, query her as to the actual state of the market. Knowing nothing, she gives facetious answers with a straight face and finds herself first causing a panic of buying and then one of selling. She also gets involved with the so-called common man and makes friends with a select handful, portrayed by such experts of comedy as Alberni, Franklin Pangborn, William Demarest, Barlowe Borland, and Andrew Tombes. Mary Smith is a nice, sensible girl who is no fool, accepting everything she is offered; and, like many another nice, sensible girl, she ends up marrying the millionaire's son. Both the millionaire and his eccentric wife are proud to have her as their daughter-in-law. She has brains, and there is a deficiency of that commodity among the Balls.

Easy Living was quickly recognized as one of the freshest comedies on the market, and although some critics dissented, taking a dim view of its wacky goings-on, the public loved it, and everybody had a good time. Paramount did well with a series of zany comedies during that decade. They not only had Leisen and Sturges under contract, but they also had commitments with the best of the stylish comediennes of the era, such as Arthur, Carole Lombard, Claudette Colbert, and Barbara Stanwyck. Paramount also had such leading men as Milland, Fred MacMurray, and Henry Fonda, to say nothing of "gentlemen" comic stars such as Bing Crosby, Bob Hope, and W. C. Fields. A Paramount motion picture might be not only the best show in town, but it might also be the funniest.

Arthur was one of the brightest of all screen comediennes; she remains a favorite in the public memory because she looks and talks as ordinary people do. Actually, she is an unusually pretty girl who can be glamourous if the part requires it. She also possesses one of the most individual voices in the business—low-pitched, husky, with a charming little crack or break in it. She received her first contract at Paramount during the silent era, but, unable to crash through to more important roles, she went to New York and became a hit in a few plays. She then returned to Hollywood, where her services were divided mostly on a commitment basis between Paramount and Columbia. She is the best example of the old adage that if an actress can play comedy, she can play anything. Arthur not only shone in farces such as *Easy Living*, stylish black humor comedies such as *A Foreign Affair* (1948), Frank Capra comedies such as *Mr. Deeds Goes to Town* (1936), *You Can't Take It with You* (1938), and *Mr. Smith Goes to Washington* (1939), and George Stevens comedies such as *The More the Merrier* (1943) and *The Talk of the Town* (1942), but she also proved to be an effective dramatic actress in *Diamond Jim* (1935) and *History Is Made at Night* (1937). She also handled Western roles capably in a variety of films, such as *Arizona* (1941) and *Shane* (1953). She was excellent as Calamity Jane, with Gary Cooper in Cecil B. De Mille's *The Plainsman* (1936). She has always been one of the most versatile actresses on stage or screen, and it is regrettable that since *Shane*, she has chosen to stay away from the screen, preferring to lecture in the Drama Department of Vassar and at Stephens College. Like Barbara Stanwyck and Irene Dunne, however, she has never really officially retired, so there is always the possibility that if the right property and the right director came along, she might take another turn before the cameras. Her timing has always been the best; she is a film editor's delight. *Easy Living*, is a perfect example of how effortless and how varied her style of playing can be.

Leisen, who directed *Easy Living* and many other smart comedies for Paramount, was trained as an architect and went originally into interior design and costuming in his early Hollywood career. From 1919 to 1933 he worked as a costumer for De Mille and Douglas Fairbanks; when De Mille set up his own company, Leisen went with him as an art director. Back at Paramount in 1933, he worked briefly as an assistant director, and in that year directed his first feature film, *Cradle Songs*, a delicate drama of nuns in a convent who rear a baby orphan to womanhood. Neither it nor *Death Takes a Holiday*, a fantasy he directed in 1934, gave any indication that he could direct a series of bright farces, culminating in *Easy Living*.

Sturges, during his youth, flitted around Europe, his mother being a close friend and confidante of dancer Isadora Duncan. He was always a nonconformist who secretly wanted to be a successful stockbroker. He first wrote a most engaging Broadway comedy, *Strictly Dishonorable*, and then, because he had a way with words, he had no trouble getting work as a screenplay writer in Hollywood, where he worked behind a typewriter from 1930 to 1938. Paramount gave him his first chance to direct the scripts he wrote, and a brilliant series of extraordinary comedies followed from 1940 through 1944, giving sparkle to the war years. He then left Paramount, but his subsequent work showed little evidence of the fresh comic touch that had blessed his Paramount films. In *Easy Living* he was at his zany best. He had in Leisen a director who understood him and knew exactly how to interpret his script; and in Arthur he had a real artist, a woman who could play comedy or drama with equal ease. *Easy Living* represents the only time the three of them worked together. That is unfortunate, because they were a trio of professionals who seemed to bring out the best in one another.

DeWitt Bodeen

EDGE OF THE CITY

Released: 1957
Production: David Susskind for Metro-Goldwyn-Mayer
Direction: Martin Ritt
Screenplay: Robert Alan Aurthur; based on his television play *A Man Is Ten Feet Tall*
Cinematography: Joseph Brun
Editing: Sidney Meyers
Running time: 86 minutes

Principal characters:
Axel North	John Cassavetes
Tommy Tyler	Sidney Poitier
Charles Malik	Jack Warden
Ellen Wilson	Kathleen Maguire
Lucy Tyler	Ruby Dee
Mr. Nordmann	Robert Simon
Mrs. Nordmann	Ruth White

Sidney Poitier was the dominant black actor of the 1950's, the first of his race consistently to win starring roles in films. While Poitier was no carbon copy of Clarence Muse or Stepin' Fetchit, however, his films still show him as a black in a white society who willingly sacrifices his cultural heritage and blackness to be accepted by whites and on white terms. To gain this approval, he had to be no less than perfect. The cinematic Poitier was intelligent, refined, and sexually neutral; he remained calm when harassed; any complaining came from reason rather than rage. His characterizations fostered a new stereotype, and he became the "Good Negro" to white audiences. To black audiences, who were still attempting to meet white middle-class standards, the neat, deghettoized actor was an acceptable if unreal role model. *Edge of the City*, one of his best films of the decade, offers a representative Poitier characterization.

Edge of the City was adapted from *A Man Is Ten Feet Tall*, a drama written by Robert Alan Aurthur which had previously been produced for television. Poitier also had starred in that version, and won a Sylvania Award as best television actor during the 1955-1956 season. The plot, a sort of integrated *On the Waterfront* (1954), centers on two men: Tommy Tyler (Sidney Poitier), a noble, happy-go-lucky railway yard worker on New York City's West Side; and Axel North (John Cassavetes), a rebellious, bewildered army deserter who is befriended by Tyler. Tyler secures a job for North alongside him and soon invites him home to meet his family. He becomes North's mentor, protector, and friend. Charlie Malik (Jack Warden), a bullying boss, persistently insults both men because North always prefers working with the black man.

When North refuses to fight Malik, Tyler must take his place. Although he is winning, Tyler begs his adversary to stop. As he turns his back, Malik stabs him with a baling hook, and the Christ-like Tyler dies in North's arms. Predictably the white man avenges his black friend's death, and by this heroic act, he finds himself acknowledging his responsibility as a human being.

The relationship between Poitier's Tyler and Cassavetes' North in *Edge of the City* is intriguing. Despite the liberation of Poitier from shuffling feet, a pullman porter profession, and a "dees/dems/does" dialect, Cassavetes' character remains the master to Poitier's servant. Tyler, good, clean, and perfect, is still an idealized black as envisioned by his white "brother." The footloose North rebelliously confronts and rejects the hypocrisy he perceives in white society. He is more at home with the outcast Tyler, on the outside simply because of the color of his skin, than with those of his own race. Tyler is sympathetic to North and serves as ego support for his rebellion, but he never dares to compete with the white man for attention. Eventually, he dies out of loyalty to his friend, and the white man must avenge his demise. Tyler is merely an instrument in the catharsis of North from rootlessness to responsibility.

Despite these shortcomings, Tommy Tyler is one of Poitier's finest, most humanistic roles of the decade. Although he remains subservient to North, it is Tyler, the black man, who extends his hand to lift the white man out of his troubles. He is a three-dimensional character, strong, sensitive, and humane, a man of conscience. He is no caricatured black, but a symbol of brotherly love.

Edge of the City is also noteworthy as the directorial debut of Martin Ritt. Ritt is an *auteur* of social consciousness. From *Edge of the City* through *Paris Blues* (1961), in which jazz musicians Poitier and Paul Newman romance tourists Diahann Carroll and Joanne Woodward on the Left Bank; *Conrack* (1974), which tells the story of white educator Jon Voight who teaches at a rural black school; and more recently, *Norma Rae* (1979), about a Southern cotton mill worker, Sally Field, and a New York Jewish labor organizer, Ron Leibman, who unionize a factory, Ritt's characters clasp hands in friendship and trust despite their ethnic or cultural differences. His themes and denouements may be seen by some as overly idealized, but they are certainly not without merit.

Edge of the City is a well-acted film; two decades after its release, the performances remain fresh and poignant. Of particular note in the cast is Ruby Dee, who renders a fine supporting performance as Poitier's loyal wife, Lucy. She is especially moving when she breaks down after learning from North of her husband's death, telling him to get away from her with his "white money" when he offers to help her. Poitier and Dee appeared together as husband and wife in no less than five features: *No Way Out* (1950), *Go, Man, Go* (1954), *Virgin Island* (1959), and *A Raisin in the Sun* (1961), as well as

Edge of the City. The film was favorably reviewed by the critics; consistently cited were the scenes between Tyler and North as their friendship flourishes.

Edge of the City (along with *The Defiant Ones*, 1958, in which Tony Curtis costars as an escaped convict shackled to fellow prisoner Poitier, who sacrifices his freedom to come to the rescue of his newly found white "brother," and for which Poitier earned his first Oscar nomination) helped to affirm the actor's status as a talented performer and Hollywood star. During the next decade, he reached his zenith, winning an Academy Award in 1963 for *Lilies of the Field*. In 1967 he starred in no less than three blockbusters: he was the Nobel Prize candidate/fiancé of white Katharine Houghton in Stanley Kramer's *Guess Who's Coming to Dinner*; a schoolteacher who tames a brood of rebellious British teenagers in the entertaining *To Sir with Love* and a police officer from the North who solves a murder case and wins the respect of a bigoted Southern sheriff played by Rod Steiger in the Academy Award-winning *In the Heat of the Night*.

Black films of the following decade were made expressly for black audiences. Such motion pictures as *Super Fly* (1972), *Black Caesar* (1973), *The Spook Who Sat by the Door* (1973), and *Mandingo* (1975) are violence-oriented, reverse racist diatribes in which all blacks are "supercool" studs hustling to survive in a white world of oppression. Far more positive are films such as *Shaft* (1971), *Sounder* (1972), *Cooley High* (1975), and *A Hero Ain't Nothin' But a Sandwich* (1978). These features either attempt to deal with the black experience and the problems of black survival in a serious, humanistic manner or depict blacks as real, identifiable heroes/heroines in nonmessage stories meant to be pure entertainment.

The Poitier screen *persona* may be as unreal as it is outdated, but he nevertheless filled a role that was necessary in the break from the traditional, shuffling stereotyped Uncle Tom. His early portrayals marked a major step toward insightful characterizations and away from the blatant racism which dates back to *The Birth of a Nation*, (1915), and his later roles have shown him to be one of the major acting talents of the 1960's and 1970's.

Rob Edelman

THE EGG AND I

Released: 1947
Production: Chester Erskine and Fred F. Finklehoffe for Universal-International
Direction: Chester Erskine
Screenplay: Chester Erskine and Fred F. Finklehoffe; based on the novel of the same name by Betty MacDonald
Cinematography: Milton Krasner
Editing: Russell Schoengarth
Running time: 108 minutes

Principal characters:
Betty .... Claudette Colbert
Bob ....Fred MacMurray
Ma Kettle .... Marjorie Main
Harriett Putnam .... Louise Allbritton
Pa Kettle .... Percy Kilbride
Tom Kettle .... Richard Long
Birdie Hicks .... Esther Dale

Betty MacDonald's humorous memoir of life with her first husband, Robert Heskett, on an egg ranch in the Pacific Northwest in the late 1920's was serialized in *Atlantic Monthly* in 1945. When *The Egg and I* came out as a book later that year, the publisher, J. P. Lippincott, ordered five printings totalling sixty-one thousand copies within the first ten days. A year later, sales had passed the one million mark; the book seemed permanently installed at the top of every best-seller list; and MacDonald and her second husband, Donald, had received that ultimate accolade of mid-twentieth century celebrity, a "visit" from *Life* magazine, which was duly recorded in the issue of March 18, 1946.

A movie sale for *The Egg and I* was inevitable. What may have surprised some people, however, was that the book was sold, not to Warner Bros., M-G-M, or one of the other "major" studios, but to Universal-International, the newly formed amalgamation of Universal Pictures, one of the oldest studios in Hollywood, and William Goetz's International Pictures, an independent production company that had been responsible for such highly regarded films of the preceding few years as *The Woman in the Window* (1944) and *Scarlet Street* (1945), both directed by Fritz Lang, *The Dark Mirror* (1946), directed by Robert Siodmak, and *The Stranger* (1946), directed by Orson Welles. Under its founder, Carl Laemmle, and his brilliant young assistant, Irving Thalberg, Universal had once been an industry leader, with stars such as Eric von Stroheim and Lon Chaney under contract, and such films as *Foolish Wives* (1922), *The Hunchback of Notre Dame* (1923), *The Phantom of the Opera* (1925), and *All Quiet on the Western Front* (1930) to its credit. By the 1940's, however, after many reorganizations and years of mismanagement by Laemmle's son, Carl, Jr., the studio was known chiefly for Bud Abbott and Lou Costello comedies, the Basil Rathbone-Nigel Bruce Sherlock Holmes mysteries, desert spectaculars starring Maria Montez and Jon Hall, and the increasingly ludicrous sequels to its classic horror films of the early 1930's, *Frankenstein* (1931), *Dracula* (1931), and *The Mummy* (1932).

The merger with International, and the new company's purchase of a bestseller such as *The Egg and I*, were signs that Universal was determined to recapture some of its former glory. Two stars with established reputations in the field of light comedy, Claudette Colbert and Fred MacMurray, were signed for the parts of Betty and Bob. Betty and Bob Heskett were divorced in 1931. Some early reviewers of *The Egg and I* had described the "MacDonalds' " struggle on their ranch—a natural mistake, since Betty had not written of her divorce or called her husband anything except Bob. Possibly out of a desire to protect Robert Heskett's privacy, this mistake was perpetuated in the movie. Another case of popular misinformation was occasioned by the circumstance that Colbert and MacMurray had both just ended long-term associations with Paramount. As a result, many people today think that *The Egg and I* was a Paramount picture. The screenplay was written by Chester Erskine, a former playwright with many years of theatrical experience, and Fred F. Finklehoffe, a seasoned screenwriter whose previous films included the successful *Brother Rat* (1940), *Babes on Broadway* (1941), and *Meet Me in St. Louis* (1944). The two men were allowed to produce their own screenplay, and Erskine, who had directed plays for Charles Frohman, the Schuberts, and the Theatre Guild, made *The Egg and I* the vehicle for his debut as a motion picture director.

The result was justly condemned by Bosley Crowther in his *New York Times* review of April 25, 1947, as a "watered-down rewrite" that failed completely to capture the "earthy tang" of the book. (Some of MacDonald's experiences had been "earthy" indeed, such as her encounter with a neighbor who, at their first meeting, had offered to perform an abortion on her, for a small fee, whenever she asked him to. Given the restrictions of the Production Code that was still in effect in 1947, there was no way Erskine and Finklehoffe could have worked that incident into their script.) Instead of the ruggedly beautiful Olympic Peninsula scenery that MacDonald had described so evocatively, the film offered only a few prop pine trees standing in front of a cyclorama to suggest a vaguely Northwestern locale. The period was updated to 1946, to emphasize the similarity of Heskett's dream of owning his own farm with the dreams of many returning servicemen after World War II.

The book's "plot" had consisted of episodes from young Betty's continual struggle with such unpleasant facts of rural life as the absence of electricity and modern plumbing, and her difficulty in adjusting to the ways of her mountain neighbors. Betty was a precocious eighteen-year-old when Heskett married her out of college in 1927, and, one suspects, a terrific snob. A few of these incidents (chiefly Betty's difficulty in learning to cook on an antiquated cast-iron stove) formed the basis for situation comedy-style "gag" sequences in the film; but Erskine and Finklehoffe relied on a character of their own invention to provide them with material for a conventional dramatic crisis.

In the film, one of Betty and Bob's first callers at the ranch is a glamorous divorcée, Harriett Putnam (Louise Allbritton), who arouses Betty's jealousy because she owns a ranch equipped with all the latest conveniences, and because she is obviously attracted to Bob. Near the end of the story, Bob meets with Harriett to discuss buying her ranch, but without telling Betty because he wants to surprise her. Betty, who has just discovered that she is pregnant, learns of the meeting, and furiously comes to the conclusion that Bob and Harriett are having an affair behind her back. She goes home to her mother without giving Bob a chance to explain, and somewhat implausibly goes through the full term of her pregnancy and gives birth to a baby girl without reading any of Bob's frantic letters or having any communication with him at all. Finally, at her mother's urging, she returns with the baby intending to surprise him. Betty is the surprised one, however, when her cab driver stops at the Putnam ranch (which Bob had bought after all), and she sees Bob's old car parked next to Harriett's sleek station wagon. Betty is furious all over again, and only calms down long enough to learn that Harriett is gone in time for the inevitable happy ending.

As Crowther said, the general tone was of "a quaint and cozy cut-up for the reliable women's trade"; and perhaps the most surprising thing about the film was that it not only repeated the book's success, but was also reissued profitably in 1955. Profitability alone would not justify an article about *The Egg and I* in this reference work, however; many films are released every year to equally great success that are forgotten a few years later by everyone except specialists in film history. What gave *The Egg and I*, as a book and as a film, a special place in cultural history was its introduction of two memorable characters—in fact, a whole family—into the gallery of American folklore.

In the book, MacDonald had described how she looked with dismay at her first batch of home-baked bread, which was "pale yellow" in color and tasted like "something we had cleaned out of the cooler," and, at Bob's suggestion, had taken a sample loaf to a neighbor, Mrs. Kettle, for her diagnosis. As it happened, Mrs. Kettle, a mountainous woman from whose "pretty head cascaded a series of breasts and stomachs which made her look like a cookie jar shaped like a woman," was just taking out of the oven "fourteen of the biggest, crustiest, lightest loaves of bread" that Betty had ever seen. Mrs. Kettle amiably wiped her hands on her dirty housedress, tasted Betty's bread, and pronounced her verdict: "Goddamn stuff stinks."

Mrs. Kettle, her shiftless husband, and their brood of fifteen children were easily the most memorable of the many memorable characters that Betty and Bob Heskett encountered during the two years they lived on their ranch. (Betty's neighbors as described in her book were undoubtedly all fictionalized composites, but the general accuracy of her recollection may be judged from the circumstance that she was later sued by members of two separate families who claimed that she had libeled them as the "Kettles.") In the film, Mrs.— or Ma—Kettle was played by the veteran character actress Marjorie Main, who had already created a long screen gallery of motherly landladies and bad-tempered domestics. Her physical appearance was not as grotesque as MacDonald's description of Ma, but she fully conveyed the good-heartedness that won Betty over in spite of Mrs. Kettle's slatternly appearance and earthy ways. (Needless to say, Mrs. Kettle's profanity and gossip about her neighbors' sex lives did not make it to the screen, nor did her comfortable habit of receiving visitors while seated in her doorless privy.) In the book, Betty described Pa Kettle as a close cousin to Erskine Caldwell's Jeeter Lester (in *Tobacco Road*, 1932): a dirty, lazy Northwestern hillbilly who spoke with a pronounced lisp through a thick black mustache. Someone like Henry Hull— who created the part of Jeeter on the stage—would probably have made a screen Pa Kettle who closely matched Betty's conception; but the role instead went to Percy Kilbride, a gentle, soft-spoken New Englander who created an indelible image of low-keyed guile that brought him his first real public notice after years in small parts (including a role as a handyman in *George Washington Slept Here*, 1942, that was like a sketch for his performance as Pa Kettle).

As played by Main and Kilbride, Ma and Pa Kettle stole the movie of *The Egg and I* as easily as they had stolen the book. (Main, in fact, received the film's only Academy Award nomination, although she lost in the Best Supporting Actress category to Celeste Holm in *Gentleman's Agreement*.) The Kettles were naturals for their own series of second-feature comedies, a fact that was not lost on the management team at Universal-International, which never entirely abandoned the old Universal's commitment to dependably profitable "bread and butter" filmmaking. (One could argue, in fact, that Universal's present eminence as a leading producer of motion pictures and filmed series for television is a continuation of this policy.) In 1949 the studio released *Ma and Pa Kettle*, the first of nine sequels to *The Egg and I*. Bob and Betty MacDonald did not appear as characters in this or any of the subsequent Kettle films, which instead relied on such devices as having Pa Kettle win a modern, fully equipped "dream house" in a contest to engineer the city versus country confrontations that lay at the heart of their comedy. The Kettle series was produced by Leonard Goldstein and, after his death, by Richard Wilson and Howard Christie. The directors included Charles

Lamont, Edward Sedgwick, Charles Barton, Lee Sholem, and Virgil Vogel, who kept the Kettles in motion at an increasingly farcical pace without disappointing their fans or, it must be said, stamping any film in the series with something that could be recognized as a personal point of view.

An important subplot in *The Egg and I* had concerned the oldest Kettle son, Tom (Richard Long), a bright boy who was encouraged by Betty to fulfill his dream of going to college. In *Ma and Pa Kettle*, Long returned with a magazine-writer girl friend (Meg Randall), whom he subsequently married (in *Ma and Pa Kettle Go to Town*, 1950). Long and Randall dropped out of the series after *Ma and Pa Kettle Back on the Farm* (1951), but their place as the "normal" members of the Kettle family was taken by Lori Nelson, who played the oldest Kettle daughter in *Ma and Pa Kettle at the Fair* (1952) and in *Ma and Pa Kettle at Waikiki* (which was filmed in 1953 but not released until 1955). Other recurring characters included a pathologically tidy farm woman named Birdie Hicks (Esther Dale), who had been Ma's natural rival as early as *The Egg and I* (like the Kettles, Mrs. Hicks had also been a character in MacDonald's book), and Meg Randall's stuffy parents, played by Ray Collins and Barbara Brown. Collins and Brown were perfect foils for Main and Kilbride in *Ma and Pa Kettle Go to Town* and *Ma and Pa Kettle on Vacation* (1953). (In this last film, the two ill-matched sets of in-laws wound up in Paris together.)

Percy Kilbride decided to retire after *Ma and Pa Kettle at Home* (1954), but the producers announced that the series would continue without him. In *The Kettles in the Ozarks* (1956), Main journeyed south without Pa to cross swords with his equally shiftless hillbilly cousin, played by Arthur Hunnicutt. By this time, even the usually friendly trade press was reporting (in the words of *Daily Variety*), that the " 'Kettles' series [was] beginning to wear thin"; but the studio released one more film, *Ma and Pa Kettle on Old MacDonald's Farm*, to end the series in 1957. Parker Fennelly, who had played "Titus Moody," another rural con man with a New England twang, on Fred Allen's radio show, took the part of Pa, but he was unable to erase the image created by Kilbride in the role. In a sense, the last film took the series full circle by having the Kettles return, not to their own ramshackle farm, but to Bob and Betty MacDonald's old ranch, where Ma promoted a match between a lumberjack (John Smith) and a spoiled rich girl (Gloria Talbott), whom she undertook to instruct in the duties of a proper farm wife, just as she had coached MacDonald ten years before.

It was suggested as a reason for the series' demise that movie audiences of the late 1950's were too sophisticated for the Kettles' brand of rural humor; but it seems fairer to say that Ma and Pa Kettle—along with Francis the Talking Mule, the Bowery Boys, Blondie, and all the other once popular second-feature characters—were victims of television, which had captured the regular movie audience in small towns where the "B"-picture series had always been strongest. That the basic appeal of rural comedy had not diminished was indicated by the success a few years later of such television series as *The Beverly Hillbillies*, *Petticoat Junction*, and *Green Acres*. This last show, in fact, with its theme of a city couple (played by Eddie Albert and Eva Gabor) who were constantly being outwitted by a country bumpkin (Pat Butram), was nothing more than a reworking of the basic situation that audiences had laughed at in *The Egg and I*.

Charles Hopkins

THE ELECTRIC HORSEMAN

Released: 1979
Production: Ray Stark for Ray Stark-Wildwood; released by Columbia and
  Universal
Direction: Sydney Pollack
Screenplay: Robert Garland; based on Robert Garland and Paul Gaer's adapt-
  ation of an original story by Shelly Burton
Cinematography: Owen Roizman
Editing: Sheldon Kahn
Running time: 120 minutes

Principal characters:
Sonny Steele	Robert Redford
Hallie Martin	Jane Fonda
Wendell	Willie Nelson
Hunt Sears	John Saxon
Charlotta	Valerie Perrine
Fitzgerald	Nicolas Coster
Gus Atwater	Will Hare
Leroy	Timothy Scott
Danny Miles	Allan Arbus

The Electric Horseman, a likable and well-made romantic comedy with a
minor antiestablishment theme, is in the tradition of Frank Capra's Oscar-
winning *It Happened One Night* (1934). As in the Capra film, the chief virtues
are the superb but easy acting of the stars and the witty dialogue of the script.
The Electric Horseman, however, introduces some modern variations on the
conventions of the romantic comedies of the 1930's and 1940's.

With great artistry and economy, the shots under the credits portray the
career of five-time world champion cowboy Sonny Steele (Robert Redford).
He wins his rodeo championships, suffers a few broken bones along the way,
and is signed by Ampco Corporation to promote its Ranch Breakfast cereal.
The beginning of his career with Ampco is shown through a shot of a commercial artist adding a moustache to Sonny's picture, a photography session
with Sonny now wearing a moustache, and a series of posters advertising
Sonny's appearances as the Ranch Breakfast Cowboy. There is not a word
of dialogue during this sequence, only the voice of country singer Willie
Nelson singing "My Heroes Have Always Been Cowboys."

As the credits end, we find out what the job of Ranch Breakfast Cowboy
has become. Sonny is intoxicated and late for an appearance as his sidekicks,
Wendell (Willie Nelson) and Leroy (Timothy Scott), struggle to dress him in
his special costume. Once he is dressed and mounted on a horse, he rides
onto a darkened football field as part of a half-time show. His flashy cowboy

costume is electrified so that he is outlined in lights (hence the title), and he holds up a giant box of Ranch Breakfast as he rides around the field, but this time he is too drunk to stay on the horse and he falls off. Now we hear Willie Nelson singing again, but this time the song is "Mama, Don't Let Your Babies Grow Up to Be Cowboys."

The central action of the plot begins in Las Vegas, where the Ampco conglomerate is holding a convention and media event at Caesar's Palace. The Ampco people are trying to buy a bank and want everything to go smoothly. Hallie Martin (Jane Fonda) is a television reporter looking for a story, and when the Ampco public relations man, Fitzgerald (Nicolas Coster), suggests that she not interview Sonny, Hallie decides that there is something to hide and that Sonny will be her story. Sonny meanwhile has found that Ampco has bought a twelve-million-dollar thoroughbred horse, Rising Star, to be another of its "corporate symbols." He is upset when he sees the animal on display in the Caesar's Palace parking lot and even more upset when he finds that various drugs have been administered to keep the horse tranquil enough to take part in a stage show but that its inflamed tendon has not been properly treated because Ampco does not want the horse to appear with a bandage on its leg.

Sonny confronts the head of Ampco, Hunt Sears (John Saxon), with his complaints about how the horse is being treated, but Sears tells him that he is not to interfere in corporate policy. "Sir, I used to rodeo," Sonny says. "I was good at it." Sears merely replies, "That's irrelevant."

Sonny is therefore forced to take matters into his own hands. During the "Disco Magic" portion of the Ampco stage show, he mounts Rising Star, turns on his electrified costume, and rides the horse across the stage, through the casino, and off down the street. In his electric cowboy suit riding down the garish Las Vegas strip, Sonny is an impressive sight, but the director of the show, Danny Miles (Allan Arbus), is upset because he has ruined the "whole concept" of the show, and Sears is afraid the publicity will ruin his three-hundred-million-dollar merger with the bank. "One drunken cowboy," he mutters.

The emphasis of *The Electric Horseman* then shifts from the "liberation" of both Sonny and the horse to the relationship between Sonny and Hallie. It begins as romances always do in the old-fashioned romantic comedies, with two people of different backgrounds battling each other. In the 1930's the battling would have lasted until the final part of the film when the two would have recognized their love, gotten married, and presumably lived happily ever after. In *The Electric Horseman* the romance comes sooner and the two separate at the end, but the attention to characterization and subtlety of feelings is the same as in the older films.

Hallie had already confronted Sonny at a press conference with questions about why he was late for the conference and whether he actually ate Ranch

Breakfast cereal, and—referring to the fact that he had been a cowboy and was now a cereal salesman—had asked the universal television reporter's question: "How do you feel about that?" Now she finds that Sonny is a bigger story than she could have imagined. In an effort to find Sonny she interviews Leroy and replays a tape recording of her earlier interview with Wendell. Through these interviews she finds Gus Atwater (Will Hare), a somewhat demented friend of Sonny who lives in the desert, and through Gus she finds Sonny.

When Hallie finds Sonny, he attacks her both physically and verbally. He is startled by her sudden appearance in the dark, afraid that she has told others where he is, and angry at her desire for a story, "any story." Sonny finally persuades her to leave, but the next day as he buys some supplies at a small store he sees her on television reporting what she learned from a "wide-ranging conversation" lasting "many hours." Sonny then decides that if he is going to be on television he wants to tell his story himself; so he telephones Hallie and tells her to bring a camera and to meet him alone at a remote location. There he explains on camera that the stallion has earned a better life, tells Hallie that he is going to set the horse loose, and sends Hallie away with the videotape. He has not gotten rid of her, however, because she soon returns to warn him that the police are waiting for him and that she must go with him or she will be legally forced to tell all she knows. She has already told her network to meet her at Rim Rock Canyon, where she has deduced Sonny is taking the horse, but she of course does not tell Sonny that. She still sees him merely as a big and exclusive story for herself.

Gradually their hostility toward each other changes to more tender feelings. As they finally embrace, a slow dissolve takes us to the next morning. Their romance is based on a mutual respect as Hallie begins to understand what Sonny is doing and why he is doing it and Sonny appreciates that Hallie is good at her job. Now Hallie regrets telling the network to have a camera crew waiting at Rim Rock Canyon, and she tries unsuccessfully to get word to her boss to cancel that plan. That night she tells Sonny what she has done and that she lied about having to stay with him or face legal troubles. The news does not change his plans, however; the next day when they reach a quiet secluded valley, he releases Rising Star, telling him, "make something out of yourself now." Hallie is amazed that the network crew is not there, but Sonny is not because they are in Silver Reef. He had never intended to go to Rim Rock Canyon; that was Hallie's mistaken assumption.

The film cuts from Rising Star running free to a small coffee shop and bus station. Hallie is taking a bus and going back to her job; Sonny is going to look for something simple to do. As he sees her off, Sonny says, "I keep wanting to thank you—but then I keep wondering what for." The film ends with Hallie reporting on television from New York while Sonny walks along a road halfheartedly trying to hitch a ride.

Credit for the success of *The Electric Horseman* belongs primarily to the script and the acting. The script, by Robert Garland from a screen story by Garland and Paul Gaer that is based on a story by Shelly Burton, is both unhurried and packed with information that reveals both plot and character. These details of both plot and characterization are continually revealed, but they are never overemphasized. The result is a coherent narrative that gives the audience credit for the intelligence to follow it without having every point underlined. The dialogue is also witty but unforced. The Ampco personnel are characterized less subtly than the others, however; in addition, some pertinent points about the media in our society are made even if they are not deeply explored. The main points concern the all-too-frequent desire of reporters to find a story rather than the truth and the fact that a person may become more famous and rich as a "corporate symbol" than for what he does well that made him celebrated in the first place. An example of this is the fact that Joe DiMaggio may be known to more people today as a spokesman for a coffee machine than as a star baseball player. The only bad sequence in the film is a chase in which Sonny, who is riding Rising Star, incredibly escapes from several police cars and motorcycles.

The acting is superb. Both Redford and Fonda play their roles with an ease that makes them credible but with perfect timing so that nothing in the script is lost and much is added. Redford and Fonda may be major stars, but they are also excellent actors. They are well supported by virtually every member of the cast, with country singer Nelson as Wendell and Valerie Perrine as Sonny's ex-wife deserving special notice. *The Electric Horseman* is skillfully made and enjoyable enough to reward repeated viewings, but some reviewers faulted the film for not being what they expected. Other reviewers, however, recognized its virtues, as did the public, which made it one of the ten most popular films of the year.

Timothy W. Johnson

THE ELEPHANT MAN

Released: 1980
Production: Jonathan Sanger for Paramount
Direction: David Lynch
Screenplay: Christopher DeVore, Eric Bergren, and David Lynch; based on the book *The Elephant Man and Other Reminiscences* by Sir Frederick Treves and in part on *The Elephant Man: A Study in Human Dignity* by Ashley Montagu
Cinematography: Freddie Francis
Editing: Anne V. Coates
Music: John Morris
Running time: 125 minutes

Principal characters:
Frederick Treves	Anthony Hopkins
John Merrick	John Hurt
Mrs. Kendal	Anne Bancroft
Carr Gomm	John Gielgud
Mothershead	Wendy Hiller
Bytes	Freddie Jones
Mrs. Treves	Hannah Gordon

The Elephant Man, a stirring paean to the dignity of the human spirit, derives its greatest impact from its real-life origins. This highly original film tells the touching story of John Merrick, one of the most hideously deformed men who ever lived. A Victorian-era victim of the disease neurofibromatosis, Merrick had a twisted spine, a useless right arm, and a head swollen to twice the normal size. Sir Frederick Treves, the surgeon who befriended Merrick, described him as "the most disgusting specimen of humanity that I have ever seen. . . . From the brow there projected a huge bony mass like a loaf, while from the back of the head hung a bag of spongy, fungous-looking skin . . ."

The film opens on a note of anticipation as Frederick Treves (Anthony Hopkins) makes his way through a dank circus sideshow. As he shuffles through the twisting passageways, the audience shares his voyeurism. When he at last confronts the show's main attraction, billed as "The Terrible Elephant Man," the camera pulls away; instead of seeing the deformed Merrick (John Hurt), the audience sees the doctor's reaction to him: tears glisten in his eyes. "I pray to God he's an idiot," Treves says upon first seeing Merrick; but after summoning him to his clinic for closer examination, he is shocked to discover that his subject has a kind and gently inquisitive demeanor. *The Elephant Man* goes to the heart of the eternally popular Frankenstein theme by examining the man within the monster; for while Merrick is a kindly soul (he knows his Book of Common Prayer), given to childlike wonder, others to whom nature has been kinder harbor monstrous personalities.

The revelation of beauty within the beast comes as the film studies the friendship between Treves and Merrick. For Treves, Merrick is initially a creature of curiosity. When he lectures about Merrick to members of the London Pathological Society and exhibits the deformed young man, he garners notoriety. Still the camera refrains from showing Merrick, although we do hear the startled gasps of the doctors assembled, and Merrick's crippled frame is seen, silhouetted against a screen. Later, when Merrick is viciously beaten by his "owner," Bytes (Freddie Jones), Treves has him admitted to London Hospital. Although Carr Gomm (John Gielgud), chairman of the hospital committee, questions Treves's motives, warning that the hospital cannot house incurables, the Elephant Man is given a room temporarily.

It is at this point, after audience expectations have grown, that Merrick's grotesque face and body are at last seen. Although the initial impact is shocking, it is a sign of the film's great sensitivity that the hideousness of the features soon diminish as the viewer comes to care for the man's feelings and situation; acceptance of the Elephant Man comes, in part, through the gradual understanding achieved by those about him. Carr Gomm, anxious to prove the man an imbecile so that the hospital can be done with him, is startled to hear Merrick, in his wheezing voice, reciting the Twenty-third Psalm. The hospital's head matron, Mothershead (Wendy Hiller), who once looked at Merrick sternly, begins to hover protectively over him.

In one of the film's most moving sequences, Treves invites Merrick to his home for tea. Startled by his disfigurement, Mrs. Treves (Hannah Gordon) can barely conceal her horror. When Merrick sees the family photographs clustered on the mantle and comments on them, however, she discovers that she shares a common link with this man: love of family. "They have such noble faces," he says, pointing to a picture. Then, after reaching into his pocket, Merrick produces his own family portrait—a small photograph of his (beautiful) mother, "She had the face of an angel," says Merrick, adding, "I must have been a great disappointment to her. I tried so hard to be good. . . ."

When the newspapers learn of London Hospital's unique resident, Merrick becomes something of a social celebrity, to the consternation of Mothershead, who feels he is being exploited. Treves is also beginning to doubt his motivations, since the Elephant Man has brought him such fame. Yet Merrick, as portrayed here, seems to delight in his new life. Among his new friends is the celebrated stage actress, Mrs. Kendal (Anne Bancroft). During their first encounter Mrs. Kendal is so shaken by Merrick's appearance that she draws upon her dramatic abilities to sustain herself. Upon discovering that Merrick enjoys Shakespeare, however, she reads some passages with him from *Romeo and Juliet*. "Oh Mr. Merrick, you aren't an elephant man at all.

You are a Romeo," says Mrs. Kendal, conscious of a new dimension to this much-heralded man.

While Merrick enjoys his newfound celebrity by day, at night he is victimized by a cruel porter who sells visits to his room. The macabre visits find the terrified Merrick being joustled and fondled by the converging mobs. One night, Bytes is among the visitors, and angry over the loss of his sideshow attraction, he forces Merrick away. Once again, Merrick is caged, treated like an animal, and exhibited to the curious, this time at a circus in Belgium. Bytes, never before so cruel, displays such viciousness that the show's other "freaks" band together to save the pathetic Merrick. In what is perhaps the film's most beautiful scene, the parade of human oddities spirits Merrick away in the dead of night, with the lakeside procession reflected in the shimmering waters. When Merrick, masked and robed, later arrives at the Liverpool Street Station enroute to his hospital home, prankish boys send him running. An excitable mob gathers and grows, dispersing only after Merrick pleads, "I am a human being!"

After his return to the hospital and a tearful reunion, Merrick is revitalized by an invitation from Mrs. Kendal to attend the theater. Seated in the Royal Box with Princess Alexandra, the Princess of Wales, Merrick watches an enchanting production of the Christmas pantomime, "Puss in Boots." At the performance's end, Mrs. Kendal goes to the stage and dedicates the performance to Merrick, after which the audience rises in a standing ovation. The Elephant Man's most triumphant night is also his last, for when he returns to his room after leaving the theater, he chooses to ignore his usual sleeping position. Because of his deformity, he must sleep upright, but this night, after glancing at the beloved portrait of his mother, he decides to sleep lying flat knowing that death is a result.

One of the year's most acclaimed films, *The Elephant Man* was praised for its dignified treatment of a subject that could have easily been treated in a grisly, exploitative manner. Named to numerous critical "top ten" lists (in doing so, *Time* magazine called it "the year's sweetest movie"), *The Elephant Man* earned eight Academy Award nominations, including one for Best Picture. Although the film did not win any Oscars, with *Ordinary People* dominating the year's awards, it stands as an awesome effort for director Lynch as well as for actor Hurt. Prior to directing this, his first major studio release, the thirty-three-year-old Lynch was known chiefly on the "midnight circuit" for his 1977 cult film *Eraserhead*, a bizarre study of a mutant child. Lynch, a graduate of the American Film Institute, has admitted his interest in unique, unsettling film subjects. "I want to get into areas people haven't been before, and still make people want to see them," he has stated.

The uncompromising talents of Hurt are also amplified by the film. As the Elephant Man, Hurt is barely recognizable, due to an exhaustive (seven-hour) makeup session. Regardless of his character's physical appearance, however,

Hurt is able to create a man who is at once real and sympathetic, despite a tragic deformity. In discussing the challenging role, Hurt has noted, "I found that I had quite literally to give my soul to the part. It is so far beyond any ordinary human experience. I don't want to sound pretentious, but I would find myself praying, to God and to Merrick—wherever he might be—to help me." An actor of diverse range, Hurt has appeared in films including *Midnight Express* (1978), for which he was nominated for an Oscar, and *Alien* (1979). His television appearances include the acclaimed British programs *I, Claudius*, *The Naked Civil Servant*, and *Crime and Punishment*. His role in *The Elephant Man* earned him a second Academy Award nomination.

Hopkins is superlative as Merrick's benefactor, Treves, ingratiating, sometimes opportunistic, and always a staunch friend. Hopkins' recent film credits include *Magic* (1978), in which he plays a ventriloquist seemingly tormented by his dummy, and *A Change of Seasons* (1980), a Bo Derek film which examines middle-aged sexual mores. The release of *The Elephant Man* came in the aftermath of a successful Broadway production which also is called *The Elephant Man*. For that reason, Paramount and Brooksfilms, headed by Mel Brooks, stressed that the film version was totally unrelated to the stage play, although the subject of both is the same. Such a distinction, however, is not really necessary, for *The Elephant Man* stands as a highly original cinematic work in theme, tone, and delivery.

Largely responsible for the film's exquisite craftsmanship is the cinematography by Freddie Francis, the black-and-white master who filmed *Room at the Top* (1959), *Saturday Night and Sunday Morning* (1960), and *Sons and Lovers* (1960), for which he earned an Academy Award; he demonstrates an ingenious photographic artistry which includes an infatuation with odd camera angles. In addition to his revered cinematography, Francis is something of an *auteur* in his own right; as a director for Hammer Films, his credits include *Nightmare* (1964), *The Evil of Frankenstein* (1964), *Tales from the Crypt* (1972), *The Creeping Flesh* (1972), and countless other titles which have popularized him with horror-film fans.

Pat H. Broeske

THE EMPEROR JONES

Released: 1933
Production: John Krimsky and Gifford Cochran; released by United Artists
Direction: Dudley Murphy
Screenplay: DuBose Heyward; based on the play of the same name by Eugene
O'Neill
Cinematography: Ernest Haller
Editing: Grant Whytock
Running time: 72 minutes

Principal characters:
Brutus Jones	Paul Robeson
Smithers	Dudley Digges
Jeff	Frank Wilson
Undine	Fredi Washington
Dolly	Ruby Elzy
Lem	George Haymid Stamper

Based on Eugene O'Neill's 1920 stage *tour de force*, the film version of *The Emperor Jones* opens up the play, principally by picking up the bits of Jones's earlier life from the flashes given in his jungle flight and restructuring the first half of the film upon an expanded version of these events. Thus, O'Neill's play begins with Jones's exodus from his palace, while the film begins with his foray into the white man's world as a Pullman porter. Particularly fascinating is the film's addition of the mirror motif: it is through this image in a series of mirrors that we see the gradual transformation of Brutus Jones (Paul Robeson) from self-satisfaction as a porter to his eventual personal belief in himself as "Emperor."

Robeson's portrayal of Jones is masterful, whether he is singing, "travellin,' " or playing the penny-ante island ruler. After graduating from Princeton, Robeson played the Brutus Jones role on the stage, went on to do a series of musical plays in New York and in Britain, and finally agreed to do the film version of the play, his first sound film, in 1932. *The Emperor Jones* was one of the few films of which he was proud. Independently produced, the film was a reasonable financial success, although it did bear the period stigmata of being an "art film." The director, Dudley Murphy (assisted by William C. De Mille, who apparently finished the film), had collaborated with Fernand Leger on the classic experimental film *Ballet Mecanique* in 1924, then went on to direct Bessie Smith in *St. Louis Blues* (1929).

The credits of *The Emperor Jones* are superimposed over a group of dancing natives; this shot slowly dissolves into a marvelous down-home gospel meeting alive with dancing and hand-clapping. As the minister intones a benediction for brother Brutus Jones, who is about to leave for the big world, the film cuts to Brutus admiring himself in front of the mirror in his new Pullman porter uniform. The film then cuts back and forth between the church and Brutus' departure from his home and wife Dolly (Ruby Elzy). The couple stop by the church to receive farewell congratulations, allowing Brutus the opportunity to sing "Now Let Me Fly." Suddenly, he is on his way, and fellow porter and friend Jeff (Frank Wilson) gives Brutus his first lecture on "high finance"—how to get the biggest tips by analyzing passengers' shoes while polishing them.

To the background of "The St. Louis Blues" Jeff introduces Brutus to his first Harlem club and also to his girl friend Undine (Fredi Washington), whom Brutus proceeds to steal. There follows a montage of the totally unprincipled Brutus' climb up through the Pullman heirarchy. Always humming and singing snatches of "I'm Travellin,' " he is transferred to "The President's" private car, where he tries his hand at a little financial blackmail. Over his head in the white man's world of high finance, Brutus is promptly demoted, but when the more sensible Undine points out this fact, he drops her. Later, in another Harlem club, Brutus and his new date Belle meet Jeff and Undine. Still in love with him, Undine attacks Belle in the middle of the dance floor and Brutus walks out again, "travellin' light."

Another train montage takes Brutus to a Savannah poolroom where heavy betting between himself and Jeff turns up loaded dice. Jeff pulls a knife but is killed by Brutus in the ensuing fight, and Brutus takes flight. The film cuts to Brutus on a chain gang, breaking rocks between breathtaking renditions of "John Henry" and "Water Boy." When a guard tries to harass him into beating a fellow convict, Brutus escapes, to return briefly to his wife for aid.

Always moving, Brutus ends up shoveling coal in a freighter's boiler room, jumps ship, and heads for an inhospitable island (based on Haiti) where he is quickly captured, condemned to jail by the dissolute black leader, and saved by being sold to the sly white trader Smithers (Dudley Digges). Teaching the natives to. play dice, Brutus quickly gambles his way up to a partnership with Smithers.

On a routine trip to the island palace to further bilk the ruling "General," Brutus purposely provokes the palace guard into shooting him. Since the bullets prove harmless to him (he had filled all the guns with blanks), he is able to promote the myth that he is invincible except to a silver bullet. Thus, cowing the superstitious guards, Brutus pulls off a bloodless *coup*, and, admiring himself in a palace mirror, dubs himself "The Emperor Jones."

Brutus is next seen after a two-and-a-half-year period during which he has decorated the palace in mirrors, dressed himself and his attendants in eighteenth century finery, and bled the natives dry and to the edge of revolt. One day, after perpetrating a particularly vicious bit of punishment on the natives, Brutus is awakened by Smithers to find an empty palace, his court and guards having fled during the night. Brutus instantly "resigns the job of Emperor" and takes off to the hills in an attempt to escape to the sea before the native revolutionaries capture him. Dressed in his imperial uniform and carrying only a revolver loaded with six bullets—five lead, and one silver, the latter his charm—Brutus enters the jungle to the steady background beat of the natives' drum.

A masterful monologue by Brutus during his tortuous flight through the jungle keeps the second half of the film very much alive with excitement. As the darkness descends and Brutus cannot find his food stash, the drum beat begins to effect him, and his composure disintegrates. Vignettes from his past life appear to haunt him, and he begins to shoot at his fears: "wild pigs," a crap-shooting Jeff, and the chain gang guard. Hallucinating a service in his old Baptist church, Brutus sings "Daniel in the Lion's Den" and prays for forgiveness. Finally, he imagines he sees a witch doctor who conjures up a crocodile, at which Brutus shoots his last bullet—the silver one. Maddened and shorn of his fine clothes, Brutus is finally driven by the drums into a native ambush. Only when he is killed by a series of silver bullets does the drum stop beating. After expiring in the natives' camp in the presence of their leader, Lem (George Haymid Stamper), and the white trader, Smithers takes his hat off to Brutus, commenting that "yer died in the 'eighth o' style."

Although *The Emperor Jones* may be somewhat dated in its presentation of a black man, it is still tremendously effective as a view of everyman meeting his primal fears and trying to deal with them. It is really a one-man show, however, and Robeson's bravura performance holds the film together and makes it ageless.

The Emperor Jones is acknowledged to be Robeson's finest American film. Because Robeson wanted to break away from the stereotyped roles which he was offered in American films, he began making films in Europe in the 1930's, most notably *Sanders of the River* (1935), produced by British impressario Zoltan Korda. Because even these films turned out to be, in essence, the same type of exploitive films which were made in the United States, Robeson became disenchanted with them as well. His well-publicized affiliation with the Communist Party beginning in the 1930's and other problems created a furor around him which badly hurt his career. His last film was *Tales of Manhattan* (1942), and he died in relative obscurity in 1976 in Philadelphia.

Kathleen Karr

THE ENEMY BELOW

Released: 1957
Production: Dick Powell for Twentieth Century-Fox
Direction: Dick Powell
Screenplay: Wendell Mayes; based on the novel of the same name by D. A.
  Rayner
Cinematography: Harold Rosson
Editing: Stuart Gilmore
Special effects: Walter Rossi (AA)
Running time: 98 minutes

Principal characters:

Captain Murrell	Robert Mitchum
Von Stolberg	Curt Jurgens
Lieutenant Ware	Al (David) Hedison
Schwaffer	Theodore Bikel
Doctor	Russell Collins
Von Holem	Kurt Kreuger
Ensign Merry	Doug McClure

Films featuring men in war most often focus on the direct, face-to-face confrontation aspect of combat, rifles, machine guns, and grenades. Shots of soldiers blowing each other to oblivion make for visually exciting cinema. Often, however, real war can be a game of nerves, of wait-and-see or think-and-outthink-your-adversary strategy. *The Enemy Below*, released in 1957, is not a standard war film since the scenario stresses the strategical, chess-game aspect of war. Outwait the enemy, anticipate his moves, plan a strategy, try to outwit him, and, then, hopefully, checkmate him.

The film is not devoid of violence, as an American destroyer and German U-boat do fire torpedoes and depth charges at each other. Still, it is closer in content to Jean Renoir's *Grand Illusion* (1937), considered by some the greatest film ever made. *The Enemy Below* stresses the respect that two dedicated soldiers can have for each other, even though they are on opposite sides of the battle lines.

Robert Mitchum stars in the film as Murrell, the calm, cool, but haggard captain of the United States destroyer *Haines*. Murrell's nemesis is Von Stolberg (Curt Jurgens, in his American film debut), the war-weary commander of the U-boat. While on patrol in the South Atlantic, the *Haines* makes radar contact with the U-boat, headed for a rendezvous with a Nazi surface raider. Von Stolberg becomes aware of the contact and sets his ship on a zig-zag course in order to evade the *Haines*'s pursuit. Murrell, anticipating Von Stolberg's strategy, holds a steady course. The German thinks he has escaped, but the *Haines* has stayed with the U-boat. Murrell baits Von Stolberg into firing two torpedoes that miss. In response, depth charges are dropped from the *Haines*, but they do not hit their target either. The U-boat sets its course, but the destroyer follows and overtakes it. Von Stolberg lowers his ship to a dangerous depth of 310 meters after more depth charges are dropped. Murrell in turn stops the *Haines*. Both skippers wait out each other in silence.

Finally, Von Stolberg moves. His submarine is followed by the *Haines*, which drops additional depth charges at intervals. The German anticipates the destroyer's position and fires its four remaining torpedoes. One torpedo hits the *Haines*. Murrell orders his crew to set fake fires, assuming correctly, that Von Stolberg will be tricked into surfacing. According to Murrell, this is the "first foolish thing he's done." Now, both ships shoot at each other; both are hit hard and are doomed. The *Haines* finally rams the U-boat, and both Americans and Germans end up sharing the same life boats. Murrell and Von Stolberg face each other from the decks of their respective ships and salute. Murrell helps his adversary escape his sinking boat by throwing him a rope, but Von Stolberg fails to save his mortally wounded second-in-command, Schwaffer (Theodore Bikel). The life boats are picked up by another American destroyer and, at the finale, the two skippers share a cigarette as they gaze out at the sea.

The Enemy Below is based on an actual incident which occurred during World War II. As a suspense drama it is first-rate, with director Dick Powell and screenwriter Wendell Mayes keeping the viewer fully engrossed in the proceedings. The film is primarily noteworthy for its depiction of the German, Von Stolberg, who is not merely the "enemy," an anonymous Nazi submarine commander. As conceived by Mayes and portrayed by Jurgens, he is a fully three-dimensional character, a career soldier trying to do his job to the best of his abilities. Because of this interpretation, *The Enemy Below* could never have been made during the war years when Germany had not yet been defeated. At that time, to keep up morale, Hollywood's war films were propaganda, with patriotic scenarios depicting the Germans and Japanese as dirty "Krauts" and "Nips," vicious sadists killing and maiming eighteen-year-old American draftees who, six months before, had been playing high-school football and who had never set foot east of Kentucky or west of Kansas. By 1957, twelve years after the war had ended, enough time had passed for a German soldier to be presented in an American film as a human being, not a caricature who stomps around yelling "Heil Hitler." Incidentally, the Germans, and Von Stolberg in particular, are no Nazis; the commander is simply a navy man and even spouts some anti-Nazi rhetoric about "the new Germany, a machine." The manner in which the sailors from each ship assist one another in abandoning their respective vessels to the safety of the lifeboats—despite the fact that they are at war and should be killing one another—is touching. Whether by choice or by chance, *The Enemy Below* is an effective commentary on the stupidity and wastefulness of war.

Powell, star of musicals during the 1930's and of mysteries during the mid-1940's, began his career as a director in 1953 with *Split Second*. His other films are *The Conquerer* (1956), *The Hunters* (1958), and *The Enemy Below*. Powell's work is adequate (with the exception of the laughable *The Conquerer*), and *The Enemy Below* is easily his best effort. In particular, he intercuts easily between scenes juxtaposing the commanders of both ships.

Jurgens, Mitchum, and the other members of the all-male cast offer fine performances. Mitchum is a vastly underrated actor who has managed to remain a top star for more than thirty-five years. This film is the first of two he made with Powell. In the other film, *The Hunters*, he plays an ace fighter pilot in the Korean War. Jurgens, originally a journalist in his native Germany, first gained recognition in America playing a Nazi officer who rebels against his party in *The Devil's General* (1955), a role that is not dissimilar to his Von Stolberg. He is a star of the European stage and has become a star and supporting actor in international films.

The Enemy Below was unfortunately a box-office failure, not even ranking among the top ninety-seven grossing films of 1957, according to *Variety*, and earned less than one million dollars. The reviews were good, however; the National Board of Review even named the film to its ten-best list, and *Time* magazine selected it as one of the twelve best films of the year. Also, Walter Rossi's excellent special effects earned him an Academy Award.

Rob Edelman

ENTER THE DRAGON

Released: 1973
Production: Fred Weintraub and Paul Heller; released by Warner Bros.
Direction: Robert Clouse
Screenplay: Michael Allin
Cinematography: Gilbert Hubbs
Editing: Kurt Hirschler and George Watters
Running time: 98 minutes

Principal characters:
Lee .... Bruce Lee
Roper .... John Saxon
Williams ....Jim Kelly
Han .... Shih Kien
Oharra .... Bob Wall
Tania ....Ahna Capri
Su-Lin .... Angela Mao-Ying

Legendary Oriental superstar Bruce Lee made his final screen appearance in *Enter the Dragon*, the first United States-produced martial arts film. Because of Lee's untimely death at the age of thirty-three and the film's status as the most lavishly produced film of its genre (and the first one to be filmed in English), *Enter the Dragon* has come to be regarded by critics and audiences alike as the definitive martial arts film. Its fame has been compounded by the fact that it has attained both cult status and phenomenal box-office success, with worldwide earnings reportedly in excess of one hundred million dollars. Its story line is slim, with an accent on action, notably battles involving the Oriental arts of self defense; the film is also marked by surprisingly strong production values and a capable cast, led by the indomitable Lee.

Appropriately, the film opens with a look at Lee in action, as he displays his pantherlike grace, coupled with deadly skill, during an exhibition. Cast simply as "Lee," a member of an Oriental temple, he is visited by a representative of an agency that "functions as gatherers of information—evidence upon which interested governments can act." Lee, who has been sought out because of his command of the martial arts, is asked to enter an upcoming tournament which will be held on an island fortress. The event's sponsor is Han (Shih Kien), who is suspected of dealing in white slavery and opium, and Lee is asked to locate evidence against him.

For Lee, the assignment is a vendetta. At one time, Han was a member of Lee's temple. By leaving it, Lee feels Han has insulted both the temple and its teachings. Most important, however, is the fact that Han's henchmen were responsible for the death of Su-Lin (Angela Mao Ying), Lee's sister.

En route to the island, which is located near Hong Kong, Lee comes in contact with fellow tournament hopefuls. Through a series of flashbacks delivered in lapse dissolve effects, the audience sees why the principal characters have chosen to participate. Roper (John Saxon), an American with a penchant for gambling, left the United States because of gambling debts totaling $175,000—and a bank account of only $64.43. Williams (Jim Kelly), an American black, had been involved in a fracas with bigoted police officers. For both Roper and Williams, therefore, the tournament provides temporary escape, with the added possibility of financial reward, should they win their bouts. Lee's flashback involves the beautiful Su-Lin, herself a martial arts expert, as she bravely battles to the death. Leading the horde of attackers against the diminutive young woman is Oharra (Bob Wall), Han's right-hand man. Before she dies, Su-Lin is able to scar Oharra's cheek.

Once at the island fortress, tournament participants are feted at an opulent, colorful banquet, complete with Sumo wrestlers. The event is brought to a dramatic, virtual standstill when Han, accompanied by a group of attractive women, makes his entrance. At Han's command, the women display remarkable and deadly dart-throwing skills. Lee recognizes one of the women as an operative for the agency that has hired him.

He is able to talk with the girl personally later that night, after Tania (Ahna Capri), Han's hostess, visits the guests to make sure they are comfortable. Among the pleasures she offers is women. Williams matter-of-factly chooses four women as companions for the night; Roper requests that Tania stay with him, and she is happy to oblige. Lee asks to see the young woman who threw the darts. His interest is strictly professional, and after being summoned to his room, the girl confesses that she has been unable to compile evidence against Han.

It remains for Lee to do the investigating, despite the fact that Han has issued orders that strictly forbid the guests from moving freely about the grounds. Lee's nighttime discoveries lead to a shaft which enters an underground chamber. After lowering himself inside, he locates opium-making facilities. His search is interrupted by the arrival of several guards, but they are overcome by the deft Lee.

Han retaliates the following day during tournament activities. At this point, the viewer has witnessed the considerable skills of Roper and Williams (Williams' style is labeled "unorthodox but effective"), but Lee's talents and reputation remain a mystery to the tournament contenders and Han's soldiers. Lee's skills fairly burst into view when he is paired in deadly battle against Oharra, who bears the ugly scar inflicted by Su-Lin. Although the menacing Oharra dwarfs Lee, Lee moves swiftly, with deadly aim. He culminates the battle by stomping Oharra to death in front of a startled crowd, satisfying his own vengeance. The gory scene, with its combined acrobatics, balletlike beauty, and undeniable violence, gives credence to Lee's statement about his fighting style, "you can call it the art of fighting without fighting."

Following the day's startling competition, Williams is summoned to Han's office. There Han reveals that his tournaments are actually fronts to find salesmen to peddle his illegal wares. "Man, you come right out of a comic book," says a disbelieving Williams. Unwilling to work for Han, Williams then comes up against Han's martial arts prowess. Caught off-guard by a blow from the steel hand worn by Han, Williams is killed. Han next introduces Roper to his illegal operations. On a tour of the underground facilities, Roper is witness to the manufacture of opium, as well as the enslavement of young women who are being forced into drug addiction. Han also escorts Roper through a bizarre, museumlike hall which showcases various vicious murder implements, including a number of "attachments" for Han's hand. Roper shows little emotion during the tour, but he shows his basic goodness when he rescues a cat from death by a guillotine in the museum. After seeing the mutilated body of Williams, he turns against Han, insisting he will never align himself with him.

Through Roper, Lee learns of the workings of Han's organization. Convinced he has the evidence he needs, he decides to send word to the agency, which has promised retaliatory troops. To get a message through, Lee must get into Han's "control room." He accomplishes the mission by slipping a cobra into the room. After the frightened attendants flee, Lee sends word.

Afterward, he is confronted by Han's men—literally dozens of them—all of whom Lee successfully and incredulously battles. The entire island then becomes a battleground after Lee sets free legions of men who have been unjustly imprisoned by Han (they are described as "the refuse found in water-front bars"). Han's prisoners, clad in black, battle his soldiers, who ironically wear white. Roper is among those battling Han's soldiers.

The inevitable battle between Lee and Han follows. It is a grueling, drawn-out affair during which Han (unfairly) replaces his steel hand with a "claw." After a flurry of lightning-fast moves, the claw leaves its mark across Lee's face and bare chest. Prior to a last angry assault, Lee runs his fingers across his wounds. After bringing them to his mouth and dramatically tasting his own blood, he lashes out against Han. The fight, which has taken place in Han's unsettling exhibit hall, comes to an end as Han is impaled on one of his own spears. At film's end, Lee and Roper are the only principals to have survived the bloody melee. The final seconds are devoted to a lingering close-up of the insidious claw worn by Han.

With its liberal dose of blood and gore, along with its rather tawdry qualities, including the white slavery subplot, *Enter the Dragon* is a decidedly exploi-tative work; however, under the taut direction of Robert Clouse, who has wisely chosen to emphasize action and Lee's role, the film emerges as a polished work. For fans of its genre, it is highly diverting, and the martial arts encounters which form the basis of the film are carried out with imagi-native flair. One of the film's most intriguing scenes takes place in a hall of mirrors, during the battle between Lee and Han, which has the antagonist as well as the viewer confused by the multi-image effect. This stunningly-photographed sequence was obviously copied from the mirror funhouse scene of Orson Welles's *Lady from Shanghai*, (1948), but with a clever twist. *Enter the Dragon* also blatantly borrows from other films, including the James Bond series, for in addition to Lee's super-agent status, Han carries a white persian cat, imitative of Bond's archvillain, Ernst Stavro Blofeld. Since directing *Darker than Amber* in 1970, Clouse has come to be known for his fast-paced action films, and in fact has called himself "the poor man's [Sam] Peckinpah." In *Enter the Dragon*, he proves himself particularly adept at showcasing martial arts battles.

Although the film's characterizations are meager, performances are adequate. Saxon, who portrays Roper, has long been underrated, despite his convincing portrayals (often as the heavy, because of his dark, rather sinister good looks), which have been relegated mostly to "B"-pictures. Kelly, in his acting debut as Williams, also proves suitable, coming to the role after establishing himself as a martial arts expert (he was International Middleweight Karate Champion of 1971).

The indisputable highlight of the film, however, is Lee. Hardly an imposing figure in terms of size, with no commanding ability in dialogue delivery (in fact, he speaks with a slight lisp), Lee nevertheless possesses a charismatic screen presence. Audience response to a Lee performance is probably highest when he lets loose one of his famed shrieks (signifying impending attack), and soars across the screen, displaying his prowess with karate, judo, hapkido, tai-chih, or kung fu.

Lee's death of an edema (swelling) of the brain came at the height of his career, thus assuring his cult status, as well as enduring rumors regarding the cause of his death. Ironically, the man who by his very name defined the martial-arts genre was an American by birth, a one-time waiter in a Chinese restaurant and a 4-F army reject.

Lee's credits include a string of Hong Kong-produced films, often made for famed Oriental producer Raymond Chow, including *Fists of Fury* (1972) and *The Chinese Connection* (1973). He also appeared as Kato in the 1966 ABC-television series, *The Green Hornet*. Lee, who staged the impressive fight sequences for *Enter the Dragon*, also supervised stunts and karate sequences in American feature films, including *Marlowe* and *The Wrecking Crew* (both in 1969).

Years after his death, the Lee legend persists. Numerous martial arts films have attempted to summon up the Lee presence, including *The Black Dragon Revenges the Death of Bruce Lee* (released in London in 1979). Perhaps the most peculiar "Bruce Lee film" is *Game of Death*. Released six years after Lee's death, the film contains fight footage of the actual Lee, but story line sequences utilize two Lee look-alikes. Films such as this one give impetus to the various Lee myths, especially the one that proclaims that Lee still lives.

Pat H. Broeske

THE ENTERTAINER

Released: 1960
Production: Harry Saltzman for British Lion Films in association with Bryanston Films
Direction: Tony Richardson
Screenplay: John Osborne and Nigel Kneale; based on the play of the same name by John Osborne
Cinematography: Oswald Morris
Editing: Alan Osbitson
Music: John Addison
Running time: 96 minutes

Principal characters:
Archie Rice	Laurence Olivier
Phoebe Rice	Brenda De Banzie
Jean Rice	Joan Plowright
Billy Rice	Roger Livesey
Frank Rice	Alan Bates
Graham	Daniel Massey
Mick Rice	Albert Finney
Tina	Shirley Anne Field

The Entertainer is a controversial film and the only X-rated one in which Laurence Olivier has appeared. Its representation of the death and decay of vaudeville in the person of Archie Rice (Laurence Olivier) can be seen as an allegory for the decay of Great Britain in the 1950's.

Set in a seedy coastal resort in the south of England, the film opens with Archie's daughter Jean (Joan Plowright) down from London on a visit to her father, a down-and-out vaudeville performer, her stepmother Phoebe (Brenda de Banzie), who is losing herself in movies and gin, and her grandfather Billy Rice (Roger Livesay), a has-been who was once a famous and talented vaudevillian. A fight with her fiancé Graham (Daniel Massey) has prompted Jean's sudden visit. Jean's stepbrother Mick (Albert Finney), away at war, had been taken prisoner but is now being released. This incident sets up an emotional crisis in the family, but also brings them all together for a few days. The nightly parties celebrating Mick's release and pending return turn into ugly, drunken rows, reminiscences of better times, and bitter reprisals for the current state of affairs.

Each member of the family has his or her memories and disappointments. Phoebe, who is bored and frustrated by Archie's continual affairs and escapes the drudgery of daily life through drink, desires nothing more than to be treated kindly and live among people who are not destitute and disillusioned. Billy, the ex-vaudevillian, spends his time reading the evening paper, smoking cigarettes, sighing for "the good old days," and suffering the patronage of his son, Archie. Archie, perhaps, is the most frustrated one of them all. A mediocre talent living under the shadow of his famous father, Archie is desperately trying to subsist in a third-rate show entitled *Rock and Roll New'd Look*. In the numerous variety-hall numbers, we are allowed to see that Archie has no rapport with his working-class audience. What he desires most is to get up on stage and make a beautiful, spontaneous, joyful "fuss," just like a blues singer he had once seen. He feels that if he could do something that good just once in his life, it would make everything else worthwhile. Meanwhile he spends his days drinking, having affairs, and feeling degraded.

At one of the nightly parties, one of the most heartrending scenes occurs. Billy, feeling hungry, heads into the kitchen and eats a piece of cake. Unfortunately, that cake was one which Phoebe had bought with her scanty savings for Mick's return, and the verbal abuse and pain which follow are typical of the entire movie.

With the unexpected death of Mick overseas, Archie crumbles. This, however, provides the emotional release which enables him finally to sing the blues, to make a beautiful "fuss." Mick's death and the approaching threat of the tax man becomes too much for him, however, and in a desperate attempt to escape, Archie becomes involved with a young local girl named Tina (Shirley Anne Field), the second-prize winner in a beauty contest for which he is master of ceremonies. Thoughts of marriage even enter Archie's head, but his feelings of hope are shattered when Billy informs the girl's family of Archie's wife and three children. As atonement, Billy provides an alternative means of escape. He agrees to go back into show business, with the hope that his name will provide the necessary draw to bolster Archie's sagging show and ward off the creditors. Billy's return proves too much for him, however, and he dies in the wings without ever making an appearance.

Archie is left to face the tax man alone. Although he has an opportunity to manage a hotel in Canada, Archie feels that Canada would be too far removed from everything he has ever known and chooses to remain an entertainer and perhaps retain a little honor.

The Entertainer was first a stage play written by John Osborne, one of England's "angry young men" and a very anti-Establishment writer. *The Entertainer* was chosen by the English Stage Company (founded in 1956 and housed in the Royal Court Theatre) as one of the new plays it wanted to produce. George Devine, a founder of the company, was a good friend of Olivier, and it was through him that Olivier approached the idea of appearing in Osborne's play.

This move required considerable courage on Olivier's part because it caused a good deal of furor. Olivier's appearance in a non-Establishment play might have cost him the approval of his influential and highly placed friends. Although he was warned of the risk of placing his reputation in the care of relatively inexperienced talents, however, Olivier was nevertheless ready to gamble on a dramatic change of direction. It is Olivier's involvement which gives an air of respectability to Osborne's play.

In addition to the disapproval he had to face, Olivier had to counter doubts as to whether an actor of his power and prestige could convincingly play a broken-down, third-rate vaudevillian. To dispel these doubts, Olivier, who already had a keen sense of identification with the character, frequented the old Collins Music Hall in Islington, watching the variety show of nudes and rock-and-roll and quizzing the showgirls. The owners were so honored that they put up a commemorative plaque.

At one point, Olivier's wife Vivien Leigh was considered for the part of Phoebe (she was to wear a rubber mask to disguise her good looks), but the idea was abandoned, perhaps because of Olivier's crumbling marriage. In 1961, the year after the film was released, they were divorced, and Olivier married Joan Plowright, who plays Jean in the film. De Banzie was eventually chosen to play Phoebe, reviving her role from the original stage version.

The film's director, Tony Richardson, also directed the play *The Entertainer*, which opened at the Royal Court Theatre in London in 1957. A comparatively young, inexperienced, and unknown talent, Richardson had previously directed the stage version of Osborne's *Look Back in Anger* and would go on to direct the 1969 stage version of *Hamlet* and such films as *The Loneliness of the Long Distance Runner* (1962) and *Tom Jones* (1963). The latter film again teamed Richardson with the composer John Addison and with actor Albert Finney, who had a bit part as young Mick Rice in *The Entertainer*.

Osborne's play was considerably expanded for the film version. The part of Jean was developed more, while the addition of the character Tina, created cinematic allure. The fact that Osborne wrote the script for the film assured that the film's changes would be in keeping with the original tone of the play. The result was an incredibly poetic and literate script which is one of the outstanding features of the movie.

Production values for *The Entertainer* are excellent; meticulous care was taken with every aspect of the film. The music, cinematography, sets, and costumes all combine to produce a very real atmosphere of seediness, despair, and decay. Olivier's makeup, as usual, is impressive. The character becomes a leering, sad, broken-down old man in a tacky checked suit and bow tie. Olivier, it was rumored, even went to the extreme of having his own teeth filed down to achieve the very odd set of teeth belonging to Archie. The makeup and physical aspect of Archie was so important to the story that even twenty years later, a photograph of Olivier in costume for the film is immediately identifiable.

It is Olivier's acting, however, which above all dominates and carries the film. It is a widely held opinion that Archie Rice is one of Olivier's greatest performances outside of the classics. Olivier himself has named it one of his favorites. Certainly, he manages to capture the essence of Archie, making him a credible, understandable, and sympathetic character, even if a pitiable one. Olivier even captures the mediocrity of the music-hall numbers, the possibility of talent numbed by fatigue and disillusionment, and he gives the audience the real man behind the entertainer, a man frustrated, disappointed, tired, and broken-hearted.

Standing up under Olivier's almost overpowering presence is an outstanding supporting cast. Headed by such well-known British character actors as de Banzie and Livesey, excellent as Phoebe and Billy, the cast also boasts an array of talented young newcomers who were to go on to become stars in their own right, including Plowright, Alan Bates (as Jean's stepbrother Frank), and Finney.

It was Olivier, nevertheless, who received most of the attention of the critics. Reaction was very strong; critics either loved Olivier and hated the film, or the reverse. Olivier's performance was powerful enough to earn him an Academy Award nomination, although he lost to Burt Lancaster for *Elmer Gantry*.

A later televised version of *The Entertainer* starring Jack Lemmon as Archie Rice, Ray Bolger as Billy, Sada Thompson as Phoebe, and Tyne Daly and Michael Christopher as the children is excellent on its own but does not stand up to the level of the 1960 film, which is undeniably a classic, owing to Olivier's monumental performance.

Grace Anne Morsberger

ENTERTAINING MR. SLOANE

Released: 1970
Production: Douglas Kentish for Canterbury Films/Anglo-Amalgamated-EMI
Direction: Douglas Hickox
Screenplay: Clive Exton; based on the play of the same name by Joe Orton
Cinematography: Wolfgang Suschitzky
Editing: John Trumper
Running time: 94 minutes

Principal characters:
Kath .... Beryl Reid
Ed .... Harry Andrews
Mr. Sloane .... Peter McEnery
Kemp ('Dadda') .... Alan Webb

"It's just a *play*," author Joe Orton declared about his 1964 work, "which happens to make people laugh about sodomy and nymphomania." *Entertaining Mr. Sloane* opened in a London fringe theater in May of 1964 and quickly transferred to the West End, where it was a great commercial success and won the 1964 "Best Play" award. Even in the "swinging sixties," sodomy and nymphomania were not really the safest of subjects for discussion, let alone for a comedy, and it was another five years before the movie version of *Entertaining Mr. Sloane* went into production. In the meantime Orton had been battered to death in his sleep by what the press cautiously called his "room-mate," who then went on to commit suicide himself. This event, together with the movie's calculatedly outrageous theme, may well account for the reason that *Entertaining Mr. Sloane* became something of a cult success in the United States.

In Britain, the film opened to polite but unenthusiastic reviews, somewhat overshadowed by the simultaneous opening of Luigi Visconti's much-heralded *The Damned*, which handled similar themes in a much more artistic fashion, and ran for only three weeks in the West End despite the prestigious (but under the circumstances slightly inappropriate) send-off of a Royal Premiere in the presence of Princess Margaret. In New York, however, where the stage production had run for a mere thirteen performances, the movie opened in July, 1970, to excellent notices. Roger Greenspun in *The New York Times* spoke of "a production of an excellence that in this world not even the intellectually fashionable can normally expect"; Penelope Gilliatt devoted her entire *New Yorker* column to it, and Stefan Kantner in *Time* called it a "savagely witty success." Like a later cult movie, *The Rocky Horror Picture Show* (1976), *Entertaining Mr. Sloane* triumphed on the stage and flopped in the cinema in its native Britain, but flopped on the stage and became a cult movie success in the United States.

Screenwriter Clive Exton has done some judicious pruning of Orton's stage original, opening it up a little—notably at the beginning and the end—and adding a few lines of his own which are largely indistinguishable from Orton's. He has preserved almost intact the flavor of Orton's language, a wonderfully stilted flow of florid verbiage which buries the most perverted of concepts beneath a frosting of genteely proper euphemisms. Orton professed himself an admirer of playwright Oscar Wilde, and lines such as Kath's fanciful description of her supposedly sheltered childhood ("I'd the upbringing a nun would envy and that's the truth. Until I was fifteen I was more familiar with Africa than with my own body") or the equally fanciful picture Sloane gives of the pastimes of his departed parents ("You know, H. P. debts. Bridge. A little light gardening. The usual activities of a cultured community") have very much the ring of a mid-twentieth century Oscar Wilde.

Kath (Beryl Reid), a "mature" blonde given to wandering around the cemetery adjacent to her home in a diaphanous dress, one day comes across Mr. Sloane (Peter McEnery), a very decorative young man sunbathing on top of a tombstone. Leaning across him in casual provocation—"I'm quite *eminent* above the waist, as I expect you've noticed" (an Exton line)—Kath invites Sloane back and offers him a room in the house. Sloane encounters immediate hostility from Kath's father, Kemp (Alan Webb)—known as "the Dadda"— a totally disgusting old man whose appetite for vice has largely wilted, but who thinks he recognizes in Sloane the man who murdered his former boss, a porno photographer. Tormented by Sloane (who knows the Dadda's eyesight is too poor for his identification ever to be a real threat), Kemp lances him in the leg with a garden fork. Kath soon has Sloane's jeans off to tend the wound, noting with innocent awe that the hair on his leg (brown) is a different color from that on his head (blonde): "Isn't nature wonderful?" she marvels. The idyll is interrupted by the arrival of Kath's brother Ed (Harry Andrews), a successful businessman to whom the Dadda has not spoken in twenty years, ever since, shortly after Ed's seventeenth birthday, he "had cause to return home unexpected and found him committing some kind of felony in the bedroom." Ed is firmly opposed to the idea of Kath taking in a lodger until he actually catches sight of Mr. Sloane. Sloane is quick to reassure him about his healthy athletic interests, and before long Ed, too, is under his spell, solicitously inquiring whether he ever wears leather "next to the skin? Leather jeans, say? Without . . . . aah . . . ." "Pants?" supplies Sloane helpfully. Ed offers him a job as his chauffeur.

Sloane happily settles into his new home, playing both ends against the middle, but he has misjudged his "victims." Ed is unhappy about Sloane's tendency to go joy-riding in his "motor," but easily mollified by Sloane's offer to move in with him—until the Dadda breaks his twenty-year silence to tell him that Kath is pregnant. At first much put out by the news—"What attracted you? Did she give trading stamps?"—Ed is won round by Sloane's repentance. Left alone with the old man, Sloane thoughtfully kicks him to death. This brings the battle to "entertain" Mr. Sloane to a head: if Sloane goes off with Ed (whose grief at his father's death is soon assuaged by a gently reassuring hand on the knee from his chauffeur), Kath will report the murder to the police, but if Sloane stays with Kath, Ed will report it.

In the end they come to the perfect solution. The Dadda "fell downstairs" (Kath thoughtfully polishes the linoleum at the stairhead and puts the Dadda's new shoes with the slippery soles on the corpse), and Kath and Ed agree to share Mr. Sloane on a half-yearly basis until he is no longer serviceable. Sloane's schemes collapse around him. The movie ends with a marriage ceremony (not in the original play) in which, with the aid of a prayer book wrested from the rapidly stiffening fingers of the Dadda, Ed solemnizes Sloane's marriage to Kath, and Kath his marriage to Ed, after which they plant kisses on opposite cheeks.

In his feature debut (and his only film to win much acclaim), director Douglas Hickox has managed the business of bringing Orton's play to the screen with skill and inventiveness. *Entertaining Mr. Sloane* is, of course, a very talky film, but Hickox captures for most of the time the balance between the overblown dialogue and the rather ordinary British middle-class settings. He is enormously helped in this by Michael Seymour's main set, a cozy Gothic villa whose exterior is to be found in real life nestling amid the gravestones of London's Camberwell Old Cemetery. Hickox's style is very much marked by his television advertising experience, showing a fondness for extreme close-ups, accelerated editing, and idiosyncratic camera set-ups. Often this blends in very nicely with the baroque extravagance of Orton's language. Particularly effective is the opening scene in the cemetery. In long shot we solemnly observe a vicar officiating at a funeral. The solemnity is somewhat undermined when the damp earth sticks to his fingers as he tries to sprinkle it on the coffin, but is still preserved as the camera pans across to a piously heaving female bosom with a little gold cross suspended on it. At this point the pious solemnity is broken forever as a phallic red popsicle comes suddenly up into focus and precedes upward, to the deafening crunch of Kath's teeth being sunk into it. Less successful, however, are the frenzied angles and distortions of the scene in which Sloane murders the Dadda—a moment which tips *Entertaining Mr. Sloane* dangerously close to horror.

In the final analysis, *Entertaining Mr. Sloane* is an actor's movie. In this respect it is beyond reproach. McEnery is seductively murderous as Sloane, while Webb is the exact opposite—innocent, but totally repulsive—as the vindictive old Dadda. Andrews, an actor whose reputation was, and is, based on tough military roles, is perfect as Ed, never giving way to a temptation to campiness. Above all, Reid carries the film with her hideously rounded vowels, her archly suggestive looks, and her appearance, as one critic put it, of "a blancmange struggling for the respectable status of apple pie."

Entertaining Mr. Sloane is unlikely to be a film that will ever appeal to everyone, but it is also never a film for specialist tastes: in no sense does it belong in the sexual ghetto. It is a wittily scripted, solidly directed, and superbly acted comedy which "happens to make people laugh about sodomy and nymphomania."

Nick Roddick

EVERGREEN

Released: 1934
Production: Michael Balcon for Gaumont British
Direction: Victor Saville
Screenplay: Marjorie Gaffney; based on the play *Ever Green* by Benn W. Levy and adapted with dialogue by Emlyn Williams
Cinematography: Glen MacWilliams
Editing: Ian Dalrymple
Art direction: Alfred Junge
Costume design: Berleo
Choreography: Buddy Bradley
Sound: A. F. Birch
Music direction: Louis Levy, with the Gaumont British Studio Orchestra conducted by Bretton Byrd
Music: Harry Woods, Richard Rodgers, and Lorenz Hart
Running time: 90 minutes

Principal characters:
Harriet Green/Harriet Hawkes	Jessie Matthews
Leslie Benn	Sonnie Hale
Maudie	Betty Balfour
Tommy Thompson	Barry MacKay
Marquis of Staines	Ivor Maclaren
George Treadwell	Hartley Power
Lord Shropshire	Patrick Ludlow
Mrs. Hawkes	Betty Shale
Marjorie Moore	Marjorie Brooks

Evergreen was old-fashioned even in 1934, and time has not been kind to its ancient plot. On the night that music-hall star Harriet Green (Jessie Matthews) retires from the stage to marry the Marquis of Staines (Ivor MacLaren), George Treadwell (Hartley Power), the father of the daughter she has kept hidden from the public, turns up to blackmail her. She flees to South Africa where she eventually dies. Twenty-five years later, the daughter, Harriet Hawkes (also Jessie Matthews), arrives at a London theater to audition for a spot in the chorus. Her resemblance to her famous mother is spotted immediately by Tommy Thompson (Barry MacKay), a publicity man desperate for an angle to draw attention to a new show by Leslie Benn (Sonnie Hale). Despite the fact that the real Harriet Green would be almost sixty, Harriet is passed off with no trouble as her own ever-youthful mother to a public clamoring to see their favorite star again. The aged Marquis of Staines turns up to resume his courtship, believing that Tommy is the child Harriet told him she was leaving him to care for. The Marquis rents a house for them to share, a situation which causes Tommy and Harriet a certain amount of embarrassment. *Harriet Green and Son*, Benn's new review, opens with Tommy singing and dancing alongside his "mother." The Marquis confesses that he was not fooled by Harriet's masquerade—he was just delighted to see her again, and as Harriet dances and sings to "Over My Shoulder," she "strips" away her disguise and is revealed at last as Harriet Hawkes to the very real pleasure of the audience. Harriet is tried for attempting to defraud the public, but her lawyer proves that since she performs as well as her mother and her name really *is* Harriet Green, no deception has taken place. Harriet wins her case and is free to marry Tommy.

Musicals have never been the kind of thing at which British filmmakers excel; they are more successful with psychological melodramas (*The Seventh Veil*, 1946, and *Dead of Night*, 1946), comedies (the Alec Guinness films of the 1950's), and romances (*I Know Where I'm Going*, 1947, and *The L-Shaped Room*, 1963). This musical is leaden and awkward except when Matthews is onscreen, and even she is not used very effectively until she wafts her way through the "Dancing on the Ceiling" number. Matthews carries the entire film with her charm, perkiness, and resilience, her round face, wide eyes, and cupid's bow mouth pouting over prominent teeth. Her singing is not great, but she dances like a feather in the wind, and her apotheosis comes in "Dancing on the Ceiling." Flinging her legs into the air, arching her back, and twirling through the cavernous house MacLaren has rented for her, she is girlishly, seductively innocent. It seems there is nothing her body cannot do, yet her antics are not contorted or bizarre; they appear to be the natural expression of her youthful high spirits. She is like an English Ann Miller, more ladylike, less vulgar, good-humored, plucky, and ready for anything. The other numbers, from "Daddy Wouldn't Buy Me a Bow-Wow" to "Over My Shoulder" (the title of Matthews' autobiography), are rather ridiculous by modern standards.

The supporting cast is predictable. Hale (Matthews' husband) looks like a British Harpo Marx from his floppy blond curls to his maniacally toothy grin, but his age makeup for the scenes set in the present is unfortunately obvious. MacKay is the perfect male ingenue, dim-witted, ambitious, stalwart, and greedy. He has a male mannequin's good looks and the personality of a newt. Betty Balfour is chirpily helpful as the heroine's best friend, and MacLaren is an appropriately doting old fogey—all good intentions and sexless adoration—as the abandoned fiancé.

The musical numbers are strange. "When You've Got a Little Springtime in Your Heart" is separated into several sections divided by the whirling of a huge hour glass. One part is like a dance version of *Metropolis* (1926) with robots on an assembly line standing inside halves of enormous torpedoes. A huge bomb apparatus descends to enclose myriad girls parading on the line and ascends to reveal each one transformed into a soldier. It is a ballet-mechanique, soulless, unmusical, and pointless. Matthews rehearses "Tinkle,

Tinkle, Tinkle" in pleated tulle, bouncing madly around a rehearsal room, and in "Over My Shoulder" a queue of plump-thighed chorines clunk in circles in an imitation of a Busby Berkeley ballet. The set is huge, but the choreography is almost boring, and nothing can animate it until Matthews whirls onstage to reveal herself as Harriet Hawkes. Compared to the inspired, lunatic work the real Berkeley was doing in this country at the same time, or the effervescent and by now immortal routines of Fred Astaire and Ginger Rogers, *Evergreen*'s numbers seem to be performed by elephants and staged by automatons. (Oddly enough, producer Michael Balcon had wanted Fred Astaire, who was appearing in London at the time, to star with Matthews in *Evergreen*, but his American studio, RKO, would not release him from his contract. Had Astaire been in the film it would certainly have had a different look, since he left his indelible mark on any film in which he danced.)

Only when the magical Matthews is onscreen is *Evergreen* truly alive. Matthews, who was known as "The Dancing Divinity," was one of the biggest musical stars of the British theater, and later of British films. Her success in *Evergreen* led to a contract offer from M-G-M to come to the United States, but obligations in England made that move impossible.

The box-office success of *Evergreen* seems rather odd now because of the trite story and unusual staging, but the appeal of Matthews, coupled with a handful of good Richard Rodgers and Lorenzo Hart tunes, made it a success, if not a classic.

Judith M. Kass

EXCALIBUR

Released: 1981
Production: John Boorman for Orion
Direction: John Boorman
Screenplay: John Boorman and Rospo Pallenberg; based on the chronicle *Le Morte d'Arthur* by Sir Thomas Malory
Cinematography: Alex Thomson
Editing: Donn Cambern
Production design: Anthony Pratt
Running time: 140 minutes

Principal characters:
King Arthur .... Nigel Terry
Morgana .... Helen Mirren
Lancelot .... Nicholas Clay
Guinevere .... Cherie Lunghi
Perceval .... Paul Geoffrey
Merlin ....Nicol Williamson
Mordred .... Robert Addie

In the wake of the space epics that domninated film theater marquees and box-office figures in the late 1970's, a return to the medieval myths and legends which had spawned them seemed almost inevitable. Yet the chronology is misleading, since *Excalibur* had been a cherished project for producer-director John Boorman for nearly a decade. The film bears very much the appearance of a personal work—too personal, some critics felt. Unlike more or less calculated exploitation pieces such as *Dragonslayer* (1981) which were released around the same time, its commercial timeliness was largely fortuitous. Not, of course, that this did any harm to *Excalibur's* box-office prospects: opening in March, 1981, to slightly mixed notices, it was nevertheless one of the runaway commercial successes of the spring season.

The film deals with the legend of King Arthur and the Knights of the Round Table. It is not, of course, by any means the first film to do so. Among others, there was a musical version of Mark Twain's *A Connecticut Yankee at King Arthur's Court* with Bing Crosby in 1949; a sword and shield epic, *Knights of the Round Table*, with Robert Taylor in 1953; a tepid film version of the Alan Jay Lerner and Frederick Loewe musical *Camelot* in 1967; and an austerely beautiful *Lancelot du Lac* by French director Robert Bresson in 1974. With the exception of Bresson's film—to which *Excalibur* bears a certain resemblance—almost all the versions have tended to treat the legend as a romantic fairy tale with bold knights, beautiful damsels, and courtly dancing. The Knights of the Round Table had become the ultimate repository for nostalgia, denizens of a lost age when values were still pure and decisions made with clarity and honor. Boorman's *Excalibur* could not be further removed from this world of pop-up picture books: a brooding, violent, shimmeringly beautiful film, it deals with the raw material of legend. Partly inspired by Boorman's reading of J. R. R. Tolkien's classic novel *The Lord of the Rings*, it is a journey into the dream time, and, like most dreams, its images and discoveries are as often dark as they are light.

The first screenplay was a solo effort by Boorman himself, based on *Le Morte d'Arthur* by Sir Thomas Malory. Malory was, in Boorman's words, "the first hack." Commissioned to write something for the English printer William Caxton, he pieced together a string of familiar myths and legends. Boorman's screenplay tackled this built-in element of myth. His *Excalibur* does not simply tell a story, it tells a story which has meant a great deal to numerous people over a long period of time. More than an adventure yarn, it is one of the sources of human memory. After the disappearance of Merlin near the end of the film, Arthur says: "Merlin lives. He lives in our dreams now." It could be the theme for the entire film.

The final screenplay of *Excalibur* is jointly credited to Boorman and Rospo Pallenberg, a former collaborator who helped him with certain insuperable problems. It consists of four fairly distinct parts, with little or no indication of the passage of time: we move forward fifteen or twenty years without any of the usual transitional devices, often without either a cut or a dissolve. In a kind of prologue, Uther Pendragon agrees to make peace with his enemy the Duke of Cornwall in return for a magic sword, Excalibur, from his necromancer Merlin (Nicol Williamson). The peace is broken, however, when Uther lusts after Cornwall's wife, Igrayne. He persuades Merlin to spirit him into Cornwall's castle transformed into Igrayne's husband. Merlin's price is the child of the union, which he duly exacts nine months later. Uther is killed in an ambush, and as he dies, he buries Excalibur in a stone. Years later, in the first part of the legend proper, young Arthur (Nigel Terry), who is now squire to an impoverished knight, effortlessly extracts the sword from the stone and is hailed as king. With Merlin's help, he pacifies the land and takes Guinevere (Cherie Lunghi) as his queen. Invincible because of Excalibur, Arthur is nevertheless almost bested by a young French knight, Lancelot (Nicholas Clay), and in the end has to abuse Excalibur's power to avoid being defeated. The sword shatters. Horrified by his own trickery, he begs forgiveness. The sword is restored to him by the Lady of the Lake, and Lancelot becomes his champion.

In the third part of the film, the peace and stability of the Court of the Round Table is threatened by inactivity and purposelessness. Lancelot falls in love with Guinevere and they make love, but he leaves rather than threaten his best friend, Arthur. At the same time, Arthur's half-sister Morgana (Helen Mirren), Igrayne's legitimate daughter, is beginning to realize her own magic powers and ends by vanquishing Merlin. Disguised as Guinevere, she also seduces Arthur and conceives a child by him. The final part of the film concerns the Quest for the Grail (the cup from which Christ drank at the Last Supper). By the time that Perceval (Paul Geoffrey) returns with it and its secret—that Arthur and the land are one—Camelot has crumbled into ruin, Guinevere has retired to a convent, and Morgana and her son Mordred (Robert Addie) are the power in the land. Regenerated by the Grail, Arthur rides out with his remaining knights, to be joined at the final moment by Lancelot. Both Arthur and Mordred are killed in the battle, and, as Arthur's body is borne off on a boat into the sunset, Perceval obeys his command to return Excalibur to the Lady of the Lake—until "one day a king will come and the sword will rise again."

Filmed entirely on location in Ireland, *Excalibur* is one of the most beautiful films ever made. Its beauty, however, unlike many of the cinematically beautiful films of the 1970's, comes from altering and enhancing the shades and textures of nature, not from merely capturing them. Each scene has a dominant color value, whether it be the steam-filled orange of the opening skirmish; the clear, shimmering light of the Round Table scenes; or the lowering red of the final confrontation between Arthur and Mordred, a twisted mound of horses and humans. Enormous attention has been paid to details of setting and costume, especially to the knights' armor, which glints beautifully in the candlelight of Arthur and Guinevere's wedding without ever giving the impression of being anything other than heavy, inflexible metal. One scene, perhaps, sums up Boorman's control of the visual imagery of the film. Shortly after pulling the sword from the stone, Arthur follows Merlin off into the forest for advice. Merlin tells him about the dragon which, in Boorman's version, seems to owe more to Japanese mythology than to the usual medieval legend. It is not a single, fearsome creature, but is "in everything and is everything," an ever-present pantheistic force of good *and* evil. The dragon, indeed, symbolizes the old gods who are being forced out of the world by the one God. *Excalibur* is set at the dawn of Christianity. As Merlin sits in the nighttime forest, his eyes glow red and the forest comes alive. A snake coils down from a tree, an owl stares at Arthur, and insects move across the bark. The imagery of *Excalibur* is as rich as that of a medieval Book of Hours.

In some ways, the characters in the film are submerged into the legend: "I was not born to live a man's life but to be the stuff of future memories," Arthur tells Perceval when he has understood the lesson of the Grail. Until this is understood, the characters seem to be well below our expectation of the figures of myth and legend: Arthur is an uncoordinated youth given to outbursts of anger, Perceval is an eager, gangling lad, and Merlin often seems no more than a rather fey court entertainer. Yet Boorman's direction of actors here, as in *Zardoz* (1973), is designed to show ordinary, not especially impressive people becoming the figures of legend through the intervention of extraordinary outside forces (Merlin, Excalibur, the Grail).

Gradually and inexorably, *Excalibur* creates the world of myth before our eyes. Although absent in the opening scenes, by the end it suffuses the entire frame. It is not the adventure-packed world of the Saturday afternoon matinee so frequently pastiched by American directors of the 1970's generation, but a world apart: the "Dark Ages," a view of "what was and the dream of what could be" which Arthur rides out to defend at the end. *Excalibur* relates to many other Boorman films, in which time and again the central characters are forced to rise above circumstances that they had vaguely foreseen but had in no sense truly anticipated. *Deliverance* (1972) is the most obvious example, but all of his prior films contain elements of the same growth. *Excalibur* is perhaps the logical outcome, showing men in extreme circumstances rising to heights which will become "the stuff of future memories." Like all memories, *Excalibur* exists simultaneously in the present and in the past: with the thing remembered and with the process of remembering. Dealing explicitly with the sources of the legend *and* its ramifications, it is probably the definitive Arthurian film.

Nick Roddick

EXECUTIVE SUITE

Released: 1954
Production: John Houseman for Metro-Goldwyn-Mayer
Direction: Robert Wise
Screenplay: Ernest Lehman; based on the novel of the same name by Cameron Hawley
Cinematography: George J. Folsey
Editing: Ralph E. Winters
Running time: 104 minutes

Principal characters:
McDonald Walling .... William Holden
Mary Blemond Walling .... June Allyson
Julia O. Treadway .... Barbara Stanwyck
Loren Phineas Shaw .... Fredric March
Frederick Y. Alderson .... Walter Pidgeon
Eva Bardeman .... Shelley Winters
Josiah Walter Dudley .... Paul Douglas
George Nyle Caswell .... Louis Calhern
Jesse Q. Grimm .... Dean Jagger
Erica Martin .... Nina Foch

The film *Executive Suite* introduced a new direction in post-Depression era success or corruption stories. American audiences had grown familiar with the stories of individuals born into families ravaged by economic chaos who, with intelligence and hard work, rose to success. Unlike the cynical examination of one man's rise to success and power such as Orson Welles's *Citizen Kane* (1941), *Executive Suite* concerns a team of men. This new theme was consistent with the shape of big business two decades after the Depression. Seldom before had there been a motion picture that had exploited the rivalries and the jockeying for position among the highest executives of American corporate business as in this film.

Ernest Lehman wrote the screenplay, based on a Cameron Hawley novel. Hawley had been the advertising director of the Armstrong Cork Company in Pennsylvania until he left his job, apparently, to write the book. The novel offered the reader an inside look at the workings of big business. After Metro-Goldwyn-Mayer acquired the screen rights, producer John Houseman enlisted the directional talents of Robert Wise and amassed a crowded billing of big-name stars. Houseman's previous hits, *The Bad and the Beautiful* (1952) and *Julius Caesar* (1953), were also made with large star casts, and it was all part of a relatively new Hollywood trend designed to increase box-office potential in the new television age.

In the opening scenes, the president of Treadway Corporation, Avery Bullard, having sent a telegram calling for a 6:00 P.M. Executive Board meeting, walks out of the office and promptly falls down dead. Although Treadway is a fifty-year-old company and America's third largest manufacturer of fine furniture, Bullard had been running a one-man operation and had never appointed an Executive Vice President. Suddenly, the one-man company is left without its one man, and the situation sets off a competitive search for a successor among the Board of Directors. The ensuing drama brings together seven diverse personalities, and virtually all of the action occurs within a twenty-four-hour period between two 6:00 P.M. meetings.

The audience is introduced to the directors at the meeting originally called for by the deceased president. George Caswell (Louis Calhern) is the cynical member. He had witnessed Bullard's death and immediately ordered his broker to sell the bulk of his Treadway stock short before the market closed; he thinks that he will make a huge profit when he buys it back after the price drops. Fred Alderson (Walter Pidgeon) is an old, seasoned Vice President. He was around from the beginning and helped to build the company as Bullard's right-arm man. Another old-timer, Production Manager Jesse Grimm (Dean Jagger), originally built the factory. He is now disheartened, and, had Bullard been present, he would have resigned at the meeting. Walter Dudley (Paul Douglas) is Chief of Sales, and a rather ineffectual person who is threatened by his position. He is having an affair with his secretary, Eva (Shelley Winters). Julia Treadway (Barbara Stanwyck), whose father founded the company, is the major stockholder. Threatening to dispose of her holdings has been the only way she could capture the attention of Bullard, with whom she had been in love for many years, although they never married. Loren Shaw (Fredric March) and Don Walling (William Holden) are the two most fully-developed characters. Shaw is the champion efficiency expert who devotes himself to convenience and improved earnings. The young Chief of Design and Development, Don Walling, is the spokesman for corporate morality. He wants to rebuild the earliest dreams of the company: to make the best product.

The plot proceeds rapidly. It is revealed to the viewer that Loren Shaw is fighting the most aggressively for the top position. Shaw is mechanical and conniving; he understands each man's weaknesses and he plays on them. Because of his unsympathetic yet efficient actions, Treadway lost no money after Bullard's death. George Caswell, therefore, lost a great deal by selling his stock. Shaw knows this and buys Caswell's vote with a promise of a large stock gift. He knows about Walt Dudley's affair with Eva, and, with an unstated threat of exposure, secures Dudley's vote as well. In another display of conniving, he gives fatherly sympathy to the distraught Julia Treadway and obtains her proxy. The others are vehemently opposed to his obvious aspiration, but cannot find another nomination.

It becomes understood that Fred Alderson is a perennial second man. He has always been number two, and is by his nature of that caste; he knows that Avery Bullard never considered him as a candidate. Don Walling maintains ideological contentions that are similar to Alderson's, and the two men band together. They fail to make a candidate of Jesse Grimm when they learn of his intention to resign, and they soon discover that Shaw has manipulated their second choice, Walter Dudley. Don Walling, the obvious choice from the start, is the only man left. Grimm, who does not like Walling, supports him to prevent the election of Loren Shaw. Walling has an argument with the indifferent Miss Treadway, and, for the first time ever, she appears at the six o'clock meeting. Without her proxy, Shaw's three votes are not enough to elect. In the end, Don Walling's passionate, idealistic oration wins Julia's approval, and her vote elects him, while causing the corporate demise of Mr. Shaw.

The fast-paced, highly involved plot is emblematic of the production's overall slickness. George Folsey's cinematography is unobtrusive, merely recording each portrait of a conversation, and it was nominated for an Oscar. There is neither a musical score nor any vigorous action, making the production rely almost entirely on the dialogue and the actors' abilities to pull it off. Dramatically, the film is fairly successful. March's portrayal of Loren Shaw, subtle and unnerving, commands attention throughout the film. Calhern also offers a notable performance. Nina Foch, Stanwyck, Holden, and Pidgeon give very adequate performances as well, but, like many star-studded films, the script does not live up to the actor's dramatic capabilities. In this way, the film is shallow. Don Walling's less-than-believable speech on quality and employee self-respect is anticlimactic, as the viewer had heard it all through the film. The female characters typify embarrassingly empty personalities, and the part of Walling's wife, as played by June Allyson, seems an unnecessary addition to the film. The only acting nomination by the Motion Picture Academy, however, did come to one of the women, Foch, in a supporting role.

As predicted by the studio and the producer, the film was a relative hit at the box office. More important, it set the stage for a growing interest in group, or team, dramas. It also prepared the way for a number of mid-1950's "corporate" dramas of a similar ilk such as *A Woman's World* (1954) and *Patterns* (1956), which further explored power struggles, business scruples, and the American executive. In 1976, an unsuccessful television series based on *Executive Suite* was produced by Stanley Rubin and Norman Felton.

Ralph Angel

A FACE IN THE CROWD

Released: 1957
Production: Elia Kazan for Warner Bros.
Direction: Elia Kazan
Screenplay: Budd Schulberg; based on his short story "Your Arkansas Traveler"
Cinematography: Harry Stradling and Gayne Rescher
Editing: Gene Milford
Running time: 125 minutes

Principal characters:
Lonesome Rhodes .... Andy Griffith
Marcia Jeffries .... Patricia Neal
Joey Kiely .... Anthony Franciosa
Mel Miller .... Walter Matthau
Betty Lou Fleckum .... Lee Remick
J. B. Jeffries .... Howard Smith

Since the release of *A Face in the Crowd* in 1957, public events have continued to bear witness to the prescience of Elia Kazan and Budd Schulberg. The film is an exploration of the function of television in American society and was, as director Kazan has observed, "ahead of its time." At the time of its release, reception and reviews of the film ranged from positive to mixed to negative. Both its style and content were criticized as exaggerated. In terms of style, the film is in fact an uneasy combination of satire and melodrama. Its treatment of television, however, has proved to be far from exaggerated. Payola, TV quiz scandals, the book *The Selling of the President*, and a brief glance at the Top Ten shows in the Neilson ratings attest to, if anything, the film's restraint in exploring television as a powerful and inevitably corrupt medium.

A Face in the Crowd portrays the birth, rise, and fall of a media "hero." During the hero's rise to fame, television as a vehicle for advertising and selling products and the manipulation of the medium for political purposes are dealt with; during his decline (which is abrupt) it is the power and intelligence of the American people which are affirmed. From the film, it is obvious that Kazan and Schulberg were convinced of the power of advertising and hopeful about the intelligence of the American viewing public when subjected to ad agencies' tactics.

This film was the second successful collaboration of writer Schulberg and director Kazan following the highly effective and Academy Award-winning *On the Waterfront* (1954). Kazan, as a veteran theater director, was an actor's director and comfortable with eliciting performances from actors; moreover, as he moved away from Hollywood studio productions, he was developing a fluid, highly realistic visual style. Schulberg had an eye for satire and had written about another fictional monster/victim of the world of entertainment; Sammy Glick in *What Makes Sammy Run?* Their combined skills in directing actors and creating characterizations, as well as shared attitudes toward their work (which caused them to spend months researching the domain of advertising), contribute to the impact of *A Face in the Crowd.* The film's satire is grounded firmly in reality, both visually and verbally.

The film was shot on location in Arkansas, Memphis, and New York City, following the trail of Lonesome Rhodes (Andy Griffith), the folksy media hero. The talents of "real" people in all the locales is utilized, including current television personalities. For the principal characters, Kazan looked mainly to Broadway for talent, and the film marked the successful screen debuts of Griffith, Lee Remick, and Anthony Franciosa. Patricia Neal returned to the screen for one of her best roles after a four-year absence from Hollywood.

The film is extremely well-structured and, in fact, in the first half hour contains all of the elements which will later be explored and amplified. We see flashes of the corruption and corruptibility of the unknown Lonesome Rhodes and the relationship among business, politics, and the media in a very small town. The structure of Piggott, Arkansas, and New York City are exactly the same; only their sizes are different.

Lonesome Rhodes is discovered in Piggott, Arkansas, by Marcia Jeffries (Patricia Neal), an Eastern college-educated woman who works for the radio station owned by her uncle, J. B. Jeffries (Howard Smith). Her businessman uncle not only owns the town radio station, but also the newspaper and the printing press. Larry Rhodes is in jail for drifting. Marcia puts him on her interview program on which he proves to be a seductive (in more ways than one) natural talent, playing the guitar, spouting folk tales and wisdom, and showing his identification with the lives of the "little" people. He rises to the top at KGRK; housewives are charmed into sending him cookies, while sponsors are charmed into buying time on his program. After Lonesome ridicules a candidate out of office on the air, he gets the glimmer of potential power in his eye. He is delighted to leave the small town for Memphis television with Marcia in tow, and she, who has been charmed by his "down-to-earth" qualities, gets her first clue that his raunchy ingenuousness might be but another aspect of his performing talent.

As the performing domain of Rhodes widens, so does the frenzy of the film increase. The pace quickens in Memphis as he perfects his "little people lost in the big city" act, derides his sponsors, and watches sales climb. He is sold to New York's highest bidder by a kindred spirit, an opportunist named Joey Kiely (Anthony Franciosa). Once in New York, on national television, Lonesome's powers as a shrewd manipulator of the medium come to full flower. He sells himself to the viewers, and he sells products. In several chilling montages we see the creation of Lonesome Rhodes as an institution: public relations tours, telethons, dedications, political events, and a marriage made in media heaven to a drum majorette. As Lonesome becomes increasingly attracted to the arena of right-wing politics, the contradictions inherent in his character and his position emerge. While masquerading as the folksy friend of the people, he drops a lot of bodies along the way, including an unmentioned first wife; a gullible young second wife; Marcia, the woman who gave him his start and organized his television programs; and various ulcer-prone television writers and ad executives.

Lonesome links up with the right-wing purveyors of a product which is an empty package: a political candidate with only a good profile who is looking for an image to attract the constituency which Lonesome describes as "rednecks, housewives, shut-ins, peapickers . . . everybody who's got to jump when somebody else blows the whistle." Marcia Jeffries blows the whistle on Lonesome by not pulling the plug while he is engaging in his usual postbroadcast derision of his loyal fans, the "trained seals who watch his program and listen to his advice." From that point on, he quickly falls to the bottom, ending at a political rally with no one in attendance except a few "little" people—the black waiters who are paid to be there.

If *A Face in the Crowd* ends in melodrama, it is nevertheless highly effective satire, exposing the actual workings of an industry which has continued to demand attention for sparse entertainment and high levels of abuse.

Connie McFeeley

FACES

Released: 1968
Production: Maurice McEndree for Continental
Direction: John Cassavetes
Screenplay: John Cassavetes
Cinematography: Al Ruban
Editing: Maurice McEndree
Running time: 130 minutes

Principal characters:
Richard Forst	John Marley
Jeannie Rapp	Gena Rowlands
Maria Forst	Lynn Carlin
Chet	Seymour Cassel
Stella	Elizabeth Deering
Freddie	Fred Draper

John Cassavetes is an American writer-director who is difficult to pigeon-hole into a specific style, theme, or influence. A very personal filmmaker, he has been described as the father of the American New Wave and variously as a maverick, renegade, and iconoclast. His intuitive, improvisational approach to film does not fit into the "system" of the motion picture industry; in fact, the industry avoids Cassavetes as much as Cassavetes avoids the industry. His films have been glowingly praised and voraciously panned, but it is impossible to come away from a Cassavetes film without feeling the emotional impact of what he puts on the screen. The ability to capture on screen the raw, exposed nerve endings of daily life and the uncanny facility for making actors come "alive" are Cassavetes' greatest attributes as a director. Cassavetes insists that he is "basically not a director," but adds that "I'm a man who believes in the validity of a person's inner desires," and goes on to explain that his purpose as a writer-director is to get on the screen those varied human emotions no matter how "ugly or beautiful" and to have audiences respond to them for the reality they possess.

Cassavetes was born in New York City on December 9, 1929, and is of Greek heritage. He attended Colgate University, where the plays of Robert E. Sherwood inspired him to study acting at the American Academy of Dramatic Art in New York City. After graduating from the AADA in 1953 (where he met his wife, actress Gena Rowlands), he acted in television and in films. His screen credits as an actor have included *Edge of the City* (1957), *The Killers* (1964), *The Dirty Dozen* (1967), *Rosemary's Baby* (1968), *Brass Target* (1979), and roles in such productions of his own as *Husbands* (1970), *Minnie and Moskowitz* (1971), and *Opening Night* (1978).

Cassavetes' writing-directing debut occurred in 1960 with *Shadows*, and in the years since, he has directed only eight more films. *Shadows*, which remains his favorite film, and which received the Critics Award at the Venice Film Festival, is a *cinéma vérité* rites of passage depiction of three orphaned blacks. *Too Late Blues* (1961), a commercial spin-off of *Shadows* produced for Paramount and starring Bobby Darin and Stella Stevens, Cassavetes regards as a failure. His third film was *A Child Is Waiting* (1962) starring Burt Lancaster and Judy Garland, a semidocumentary about retarded children, which Stanley Kramer produced for United Artists from a script which Abby Mann wrote, based upon Cassavetes story idea. Cassavetes regards this film as a failure because of Kramer's sentimentalizing it via the editing.

Faces (1968) was Cassavetes' fourth film, and was followed by *Husbands*, the story of three married buddies who set out on a binge following the funeral of one of their good friends. The film starred Cassavetes' close friends Ben Gazarra and Peter Falk and is considered one of his best films. *Minnie and Moskowitz*, which Cassavetes calls his "entertainment" outing, chronicles an unconventional romance between a blonde WASP (Gena Rowlands) and a long-haired hippie who parks cars for a living (Seymour Cassel).

A Woman Under the Influence (1974) is probably Cassavetes' best film and contains one of the screen's most extraordinary female performances—that of Rowlands as a lower-middle-class housewife who has a mental breakdown. For this wonderful, inventive portrayal Rowlands received the National Board of Review of Motion Pictures Award and the Golden Globe as Best Actress of 1974. Cassavetes' next film was *Opening Night*, a compelling depiction of the disintegration of an alcoholic actress with another marvelous performance by Rowlands. The film, which could use some editing despite Cassavetes' reluctance to do so, earned praise at the Berlin Film Festival but failed to gain a wide release in the United States. His 1980 film *Gloria*, again starring Rowlands, is probably his most financially successful film.

All of Cassavetes' films deal with emotional alienation in modern society and a (often subconscious) desire to change one's life, break out of the emptiness of life and gain emotional freedom. This search is the crux of *Faces*— which, simplified, is the story of two middle-class, middle-aged marrieds who endeavor to overcome the hollowness of their marital existence through infidelity. It is Cassavetes' rejection of the dull, phony convention of modern life and not without its own sense of prescience in that this film was made several years before it became fashionable to participate in "open marriage."

Faces is a two-hour-and-ten-minute film which took eight months to make and nearly four years to edit, after Cassavetes' first cut ran six hours. The film cost an incredibly meager $200,000 and was shot mostly in the Cassavetes' own home. Its leading characters, Richard Forst (John Marley) and his wife Maria (Lynn Carlin), are veterans of a childless, fourteen-year marriage. Both are fed up with the superficial pretense of their lives and yet see little they can do to change it constructively. Forst is a successful television producer, and he and his wife live in middle-class luxury bored with the emptiness and banality of their existence.

Forst leaves work one evening and goes to a bar with a male companion where they pick up a call-girl named Jeannie Rapp (Gena Rowlands) and there begins a thirty-six-hour disintegration of a marriage. Forst and his friend Freddie accompany Jeannie to her apartment where they obscure their sexual desire behind silly jokes and sillier songs ("I Dream of Jeannie") until Freddie snidely refers to Jeannie as a cheap pick-up and leaves.

While the attraction between Forst and Jeannie is mutual, he also leaves and goes home to his wife. Their confrontation over dinner and an aborted attempt at lovemaking is likewise veiled in endless jokes, neither of them saying what they mean until finally Forst exclaims, "I want a divorce," and returns to the bar where he had picked up Jeannie. From the bar he telephones Jeannie who is by now entertaining several friends of both sexes. Forst joins them and ends up spending the night with Jeannie.

In the meantime Maria has joined several of her friends for a night of dancing, during which they pick up a congenial, aging surfer-gigolo named Chet (Seymour Cassel), who, like the middle-aged women, is searching for an emotional haven. They all make fools of themselves vying for his sexual favors, and Maria invites them all back to her home. One of the most poignant scenes occurs when Stella (Elizabeth Deering), an overweight "Jewish mother" type of woman, embraces Chet and begs him to take her home. He does so but returns to spend the night with Maria.

Throughout these obviously clichéd happenings, Cassavetes reveals the pain and anxiety of each of his characters by focusing his hand-held camera endlessly on his actors—their faces—in focus and then distorted. He focuses on their hands and legs, capturing all of their embarrassing and pathetically vulnerable body language, groping with his lens on them as they grope for their lives. All the while the camera is peeling off their façades, layer by layer, to expose their real faces underneath. One of Cassavetes' directorial credos is that while his scripts are written, the "acting" is not. He instructs his actors by saying, "Listen, we've got to go further and we've got to go underneath." It is this probing camera which lifts Cassavetes' rather ordinary situations into emotionally moving theatrical experiences. Just when we think the camera has stayed too long on one shot or one actor, something marvelous and spontaneous occurs which makes the wait worthwhile.

The film ends the next morning after both husband and wife have committed adultery. Chet is trying to revive an almost catatonic Maria, who in guilt over her indiscretion has taken an overdose of sleeping pills. Chet manages to revive her, then hears Forst returning home, and with the comic flourish of a swashbuckler, jumps out the window of the one-story house and races across the lawn—but not before Forst sees his departure. The final scene shows both husband and wife sitting on the staircase in embarrassed silence. Cassavetes seems to indicate that somehow there is communication between the two because somehow they are survivors.

The hallmark of *Faces* is the excellent ensemble acting. Marley as Forst received the Best Actor Award at the Venice Film Festival, and Rowlands gives another of her wonderfully vulnerable performances as Jeannie the prostitute. Carlin, here making her acting debut, is exquisite—a cross between the graceful beauty of Loretta Young and the sensuousness of Ava Gardner.

The film provides no answers regarding marriage. In fact, Cassavetes said it best in an interview: "I don't know anything about marriage at all. I've been married a long time. But I don't know anything about marriage. I don't know anyone who does."

Ronald Bowers

THE FALLEN IDOL

Released: 1949
Production: Sir Carol Reed for Selznick Releasing Organization
Direction: Sir Carol Reed
Screenplay: Graham Greene, Lesley Storm, and William Templeton; based
  on Graham Greene's short story "The Basement Room"
Cinematography: George Perinal
Editing: Oswald Hafenrichter
Music: William Alwyn
Running time: 94 minutes

> *Principal characters:*
> Baines .... Ralph Richardson
> Julie .... Michele Morgan
> Felipe .... Bobby Henrey
> Mrs. Baines .... Sonia Dresdel
> Inspector Crowe .... Denis O'Dea
> Doctor Fenton .... Walter Fitzgerald

Short stories often make better films than full-length novels do, perhaps because, in the words of British author Graham Greene, "condensation is always dangerous while expansion is a form of creation." Greene is in a position to know this, since his novels have been as much a victim of sensationalistic adapters and Hollywood "improvements" as any writer's, while his short stories have resulted in several excellent features and a fine British television series. A perfect, although on first thought unlikely, example is "The Basement Room," which in 1949 reached the screen under the title, *The Fallen Idol.*

Even Greene admits that the story certainly seemed unlikely film material, containing "a murder committed by the most sympathetic character and an unhappy ending." More to the point, however, it was about a young boy's disillusionment when rudely confronted with the contrary passions of adults, and it was told completely from the boy's point of view. Young Phillip is a rich man's son temporarily stranded in a London mansion with only the company of the butler Baines and his housekeeper-wife. Phillip adores Baines, who tells him genteel fabrications about past exploits in Africa, but as Phillip follows his idol around, he begins to uncover larger and larger flaws in his character. The man and his wife have a permanently soured marriage, so much so, in fact, that Baines has been having an affair with a "niece" on the side. Caught between Mrs. Baines's jealousy and Baines's congeniality and then increasingly forced to share little secrets that he really cannot keep, Phillip's problems come to a head when Mrs. Baines sneaks back into the house after going on a sudden trip, has a huge argument with her husband,

and is thrown to her death over a bannister. His confusion over events taking precedence over his love for Baines, Phillip takes refuge in the truth and stumbles his way into thoroughly implicating the butler before the police. As his beloved Baines is led away, the boy inwardly swears never to let anyone or anything touch him again.

As film material, it was sour, difficult, and depressing. The man who made it work, who changed it around until it became one of the better intimate suspense films to come out of Britain, was, again in Greene's words, "the only director I know with that particular warmth of human sympathy, the extraordinary feeling of the right face for the right part, the exactitude of cutting and not least important the power of sympathising with an author's worries and the ability to guide them," Sir Carol Reed.

Reed, after a long prewar apprenticeship, had finally had an international success in 1946 with *Odd Man Out* when Alexander Korda, anxious to get him under contract to London Films, introduced him to Greene with the idea of a joint collaboration. The friendship was immediate, the mutual respect immense, and it resulted after *The Fallen Idol* in the even more acclaimed *The Third Man* (1949).

It was during those initial conferences that the plot was altered and "the subject no longer concerned a small boy who unwittingly betrayed his best friend to the police but dealt instead with a small boy who believed that his friend was a murderer and nearly procured his arrest by telling lies in his defense." That was not the only change, however; in the film, Baines (Ralph Richardson) has not murdered his wife (Sonia Dresdel)—she has fallen off a window ledge accidentally—but the boy still thinks Baines has committed the murder. The setting is now a foreign embassy; Phillip is Felipe (Bobby Henrey), who is French, and the other woman is a sympathetic embassy typist named Julie (Michele Morgan) whose affair, particularly in a sequence in which Felipe stumbles upon the pair in a grubby teashop, has touching *Brief Encounter* (1945) overtones. To effect a happy ending, some crucial bits of evidence have been added: a telegram that contradicts Baines's somewhat fabricated story about the death and a telltale footprint near the window ledge. Most important, however, there is much more irony and suspense in Felipe's attempts to grapple with truth and falsehood.

The film revolves around this puzzlement. "There's lies and lies," Baines murmurs early in the film. "Some lies are just kindness." It is a distinction Felipe cannot grasp yet, and so each time he tries to do his best for Baines, he manages instead to do the worst thing possible. Convinced that he "must think of lies and more lies and tell them all the time" to save Baines, his words only wreck Baines's carefully prepared statement. After Julie has pleaded with him to tell the truth, Felipe tries that. By this time the police have discovered the footprint which only Felipe knows was actually made by Mrs. Baines on the day before her death. His attempts to tell that truth imperil Baines all over again (or would if the police now paid him any attention).

They do not, the happy ending is preserved, and it is indicative of the film's somewhat lighter treatment of the story's themes that the duplicity and contradictions of all these events bother Felipe not in the least. By rubbing out the bothersome footprint at the film's end, he seems to rub out all that has gone before. Greene disliked the film's title, and it is also rather inappropriate, as Felipe's devotion to Baines seems as strong at the end of the film as it was in the beginning.

Aside from this, the film is a cogent and probing examination of a child's view of things. Many scenes and more than a few camera angles quite literally express only what a child could see and hear (although this approach is occasionally abandoned in order to convey better the fairly complicated plot). The film is especially interested in the way adults approach children, talking down and condescending to them in some painfully obvious ways. Here, once again, the film has its quiet ironies. Although Baines has the most genuine attachment to Felipe of anyone in the film, he also continually underestimates the boy's ability to understand what is happening, and, as the film progresses and the pressures on him build, he even gets a bit insulting in his offhand comments about Felipe to both Julie and the police. Mrs. Baines, on the other hand, although she has no idea how to handle Felipe and quite dislikes him, is the only one to judge his perspicacity correctly and not treat him like an infant. "You're not such a child as you pretend to be," she snaps during one vindictive moment. "You've got a nasty wicked mind." Both suggestions turn out to have more than a grain of truth to them.

Reed is equally good with a number of not-so-child-oriented moments. As the illicit lovers he cast the actors against type. Morgan seems both too mysteriously gorgeous and too heroically serene for the part of a little working-girl émigré, but she gives her performance a tart Gallic dignity that adds to the part. As Baines, Reed cast the one major British actor not known for romantic leads. Richardson had made his name playing Falstaff, Uncle Vanya, and sophisticated comedy or character parts. Prior to this film he had been Olivia de Havilland's stern father in *The Heiress* (1949) and Vivian Leigh's equally cold husband in *Anna Karenina* (1947), and he brought what one English critic called "a gentleman's gentleness to the part of a gentleman's gentleman." His fumbling, quiet attempts to assuage the tormented Julie in the teashop are beautifully conveyed, and the scene ends with a surprisingly poignant bit of symbolism: the "closed" sign banging on the back of the teashop door as Julie runs out, putting an end to their affair.

Reed also knows how to set up moments that would make even Alfred Hitchcock smile. The all-important telegram is turned into a paper airplane and sent swirling around everyone's head until it strikes just the one man who should not see it. A game of hide-and-seek played out among dust-covered furniture manages to sweep up the stealthily returning Mrs. Baines without any of the others realizing it. The final and most damning interrogation of Baines is held with the dormer window, its part in Mrs. Baines's death still undiscovered, highlighted in the background of each shot as the film cuts from the fumbling, now desperate butler to the implacably self-assured Inspector Crowe (Denis O'Dea). Even the comic relief gets neatly offbeat. A little streetwalker in the police station, finally informed of who Felipe is, bursts out with "Oh, I know your Daddy," and two charwomen carefully examine the accident site hoping against hope that even a simple broken neck might leave a sensationalistic trace of blood somewhere.

Reed's main accomplishment, however, is with Henrey as Felipe. A French child who had spent the Occupation years in England, the boy's quizzical eight-year-old face, his unruly blond hair, and his sturdy but not quite coordinated limbs are a fine embodiment of the role. Still, it is Reed's skill that saw to it that Henrey never hits a false note; no fake endearing grins, no cloyingly obvious bids for sympathy in the patented manner of other child actors such as Jackie Cooper or Margaret O'Brien. Instead, what is shown is a little boy constantly at work to understand what is going on around him, beset by sudden bursts of confidence that are usually followed by equally sudden nervous withdrawals. Reed has stated that one way he kept the boy's performance natural was to give him as little dialogue as possible in group takes so that all he had to do was concentrate on the others. Whatever he did, it worked. Henrey has a virtuoso's ability of never saying the name "Baines" in the same way twice. His look of sudden wonder and confusion at the end of the film when he has to confront something entirely new (his mother returned home after a long illness) is so endearing and definitive of childhood that it nearly erases the rest of the film from our minds.

The Fallen Idol came in the middle of Reed's—and the British film industry's—most productive period, and it has often tended to be ignored next to the more florid splendors of *Odd Man Out*, *The Third Man*, and *Outcast of the Islands* (1951). As a drama of childhood, it is certainly on par with *Forbidden Games* (1951), *The Little Kidnappers* (1954), and François Truffaut's *Small Change* (1946), and as a work of suspense on an intimate scale it ranks with *Shadow of a Doubt* (1943) and *Diabolique* (1955). That it could have come from two men hitherto known for espionage "entertainments," theological novels, and social dramas is itself a surprise of major amplitude.

Lewis Archibald

A FAMILY AFFAIR

Released: 1937
Production: Lucien Hubbard and Samuel Marx for Metro-Goldwyn-Mayer
Direction: George B. Seitz
Screenplay: Kay Van Riper; based on the play *Skidding* by Aurania Rouverol
Cinematography: Lester White
Editing: George Boemler
Running time: 69 minutes

Principal characters:
Judge James Hardy	Lionel Barrymore
Andy Hardy	Mickey Rooney
Mrs. Hardy	Spring Byington
Marion Hardy	Cecilia Parker
Joan Hardy	Julie Haydon
Bill Martin	Allen Vincent
Wayne Trant	Eric Linden
Polly Benedict	Margaret Marquis

A Family Affair was the first of the Andy Hardy films, which were popular in the 1930's and 1940's. They portrayed that era's ideal America: small-town life, a close-knit family, the virtues of honesty and perserverance, and, most importantly, justice triumphant in the end. Plots varied throughout the series as Andy grew up and went away to college, but the films always featured the light comedy of Andy's romantic misadventures set against a story of Judge Hardy's integrity in the face of political expediency.

A Family Affair opens in Carvel, California, whose population is twenty-five thousand. Three of the town's most powerful men (the head of a local engineering firm, the editor of the town newspaper, and Judge Hardy's campaign manager) confront Judge James Hardy (Lionel Barrymore) in his chambers. They are angry because he has granted a restraining order against the new thirty-million-dollar aqueduct that is about to be built near Carvel. The three argue that the aqueduct will be a tremendous boon to the area's economy in this, the Depression, and that the Judge is hurting Carvel by not letting the construction proceed. Judge Hardy listens patiently and then calmly explains that, according to the law, he had no choice about signing the restraining order, since legitimate litigation is pending. Not satisfied by his explanation, the three men threaten the Judge with a challenge to his reelection in the next primary, but he remains unperturbed. Judge Hardy is the film's anchor, and director George B. Seitz wastes no time in establishing his character. In the opening scene we learn of his professional integrity and of the powerful sense of self-confidence that enables him to retain his serenity in the face of adversity, something that will be tested throughout the film.

At the Hardy home, the news is that daughter Marion Hardy (Cecilia Parker) is coming home after a year at college, and the family will be reunited again. Teenage son Andy (Mickey Rooney) still lives at home, and another daughter, Joan (Julie Haydon), is married to Bill Martin (Allen Vincent). As we soon learn, however, all is not well between Bill and Joan. Outside the Hardy home, Bill tells Joan that their marriage is finished, and Joan must go to the Hardy reunion dinner alone. Andy has a problem too, albeit a considerably less serious one. His mother insists that he attend a party, whereby he complains, "Holy jumpin' Jerusalem, a party with girls?" Marion, meanwhile, has met a young man named Wayne Trant (Eric Linden) on the train to Carvel, and the two are quite smitten with each other. Marion agrees to see Wayne after the dinner, although she is a bit nervous about introducing to her parents a man with whom she has spent an unchaperoned train ride.

The dinner commences, with Joan making an excuse for Bill's absence. Marion introduces Wayne to the family, and although Mrs. Hardy (Spring Byington) is a bit uneasy over the story of their train ride, Judge Hardy calms her fears, and the young man makes a good impression. He has come to Carvel, it develops, to work on the new aqueduct. Thus the filmmakers place additional moral pressure on the Judge, since his decision to delay construction on the aqueduct will now have a direct effect on a member of his own family. He keeps this knowledge to himself for the time being, however, to avoid spoiling his family's evening.

Andy's troubles appear to deepen when his mother volunteers him as an escort for Polly Benedict (Margaret Marquis), a girl whom he has not seen since grade school, to the party he is already attending with great reluctance. Andy is a well-meaning but overexuberant young man in his early teens. Although his problems are real enough to him, they are absurdly trivial compared to the difficulties faced by the other Hardys. Director Seitz uses his overreactions to provide comic relief from the film's more serious moments. It is a dispirited Andy Hardy who arrives at Polly Benedict's doorstep. His spirits lift, however, when she answers his knock. During her years away from Carvel, she has grown into a lovely young lady, and Andy is quite taken with her.

Meanwhile, at the Hardy home, Joan breaks down, announcing that she and Bill are separating. He had been neglecting her, she explains, and she went with a male friend to a dive called the Blue Rabbit Inn, where, after drinking too much champagne, the pair began necking. It was just a harmless flirtation, she swears, and it went no further, but Bill found out about the incident and is insisting on a divorce. Although Joan apologizes to her parents for bringing this trouble upon them, the Hardys are very supportive. "What's a mother and father for if they can't stand by in times of trouble," asks the Judge. Although his own problems are escalating, Judge Hardy is still able to offer comfort to his family.

Just how serious his political problems are is revealed by the headline on the next morning's newspaper, which reveals a move by outraged citizens to have the Judge impeached. Hardy remains calm, preferring to tease Andy about the lipstick on his collar, but the situation is clearly deteriorating. By the end of the day, he has been offered a bribe to withdraw his restraining order against the aqueduct (he angrily throws the man out of his office), and the only ones in town left on his side are his family and his campaign manager, who has decided to stick with the Judge even though his instinct tells him that the Judge's stubborn integrity may mean political suicide for both of them.

Support for the Judge's position begins to erode even within his own family, as illustrated in the next few scenes. Marion and Wayne, parked on a country road, argue about her father's role in blocking construction on the aqueduct. Although Marion at first takes her father's side, she realizes how much Wayne means to her and vows to persuade the Judge to relent. Meanwhile, Polly Benedict's father has refused to let his daughter see Andy on account of the Judge's controversial decision, and the Hardys' neighbors will not speak to the Judge as he walks down the street. Andy and Marion both confront their father, who insists that he is only doing his duty, which is to carry out the law. Marion calls him an old fogey and leaves the room in tears, but Andy, although younger, is more reasonable. He agrees to read the Judge's oath of office and consider the matter. After mulling over the implications of the oath, Andy is persuaded that his father is right.

The sternest test of the Judge's willingness to stand behind his convictions comes when the editor of the town newspaper finds out about Joan's marital difficulties. He threatens to print the story of Joan's escapades at the Blue Rabbit Inn unless Judge Hardy lifts his restraining order against the aqueduct. Once again, however, the Judge stands firm. Despite all of the adversity besetting him and his family, including Joan's discovery that she is pregnant with her estranged husband's child, the Judge remains relentlessly good-humored and optimistic, assuring everyone concerned that all will work out for the best.

The film's denouement begins later that night when Judge Hardy receives a mysterious phone call. He leaves a note ordering his wife and Joan to appear at the political convention being held the next day (at which the Judge's renomination for office is being contested), but offering no explanation for his disappearance. He then visits Joan's husband Bill. Again offering no explanation, he asks Bill to accompany him on an urgent mission relating to the aqueduct, and Bill reluctantly agrees to come.

At the convention the next day, his opponent's nomination is cheered wildly, but when the Judge's campaign manager attempts to defend the Hardy record, his efforts are met with boos and catcalls—both about the aqueduct and about the incident at the Blue Rabbit Inn, which has been published in the newspaper in a thoroughly distorted manner. Joan and Mrs. Hardy sit cringing through the whole process.

Suddenly Judge Hardy strides through the crowd, takes the floor, and forces the crowd to listen. He exposes the newspaper's blackmail attempt, and, in a dramatic moment, produces Joan's husband Bill, who embraces his wife and denies that they are about to get a divorce. Then the Judge turns to the matter of the aqueduct. It turns out that the previous night's mysterious phone call was from a respected firm of geologists in Denver. Their intensive study of the plans for the aqueduct reveal it to be nothing more than an elaborate attempt to divert all of Carvel's water to a large California city, leaving Carvel and its sister towns literally high and dry and bringing economic ruin to the entire area. Amid cheers, Judge Hardy makes the restraining order against the aqueduct permanent, and he is renominated to the judgeship by acclamation as his political enemies stand by helplessly.

In the final scene, the entire family crowds around the Judge, their problems solved. Joan and Bill are reunited; Polly Benedict rushes up to apologize to Andy; and the Judge assures Wayne Trant that the state legislature will soon pass a law authorizing the construction of a legitimate aqueduct program on which Wayne will be able to work. By doing his duty and standing up for what he believes in, Judge Hardy has brought about a happy ending.

A Family Affair is undeniably simplistic in many respects, but its obvious sincerity allows it to rise above the level of cliché. Many of the characters are stock types which function more as symbols than as real people, but two of them stand out. Barrymore is outstanding as Judge James Hardy. He constantly projects an image of warmth, serenity, and optimism and is eminently believable as the film's pillar of strength. It is Andy Hardy, however, who caught the audience's imagination; and, although Rooney's part in *A Family Affair* is a relatively small one, he plays it for all it is worth. His "gee-whiz," slightly off-center portrayal of the almost All-American Boy became the prototype for many comic adolescent heroes, from Henry Aldrich to Beaver Cleaver.

As the Andy Hardy series developed, Lewis Stone replaced Barrymore as the stern but loving Judge Hardy, and Andy's misadventures came to dominate the films. The basic theme, however, remained the same: the American family pulling together and winning. Ultimately, *A Family Affair* is the cinematic equivalent of Norman Rockwell's *Saturday Evening Post* covers—an idealized reflection of an era when the virtues of hearth and home were defended unquestioningly. The Academy of Motion Picture Arts and Sciences, recognizing the strengths that the Andy Hardy series embodied, gave the series a special Academy Award in 1942 "for its achievement in representing the American way of life."

Robert Mitchell

THE FAMILY WAY

Released: 1966
Production: John Boulting and Roy Boulting for Warner Bros.
Direction: Roy Boulting
Screenplay: Bill Naughton; based on his play *All in Good Time*
Cinematography: Harry Waxman
Editing: Ernest Hosler
Music: Paul McCartney
Running time: 115 minutes

Principal characters:
Jenny Fitton	Hayley Mills
Arthur Fitton	Hywel Bennett
Liz Piper	Avril Angers
Leslie Piper	John Comer
Ezra Fitton	John Mills
Lucy Fitton	Marjorie Rhodes
Uncle Fred	Wilfred Pickles
Geoffrey Fitton	Murray Head

With sensitivity and a gentle touch of humor, *The Family Way* examines marital impotence. The British-made film is the story of a bride and bridegroom who have difficulty consummating their marriage, but it also has a background story involving conflict between the young man and his father, and these background facts ultimately give credence to the sexual problems. The story takes place in a small, industrial town in England's North County. The wedding ceremony is performed against the opening credits, with special emphasis placed on the vicar's words that marriage is "a remedy against sin and to avoid fornication." Arthur Fitton (Hywel Bennett), projectionist at a local movie theater, has married Jenny Piper (Hayley Mills), a counter assistant in a gramophone shop. He is intelligent and serious, with a penchant for Beethoven and books. She generally likes the same things, but she also tends to be less serious. She is a virgin, but Arthur's sexual past is never detailed.

The stern wedding is followed by a reception at the local pub where ribald jokes concerning the young couple's wedding night flow as freely as the ale. Arthur and Jenny have arranged for a "package" honeymoon trip, but their first night together will be spent in Arthur's room, at the Fitton home. The couple is understandably taken aback when the rowdy reception crowd moves from the pub to the Fitton home. There, Arthur endures off-color jokes and Jenny receives advice (one sexy-looking blonde tells her not to show pleasure while performing her "duty"). After escaping the crowd and going upstairs, the two undress shyly, then get into the bed, which has been rigged and collapses. While Jenny laughs at the predicament Arthur is incensed by it all. That night he is unable to consummate the marriage.

Ezra (John Mills), Arthur's crude, brawling father, was partially to blame for the noisy reception and blue humor. He is a hard-drinking man who seems to epitomize the lower levels of the working class. Simple and straightforward, he is at odds with Arthur, his oldest son, and is, in part, threatened by Arthur's sensitivity. Although unable to compete with his son's intelligence, Ezra is physically the stronger of the two and during the wedding reception rankles his nervous son by challenging him to a game of strength, "the elbow game." The assembled crowd applauds the event heartily, but to Arthur and Ezra, the competition is serious, and their faces during the "game" reveal their strained relationship. Ezra's eventual victory allows him to torment his son further. The out-of-control reception and the unfortunate "game" between Arthur and Ezra signify the problems inherent in the Fitton household. They are only some of the barriers, however, real and imagined, to come between Arthur and Jenny during their young marriage.

Following the uneventful wedding night in the collapsed bed, Arthur and Jenny look forward to their honeymoon trip to Majorca. There is a grim surprise awaiting the couple when they go to take their bus to the airport, however; their trip has fallen through because a scheming travel agent has absconded with their funds. Because of a housing shortage, Arthur and Jenny must continue to make their home in the Fitton house. The situation is uncomfortable, compounded by paper-thin walls and the remarks of the insensitive Ezra, who continues to irritate Arthur. Elements of soap opera as well as situation comedy are woven throughout the story. The couple goes back to work, but Jenny works days and Arthur works nights, allowing them little time together. Arthur is intensely disturbed that the marriage remains unconsummated, but Jenny soothingly replies "One doesn't miss what one's never had." Her words grate on Arthur, however, and the two, with doubts about themselves and each other, begin to bicker.

A month passes, and the couple decides to turn to outside help. When Arthur visits a marriage guidance counselor, his session is overheard by a cleaning woman who happens to live in his neighborhood. Jenny, in the meanwhile, is beginning to act troubled. Although she has promised Arthur she will tell no one of their problem, she reveals the truth to her mother (Avril Angers). Between the cleaning woman and Mrs. Piper, word that "their marriage hasn't taken on yet" spreads. At the urging of her mother, Jenny goes to visit her Uncle Fred (Wilfred Pickles), a male nurse who raises rabbits. Finally, the concerned Pipers pay a visit to the Fittons (Jenny and Arthur do not know that they all know). Everyone, it seems, wants to help the consummation of the marriage.

Arthur's mother (Marjorie Rhodes) patiently maintains, "Nature always finds a way. That's what it's there for." Although she tolerates her crude husband, she has a special understanding of her sensitive son, who is not at all like Ezra. The night Jenny's parents come to visit, Mrs. Fitton makes a revelation that is central to the story of *The Family Way*. Reminiscing about her own honeymoon, she reveals that Ezra had had a dear friend named Billy, whom he always insisted on bringing along, even on the wedding trip. In gentle dialogue, Mrs. Fitton recounts her own sexual awakening—not with the boisterous Ezra, but, unknown to Ezra, with the sensitive Billy. Her husband, she says, never understood why his best "mate" took off after the honeymoon and the two men never saw each other again. Arthur, then, is revealed to be Billy's son. Although Arthur and Ezra are unaware of the truth, they are constantly alert to the conflict between them. The two men are at odds with each other, and much of the problem lies with their perceptions of what manhood is. "You can do yourself a damage, reading all those books," says Ezra thoughtlessly to his son, and Arthur similarly has no desire to understand his coarse father.

The rumors about Arthur and Jenny continue to spread until finally they reach Arthur. Already angry with Jenny because she has been spending her free time with his more free-spirited younger brother, Geoffrey (Murray Head), Arthur starts a fist-fight when his employer cracks a joke about his sexual inability. After fighting it out, Arthur storms off, in the middle of the afternoon, and goes home. Finding Jenny at home, too, he accuses her of spreading the rumors. She yells back, and the issue becomes a physical jostle. The small room cannot accommodate a major battle, however, and after falling onto Jenny on the bed, Arthur's anger becomes affection. The quiet house lends itself to the couple's lovemaking. Afterward, a host of nosey neighbors, peering up at their window, are puzzled to hear the loud strains of Beethoven coming through the air. With the marriage consummated, Arthur and Jenny have a newfound determination. Their honeymoon money has been returned, and they decide to try another trip. Arthur has also heard of a place for rent, and, with difficulty, he asks his father for financial assistance. Ezra, ashamed of past bad feelings toward his son and pleased to be asked to help, gives a positive response and then weeps, his first real display of sensitivity in the film.

A bittersweet comedy, *The Family Way* offers wry observations about marriage and family life. The Boulting brothers have also included jabs about the English working class and the battle between brawn and intellect. When first released, *The Family Way* received much attention from the press because, in her first "grown-up" role, Hayley Mills as Jenny has a brief nude scene (she is bathing when Geoffrey walks in on her). What distinguishes this film, however, is not its notoriety, but its careful look, including some of the psychological reasons behind brief marital impotence. Bennett as Arthur has an almost effeminate quality, a trait that works to his advantage, considering Arthur's predicament. Mills (Hayley Mills's own father) is especially effective as the working-class Ezra. Showing his versatility as an actor, Mills can play brutes or genteel aristocrats with equally excellent results. In fact, during his younger days, he played several characters more similar to Arthur than Ezra, such as Willie Mossop in *Hobson's Choice* (1954) and Pip in *Great Expectations* (1947). Finally, adding to the overall enjoyment of the film, is the musical score composed by then-Beatle Paul McCartney.

Pat H. Broeske

FANNY

Released: 1961
Production: Joshua Logan for Warner Bros.
Direction: Joshua Logan
Screenplay: Julius J. Epstein; based on the play of the same name by Joshua
    Logan and the French trilogy *Marius*, *Fanny*, and *César* by Marcel Pagnol
Cinematography: Jack Cardiff
Editing: William Reynolds
Music: Harold Rome
Running time: 133 minutes

Principal characters:
Fanny .... Leslie Caron
Panisse .... Maurice Chevalier
César .... Charles Boyer
Marius .... Horst Buchholz
Honorine .... Georgette Anys

The 1961 *Fanny* was the third filmed version of the same story. French
novelist and director Marcel Pagnol first introduced the character of Fanny
to the screen, along with her charming family and friends, in his classic trilogy
about Marseilles made between 1931 and 1936: *Fanny*, *Marius*, and *César*.
These films, adapted from Pagnol's plays of the same names, became very
successful in France and were also highly acclaimed in the United States,
where they continued to be shown in "art" film houses for more than two
decades. In 1938, American director James Whale made yet another version,
Port of Seven Seas; but the story was greatly changed and was almost unre-
cognizable as Pagnol's.

In 1954 Joshua Logan and S. N. Behrman wrote a Broadway musical of
the story, with music and lyrics by Harold Rome. The play *Fanny* was a smash
hit and inspired Logan to attempt another screen version of the Marseilles
melodrama. Logan and screenwriter Julius Epstein went back to Pagnol's film
for the new project, combining all three stories from the trilogy into one film,
Fanny. The new picture was not a musical, although Harold Rome's music
was used as background. What finally emerged was something between Gallic
sophistication and Hollywood romanticism. The cast was appropriately European, mostly French, with Maurice Chevalier and Charles Boyer as the two
older gentlemen who are close to Fanny, and Leslie Caron and Horst Buchholz
as the young couple, Fanny and Marius.

The story turns on the pathetic predicament of Fanny, the daughter of
fishmonger Honorine (Georgette Anys). She has been in love since childhood
with Marius, the son of César. Marius is a handsome youth who helps his
father in his small waterside café, but longs to go to sea and has made secret

arrangements to sail on a schooner bound for "the isles beneath the sea." The sea is everywhere in the film: it is the setting for all of the characters' lives; it is the enemy for Fanny and, ultimately, for Marius; and it provides a livelihood for the residents of Marseilles. Fanny and Marius are deeply in love as the film opens, but Marius is torn between his love for her and his terrible aching for a life at sea. Counterpoised with the two lovers are their parents and their friends of the waterfront, who offer them support and advice. The night before Marius is to depart, he and Fanny confess their love to each other and spend the night together. When morning comes, Marius offers to stay behind and let his ship leave without him; but Fanny, knowing he will never be happy on land, sends him away.

Marius' departure marks the end of the first "act" of the film. The second part begins with Fanny's realization that she is going to have Marius' child. César and Honorine do their best to console her, but Fanny is desolate. Hearing of their plight, Panisse, a wealthy sail merchant and good friend of both families, offers a way out. A lonely widower, he has always admired Fanny and offers her marriage with the understanding that the child, if a son, would bear his name and some day take over his business. At first César is against the idea of his grandson having such an old father, but he reconsiders when Honorine points out that the child may stand to inherit a very large fortune some day. Fanny also reluctantly agrees to the plan. She respects Panisse and knows that he is aware that she does not love him. The marriage takes place, and several months later a son, Cesario, is born.

In the third and final part of the film, Fanny is confronted with her past. A year goes by. Fanny is reasonably happy and has learned to care for Panisse, for he is generous to her and the boy, making sure they want for nothing. César acts as godfather and Uncle to Cesario, but is as close to him as a grandfather would be. Then the inevitable happens and Marius returns home. Completely disillusioned by his experiences at sea (his beloved isles turned out to be volcanic ash), he seeks out his father who tells him of Fanny's new life and warns him not to make trouble for the family of Panisse. When Marius confronts Fanny while Panisse is away, she considers running off with him, but soon realizes that they could never be happy that way. Embittered, Marius leaves and finds a job as a garage mechanic in a nearby town.

Nine years pass. Cesario grows up fascinated by the sea, causing Fanny to worry that he is his father all over again. A friend takes the boy to see Marius, and they become great friends. When Fanny learns of this, she is furious and confronts Marius. They find they still love each other, but Fanny will not leave Panisse. After much persuasion by Cesario, Fanny invites Marius to the boy's ninth birthday party. At the party, Panisse sees the affection that the boy has for his natural father and also sees in Fanny's eyes that she still cares for Marius. Panisse becomes very ill, and Fanny is truly worried that she will lose him. He becomes worse and calls all of his friends, including Marius, to his bedside. From his deathbed, the old man dictates a letter to César in which he asks Marius to marry Fanny when he is gone, and the film ends on this bittersweet note.

Fanny manifests great spirit and reverence for life. Although it is an American film, it has a distinct European flavor. There is overemphasis on broad comedy in some of the scenes and some rather stiff staging, but the truth of the characters that Pagnol created some thirty years ago still asserts itself, and the honesty of their emotions comes through. The acting is uniformly excellent, but does not always mesh well. Both Boyer and Chevalier, suave charmers in films for years, seem a bit out of place in Marseilles, especially Boyer as a saloon keeper. Chevalier is his own delightful self, and when pitted against the sullen behavior of Bucholz's Marius, it is a bit hard to understand Fanny's dilemma. Caron is radiant as Fanny. She had been exhibiting her gamin charm in American films since *An American in Paris* (1951), and brought a naturalness and warmth to the role of Fanny that made it her best performance since the 1958 Academy Award-winning *Gigi*. The film was well received by critics and brought Boyer an Oscar nomination for supporting actor. Although the familiar songs were missed by fans of the Broadway musical, the sound track of the original score at least evokes the atmosphere of Logan's play, and the beautiful cinematography of Jack Cardiff evokes the Marseilles waterfront to perfection. The one unfortunate result of the film was that the original Pagnol trilogy was withdrawn from circulation in America for many years, and only recently has it been possible to see it again in revival houses.

Joan Cohen

THE FARMER'S DAUGHTER

Released: 1947
Production: Dore Schary for RKO/Radio
Direction: H. C. Potter
Screenplay: Allen Rivkin and Laura Kerr; based on the play *Hulda, Daughter of Parliament* by Juhri Trevataa
Cinematography: Milton Krasner
Editing: Harry Marker
Costume design: Edith Head
Running time: 97 minutes

> *Principal characters:*
> Katrin Holstrom .... Loretta Young (AA)
> Glenn Morley .... Joseph Cotton
> Clancy .... Charles Bickford
> Mrs. Morley .... Ethel Barrymore
> Adolph Petree .... Rhys Williams
> Mrs. Holstrom .... Anna Q. Nilsson
> Anders Finley .... Art Baker

Based on the Scandinavian play *Hulda, Daughter of Parliament* by Juhri Trevataa and originally entitled *Katie for Congress*, *The Farmer's Daughter* stars Loretta Young as Katrin Holstrom a beautiful Swedish girl from a Minnesota farm who goes to the big city and eventually finds herself running for Congress. Katrin leaves her home and the comfortable security of her loving family, which includes several brawny brothers, and heads to "Capital City" to begin her study of nursing. To save bus fare, she accepts a ride with itinerant worker Adolph Petree (Rhys Williams), who has just painted her father's barn, but the man soon tricks her when an accident forces them to spend the night in a tourist camp. After he borrows all of Katrin's money for repairs, Adolph claims he is unable to repay her, and she must find her way to the city herself.

Without any money, Katrin is forced to take a job as a maid. She finds employment with Glenn Morley (Joseph Cotton), a young, handsome Minnesota congressman, and Mrs. Morley (Ethel Barrymore), his rich and politically influential mother, who is the widow of a famous United States senator. Intelligent and efficient, Katrin soon becomes indispensable to the Morley household, and at one point when the skating congressman falls through the ice, Katrin even gives him a rub-down with her Swedish massage technique. At the same time, the housemaid surprises her employees with her interest in politics; for the public-speaking class in which she has enrolled, Katrin practices elocution with Woodrow Wilson's comments on democratic principles. Soon, without invitation, she enters the family's political discussions, and for Glenn, she becomes an amusing, then annoying problem, when she expresses political opinions contrary to his own. Katrin, however, thinks clearly and independently and Glenn finds his irritation turning into interest and infatuation.

When a congressman from a neighboring district dies, a meeting of party leaders is held at the Morley house in order to select new candidates to fill the vacated seat. Anders Finley (Art Baker), whom the Morley's reluctantly accept, is chosen, but the outspoken Katrin vehemently disapproves and airs her protesting convictions at a political rally. After these verbal attacks and objections, the favorably impressed opposition persuades Katrin to accept their Congressional nomination against Finley. She agrees, quits her job as housekeeper, and says good-bye to the angry Glenn Morley and his more sympathetic mother. Following a smear campaign by Adolph Petree against Katrin which almost ruins her, the Morleys uncover the tourist camp facts and discover that Finley paid Petree to defame Katrin, and the scandal is published. With Glenn Morley now on her side, Katrin easily wins the election by a landslide. Glenn and Katrin decide to get married, and the two congresspeople go off together to Washington, D.C. A socially conscious comedy-drama, *The Farmer's Daughter* is an entertaining exposé of political shenanigans. It not only provides funny commentary about the peculiar voting habits of many American citizens, but it also presents, with good humor, the view that truth is above politics. Indeed, the film is a positive statement about United States democracy and patriotism.

Young plays the fiery reformer with intelligence and charm and convinces us with her character's rare political honesty. As the blunt-questioning political Cinderella, Young's peasant Swedish accent is also believable. Interestingly, *The Farmer's Daughter* was originally intended as a starring vehicle for Swedish actress Ingrid Bergman, but Bergman turned the part down following a falling-out with independent producer David O. Selznick. Later Dore Schary took over as producer, and Young won the Academy Award for Best Actress for the part, in competition with Joan Crawford in *Possessed*, Susan Hayward in *Smash Up*, Dorothy McGuire in *Gentleman's Agreement*, and Rosalind Russell in *Mourning Becomes Electra*.

At the age of thirty-six when she made *The Farmer's Daughter*, Young had been in films for almost twenty years. She was featured as a young teenager in several silent films, most notably *Laugh Clown Laugh* (1928) with Lon Chaney, and had gradually become a major star by the mid-1930's when she began contract work for Twentieth Century-Fox. From that time until she retired from films to begin her long-running television anthology, *The Loretta Young Show*, she was a successful film star. Usually playing up her beautiful features and elegant mannerisms, she starred in a number of successful films with other Fox stars such as Don Ameche and Tyrone Power. Interestingly, the three films in which she gives perhaps her best performances, *The Farmer's*

Daughter, Rachel and the Stranger (1948), and *Come to the Stable* (1949), gave her the opportunity for parts which went against her usual screen image.

Cotton is also excellent as Congressman Morley. An actor who has moved among starring and character parts throughout his long career, Cotton has always given competent performances in a wide variety of roles. His light comedic touch here is as pleasing as was his penetrating performance as the psychotic killer in Alfred Hitchcock's *Shadow of a Doubt* (1943). Barrymore, as the dry and witty matriarch of a political family, is also enjoyable to watch as she masterfully delivers some of the best lines in the film, next to Young's. Charles Bickford as the hard-nosed yet devoted Clancy, who becomes Katrin's mentor and strongest supporter, won an Oscar nomination for his role, losing to Edmund Gwenn for *Miracle on 34th Street*. The rest of the cast, which consisted of many well-known character actors such as Williams, Baker, and former silent screen star Anna Q. Nilsson as Katrin's mother, is equally good in small roles. As a historical footnote, three of Katrin's strapping brothers are played by actors who would later become famous: Lex Barker, Keith Andes, and James Arness, using his real name, James Aurness.

Although there are some rather implausible moments in the film—especially when the politically powerful Morleys switch allegiances during the middle of Congressional campaign—the film still presents a solid case for the future of democracy and is a highly enjoyable film as well.

Janet St. Clair

FAT CITY

Released: 1972
Production: Ray Stark for Columbia
Direction: John Huston
Screenplay: Leonard Gardner; based on his novel of the same name
Cinematography: Conrad Hall
Editing: Margaret Booth
Running time: 100 minutes

Principal characters:
Billy Tully	Stacy Keach
Ernie Munger	Jeff Bridges
Oma	Susan Tyrell
Faye	Candy Clark
Ruben	Nicholas Colasanto
Earl	Curtis Cokes
Lucero	Sixto Rodriguez

After a ten-year self-imposed exile filled with flawed and abandoned projects, John Huston was to direct *Fat City* as a labor of love. *Night of the Iguana*, released in 1964, proved to the Hollywood film industry that the "Monster," as he was affectionately called by his late pal Humphrey Bogart, had not lost his touch. That had been eight years earlier, however, and by 1972, Huston's "bankability" was again in question. When he discovered Leonard Gardner's lean, gritty novel chronicling the lives of would-be and has-been fighters drinking and killing time in Stockton, California, Huston knew that he wanted to film it. The down-and-outer has always been a prominent figure in Huston's work; at seventeen, he had himself been a fair welterweight and had traveled the tanktown circuit in California which included towns like Watsonville and Stockton.

Taking along cinematographer Conrad Hall (*Cool Hand Luke*, 1967, and *In Cold Blood*, 1967), he set about re-creating the feel and smell of the place. Anyone who has seen *Fat City* can bear witness to how well the pair succeeded. Originally Huston had wanted Marlon Brando for the role of Billy Tully (the two men had gotten along and Brando had delivered a brilliant performance in Huston's adaptation of Carson McCullers' *Reflections in a Golden Eye*, 1967); but he had proved to be unavailable, and Stacy Keach was engaged to portray Billy Tully, a man who has seen his dreams dashed and, at twenty-nine, considers his life to be over. Much less well-known to the public than Brando, it would be difficult to think of an actor who could have handled the role better than did Keach.

Billy Tully is a fighter who has taken one punch too many. One of the walking wounded, a form of entropy has taken over his life. Partially, this is because of his wife's decision to walk away from the dead end of their life together; partially it is because, outside of boxing, there are few places Billy can go. At the beginning of the film he is dividing his time between halfhearted workouts at the YMCA with the dim notion of a comeback in mind, and the fields of the San Joaquin Valley where he earns enough money picking fruit to pay for wine and a cheap room.

One day at the YMCA he begins sparring with a young man named Ernie Munger (Jeff Bridges). Billy is surprised at Munger's prowess and suggests that he look up Ruben Luna (Nicholas Colasanto), a promoter who had once managed his own career. Billy sees in Ernie the cocky kid that he used to be. The youth is both an inspiration and a threat: an inspiration because he is the catalyst that causes Billy to begin training in earnest and a threat because he is a reminder to the older man of how much his reflexes have deteriorated during his absence from the ring. Billy trains, but cannot help wondering whether his best days are not gone forever and his dream of a comeback sheer folly. Ruben Luna also sees in Ernie the potential Billy had had before his marriage went on the rocks; yet he also retains enough faith in Billy as a fighter to want to manage him again if he is genuinely serious about training.

The lives of Billy and Ernie also intersect romantically. Ernie is trapped into marriage with Faye (Candy Clark), and Billy meets Oma (Susan Tyrell) in a Stockton dive. When Billy and Oma first see each other, she is involved in a stormy affair with a black man named Earl (Curtis Cokes). She bends Billy's ear with diatribes about the decline of the white race, at the same time berating Earl, who impassively absorbs her verbal abuse. When Earl is arrested on some minor charge, Oma continues arguing and drinking in the same bar, and eventually mutual loneliness brings Oma and Billy together after one of the most off-center, pugnacious courtships in film history. In order to prove his inarticulate need for her, Billy smashes his head against the glass-topped jukebox. Suddenly, in Oma's eyes, he is transformed into a battered Romeo ("the only sonofabitch worth a shit in this place"). The pair exit like drunken lovebirds. Yet all the while they are together, the cardboard carton containing Earl's possessions sits in Oma's closet as a reminder of the transience of her relationship with Billy. Billy realizes that the relationship is an impossible one, but his desperate loneliness compels him to try to make it work. He suffers her abuse as Earl did, attempts to get her to cut down on the drinking which is destroying her, and even cajoles her into eating. His reward is almost always a curse.

Ruben sets up a match for Billy, who has been training in earnest for his reentry into the ring against a fighter named Lucero (Sixto Rodriguez) in the Stockton Memorial Stadium. Lucero travels by bus from Mexico, arriving in town alone. He is a calm, taciturn man more reminiscent of a gunfighter or a matador than of a prizefighter. Perhaps because he is not good enough any more, or because his life has turned into an endless series of losses, Billy is no match for Lucero.

His ultimate defeat, however, does not take place in the ring. Upon Earl's release from jail, he is taken back by Oma, and Billy is once again shut out from what is most probably his last chance for a measure of happiness. He sees Ernie off to travel the same punchy circuit that he himself has traveled.

Fat City is the dark side of *Rocky* (1976). It is a story of the "bottom dogs" that Edward Dahlberg and Nelson Algren once wrote about. The expression itself is a metaphor for whatever a man's dream might be. The film opened late in 1972 to excellent notices and poor box office. The same, however, was true of what is possibly Huston's greatest work, *The Treasure of the Sierra Madre* (1947); and, like the earlier film, *Fat City* is gradually being recognized as the important work that it is. Bridges as Ernie plays well opposite Keach. Tyrell was nominated for an Academy Award for Best Supporting Actress for her portrayal of Oma, and, although she has not become a major star, she remains in demand and often dominates the usually high-quality projects in which she appears. As with all Huston films, even the casting of minor characters was meticulous. Rodriguez, a professional boxer, brought total authenticity to the role of Lucero, and the assemblage of battered pugs made it clear that the fight game breaks far more men than it elevates.

If there is a recurring theme running through the fabric of Huston's work, it is that dreams are elusive and that man is, often unwittingly, his own opponent. The broken, uncomprehending face of Billy lingers long in the mind of anyone fortunate enough to see this remarkable film.

Michael Shepler

FATHER GOOSE

Released: 1964
Production: Robert Arthur for Universal
Direction: Ralph Nelson
Screenplay: Peter Stone and Frank Tarloff (AA); based on the short story
"A Place of Dragons" by S. H. Barnett (AA)
Cinematography: Charles Lang
Editing: Ted Kent
Song: Cy Coleman and Caroline Leigh
Running time: 115 minutes

Principal characters:
Walter Eckland	Cary Grant
Catherine Freneau	Leslie Caron
Commander Frank Houghton	Trevor Howard
Stebbings	Jack Good
Elizabeth	Stephanie Berrington
Harriet	Jennifer Berrington
Kristina	Verina Greenlaw
Angelique	Laurelle Felsette
Dominique	Nicole Felsette
Anne	Pip Sparke
Jenny	Sharyl Locke

If *Father Goose* qualifies as a classic for any one reason, it would have to be the presence of Cary Grant. It was primarily through his interest in the original property that the film was made; it represented a new departure for him in terms of characterization, and it ended up being his penultimate film. He made *Walk, Don't Run* the next year, and then retired to pursue business interests and rear his daughter.

The title *Father Goose* is figurative and indirect but also quite appropriate. Walter Eckland (Cary Grant), a late 1930's dropout bumming around the South Pacific, is commandeered by his friend in the British Navy, Frank Houghton (Trevor Howard), to perform the job of "coast watcher," which consists of observing enemy sea and air movements from a remote island just after the beginning of World War II. His code name is "Mother Goose." He is not at his job very long before his solitary life becomes interrupted by a gaggle of tiny schoolgirls and their headmistress, Catherine Freneau (Leslie Caron), who are escaping from the approaching Japanese. Since the British are occupied with the war effort, Catherine and the girls are left in Walter's care indefinitely, a prospect that chills her and mortifies him. She hides his liquor, since it sets a bad example for the children, and criticizes his loutish behavior and unshaven appearance. He calls her a hypocrite, exactly the type of falsely proper, preachy moralist that caused him to drop out of the rat race.

Circumstances, however, dictate that they stay together. The islands are now swarming with Japanese troops, and there are any number of close calls in which both Walter and Catherine have to act calmly in order to protect the children. She proves more adaptable to the primitive living conditions than expected, and, for his part, he demonstrates a knack for communicating with the little girls. In one instance he is able to get one who had been traumatized into muteness to speak. By the time of the film's climax, Walter and Catherine have confessed their love for each other. They court very briefly, marry by radio from headquarters, and are attacked by the Japanese from the air in the middle of the ceremony, so everyone must dash back and forth from cover to the microphone. The ceremony ends just as the Japanese infantry lands on their beach. Catherine takes the small motorboat, escaping with the girls, and Walter pulls out as a decoy in the cruiser. There is a tense climax as he encounters and lures a Japanese ship out into the open sea, where he knows an American submarine is waiting. He nearly gets killed in the torpedo fire, but survives and joins the girls and his new bride. At the end, they are all rescued together.

Universal Studio's promotional material touted *Father Goose* as a radical break from Grant's traditional *persona*, stating: "Gone is the clean-shaven face; gone the impeccable tailoring that has distinguished Cary Grant throughout his long career." The part of Walter Eckland, however, was not a departure in the deepest sense. The Grant screen *persona* always resents the intrusion of anyone, whether they are crooks, liars, unimaginative cops, flighty and/or mysterious women, wealthy people of both sexes or plain ordinary citizens. His surliness forms the cornerstone of his charm. No one else has ever made his distaste seem quite so personal, or likable, except perhps W. C. Fields. Yet, whereas Fields was puffy and vaudevillean, often seeking to cheat first rather than be cheated, Grant is debonair, handsome, and very much the lady's man who merely does not want to be cheated at all. The winning aspect of his misanthropy in *Father Goose* is that he manages to be so honorable about it at the same time. These qualities are simply externalized for the first time here and to a maximum degree. As a result, even though he looks grubby clad in his oily jeans, his dapper magnetism comes across.

Caron is the film's other great asset. French, lithe, and very beautiful, she has a unique presence that is striking, but not altogether unprecedented in the gallery of Grant heroines. Caron's almond eyes and high cheekbones offset his soft, clefted features in much the same way Katharine Hepburn's did in her early films with Grant. Her performance invites comparison with the best leading ladies. There is a scene, the crucial one in bringing the lovers' feelings about each other into the open, in which Caron's particular brilliance is made very clear. Catherine believes, mistakenly, that she has been bitten by a snake. Because the only breeds in the islands are deadly poisonous,

Walter thinks he is helping her to die as he gets her drunk and tucks her in. The drunkenness is a first for Catherine. Caron's slinky, balletic movements as her limbs wind in and out of each other in the lotus position, simply to bring a cup to her lips, tell far more about her character than the dialogue does.

The script, based on a story by S. H. Barnett and constructed originally by Frank Tarloff, was taken through its last draft by Peter Stone, who had earlier worked with Grant on *Charade* (1963). *Father Goose* is no less believable for being a star vehicle, although much of its comic tone—Walter Eckland trading popeyed looks with everyone from pelicans to children—simply would not have been effective with anyone other than Grant. Even the dialogue seems made to order. A good example is Walter's reply when Frank tells him he needs a "volunteer" for the coast-watching service. He says, "Oh, I'd love to, Frank, but I've already volunteered for another watching service—the 'Watch Out for Walter Eckland Service'—it's damned important work, too."

The storytelling itself is well structured. From the opening scene, in which Walter sails his boat along idly, ignoring the explosive air attack taking place on a nearby island and switching the channel on his radio from war reports to the film's musical theme, "Pass Me By," no detail is superfluous. Everything is constructed with a purpose that pays off somewhere, either in the film's dramatic climax or in delineation of the central themes. There is also a system of confidantes and foil figures employed in various scenes. Frank has an assistant, Stebbings (Jack Good), to whom he has to explain everything; the little girls, playing with the radio, confide their troubles (which include progress reports of Walter and Catherine's relationship) to Frank, who in turn, needing Walter's help, but unable to relieve his bitterness at having so many demanding women on his hands, is forced to confide in Catherine; Catherine, at one point, drunk and thinking she has been snake bitten (it turned out to be a two-pronged branch instead) confides in Walter, who, thinking she is about to die, also confides in her. Like all of the best Cary Grant films, the story moves, sometimes meanders, but is never boring.

Ralph Nelson, who also directed *Lilies of the Field* (1963) and *Charley* (1968), is equal to the script. The supporting cast—Howard, Jack Good, and the little girls, Verina Greenlaw, Pip Sparke, Sharyl Locke, Stephanie and Jennifer Berrington, Nicole and Laurelle Felsette—are all excellent. The special effects—matte work, miniatures and opticals (to turn large Bahaman islands into small South Pacific ones, and render a realistic cameo of the Japanese Navy)—are extremely well done.

Father Goose opened as the Christmas show at Radio City Music Hall and went on to become a worldwide hit, gaining an Oscar for Best Screenplay. The critical reaction, on the other hand, was either condescending or negative. Arthur Knight of the *Saturday Review* saw it as suited "for the smaller fry," but "far removed from great comedy, which needs a good pinch of vulgarity."

Brendan Gill of *The New Yorker* similarly lamented the bygone era of *Bringing Up Baby* (1938) and its like. Although it is clear that these critics have, to some extent, a valid point (the most substantial being tht the film lacks spontaneity and draws heavily on the basic premise of *The African Queen*, 1951), one must bear in mind that 1964-1965 was a curious time. It was a watershed year in both American history and Hollywood filmmaking. Readiness among viewers and critics for more candid treatments of human (particularly sexual) relationships was in conflict with the traditional box-office ideal of "the film for the whole family." Thus, *Father Goose* was particularly appropriate as it was a sophisticated family comedy, and, as such, probably the last really successful film of its kind. *Father Goose* is a small gem that will endure.

F. X. Feeney

FATHER OF THE BRIDE

Released: 1950
Production: Pandro S. Berman for Metro-Goldwyn-Mayer
Direction: Vincente Minnelli
Screenplay: Frances Goodrich and Albert Hackett; based on the novel of the same name by Edward Streeter
Cinematography: John Alton
Editing: Ferris Webster
Running time: 93 minutes

Principal characters:
Stanley T. Banks	Spencer Tracy
Ellie Banks	Joan Bennett
Kay Banks	Elizabeth Taylor
Buckley Dunstan	Don Taylor
Doris Dunstan	Billie Burke
Herbert Dunstan	Moroni Olsen

In 1950 Vincente Minnelli directed a quick comedy while he waited to begin production on *An American in Paris* (1951). That quickly made comedy became a classic film in its own right and a large financial success for M-G-M. *Father of the Bride* scrutinized all the little courtesies, frustrations, and complex displays of good manners required in putting on a wedding. The bride, Kay Banks, is played by Elizabeth Taylor, but as the title of the film indicates, this is not really her story. Her character is fairly sketchy, delineated only enough to let us know that she is a typical idealized American girl from a steady family in a small town in the late 1940's. She is in love and wants to get married. This story is about the effects of the wedding on her family, particularly Spencer Tracy as Stanley Banks, the father of the bride.

If the goal of every young girl is to be married, as this film implies, then what is the goal of every young girl's husband? To be the father of the bride, suggests this film. There is no one prouder than Stanley from the moment that his daughter announces her intentions at the dinner table to the moment that she and her new husband drive down the road on their honeymoon. There is also no one more confused or more surprised and unlucky than the man who is about to lose his "baby girl" to a strange boy. At best, Stanley is filled with extremely mixed emotions, all of them funny and quite touching. After all, Stanley is digging into his own pocket to finance the loss of his daughter, a girl for whom nothing is good enough.

The opening image of the film offers a very broad clue to its general intent. The camera slowly moves past the debris which remains of the wedding reception, pausing when it comes across a pair of feet belonging to Stanley. Sunk in his chair with weary satisfaction, he turns directly to the camera to inform the viewer that he is in his current privileged position because he is the father of the bride. Stanley knows exactly what that means and is determined to share his knowledge. It means having a quiet family dinner shattered one night with your daughter's announcement of her marriage plans. Stanley does not even know the boy, whose name is Buckley Dunstan (Don Taylor), so he waits nonchalantly by the window the next time the boy comes to call and peeks through the pane to give him the once-over. He is not good enough; Stanley winces to look at him. Every time Stanley tries to worry about Kay's decision with his wife Ellie (Joan Bennett), however, she tells him to calm down and go to bed.

The father of the bride carries a heavy burden, at least in his own mind. He has to check the boy out. A painful interview ensues. Minnelli conveys the slow passage of time with the detail of a close-up of the ashtray placed near Stanley's chair. As Stanley nervously drones on, the ashtray fills with matches. Finally Minnelli pulls his camera back to reveal Buckley's bored face. That interview with the intended is followed by Stanley's next determined effort to do the right thing when Buckley's parents get the once-over. This interview, at least, is reassuring for Stanley. As he and his wife drive up to the house, which is quite large, Stanley observes that these people are all right; they have money. Herbie (Moroni Olsen) and Doris Dunstan (Billie Burke) are gracious hosts with thoughtful decanters of liquor on the coffee table. Ellie is also gracious, but Stanley first warms to the task of drinking the host's liquor, becoming quite talkative with his captive audience, and then falls asleep. Another interview has not quite gone according to plan. This same pattern of confident expectation and humorous realization follows Stanley from the party he throws to celebrate the engagement announcement, to meetings with the caterer, to church rehearsals for the wedding. At one point Stanley gets a little desperate with the weight of his ceremonial duties and offers his daughter some money to elope. His family quickly brings him back to the realization of his duties, however, and he is back with the caterer's bills and his good suit.

By the night before the wedding, Stanley is quite nervous, and his anxiety provides Minnelli an opportunity for a surreal dream sequence in which a distorted Stanley bounces down the aisle, his shoes sticking to the floor. Grotesque, horrified faces look on, overlapping in close-up. The organist is a goblin reminiscent of the terrors of old horror films. The bride screams in fear at her father's *faux pas*. Stanley awakens from the nightmare and heads for the kitchen. There he finds his daughter, also unable to sleep. Father and daughter touchingly reassure each other about the day to come, eating sandwiches and milk.

Because Stanley has already faced the worst in his nightmare and worked through his nervousness over sandwiches and milk in the kitchen, the actual wedding day finds him relatively calm. He is a rock of Gibraltar in the midst of pandemonium at home and confidently plays his part in a beautiful church ceremony. Only during the reception does he finally realize the terrible fact of his daughter's departure. He tries to find her to say good-bye, but cannot make his way through the press of the reception crowd. As he watches from a distance, the newlyweds' car pulls away.

All these events bring the story back to a disconsolate Stanley, surveying the mess of the reception's aftermath. As he ponders the wreckage, the phone rings. It is Kay, calling to thank her father and mother before she leaves on her honeymoon. After talking with her, Stanley turns to his wife, feeling much better. "My daughter's my daughter all of her life—our life," he tells her. Then the two of them have a sentimental dance in the midst of the party debris. The last shot of the film pulls away from the two in the dark, through a doorway which frames them dancing. In that silhouetted tableau it's possible to see the husband of the bride become the father of the bride.

Clearly, *Father of the Bride* is not the story of the romance of bride and groom. It is the comedy of manners, a courtship of social flagbearers. Along with conveying the humor of wedding preparations, however, from in-laws to decorators, involving church, home, and painful finances, the film depicts the poignant position of those involved in the ceremony. Stanley is funny but also quite touching, a man who is in a very real sense about to lose his daughter. What the father of the bride learns is to place his relationship to his daughter in a new framework. Now he is not simply daddy, but the father of the bride. All of the comedy and the lovely sentimental quality of the film derives from the title Stanley assumes and the education he acquires from his new status. The sympathy that the audience feels for Stanley is in no small part due to Tracy's delightful performance. Although the others in the cast are good, his at times wise, at times befuddled, Stanley is the highlight of the film.

The success of *Father of the Bride* led to a sequel, *Father's Little Dividend* (1951), which picks up where the first film ended. The sequel relies much more on the relationship between Kay and Buckley as they endure a first year of marriage and a first child. By this time Taylor was becoming a more popular star, and it was perhaps for this reason that the relationship between the newlyweds became the central focus of the plot. This was unfortunate, however, as the sequel did not stand up at all well to the original film either as a comedy or box-office moneymaker. Eventually the story led to a short television series in the early 1960's, but despite the appearance of M-G-M stock player Leon Ames as the father, it had little of the sparkle of Minnelli's original film.

Leslie Donaldson

FEAR STRIKES OUT

Released: 1957
Production: Alan Pakula for Paramount
Direction: Robert Mulligan
Screenplay: Ted Berkman and Raphael Blau; based on the autobiography of the same name by Jimmy Piersall and Al Hirshberg
Cinematography: Haskell Boggs
Editing: Aaron Stell
Running time: 100 minutes

Principal characters:
Jimmy Piersall (older) .... Anthony Perkins
John Piersall .... Karl Malden
Mary Piersall .... Norma Moore
Mrs. John Piersall .... Perry Wilson
Doctor Brown .... Adam Williams
Joe Cronin .... Bart Burns
Jimmy (younger) .... Peter J. Votrian

Real-life sports figures have often inspired good cinema—*The Pride of the Yankees* (1942, about baseball's Lou Gehrig) and *Knute Rockne—All American* (1940, about Notre Dame's famous football coach) are two obvious examples. In almost every such film that comes to mind, the subject is someone whose skills had taken him to the top of his sport. This is not the case with Robert Mulligan's *Fear Strikes Out*, however, a film based on Jimmy Piersall's autobiography.

The Baseball Encyclopedia reveals that Jimmy Piersall spent seventeen years in major league baseball, most of them with the Boston Red Sox. His lifetime batting average of .272 is well under the magic .300 mark that separates the potential Hall of Famers from the journeymen. Nevertheless, Piersall had a remarkable career—one that fully warranted an autobiography and film biography of a mediocre athlete still in his twenties. For Piersall in his heyday (the early 1950's) was one of the best-known and most controversial figures in baseball. He was an inveterate clown, umpire baiter, and brawler. Indeed, Billy Martin's fight with Piersall in 1952 was the first in a long line of that celebrated player-manager's celebrated bouts of fisticuffs. Midway into the 1952 season, Piersall was clearly losing control. At twenty-three, he suffered a complete, and very public, mental breakdown. *Fear Strikes Out* is the story of this breakdown and of Piersall's recovery from it.

Mulligan establishes the root causes of Piersall's anxieties early. In the film's first scene, John Piersall (Karl Malden) arrives home from work early because he has lost his job in a quarrel with his foreman. He quickly shrugs this off as a minor irritant, however, and turns his attention to his twelve-year-old son (Peter J. Votrian), who is practicing hook slides in the yard. The elder Piersall had been a semiprofessional ballplayer in his younger days, and he is obsessed with the idea that his son will someday star in the big leagues. Young Jimmy is desperate for his father's approval, but John Piersall offers only criticism. Jimmy can never do well enough to please him.

The first scene ends with a game of catch between Jimmy and his father. The elder Piersall is throwing the ball much too hard, and the boy begins to weep silently in pain, although he never stops returning the throws. The camera follows the flight of the ball, and suddenly the scene changes. The ball hurtles over a real baseball diamond, cutting down a runner sliding towards home plate. Mulligan has neatly moved the action into Jimmy's late adolescence.

The scene shifts to five years later, as Jimmy (Anthony Perkins), a high school junior, has just helped his team win the state championship with a great throw. Elated, he runs to share the moment with his father, only to be rebuffed. Every word of praise John Piersall utters is countered by two of criticism; he recites a litany of every slight mistake Jimmy made during the game. Obviously, nothing has changed between Jimmy and his father in the past five years. The poisonous nature of their relationship is gradually driving the younger man close to insanity. He slouches into the dressing room, gulps a handful of aspirin, and lurches, fully dressed, into the shower.

The Boston Red Sox hold Jimmy in higher esteem than does his father; they scout him extensively during his senior year. Although Piersall spends most of that season a nervous wreck—his attention is more on his father in the stands than on the game—he plays well enough to earn a contract with the Red Sox, who send him down to their minor league farm club in Scranton, Pennsylvania.

In Scranton, Jimmy does well. He is third in the league in batting average (his father carps that he should have been first), and, more importantly, his social life blossoms away from the influence of John Piersall. He meets Mary (Norma Moore), a pretty nurse, and the two fall in love. Jimmy's sense of humor, something that has not been revealed up to this point, asserts itself. Piersall seems on his way to becoming a well-rounded human being; but then the season ends, and it is time to return home. By this time, he and Mary have wed, and they move in with Jimmy's parents.

The next year is mixed for the young Piersalls. They have a baby daughter, and Jimmy does well the next season in Louisville (the Red Sox's highest minor league team), but his father fumes continually because Jimmy is "rotting" in the minor leagues. The decision of whether or not to buy a house sends Jimmy into hysterics; clearly he is losing his grip on reality. His deterioration continues during spring training, when he is given a slot on the major league club as a shortstop. Jimmy is stunned: all of his training, all of the programming by his father, has been for the outfield. He becomes literally paranoid about the switch, convinced that the Red Sox want him to fail and disgrace himself in front of his father.

John Piersall finds his son crying under the bleachers at his old high school. Blind to his son's distress, he lashes out: "You want them to call you yellow? If that's what you want, then you're no son of mine." His father's taunts pull Jimmy out of hysterics, but not back into any semblance of normality. Instead, he becomes an automaton, mumbling under his breath and raging at his teammates, whom he considers slackers. Finally, he picks a fight with one of them and is suspended from the team by his manager, Joe Cronin (Bart Burns). Mulligan makes it clear that Piersall is unconsciously hoping to get thrown out so that he will not have to risk failure at shortstop.

After his father intercedes, Cronin reinstates Jimmy as an outfielder. This time, he has no excuse for failure. The game in which Jimmy returns to the team is one of the most shocking and effective scenes in the whole film. It is a night game. Jimmy stands, alone and intent, in the outfield, his isolation intensified by the darkness surrounding him. The press had labeled him a "problem boy," and the crowd is unsympathetic. The soundtrack pulses with noise as the tension mounts.

Finally it is Jimmy's turn at bat. His father is in the stands, and the pitcher stalls, feeding his anxiety. Jimmy swings futilely at the first two pitches, but on the third, he hits a home run. The audience relaxes momentarily, thinking that the tension has lifted. As Jimmy crosses home plate, however, he continues to run. Charging towards his father's seat in the stands, he screams "I showed 'em," over and over again, and attempts to climb over the screen and into the grandstand. Dragged into the dugout by his teammates, he grabs a bat and begins swinging wildly. He has finally snapped under the pressure that has been building for more than a decade. This scene is the dramatic highlight of the film. Shocking and yet utterly convincing, it is the logical culmination of all that came before it in the film. *Fear Strikes Out* is only half over, however, with the story of Jimmy Piersall's recovery yet to be told.

The next scene takes place in a hospital. A Dr. Brown (Adam Williams) is explaining Jimmy's mental breakdown to the Piersalls. "You'll handle Jimmy easy, won't you," his father pleads—an ironic touch on the part of screenwriters Ted Berkman and Raphael Blau, since John Piersall never handled his son gently in his entire life. It is only after electroshock therapy that Jimmy begins to struggle back from his illness. Under Dr. Brown's careful tutelage, he begins to examine the corrosive relationship with his father that led to his problems. Initially, he resists blaming his father: "Why, if it hadn't been for him pushing me, I wouldn't be where I am today," he exclaims. Realizing the irony of those words—they are, of course, quite literally true— he bolts from the psychiatrist's office. When he returns moments later, he is on the road to recovery.

The elder Piersall also comes to understand his failure as a father through the course of Jimmy's illness. When his son finally confronts him with the words "All my life I've been splitting my gut to please you, and I never could. You're killing me," John Piersall goes home and cries. The two are reconciled later; Mulligan establishes this reconciliation neatly. Father and son, after a bit of nervous small talk, begin playing catch. In contrast to the similar scene early in the film, however, there is no tension or pain involved; this time, it is just a pleasant game.

The film ends as Jimmy is about to make his comeback with the Red Sox. Once more, his family is in the stands; for once, however, they are more nervous than he is. He embraces his wife and assures her that, although he is a bit frightened, he is ready to play ball for himself, not for his father. "I want to. I wanna play," he grins. The final shot is of a relaxed and confident Jimmy Piersall walking towards the field.

Mulligan's decision to end the film before his protagonist returns to the fray is both significant and sound, for Mulligan is aware that his film, and Piersall's biography, were only incidentally about baseball. The real story was that of a mind in torment, how it got that way, and how it recovered. Piersall's recovery is complete when he makes the decision to play because *he* wants to. His success or failure, while obviously not a trivial matter, is secondary to the fact that he decides to try.

Since *Fear Strikes Out* is centered on the relationship between Jimmy Piersall and his father, Perkins and Malden carry the bulk of the acting load, and they do so commendably. Malden has been a distinguished character actor for years, winning an Academy Award as Best Supporting Actor in Elia Kazan's *A Streetcar Named Desire* in 1951. The character of John Piersall is fairly one-dimensional as written; his main function in the film (perhaps, to be fair to the screenwriters, simply mirroring his role in Jimmy's life) is to intimidate his son. Even Malden's acting skills could not have turned the elder Piersall into a well-rounded human being, but by the end of the film, Malden is able to inject into his character a certain amount of sympathy. An occasional moment of tenderness surfaces before the gruffness takes over. These moments pave the way for John Piersall's reconciliation with his son at the end of the film.

Perkins, on the other hand, was a relative newcomer to the screen, and *Fear Strikes Out* marked the first full flowering of the acting skills that would characterize his career from then on. He excelled at playing troubled young men (with his role as Norman Bates in Alfred Hitchcock's *Psycho* in 1960 representing the apex of his career), and his portrayal of Jimmy Piersall gave him ample opportunity to convey his character's mental anguish. His angular, expressive face clearly reflects the torment in his character's soul. Among the other actors, Williams was fairly wooden as Dr. Brown, Jimmy's psychiatrist; but Moore was appealing in her role as Mary Piersall, Jimmy's understanding wife.

Fear Strikes Out marked the directorial debut of Mulligan. Mulligan went on to direct a wide variety of films—such a wide variety, in fact, that he has been criticized for lacking any distinguishing point of view. There has been, however, at least one recurring theme in many of Mulligan's films, such as *To Kill a Mockingbird* (1962), *Summer of '42* (1971), and *The Other* (1972): that of youth under stress. *Fear Strikes Out* was perhaps atypical of the best of these films, for it was based on fact.

There are two primary criticisms to be made of *Fear Strikes Out*. First, the film offers only a hint—mostly in his courtship of Mary—of Piersall's renowned sense of humor. His antics on the field made him a great crowd favorite, and his colorful personality paved the way for his career in broadcasting after his playing days were over. Mulligan evidently decided that an examination of this aspect of Piersall's life would have distracted from the seriousness of the film. He may have been correct, but *Fear Strikes Out* might have benefited from an occasional comic moment to relieve the tension. Second, and perhaps inevitably, the portion of the film dealing with Piersall's recovery is less interesting than that dealing with his breakdown. The slow, steady process of healing is always difficult to dramatize.

Despite these cavils, however, *Fear Strikes Out* remains an interesting and worthwhile film. It showcases the acting talents of Perkins and Malden and presents a sympathetic view of mental illness to a portion of filmdom's audience—the sports fans—to whom such a view may have been unfamiliar. Indeed, *Fear Strikes Out* is noteworthy primarily because it presents a view of a sports figure as a real person, not simply as an on-the-field hero.

Robert Mitchell

FFOLKES

Released: 1980
Production: Elliott Kestner for Universal
Direction: Andrew V. McLaglen
Screenplay: Jack Davies; based on his novel *Esther, Ruth and Jennifer*
Cinematography: Tony Imi
Editing: Alan Strachan
Special effects: John Richardson
Running time: 99 minutes

> *Principal characters:*
> ffolkes .... Roger Moore
> Admiral Brinsden .... James Mason
> Kramer .... Anthony Perkins
> Shulman .... Michael Parks
> British Prime Minister .... Faith Brook
> Sanna .... Leah Brodie

On hiatus from his starring role in the adventures of James Bond, Roger Moore chose to star in an extremely exciting high-seas caper, known as *North Seas Hijack* in England but titled *ffolkes* in America after its hero's surname. It would have been wiser to release it here as *North Sea Ransom* as was first intended, because although the film got enviable notices when it was released in April, 1980, potential audiences stayed away in droves. This occurred in spite of the fact that James Mason and Anthony Perkins were also featured with Moore, a big draw in his own right, and the supporting cast boasted some of the biggest names in British films.

The taste of the American film public is fickle at best, and their lack of interest in a thriller as exciting as *ffolkes* is simply indicative of their inability to be reached consistently by film reviews. The title alone might have thrown them off since it conjured up visions of something "folksy," even though the names of the three principal players should have lured them to the box office. Universal quite rightly did not want to release the film as *Esther, Ruth and Jennifer*, which is the title of the novel from which Jack Davies adapted his own screenplay, especially since the film has few women in the cast.

In this case, *Esther* is the name of a Norwegian ship which carries supplies to "Ruth," a drilling rig in the North Sea, and "Jennifer" is the sister production platform which produces millions of dollars worth of oil for Great Britain. James Excalibur ffolkes (Roger Moore) is the full name of the leader of a frogman-commando squad (known as "ffolkes ffusiliers") patrolling the North Sea. His frogmen are the best in the British Isles, and he drills them mercilessly.

In this role, Moore has completely eschewed the perfect stylish tailoring worn by agent "007." He dresses, not as a modern, urbane hero, but in baggy woolens, wearing a warm knitted cap over his usually fastidiously combed hair. He sports a scruffy beard and wears a pair of granny glasses most of the time, peering over them with his sea-blue eyes. He is, in short, weatherbeaten and a curio among captains, for his only hobby is working on needlepoint, which gives him a chance, he claims, to think clearly and logically. He drinks the best scotch, "neat" (straight up). Because of earlier events in his personal life, he loathes all women and is hardly civil to them; but he adores cats, which are his only friends. When he leads his frogmen, he wears a lumpy red wetsuit and requires that his crew be as adept with spear, knife, and gun as he, which they are, or they would not stay long under his command.

A group of seven hijackers led by a neurotic homosexual named Kramer (Anthony Perkins) and his lover, Shulman (Michael Parks) take over *Esther*, with her captain and crew, and plant explosives on both "Ruth" and "Jennifer," demanding twenty-five million pounds sterling as ransom from the British Government. They warn the Prime Minister (Faith Brook) that unless their monetary demands are met within a short period of time, both "Ruth" and "Jennifer" will be blown apart.

It is at this point that ffolkes and his crew are called in to detonate "Ruth" and "Jennifer" and capture *Esther* with the terrorists and their hostages. First ffolkes has himself and his men concealed on a British supply ship near *Esther*. The British government then contacts the captured ship and refuses to pay the ransom. Kramer orders the oil platform "Ruth" blown up to show that he is serious about his threats. Ffolkes's frogmen, having discovered the real location of the bomb, however, fake an explosion of considerable magnitude to make Kramer believe that "Ruth" actually has been destroyed in compliance with his orders. He is now confident that the British will bow to his ransom demands. In the meantime, several crew members of the captured *Esther* attempt to murder Kramer and his men by serving them poisoned coffee. Kramer discovers their plan, however, and forces one of the crewmen to drink the coffee, then has his body thrown over the side. In the confusion, Sanna (Leah Brodie), the only female member of the crew, disappears, and it is assumed that she too has gone over the side.

The next morning, Admiral Brinsden (James Mason) contacts *Esther* and tells Kramer that England will pay the ransom. He agrees to come aboard Kramer's ship because the hijackers want to be certain that the ransom is not booby trapped. Ffolkes accompanies him disguised as his aide and plans to shoot Kramer when the admiral distracts him by dropping a cigarette. Kramer suspects a trap, however, and will not let ffolkes remain on the ship.

That night ffolkes dons a wet suit, swims over to *Esther*, and sneaks on board. His men arrive soon after and attempt to take over the ship. When the fighting starts, ffolkes is almost killed when one of the hijackers sneaks up behind him, but he is saved by Sanna, who had been hiding on the ship all the time. As a lifelong woman-hater, ffolkes is now forced to admit that a woman has actually been helpful in a dangerous situation, and he offers her his thanks. The frogmen then succeed in recapturing the ship, and they kill the hijackers. When the seven villains are annihilated, ffolkes is properly rewarded. Knowing that he would shun monetary reward or any titular honor, the Prime Minister herself presents him in the name of Her Majesty with a handsome box containing three lovely all-white kittens, a delightfully soft ending to a tense adventure film.

Moore and the entire supporting cast turn in excellent performances. One of the most believable members of the company is Brook as England's prime minister. With her character obviously patterned after Prime Minister Margaret Thatcher, Brook is direct, intelligent, and becomingly efficient. The daugher of the late British actor Clive Brook, she carries on nobly in the acting tradition set by her father. The film is expertly directed by Andrew V. McLaglen, who, after a long career in television, has directed a number of adventure films with international casts which are aimed primarily at the world market, not merely that of the United States. *The Wild Geese* (1978) with Moore, Richard Burton, and Richard Harris was this same type of film. John Richardson's special effects are impeccable and add to the sense of realism in the film.

This film is an example of an excellent motion picture that can fail totally at the box office for no particular reason. American moviegoers have turned their backs upon it, and it apparently has not been released in many of the larger cities because of the disastrous fate it suffered in the Los Angeles area. It went to cable television within a year of its release and will probably be a staple of late-night television. The story is contemporary, but certainly will not age quickly. In fact, the universal oil situation will probably make it more timely as years go by and petrol shortages worsen. The film's fate in England as *North Seas Hijack* was a happier and more successful one, indicating more certainly that whoever titled the motion picture *ffolkes* does not understand American film audiences. The title gives no clue as to what an enthralling melodrama this is, and thus handicaps the film's potential as an audience-drawing thriller. Regardless of its title, *ffolkes* is the most original and suspenseful thriller to have come to the screen in a long while, and it proves conclusively that Moore is one of the best English male stars, deserving of a lengthy career beyond the five James Bond thrillers with which he has delighted moviegoers.

DeWitt Bodeen

A FINE MADNESS

Released: 1966
Production: Jerome Hellman for Pan Arts; released by Warner Bros.
Direction: Irvin Kershner
Screenplay: Elliott Baker; based on his novel of the same name
Cinematography: Ted McCord
Editing: William Ziegler
Running time: 104 minutes

Principal characters:
Samson Shillito	Sean Connery
Rhoda Shillito	Joanne Woodward
Lydia West	Jean Seberg
Dr. West	Patrick O'Neal
Dr. Kropotkin	Colleen Dewhurst
Dr. Menken	Clive Revill
Dr. Vorbeck	Werner Peters
Daniel Papp	John Fiedler
Secretary	Sue Ann Langdon

The screenplay for *A Fine Madness* was written by Elliott Baker, adapted from his novel of the same name. The film is a satirical comedy about a bullheaded Bohemian poet named Samson Shillito and his nonconformist life-style. Feeling battered and bruised by a heartless, uncaring society, he clings tenaciously to his dream of writing the greatest poem of his career. Although his creative juices have dried up some five years earlier, he never wavers in his belief that they will flow again, given time, inspiration, and the proper working conditions. The poem becomes his obsession, a goal to be defended against all odds. He is the talented intellectual down on his luck, fighting against impossible odds.

As the film begins, Samson Shillito (Sean Connery) is seen moodily hunched over a kitchen table in his seedy Manhattan apartment. His wife, Rhoda (Joanne Woodward), is fixing a hasty breakfast before rushing off to work. Almost immediately the audience is interested in how these two people with conflicting personalities ever got together in the first place. They are a classic example of the old adage of opposites attracting, for good-hearted Rhoda is an uneducated, gum-chewing, hard-working waitress and Samson is, by contrast, a brooding, frustrated intellectual. About all they have in common are their impetuous, violent tempers and their shared goal of Samson's creating a masterpiece.

Producer Jerome Hellman has chosen his settings well, shooting the entire film on location in New York amid grubby brownstone tenements and swank Park Avenue high-rises that provide the perfect background and atmosphere for the struggling poet. Indeed, the colorful, bustling New York backdrop compensates for some unevenness in the film, injecting a note of reality into the rather bizarre symphony of events that is being acted out.

As the story progresses, Samson, wearing the uniform of the "Athena Carpet Cleaning Company," wends his way toward a posh office building in downtown Manhattan. En route, he is beset by two zealous alimony process servers who threaten him with legal action if he continues to ignore his financial obligation to his former wife. This is the first of many such encounters; Samson is plagued by these dogged zealots throughout the film. Subsequent episodes lose some of their freshness and pointed humor but serve the important function of bringing home to the audience a keen sense of Samson's helplessness and frustration. While busily shampooing carpets, Samson's eye is caught by a blonde secretary (Sue Ann Langdon). In the hilarious debacle that follows, he proceeds, amid a torrent of bubbles and aghast onlookers, to demolish the reputation of both the "Athena Carpet Cleaning Company" and the blonde secretary.

Losing his job with the cleaning company, Samson intensifies his search for three hundred dollars with which to pay his back alimony. He enlists the aid of a friend who reluctantly arranges for Samson to give a poetry reading for a women's league composed of stuffy, rich, middle-aged "patrons of the arts." His railings against motherhood and practically every other subject sacred to the hearts of these pillars of society provide one of the funniest sequences in the movie. When he describes them as red roses who should open their corsets and bloom, it is more than they can bear. Shedding their veneer of civility and sophistication, they attack him with gusto. The ever-faithful Rhoda arrives barely in time to rescue him from the vengeance of this enraged mob of solid citizens. A most enterprising woman, she not only secures Samson's safety, but also extracts payment for the ill-fated poetry reading.

Rather than using the money to pacify the alimony servers, however, Rhoda engages the services of a polished Park Avenue psychiatrist, Dr. Oliver West (Patrick O'Neal), whose specialty is rejuvenating dried-up geniuses. O'Neal is perfect in his tongue-in-cheek portrayal. The psychiatrist is smooth-talking, nattily dressed at all times, and blessed with all the trappings of success. He has a home on Long Island with a kidney-shaped swimming pool, two late-model cars, two spoiled children, and a bored, unhappy wife, Lydia (Jean Seberg), who tries to fill her empty days with harp, ballet, and macrame lessons.

Director Irvin Kershner keeps the action going at top speed, rushing from one sequence to another, barely giving us time to grasp the impact of what is happening before he bowls us over again. Indeed, as the main characters scurry madly in and out of tenements, office buildings, training gyms, and sanatoriums, one has the peculiar feeling that the entire film is really a series of isolated incidents glimpsed through the window of a runaway train. Yet they represent exactly the type of life that Samson is living. We realize that his own misguided energy is precisely the reason for his failure as a poet.

Eventually, Samson is convinced by Dr. West to commit himself to a private sanatorium where he will be treated and also will have the peace and quiet to work on his poem, while out of the reach of the alimony servers. All goes well until he is discovered by Dr. West frolicking in the hydrobath with the doctor's wife, who is visiting the sanatorium. As a result, Samson is given a lobotomy to curb his antisocial behavior, a solution which the enraged Dr. West had previously opposed, along with Dr. Kropotkin (Colleen Dewhurst), another of Samson's romantic conquests and ardent admirers.

Clive Revill as Dr. Menken and Werner Peters as Dr. Vorbeck add a sinister, "mad-scientist" air to the hospital scene. These overzealous doctors are in the habit of performing unorthodox experimental operations on their patients in the name of scientific research. They provide the perfect excuse for Baker to poke a satirical finger at the so-called "experts" in the field of mental health care. Having performed the lobotomy, meant to curb the violent side of human nature and thus return its recipient to an active, useful role in society, they are confronted with a patient in the person of Samson Shillito who comes out of the anesthesia in a fit of rage and promptly proceeds to demolish everything and everybody blocking his exit from the sanatorium.

All is not lost, however; Lydia, feeling guilty over the part she has unwittingly played in precipitating the ill-fated operation, writes Samson a check that brings his alimony payments up to date. In the final scene, we find Rhoda timorously confessing that she is four months pregnant and begging Samson not to be angry. He blusters; but one is left with the impression that he is not, perhaps, too furious.

Connery runs rampant through *A Fine Madness*. As James Bond, a role closely associated with his name, Connery had already shown a flair for light comedy and a capacity for depicting violence. In *A Fine Madness*, he reveals a previously unsuspected talent for both slapstick comedy and raw emotionalism, evoking a range of emotions from poignant and sad to utterly hilarious. Woodward, his long-suffering albeit loving wife, manages to add a certain credence and dimension to the character of Rhoda despite the confines of a relatively unimportant and stereotyped role. All in all, *A Fine Madness* is a fine film.

D. Gail Huskins

FIVE FINGERS

Released: 1952
Production: Otto Lang for Twentieth Century-Fox
Direction: Joseph L. Mankiewicz
Screenplay: Michael Wilson and Joseph L. Mankiewicz (uncredited); based on the novel *Operation Cicero* by L. C. Moyzisch
Cinematography: Norbert Brodine
Editing: James B. Clark
Music: Bernard Herrmann
Running time: 108 minutes

Principal characters:
Ulysses Diello ("Cicero")	James Mason
Countess Anna Staviska	Danielle Darrieux
George Travers	Michael Rennie
Sir Frederic	Walter Hampden
L. C. Moyzisch	Oscar Karlweis
Colonel Von Richter	Herbert Berghof
Count Von Papen	John Wengraf

When *All About Eve* won the Academy Award for Best Picture of 1950, the Oscar, as was customary, was accepted by the producer of the film, Darryl F. Zanuck of Twentieth Century-Fox. Zanuck was only too aware, however, that the real winner that evening was Joseph L. Mankiewicz, who for the second year in a row had won Academy Awards for Best Original Screenplay and Best Direction. Mankiewicz's 1949 Oscars were for *A Letter to Three Wives*, although the picture itself was passed over by the Academy voters in favor of *All the King's Men*. Shortly after *All About Eve* was released, and while Mankiewicz was still preparing *People Will Talk* (1951), his next project, Zanuck wrote Mankiewicz a confidential memo informing him that his films for the studio would no longer be released as Zanuck productions. Zanuck later relented and accepted credit as the producer of *People Will Talk*, but Mankiewicz had already reached the conclusion that it was time he left Twentieth Century-Fox, where he had been under contract since 1943 after years of experience as a writer and producer at Paramount and M-G-M.

While casting about for a project that would enable him to work out his contract without the sort of major creative effort called for by *All About Eve*, Mankiewicz came across a completed screenplay by Michael Wilson which was just about to go into production. Wilson's script, which at that point was still called *Operation Cicero* after the title of the book by L. C. Moyzisch on which it was based, was a fictionalized account of the means whereby the valet to the British Ambassador to Turkey during World War II was able to photograph and sell to German intelligence copies of most of the Allies' top secret documents, including the final plans for the Normandy invasion of 1944. Moyzisch had been an attaché with the German embassy in Turkey, and Cicero was the code name given the valet by German intelligence. In Mankiewicz's revised screenplay for *Five Fingers*, the cynical German Ambassador, Von Papen, remarks that what has surprised him about his superior's choice of the name of the famous Roman orator and statesman was that they had even heard of him. Mankiewicz enthusiastically wrote Zanuck that he thought the script had "more than just potentialities—it is *on the verge* of being superb." The picture had already been assigned to Henry Hathaway, but Zanuck gave *Operation Cicero* to Mankiewicz with the stipulation that he not take a writer's credit for his script revisions, and that he accept Zanuck's friend, Otto Lang, as nominal producer. According to Mankiewicz's biographer Kenneth L. Geist, Lang was a former ski instructor who was learning the picture business from Zanuck in return for his tutelage on the slopes. Mankiewicz began by going through Wilson's script and, without changing his outline of the action, replacing most of the original dialogue with new lines of his own invention. Wilson has since contended that "no more than twenty-five to thirty lines" were rewritten by Mankiewicz, although textual comparisons of the Wilson and Mankiewicz screenplays prove otherwise.

Operation Cicero had been planned as a late entry in the well-received series of semidocumentary films Fox had produced since the war. At Zanuck's insistence, the title was changed to the meaningless *Five Fingers* because three of the studio's biggest hits in the genre had also had numerals in their titles: *The House on 92nd Street* (1945), *13 Rue Madeleine* (1946), and *Call Northside 777* (1948). A Fox-produced television series called *5 Fingers* also ran for a short time on NBC in 1959; but except that it was concerned with espionage, it bore no other resemblance to Mankiewicz's film. Most of the semidocumentaries carried full-frame titles proudly announcing that they were based on fact and had been filmed in the locales where the events depicted had originally taken place. Mankiewicz and a camera crew spent seven weeks in Ankara and Istanbul shooting exterior scenes with doubles for the actors who would appear in the interiors to be shot after they returned to Hollywood. While Mankiewicz was in Turkey, he arranged a series of meetings with Eliaza Bazna, the real-life "Cicero" of the story. Bazna offered to sell Mankiewicz some additional information that Moyzisch had not included in his book. Mankiewicz refused Bazna's offer "on principle," according to Geist, but he arranged to have their meetings photographed by a man with a hidden camera. The pictures thus obtained provided useful publicity when they were featured in an article in *Life* magazine.

Mankiewicz later described Bazna as "the most obvious-looking villain I've ever met. He was almost bald, with wisps of hair across his head, gold teeth, and two different-color eyes." In the film, Bazna, called Diello, is played by the darkly handsome James Mason, who nevertheless conveys the moral ugliness of a man who is willing to sell the Nazis information which could help them win the war. With the utmost self-confidence, Diello arrogantly stops Moyzisch (Oscar Karlweis) outside his quarters in the German embassy in Ankara and demands to speak to him alone. He tells Moyzisch that, in exchange for £20,000 the first week and £15,000 a week thereafter, he will supply him with rolls of film containing photographs of every top secret document that crosses the British Ambassador's desk. Moyzisch reports Diello's offer to Von Papen (John Wengraf), who in turn informs his superiors in Berlin. German intelligence agrees to pay Diello the sums he has asked, but they are too mistrustful to make proper use of the information he gives them.

Diello's motive in asking for so much money is revealed in his scenes with the Countess Staviska (Danielle Darrieux), the beautiful but impoverished widow of his previous employer, a Polish count. Since the start of the war, the Countess has been living in exile in Turkey, where Diello had met her again after his arrival with the British Ambassador. On the night that he receives his first payment from Moyzisch, Diello stops by her squalid apartment with a proposition: he will give her £5,000 and extra money to set up a decent establishment if she will occasionally allow him to use her house as a place in which to conduct the mysterious "business" that provides him with his handsome income. He tells her that when he has accumulated £200,000 he plans to escape to Rio de Janeiro where, at last, he can live as the gentleman he has always dreamed of becoming. He suggests that she might like to continue sharing his wealth, at which point she slaps his face "because, in the manner of an inferior, you tried to buy something you didn't think you merited on your own." The character of the Countess had no counterpart in Bazna's life, but was invented by Wilson in his original screenplay. The dialogue for Diello's scenes with her was the most heavily reworked by Mankiewicz of any part of Wilson's script. The interaction of Diello's snobbery and the Countess' need for money crackles with an energy and tension far stronger than any motive of physical desire.

British intelligence soon gets wind of the security leak in the Turkish embassy, and special agent George Travers (Michael Rennie) flies to Ankara to alert Diello's employer (Walter Hampden). Travers has the embassy safe wired so that a loud alarm will sound if anyone tries to unlock it without letting him know first. In the meantime, Colonel Von Richter (Herbert Berghof), a Gestapo agent who has taken over from Moyzisch as the Nazis' contact with Diello, has become curious about repeated references he finds in Cicero's documents to a mysterious Operation Overlord. He suspects, correctly, that Overlord is the Allies' code word for their inevitable invasion of Nazi-occupied Western Europe, the so-called Second Front. He asks Diello to bring him copies of every document he can find containing references to Overlord. Diello agrees, but when he realizes that Travers is having him watched he decides to quit while he is ahead and flee to South America with the Countess, whom he now freely addresses as Anna. She obtains the forged passports and other papers they will need; but, on the day planned for their getaway, Diello learns from Travers that his former employer's widow has withdrawn the balance of £130,000 from her bank account, which she had opened at Diello's request so that he would have a place to hide the money the Germans gave him, and has left suddenly for Switzerland. The now penniless Diello tells Von Richter that he will get copies of the Overlord documents for him after all, in exchange for £100,000 in cash. He silences the safe alarm by removing a fuse; but, while he is taking his photographs, a cleaning woman replaces the fuse so that she can run her vacuum cleaner. The alarm goes off when Diello tries to replace the documents and he is forced to flee with Travers and his men in hot pursuit. He reaches Istanbul, where his ship for South America is waiting, and hands the roll of film over to Moyzisch before making his final escape both from the British and the Gestapo men who want to kill him now that his usefulness as a spy is ended. Von Richter has the information about Operation Overlord that he wants, but he angrily tears it up when Von Papen tells him that he has received a letter written by the Countess Staviska on the day of her flight denouncing Diello as a British agent. A brief epilogue reveals that Anna, who double-crossed Diello, and Diello, who double-crossed his British employer, were both double-crossed by the Nazis, who paid Diello the exorbitant sums he asked for entirely in counterfeit bills.

The previously mentioned Fox semidocumentaries had been straightforward melodramas, seriously intended, with a narrator on the sound track to remind audiences that they were watching a true story. *Five Fingers* opens with just such a narrator describing the political situation in neutral Turkey during the war, but Mankiewicz quickly punctures this balloon of solemnity with a scene between Von Papen and the Japanese ambassador at a diplomatic reception. The two men have been patiently enduring an after-dinner recital by a loud soprano when Von Papen excuses himself by whispering that he has a headache. "Besides," he adds, "I hate Wagner." "Count Von Papen," the other ambassador delightedly whispers back, "You are the only unpredictable German I have ever met." Rennie as Travers plays his usual droll self, but under Mankiewicz's direction the rest of the principal actors in the film approach their roles in a spirit of comic exaggeration. The result is that they more nearly resemble the character types in a Lubitsch comedy of the 1930's than the naturalistically conceived figures in typical postwar spy films such as Hathaway's *Diplomatic Courier* (1952). Even Diello and the Countess, as they spar and play their tricks, remind one of the crooked hero and heroine of Lubitsch's *Trouble in Paradise* (1932), that charmingly amoral comedy about two thieves who are last seen picking each other's pockets as they ride off together in a taxi. The other relevant comparison, of course, is between

Five Fingers and one of Alfred Hitchcock's comedy thrillers. Mankiewicz does not have Hitchcock's skill at staging physical action, but the whole atmosphere of cross and double-cross is distinctly in the Hitchcock tradition, as is Bernard Herrmann's witty and romantic score. The film was nominated for Academy Awards in two categories: Best Direction (which Mankiewicz lost to John Huston for *Moulin Rouge*) and Best Screenplay (which Wilson, and, by proxy, Mankiewicz, lost to Charles Schnee for *The Bad and the Beautiful*).

Charles Hopkins

FIVE GRAVES TO CAIRO

Released: 1943
Production: Charles Brackett for Paramount
Direction: Billy Wilder
Screenplay: Charles Brackett and Billy Wilder; based on the play *Hotel Imperial* by Lajos Biros
Cinematography: John F. Seitz
Editing: Doane Harrison
Interior decoration: Hans Dreier, Ernst Fegte, and Bertram Granger
Running time: 96 minutes

Principal characters:
John J. Bramble .... Franchot Tone
Mouche .... Anne Baxter
Farid .... Akim Tamiroff
Field Marshal Rommel .... Erich Von Stroheim
Lieutenant Schwegler .... Peter Van Eyck
General Sebastiano .... Fortunio Bonanova

The first time Charles Brackett and Billy Wilder combined their talents to work as a writing team, one of whom also worked as producer and the other as director, was for *Five Graves to Cairo* at Paramount. This arrangement was a writer's dream come true, for it allowed them to control the production and the script. Their ensuing pictures included some of the brightest and most important films of the 1940's and the 1950's. Then Brackett moved to Twentieth Century-Fox to continue as a solo producer for a long list of films before he died, and Wilder is still working as an independent director, writer, and producer.

Five Graves to Cairo had been filmed twice before, both times as *Hotel Imperial*, the title of the Lajos Biros play from which it was adapted. The first time (1927) was as a silent, when it was one of Pola Negri's better features; the second time (1939) it presented Isa Miranda to American audiences in support of Ray Milland. Miranda never really made it as a star in the United States, although Milland was only six years away from winning an Oscar for *The Lost Weekend.* This second production had been planned two years previously as a vehicle for Marlene Dietrich and Charles Boyer to be called *I Loved a Soldier*, but Dietrich had walked out on the production and was replaced by Margaret Sullavan, who worked only a few days before she stumbled over a cable and injured her foot. The production was thereupon shelved and only revived in 1939 as a vehicle for the studio's new import, Miranda; it probably should have been left on the shelf, for it did not open the doors to a starring career at Paramount for her, and it was never anything more than a run-of-the-mill vehicle for Milland.

Brackett and Wilder only used the plot basis from *Hotel Imperial* as a jumping-off place for a brand new story line, which they called *Five Graves to Cairo*. Because World War II was in progress, the action of the piece was moved up to contemporary times, involving the conflict in Africa, with Rommel playing the key villain in an actual move he made in his North African campaign that nearly won victory for the Nazis. Brackett and Wilder turned the story into a tight, skillfully made thriller, loaded with suspense and as timely as the headlines of the day.

Five Graves to Cairo tells the story of a British corporal, John J. Bramble (Franchot Tone), the sole survivor of a tank battle during the fall of Tobruk. He manages to make his way to the Libyan border, only to discover that his regiment has moved on and the hotel where the English had made their headquarters is now held by the Nazis. The hotel's staff has run away except for the Egyptian owner, Farid (Akim Tamiroff), and his Alsatian maidservant, Mouche (Anne Baxter). Reluctantly at first, they give Corporal Bramble shelter, and he assumes the identity of a crippled manservant who was killed in a recent air raid. He and Mouche work to get information from Rommel (Erich Von Stroheim) and his officers. Bramble soon discovers that the man he is now impersonating had been in the pay of the Nazis, and Rommel divulges that seven years earlier the Germans had hidden huge supplies of gasoline, ammunition, and water in the desert; the key to the whereabouts of those hidden supplies lies in the position of the letters on the map spelling out the country's name, "Egypt." Those five letters become the titular five graves to Cairo, and it is Bramble's task to relay that information back to the British in Cairo. He manages only with the aid of Mouche, who gives her life to save him when his machinations are nearly discovered by Rommel and his officers. The British are able to locate the "five graves to Cairo" and usurp them, thanks to the information transmitted by Corporal Bramble, and Rommel and his officers are forced to make a hasty retreat from Africa.

The excellent dialogue and crisp story line elicit top performances from the cast. Franchot Tone, who never really got a great part from his home studio, Metro-Goldwyn-Mayer (outside of *Mutiny on the Bounty*, 1935), gives what is probably his finest acting performance in *Five Graves to Cairo*; and Anne Baxter, the only woman in the film, on loan-out from Twentieth Century-Fox, is spirited, sexy, and intelligent and gives the kind of performance that should have made her a top star. She did some of her best work in roles in which she had to use an accent (as in *Walk on the Wild Side*, 1962); she is always believable and dramatic. Erich Von Stroheim as Rommel gives one of the best performances of his long career. He fits his character to his own unique cinema personality and is wonderfully, Teutonically villainous, just he was later for Brackett and Wilder in *Sunset Boulevard* (1950). Akim Tamiroff plays the Egyptian hotelkeeper with a kind of catlike grace, and Peter Van Eyck, as a Nazi lieutenant who is attracted to Mouche, the maidservant, is a handsome addition to the cast, just as Fortunio Bonanova, as an Italian general snubbed and often snarled at by Rommel, is amusing and makes the most of the sharp, bitter dialogue assigned him.

The film should have won major nominations from the Motion Picture Academy members, but this was the year of *Casablanca*, also set in North Africa, which captured three Oscars and four other nominations. Academy members did at least acknowledge *Five Graves to Cairo* by giving it three nominations, recognizing its outstanding and dramatic black-and-white cinematography, its interesting interior decoration, and the superior job of film editing which never once lets the mood of tenseness lapse.

Brackett and Wilder were to go on to more popular collaborative efforts. Their films at Paramount—*Double Indemnity* (1944), *The Lost Weekend* (1945), *A Foreign Affair* (1948), and *Sunset Boulevard* (1950)—were especially honored. *Five Graves to Cairo*, however, began their collaboration, giving a promise for further work from two men who knew what they were doing and worked in complete harmony together.

DeWitt Bodeen

THE 5,000 FINGERS OF DOCTOR T.

Released: 1953
Production: Stanley Kramer for Columbia
Direction: Roy Rowland
Screenplay: Dr. Seuss and Allan Scott; based on an original story by Dr. Seuss
Cinematography: Franz Planer
Editing: Al Clark
Music: Frederick Hollander
Running time: 88 minutes

Principal characters:
Arthur Zabladowski .... Peter Lind Hayes
Mrs. Collins .... Mary Healy
Dr. Terwilliker .... Hans Conreid
Bart Collins .... Tommy Rettig
Uncle Judson .... Robert Heasley
Uncle Whitney .... John Heasley
Sergeant Lunk .... Noel Cravat
Stroogo .... Henry Kulky

To the average adult, *The 5,000 Fingers of Doctor T.* may very well appear to be, as Bosley Crowther stated in *The New York Times* upon the film's premiere, "a strange and confused fabrication . . . with little or no inspiration or real imagination . . . abstruse in its symbols and in its vast elaboration of reveries, but also dismally lacking in the humor or enchantment such an item should contain."

To a small child, however, one whose eyes are not yet jaded and whose brain has not as yet become sophisticated enough to see through the rather elementary Freudianisms that are liberally spread over the film's eighty-eight minutes, viewing *The 5,000 Fingers of Doctor T.* can be an extremely frightening experience. For while most adults have worked through, exorcized, or repressed the many childhood fears brought to light in this film, children have not yet had the chance to do so. *The 5,000 Fingers of Doctor T.* illuminates many of the most basic childhood fears; forces children to come to grips with the possibility of these fears becoming reality; and finally provides an ultimate victory over their influence—a victory of good over evil, of courage over cowardice, of action over passivity, and of the young over the old.

The plot of *The 5,000 Fingers of Doctor T.* is very much like a child's nightmare, and the outlandishly surreal sets inspired by the well-known children's author/artist Dr. Seuss give the film the look of one as well. It opens with a young boy, Bart Collins (Tommy Rettig, who was later to star in television's *Lassie* series) wandering lost through a dream world of huge metallic balls and mounds set on a slick, gunmetal floor. As he moves over this oddly constructed universe, he is attacked from all sides by a group of darkly clad men wielding colorful nets just the right size for ensnaring small boys. As the pursuers close in on him, the picture fades out and in again to reveal the boy, asleep at a piano. As he screams for the nightmare to vanish, he is awakened by his piano teacher, Dr. Terwilliker (Hans Conreid), a mean, pedantic dictator whose only concern seems to be preparing his students for an upcoming recital, and who will not let "one dreary little boy" humiliate him. He further demands that Bart practice, practice, and practice until his technique is perfect.

After Dr. Terwilliker stamps out the door, Bart turns and addresses the camera directly, an act which draws us into his own level of experience, forcing us to confront his predicament head on. "Well, that's my problem," Bart tells us. "Dr. T. is the only enemy I've got." He further explains that he accepts this horrid situation only because it pleases his mother, who is having a difficult enough time of it since the death of his father. He goes on to say that sometimes it seems as though Dr. Terwilliker has his mother hypnotized, a fear emphasized by her ultimatum that he *will* learn the piano even if she has to keep him at the keyboard forever.

After this introduction to Bart's unenviable situation, to his lovely young mother (Mary Healy), and to a handsome plumber named Zabladowski (Peter Lind Hayes), the boy again lapses into dreamland as the film's main action begins.

Another fade takes us out of the Collins' home and into the Terwilliker Institute, a surreal environment whose labyrinthian corridors, trap doors, leering gargoyles, and other assorted oddities look familiar enough to anyone who has ever delighted in the remarkable world of the Dr. Seuss books. It is a world both frightful and wonderful, a Technicolor playground which doubles as a cage.

Bart is now a prisoner in Terwilliker's "Happy Finger Institute." He lives in a cell, is forced to wear the horribly absurd "Happy Fingers" beany (a skull cap topped by a bright yellow outstretched hand), and will, as of the next day, become an unwilling participant in the fulfillment of Dr. Terwilliker's lifelong dream. For tomorrow is to be the official grand opening of the Institute, and five hundred little boys, five thousand little fingers, will be forced to practice the piano twenty-four hours each day, 365 days a year.

Another inhabitant of Bart's nightmare world is the plumber Zabladowski, employed by Terwilliker to install fixtures in the five hundred cells to be occupied by the soon-to-be-arriving boys. Most horrifying to the boy, however, is the presence of his mother, who, under the tyrannical doctor's hypnotic spell, serves as the Institute's second-in-command. To make matters even worse, she is to wed the Doctor immediately following the grand opening.

With this horrific scenario in place, Bart's duty is clear. He must first enlist the aid of the kindly Zabladowski, after which the two will free his mother; foil both Terwilliker's grand opening and his marriage plans; liberate five hundred boys from the Doctor's iron clutches; and finally, see to it that his mother and the plumber discover their love for each other, thus insuring Bart a stable home life and a normal family.

Bart accomplishes all of the above-named tasks entirely through the use of his own resources. He bring's Terwilliker's world crashing down around the befuddled tyrant by inventing a "music fix," a hastily fashioned device that seems to draw sound out of the air like a room deodorizer. He frees the other boys from a life of slavery and finally brings Zabladowski and his mother together. He awakens to discover that again he has only been dreaming, but happily finds that Zabladowski is driving his mother downtown (we can only assume that their marriage is just around the corner). Upon their departure, Bart grabs his baseball and glove and races into the street, freed at last from the horrors of the piano and of Dr. Terwilliker.

During the course of the film the viewer is presented with a number of situations which provoke in children terrible fears and insecurities. As the young son of a pretty widow, Bart must both grow up himself and watch his mother get along without a man around the house, without a father/husband to guide and protect a weakened family structure through the hazards of daily life. Add to this the prospect of an unloving stepfather, and real fright results. Bart's worries along these lines are clearly manifested throughout the narrative. He sees that Dr. Terwilliker has a certain influence over his mother and concludes that he has hypnotized her, that he has turned her into an alien being unable to love or to think independently.

The film also brings to light the fact that children often see that adults do not take them seriously, that childhood perceptions are deemed discountable and illegitimate. Bart senses this when he tries to convince Zabladowski that Dr. Terwilliker is a tyrant, and it is only after the plumber is shown tangible proof that he is to be killed when his services are no longer required, that he decides to aid the boy.

Perhaps the most important message imparted by *The 5,000 Fingers of Doctor T.* is that while many situations are indeed frightening and are filled with uncertainty, anyone, including children, can take matters into his own hands, deal with problems and fears, and provoke effective, long-lasting change. Demons, once defined, can be exorcized. Wrongs can be righted. The world can be made whole once again.

We all need to be reminded of our own power from time to time, and film is just one mechanism by which we can do so. With so many films telling us that we are helpless tools in the palms of massive and uncaring power structures, it is comforting to see that *The 5,000 Fingers of Doctor T.* is more than a simple children's fairy tale. Rather, it operates, as do all great fantasies, on a variety of levels, the most important of which reveals us to ourselves and instructs us on how best to live our lives in times of great difficulty.

Daniel Einstein

FLASH GORDON

Released: 1936
Production: Henry McRae for Universal
Direction: Frank Stephani
Screenplay: Frank Stephani, George Plympton, Basil Dickey, and Ella O'Neill; based on the cartoon strip by Alex Raymond
Cinematography: Jerry Ash and Richard Fryer
Editing: no listing
Running time: 97 minutes

Principal characters:

Flash Gordon	Buster Crabbe
Ming the Merciless	Charles Middleton
Dale Arden	Jean Rogers
Dr. Hans Zarkov	Frank Shannon
Princess Aura	Priscilla Lawton
Prince Barin	Richard Alexander
King Vultan	John Lipson
Prince Thun	James Pierce

Flash Gordon made his first appearance in 1934 in a comic strip by Alex Raymond. A Depression-weary America took an instant liking to this dashing science-fiction hero and his incredible adventures on the fantastic planet of Mongo. The tremendous public affection for this harmless bit of fantasy did not escape the notice of Universal. In 1936, the studio gave its veteran producer Henry McRae the then-incredible sum of one million dollars to create a thirteen-episode serial out of the best of Flash's comic-page derring-do.

McRae was able to stretch his lavish budget even further, thanks to the settings and costumes that artist Raymond had drawn for his strip. Aside from the outlandish monsters and a bit of futuristic machinery, Raymond had created a world that was littered with the artifacts and architecture of ancient earthly civilizations—primarily Chinese and Roman. Through the judicious use of props and stock film footage (from such films as *Frankenstein*, 1931, *The Invisible Man*, 1933, *The Invisible Ray*, 1936, and Twentieth Century-Fox's *Just Imagine*, 1930, among others), McRae was able to cut a number of corners on backgrounds and special effects. Curiously, this heavy interpolation of borrowed material into the *Flash Gordon* serial is not as distracting as it sounds; certainly the audiences of the day were happy with the results.

McRae turned the film over to director Frank Stephani, who wrote the screenplay along with George Plympton, Basil Dickey, and Ella O'Neill. The script followed the story developed by Raymond in his comic strip, and the film began with mysterious celestial disasters befalling the planet Earth. The disasters resulted from the approach of the planet Mongo, ruled by its diabolical emperor, Ming the Merciless (Charles Middleton), who is intent on destroying Earth, after first toying with it a bit. Ming causes comets and meteors to be hurled at the helpless Earthlings, two of whom—Flash Gordon (Buster Crabbe) and Dale Arden (Jean Rogers)—are forced to bail out of an airplane when it is struck by a bit of cosmic debris.

Flash and Dale land safely, but are captured by the brilliant-but-eccentric scientist, Dr. Hans Zarkov (Frank Shannon), who forces them at gunpoint to board his rocket ship. Zarkov plans to defeat Ming by crashing his vehicle into Mongo. The suicidal plan fails, however, as Ming's henchmen capture the trio before they can do any damage. The three are brought before Ming; the lustful tyrant takes a fancy to Dale, and Ming's daughter, Princess Aura (Priscilla Lawton), is similarly attracted to Flash. The remainder of the plot features one instance after another of Flash trying to save Dale, imperiled by one of Ming's monsters, only to be saved at the last moment (one episode would end with Flash facing what seemed to be certain death; the next would begin with his rescue) by the lovestruck Aura or by the brilliant Zarkov. Dr. Zarkov has a less complicated love life, but he is important to the plot, for it is he who persuades Ming not to destroy Earth immediately. Thus Zarkov and Flash have time to develop a plan to thwart Ming.

Meanwhile, Mongo teems with an incredible array of beasts and manlike creatures against which Flash must test his mettle. Needless to say, he is equal to the task. In a few instances, he not only defeats his adversaries but also succeeds in persuading them to join his crusade against Ming the Merciless. Among his new allies are Prince Thun (James Pierce) and his maned Lion Men, King Vultan (John Lipson) and his winged Hawk Men (who live in Sky City, a metropolis suspended by beams of light), and Prince Barin (Richard Alexander), who dresses like a Roman centurion and is in love with Princess Aura.

When Flash and his comrades launch their final attack, the forces of Mongo are defeated. Ming flees into the Sacred Palace of the Great God Tao, a holy-of-holies from which no one has ever escaped alive. Prince Barin marries Princess Aura, and Flash, Dale, and Dr. Zarkov return to the now safe planet Earth.

The plot may have been hokey, but the whole thing was irresistible, not the least because *Flash Gordon* featured inspired casting, especially in the choice of Crabbe and Middleton. Crabbe was an athlete before he was an actor. He won the Olympic four-hundred-meter freestyle swimming event in 1932, breaking the record held by another athlete-turned-actor, Johnny Weissmuller. His good looks and ambition took him to Hollywood, where, among his other roles, he took the perhaps inevitable shot at succeeding Weissmuller as Tarzan. He had made eight films before *Flash Gordon* made him famous. The virile Crabbe specialized in action and adventure films, including two more Flash Gordons, sandwiched around a Buck Rogers serial (based on another science-fiction hero from the comic strips) in 1939. He tried television briefly with *Captain Gallant of the French Foreign Legion* in the early 1950's, and retired from acting in 1965. None of his many roles brought him as much reknown as that of Flash Gordon.

Middleton was a veteran character actor who also reached the epitome of his career in the *Flash Gordon* serials, although he also played in such out-standing films as *Abe Lincoln in Illinois* (1940) and *The Grapes of Wrath* (1940). His Ming the Merciless appears to be the incarnation of evil; a more thoroughly dastardly character would be hard to find. In the other male roles, Shannon plays a relatively subdued Hans Zarkov; Alexander is a handsome Barin; Pierce is appropriately leonine as Prince Thun; and Lipson stands out as the barrell-chested King Vultan. The two female leads, Rogers (as Dale; she dyed her hair blonde for *Flash Gordon*, but appeared as a natural brunette in the sequel) and Lawton (as Princess Aura), are quite fetching.

Given the popularity of Flash and the other characters, a sequel was inevitable. 1938 found Ming the Merciless on the planet Mars (Universal capitalized on the Mars fever that gripped the nation that same year when Orson Welles terrified the populace with his radio broadcast of H. G. Wells's "The War of the Worlds"). Flash, Dale, and Dr. Zarkov investigate—Ming had been hitting Earth with a mysterious ray that deprived plants of nitrogen—and once again save their planet. *Flash Gordon's Trip to Mars* was the longest of the Flash Gordons, at fifteen episodes.

Flash came back for a final bow in 1940, in *Flash Gordon Conquers the Universe*. Crabbe and Middleton were back in their customary roles, but many other characters featured new actors. Carol Huges was Dale Arden, Roland Drew was Prince Barin, and Shirley Deane played Princess Aura. In this twelve-episode tale (which used a good deal of footage from Universal's 1930 feature *White Hell of Pitz Palu*), Ming is back on Mongo calling himself "the Universe"; hence the film's title, as Flash and his comrades fly once more into the breach to prevent the spread of a mysterious, Ming-inflicted plague called The Purple Death. Ming is defeated for what proved to be the last time.

Although the Flash Gordon serials were gone after 1940, they were not forgotten. Spliced together into single films, the three Flash Gordons appeared on television late shows throughout the 1950's and 1960's, inspiring a new generation of fans. One of these fans was director George Lucas, whose memories of the Flash Gordon serials prompted him to launch the epic *Star Wars* (1977) saga. *Star Wars*, in turn, sparked a boom in big-budget science-fiction films in the late 1970's, and the wheel came full circle in 1980, with the release of a new and lavish feature film entitled *Flash Gordon*. The 1980 version of the Flash Gordon saga was pleasant enough, and remarkably unpretentious, given the enormous size of its budget, but most critics agreed that it suffered in comparison with the original. Although they may never make anybody's ten-best list, the Crabbe–Middleton Flash Gordon films deserve to be remembered as an example of popular filmmaking at one of its apexes. Among the scores of cliffhanging Saturday matinee serials, *Flash Gordon* reigned as the undisputed king.

Robert Mitchell

FOOTLIGHT PARADE

Released: 1933
Production: Warner Bros.
Direction: Lloyd Bacon
Screenplay: Manuel Seff and James Seymour
Cinematography: George Barnes
Editing: George Amy
Music direction: Busby Berkeley
Song: Harry Warren and Al Dubin
Running time: 104 minutes

> *Principal characters:*
> Chester Kent .... James Cagney
> Nan Prescott .... Joan Blondell
> Bea Thorn .... Ruby Keeler
> Scotty Blair .... Dick Powell
> Silas Gould (Kent's partner) .... Guy Kibbee
> Harriet Bowers Gould .... Ruth Donnelly
> Vivian Rich .... Claire Dodd
> Cynthia Kent .... Renee Whitney

The year 1933 was an important one for the film musical and for Warner Bros. The studio, which had pioneered the sound film in 1927 with *The Jazz Singer*, was in some financial trouble. Three smash hit musicals in that year solved their money problems, however, and marked the emergence of an important new talent in the world of the cinema musical: Busby Berkeley. *Footlight Parade* was the third, and in some ways the most impressive, of these films. Lloyd Bacon's fast-paced direction, James Cagney's superlative performance, and a good script with plenty of snappy dialogue and well-drawn characters combined with some of Berkeley's best musical extravaganzas to make *Footlight Parade* an excellent backstage musical.

The opening shot of the film is of an electric newsstrip on the Times Square Tower proclaiming that stage shows are dead—only talking pictures will be made in the future. Chester Kent (James Cagney), a producer of stage musical comedies, does not believe it, but he soon finds that his employers do not agree with him. They explain that they want no more such productions because they can make more money from films than from stage presentations. "Breadline, I hear you calling," Kent responds. Then he finds that his wife Cynthia (Renee Whitney) wants a divorce now that he cannot buy her the good clothes and good times that she is accustomed to having.

At this low point Kent decides to use his stage experience to make prologues, short stage musicals to precede the films in large motion picture theaters. He plans to have many units and book them into hundreds of theaters. We know that the idea is a success when we see a large sign advertising Chester Kent Prologues, and then a crowded waiting room.

Behind that waiting room we find that the company is, in fact, much like a factory. Dozens of prologues are being rehearsed simultaneously, and in the middle is Chester Kent. Under constant pressure to come up with new ideas, he also auditions performers, supervises rehearsals (sometimes demonstrating dance steps), works on promotion, and worries about a competitor who keeps stealing his plans. When Nan Prescott (Joan Blondell), his personal secretary, tells him she thinks his partners are cheating him, Kent says that he is too busy to investigate.

The pace never flags as we are introduced not only to Nan, who is a wisecracking blonde in love with Kent even though he does not notice it, but also to Bea Thorn (Ruby Keeler), Scotty Blair (Dick Powell), and Vivian Rich (Claire Dodd). Bea is a mousy office secretary; Scotty is an aspiring singer who is the protégé of the rich Mrs. Gould (Ruth Donnelly), the sister of one of Kent's partners; and Vivian is Nan's rapacious friend who has designs on Kent. Among this group there is a great deal of rapid-fire dialogue and witty banter that always makes a point, advances the plot, or furthers characterization.

Kent admires Bea, with her glasses and lack of makeup, because she has brains—she is not interested in show business; but when Scotty tells her that she is not alive, "not a bit feminine—all you need is the *Atlantic Monthly* tucked under your arm," Bea goes to Nan for help, and soon the drab secretary blossoms into a beautiful dancer and becomes a star in the company. Meanwhile, despite the efforts of Nan to warn him of Vivian's true character, Kent has fallen in love with Vivian and wants to marry her. All of these plot intricacies move briskly along under the direction of Bacon and are carried off with style and verve by the principal performers. Needless to say, all plot complications are resolved happily. Vivian is exposed as the cold-blooded gold digger she is, Kent finally realizes he loves Nan, and Bea and Scotty decide to sing and dance their way through life together.

The film vividly conveys the backstage atmosphere which is so important an element in the plot. It presents show business as tough, frantic, exhausting, and exciting. At one point Kent is shown falling asleep in his office after working all night; and always in the background are the constant rehearsals. Some of the numbers being rehearsed are full-scale production numbers seen at the end of the film, but one musical number, "Sitting on a Backyard Fence," is seen only in dress rehearsal in an empty hall. Unlike most Berkeley numbers, this one could conceivably have been done on an actual theater stage, except for one or two overhead shots.

In the film's denouement Kent must present three different prologues in as many theaters on the same night in order to secure a valuable contract with the owner of a large chain of theaters. To prevent his rivals from stealing his ideas, he keeps everyone in the rehearsal hall until the big night finally arrives. Then the company is loaded on buses and hurriedly shuttled from one theater to another. There are many shots of the chorus girls changing costumes on the buses, running in and out of theaters, and scurrying around backstage. All of this successfully conveys the tension, urgency, and pressures of an opening night. Director Bacon, as he had earlier demonstrated in *42nd Street* (1933), was an expert at capturing backstage atmosphere.

As might be expected in a film involving Berkeley, the musical numbers are the chief attraction. The three prologues, as directed by Berkeley, bear no resemblance to stage pieces; instead they are full-fledged musical numbers in which he utilizes all of his celebrated techniques. Although famous for his use of the moving camera, overhead shots, huge, elaborate sets, and dancers forming patterns, Berkeley never surpassed the numbers he staged for *Footlight Parade*. All are classics and show various aspects of his technique at its best. Each detail, as it unfolds, reveals his creative genius.

The first prologue is "Honeymoon Hotel," which in style and character is a variation of "Shuffle Off to Buffalo" in *42nd Street*. It opens in the standard Berkeley manner with Scotty singing the lyrics to Bea, followed by a close-up of a hotel doorman in a newspaper advertisement, taking the viewer into the actual number. The photograph turns into a real doorman who sings a line of the lyrics. Then the camera moves on to a clerk, a bellhop, a cocktail waitress, the house detectives, and the switchboard operator, each of whom sings a line of the lyrics. This is another typical Berkeley device. At this point Scotty and Bea arrive and are shown to their room, where they find a welcoming party consisting of Bea's parents and relatives. Next, a shot of the hotel in cross-section shows a pretty girl in a negligee in each room. After a scene showing Bea with Scotty in a double bed quarreling and making up, the camera moves in for a close-up of a magazine whose pages turn until they stop at a baby's picture. Although there are many indications that the Honeymoon Hotel is not very respectable, the number is performed with such a naïve air of fun and innocence that it is inoffensive.

The next number, "By a Waterfall," is one of Berkeley's most lavish and dazzling musical fantasies. As Chester Kent says, "If this doesn't get them, nothing will." Running nearly fifteen minutes, it uses two huge sets and was supposedly inspired by Kent's seeing black children playing in the water from a fire hydrant. The number begins modestly and builds gradually through one stupendous effect after another.

After singing the lyrics to Bea, Scotty goes to sleep. Seeing a few girls in bathing suits by a waterfall, Bea quickly changes so that she too can frolic in the water. Soon there are many girls by the waterfall, and then the camera moves in closer as the girls perform an intricate aquaballet. There are underwater shots, overhead shots, and close-ups, as Berkeley photographs the swimmers from almost every conceivable angle while they form kaleidoscopic patterns, break apart, and regroup. At one point the setting changes from the sylvan to an art deco Roman bath, and the dazzling variations continue. In addition to using a variety of shots, Berkeley continually changes the lighting for added emphasis and diversity. Sometimes the swimmers are dark silhouettes in the lighted pool, and then the effect is reversed, with the pool dark and only the girls lighted. At one point they form chains that become snakes, a Berkeley trademark, then butterflies, then a mandala in a continuous fluid series of movements. For the ending, the girls perch on a huge tiered fountain that revolves and spouts water, and the effect is that of a gigantic fountain composed of human bodies. The ending of the number brings us back from the realm of fantasy to reality as Bea sprinkles water on Scotty's feet to awaken him.

The final number, "Shanghai Lil," is the most dramatic and in many ways the most impressive number in the film. It is unique among Berkeley's creations because it is dominated and shaped by the vitality, singing, and dancing of its star, Cagney. The number tells a dramatic story before ending with some spectacular Berkeley patterns. In the time-honored tradition of backstage musicals, Chester Kent goes on at the last moment to save the show. Pushed down a short flight of stairs by the drunken leading man, Kent is literally forced into the number. We have already been prepared for his ability to handle the role because we have seen him rehearsing the various prologues and showing the chorus girls how to do the steps. The camera follows Kent as he threads his way among the tables of a barroom looking for his sweetheart, Shanghai Lil. The lyrics are half sung, half spoken by various people in the room as Kent makes his way to the bar, where he gets a bottle and sings about Shanghai Lil. There we see different types of people: a black, several Orientals, a number of sailors, and a British army officer. Each is assigned a single line of the lyrics.

Still searching for Shanghai Lil, Kent goes into a romanticized and extremely stylized version of an opium den filled with beautiful, long-haired girls reclining languorously on shadow-barred couches. Kent continues searching until, after a huge barroom brawl that seems almost choreographed, he comes out from behind the bar in a sailor's uniform while Shanghai Lil, played by Bea in a black wig and satin pajamas, appears from the other end. They sing the lyrics to each other, Bea does a tap dance on top of the bar, and Kent joins her. Suddenly a bugle call is the signal for sailors to form ranks and march off to their ship as crowds cheer. They go through various weapons drills before being joined by their Chinese girl friends. The situation is being reversed and it is Shanghai Lil who is looking for Kent and begging him to take her with him when he leaves. In the closing sequence the marching sailors, using placards, successively form pictures of the American flag, Franklin D. Roosevelt's face, and the National Recovery Act eagle. In the last shot we see Lil, now dressed in a sailor's uniform, marching off with Kent to board the ship.

Although Cagney is famous for his gangster roles, he himself is prouder of his musical films. *Footlight Parade* abundantly shows why. Indeed, the talents of Cagney and Berkeley dominate the film and make it a classic of musical cinema.

Julia Johnson

FORBIDDEN PLANET

Released: 1956
Production: Nicholas Nayfack for Metro-Goldwyn-Mayer
Direction: Fred McLeod Wilcox
Screenplay: Cyril Hume; based on an original story by Irving Block and Allen
  Adler
Cinematography: George Folsey
Editing: Ferris Webster
Music: Louis Barron and Bebe Barron
Running time: 98 minutes

Principal characters:
Dr. Morbius .... Walter Pidgeon
Altaira Morbius .... Anne Francis
Commander Adams .... Leslie Nielsen

From the time of Fritz Lang's *Metropolis* (1926) to the present, science-fiction films have expressed modern man's simultaneous fascination with and fear of the growing rapidity of man's technological innovation. This genre forms the screen upon which we can project our possible futures and see, through imaginative extrapolation, the results of our present acts. These projections are not, however, the purely mathematical or even logical outgrowths of our daily circumstances; they are an almost allegorical mixture of our cultural prejudices and our present fears.

When Boris Karloff cinematically immortalized Mary Shelley's Gothic figures in James Whale's *Frankenstein* (1931), he represented far more than the embodiment of that particular character. He personified the contemporary tension between man's newly found ability to control life and the still strong Judeo-Christian injunction against an individual's creations challenging those of the Creator Himself. Thus, beneath the film's technological trappings lies a bedrock of moral and psychological concerns expressed in the original Shelley novel.

An ethical antipathy to the forces of scientific change is found throughout films of the 1930's, even those that are not explicitly science fiction. In Charles Chaplin's *Modern Times* (1936), for example, the huge surreal machines which surround the Tramp are clearly antithetical to the film's sylvan, pastoral ending when Chaplin and Paulette Goddard walk away from the amoral city and into the United States' uncluttered agricultural past. Thus, throughout the era the tension between the machine and nature grew more pronounced and could only be resolved through escapism, as in *Modern Times*, or through the death of nature's near divinity, as in King Kong's unsuccessful epic battle against the Empire State Building and the airplanes which attack him.

During the 1940's and early 1950's, director/producers such as Val Lewton

(*Cat People*, 1942; *Isle of the Dead*, 1945; and *Bedlam*, 1946) focused this general phobia against technological change and began to apply it in ways that seemed more specifically to reflect their time's ambience. Thus, Byron Haskin's *War of the Worlds* (1953) stems not only from H. G. Wells's fascinating story but also from the McCarthy era's fear of Communist invasion. Likewise, Jack Arnold's *The Incredible Shrinking Man* (1953) seems to reflect the modern person's sense of diminishing self-worth in a growing mass society which was and is constantly threatened by the destructive power of atomic weaponry.

Throughout the middle and late 1950's, the period of open-air testing and of fallout shelter mania, science-fiction films found their format in the atomic potential for destruction. Typically, a hydrogen blast would unleash a mutated or primitive natural force which would revenge the systematic abuse of nature that had been seen in the 1920's, 1930's, and 1940's, as in *Godzilla* (1954). This A-bomb/monster combination was often too predictable and too facile, however, and it was not until *Forbidden Planet* (1956) that the psychological and moral tensions between past and future found an adequate vehicle.

Forbidden Planet, unlike its predecessors, drew from the two wellsprings of science fiction: a classic moral model and a modern psychological understanding. Thus, the story is a hybrid of two unlikely sources: William Shakespeare's last play, *The Tempest*, and Sigmund Freud's concept of a tripartite psyche consisting of the id, the basic primordial animalistic instinct; the ego, the conscious awareness of self and of others; and the superego, the moral moderator which enforces social and ethical norms in the conscious mind. This apparently infelicitous marriage is not as unlikely as it might seem; but to understand it fully we must turn to the film's plot.

Commander Adams (Leslie Nielsen) and his crew have been sent by earth to investigate an apparently ill-fated colonization effort of twenty years earlier. Upon landing he is greeted by a robot named Robby who escorts him to the home of the colony's two survivors, Dr. Morbius (Walter Pidgeon) and his extremely innocent and beautiful daughter, Altaira (Anne Francis). Dr. Morbius and his daughter, as he explains, are the only members of the original landing party who were saved from an unknown malevolent nocturnal power. When the spacemen are able to turn their attention from Altaira, they begin to wonder about Dr. Morbius' plush accommodations. As they discover, Dr. Morbius draws his physical wealth and, as will later be seen, his mental prowess from the mechanical remains of an ancient and highly evolved civilization, the Krell. He takes his material needs from a two hundred thousand-year-old powerhouse and has, through a Krell I.Q. machine, greatly increased his psychic powers. All this has led to an idyllic existence for twenty years; but now the spell is broken.

While Earl Holliman, as a space age cook, provides comic relief by convincing Robby to produce endless bottles of alcohol, the nocturnal monster stalks again. As we quickly discover, this invisible demon is a product of Dr. Morbius' sleeping mind. While unconscious, his most primal fears of the spacemen emerge as a telekinetically embodied monster which is fueled not only by Morbius' mind but also by the Krell powerhouse. At this point, the demise of the wise and superintelligent Krell race is explained. Having given themselves the power to materialize thought, they were, despite all their intellect, destroyed by the irrational urges that seethe at the bottom of even the most rational mind. Thus, Dr. Morbius' living nightmare can only end when he is destroyed by the amplified forces of his own basic fears.

Now some Shakespearean parallels become clear. Dr. Morbius is Shakespeare's Prospero, the magician who controls the action in *The Tempest*, and Altaira is his daughter, Miranda. Commander Adams is the handsome Prince Ferdinand. Robby is Caliban, the earthly—and here mechanical—spirit. The monster is Ariel, the effluvial sprite who does Prospero's bidding. Even minor characters, such as the cook, fit the mold: he matches Shakespeare's Stephano, the drunken servant. Thus, all these similarities tie the movie to the play and so provide a classic base of humanity, virtue, and the values of marriage.

Each major character also plays a Freudian role. Morbius and Altaira are, in this scheme, still father and daughter, although now in the archetypal Electra pattern (the female equivalent of the Oedipus complex) in which the overly fond father drives off a more appropriate suitor (Adams). Unable to realize this desire during his conscious moments, Morbius' id comes forth in the world of dreams. Within this sphere of wish-fulfillment—unhampered by the superego—the monster of his incestuous protectiveness comes forth and is, in this case, literally embodied by his Krell-enhanced capacity for telekinesis. Ultimately, Dr. Morbius is confronted with his own primal nature, and this confrontation, as in psychotherapy, leads to the crisis.

By bringing these elements together—Shakespeare and Freud, past and present, technology and psychology—*Forbidden Planet* epitomizes the inherent structure of the science-fiction tale. It brings into conscious recognition the forces that had always been at play in this backwater genre. In doing this with some quality, *Forbidden Planet* began the trend—especially in the United States—toward cinematic development of an often abused art form.

While the acting, especially that of Pidgeon, is better than the usual "B"-grade average, it still is not the film's saving grace; rather, the attention to the supporting technology is what helps to distinguish the film. The sets—the saucer/spaceship, Morbius' home, the Krell powerhouse—are all created with an attention to detail that gives them plausibility. This realism is complemented by the art work, which must create the impression of a new world and not, as was typical for this era, of a picture filmed in Arizona. The music, too, adds to this heightened effect, using electronic music effectively for almost the first time. Finally, Robby the Robot is himself a notable addition to the genre's repertoire of devices. Robby, the urbane, knowledgeable, almost human being, formed the prototype for a generation of robots to come, leading ultimately to H.A.L. in Stanley Kubrick's *2001* (1968).

Forbidden Planet, therefore, while not the most important picture of the 1950's, made a notable contribution to film. It helped to create a film precedent for the acceptance of psychology and special effects; it opened the way for the development of serious fantasy films; and it introduced the techniques which were to be realized most fully by the mammoth productions of the late 1970's: *Star Wars* (1977), *Close Encounters of a Third Kind* (1977), and *Alien* (1979).

Daniel D. Fineman

FORCE OF EVIL

Released: 1948
Production: Bob Roberts for Enterprise; released by Metro-Goldwyn-Mayer
Direction: Abraham Polonsky
Screenplay: Abraham Polonsky and Ira Wolfert; based on the novel *Tucker's People* by Ira Wolfert
Cinematography: George Barnes
Editing: Art Seid
Music: David Raksin
Running time: 78 minutes

Principal characters:
Joe Morse	John Garfield
Leo Morse	Thomas Gomez
Doris Lowry	Beatrice Pearson
Ben Tucker	Roy Roberts
Edna Tucker	Marie Windsor
Freddie Bauer	Howland Chamberlain
Ficco	Sheldon Leonard

The critical and commerical success of *Body and Soul* (1947) paved the way for a second teaming of John Garfield and Abraham Polonsky, thus allowing Polonsky the opportunity of directing a film that he had written. Viewed upon release as somewhat of an arty gangster film, *Force of Evil* is something far more—a somber, unrelenting tale of corruption and attempted redemption.

Joe Morse, a young corporation lawyer (John Garfield), aligns himself with Ben Tucker (Roy Roberts), a smooth racketeer. Together they devise a scheme to turn a lucrative numbers racket into a legitimate business. They have discovered that superstition invariably causes thousands of nickel and dime bettors to pick 776 to win every Fourth of July. Joe and Tucker, cutthroat businessmen out to eliminate the competition, arrange for the number to hit, causing the collapse of all the small numbers "banks," which are unable to pay off. One such bank, however, is run by Joe's older brother, Leo (Thomas Gomez), a failed businessman with a weak heart. Joe owes his success to Leo, who sacrificed his own dreams by working to put Joe through school. Joe's rise from the slums to an office on Wall Street has left him with an enormous sense of responsibility and guilt. He must therefore coerce Leo into Tucker's Combination because he knows that when Leo's bank is wiped out with the rest, it will kill him.

In trying to persuade Leo to become one of Tucker's people, Joe meets his brother's secretary, Doris Lowry (Beatrice Pearson), a fresh-faced innocent in an otherwise corrupt world. Joe has never known anyone like her and is immediately attracted to her, while Doris, although disapproving of the kind of life he represents, is drawn to Joe and to the promise of excitement he offers. Meanwhile, two problems loom on the horizon for Tucker and Joe. A shadowy "special prosecutor" named Hall, whom we never see, is intent on trapping the Combination and its lawyer by tapping their telephones, and Ficco (Sheldon Leonard), Tucker's ex-partner from Prohibition days, arrives. He is a stereotypical gangster possessed of none of Tucker"s carefully acquired polish, and he is an unpleasant reminder of Tucker's past.

As the Fourth of July draws closer, Joe attempts to frighten his brother by arranging for the police to raid his bank. Everyone is arrested: Leo, Doris, Bauer, the frightened bookkeeper, and even the cleaning lady. Joe bails them out but Leo is adamant and will not join the scheme, clinging to his illusion of being a respectable paternalistic small businessman. When the number 776 hits and the small banks go under, Tucker, as a favor to Joe, allows Leo and his staff to remain in business, with Tucker running the show. When Freddie Bauer (Howland Chamberlain), terrified to see Tucker's gangsters in the office, attempts to quit, he is told that no one quits the Combination. Later, approached by one of Ficco's henchmen, Bauer is forced to arrange a meeting between Leo and Ficco. The "meeting" turns out to be a kidnaping engineered by Ficco, who is still attempting to force his way into the Combination. Leo is abducted, and Bauer, the timid Judas, is killed.

When Joe learns of the kidnaping, he bursts into Tucker's apartment demanding his brother's release. Ficco is there, now a full partner with Tucker. Joe is told that Leo has died of a heart attack and that his body has been dumped by the river. Suddenly the tension which has pervaded the film erupts into violence. A gun battle ensues, and Joe kills both men in the darkened apartment.

Leaving Tucker's apartment as the sun is rising, Joe finds Doris waiting. He runs through the empty streets until he reaches a great bridge and begins to descend flight after flight of stairs in search of his brother. He finds his brother's body where the gangsters left it on the rocks. Doris reaches his side as he turns away and leaves to surrender to the prosecuter.

Garfield's electric personality was never used to better advantage. Gomez's Leo is a remarkably defined character: a "good" man with a martyr complex that allows him to abandon his own dreams in favor of his brother's. In the kidnaping scene, for example, as he is dragged from the all-night diner to his doom, his crumpled body supported by his arms, Leo assumes the appearance of a shabby Christ. Pearson, who possessed the talent and "offbeat" beauty that might have made her a star, appeared in only one other film before disappearing from Hollywood. Chamberlain is the perfect victim as the frightened bookkeeper, first coerced into becoming a Judas goat and then slaughtered.

Force of Evil had some disturbing things to say about the law as an abstraction. Hall, the special prosecutor, is always mentioned but never seen. He is omnipresent and threatening, not unlike Ben Tucker. In initiating the wire-taps in his battle against organized crime, he presents an uncomfortable parallel to similar actions occurring during the Cold War hysteria which had already begun to cast a cloud over Hollywood. The filmmakers at Enterprise were aware of this; and, as a result, scene after scene reverberates with a palpable paranoia. The film's ending, centering on Joe's decision "to help," was, as director Polonsky admits, something of a compromise with Hollywood censors. Yet it rings true because the long descent to the bridge, "the bottom of the world," is representative of Joe reaching his nadir. He must commit himself to the destruction of the evil of which he has been a part if he is to survive at all. Far from being a noble act, it is one born out of desperation.

Force of Evil received little attention when it was released in 1948. Enterprise had lost a great deal of money in other ventures, chiefly Lewis Milestone's epic film *Arch of Triumph* (1948), and with the dissolution of that studio, M-G-M assumed distribution of the film and handling it as if it were a routine programmer. With time, however, it has grown significantly in stature. The richness of the film and its use of image and language indicate that it was somewhat ahead of its time and that audiences of the 1940's simply did not fully understand it.

Perhaps the very richness of the film is what made it so misunderstood, so inaccessible. It is a gangster film with allusions to the coming blacklist, but it is also a love story, not between a man and a woman but between two brothers who ultimately destroy each other. It is a film which dared to tell its audience that there are no easy answers—that perhaps no answers exist at all.

Michael Shepler

A FOREIGN AFFAIR

Released: 1948
Production: Charles Brackett for Paramount
Direction: Billy Wilder
Screenplay: Charles Brackett, Billy Wilder, and Richard L. Breen; based on stories by Robert Harari, Irwin Shaw, and David Shaw
Cinematography: Charles Lang
Editing: Doane Harrison
Costume design: Edith Head
Music: Frederick Hollander
Running time: 115 minutes

> *Principal characters:*
> Phoebe Frost .... Jean Arthur
> Erika von Schluetow .... Marlene Dietrich
> Captain John Pringle .... John Lund
> Colonel Rufus J. Plummer .... Millard Mitchell

The summer of 1948 saw the unexpected release of what is still considered the best "black" comedy to emerge from Hollywood, *A Foreign Affair*. It was the kind of film only Charles Brackett and Billy Wilder would have dared make on a postwar theme. It dealt with the twelve thousand American troops assigned to the American zone of Berlin, and with what came to be known as the "moral malaria" infecting them. It was remarkably witty and funny— in a sobering kind of way. *A Foreign Affair* remains one of the best of all the Brackett-Wilder comedies released by Paramount during the 1940's; and in addition to being funny, it provides food for thought, as well as a good photographic view of life as it was then being lived among the ruins of Berlin. Its exteriors were all shot in the actual occupation zone of that city.

As the movie opens, a congressional investigating committee arrives in Germany to track down the facts of what is really going on among American men stationed there. The most determined member is a spinster Congress-woman from Iowa, Miss Phoebe Frost (Jean Arthur), who is ready to be shocked by everything she learns and is equally confident that she can right all the wrongs she uncovers. Captain John Pringle (John Lund) is put in charge of showing her Berlin. He is disgruntled at first, because he himself has been involved in black market profiteering, and is reluctant to throw the first stone in an investigation. Gradually, however, she wins him over in spite of the fact that he has also been enjoying the favors of a onetime Nazi, Erika von Schluetow (Marlene Dietrich). Later, when Phoebe discovers what is going on between Captain Pringle and the lovely Erika, her annoyance and rage are boundless.

The pace never slows, in spite of such black comedy happenings as black market operations in full swing under the Brandenburg Gate by day and drunken gaieties in the cabarets by night—all patronized by the occupying armies. Driven to desperation when she tries to prove to Erika that American women are not the moral frumps that German women believe them to be, Phoebe makes the mistake of drinking too much champagne, which causes her to behave with abandon. She realizes that she has disgraced her country as well as herself; but before she returns home in shame, she wins the admiration of Captain Pringle, who recognizes that she is human after all. The audience now perceives that Phoebe is going to win Captain John, romantically. The sophisticated Erika, whose operations have been exposed, is sent to jail and placed under the guard of a handsome policeman. She proves that if a woman has something to sell in an occupied country, she can always find a willing buyer among the onetime enemy, even if it is behind bars.

Directed at a fast pace by cowriter Wilder, the motion picture's comedy never falters even under the blackest circumstances, and the cast of four principals constantly sustains the script. Lund as John Pringle has his best part ever at Paramount. The understanding Colonel is played with just the right degree of awareness by Millard Mitchell. Arthur as Phoebe Frost is cast in a role perfectly suited to her talents: she is officious and, at first, seemingly right out of the Bible belt. Then as she falls under the spell of Captain Pringle and becomes progressively more human, she turns from an ill-tempered spinster into a shy and very attractive woman.

Dietrich, as the onetime Nazi charmer, Erika, has one of her best parts. In addition to being well photographed by Charles Lang, she and Arthur have been given some very pungent dialogue as they spar for the favors of the hero. Dietrich, beautifully gowned by Edith Head, also has a chance to sing three songs in her own inimitable style. They are by Frederick Hollander, who wrote all of her best material when she was rising to fame as a top star at Paramount. In her husky style she sings "Black Market," "Illusions," and "In the Ruins of Berlin" with a wise, smiling amorality that is beguiling. Nobody else played a modern siren with the knowing sexuality that Dietrich always brought to her roles. In Germany during the 1920's she had played homewreckers and fast ladies of the evening with Emil Jannings, Willi Forst, and Fritz Kortner. The Hollywoodized Dietrich, however, proved to have unusual beauty, real chic, and a flair for high comedy rarely possessed by actresses known for their siren qualities. She had no singing voice, but she knew how to deliver a song, and Hollander knew exactly how to write for her. As she sings it, "Black Market" becomes almost a very evil ballad; the lyrics of "Illusions" have a kind of desperately resigned poignancy, while "Ruins of Berlin" is bold and boastful, exactly right as a song for one of the vanquished. When Josef von Sternberg brought Dietrich to Hollywood and made her an overnight star in *Morocco* (1930), he created a Dietrich image that had very little to do with the real actress. The last film she made for Sternberg was *The Devil Is a Woman* (1935), and that bears the full flower of the Sternberg image. By the time she made *A Foreign Affair* for Wilder, thirteen years had passed and that image had completely vanished. She went on, after *A Foreign Affair*, to play *Witness for the Prosecution* (1957) and *Judgment at Nuremberg* (1961), both of which had even less to do with the former Dietrich image.

Arthur, who has top billing in *A Foreign Affair*, actually displays a greater variety of acting talents than Dietrich does. She was under contract to Paramount during the silent era and rarely had anything to play except nice ingenues and breezy leading ladies. She established a very "becoming" image of herself with her healthy, good-natured characterizations of ordinary girls, made memorable by her husky, broken voice and completely honest portrayals. She could make almost any character she chose fit that mold, and she swiftly became a star. In one of her first talking features, *The Greene Murder Case*, she was able to confuse most people as to her identity as the real, more than slightly insane, murderess, simply because she was so affable, charming, and clever in her performance. Many a director has agreed that he would rather have Arthur play his leading female role than any other star, because audiences not only empathize with her, but they also really love her. Those same audiences, on the other hand, have always admired Dietrich, but only at a distance, because of her timeless, aloof glamour, which keeps them at a distance.

Viennese-born Wilder and Brackett, his collaborator in *A Foreign Affair*, were in an enviable situation as a team. They wrote their screenplays together; Brackett produced and Wilder directed, so they never really relinquished control over their property. A Brackett-Wilder motion picture is immediately identifiable because it is not only thoroughly professional, but also possesses an ironic humor that is inimitable. In *A Foreign Affair,* for example, when the camera pans down a Berlin street lined with its ruins, it is done to the melody on the soundtrack of "Isn't It Romantic?" They were fond of *A Foreign Affair*, although their most popularly successful collaboration was *Sunset Boulevard* (1950), and their own favorite film seems to have been *Double Indemnity* (1944).

More than thirty years have passed since *A Foreign Affair* was released. There is a new Berlin now, West and East, and the ruins have long since been cleared away. At any revival of this film, however, one finds audiences still intrigued by the fortunes of Congresswoman Phoebe Frost, Nazi sophisticate Erika von Schluetow, and American Army Captain John Pringle.

DeWitt Bodeen

FOREVER AND A DAY

Released: 1943
Production: RKO/Radio
Direction: René Clair, Frank Lloyd, Victor Saville, Edmund Goulding, Robert Stevenson, Herbert Wilcox, and Sir Cedric Hardwicke
Screenplay: Charles Bennett, C. S. Forester, Lawrence Hazard, Michael Hogan, W. P. Lipscomb, Alice Duer Miller, John Van Druten, Alan Campbell, Peter Godfrey, S. M. Herzig, Christopher Isherwood, Gene Lockhart, Emmet Lavery, R. C. Sherriff, Claudine West, Norman Corwin, Jack Hartfield, James Hilton, Frederick Lonsdale, Donald Ogden Stewart, and Keith Winter
Cinematography: Robert de Grasse, Lee Garmes, Russell Metty, and Nicholas Musuraca
Editing: Elmo Williams and George Crone
Running time: 104 minutes

Principal characters:
Gates T. Pomfret	Kent Smith
Lesley Trimble	Ruth Warrick
Admiral Eustace Trimble	C. Aubrey Smith
Bill	Ray Milland
Squire Pomfret	Claude Rains
Mildred Trimble	Jessie Matthews
Bellamy	Charles Laughton
Jenny	Ida Lupino
Jim	Brian Aherne
Marjorie	Merle Oberon
Barringer	Roland Young
Mrs. Barringer	Gladys Cooper
Spavin	Victor McLaglen
Dexter Pomfret	Ian Hunter
Mrs. Ismay	Una O'Connor
Dabb	Sir Cedric Hardwicke
Sentry	Ray Bolger
Plumber	Buster Keaton

Films scrutinizing the branches of family trees have included the Academy Award-winning *Cavalcade* (1933), covering three decades in the lives of the Marryot family of England, and the Emmy Award-winning *Roots* (1977), tracing the ancestry of writer Alex Haley through seven generations. *Forever and a Day* is not as honored as *Cavalcade* or *Roots* but it does feature a large and unique cast in a once-in-a-lifetime venture. In 1943, the year in which *Forever and a Day* was released, England was battling for survival in World War II. The film was conceived as a tribute to the nation's courage and tenacity and to the spirit of a people willing to fight and to die for their country.

The film chronicles the lives of two English families, the Trimbles and the Pomfrets, through several generations, beginning with the early 1800's and ending with the London Blitz of 1940. The principal setting is a sturdy old house constructed on the outskirts of London by Admiral Eustace Trimble (C. Aubrey Smith) as a shelter against a threatened Napoleonic invasion (a parallel to the similar events of World War II, 140 years later). The loves and lives of each generation are depicted in episodic fashion. The film opens during a Nazi air raid and then leaps back to the real beginning in 1804. The two "modern" protagonists, Gates T. Pomfret (Kent Smith) and Leslie Trimble (Ruth Warrick), the admiral's great-great-great-great grandchildren, narrate the story and tie the various episodes together. Pomfret is an American reporter whose London-born father still owns the old house. Lesley Trimble is an English girl who was born and reared in the house and who now wants to buy it.

The house was built in 1804 by Admiral Trimble, who hoped that it would house future generations of Trimbles. Among its first tenants were the Admiral's son Bill (Ray Milland), who eventually died at the battle of Trafalgar. By 1821, however, the Trimble family becomes impoverished, and the house passes into the hands of Squire Pomfret (Claude Rains), a scheming industrialist. Bill Trimble's granddaughter, Mildred (Jessie Matthews), soon returns to the house, marries Dexter Pomfret (Ian Hunter), and rises to prosperity during the reign of Queen Victoria. At this point in the film, Charles Laughton portraying Bellamy, the family butler, interacts with Matthews' character in a series of incidents. Also, Sir Cedric Hardwicke and Buster Keaton—one of many odd casting combinations—are hilarious as a pair of plumbers installing a bathtub. The film falters during the final scenes, with the exception of a sparkling performance by Ida Lupino in the role of Jenny, a Cockney maid confronted with problems in her love life.

By the turn of the century, the house has become a hotel. During World War I, it becomes more of a boarding house. By the start of World War II, however, it has become a public air raid shelter. Gates T. Pomfret arrives at the house as it is finally demolished by Luftwaffe bombs. (It took three art directors for the sequence, and then fifty workmen several days to build a set that one aerial bomb would destroy in five seconds.) Gates and Lesley decide to rebuild it together, and hope that it will flourish in a world without war and suffering.

Forever and a Day is a nostalgic, mawkish soap opera. The story is hackneyed and predictable, overly sentimental, and lacking cohesion; indeed, seven directors worked on the film, so a lack of structure is no surprise. No one actor dominates—the true star of *Forever and a Day* is the house, which still stands as each generation dies off and is replaced by the next. Still, the performances by some of Hollywood's top stars appearing in small roles—

sometimes even bits—are generally excellent. In addition to Laughton, Matthews, Hardwicke, and Keaton, Roland Young and Gladys Cooper as Mr. and Mrs. Barringer shine in the film's most touching sequence, when they learn during a festive evening of the death of their aviator son during World War I.

Forever and a Day, allegedly the brainchild of Hardwicke, was almost two years in the making. Originally, it was scheduled to be a British film, with proceeds to go to British war charities, but plans were changed after Pearl Harbor. Almost the entire British film colony appeared in the film, from Brian Aherne to Young, with the addition of American-born actors from Robert Cummings to Warrick. "Seventy-Eight Stars in One Great Picture," proclaimed the ads. The directors include Frank Lloyd, in charge of the opening and closing sequences, and Herbert Wilcox, Robert Stevenson, Victor Saville, Edmund Goulding, Hardwicke, and René Clair (replacing Alfred Hitchcock). In addition, thirty-one writers contributed to the script; among them were James Hilton, C. S. Forester, Christopher Isherwood, and Donald Ogden Stewart. One unique aspect of the casting is the appearance of a number of well-known stars and featured players acting against type, among them, Victor McLaglen as a London hotel doorman; Merle Oberon as a bespeckled boarding-house clerk; Aherne as a coal miner; Ray Bolger as a sentry; and Una O'Connor, usually cast as a servant, as the mistress of the house.

Most of the actors, writers, and directors donated their services to the project, with the profits from distribution in each country set aside for donation to charity. In the United States, monies went to the National Foundation for Infantile Paralysis. The film, which received reviews that may best be described as complimentary, earned more than one million dollars for the respective charities. *Forever and a Day* is not an outstanding film, but it is special nevertheless, unique for its incredible cast.

Rob Edelman

THE FORTUNE COOKIE

Released: 1966
Production: Billy Wilder for the Mirisch Corporation; released by United Artists
Direction: Billy Wilder
Screenplay: Billy Wilder and I. A. L. Diamond
Cinematography: Joseph LaShelle
Editing: Daniel Mandell
Music: André Previn
Running time: 125 minutes

Principal characters:
Harry Hinkle ....Jack Lemmon
Willie Ginrich .... Walter Matthau (AA)
Luther "Boom Boom" Jackson .... Ron Rich
Sandy .... Judi West
Perkey .... Cliff Osmond

The general popularity and critical esteem enjoyed by writer-director Billy Wilder reached a peak at around the time of *Some Like It Hot* (1959) and *The Apartment* (1960), the first two films with the actor who was to become his favorite, Jack Lemmon, and among the first with I. A. L. Diamond as his writing partner. Subsequently, Wilder seemed to fall out of favor, but it is retrospectively evident that *The Apartment*, rather than representing the last surge of his full creative powers, marks the beginning of the most rewarding phase of his career. With the exception of *Fedora* (1979), all of these late films are comedies, but they reveal a touching romanticism which characteristically had been concealed in Wilder's earlier films. This development creates a fruitful tension with his still cynical surfaces, most memorably in his most personal film, *The Private Life of Sherlock Holmes* (1970), in which the conclusion is explicitly poignant without a trace of derision.

The richness of Wilder's artistry in this period is brilliantly manifested in *The Fortune Cookie*, an often savagely witty film, but one with unexpected moments of mellowness and melancholy. The pretext is fraud against an insurance company, and it is a measure of Wilder's shrewd judgment of the range of his talent that this comedy has as much moral bite as his earlier *film noir* classic, dealing in part with insurance fraud, *Double Indemnity* (1944).

The screenplay is cleverly divided into a number of episodes, some long and some short, each providing an additional twist to the story. Each of these episodes is introduced by a written title, like that of a chapter in a book, and as the pattern of the film becomes apparent, the audience looks forward to discovering the additional element which has been added to the narrative and the characterizations. The first chapter introduces the protagonist, Harry

Hinkle (Jack Lemmon), a television cameraman covering a Cleveland Browns football game, and presents an accident in which a massive football player, Luther "Boom Boom" Jackson (Ron Rich), inadvertently slams into Hinkle and knocks him cold. Here Wilder delights in satirizing the stop-motion playbacks beloved of television coverage by showing the accident a second time with Hinkle looking ridiculous as he falls backward over a rolled-up tarpaulin, but the sequence then concludes straightforwardly as the worried Jackson looks back at Hinkle being carried from the field by ambulance.

The second chapter introduces the principal antagonist, "Whiplash" Willie Ginrich (Walter Matthau), a lawyer of dubious character who happens to be Harry's brother-in-law. Although Harry has not been seriously hurt, Willie seizes on an old back injury the other had sustained as a boy and starts to plan a spectacular lawsuit. Willie is an arresting presence from his first appearance, which finds him pacing the hospital corridor like a cartoonist's interpretation of a Machiavellian figure, by turns scowling, scheming, and feigning innocence. Again, the opportunity is not lost for a wickedly humorous moment. Ginrich's daughter has asked him for a dime to put into a collection box for unwed mothers, prompting him to say, "I'm for that" as he gives her the coin. Afterward, finding he needs the dime for the telephone, he stealthily retrieves it from the box.

The third chapter develops the character of Boom Boom Jackson, who begins to suffer from an overwhelming feeling of guilt because he believes that Harry is paralyzed as a result of the accident. If Harry is basically a decent man, enticed into Willie's scheme by the prospect of winning back his estranged wife Sandy (Judi West), Boom Boom is something else, an almost insufferably good and selfless human being who believes only the best of Harry. He begins to take care of Harry at the expense of his football career, and the fact that he is black adds disturbing implications to this servitude. Boom Boom, however, is not quite so simple as he appears and becomes the catalyst for the ultimate resolution of the story.

Another chapter introduces Sandy, who is as conniving and unscrupulous as Willie. Boom Boom, who picks her up at the airport, is immediately confused and troubled by her obvious ambivalence to Harry, beautifully reflected in his silent reactions as she speaks. Willie, however, knows her for what she is. It is he who has persuaded her to come to Cleveland with the prospect of a share of the money. As they pass each other on the stairway, he slaps her backside and mutters that she has lost weight, figuring the exact number of pounds. The innuendo of this meeting is never explored, but a number of viewings seem to confirm the subtle suggestion that Sandy was unfaithful to Harry with Willie, which adds tension to the central relationship between Harry and Willie.

Despite setbacks, Willie ultimately has his way with the insurance company, but the tragic cost has already taken a toll on Harry. Overwhelmed by guilt and unable to bear Sandy's manipulation of Harry, Boom Boom starts drinking, is suspended from the team, and finally is arrested for initiating a drunken brawl. Harry has become a saddened and passive participant in the scheme when Willie arrives with the settlement check. Perkey (Cliff Osmond), the detective who has been bugging Harry's apartment for the insurance company, pretends to have given up and comes to the apartment to get his equipment, but with instructions to his associate to keep the camera rolling. Realizing that Willie has been too smart for him, Perkey takes a new tactic in this chapter, stingingly designated "The Better Mousetrap." He baits Harry with racial slurs about Boom Boom, and Harry gives up feigning paralysis so that he can leap from his wheelchair and hit Perkey. Harry then denounces both Willie and Sandy and heads for the empty football stadium where he finds the dispirited Boom Boom lighting matches in a bleak travesty of what was to be Harry Hinkle Night.

The story ends on a sentimental note, with Harry and Boom Boom tossing a football back and forth in the deserted stadium. This ending has drawn some criticism, and it is true that it is lacking in credibility. Boom Boom Jackson is a weak man, and the thrust of the story has been partly to show him being crushed by this weakness. The ending, however, is not altogether unsatisfying. For one thing, Harry's example in overcoming his own worst instincts keeps the movie from being too bleakly cynical, and for another, the beginning of a renewed sense of self-worth in Boom Boom and a sense of solidarity between the two men overcomes the sense of tragedy and desolation which would have been unsuitable to this particular comedy. *The Fortune Cookie* has a fundamentally realistic sense of modern life, and for this reason, the traditional form of comedy, with a happy ending optimistically resolving implied tragedy, is appropriate.

This does not make Boom Boom an any less remarkable character. At certain moments, he is presented with a pathos that is rare and daring in a comedy. The only comparable character to be found in a 1960's comedy is the spoiled rich boy played by Pat Boone in *Goodbye Charlie* (1964). In that film, director Vincente Minnelli used a tactic opposite to that employed by Wilder. The Boone character is played for laughs until his final scene, when he is movingly revealed as a pathetic figure in the story he tells to the Debbie Reynolds character about his attempt as a boy to run a lemonade stand from inside his gilded cage. Because *Goodbye Charlie* has a different frame of reference from that of *The Fortune Cookie*, being essentially a fantasy, it is possible to leave Boone at this point, but in both films, the characters in question are secondary and would be unimaginable as protagonists.

Boom Boom is at his most compelling in two scenes which are among the film's finest. The first follows the dinner he makes for Harry and Sandy, in which he becomes progressively more unhappy over the woman's insincerity and Harry's misguided love for her. The final shot of this sequence, directed with masterful economy, simply shows Boom Boom opening a cupboard door in the kitchen, which obliterates his face, taking a drink of the whiskey he is hiding and setting down the empty glass. In the second scene, a short chapter with the cruelly witty title "The Other Blonde," Boom Boom is sitting in his father's bowling alley drinking when he encounters a black woman who has dyed her hair blonde in an inadvertent grotesque parody of Sandy. It is this encounter which triggers Boom Boom's violent attack on several men which leads to his arrest.

Although used primarily for dramatic purposes, Boom Boom is not exempt from the wry satire enjoyed by Wilder and Diamond. He drives a white Cadillac and is almost ludicrously soft-spoken and well-mannered. Similarly, the comic characters who dominate the story are not simple types. Whiplash Willie, who is responsible for much of the humor of the film and is often the dominant figure, is never a lovable figure of fun. Matthau's performance has been deservedly celebrated, and one of the reasons he is so memorable is that the sweetness which so often disfigures his later comic roles is avoided. *The Fortune Cookie* remains the film which displays Matthau's cynical screen personality at its purest and funniest. In one of the most outrageous moments, Willie's children are running noisily around in the background of his home as he tries to speak on the telephone in the foreground. He interrupts his conversation to yell at them, "Why don't you kids go play on the freeway?" As Matthau delivers the line, it sounds like Willie means it.

The irresistible malevolence of Matthau's characterization should not obscure Jack Lemmon's equally fine performance as Hinkle. For Wilder, Lemmon is an archetype of the modern comic figure, endearing in his vulnerability, credible in his moral vacillations, and ultimately sympathetic in his human completeness. Amusing in such chapters as "The Snake Pit," in which Hinkle is examined by skeptical doctors, Lemmon is also quietly moving in such sequences as the one in which Harry reminisces about his marriage to Sandy. No one appreciates the versatility and appeal of Lemmon more than Wilder, who has utilized the actor with maximum effectiveness in a half dozen films.

Wilder's later works also benefit from the contributions of other loyal contributors. Joseph LaShelle photographed four of these films, three of them, including *The Fortune Cookie*, in black-and-white CinemaScope, a format which would become completely out of fashion within the next few years. The mood achieved in LaShelle's lighting immeasurably enhances the director's skill with direct and uncluttered compositions and fluid camera movements. André Previn also worked often with Wilder in this period. In *The Fortune Cookie*, he adeptly contrasts three major themes—the old standard "You'd Be So Nice to Come Home To" for Harry, a humorously sinister theme for Willie, and a poignant blues theme for Boom Boom.

Finally, there is I. A. L. Diamond, who has been steadfastly involved on every screenplay for a Wilder film for more than twenty years. Wilder was always a great writer, even if his full gifts as a director were not consistently evident until these mature works of the 1960's and 1970's. It would appear to be indisputable that Diamond has been crucial in helping to bring out the finest personal qualities of Wilder. Diamond has a sardonic wit that is equal to that of his partner. With an "alter ego" who can so readily provide the acidly witty dialogue and clever narrative twists which he enjoys, Wilder has become free to express the warmth and tenderness which he once had the instinct to repress. The resulting richness of tone, so evident in *The Fortune Cookie*, shows the Wilder-Diamond relationship to be an uncommonly creative one.

Blake Lucas

FOUL PLAY

Released: 1978
Production: Thomas L. Miller and Edward K. Milkis for Paramount
Direction: Colin Higgins
Screenplay: Colin Higgins
Cinematography: David M. Walsh
Editing: Pembroke J. Herring
Running time: 115 minutes

Principal characters:

Gloria Mundy	Goldie Hawn
Tony Carlson	Chevy Chase
Mr. Hennesey	Burgess Meredith
Delia Darrow/Gerda Casswell	Rachel Roberts
Stanley Tibbets	Dudley Moore
Fergie	Brian Dennehy
Stiltskin	Marc Lawrence
Bible Salesman	Billy Barty
Bob Scott	Bruce Solomon
The Albino, Whitey Jackson	William Frankfather
Sally	Barbara Sammeth
Attacker	Don Calfa
The Turk	Ion Teodorescu
Manager	Chuck McCann
Pope	Cyril Magnin
Archbishop's brother	Eugene Roche
Japanese tourists	Rollin Moriyama and Mitsu Yashima

Colin Higgins, the writer and director of *Foul Play*, began his career making student films at UCLA and progressed to writing the scripts for the delightful cult film *Harold and Maude* (1972) and the quite profitable *Silver Streak* (1976). The financial success of the latter apparently gave him the opportunity to direct his next script, *Foul Play*. That script combines the detective thriller with the romantic comedy and reveals its author as an admirer and student of films of the past. It uses both general conventions of the thriller genre, such as the innocent person being caught up in a murder plot, reminiscent of the films of Alfred Hitchcock, and references to specific films, such as *Bullitt* (1968) and *Dial M for Murder* (1954). It is probably the best of the so-called "imitation" genre in which homage is paid to a style of filmmaking that has disappeared.

The film has two important scenes before the credits are finished. The first is a shocking image, the meaning of which does not become clear for some time; it does, however, establish the tone of the film. A religious figure (whom we later find is the Archbishop of San Francisco) looks in a mirror and sees someone who is dressed exactly as he is. Before he can utter a sound, he is killed by a knife, as a recording of Gilbert and Sullivan's *The Mikado* plays in the background. We then meet Gloria Mundy (Goldie Hawn) and find that she is a librarian who has recently been divorced. At a party, her friend Sally (Barbara Sammeth) is encouraging her to be more outgoing, to take a chance. Sally says Gloria should be more like the cheerleader she used to be than the repressed librarian hiding behind her glasses that she has become. Another guest at the party, Tony Carlson (Chevy Chase), reveals that he has been eavesdropping and tells Gloria that he agrees with Sally. Gloria is not amused.

Some time later, however, as Gloria is driving along the coast highway toward her home in San Francisco, she seems to heed the advice of Sally, Tony, and the theme song of the film, which we hear on the soundtrack, "Ready to Take a Chance Again." When she sees a young man standing by his disabled car, she picks him up. She finds that his name is Bob "Scottie" Scott (Bruce Solomon), and soon after he gets in her car, Gloria removes her glasses—without affecting her ability to drive. When he looks behind them, Scottie notices that they are being followed by a black limousine. He tells Gloria nothing about this, but when they reach the city he surreptitiously slips a roll of film into a box of cigarettes, asks her to keep it for him, and says he will meet her later at a movie theater.

Thus Gloria has unsuspectingly been drawn into the thriller plot. She does not even know that she possesses anything more than a box of cigarettes given to her by a hitchhiker who says he is trying to quit smoking; we in the audience know that the box is more important than that, but we have no idea why or to whom. We will soon find that certain people will go to any lengths to get the roll of film that the box contains.

At the movie theater, which is showing two old murder mysteries, Gloria has to go in by herself because Scottie is not there, but he soon joins her. He is wounded and bleeding, but she does not notice, and when he tries to tell her about the murder plot he has discovered, she thinks he is talking about the film they are watching. Finally he says to her, "Beware of the dwarf," and slumps over dead. By the time Gloria gets the manager (Chuck McCann) to stop the film and turn on the lights, the body is gone. She is then unable to convince anyone that the murder actually happened. Even her kindly old landlord, Mr. Hennesey (Burgess Meredith), tells her that Scottie was only playing a trick on her.

Gloria soon discovers that this "trick" was not an isolated incident. The next day, as she is closing up the library where she works, she is attacked by an albino (William Frankfather). She escapes by hitting him with her umbrella and dashing into a nearby singles bar. When the albino follows her, she asks the nearest man, Stanley Tibbets (Dudley Moore), to take her home. He is quite happy to agree, but he of course misunderstands the reason for her request. Gloria watches from Stanley's window until she sees the albino leave in the black limousine and then finds that Stanley has outfitted his apartment with every device he imagines a "swinger" should have, including flashing lights, a projector showing pornographic films, and life-sized inflated female mannequins. Gloria literally deflates a mannequin and figuratively deflates Stanley himself. She then returns home.

At her apartment, however, she is attacked by a large man with a scar on his face (Don Calfa) who wants her to give him whatever Scottie gave her. After he gets the box of cigarettes and sees that it has a roll of film in it, the man tries to strangle Gloria, but she stabs him with her knitting needles, in a scene reminiscent of Hitchcock's *Dial M for Murder*. She thinks she has killed him and calls the police. While she is telephoning, however, the man gets up and starts toward her with a poker in his hand. Before he can reach her, he is felled by a knife thrown by the albino. All this is too much for Gloria, and she faints.

When she awakens, Gloria finds Tony Carlson talking to her. It turns out that Tony is a policeman and that he and his partner, Fergie (Brian Dennehy), have answered her report of a murder in her apartment. Once again, however, there is no body. Neither Tony nor Fergie takes Gloria seriously, although Tony continues to be romantically interested in her. Tony, we find out, is currently on suspension in the police department for arresting the mayor for speeding and putting him in handcuffs. What this suspension entails, however, is never made clear, for he continues to work.

Gloria is still not safe because the cigarette box remains in her apartment, dropped by the scarfaced man after he was wounded. The next day she is abducted as she leaves the library in broad daylight. Although she is taken to an empty room where she is guarded by the Turk (Ion Theodorescu), she manages to escape and reach the police station. She is once again in the position of having no proof that anything happened.

The pieces of the puzzle finally begin to come together. Tony finds that Scott was an undercover policeman trying to find information about a tip that an assassination would take place in San Francisco. Then we gradually learn the whole plot. Delia Darrow (Rachel Roberts) and several other members of the Tax the Churches League have decided to assassinate the Pope as a protest against the government's nontaxation of churches. They murder the Archbishop of San Francisco and replace him with his twin brother (Eugene Roche), who is participating in the plot, and establish Darrow as Gerda Casswell, assistant to the Archbishop. The assassin is to be Stiltskin (Marc Lawrence), whose alias is The Dwarf.

While we and the protagonists are learning these facts, Tony and Gloria have fallen in love and spent a night together, but Gloria's adventures continue. The villains capture Fergie and through him lure Gloria to an out-of-the-way building. When he manages to warn her at the last minute, she escapes by ducking into the employee's entrance of a massage parlor. In one of the massage rooms she finds Stanley Tibbetts, waiting for a "massage." She enlists his help, but he cannot save her. After she is taken to the Archbishop's residence, Tony deduces that she is there and goes to help her. He kills Stiltskin but then is captured himself. Darrow explains to them that the Pope (Cyril Magnin) will be assassinated by the albino at the end of the first act of the opera he is attending at that very moment. Suddenly Hennesey, who had come with Tony, attacks the two villains. He dispatches the false Archbishop with a thrown bottle and bests Darrow in a wild karate fight.

Hennesey then releases Gloria and Tony, who set off on a wild race across the city to prevent the murder. It is a car race through San Francisco streets reminiscent of the one in *Bullitt* with an added touch being that the last part of the trip is in a commandeered limousine with two elderly Japanese tourists (Rollin Moriyama and Mitsu Yashima) in the back seat waving American flags and shouting "Kojak!" Tony and Gloria arrive at the opera house before the end of the first act of *The Mikado*, and after a frenzied chase and shootout behind the scenes, they kill the albino and save the Pope. This sequence is roughly patterned after the climax of Hitchcock's *The Man Who Knew Too Much* (1956), which takes place in the Albert Hall in London during a stirring concert. Finally Tony and Gloria embrace in the middle of the stage as the curtain is raised for the cast to take a bow. When they finally notice the applauding audience, they, too, turn and bow, as does a sheepish Stanley, who turns out to be the orchestra's conductor.

Critical reaction to *Foul Play* was mixed. Indeed, almost all reviewers praised some aspects of the film and criticized others. Moore's scene as the ultimate swinger with an apartment seemingly equipped with every possible sexual device was generally regarded as overdone and not in keeping with the rest of the film. Also excessive is the scene in which a dwarf Bible salesman, played by Billy Barty, visits Gloria's apartment. Gloria thinks that he is the dwarf she has been warned about and pushes him out her window. He falls into a garbage can, rolls down a hill, and ends up falling down a manhole. Indeed, the chief weakness of Colin Higgins' debut as a director is that he tends to excess in the effects and in the length of the scenes. The film could have been even more effective had it been more subtle and fast-paced.

Hawn has remarked that her role was not especially demanding, but both she and Chase are pleasant and likable in the film, and it is undoubtedly their performances that contributed the most to the enormous success of *Foul Play* at the box-office, placing it in the top ten of 1978. The film also led to a television series in the fall, 1980, season, but it was a short-lived failure. As an ironic footnote to the film, when *Foul Play* was scheduled for a prime-time television appearance in the spring of 1981, it had to be removed because the real Pope had just had an attempt made on his life in Rome. NBC network officials thought it ill-advised to show a film with *Foul Play*'s plot at that time.

Marilynn Wilson

THE FOUNTAINHEAD

Released: 1949
Production: Henry Blanke for Warner Bros.
Direction: King Vidor
Screenplay: Ayn Rand; based on her novel of the same name
Cinematography: Robert Burks
Editing: David Weisbart
Running time: 114 minutes

Principal characters:
Howard Roark .... Gary Cooper
Dominique .... Patricia Neal
Gail Wynand .... Raymond Massey
Peter Keating .... Kent Smith
Ellsworth Toohey .... Robert Douglas
Henry Cameron .... Henry Hull
Roger Enright .... Ray Collins
The Dean .... Paul Stanton

Hollywood likes to make films based on best-selling books because it can count upon virtually millions of people who have read or heard about the book wanting to see the film. Therefore, when Ayn Rand's novel *The Fountainhead* became a best-seller in 1943, Warner Bros. bought the screen rights to the work. *The Fountainhead* is, however, not the usual popular novel; it is a novel of ideas in which the thesis is often more important than the characters or the plot. The fact that Rand was hired to write the screenplay from her own book ensured that the studio could not follow the all-too-frequent practice of drastically changing the original material. Accordingly, *The Fountainhead* is a distinctly unusual film in which such customary Hollywood attributes as romance, spectacle, and characterization are subordinated to the development of the idea expressed, the importance of individualism.

In Rand's view it is individuals working without regard for the ideas and opinions of the public who produce "the constant stream of ideas" without which a culture cannot exist. She scorns "collectivism," the belief in subordinating oneself to the standards of the majority. In *The Fountainhead* she has constructed characters to represent various elements of this argument. Representing pure individualism is an architect, Howard Roark, and representing pure collectivism is a newspaper architecture critic, Ellsworth Toohey.

The film begins with Roark (Gary Cooper) being dismissed from a school of architecture by a dean (Paul Stanton) who tells him he cannot be so individualistic because there is "no place for originality in architecture." Roark then spurns the advice of a fellow student, Peter Keating (Kent Smith), that he compromise so that he can be successful. Keating says that he himself will give the public what it wants and predicts that he will soon be a successful architect. Roark instead goes to work for the only man he respects, Henry Cameron (Henry Hull), a character apparently meant to represent real-life architect Louis Sullivan, just as Roark himself is to some degree meant to suggest Frank Lloyd Wright, Sullivan's brilliant pupil. Cameron, although he is an independent man himself, does not encourage Roark on the road he has chosen because Cameron knows how difficult that road is; he urges Roark to compromise.

Roark, however, follows Cameron's example rather than his advice and takes over Cameron's office when the old man retires. He has very little success, just as everyone predicted. Indeed, Cameron comes to see him one day to urge that he give in to public taste. He contrasts Roark's lack of success with the newspaper *The Banner*, which has made its publisher a powerful man by giving the public the cheap, tawdry product it wants. Roark remains unmoved, and when Cameron asks if he knows what the people on the street think of architecture, Roark replies calmly, "I don't care what they think of architecture or anything else."

The next scene is perhaps the best in the film. Cameron has collapsed and Roark is riding with him in an ambulance. We see the city buildings through the ambulance windows as Cameron points out the folly of trying to make a totally new kind of building, the skyscraper, look like a Greek temple or some other design from the past. Cameron also notes one of his own buildings as they pass it, a building in which the form follows the function rather than copying the past. "Every new idea in the world comes from the mind of some *one* man," Cameron says, but once again he warns Roark of the difficulty of his chosen road; then he dies.

The next day Peter Keating visits Roark with the news that he has just been made a partner of Guy Francon, one of the city's most successful architects. While Keating is there, Roark gets a telephone call, but it is a wrong number that only emphasizes the contrast between the successful Keating and Roark, who has had no clients for eighteen months. Roark soon does get a chance for a commission, but he refuses when he finds that he would have to change his design to make it more conventional. He would, he tells the board asking him to compromise, rather work as a day laborer. We find that the attempt to get Roark to compromise was engineered by Ellsworth Toohey (Robert Douglas), the architecture critic for *The Banner*. He then recommends Peter Keating for the commission, because "artistic value is achieved collectively," and Keating's work has no individual personality stamped upon it.

Thus the main themes and characters have been established, but the plot and the argument are further thickened by the introduction of two more characters: Gail Wynand (Raymond Massey) and Dominique Francon (Patricia Neal). Wynand, the publisher of *The Banner*, has made himself rich and powerful by appealing to the taste of the masses even though he despises that taste. Dominique is the daughter of Guy Francon and is engaged to Peter Keating. We are introduced to her as she melodramatically drops a statue out the window of her high-rise apartment because she does not want to love anything in a world in which the masses rule. Wynand, who is in love with Dominique, offers Keating the commission for an important building if he will break his engagement, and Keating accepts. Dominique and Roark meet when she sees him working as a day laborer in her father's quarry in Connecticut. She does not know he is an architect but is attracted by his dynamic presence. She attempts to seduce him by asking him to come to her bedroom to replace some broken marble in the fireplace, but he ignores her obvious intention only to return at night and take her by force.

It is not until Roark has designed a building for Roger Enright (Ray Collins), a fiercely independent man who recognizes his talent and does not care what the public thinks of his building, that Dominique learns that Roark is an architect. She greatly admires his work, but she tries to persuade him to abandon architecture so that he will not be destroyed by the world as represented by Toohey, who gives the building a bad review in *The Banner* even though he knows it to be a great achievement. Roark, of course, refuses.

All the threads and themes come together dramatically in the last third of the film. Dominique has married Wynand although she does not love him, and Keating has come to Roark for help in designing a housing project. Roark agrees to design the project and let Keating receive all the credit on the strict condition that no detail of his plan shall be changed. The design is changed, however, over Keating's strenuous objections, and the resulting building is a monstrosity, a tasteless mixture of conflicting designs. Unwilling to accept this perversion of his work, Roark destroys the housing project with dynamite, then says he will explain nothing until his trial.

Wynand then tries to use the power he believes he has by supporting Roark in *The Banner* after firing Toohey, who continues to maintain that man can exist only to serve the wishes of others. Neither the public nor the staff of the newspaper will follow Wynand's lead, however; the paper is reviled and boycotted, and least credible of all, the staff of *The Banner* refuses to work until Toohey is rehired. After fighting for a while, Wynand finally gives in and denounces Roark, realizing that the "power" he achieved by following public opinion cannot be used against that same opinion.

Roark, therefore, must depend entirely upon his courtroom speech to the jury for his vindication. It is a long, didactic speech in which he states that all great creators stood alone and his idea is his property. He rejects collectivism, saying "The world is perishing in an orgy of self-sacrifice." Incredibly, even though we were led to believe that the entire city was against him, this speech convinces the jurors to find Roark not guilty.

After the trial, Wynand gives Roark a contract to design a massive building to commemorate his achievements, and then commits suicide. The film ends with Dominique, who had decided to leave Wynand for Roark even before he dynamited the housing project, riding a construction workers' elevator to the top of the new Wynand Building where Roark stands dramatically waiting for her.

The vindication of Roark's destruction of the project that did not follow his plans upset some critics and viewers, as well as the film's director, King Vidor. The film industry, after all, has very seldom let a director or a writer insist that his or her idea be followed to the letter; studio executives have nearly always made changes in films before, during, and after they were shot. Vidor says that he suggested to Jack Warner, the head of the studio, that he (Vidor) could burn the film if anyone changed it, but Warner did not agree. Also somewhat ironic is the fact that Rand specified in the script that Roark's buildings in the film should resemble those of Frank Lloyd Wright, since he was both modern and popular. "We must make the audience admire Roark's buildings," she wrote, even though that is the opposite of what Roark says throughout the film.

Another difficulty with the film is its incessantly didactic tone. The characters do not talk to one another; they state positions, giving much of the film the feeling of a dramatized debate rather than a drama of realistic characters. This difficulty is a great challenge for the actors, and one that none of them fully overcomes. Perhaps Hull, in the fairly small part of Roark's mentor Henry Cameron, is best because his character has some ambivalence. In the main roles, Cooper as Roark never seems quite comfortable having continually to utter such speeches as, "A building has integrity just like a man—and just as seldom," and Neal as Dominique has much the same problem, having at one point to say, "If it gives you pleasure to know that you are breaking me down, I'll give you greater satisfaction—I love you."

The film is by no means a total failure; it simply illustrates the difficulties of making a convincing film that is also explicitly didactic. Even such talented screen professionals as Cooper, Neal, and Vidor were not able to realize completely such an ambitious undertaking.

Julia Johnson

FOUR DAUGHTERS

Released: 1938
Production: Hal B. Wallis for Warner Bros.
Direction: Michael Curtiz
Screenplay: Julius J. Epstein and Lenore Coffee; based on the short story "Sister Act" by Fannie Hurst
Cinematography: Ernest Haller
Editing: Ralph Dawson
Music: Max Steiner
Running time: 90 minutes

Principal characters:
Ann Lemp	Priscilla Lane
Kay Lemp	Rosemary Lane
Thea Lemp	Lola Lane
Emma Lemp	Gale Page
Adam Lemp	Claude Rains
Mickey Borden	John Garfield
Felix Deitz	Jeffrey Lynn
Aunt Etta	May Robson
Ben Crowley	Frank McHugh
Ernest	Dick Foran

A sentimental tale about small-town life, *Four Daughters* was widely heralded at the time of its release for its casting of three real-life sisters as the principal players. Soon after the film opened, however, Priscilla, Rosemary, and Lola Lane found themselves sharing the spotlight with a virtual screen newcomer, John Garfield. With his darkly cynical portrayal of a young fatalist, Garfield intensified an otherwise standard 1930's era soaper, giving a rough, thought-provoking edge to the film's gentle story.

Based on "Sister Act," a short story by Fannie Hurst, *Four Daughters* tells the story of Adam Lemp (Claude Rains) and his four daughters, Ann, Kay, Thea, and Emma (Priscilla Lane, Rosemary Lane, Lola Lane, and Gale Page, respectively), and of their life in a small Connecticut town. Lemp is a musician who frequently conducts his four musically inclined daughters in a family quintet. It is a close-knit, loving family, as evidenced by Ann's idealistic pledge to Emma that "neither of us shall marry, but just live like the happy family we are, forever." Ann, the youngest of the four daughters, feels threatened by the beaus who call on her sisters, for she does not want the family to break up. When a handsome stranger comes to town, however, even Ann is captivated by his charms.

Felix Deitz (Jeffrey Lynn) is a young composer from the West Coast who has come to town to vie for a thousand-dollar music prize. Adam invites Felix to board at the Lemp home, and all four girls are immediately taken with him, although he must put extra effort into winning over the family's spinster aunt, Aunt Etta (May Robson). The uplifting, engaging quality of the story is broken by the appearance of Mickey Borden (John Garfield), Deitz's orchestrator. Mickey has dark, tousled good looks, dresses carelessly, smokes constantly, and renounces almost everything that he encounters. His fatalistic views are the result of an orphaned youth spent in the big city. Mickey, who is uneasy in the quaint, small-town surroundings, immediately captures Ann's interest. She is attracted by his looks and startling demeanor, as well as the fact that she has never known anyone like him.

A key scene underlining the differences between the two takes place at the Lemp piano, where Mickey is playing a haunting piece. When Ann expresses her feelings about the music's beauty, Mickey retorts, "It stinks. It hasn't got a beginning or an end. Just a middle." When Ann asks why he does not complete the work, an angry Mickey responds, "What for? The fates are against me. They tossed a coin—heads, I'm poor, tails I'm rich. So what did they do? They tossed a coin with two heads." Although Ann is enamored of Felix, she is also determined to cheer the sardonic outsider. Indeed, Mickey does find himself touched by her sincerity and warmth. His near-optimism is depicted in a charming moment which finds Ann in the kitchen baking gingerbread men. With Mickey watching, she wipes away the sad, drooping mouth of the gingerbread man bearing his name and replaces it with a smile.

Mickey's changing attitude is shattered, however, when Ann accepts a marriage proposal from Felix. Her sisters are also caught off-guard by Ann's decision, for each had had a "crush" on the handsome composer. Ann's marriage plans force the other sisters to make decisions about their own lives. In a sense, it is the film's turning point. Kay, a promising singer, at last decides to pursue a scholarship in Philadelphia. Thea, who has always been impressed by money, agrees to marry wealthy Ben Crowley (Frank McHugh). Emma, however, who had been especially enamored with Felix, remains hurt and perplexed by Ann's plans. Mickey, who is equally upset, notices this.

When he at last reveals his own love to Ann, he also insists that Felix is the man Emma loves. Ann is doubly shocked. Caught up in Mickey's spell, she is also concerned for the feelings of her beloved sister. Thus, on the day she was to have married Felix, Ann elopes with Mickey. The Lemp family learns of the elopement as they are gathered for the wedding. They are so stunned by the news that it remains for family friend Ernest (Dick Foran), the town's florist, to deal with the wedding guests. Ernest's new, take-charge manner impresses Emma, who later realizes it is Ernest she truly loves (and will marry). Following the crisis, a jilted Felix leaves for Seattle.

The film now focuses on life for Ann and Mickey, which seems filled with constant disappointments, made worse by Mickey's belief that he cannot rise above the fates. Ann is encouraging and is hopeful that a Christmas visit back home will lift Mickey's spirits. The two are warmly welcomed by the family, and Felix, who is also visiting for the holidays, proves he is no longer angry with them when he offers Mickey financial assistance. Mickey, however, the "born loser," now realizes that he is wrong for Ann. Hoping to free her from his spell, he causes his own death by crashing his car into a tree.

Tragedy finally gives way to hope and new love in the spring. As the touching story comes to a close, Ann is reunited with Felix, and all four daughters, conducted by their father, again perform in the family home.

Four Daughters, which is effectively directed by the prolific Michael Curtiz, proved an immediate success following its August 9th opening at New York's Radio City Music Hall. Many critics of the day likened the film to an updated *Little Women* (1933). Nearly all were impressed with Garfield's performance and characterization, although several noted that his dark intensity nearly threw the charming film off balance. One of the year's most popular films, *Four Daughters* was nominated for five Academy Awards, including Best Picture, Best Director, Best Screenplay, and Best Supporting Actor. Garfield lost the Oscar to Walter Brennan, who won for *Kentucky*.

Four Daughters also inspired two sequels. *Four Wives* (1939), also directed by Michael Curtiz, included an appearance by Garfield as the ghost of Mickey Borden. *Four Mothers* was released in 1941. The huge success of *Four Daughters* and Garfield's portrayal also inspired a film which is nearly a clone of the original: *Daughters Courageous*, released less than a year after the first film, again starring Claude Rains, the Lane sisters, and Garfield, and directed by Curtiz. Garfield was once again paired with Priscilla Lane, and again, he played a world-weary cynic. This time around, he did not die—but neither did he get the girl. *Four Daughters* was also remade in 1954 as *Young at Heart*, a semimusical with Gordon Douglas directing. Doris Day, Dorothy Malone, and Elizabeth Fraser portray the film's sisters (this film featured only three), with Frank Sinatra cast in the Garfield role (the character was renamed Barney). This version, however, has an upbeat ending, with Barney, who does not die in the car crash, losing his cynicism; the final moments depict his happy reunion with Day. The story line changes were made because Sinatra had already "died" in his two previous films, *From Here to Eternity* (1953) and *Suddenly* (1954).

Garfield's career was forever marked by downbeat characterizations. In fact, the social unrest of the post-Depression era was often depicted by his work. Thus, in addition to providing a springboard for the actor's distinguished career, the *Four Daughters* characterization also came to personify his most famed roles. Particularly brilliant among Garfield's stirring depictions of men at odds with society and fate are *Humoresque* (1945), *The Postman Always Rings Twice* (1946), *Body and Soul* (1947), and *Force of Evil* (1948). His characters struggle against the darker side of human nature. The only traditional hero the actor ever portrayed was real-life Marine hero Al Schmid, in the patriotic *Pride of the Marines* (1945).

Generally regarded as the screen's first "angry young man," Garfield epitomized the man beset by inner conflict as well as a stacked deck. As Archer Winston once noted of the actor's grim characterizations, "He is fate's whipping boy, a personification of the bloody but unbowed head, and the embittered voice of the dispossessed." It is unfortunate that Garfield died from a heart attack in 1952 at the age of thirty-nine, not long after refusing to testify before the House UnAmerican Activities Committee, and at the low point of his career.

Pat H. Broeske

THE FOUR POSTER

Released: 1952
Production: Stanley Kramer for Stanley Kramer Company; released by Columbia
Direction: Irving Reis
Screenplay: Allan Scott; based on the play of the same name by Jan de Hartog
Cinematography: Hal Mohr
Editing: Henry Batista
Running time: 102 minutes

> *Principal characters:*
> John Edwards .... Rex Harrison
> Abby Edwards .... Lilli Palmer

The Four Poster covers several decades, has only two characters, and has only one setting. By taking on all these self-imposed difficulties and restrictions, the filmmakers ran the risk of making the audience constantly aware either of the film's limitations or of the ingenious means used to overcome these limitations. Fortunately the film does not use techniques such as heavy makeup that call attention to themselves. Only one obvious device is used—that of animated sequences between the episodes—and it works quite well.

The single setting of the film is a bedroom, which contains the four-poster bed that gives the film its title. The two characters are John Edwards (Rex Harrison) and his wife Abby (Lilli Palmer). The time covered is from the couple's marriage in the last years of the nineteenth century until John's death nearly fifty years later. We visit the bedroom eight times during that period to see the high and low points of the lives of the two and of their relationship with each other.

To provide a transition between the scenes and to convey some information about the life of the characters between times as well as about events in the outside world, producer Stanley Kramer decided on the idea of what filmmakers came to call "mood painting interscenes." These are animated sequences produced by Stephen Bosustow, whose company had won an Oscar for *Gerald McBoing-Boing* (1950), and directed by John Hubley, who had worked on Walt Disney's most famous animated films and would go on to win Oscars for two of his own animated shorts—*Moonbirds* (1959) and *The Hole* (1962).

The interscenes are imaginative without being precious, and informative without distracting us from the live action episodes which are the essence of the film. Indeed, it is one of the animated sequences that opens the film and quickly and skillfully sets up the first episode—the arrival of the newlyweds at their first home. Other such sequences establish the fame of John as an author and lecturer; portray the 1920's of flappers, flagpole sitters, and Herbert Hoover; and depict the second honeymoon of John and Abby. The most creative and moving interscene conveys World War I and the death of John and Abby's son in that war. It begins by showing a foggy forest as military music plays on the sound track and ends with a picture of a single helmet and the sound of "Taps."

It is, however, the human drama of the lives of John and Abby as portrayed by excellent actors that is the main substance of *The Four Poster*. Indeed, the only serious criticism of the acting is that Harrison and Palmer are so obviously accomplished and sophisticated that they are unable to make wholly convincing the early scenes in which they are supposed to be young and naïve. They are not aided by the script, which gives unnecessary prominence to the young wife's reluctance to go to bed with her new husband, an idea which could have easily been conveyed in much less screen time. Once the first episode or two are past, even that one criticism is behind them, and Harrison and Palmer—who were married to each other at the time and had worked together in films previously—are completely credible and affecting.

As the years pass, we see many aspects of John: unsuccessful poet, successful novelist, briefly unfaithful husband, overconcerned father, devoted husband, and finally weary old man. Abby similarly progresses through many stages. At one point John says that he thought he was marrying a fairy queen but instead found Abby to be a "friend, comrade, and wife." She not only gives him support and helpful advice, but she also criticizes the egoism that makes him a "ham actor" instead of a writer after his success. When he tells her that there is another woman, she frustrates him completely. She refuses to get upset, intimates that she too has found someone else and locks him out, forcing him to climb in a window during a rainstorm. Finally they reconcile, but it is primarily on her terms, not his. Her biggest crisis, however, comes the day their daughter is married. With no children left in the house she feels "empty, as if I'm dangling in the air somewhere." She feels that she went so quickly from being a girl to being a mother that she was never able to be herself. Now she wants to leave John because she can no longer "die behind the stove like a domestic animal." Abby's plight and Palmer's portrayal of it are poignant and persuasive. (The resolution, in which John solves her problem with a second honeymoon in Europe, is less credible.)

Indeed, the chief weaknesses of *The Four Poster* come from its script, which tends to be overly sentimental and melodramatic. When, for example, John discovers that Abby has a fatal and painful disease, he prepares poisoned brandy for them both, but at the last moment he knocks the brandy snifter out of Abby's hands. The last episode, in which Abby comes back from the grave to visit John (or his subconscious) is especially weak and unnecessary.

Director Irving Reis and cinematographer Hal Mohr are masterful in handling the restricted setting so that the emphasis is on the actors rather than on the cleverness of the men behind the camera. Only two exceptions stand out. One is a particularly jarring shot in which the camera seems to be inside the fireplace. The other is more imaginative and effective: after their son's death Abby spills a basket of his childhood toys and they suddenly begin moving on their own while making bizarre noises. Thus a sentimental scene becomes surrealistic.

The Four Poster is, all in all, a first-class treatment of a good but occasionally overly sentimental or melodramatic script. The original Jan de Hartog play was very popular as a stage production in both the United States and Great Britain, and has often been revived in small theater groups. Years after the success of the play and the film, a musical version of the story entitled *I Do, I Do*, written by Meredith Willson, became a popular stage success. The musical numbers added to the story brought an added dimension to the two-character story which enhanced its original appeal. As a result, *I Do, I Do* can be seen as a summer stock production in various parts of the United States almost every year. The national touring company of the musical starring Rock Hudson and Carol Burnett was immensely successful in the late 1970's and probably brought the original story its greatest popularity.

Sharon Wiseman

FRANCIS IN THE NAVY

Released: 1955
Production: Stanley Rubin for Universal-International
Direction: Arthur Lubin
Screenplay: Devery Freeman
Cinematography: Carl Guthrie
Editing: Milton Carruth and Ray Snyder
Running time: 80 minutes

Principal characters:
Lieutenant Peter Stirling/
Slicker Donevan .... Donald O'Connor
Commander Hutch .... Jim Backus
Jonesey .... Clint Eastwood
Francis' Voice .... Chill Wills

The New York Times critic Bosley Crowther once complained, half-jokingly, that 1950 was turning out to be the year of the mule. First there was Frankie Laine's pop record hit "Mule Train," and then came the movie *Francis*, which became the first in a long line of films based on the fictional adventures of Francis the Talking Mule. Based on the novel *Francis* by David Stern (who also wrote the screenplay for the series' opener), most of the Francis films were directed by Arthur Lubin and featured Donald O'Connor as the bumbling but enthusiastic Lieutenant Peter Stirling. Chill Wills provided the gravelly voice of the title creature.

The original *Francis* was set in the jungles of Burma during World War II. Peter Stirling (Donald O'Connor) stumbles across an old army mule named Francis who has the power of speech; Stirling is incredulous at first, but cannot deny the evidence before his eyes and ears, and the two become friendly. Francis is a patriotic mule and takes to spying on the Japanese, who never suspect that the traitor in their midst is a jackass. Francis relays the secrets to Stirling, who passes them on to his superiors.

All is well until Stirling is questioned about the source of his information. He tells the truth, and ends up in a psycho ward. Francis, it seems, wants to avoid the notoriety that would surely attend a talking animal and stubbornly refuses to talk to anyone but Stirling. It is from this situation that most of the film's laughs derive. Finally, however, Francis relents. He rescues his friend by talking to the General and holding a press conference in the bargain.

The film proved to be an immense popular success and begat successors annually for the next six years. *Francis Goes to the Races* appeared in 1951; *Francis Goes to West Point* surfaced in 1952; *Francis Covers Big Town* was 1953's entry; *Francis Joins the WACs* came along in 1954; 1955 brought *Francis in the Navy*; and the series ended with *Francis in the Haunted House* in 1956.

Each film follows a fairly set formula. The mule, a feisty animal with a love of practical jokes, involves himself and his human friend in some unlikely situation. Peter Stirling proceeds to flounder ineptly for the next hour or so, until Francis finally pulls his chestnuts out of the fire. Along the way, Universal inserts some of its older character actors and some of its new faces into the lineup for exposure. ZaSu Pitts, Gale Gordon, Jim Backus, Clint Eastwood, Piper Laurie, David Janssen, Mamie Van Doren, and Martin Milner all graced one or more of the Francis productions in this fashion.

Francis in the Navy is typical of the Francis series, except that O'Connor plays two roles—Stirling and his look-alike, Bosun's Mate Slicker Donevan. In his studio biographies, O'Connor often expressed his admiration for William Shakespeare's *A Comedy of Errors*, in which doubles and mistaken identities form the basis of the plot; and *Francis in the Navy* seems to have been tailored to provide O'Connor with an opportunity to interpolate this plot device into the Francis series.

It seems that Francis has somehow been transferred to the Navy, where he is about to be sold as surplus property. Stirling heads for the auction at San Diego's Coronado Naval Base, where he is mistaken (first by a pretty WAVE, and next by seemingly every sailor in the port) for Slicker Donevan, to whom he bears an uncanny resemblance. Since Donevan is given to spells of irrationality, Stirling's denials are routinely shrugged off by his solicitous pals. Donevan himself figures out what is going on and decides to take advantage of the situation by going on vacation for a few days.

Peter Stirling again winds up in a strait jacket, and Francis enjoys the whole spectacle immensely. The film ends with Stirling singlehandedly disrupting a complicated Navy training exercise as he attempts to handle Donevan's duties. "Francis, don't just stand there! Throw me a line," he cries. "I would, if I could think of one," deadpans the mule.

Arthur Lubin, who directed six of the seven Francis films, may not have been the world's greatest director, but he knew how to give the public what it wanted, specializing in lightweight, low-budget comedies. In the 1940's, he directed several Bud Abbott and Lou Costello films, including their best, *Buck Privates*, in 1941. In the 1950's, he repeated his successes with the Francis series. Likewise, O'Connor's tour of duty as Lieutenant Peter Stirling may not have been great acting—O'Connor's memorably acrobatic "Make 'Em Laugh" number in Gene Kelly's and Stanley Donen's *Singin' in the Rain* (1952) will probably stand as his finest screen moment—but he did his best with material that was at times admittedly thin. The star of the show was Francis the Talking Mule himself. The animal Francis was a remarkably expressive beast, with a penchant for rolling his eyes, twitching his ears, and smacking his lips in a very anthropomorphic fashion. Wills's gravelly voice suited the "character" perfectly.

After *Francis in the Navy*, however, most of the principals associated with the series seemed to tire of it and walked away *en masse*. In 1956, Charles Lamont picked up the Francis concept for one last film, with Mickey Rooney as Francis' new pal David Prescott and Paul Frees as the voice of the mule. The result, *Francis in the Haunted House*, was poor, even for the Francis series, which was never very deep to begin with; and that was the end of Francis, at least in his first incarnation.

Francis, however, did not entirely vanish in 1956. Lubin resurrected the basic concept in 1958 with his television series *Mr. Ed*, about a talking horse; the series lasted for six seasons and is still seen in syndication today. Finally, in the spring of 1980, *Variety* reported that O'Connor himself was on the verge of putting together a deal to produce an entirely new film entitled *Francis Goes to Washington*.

Critics found the first Francis film mildly amusing, although a bit too reliant on a single joke. Its successors only exacerbated this attitude. Critical scorn, however, did not hurt the popularity of most of the films or keep them from making money for their creators. Although never even within shouting distance of great art, the Francis films were good escapist entertainment. Further, they were all family films, an attribute not to be underestimated in an era that valued praying together, playing together, and staying together. The Francis series warrants our attention today primarily as an example of popular film fare of the Eisenhower Era.

Robert Mitchell

FREAKS

Released: 1932
Production: Metro-Goldwyn-Mayer
Direction: Tod Browning
Screenplay: Willis Goldbeck and Leon Gordon, with dialogue by Edgar Allan
    Woolf and Al Boasberg; based on the short story "Spurs" by Tod Robbins
Cinematography: Merritt B. Gerstad
Editing: Basil Wrangell
Running time: 64 minutes

Principal characters:
Phroso	Wallace Ford
Venus	Lelia Hyams
Cleopatra	Olga Baclanova
Roscoe	Roscoe Ates
Hans	Harry Earles
Frieda	Daisy Earles
Hercules	Henry Victor
Bearded Lady	Olga Roderick

Tod Browning's *Freaks* has achieved a reputation, in the fifty years since its introduction in 1932, as a masterpiece of horror and as a milestone in surrealistic filmmaking. This stature has been gained despite, or, more probably, as a result of, the fact that it was banned for more than thirty years in most civilized countries throughout the world. In fact, when it was initially completed at M-G-M in 1932, it quickly became known around the studio as the one mad blunder of the studio's reigning boy genius, producer Irving Thalberg. According to one, unverified, story, women ran screaming from the theater during a sneak preview, and the manager later complained that the film left him with a "cleaning job."

Upon the official opening of *Freaks* in New York City, *The New York Times* suggested that the film be screened at the Medical Center instead of at the Rialto theater. Other reviews generally panned the film, and it did poorly at the box office. Thalberg, who loved the film despite its reputation, felt that it had been victimized by poor presentation. He made a futile attempt to reissue it in 1933 under the sensational title, *Natures Mistakes* with such teaser captions as "Do Siamese Twins Make Love?" and "What Sex is the Half-Man-Half-Woman?" This version of the film carried a prologue mentioning that history, religion, and folklore abounded in tales of deformed misfits who have altered the course of world history. This version did no better than had the original, and M-G-M quietly gave up on it.

Freaks surfaced occasionally in Europe during the next thirty years, slowly gaining a macabre reputation, while continuing to be ignored in the United

States. It finally gained some legitimacy in 1962 when it was selected to represent the horror film category at the Cannes Film Festival. This was a somewhat dubious distinction since *Freaks*, although a masterpiece of the "cinema of the bizarre," is, in most respects, the antithesis of the conventional horror film.

The standard horror film centers upon mankind's responses to the nonrational or nonhuman element in the world that threatens to render life meaningless. The monster, whether it is the great white shark, King Kong, or aliens from outer space, is the representative of all that is irrational or inexplicable. It is through the destruction of these beasts that the audience is freed from its own fears of the nonhuman. We therefore tend to empathize and identify with the victims of the monsters and thus remain on the edge of our seats, finding release only through the monster's ultimate death.

Director Tod Browning creates an identity crisis for the audience of *Freaks* by attempting to reverse our expectations and by portraying his "monsters" sympathetically. In an ethical sense, Browning's freaks represent the best traits of mankind: humility and tolerance. The viewer must therefore turn against the conventional images of his own kind and identify with beings that would normally be thought of as abnormal or subhuman. *Freaks* becomes the ultimate challenge to the myth that beauty is the embodiment of goodness and truth and that ugliness represents evil. The film's plot is fairly routine, with most of the interest coming from the characters, who are played by real side-show freaks assembled by the director from circuses all over the world. They include bearded ladies, Siamese twins, dwarfs, pinheads, midgets, and human worms.

Freaks opens with a carnival pitchman addressing a crowd of people at a sideshow. He escorts the group of spectators over to a pit to see a hidden special attraction, but first, he describes the origin of the creature. The story is told through flashback. Hans (Harry Earles), a midget, is engaged to another midget, Frieda (Daily Earles), but becomes increasingly attracted to a trapeze performer named Cleopatra (Olga Baclanova), a normal-size woman. She is already having an affair, however, with Hercules (Henry Victor), the circus strong man. Interestingly, Browning depicts Hans and Frieda's romance so that it appears, despite its stiff gesture and squeaky voices, to be more mature and settled than the similar but tempestuous affair of the "normal" people, Cleopatra and Hercules. Through a series of contrasting scenes Browning establishes the inversion of values that forms the core of the film. Cleopatra perversely encourages Hans because she finds a secret pleasure in ridiculing him. When she finds out that Hans has recently inherited a considerable fortune, she takes him more seriously, but plots with Hercules to marry the midget, poison him, and inherit the money. Hans succumbs to her charms and Frieda is distraught.

At the wedding feast, Cleopatra and Hercules are the only "normals" in attendance. The banquet quickly becomes a ritual—a celebration of freak culture—as a dwarf dances across the table bearing a large communal wine bowl. He leads a macabre chant "We accept her, we accept her, gobble, gobble, one of us, one of us." He offers the wine bowl at last to Cleopatra to drink from as a rite of induction into the world of freaks. She registers horror and revulsion and later retaliates by riding Hans on her shoulders in front of his friends to humiliate him.

Eventually, Cleopatra's plot to poison Hans is discovered, and the enraged freaks hunt down the two villains and mutilate them in an unforgettable climactic sequence that gave the film its reputation for horror. On a rainy night, amidst a maze of wrecked circus trailers, with lightning flashing to illuminate the muddy ooze of the ground, grotesque crawling and hopping shapes wreak their vengeance upon the bodies of Hercules and Cleopatra.

Flashing forward again to the present, the carnival man finishes the story and pulls back the cover from the pit to reveal that Cleopatra is now a freak. This final touch, however, is the film's weak spot and represents a blunder on Browning's part. Cleopatra is not so much horrifying as a freak as she is comical in her resemblance to a giant half-formed fowl. This contrived ending destroys the credibility established by the film up to this point. Browning's thesis that the freaks are more normal than the Aryan strong man and the deceitful trapeze artist becomes quickly unraveled in the ludicrous, laugh-provoking image of Cleopatra as a half-plucked chicken.

If the director's intention was, as Browning avowed, to show that these misshapen creatures are not monsters or practitioners of black magic but ordinary human beings deformed through an accident of birth, the audience is left with a puzzle at the end. Either the sideshow pitchman made up the story, since if freaks are normal, according to Browning, they could not transform a human into a monster; or the storyteller is correct and the freaks are imbued with mysterious powers. This interpretation could be supported by the rites of initiation to the world of the freaks performed at the wedding feast. The alternate version of the film, *Natures Mistakes*, supports both interpretations with its introductory preamble which indicates that freaks are human beings but do have a mysterious code which binds them together, "The hurt of one and the hurt of all." Thus, instead of hammering Browning's message home, *Freaks*'s final scene blurs it.

The excellence of the film lies in the delicate balance which provides the context for the plot. On one side are the normal members of the circus with their ignorant, cruel mockery of the freaks. One the other side are the freaks, who are eager to befriend anybody who will accept them for what they are. These two extremes are bridged by Phroso the clown (Wallace Ford) and his girl Venus (Lelia Hyams) who accept and are accepted by the freaks. They tease Schlitze, one of the pinheaded women, about her new dress and joke with the bearded lady (Olga Roderick) about the birth of her baby. These scenes establish an emotional and sympathetic link between characters and audience that enhances the horror of the climax.

The climactic finale itself is effectively staged and beautifully shot with chiaroscuro lighting. The sequence begins as Hercules and Cleopatra go about the ritual of poisoning Hans. Suddenly, eyes begin to watch, peering in at windows, looking up from beneath the carnival wagons. As the freak forces gather, a storm breaks and rain comes pouring down. As knives appear, nothing can be heard except the storm and a melancholy tune played by a dwarf with a pipe. Through the streaming rain, the thick mud appears full of crawling shapes, and in the darkness Cleopatra and Hercules run screaming in terror.

The rest of the film is more or less conventional fare apart from the freaks. The most significant scenes are those which show the daily routine and individual adjustment of the freaks to their handicaps. They are almost clinically depicted. The armless woman drinks beer from a glass clutched by a prehensile foot, and the human worm, both armless and legless, manages to light his cigarettes with his teeth. The freaks are very much able to function as part of the real world and seem to make the best of their physical shortcomings. Browning's smooth direction portrays these creatures as both objects of sympathy and yet, also very subtly, as nightmarish incarnations of the audience's fears of the nonhuman.

The warm appreciation of the freaks' humanity is first evoked when we are introduced to them during an outing in the country. The camera inching through the forest encounters, in a distant clearing, a grotesque round dance of hopping, wriggling, and crawling things. Yet as the camera draws closer, these seemingly grotesque apparitions coalesce into childlike shapes, thus becoming transformed from agents of terror into objects of audience compassion within seconds. This evocation of humanity and sympathy is bolstered by the wedding sequence when Cleopatra humiliates Hans by riding him piggyback but becomes reversed in the final scenes when the mud illuminated by lightning swarms with the grotesque crawling and hopping shapes. Our final image of the freaks in the rain depicts creatures with all humanity erased and comes around full cycle to our initial introduction. Although this last scene may have been a mistake, it was perhaps an inevitable outcome of the precarious and delicate balance maintained by Browning throughout the film.

The acting of the "tall" (as opposed to normal) characters (Ford as Phroso, Hyams as Venus, and Baclanova as Cleopatra) is pretty much undistinguished although Wallace Ford does have several poignant scenes with characters such as the pinheaded women and the bearded lady. Cleopatra and Hercules in particular have been weakened as characters by acting which appears badly dated by modern standards.

Although *Freaks* has been compared to the surreal cinema of Spanish director Luis Bunnell, it is more properly Germanic in its theme. The humiliating situations, the ritual wedding feast torn apart through drunken hatred, the atmosphere of sexual jealousy, and the method of telling the story in flashback are all hallmarks of German directors such as Friedrich Murnan and Josef von Sternberg. Bunnel would have portrayed the freaks as embodying the latent spiritual deformity in man. Browning, however, endows them with man's nobler virtues and then subjects them to Cleopatra, one of Sternberg's diabolical women.

The film is baroque, then, and not surreal. It is certainly not a horror film although the final sequence in which the freaks capture and mutilate Cleopatra and Hercules is as monstrous as anyone might conceive. *Freaks* is a virtual textbook of the baroque and certainly influenced Federico Fellini's *La Strada* (1954); Max Ophuls' *Lola Montes* (1955); Edmund Goulding's *Nightmare Alley* (1947), featuring Tyrone Power in what many consider to be his finest role; and, of course, Ingmar Bergman's *Sawdust and Tinsel* and *The Naked Night* (1953). Although seldom allowed to be shown throughout its history, *Freaks* has, in fact, become a major influence on serious modern attempts at the baroque film and continues to tell us a great deal about ourselves as human beings.

Stephen L. Hanson

A FREE SOUL

Released: 1931
Production: Metro-Goldwyn-Mayer
Direction: Clarence Brown
Screenplay: John Meehan; based on the novel of the same name by Adela Rogers St. John
Cinematography: William Daniels
Editing: Hugh Wynn
Art direction: Cedric Gibbons
Costume design: Adrian

Principal characters:
Jan Ashe .... Norma Shearer
Stephen Ashe .... Lionel Barrymore (AA)
Dwight Winthrop .... Leslie Howard
Ace Wilfong .... Clark Gable
Grandma Ashe .... Lucy Beaumont

With her films supervised by her brilliant husband, Irving Thalberg, who was head of production at M-G-M, Norma Shearer had the pick of story properties at that studio. When a novel by Adela Rogers St. John, *A Free Soul*, attracted her attention, Thalberg assigned it to her. In it, she plays Jan Ashe, a modern San Francisco girl who has been brought up in an atmosphere of freedom. She is motherless, but her father, Stephen Ashe (Lionel Barrymore), whom she adores, is a famous criminal lawyer. They are both free-thinking rebels. Stephen has just proved his courtroom genius by freeing Ace Wilfong (Clark Gable), a gambler and underworld character, from a murder charge.

Stephen has one great fault: drinking. He is drunk when he brings Ace to his mother's home for her birthday party, where Jan is waiting with her fiancé, Dwight Winthrop (Leslie Howard). The aristocratic Grandma Ashe (Lucy Beaumont) is appalled by her son's lack of taste in bringing someone like Ace into her home and lets Stephen know that Ace is not welcome. Stephen, already more than half drunk, says he will leave too, and Jan, in a sudden spirit of rebellion, leaves with him and Ace, even though it means the end of her engagement to Dwight Winthrop. Ace is flattered by Jan's attraction to him, and they have an affair. He is very attracted to Jan, and she has never known another man quite like him. Ace goes to Stephen to ask Jan's hand in marriage, and he is amazed and angry when Stephen will not give his consent to the marriage. Stephen tries hard to convince Ace that he is no husband for his daughter.

When Ace's gambling den is raided, forcing Stephen to take refuge in Ace's private quarters, he discovers Jan in a negligee with Ace. She is ashamed and goes away with her father, who realizes that in his drunken way of life he is debasing his own daughter. He makes a bargain with her: if she will agree not to see Ace any more, he will give up drinking. They go away to the mountains together on a camping trip, and for the first time there is hope for both of them. When Stephen returns to San Francisco, however, he begins drinking again, and Jan, realizing that there is no point in her keeping her part of the bargain, goes back to being Ace's mistress.

Ace, triumphant, turns brutal, and Jan contemptuously leaves him, returning to her ex-fiancé, Dwight Winthrop. One night when they are together, they encounter Ace, who boldly tries to molest Jan. Although she fights him off, Ace is relentless, causing Dwight to draw a revolver and shoot Ace. Dwight is tried for murder, and Stephen defends him in a brilliant courtroom scene in which he says that it is not Dwight who should be on trial, but he himself, who is guilty of allowing his daughter to associate with a "mongrel" like Ace. He asks the court to free Dwight and judge *him* for the act of murder. His speech is so impassioned that he collapses and has a heart attack, dying in his daughter's arms. The jury frees Dwight, and Jan turns to him for consolation, acknowledging that it is he that she truly loves.

A Free Soul was Norma Shearer's seventh all-talking release at M-G-M. Her films were all modern stories, ranging from stylish dramas to drawing-room comedies, and all styled to make her "First Lady " of M-G-M. She had won the Academy Award for Best Actress in the year 1929-1930 for *The Divorcee*, and that same year she also earned a nomination for her work in *Their Own Desire*. (It was a practice in the early years that actors could be nominated more than once in the same year.) She was nominated again in the year 1930-1931 for her role as Jan Ashe in *A Free Soul*, but lost to Marie Dressler in *Min and Bill*.

Top honors went to Lionel Barrymore in his role of Stephen Ashe, for which he won his only Oscar. It was a popular award; his was a brilliant performance, much admired, especially in its day. Adela Rogers St. John based the character of Stephen Ashe on her own father, Earl Rogers, an attorney who was notable for his ability to take over the courtroom like a star about to give his finest performance. He seldom lost a case, and the courtroom was always packed when he worked. Rogers, like Stephen Ashe, was a very free soul, also well-known for his drinking exploits. William A. Brady had presented a play version of *A Free Soul* on Broadway by Willard Mack, with Mack in the role of Stephen Ashe and Kay Johnson playing Jan Ashe. In 1953, M-G-M filmed a new version of the story entitled *The Girl Who Had Everything*, starring Elizabeth Taylor, with William Powell playing Stephen Ashe. It played well and might have been more successful had there not been many viewers around who still remembered the electricity of the 1931 version.

DeWitt Bodeen

FRENZY

Released: 1972
Production: Alfred Hitchcock for Universal
Direction: Alfred Hitchcock
Screenplay: Anthony Shaffer; based on the novel *Goodbye Piccadilly, Farewell Leicester Square* by Arthur LaBern
Cinematography: Leonard J. South
Editing: John Jympson
Running time: 116 minutes

Principal characters:
Richard Blaney	Jon Finch
Bob Rusk	Barry Foster
Brenda Blaney	Barbara Leigh-Hunt
Babs Milligan	Anna Massey
Inspector Oxford	Alec McCowen
Mrs. Oxford	Vivien Merchant
Hettie Porter	Billie Whitelaw
Johnny Porter	Clive Swift
Felix Forsythe	Bernard Cribbins
Sergeant Spearman	Michael Bates
Monica Barling	Jean Marsh

As *Frenzy*'s opening credits play, the camera closes in on London's Tower Bridge. A series of spectacular murders, in which the victims—all young and female—are choked to death by a necktie, is the talk of the city (this theme dates back to Hitchcock's 1926 silent film, *The Lodger*). A prime suspect is quickly established: Richard Blaney (Jon Finch), a former superstar RAF pilot who has just been fired from his job as a barman because the pub owner accuses him of pilfering drinks. He is nervous, bitter, and ill-tempered, and he vanishes when a friendly cop stops to chat; in his first appearance on screen, he is seen knotting a tie.

The least likely candidate is Blaney's friend, affable mother's boy Bob Rusk (Barry Foster), a Covent Garden fruit and vegetable dealer. Rusk offers his now unemployed friend a few pounds, a tip on a horse, and some grapes to cheer him up. Underneath his self-confident exterior, however, Rusk is a sexual sadist and killer. Rusk eventually strangles Blaney's ex-wife Brenda (Barbara Leigh-Hunt) and girl friend Babs (Anna Massey). "You know what happens to wicked girls who tell wicked lies?" he sinisterly queries Brenda when she puts him off. "Women—they're all the same," he announces, as he proceeds to wrap his tie around her throat. Later, in an outstanding sequence, Rusk disposes of Babs's body by stuffing it in a sack of potatoes in the back of a delivery truck. Afterward, he realizes that his tie pin remains in the clenched fist of the corpse, but as he returns to the vehicle to cut open the sack, the truck driver begins his journey to deliver the vegetables. Scores of potatoes haphazardly fall over the highway as the killer frantically searches for the evidence that will link him to his crimes.

Blaney, however, remains the logical suspect in the case. He is shiftless, and two women with whom he has been involved are victims of the strangler. In addition, Brenda's spinsterish secretary (brilliantly played by a pre-*Upstairs-Downstairs* Jean Marsh, who steals the film from her talented coactors), who had overheard her and Blaney fight the previous day, notices him outside her employer's office just before she discovers the murder. Blaney is caught, convicted, and sentenced to a long prison term. Inspector Oxford (Alec McCowen), the Scotland Yard policeman in charge of the case, however, is not thoroughly convinced of Blaney's guilt. He continues his investigation, and soon uncovers the identity of the real strangler, thus freeing Blaney.

Hitchcock's direction of *Frenzy* is impeccable, a virtual textbook of cinematic technique. His integration of overhead shots and close-ups, tracking shots and subjective camera is like a symphony—a unity of diverse images which create a flowing oneness. Some of his individual shots are among the best in his career: the opening shot, for example, is breathtaking as the camera sweeps across the London skyline. As Rusk leads Babs into his flat, he ominously informs the doomed woman that she is "my kind of woman"; in one unbroken camera movement, the director then takes us down the stairs, out the door and into the street. This incredible shot is fluid, with the camera seeming endlessly mobile and flexible.

Contained in *Frenzy* are all the cinematic elements of vintage Hitchcock. Blaney is a typical Hitchcockian "wrong man." He is jobless, helpless, and virtually alone, and is constantly in the wrong place at the right time. Rusk, who squeals to the police when Blaney hides out in his apartment, is an unlikely mass murderer: dapper, well-liked, and never without a smile or good word. Yet he is as psychotic as *Psycho*'s (1960) Norman Bates or *Strangers on a Train*'s (1951) Bruno Anthony; indeed, the relationship between Blaney and Rusk can be compared to that of innocent Guy Haines and the psychopathic Anthony.

The director can even frighten his audience by merely focusing his camera on the front of a building. After Brenda is strangled in her office, her secretary returns from her lunch break. The camera remains immobile on the building's façade as the woman routinely enters and climbs the stairs. The viewer knows what awaits her, and the seconds seem like minutes as we wait for the discovery of the corpse. Finally, a scream rings out into the street as passersby, unaware of the murder, shrug and keep on their way. Hitchcock does not show us the secretary actually reacting to the sight of her lifeless employer, but the effect is far more horrifying.

There is also an abundance of black humor in *Frenzy*. At the film's outset, a Parliament official blabs on about a government program to rid the waterways of pollution. As he rambles on with his rhetoric, a young woman—another necktie murder victim—is observed floating in the Thames. As Inspector Oxford describes how the killer broke the fingers of the corpse, whose muscles had stiffened in rigor mortis, his wife (Vivien Merchant) unthinkingly snaps a breadstick. Blaney's ex-wife operates, of all businesses, a dating agency. A bar patron casually announces that a juicy sex crime is "good for the tourist trade," as the possible murderer sips brandy several feet away. The image of the legs of the strangled Babs sticking grotesquely out of the back of the potato truck is surreal, perversely funny but ultimately frightening.

The metaphor of food is ever-present in the film, from Rusk's profession to the grapes he offers Blaney to the potatoes and breadsticks and the inedible gourmet cooking of Mrs. Oxford (these latter scenes, as the bubbly wife enthusiastically feeds her flustered husband, are beautifully acted by McCowen and Merchant). All are akin to the sexual hunger of the rapist as he squeezes the lives out of his victims; indeed, characters are depicted eating or talking of food and hunger throughout.

Playwright Anthony Shaffer's dialogue is literate. *Frenzy* ends on a particularly wry note as, at the capture of the mass murderer, Inspector Oxford can only sardonically quip: "Mr. Rusk, you're not wearing your tie." The plot line is not without flaws, however; Blaney is convicted of strangling his ex-wife and girl friend, but what evidence links him to the other necktie killings? All are obviously linked: surely he could have proved his innocence by establishing his whereabouts when the other murders were committed. Also, Blaney is curiously unmoved by the deaths of two women for whom he obviously cares. Since he is a victim of uncanny circumstances, he should be a sympathetic character—as was the musician falsely accused of murder in the aptly titled *The Wrong Man* (1957). Instead, Blaney is ill-mannered, selfish, and unsympathetic. He does not mourn the women, but only frets that he will be unable to prove his innocence.

Critics and audiences alike responded favorably to *Frenzy*, and the film was universally hailed as the director's best in a decade. It was cited as among the best English-language films of the year by the National Board of Review, and has earned a respectable $6,500,000 since its release. *Frenzy* is not top-drawer Hitchcock: it is no *Psycho*, *Shadow of a Doubt* (1943), or *Vertigo* (1958), but a three-quarters Hitchcock is better than no Hitchcock, and *Frenzy* easily outclasses most other films of its genre.

Rob Edelman

FRIENDLY PERSUASION

Released: 1956
Production: William Wyler for United Artists
Direction: William Wyler
Screenplay: Michael Wilson (uncredited); based on the short stories of Jessamyn West
Cinematography: Ellsworth Fredericks
Editing: Robert Swink
Running time: 140 minutes

Principal characters:
Jess Birdwell	Gary Cooper
Eliza Birdwell	Dorothy McGuire
Josh Birdwell	Anthony Perkins
Mattie Birdwell	Phyllis Love
Little Jess	Richard Eyer
Sam Jordan	Robert Middleton
Gard Jordan	Mark Richman
Widow Hudspeth	Marjorie Main

Based on Jessamyn West's stories about a Quaker family living in southern Indiana during the Civil War, *Friendly Persuasion* is a "family film" in two senses. First, it has a broad appeal, presenting material that would interest both adults and children. Second, it focuses on a family's relationships, among its members as well as between the family and the rest of society. Winner of the *Palme d'Or* at the Cannes Film Festival, *Friendly Persuasion* received six Academy Award nominations, including one for Anthony Perkins, who was appearing in only his second film, as Best Supporting Actor.

Setting is crucial in *Friendly Persuasion*. The physical setting, the wooded hills of southern Indiana, creates a sense of pastoral peace. As nurseryman Jess Birdwell (Gary Cooper) and his family go about the idyllic pursuits of farm life, the film projects an admiration for the traditional, family-oriented security imputed to rural life in America. The film's social setting is also important. As Quakers, the Birdwell family stands somewhat apart from others in their community. For example, a traveling salesman makes good-natured sport of their nonstandard use of the pronouns "thee" and "thou" early in the film. In fact, the very seriousness with which they take their religion, demonstrated by the position of Jess's wife Eliza (Dorothy McGuire) as a leader of the local Quaker fellowship, makes the family out of the ordinary. Furthermore, Quakerism encourages full participation in the religion by all members of the family and discourages involvement in such "worldly" activities as music, horseracing, gambling, and violence. The historical setting of the film makes the last prohibition particularly difficult to observe. It is the turbulent era of the Civil War, and the Birdwell family as well as other Quakers are pressured to join the Union cause at least to protect their lives and property from the depradations of John Hunt Morgan's Confederate guerrillas, who are raiding into southern Indiana. This historical setting creates a tension with the peaceful physical setting in which the Quaker family tries to live its tranquil life.

The film's major narrative thrust concerns the gradual encroachment of war into the life of the Birdwells. The war first becomes apparent in the film when a Union soldier interrupts the Quaker meeting to appeal to the worshipers' patriotism and to urge the menfolk to enlist in the Union Army. The war and its effects become personified for the Birdwells especially in Gard Jordan (Mark Richman), the son of a neighbor who serves in the army. Wounded slightly on the battlefield, Gard comes home on furlough to win the heart of Mattie Birdwell (Phyllis Love) and the admiration of her brother Little Jess (Richard Eyer). As Morgan's Raiders move ever closer to the Birdwell property, they begin to see other signs of war such as billows of smoke from burning farmsteads in the distance.

The ultimate encroachment of war occurs when Josh Birdwell (Anthony Perkins) joins the local militia to help to repel the Confederate intruders. Josh's defection from Quaker teachings generates a family crisis. His decision is the result of his own inner crisis as he has agonized over whether his refusal to fight in the war results from his Quaker principles or from cowardice. Josh's struggle within himself recalls that of the protagonist of Stephen Crane's novel of the Civil War, *The Red Badge of Courage* (1895). On the battlefield Josh kills a Confederate soldier and is injured himself. When Jess sets out to find his son on the battleground, the older man also confronts a challenge to his Quaker beliefs. He finds his friend and neighbor Sam Jordan (Robert Middleton) dying from a Confederate sniper's bullet. Although the same sniper takes a shot at Jess, the Quaker allows the man to go in peace without exacting vengeance for his friend's death. Cooper's typical low-keyed acting is particularly effective and believable in his role as Jess. While Jess is away from the farm, the Confederates pillage the place. They are allowed to take what they want, Eliza resorting to defense with her broom only when the family's pet goose, Samantha, is threatened.

Although the film explores the serious issue of conflict of loyalties between religious principles and social responsibility, it also operates on a lighter level. The theme, sung by Pat Boone over the opening credits, sets up the expectation for a lighthearted film. That expectation is fulfilled in the first scene, the first of several which depict the running feud between Little Jess and Samantha, the goose who attacks the boy at particularly inopportune moments. Other scenes in the film such as the business call which Jess and Josh pay on the Widow Hudspeth (Marjorie Main) and her nubile daughters are almost totally comic. Much of the humor in the film, however, arises directly from the problems of being a good Quaker amidst the world's temptations. Members of the Birdwell family are shown humanly straying from the paths of Quaker righteousness in minor ways. For example, Jess cannot resist a horserace with his Methodist neighbor Sam Jordan even on the way to their respective churches. Mattie is vain, spending hours before her mirror despite the taunting of her brothers. Little Jess harbors thoughts of bloody revenge against his enemy Samantha. At a fair, members of the family are shown caught between the allurements of gambling, dancing, and music and the ever watchful eye of Eliza. (Significantly, Josh, who of course will later go to war, refuses to be swayed from his convictions at the fair, even when another fairgoer begins to abuse him physically.) These minor lapses from Quakerism, presented humorously for the most part, foreshadow the major lapses which occur with the advent of war.

Critical response to *Friendly Persuasion* was favorable and praised director William Wyler for his handling of what many felt to be unpromising material. The film manages to couple the quaint charm of rural American values with comedy and a serious theme, and the acting by the major characters responds nicely to the film's changing moods. *Friendly Persuasion* is a successful blending of dramatic tension with Currier-and-Ives nostalgia.

Frances M. Malpezzi
William M. Clements

THE FUGITIVE

Released: 1947
Production: John Ford and Merian C. Cooper for Argosy; released by RKO/
   Radio
Direction: John Ford
Screenplay: Dudley Nichols; based on the novel *The Labyrinthine Ways* (or
   The Power and the Glory) by Graham Greene
Cinematography: Gabriel Figueroa
Editing: Jack Murray
Running time: 104 minutes

Principal characters:
The Fugitive	Henry Fonda
The Woman	Dolores Del Rio
The Police Lieutenant	Pedro Armendariz
El Gringo	Ward Bond
Chief of Police	Leo Carrillo
Police Informer	J. Carrol Naish

The Fugitive, based on Graham Greene's novel *The Labyrinthine Ways*, is
the first film that John Ford made with his independent production company,
Argosy, which he had established in 1946. In partnership with Merian C.
Cooper and financially supported by former wartime Office of Strategic Services comrades (William Donovan, Ole Doering, David Bruce, and William
Vanderbilt), Ford hoped to free himself from the strict controls imposed on
his earlier films by the major studios. Being an independent enabled Ford to
indulge his artistic ambitions and to produce what he would later refer to as
his only perfect film. *The Fugitive* was a commercial failure, however, and in
spite of some favorable reviews at the time of its release, most critics now
agree that it is one of Ford's worst films. Given his genius and the remarkable
achievement of the majority of his work, it is instructive to examine the film
in order to understand better why Ford's other films are so satisfying on so
many different levels.

The central figure of the book is a priest in the state of mortal sin. Pursued
by the authorities from village to village, the "whiskey priest" is also being
tracked down by his own conscience through the labyrinthine ways of his own
mind. Guilt wrenches him like a vice, leaving nothing but a yearning to do
God's will—if only he were priest enough. When at last he dies, the hardship
and the guilt have left very little of him still alive.

The film abandons the internal moral dilemma of the novel for a relatively
routine plot that does not attempt to delve into the book's complex philosophical issues. It is set in an unspecified Latin American country which bears
a strong resemblance to the Mexico of the 1920's and 1930's and its purges

of the Roman Catholic churches and clergy. As it begins, a voiceover explains that the story is timeless, a story first told in the Bible. A man (Henry Fonda) approaches an imposing church on a hill and enters, pausing as he pushes open the doors and forming a shadow in the shape of a cross. He finds that the church has been vandalized and desecrated and notices that a woman (Dolores Del Rio) and her child are hiding inside. The man asks her why she is here, and she replies that she has no home and no husband to go to. Learning that the stranger is the former priest of this parish, the woman begs him to baptize her child. Although the priest is afraid, he agrees to perform the rite for her and for the other villagers. In the film, as well as in the original story, this priest proves, in spite of his giving way to temptation, that he is not a coward but a man overwhelmed by love for his fellow men. In a beautifully photographed sequence, the villagers enter the church and restore the baptismal font. The priest then blesses and baptizes the children of the village, beginning with the illegitimate child of the woman who had been hiding in the church.

By the next day the police have learned of the ceremony. They ride to the village, where they destroy the stalls and goods in the marketplace, thoroughly frightening the people. The lieutenant (Pedro Armendariz) rides into the church, where he finds the woman who befriended the priest. He recognizes her, and it is revealed that they had been lovers and that he is, in fact, the father of her child. He is startled to learn that she now works in the cantina, but is satisfied that his dedication to the revolution is more important than are his responsibilities to this woman and her daughter.

The police herd the villagers into the square, where the lieutenant urges them to reveal the identity of the priest. If they do not do so, the police will take hostages until the priest is found. When the lieutenant takes the mayor as the first hostage, the priest, disguised as a peasant, volunteers to replace the mayor. Ironically, he is refused as an unworthy substitute.

When the police leave, the woman helps the priest to escape the village. On his way, he passes El Gringo (Ward Bond), an American thief and murderer who has arrived by ship and is attempting to hide in the village; he too is a fugitive. Further on, the priest encounters a servile, cunning man (J. Carrol Naish) who insists on accompanying him to the port city. The man is an informer who has recognized the priest from a wanted poster and plans to betray him to the police. When they stop for the night, the informer gets drunk on the sacramental wine that the priest is carrying and passes out, enabling the priest to escape. Reaching the city, the priest buys a ticket for a departing ship, but before he can board, he is recognized by a small boy who begs him to give the last rites to his dying mother. The priest agrees to see her, thereby dooming his escape.

After administering last rites to the dying woman, he is asked to say a mass for all of the mourners but he needs wine for the mass and his supply is gone.

Because the state has prohibited the sale of wine, the priest must buy it from the corrupt cousin of the governor. Once he has paid for the wine, he is forced to drink brandy and share his wine with the black marketeer and the equally corrupt chief of police. He eventually escapes with the remaining brandy, but is arrested by the police for drunkenness. Once again the lieutenant does not recognize him, even though the informer, who is, by now, also jailed, tries to tell the lieutenant who he is. In jail, the priest must watch the hostage mayor march to his death.

The priest is subsequently released from prison and returns to the woman from the church. El Gringo is there and befriends the priest, paying for his supper. Soon the police arrive, and the woman hides the priest until she can persuade them to leave. The priest is seen as he tries to flee, but El Gringo shoots several of the policemen so that he can get away. The woman then helps the priest to cross the border where he is welcomed at a hospital.

The informer tracks him to the hospital and persuades him to return to the country because El Gringo is dying and needs his help. The priest agrees to go, but when they arrive, El Gringo says that he did not send for him. The priest tries to pray for him and urges him to confess his sins and repent, but El Gringo refuses, and as he dies, the police arrive to arrest the priest.

In prison, the lieutenant attempts to convince the priest to renounce his faith and to tell the people that he was a liar. The priest refuses. The woman brings him a crucifix, and the priest is marched to his death. At the sound of the guns, the lieutenant recoils as if hit himself and involuntarily crosses himself. In the last scene, the people are in the church praying when suddenly the doors open, and a man in the doorway announces that he is the new priest.

The Fugitive is the most consciously artistic film Ford ever made. Other films, among them *The Informer* (1935), *The Grapes of Wrath* (1939), *She Wore a Yellow Ribbon* (1949), and *The Quiet Man* (1952), are beautifully photographed with expressive camera angles and striking compositions; but in no other film is the attempt for artistic effect quite as obvious as it is in *The Fugitive*. The great Mexican cinematographer Gabriel Figueroa, who would later shoot many of Luis Buñel's Mexican films, produces a series of stunning visual effects. The people in the film are photographed like heroic Russian peasants, and whereas Russian director Sergei Eisenstein had, for example, glorified the citizens of his films in order to exalt the state, Ford glorifies his devout throngs to exalt the Church. Unlike Eisenstein, Ford is unable to combine those gorgeous but static images into a montage that is vibrant and alive. The audience is left with a film of visual richness, but one with a narrative that is full of implausible coincidences, pious but murky allegories, and actors portraying symbols rather than characters.

Given the limitations of the script, the actors are effective in their roles. Del Rio and Armendariz are particularly successful in lending some depth to parts that are essentially one-dimensional. Naish's obsequious hysteria is discordant when surrounded by other actors underplaying their roles. Fonda is almost immobile as the central character. One facet of Fonda's talent as an actor is the ability to convey a stillness, a quiet center to which other characters must respond. Ford uses that passivity in this film so that the fate of the priest is preordained from the beginning; as a fugitive priest who will not run from his duty in a hostile country, his martyrdom is inevitable. Thus, there is not the degree of dramatic tension in the film that there was in the novel since a certain inner conflict is lacking. The priest cannot save himself, and the audience loses interest in his passive journey toward death.

Ford is responsible for the failure of *The Fugitive*. The absence of studio control in his first independent effort became a license for self-indulgence, but Ford would not repeat his mistake. Other films made for Argosy would be commercial successes, and three or four would be masterpieces acclaimed by film scholars. *The Fugitive* contains some traits that would later be controlled in other films, but are freely expressed in this film, much to its detriment. The director's religious beliefs are evident in every frame. Pious Catholics may be inspired by the film; in fact, the Catholic magazine *The Sign* gave the film its 1947 award for the outstanding picture of the year. Yet general audiences are not persuaded by the religious aura, and many critics have objected to the heavy-handed symbolism of permitting Fonda's shadow to assume the form of the crucifix or of showing his sandled feet walking rough cobblestones to his execution. Other artistic objections center on the film's ending in a gratuitous miracle with the cross glowing in the darkness like a neon light. At the same time, Ford's chauvinist views of women are also given free rein, reducing Del Rio's character to a solemn caricature of woman as a combination of the Virgin Mary and Mary Magdalene.

Several critics have faulted Ford for not being more faithful to Greene's novel, saying that the film removes the "stink of humanity" which Greene had so powerfully conveyed in his book. The problem with the film is that Ford removes the humanity as well as the stink, and produces instead lugubrious, albeit beautiful, tableaux that lack the warmth and vitality which enliven so many of Ford's other films. It is ironic that when Ford consciously strived to produce an artistic film, he failed miserably, but when he tossed off "a piece of work," he gave the world such masterpieces as *The Searchers* (1956) and *The Quiet Man*.

Don K Thompson

FUNNY FACE

Released: 1957
Production: Roger Edens for Paramount
Direction: Stanley Donen
Screenplay: Leonard Gershe; based on his unproduced musical play of the same name
Cinematography: Ray June
Editing: Frank Bracht
Costume design: Edith Head and Hubert de Givenchy
Dance direction: Eugene Loring
Music: George and Ira Gershwin
Visual consulting: Richard Avedon
Running time: 103 minutes

Principal characters:
Jo Stockton .... Audrey Hepburn
Dick Avery .... Fred Astaire
Maggie Prescott .... Kay Thompson
Professor Emile Flostre .... Michel Auclair
Paul Duval .... Robert Flemyng

Funny Face was a stage musical in the 1920's starring Fred Astaire and his sister Adele, but the film of the same name made in 1957 used no more of the original than the name, several of the songs by George and Ira Gershwin, and Astaire as the star. In the film Astaire plays Dick Avery, a fashion photographer. When Maggie Prescott (Kay Thompson), the editor of the magazine for which he works, decides to do a series of photographs to show that a woman can be beautiful as well as intellectual, Dick, Maggie, and a group of decidedly unintellectual models invade a small Greenwich Village bookshop, much to the dismay of the clerk there, Jo Stockton (Audrey Hepburn). She becomes especially upset when they begin moving books about as if they owned the place. When they finally leave, Dick stays behind to give her some help in straightening up the mess they have caused.

Dick finds that Jo is a student of "empathacalism," a philosophy founded by a professor in France. Although he is not interested in empathacalism, Dick is interested in Jo, but when he kisses her she responds coolly that she has no desire to be kissed. She remains unmoved until after he leaves. Then she begins to catch the mood, singing and dancing alone in the bookstore to "How Long Has This Been Going On?"

Maggie is planning to choose a "quality woman" to photograph in Paris wearing the new collection by the designer Paul Duval (Robert Flemyng). Dick suggests that they use Jo, and when Maggie looks her over she says, "She might do." "Might do what?" replies Jo. Dick convinces Jo that she can be a model, even with her "funny face," and that the trip to Paris will give her a chance to meet Professor Flostre (Michel Auclair), the founder of empathacalism.

In Paris, Maggie, Jo, and Dick are shown on a split screen singing "Bonjour, Paris!" until they end up together on the Eiffel Tower. The next day, however, Jo does not show up at Duval's salon, and Dick has to search for her, finally finding her in a Bohemian café. After they argue and make up, they get down to the fashion business as Dick photographs Jo all over Paris in various Duval creations. For each photograph he tells her the mood he wants ("Today you're Anna Karenina," for example), and after each picture is taken we see it first in black-and-white negative, then in black-and-white positive, and finally in color. It is a visually striking technique. When he is photographing her as a bride outside a small church and she confesses that she loves him, he sings "He Loves and She Loves," and they dance together.

Professor Flostre, however, continues to be an obstacle to their romance. Jo goes to hear him lecture and then to see him privately although Dick has told her that he thinks Flostre's interest in her is more physical than intellectual. When she and Flostre are alone together, Jo finds that Dick was right. "I came here to talk with a philosopher, and you're talking like a man," she says before she hits him over the head with a statue and runs from the room.

Jo appears in Duval's fashion show, and she and the collection are a success, but Dick, not knowing that Jo has rejected Flostre's advances, is discouraged and determined to leave Paris without her. At the airport, however, he accidentally runs into Flostre and learns the true story. He goes back to find her, but she has left Duval's. At Maggie's suggestion he thinks of where she was happiest and immediately goes to the small church where they danced to "He Loves and She Loves." He finds her there; they sing "'S Wonderful" and glide away into the mist on a raft.

The plot of *Funny Face* is a perfectly serviceable one despite its gratuitous antiintellectualism in portraying empathacalism as inane and its followers as foolish or hypocritical. It even contains many excellent and well-acted nonmusical scenes, especially in the first half as bookish Jo is confronted with brassy Maggie and romantic Dick. *Funny Face* is, however, most importantly a musical, and its true highlights are in its musical numbers, many of which express the feelings developed in the plot.

The first important number finds Jo alone in the bookstore after the fashion magazine people have gone. She is dressed in dark and subdued colors in the middle of the equally dark and subdued colors of the books and the bookstore furnishings. Her discovery of a long brightly colored scarf left behind by the intruders and her memory of Dick's kiss start her singing and dancing to "How Long Has This Been Going On?" The visual effect of the one bright color moving about the room is striking. The voice, incidentally, is Hepburn's own, and is engaging if not superlative. (In *My Fair Lady* in 1964, of course, the producers chose to dub in Marni Nixon's singing voice for Hepburn in a famous Hollywood imbroglio.)

Probably the best and most inventive dance number is a solo by Dick to "Let's Kiss and Make Up," danced in a courtyard as Jo looks on from a balcony above. The two have quarreled, and Dick sings to her. Then as he begins dancing, a passing vehicle with a cow in it inspires Dick to continue the dance as a bullfighter, using his red-lined raincoat and his umbrella as props. It is a truly creative and expressive dance in which the bullfight motif never seems to be a gimmick.

The dance director, Eugene Loring, was a classically trained choreographer who had worked with Astaire before. Hepburn, although not known primarily as a dancer, had extensive training in ballet, while Astaire's experience was, of course, in stage and film musicals. Loring, therefore, as he has said, had "to try to think of Fred in a fresh way." For the dances of Astaire and Hepburn together he tried to use the strengths of each so that they would complement each other rather than clash or conflict. The dance he devised for "He Loves and She Loves" is a fine combination of the two, with Hepburn dancing in a bridal dress which somewhat resembles a ballet costume.

Also notable is a fun-filled seminovelty number called "Clap Yo' Hands." When Dick and Maggie find that Jo is with Professor Flostre instead of preparing for the fashion show, they invade the Bohemian quarters of the philosopher disguised as Southern folk singers who are there to entertain the Bohemian empathacalists. They do a rousing, gospel-style singing and dancing number with Dick wearing a false beard and using some Elvis Presley-like movements. Their performance is a hit with the empathacalists, but it does not succeed in getting Jo away from Flostre.

Funny Face gained a visual distinction from its "visual consultant," the noted photographer Richard Avedon; its producer and director, Roger Edens and Stanley Donen, had been part of the golden years of the M-G-M musical; and Hepburn and Thompson gave splendid acting and dancing performances. All these virtually guaranteed a good film, and the addition of the incomparable talents of Astaire made certain that the film would be the outstanding work it is.

Judith A. Williams

GAMBIT

Released: 1966
Production: Leo L. Fuchs for Universal
Direction: Ronald Neame
Screenplay: Jack Davies and Alvin Sargent
Cinematography: Clifford Stine
Editing: Alma Macrorie
Running time: 108 minutes

Principal characters:
Harold "Harry" Dean .... Michael Caine
Nicole Chang .... Shirley MacLaine
Ahmad Shahbandar .... Herbert Lom
Emile Fournier .... John Abbott

In the early 1960's, the spy movie was a popular craze, and Hollywood obliged the public at the box office. The James Bond movies were making enormous profits, and imitation Bond movies were quick to follow. After a rash of serious spy films, the logical follow-up was a rash of spy spoof films. The spy spoof often had the advantage of supplying its audience with the best of both worlds: it preserved the forms of a thriller and the action sequences sparked by dangerous situations, but it also allowed its audience to laugh at a sometimes absurdly cool spy film hero, never at a loss for the technique needed to command any situation.

The basic point of *Gambit* is the futility of imagining that the main character, Harold "Harry" Dean (Michael Caine), could mastermind anything. To point out the difference between Dean and a "real" superspy, *Gambit* tells its story two ways, first as Dean fantasizes it in *Mission Impossible* perfection, and then in bumbling reality.

Gambit begins as Harold follows Nicole Chang (Shirley MacLaine) into the Palace of Joy, a nightclub where she is a chorus-line dancer in blue feather boas. As she bumps and grinds, Harold joins his friend Emile Fournier (John Abbott) at a table. In a flashforward, Harold lays out his plan to Emile. In the plan, Harold is the daring and self-assured cat burglar and Nicole his elegant bait. Their target is the fabulously wealthy art collector, Ahmad Shahbandar (Herbert Lom). Harold foresees him as an Eastern pushover, complete with fez, monacle, and short-tempered arrogance. Shahbandar owns a priceless sculpture, an ancient Oriental piece of art, a woman's head to which Nicole's bears a striking resemblance. Harold is sure the millionaire will be intrigued by the close resemblance, especially since his late young wife also looked like the sculpture. An invitation for both to see the sculpture is inevitable, and the theft will take only minutes. The flashforward shows Harold heisting the sculpture effortlessly, paying off a wordless, mysteriously beautiful Nicole, and escaping easily.

The crime successfully "completed," the movie dissolves back to the Palace of Joy to reveal Harry about to begin step one of the plan. Fantasy meets the complexities of immediate reality, however, when Nicole proves anything but inscrutable. Her first conversational gambit is an offer to recite a German limerick. Not only is she chatty, warm, and not mysterious, but she is also spunky. She does not jump when Harold, whom she calls Harry, beckons; she does not accept his sketchy instructions without question. Mystified but game, she does accept his offer to travel, because she needs the British passport which he offers as a bribe.

Not only does Nicole prove to have a personality, but she also repeatedly shows a street savvy and quick-witted ingenuity which Harold lacks. Harold is doubly frustrated. His beautiful, precise plan is blown from almost the moment they arrive, and Nicole has an answer for every unforeseen dilemma.

Shahbandar in person is a shrewd, modern businessman: no fez, no monacle, and no squandering of money. He is suspicious of Nicole and Harold from the moment they arrive; "Have them watched," he orders. Then we see Harold, still rehearsing his foolproof plans with Nicole. More foul-ups take place as he loses his cohort Emile in the bazaar, and Nicole outsmarts him by finding Emile. Nicole, not Harry, arranges their invitation to Shahbandar's penthouse. Once there, she manages the art connoisseur chitchat at which Harold miserably fails.

When Shahbandar proudly shows the two his prize Oriental sculpture, Nicole realizes for the first time what Harold is planning. She threatens to walk out, but for Harold's sake, goes on with the plan. She and Shahbandar go out on the town, and Harold steals his way into the penthouse. Nicole then ditches her host, returns to the penthouse, and steals the head which Harry is not agile enough to reach, using her impressively limber dancer's legs. When Harry thanks her and confesses that he loves her, however, she impulsively hugs him and inadvertantly trips the electronic alarm. She is caught at the airport, but Harry escapes.

A trick ending has Nicole set free by Shahbandar, with a message to Harry to give up the game and return the head. Harry has not taken it, however; he has merely hidden it in a Buddha inside Shahbandar's penthouse. Harry plans to sell a forgery of the sculpture, prepared in authentic detail by Emile, in the wake of publicity over the theft. Nicole tells Harry that it is her or a life of crime, and Harry dramatically smashes the fake head to prove his loyalty. Somewhat belatedly, Nicole apologizes to Emile for destroying his beautiful forgery, and the two leave a distraught Emile alone in his studio. As soon as they are gone, Emile smiles and opens a closet revealing several more fake sculptures, showing that for Emile, the plot has worked after all.

As a spy spoof, *Gambit* particularly lampooned the humorless nature of a serious spy. Harry Dean's biggest flaw is his lack of humor and self-serious cool; as a result, he cannot do anything right. Nicole is down-to-earth, inclined to make a joke of Harry's pretensions to infallibility. With the flashforward structure, *Gambit* allows us, and Harry, to indulge in a fantasy of perfect control and mastermind prowess. Because the audience is made a party to Harry's fantasy, Nicole's education of him is also a refresher course for us. The masterspy is not a grand puppeteer, pulling the strings of various conquests. Rather, the man who thinks of himself as a puppeteer is likely to be in the position of a puppet, jerkily responding to unforeseeable events.

The film gave Caine a chance to play against his own spy image, created in several successful spy movies based on Len Deighton novels, most notably *The Ipcress File* (1965) and *Billion Dollar Brain* (1967), in which he played a character named Harry Palmer. (The similarity of the names is not lost on the audience.) Caine shows a good flair for comedy here which unfortunately has seldom been able to surface. For MacLaine, the role of Nicole was a twist on her usual "hooker with a heart of gold" role; here the streetwise cabaret dancer triumphs with more brains than kook. Abbott skillfully underplays Emile as the low-key cohort who takes all, so that the ending is indeed a surprise. Ronald Neame directs with a style echoing the gloss and snapshot editing of more serious thrillers.

Leslie Donaldson

GENEVIEVE

Released: 1954
Production: Henry Cornelius for J. Arthur Rank; released by Universal
Direction: Henry Cornelius
Screenplay: William Rose; based on his original story
Cinematography: Christopher Challis
Editing: Clive Donner
Music: Larry Adler
Running time: 86 minutes

Principal characters:

Alan McKim	John Gregson
Wendy McKim	Dinah Sheridan
Ambrose Claverhouse	Kenneth More
Rosalind Peters	Kay Kendall
Hotel proprietress	Joyce Grenfell
Policeman	Geoffrey Keen
Policeman	Harold Siddons
Motorist	Reginald Beckwith
Old Gentleman	Arthur Wontner

Genevieve is an engagingly cheerful comedy, low-key in the best British tradition, but it is upper-middle-class in its tone and concerns. Along with the Alec Guinness comedies, *Kind Hearts and Coronets* (1949), *The Man in the White Suit* (1951), and other big-budget spectacles such as *Black Narcissus* (1947), *Great Expectations* (1947), and *Blanche Fury* (1948), *Genevieve* was part of Britain's postwar period of affluence. During the 1950's, the British put aside the war which had preoccupied them for so long and inaugurated a series of extremely clever, almost totally frivolous comedies which engaged their most talented actors—Guinness, Peter Sellers, Dennis Price, Kenneth More, Alastair Sim, and many others—for nearly a decade. This film represents one of the brightest examples of that period.

Genevieve takes place during the Veteran Car Club's annual London-to-Brighton rally. Every year, hundreds of vintage cars drive to the sea, bumping along, spewing exhaust, and breaking down with a vengeance. The film's central character, Alan McKim (John Gregson), operates a 1904 Darracq roadster and engages in a friendly rivalry with his good friend Ambrose Claverhouse (Kenneth More), who drives a yellow Spyker from the same year. Each time Alan's wife, Wendy (Dinah Sheridan), puts up a fuss, and each time she goes along, handing her husband tools when the car breaks down, putting up a picnic lunch, and suffering, with Alan, the wisecracks of passersby who make remarks such as "Better get a new Flint" when they spot the car collapsed by the roadside. This year, Ambrose, who hopes every time to combine the rally with a "beautiful emotional experience," has brought along Rosalind Peters (Kay Kendall), a gorgeous, svelte model, as his traveling companion, and *she* has brought her dog Susie. The film, however, focuses primarily on the McKims, an upwardly mobile couple; the attention on the journey to Brighton shifts continuously between Alan's mishaps and those of Ambrose. They delight in each other's accidents, chortling encouragement and jibes as they hurtle past each other at twenty-seven miles per hour. A disaster prevents Alan and Wendy from getting to the rally dinner on time, and Alan, who canceled their hotel booking when he thought Wendy was not coming, finds a room in a run-down hotel managed by an eccentric landlady (Joyce Grenfell) who tells them happily that there is no hot water. Their room overlooks a municipal clock which chimes the hour with a deafening racket. By now Wendy has decided to be a good sport, and this last jolt simply sends her into gales of laughter.

At the after-dinner dance, Rosalind, by now gleefully drunk, declares that she used to play the trumpet with an all-girl orchestra and proceeds to show Alan her lip. She then advances on the bandstand, commandeers a horn, and sails into a rendition of "Genevieve." Fortunately for Ambrose's ego, she is terrific. Rosalind decides to swing the tune, and the admiring band joins in, whereupon she passes out, thus denying Ambrose his "emotional experience." The next day finds Rosalind, mightily hung over, cowering behind huge sun glasses and guzzling Alka Seltzer, ready for the return run.

A not-so-friendly wager, a practice outlawed by the club, sets the tone for the trip home, which is a reprise of the catastrophes of the previous journey. Alan and Ambrose take turns playing dirty tricks on each other—stealing the top of an automobile's flow chamber, reporting a fake accident—and a pair of benevolent policemen stop them repeatedly for various infractions. There are other mishaps, and eventually they decide to call it quits; then a chance remark gets them going again, and in a last burst of desperation, they tear along to Westminster Bridge with the first one across winning. The Darracq sprouts a leak, the Spyker runs afoul of a fruit wagon, Alan is stopped by a garrulous old gentleman who courted his wife in a Darracq, and Ambrose gets his wheels stuck in the trolley tracks which swerve him away from the bridge just as he is about to win. The race finally ends with Alan pushing his car frantically while Wendy steers. They come to a stop but the brake disengages and Genevieve rolls onto the bridge alone the winner.

The film is, in reality, a character study concentrating on the two couples, particularly the similar childlike affection both men have for their vehicles, and their otherwise dissimilar personalities. McKim, a barrister, is earnest and open, a steady young chap getting along in the world; Claverhouse is a feckless, cheeky bloke, and avowed lecher who has brought a succession of "popsies" along on the rally each year. Sheridan is an English Barbara Bel Geddes type, fresh-faced, honey blonde, and cheerful. She portrays the perfect helpmate for her sincere, upright husband. Kendall of course, is tall, slinky, and gorgeous and is the sophisticated companion of Claverhouse's dreams. As she remarks to Wendy while they are observing the men haranguing each other, all Claverhouse thinks about is his car and "the other thing" (sex). Wendy replies wistfully that the only thing on Alan's mind is Genevieve. "Steady, junior," Rosalind tells Claverhouse later when his glands start racing.

Genevieve shows off many of England's remarkable company of character actors to good advantage. Grenfell makes a wonderfully mad hotel proprietress, smiling toothily at nothing with her hair done up in crazed whorls. Reginald Beckwith plays a helpful motorist who offers Gregson a tow and gets the rear of his own car bashed in for his pains. He is full of huffy outrage and reasonable chagrin, but he takes it on his stiff upper lip like a good fellow. The two policemen (Geoffrey Keen and Harold Siddons) who appear from time to time to object to McKim's and Claverhouse's transgressions do not want to penalize the men, but their patience does wear thin as each peccadillo gets worse than the one preceding it. There is also Arthur Wontner as the talkative duffer who fondly remembers his own beloved Darracq. He is sweet, blathering along about nothing and almost preventing McKim from winning; yet McKim appreciates him. When Wendy cries because she thinks that they have lost, McKim says he does not mind. He was a "wonderful old man" and he would not cut off his windy discourse for anything.

Genevieve is a film that celebrates eccentricity in the form of the two sportsmen's childish insistence that their car is the best. Although mature in other ways, these men are nothing but overgrown boys arguing over the merits of their vehicles, tinkering endlessly, and playing schoolboy pranks on each other. The women join in their madness. Much as she protests, the otherwise level-headed Wendy would not miss the annual outing for anything. Rosalind is wonderfully wacky, distending her lower lip and woozily launching into a jazz solo. Together, this motley group makes *Genevieve* one of England's most successful postwar films.

Physically the film is admirable. The color is lush, the countryside is picturesque, and the cars are delightful. There is an infinity of ancient machinery, spruced up and sparkling, leather shining, the occasional smoke stack belching black fums. Henry Cornelius is not a particularly distinguished director, but he keeps things moving along at a brisk clip, rather like an efficient traffic director, which is all a film as sprightly as *Genevieve* really needs.

Judith M. Kass

GENTLEMAN JIM

Released: 1942
Production: Robert Buckner for Warner Bros.
Direction: Raoul Walsh
Screenplay: Vincent Lawrence and Horace McCoy; based on the book *The Roar of the Crowd* by James J. Corbett
Cinematography: Sid Hickox
Editing: Jack Killifer
Music: Heinz Roemheld
Running time: 104 minutes

Principal characters:

James J. Corbett	Errol Flynn
Victoria Ware	Alexis Smith
Pat Corbett	Alan Hale
Walter Lowrie	Jack Carson
Clinton DeWitt	John Loder
Billy Delaney	William Frawley
John L. Sullivan	Ward Bond
Buck Ware	Minor Watson
Harry Watson	Rhys Williams
Father Burke	Arthur Shields
Ma Corbett	Dorothy Vaughan
George Corbett	James Flavin
Harry Corbett	Pat Flaherty
Mary Corbett	Marilyn Phillips
Governor Stanford	Frank Mayo
Colis Huntington	Henry O'Hara
Charles Crocker	Henry Crocker
Judge Geary	Wallis Clark

A good case can be made for *Gentleman Jim* as the best motion picture ever made about boxing. Many of the others, such as *The Harder They Fall* (1956) and *The Great White Hope* (1970), are primarily social criticism. Some deal with the corruption of boxing and its connection with crime. A number of them, such as *The Champ* (1979) and *Body and Soul* (1947), deal with the attempt of a defeated fighter to make a comeback. *Rocky* (1977), *Rocky II* (1979), and *Raging Bull* (1980) are more character studies than studies of boxing *per se*; the actual matches are bloody slugfests, and Rocky, or whoever the hero is, wins only because he can take more punishment than his opponent.

Gentleman Jim, the story of James J. Corbett (1856-1933), who in 1892 became the second world heavyweight boxing champion when he defeated John L. Sullivan, focuses more than any other film upon the actual skill of boxing. Corbett himself relied not on brute strength but on blocking, timing, and fancy footwork; he initiated a technique for boxing which was almost dancing. Accordingly, the fights in *Gentleman Jim* are beautifully choreographed; instead of being gory contests of survival, they are like fencing matches, with skillful feinting, parrying, and riposting. Rocky, by contrast, has hardly any guard at all; he simply absorbs punishment until he can come back with a knockout blow. Again, whereas most other boxing films have only a few vignettes of boxing and one big fight at the climax, *Gentleman Jim* has a great many scenes in the ring and focuses throughout on boxing.

It is appropriate that Errol Flynn was cast as the dapper and dancing Jim Corbett. Flynn had made his mark in films as a swashbuckler noted for his graceful acrobatics and swordplay. He also had a way with satiric repartee and impudent humor. These qualities were precisely suited to *Gentleman Jim*, for while the other boxing films (except for *The Great John L.*, 1945) are grim psychological and/or sociological dramas, *Gentleman Jim* is a light-hearted romantic comedy. A meticulous period piece, it offers a colorful, nostalgic look at the late nineteenth century, with a blend of brawling and gentility. Its director, Raoul Walsh, had just completed another romantic comedy set in the 1890's, *The Strawberry Blonde* (1941), and was perfectly in tune with the period. Earlier, he had directed *The Bowery* (1933) with a similar setting. Born in 1887, Walsh grew up in the time of *Gentleman Jim*; as a boy, he had actually met both Corbett and John L. Sullivan and had seen Corbett fight.

Walsh began his career as an actor; he had played John Wilkes Booth in *Birth of a Nation* (1914) and had portrayed young Pancho Villa while at the same time directing the real Villa in a film of the Mexican revolutionary during the actual revolution. Alternating between acting and directing (and sometimes doing both in the same film, as in *Sadie Thompson*, 1928), Walsh had made such memorable films as *The Thief of Bagdad* (1924) and *What Price Glory?* (1926). He lost an eye in an automobile accident in 1929, while playing the Cisco Kid in the first sound Western, *In Old Arizona*, which he was also directing, and thereafter he abandoned acting for full-time directing. During the 1930's, he made a series of competent but mostly unmemorable films, but when he moved to Warner Bros. in 1939, he became a major director who turned out such classics as *The Roaring Twenties* (1939) and *White Heat* (1949) with James Cagney, *High Sierra* (1941), (the film that made Humphrey Bogart a star), and seven films with Flynn that are among Flynn's best.

Gentleman Jim, the third Walsh-Flynn combination, is perhaps the best of them all. Flynn and Walsh became close friends offscreen, and Walsh evoked from Flynn more complex and fully-rounded characterizations than he had achieved in the many films he had previously made with director Michael Curtiz, which depended more exclusively upon action. In addition, *Gentleman Jim* benefits from a superior screenplay by Vincent Lawrence and Horace McCoy (author of the novel *They Shoot Horses, Don't They?*). It is supposedly based on Corbett's autobiography, *The Roar of the Crowd* (1925), but because of legal problems with Corbett's estate, many of the details are fictitious, including the names of some of the characters and a romance with a high-toned society lady named Victoria Ware.

The film opens in San Francisco in 1887, where we see some men going to an illegal prize fight. Corbett and his pal Walter Lowrie (Jack Carson) turn up, but they lack the price of admission. With characteristic brashness, Corbett gets them in by pretending that Lowrie's pocket has been picked and that the police may have to investigate if he is not admitted. The gatekeeper does not notice that Corbett is already in. The fight, between two big gorillas, is a crude slug fest with no rules and one fighter even conceals a bolt in his fist. The event is broken up by police, who club the boxers over the head and haul the spectators off to jail. There, Corbett finds himself in the same cell with Judge Geary (Wallis Clark), who complains that Barbary Coast bruisers have ruined the fight game, and therefore his aristocratic Olympic Club will sponsor fights for gentlemen. Corbett, however, wants to see the end of the brawl and incites the fighters to start it up again in the cell by telling each of them an insult that he falsely attributes to the other. Later, he gets the judge off without scandal by telling another tall tale.

Back in the Comstock bank, where he and Lowrie work as tellers, Corbett is summoned before the management. He expects to be fired but finds himself promoted instead for having rescued the bank founder's friend Geary. When Victoria Ware (Alexis Smith), an elegant lady, comes to make a withdrawal for her father who is at the Olympic Club, Corbett offers to carry the silver dollars there for her. Pretending to be a bank executive, he summons a cab, actually driven by his father (Alan Hale), from whom he borrows some money while pretending to tip him. At the Olympic Club, Corbett refuses to be dismissed and brashly bluffs his way in. From Miss Ware, he mooches a meal at the dining room, avoids paying a tip by pretending he has no cash smaller than a twenty-dollar bill, and persuades the somewhat flabbergasted Miss Ware to show him around. A rich girl who has had everything, she is amused by Corbett's ingratiating impudence. During the tour, he wants to see the gymnasium. She protests that women are not allowed there, but he waltzes her in anyway. There, he talks his way into a match with the boxing coach, who taught the Prince of Wales to fight. Leaving Miss Ware holding a lighted cigar that he has mooched, he puts on the gloves and to everyone's surprise lands several stiff punches on coach Watson (Rhys Williams), who in turn cannot lay a glove on him. Impressed, Judge Geary talks Miss Ware into sponsoring Corbett for club membership.

The club members soon find Corbett a conceited boor who has himself paged all over the premises. In fact, Corbett is a Southside boy whose brothers are longshoremen. The Corbett family regularly gets into brawls, Irish Donnybrooks, and when his brothers taunt him for putting on airs, Corbett fights them in the backyard. Back at the Olympic Club, the high-toned members arrange to have Corbett fight the former heavyweight champion of England and Australia, who they expect (and hope) will give him a drubbing. Instead, the graceful, trim Corbett dances around the champion, parries and gets through his guard with ease, and knocks him out in the second round.

At a dance afterwards, Corbett waltzes with Miss Ware. Both amused and exasperated by his cockiness, she accuses him of having a swelled head and warns him of the champagne. He counters that he can outdrink anyone in the world. She smiles sarcastically, but despite his braggadocio, she likes him and takes him into the garden, where she advises him not to let the Nob Hill snobs repress him. Although she is engaged to Clinton DeWitt (John Loder), Corbett gets carried away by the romantic moment and kisses her, whereupon she calls him an impudent upstart and hopes someone will knock his block off. His pal Lowrie, meanwhile, has become offensively drunk, and when DeWitt tries to throw him out, Corbett goes too.

The two of them wake up horribly hungover in a strange town that turns out to be Salt Lake City. They have lost all their money, so to earn train fare home, Corbett lets a prize fight manager named Delaney (William Frawley) set him up to fight a local pug. Corbett wins and decides to go professional. Back in San Francisco, Miss Ware and DeWitt see him posing beside a portrait of John L. Sullivan, heavyweight champion of the world. When Sullivan himself (Ward Bond) turns up and Miss Ware admiringly feels his biceps, Corbett calls her vulgar and says that if she were his girl, he would spank her. She responds that the last thing in the world she would be is his girl. The relationship between them has deteriorated to a sarcastic antagonism that masks their real attraction to each other.

Going professional under Delaney's management, Corbett wins bout after bout and earns the nickname Gentleman Jim both for his fancy footwork and for his swaggering *nouveau-riche* elegance. He even goes on stage as an actor, with considerable popularity, although Miss Ware mutters after one performance that she is amazed that anyone would pay to see him act. (In fact, Corbett did perform on stage, one of his roles being that of a boxer in an adaptation of George Bernard Shaw's novel *Cashel Byron's Profession*.) She is sardonically amused when Corbett informs her that he is considering playing Hamlet. Meanwhile, as he becomes affluent, Corbett buys his parents a new house on Nob Hill and sets his brothers up in business with their own saloon, in which the Corbetts boast that Jim can beat any man in the world, including John L. Sullivan.

Sullivan, however, refuses to fight Corbett, who he thinks is nowhere near his match. In order to get him to fight, Corbett swaggers into Sullivan's dressing room after seeing the pugilist perform on stage in a melodrama called *The Honest Woodsman*. He starts eating Sullivan's meal, twits him about his age, and by getting his goat, baits him into agreeing to a fight. For the forthcoming match in New Orleans, however, Sullivan insists on a side bet with Corbett of ten thousand dollars to ensure his showing up. Having spent all his money on his family, Corbett cannot raise the amount. He then meets Victoria Ware, who pages him (in mockery of his paging himself at the Olympic Club) at New York's Waldorf-Astoria. He is delighted to see her, but they quickly resume spatting after he invites her out and she insists that she is booked up for the next three weeks. Her father, who likes Jim, tells him not to worry; if he is shanty Irish, so were they; they simply have acquired a larger shanty. Victoria wants the ego knocked out of Corbett, however, and so she secretly puts up the money so that she can have the satisfaction of seeing Sullivan put him in his place.

Sullivan has a superstition against entering the ring first; Corbett also refuses to enter first, so they agree to enter together; but as they do so, Corbett holds back and tricks Sullivan into violating his taboo. When they shake before the fight, Corbett breezily warns Sullivan not to trip over his beard. As the fight begins, Sullivan tries to knock out Corbett with wild-swinging powerhouse punches that Jim easily dodges. While Sullivan slugs crudely, trying for a knockout blow, Corbett is an artist in the ring as he weaves, ducks, and virtually dances around Sullivan, dodging his heavy swings and landing quick, sharp counterpunches. The fight goes on for twenty-one rounds, with Sullivan getting progressively worn down, while Corbett remains fresh and nearly untouched. The bout is beautifully choreographed. When Corbett knocks Sullivan out in the twenty-first round, Victoria Ware surprises herself by coming cheering to her feet.

At a party afterwards, however, she presents Jim with a huge hat for his supposedly swelled head. A good sport, he laughs and tries it on. As he does so, he sees in the mirror John L. Sullivan enter hesitantly. Corbett greets him gently, "Hello, John—are you all right?" Sullivan sighs, "Just a little tired." He then gives Corbett his belt engraved for "The Heavyweight Championship of the World." Sullivan says quietly, "I've had it a long time, Jim—take good care of it." Corbett replies sincerely, "I'll do my best. The first time I ever saw you fight, I was just a kid—no man alive could have stood up to you. Tonight I was glad you weren't the Sullivan of ten years ago." Moved by Corbett's tribute, Sullivan asks, "Is that what you're thinking now?" Corbett insists, "That's what I thought when I entered the ring." Sullivan is touched by Corbett's graciousness and tells him, "it's tough to be a good loser and tougher to be a good winner. I know tonight I'm shaking the hand of the new champion and a gentleman." Moved in turn, Corbett says, "I hope when my time comes I can go out with half the friends you've got, and half the world's respect." "You will, Jim,' Sullivan assures him. "Already they're saying a great new age of boxing begins with you." "Maybe," answers Corbett, "but there'll never be another John L. Sullivan."

Corbett then goes out into the garden, where Victoria follows him, ashamed of her mocking gift after seeing his sportsmanship. She realizes there is a serious and considerate side to him, and his liking for Sullivan earns her respect. He feels sorry for Sullivan, who will never again be able to pound a bar and say that he can lick any man in the world. He then asks her if they like each other. She responds that she thinks perhaps he likes her more but that she loves him more. "Love," he says incredulously, but as they almost relapse into their antagonistic banter, he informs her that she is going to be a marvelous Corbett. As they kiss, his father and brothers break into another brawl, and Lowrie shouts again, as he did earlier in the film, "The Corbetts are at it again."

Flynn always called Gentleman Jim one of his favorite roles, and in the film he gives one of his finest performances. Because of his well-publicized offscreen shenanigans, Flynn was underrated and not taken seriously as an actor, but his performance as Jim Corbett is a splendid one, extraordinarily charismatic, full of humor, high spirits, dash, and charm. The script endows him with the gift of blarney and makes him at times a roguish, rascally liar who bluffs and swaggers his way up from obscurity but who wins fame, fortune, and the girl he loves by genuine skill. Walsh reports that Flynn was thoroughly professional and worked out strenuously in the gymnasium. A good athlete who handled his fists well, Flynn did his own fighting in the ring and worked with sportswriter Ed Cochrane, an authority on Corbett, and with fighter Mushy Callahan to recapture Corbett's style of fighting. His performance is immensely physical and energetic, and he receives fine support from Hale and Bond in possibly their best roles. Walsh directs with vigor and keeps the film moving at an almost dizzying pace. The production captures the look of the 1890's—a bit of its poverty and a good deal of its opulence. Heinz Roemheld's score consists mostly of traditional Irish reels and jigs plus some sentimental songs of the period. *Gentleman Jim* is an immensely engaging film, an example of the "movie-movie" at its best.

Robert E. Morsberger

GEORGY GIRL

Released: 1966
Production: Otto Plaschkes and Robert A. Goldston for Everglade Productions; released by Columbia
Direction: Silvio Narizzano
Screenplay: Margaret Forster and Peter Nichols; based on the novel of the same name by Margaret Forster
Cinematography: Kenneth Higgins
Editing: John Bloom
Running time: 98 minutes

Principal characters:
James Leamington	James Mason
Georgy	Lynn Redgrave
Jos	Alan Bates
Meredith	Charlotte Rampling
Ellen	Rachel Kempson

A fable of the so-called "Swinging London" of the 1960's, *Georgy Girl* reflected the increasing climate of permissiveness that began to prevail in English films during that period. At this time, four letter words, abortions, and promiscuity became almost mandatory in films that charted the lives of the emerging, outspoken youth in Great Britain. Many of the earlier films of the decade dealt with the working class, but the success of the Beatles made the world aware that there was another side to England that had nothing to do with either the landed gentry or the coal miners' problems in industrial Northern towns.

Georgy Girl takes place in the London of designer Mary Quant and Carnaby Street, but its appealing, overgrown heroine does not fit into this environment, although it is all around her. As played by Lynn Redgrave (daughter of Michael and sister of Vanessa Redgrave), Georgy is a tall, ungainly, overweight virgin who is very intelligent, but not "smart." She is warm-hearted, has a winning, self-depreciating sense of humor, and is exceedingly generous to her friends. Her parents are servants to a wealthy man, James Leamington (James Mason), so Georgy has seen life from the back stairs and knows what it is like as lived by the established upper class. She also knows another life in London as she shares a flat with a nubile young woman musician, Meredith (Charlotte Rampling), who has more men around than she can handle and fully partakes of the new freedom. Both of these worlds are documented by a camera that travels all around London, from elegant Bayswater mansions to a cheap Paddington flat.

In less capable hands than Redgrave's, *Georgy Girl* could have been a "poor Cinderella" story, but she makes Georgy so likable and endows her with so much self-knowledge and understanding that her character does not turn into an object of pity. She is ably assisted by Mason as the gentleman of the manor who wants to set Georgy up as his mistress and is the first person to recognize her value. Alan Bates is utterly charming as Jos, Meredith's boyfriend. His character is representative of the kind of English men around in the 1960's who were trying to break free of old patterns and taboos, but were not sure what to do with themselves. Jos emerges as a bit eccentric, but sensitive enough to see behind Georgy's dumpy exterior. He tells Georgy "you just missed being beautiful," but after an initial seduction, finds that she is worth two of Meredith, who is the typical London "bird."

Directed by Silvio Narizzano and written by Margaret Forster (with Peter Nichols) based on her own book, *Georgy Girl* reflects a changing scene in a world going through a transition. Its portrayal of English idiosyncrasy coupled with insights about the new generation make it a fitting document for a time that has now passed. Along with *Darling* (1965), *Morgan!* (1966), and to some extent *Charlie Bubbles* (1968), *Georgy Girl* tries to come to terms with evolving morals in a society that adapts to any kind of change slowly.

Georgy is presented at the start of the film when she emerges from a fashionable beauty salon with her hair in an elaborate beehive style that is completely wrong for her tall, gangling person. She dashes to the bathroom and dunks her head under the sink until it hangs, dripping, straight down her face, and when her father suggests that she do something with her hair, she quickly tells him that she just had it done. An unmarried virgin of twenty-two, Georgy shares a flat with Meredith, a modishly dressed young cellist who changes lovers as easily as she changes clothes. When the bedroom is occupied, Georgy returns to the Leamington house where her parents are servants and where she grew up. James generously lets Georgy use his music room to teach interpretive dancing to small children. He has been like a father to her, but as she gets older, his feelings grow less and less paternal. Georgy ignores his advances and refuses to agree to attend a large party he is giving. The night of the party Georgy returns to her flat to find that she is left to entertain Jos, Meredith's current boyfriend and sometime roommate. Georgy would willingly be seduced by Jos, but he is indifferent. When Meredith comes back and prepares to go out, Georgy relents and goes to the Leamington party, feeling it is better than spending a dull evening alone at the flat.

James takes her into his study after watching her disgrace her parents by delightfully clowning her way through a sexy song. He proposes that she become his mistress, and has even drawn up a document to seal the bargain. For a moment, Georgy responds to his embrace, but then puts him off without an answer. Georgy continues to pine after Jos as he and Meredith get more and more involved. When Meredith tells Jos that she is going to have his baby, he marries her, with Georgy radiantly in attendance at the wedding, vicariously enjoying it all. As Meredith's pregnancy advances, she becomes

more and more morose and shows no interest at all in her impending motherhood. Her behavior causes friction between her and Jos, and the night she
goes into the hospital to deliver, Georgy cooperates joyfully as Jos seduces
her. Behaving disgracefully at the hospital, Meredith refuses to look at her
baby daughter.

When she returns, Jos tells her that he wants a divorce, to which Meredith
gladly agrees, but she leaves the baby with Georgy and Jos. Georgy becomes
increasingly more interested in the baby than in Jos. He realizes this and
insists on taking them on an outing to Greening, hoping to reestablish some
of the old intimacy he had at one time with Georgy. The trip is a failure, and
Jos leaves. Meanwhile, James's invalid wife has died and he has been keeping
a keen eye on Georgy. When he finds out that her affair with Jos is over, he
proposes marriage. Georgy finally accepts—but only on her own terms. She
wants a home for herself and the baby, but no romance unless it should
develop naturally in time. In the final scene, after a lavish wedding, James
sits next to Georgy and the baby in their limousine, looking slightly perplexed
as the maternal Georgy cuddles the baby and ignores him as they drive off
to their honeymoon.

Generally liked by the critics, *Georgy Girl* was a boost for the careers of
both Redgrave and Bates. Mason was praised for adding an element of black
humor to the proceedings; his role had some similarities to the Humbert-
Humbert part he played in *Lolita* (1962). Some reviewers felt that the contrast
between the Leamington household and Georgy and Meredith's Paddington
menage ought to have been parts of two separate films, but Redgrave, they
all agreed, managed to pull them together by her performance. The film
combines the exuberance of youth with the pathos of rejection. The character
of Georgy is an unusual one for a film with such a glamorous setting, but
Redgrave manages to make her more interesting than the trendy setpieces
by which she is surrounded.

Although Redgrave has kept busy in films in the United States and England,
and is currently costarrring in the popular American television series *House
Calls*, her new slim and beautiful image somehow lacks the vibrancy of her
ugly duckling role here. It is unfortunate that her marvelous comic talent has
not been consistently utilized in good films such as *Georgy Girl*.

Joan Cohen

THE GHOST AND MRS. MUIR

Released: 1947
Production: Fred Kohlmar for Twentieth Century-Fox
Direction: Joseph L. Mankiewicz
Screenplay: Philip Dunne; based on the novel of the same name by R. A. Dick
Cinematography: Charles Lang
Editing: Dorothy Spencer
Running time: 104 minutes

Principal characters:
Lucy Muir	Gene Tierney
Ghost of Captain Daniel Gregg	Rex Harrison
Miles Fairley	George Sanders
Martha	Edna Best
Anna (older)	Vanessa Brown
Mrs. Miles Fairley	Anna Lee
Coembe	Robert Coote
Anna (younger)	Natalie Wood
Sproule	Whitford Kane
Bill	William Stelling

The Ghost and Mrs. Muir was one of many fantasy films popular in the 1940's. Whereas fantasy and supernatural films of today tend to be lavish, special effects-laden, often violent productions, fantasy films in the 1940's were more subtle. A distinction should perhaps be made between "ghost" stories and "fantasy" stories, but 1940's films such as *Here Comes Mr. Jordan* (1941) and *It's a Wonderful Life* (1946), which had spirits prominently featured in the plot, can hardly be compared to the frightening films of later years, and are thus the more akin to fantasy. *The Ghost and Mrs. Muir* is not frightening at all. Instead, it is a tender love story between two people, one alive and one dead. The main characters never kiss or embrace, and there is nothing ghoulish about their relationship. The premise is merely a flight of fancy on which to build an entertaining love story.

The story opens at the turn of the century as Mrs. Lucy Muir (Gene Tierney) tells her mother-in-law and sister-in-law that she has decided to leave their home and begin a new life for herself. Lucy is a widow with a daughter named Anna (Natalie Wood), and almost a year after her husband's death she wants to manage her own life. So she takes Anna and their faithful housekeeper, Martha (Edna Best), and moves to a small British Coastal town, hoping to support herself on income from shares in a gold mine left to her by her husband.

When they go to a real estate agent named Coembe (Robert Coote) to find a suitable house, Lucy is at first discouraged by the high rents. She decides to look at one particular property, however, when she sees that its rent is less than half the price of other similar properties. Mr. Coembe is distressed and tries to discourage her, but Lucy stubbornly refuses to be dissuaded. They visit the house, which has a beautiful view of the ocean, and Lucy is immediately enthralled with it. Unfortunately, while Lucy and Coembe are there, they hear mysterious laughter and noises and are chased outside. Coembe finally confesses to Lucy that the house is haunted by the ghost of Captain Gregg, a well-known sea captain who committed suicide four years before. Since that time no one has been able to stay in the house for more than one night, and all of the tenants have complained about the ghost. Lucy, however, is adamant; she loves the house and wants to stay.

On her first night, after the others are in bed, she has her first encounter with the house's original occupant. As she tries to light a candle which will not stay ignited because the ghost keeps blowing out the match, Captain Gregg (Rex Harrison) appears for the first time. Lucy is at first frightened and ready to faint, but gradually she regains her composure and argues with Captain Gregg about his reported suicide. He tells her that his death was an accident and that the reason he haunts the house, called "Gull Cottage," is that he wants to turn it into a home for retired seamen (not sailors, he corrects). When he realizes Lucy's determination and spunk, he promises to let her stay unmolested in the house on a trial basis. His only stipulation is that she hang his portrait in the main bedroom, which Lucy now occupies. In a very well-done scene, Lucy goes to bed after trying to hang the portrait, but is embarrassed to undress in front of it. She covers it with an afghan, then proceeds to undress and get into bed. Just as she turns out the light, however, Captain Gregg's voice is heard, telling her not to "apologize to anyone for your figure."

There seems to be a truce between Lucy and Gregg just as her mother-in-law and sister-in-law arrive to take her back to London; the gold mine in which Lucy holds shares has petered out, and Lucy will have no money coming in on which to live. While Lucy listens despondently to their entreaties to return with them, Gregg, who is visible only to Lucy, tells her to send them away—that he will do something. She does what he asks, and her wishes are reinforced by some grandstanding ghost tricks on his part which make the women vow never to return.

As time passes, Lucy begins to write a book, *Blood and Swash*, which Gregg dictates to her, based on his own colorful life as a sea captain. When she completes the book she takes it to a London publisher, Mr. Sproule (Whitford Kane), who at first refuses to see her, thinking that she is just another silly widow writing a romance. When he does read the book, however, he likes it and promises Lucy that it will bring her a considerable amount of money in royalties. Now that Lucy's finances are secure she can buy Gull Cottage.

On the way out of the publisher's office, she meets a supercilious dandy, Miles Fairley (George Sanders), who shares a cab with her and sees her to the train station. Although she seems uninterested in him, she feigns admiration for his work when he reveals that he is the noted children's author "Uncle Neddy." Gregg is jealous when he meets Lucy, whom he prefers to call Lucia, in the train. They argue, but Lucy's temper and shouts of "blast" cause the dispute to end in laughter as they frighten away a gentleman passenger.

The growing affection between Lucy and Captain Gregg soon stops because Lucy becomes infatuated with Miles and thinks that she is going to marry him. She again argues with Captain Gregg, but this time she lets him know rather obliquely that she prefers a live man who can fulfill her needs over a dead one. Gregg agrees, and in the middle of the night he visits Lucy while she sleeps and whispers tenderly to her, telling her to forget him. He tells her that all memory of him will seem like a dream, and then he leaves her.

Soon after this Lucy removes the portrait of Captain Gregg from her bedroom, not really knowing why she put it there in the first place. Because Miles cannot come down and visit her, she decides to pay a surprise visit to him after obtaining his address from their mutual publisher. When she goes to his house, he is not there, but his wife (Anna Lee) is. She kindly tells Lucy not to feel too bad, because "this isn't the first time something like this has happened." A disconsolate Lucy returns home, and we see the years passing through shots of the surf hitting against a post in the sand bearing Anna's name.

Now the action advances to about twelve years later. Anna (Vanessa Brown) is now in college and she has come home with a fiancé named Bill (William Stelling). She wants Lucy to come and live with them, but Lucy refuses because she does not want to leave Gull Cottage. While they are having tea together, Anna reveals that she, too, had had "dreams" about Captain Gregg in which they talked about the sea and played games. Lucy has had recurring dreams about the Captain over the years, but she casts aside any thoughts that Anna has concerning his reality in their lives.

After this short sequence the passage of time is again shown by the pounding surf. By now Lucy is a white-haired old woman, and she is seen standing outside her bedroom on the porch which Captain Gregg had built to view the sea. Martha, also a white-haired old lady, brings Lucy inside and admonishes her to keep warm and drink her milk to abide by doctor's orders. Lucy rather brusquely sends Martha away, and as she begins to raise the glass of milk to her lips, she drops it and dies of a heart attack. Now, for the first time since they had parted many years before, Captain Gregg appears. He reaches for Lucy's hand, and superimposed photography shows a young and vibrant Lucy rising from the body of the old Lucy. The two walk hand-in-hand down the stairs, passing the unseeing Martha. The last frames of the film show the young Lucy and Captain Gregg walking off together in the mist, now joined in eternity.

The odd premise of the film would lead one to believe that it could only be successful as a comedy, but *The Ghost and Mrs. Muir* is not that. There are some mildly funny moments which are created by the reactions of some of the minor characters to Mrs. Muir's strong language or Captain Gregg's ghostly presence, but these are few. The film is a serious romantic drama in which a woman chooses one man over another and is literally as well as figuratively haunted by her scorned lover. Although Lucy is a widow at the beginning of the story, it is revealed that she was merely fond of her late husband. It is her love for Captain Gregg, which she cannot acknowledge, for which she grieves for the rest of her life.

There are numerous allusions throughout the film to Captain Gregg's presence as it was felt by Martha and Anna as well as Lucy. Martha uses such words as "landlubber" as soon as they settle in the house, and Anna marries a Navy man. When Lucy says that Anna's fiancé is a lieutenant, Martha scoffs, "Captain's more to my liking." For all of the women the illusion of Captain Gregg has a very real influence, but for Lucy, his influence cannot alter the fact that he is dead and she is not. She cannot accept him because they are divided by death, and it is only in her own death that they can be united.

The film is a favorite on television and even fathered an updated sequel. In that popular television series of the late 1960's, starring Hope Lange and Edward Mulhare, comedy rather than romance was the thrust of the story. The original film, however, is a bittersweet love story which strongly evokes the feeling and mystery of the sea.

Tierney's popularity was just beginning to decline when she made *The Ghost and Mrs. Muir*, and this was perhaps her last good role. She never was able to capture a distinct screen *persona*, a prerequisite for so-called superstardom, but she had been a popular leading lady in the 1940's. Her two most noteworthy roles were the leads in *Laura* (1944) and *Leave Her to Heaven* (1945), the latter of which brought her her only Academy Award nomination. Although she is American and Lucy Muir is English, Tierney admirably underplays the English accent required for the role. Her soft voice and almost Oriental-looking features give her the type of mysterious quality necessary to match her rival for Gregg's affections, the sea.

Harrison, an established star of British and American films and stage, does extremely well as the ghost of Captain Gregg, who is simultaneously handsome, suave, earthy, and stern, a character reminiscent of many other seamen on film. He is so earthy, in fact, that it is sometimes hard to believe that he is a ghost. Interestingly, he seemed more ethereal in *Blithe Spirit* (1945), in which he played the live husband of a haunting first wife.

In a time of widespread cinematic violence, gore, and scare techniques in films based on the supernatural, it is refreshing to watch an old film such as *The Ghost and Mrs. Muir* which entertains and does not resort to playing on the audience's primal fears.

Patricia King Hanson

GIRL FRIENDS

Released: 1978
Production: Claudia Weill with Jan Saunders for Cyclops Films; released by
Warner Bros.
Direction: Claudia Weill
Screenplay: Vicki Polon; based on an original story by Claudia Weill and
Vicki Polon
Cinematography: Fred Murphy
Editing: Suzanne Pettit
Running time: 87 minutes

Principal characters:
Susan Weinblatt	Melanie Mayron
Anne Munroe	Anita Skinner
Martin	Bob Balaban
Ceil	Amy Wright
Rabbi Gold	Eli Wallach
Eric	Christopher Guest
Beatrice	Viveca Lindfors

Girl Friends is a small, quiet film that builds its whole effect out of individual
scenes or moments rather than through an unmistakable exposition and a
clear-cut plot line. At the beginning of the film we meet the two main characters, Susan Weinblatt (Melanie Mayron) and Anne Munroe (Anita Skin-
ner); from then on we experience the happenings and crises of their lives just
as they do, as separate events that sometimes arise out of or lead into the
next event, and sometimes do not. *Girl Friends* is not, however, a difficult
or obscure film; it merely stresses the emotions and reactions of the main
characters rather than the shaping of the plot.

Both Susan and Anne are artistic young women sharing an apartment and
a friendship as they attempt to find their way in life after college. Susan, from
whose viewpoint most of the film is seen, makes her living photographing
weddings and bar mitzvahs, but she also takes more serious and artistic photographs and tries to sell them to magazines and galleries. Anne writes poetry
and reads it for Susan's approval.

When Anne becomes involved with Martin (Bob Balaban), we do not see
him at first; we see only Anne discussing her feelings with Susan. Anne is
initially quite tentative; "I think I almost might love him," she says, and in
later discussions with Susan, she is ambivalent about whether she wants to
be independent or wants to be taken care of by Martin. A minor climax in
the film comes in an artful sequence of three scenes. Susan and Anne have
picked out a new apartment, and Susan plans to paint one wall red. Then we
see Anne in a laundromat as Susan bursts in with the news that three of her

pictures have been bought by a magazine. Sure that she is now on the way to success, Susan exclaims that she will not have to photograph weddings any more. "One more wedding," says Anne—she and Martin are getting married. Susan tries to act happy, but she says, "How can you be sure when you're so unsure?" Next we see black-and-white pictures of Anne's wedding as we hear the voices of the people at the festivities. Then, as the voices continue, we see Susan, alone, painting a wall red.

Susan has an unsatisfying experience with Eric (Christopher Guest), a man she meets at a party. (We see her leave his apartment in the middle of the night and take a taxicab home.) Then after a visit to Anne and Martin during which she sees the pictures they took on their honeymoon in Morocco and hears that they plan to go to Italy, Susan becomes depressed and goes to a hairdresser (Albert Rogers) for a new look. When he tells her that the style she has selected will not work with her face, she responds, "Will anything?" She emerges with frizzy hair but no new success in her work and no contentment in living alone. Visiting Anne and Martin again, she sees an argument break out between them and learns that Anne is going back to school because she feels so isolated.

Susan picks up a young woman hitchhiker, Ceil (Amy Wright), on the way home and offers to let her stay in her apartment since she has no other place to go. Ceil turns out to be an irritant as the weeks go by, making no effort to find her own place, but Susan does nothing about the situation. She has gone back to photographing weddings and bar mitzvahs and has a long enjoyable talk with the rabbi (Eli Wallach) with whom she works. It ends with the rabbi kissing her and arranging to have lunch with her. When Anne comes to see her soon afterward, Susan describes her relationship with the rabbi as "bordering on mad passion." Anne is not at all sympathetic, however, because he is married and much older than Susan. As it turns out, the rabbi cancels the lunch because he is going to a football game with his family.

Tearful and upset, Susan finally tells Ceil to move out. At this point she needs something good to happen to her; so she summons up her courage and guile and manages to show her work to an important gallery owner, Mr. Carpel (Roderick Cook). He does not accept her work but does recommend her to another gallery owner, Beatrice (Viveca Lindfors), who likes her work and arranges an exhibition of it. Soon she is happily anticipating her exhibition and spending most of her time with Eric, whom she has begun seeing again.

A planned dinner for the four of them at Anne and Martin's, however, precipitates another crisis. Eric does not want to go and at the last minute says he is going to stay home and watch a football game. When Susan arrives late, Anne explodes, causing an argument that brings out many of the latent feelings of both women. Susan felt betrayed when Anne left to get married and now half envies her security. Anne thinks Susan selfish because she sees her so seldom and half-envies Susan's freedom. Not long after that Susan and

Eric have an argument. Susan says that she likes herself best when she does not need him and leaves.

When Susan's exhibition opens not long after, everyone she knows comes except Anne; even Eric appears. When Martin reports that Anne left for the country that morning and that he does not know why, Susan goes to the country and finds Anne playing solitaire and ignoring the ringing telephone. Anne says that she has just had an abortion without telling Martin, and Susan says that she is afraid to move in with Eric. The two proceed to get drunk together in their first moment of camaraderie since they lived together. Then a car arrives, and we hear Martin's voice ask, "May I?" as the camera freezes on Susan's face.

A great strength of *Girl Friends* is the fact that it explores various themes—chiefly the requirements of friendship and the conflicting desires for freedom and security—without being didactic and without making each character represent a certain position. Susan gives Anne a pep talk to convince her that she can take care of herself and does not need to rush into a marriage with Martin only because he will take care of her. When Anne does marry, however, Susan has trouble convincing herself of the benefits of independence.

Girl Friends was originally planned to be a short film about the two young women living together and facing the same problems, but the creators—intrigued with the idea of exploring what would happen to the two of them, especially Susan, if Anne moved out and married—expanded the story. The chief creators of the film are Claudia Weill and Vicki Polon. After the two worked out the story line together, drawing upon Weill's earlier experience as a free-lance still photographer, Polon wrote the entire screenplay, and Weill produced and directed the film. They wisely decided to keep the film less than ninety minutes long and thus avoided dissipating the fragile effect of the work.

Working on an extremely small budget, the filmmakers were fortunate to assemble an outstanding cast in which even the small parts are well played. Mayron as Susan has the largest role and superbly portrays the young Jewish woman's vulnerabilities and strengths without making her a stereotype. Nearly everyone else in the film could be singled out for praise, especially Wallach as the rabbi. He is appropriately gentle and fatherly, but in the scene in which he tells Susan that he originally wanted to be an actor and demonstrates to her how Marcel Marceau would do the lighting of the two cigarettes scene from *Now, Voyager* (1942), he reveals more of his character rather than of his acting ability.

Weill should get major credit for her directing, which artfully uses the camera without any tricky shots, and for evoking such good performances from the actors to provide a film that lingers in the mind.

Timothy W. Johnson

LES GIRLS

Released: 1957
Production: Sol C. Siegel for Metro-Goldwyn-Mayer
Direction: George Cukor
Screenplay: John Patrick; based on an original story by Vera Caspary
Cinematography: Robert Surtees
Editing: Ferris Webster
Costume design: Orry-Kelly (AA)
Song: Cole Porter
Running time: 114 minutes

Principal characters:
Barry Nichols .... Gene Kelly
Lady Sybil Wren .... Kay Kendall
Angela Ducros .... Taina Elg
Joy Henderson .... Mitzi Gaynor
Pierre Ducros .... Jacques Bergerac
Sir Gerald Wren .... Leslie Phillips
Judge .... Henry Daniell

In the last film he made at M-G-M, Gene Kelly danced in a very sophisticated musical, *Les Girls*, directed by George Cukor. It made some immediate bows to sophistication, the music having been written by Cole Porter, known for his bright, urbane lyrics, and the setting was Paris, always a stronghold of fashionable elegance in American musicals. *Les Girls* are not fashionable ladies, however; they are low-brow hoofers scrambling their way through faintly seedy productions. The three women who are "les girls" are dancers in a burlesque show which only their manager, choreographer, boss, and dancing mainstay, Barry Nichols (Gene Kelly), imagines is a high-class act. *Les Girls'* story takes place long after the troupe has disbanded, however, in the haphazard memories of its members in a courtroom. The troupe is about to give one last performance, from a makeshift but serviceable stage. The stage is a London courtroom, the scene a libel trial, and the burlesque provided by three women who will not get their stories straight. It seems possible by the film's end, in fact, that they could not get their stories straight to save their lives.

Les Girls is artfully made up of flashbacks briefly introduced by courtroom participants. Each flashback revolves around a tragic love affair and a close call with death. Each of the stories proceeds from hilarious romantic complications to an inevitable smell of escaping gas in the apartment, a dash up the stairs, and a timely rescue. What the girls and Barry cannot agree on is their individual roles in the drama: who courted whom, who flirted, who two-timed, who was lying prostrate on the floor, and who was the stalwart rescuer.

The court has the task of deciding the truth, and so it is to the court that each witness gives his or her best performance.

Lady Sybil Wren (Kay Kendall) is the first to take her turn in the witness box. She is the defendant in the libel suit, brought against her by one of the other girls, whom she has mentioned in her recently published memoirs. According to Lady Wren's memoirs, Angela Ducros (Taina Elg), her friend and fellow dancer, once tried to commit suicide over love—and worse, over love for a man who was not her husband, Pierre (Jacques Bergerac).

Outside the courtroom that day, banner headlines proclaim, "Lady Wren tells all." The defendant pulls up to the courtroom door and takes her bows for the press and populace, elegant and smiling for the cameras. The fortunes of each witness in the box can be followed by their exit and entrance bows to this outside audience. Today, Lady Wren is a confident leading lady; tomorrow, after Angela gives her version, Lady Wren will skulk past the photographers as quickly as possible, with Angela taking the bows.

As Lady Wren narrates the first flashback, it is quickly clear that she has more to her character than the noble generosity she plays up to the judge (Henry Daniell); she also has claws. The picture she paints of Angela is sensationally immoral. Angela joins the troupe after a rollicking audition in which, dressed in a bikini, she performs an awful burlesque with a trumpet and a drum. Barry hires her only after she promises not to let her personal life intrude on her work. Angela moves in with Sybil and the other dancer, Joy (Mitzi Gaynor), arriving with steamer trunks full of tastelessly revealing outfits and giant bottles of perfume from "friends." Sybil paints Angela as a shameless golddigger hard at work in Paris, with a new boyfriend every night and an unsuspecting fiancé, Pierre, back home in the French countryside.

Sybil is not much kinder in her portrayal of her boss, Barry. Barry is soon seeing Angela on the side for "dance lessons." He is a likable heel who could never love any girl as much as his own career and who is not above getting what he can from the girls in his troupe. Sybil and Joy have kept a knowing distance, but Angela falls for him. Eventually, Angela is seriously romantic; but when she hints broadly to Barry that their union should be permanent, Barry says "I can't kiss you when you talk." Then Pierre shows up. Angela sees it as a "now or never" problem and puts the question to Barry. For Barry, it is never. He was never serious, and now Angela is suicidal. Sybil comes home later that night and, smelling gas on the apartment landing, she rushes inside just in time to rescue her friend Angela.

Lady Wren's story has clearly made trouble for Angela, who tries to mollify an angry Pierre later at their hotel. Pierre is outraged to hear details of his wife's single days in Paris which he never would have guessed, so Angela is quite eager to tell her own version in court.

Back in court Angela ascends the witness stand, and a second flashback retells the same events. These events, however, are hardly compatible with

Lady Wren's story. No longer is Angela a siren who threw herself at the boss. Now she is a goodhearted, straightforward woman who tried, with her friend Joy, to take care of Sybil, a hopeless drunk. This flashback gives Kendall wonderfully comic bits as a chronic drunk, alternately maniacally happy or apologetic for breathing. Angela and Joy try vainly to keep the apartment liquor-free, as Sybil weaves cannily through the rooms, the booze cached in a perfume atomizer. Barry is fed up with her drinking and tells Angela he is going to fire Sybil. Angela thinks of a brilliant plan to save her friend's job. She tells Barry, "Sybil drinks because she's in love with you," and his incredibly large ego accepts the explanation.

The predictable romance ensues, with predictable results. Sybil is finally spurned by the casual Barry, and one night Angela comes home and smells gas. This time it is she who dashes inside in time to rescue her friend, Sybil, lying unconscious on the floor. Now it is Sybil's turn to scurry from the courtroom, an outraged Sir Gerald Wren (Leslie Phillips) at her heels. Sybil sticks to her story, but bolsters her certainty with a drink.

The third day brings a surprise witness, Barry Nichols. Barry has come to tell the truth that neither of his two girl friends knows. Barry was actually after the third trouper, Joy. He cannot get anywhere with her, and Sybil and Angela's respective boyfriends, Sir Gerald and Pierre, visit Barry and propose a scheme which will get each man his "girl." They suggest breaking up the act so that Barry and Joy can continue as a duo, and the other two will give up show business for marriage. Barry agrees, feigns heart trouble, and the girls agree to break up the act to save Barry's health. They all get drunk at a farewell party, and finally Barry and Joy are left alone. Barry reveals the ploy. Joy is furious, and she smashes Barry with a pie and leaves. Barry chases her to her apartment. Joy is not there, but Barry smells gas. He sees a loose connection in the gas line, breaks into the apartment, and rescues a comatose Angela and Sybil. So, Barry concludes, the gas was an accident. Angela and Sybil never saw each other after that night, and each reasoned that the other must have turned on the gas. The judge is satisfied with that story, and Sybil and Angela accept it with some relief. It takes each of the girls off the hook and makes their husbands look like cads for ruining their careers. The libel suit is withdrawn, and as the Wrens and the Ducros are embracing each other, the two wives glare at each other, then tearfully embrace and make up.

The twist in the ending comes as Barry and his wife, who turns out to be Joy, leave London in a cab headed for the airport. They congratulate each other on the job Barry did in court that day, but before Barry can become too proud of himself, Joy points out that his story was convenient for everyone involved, but asks, was there no truth in the other stories? On that note, the film ends.

Sometimes the purpose of a story told from several points of view in multiple flashbacks is to establish the truth of what really happened and the reliability of each narrator. In *Les Girls*, all stories are equally plausible, and it is for the audience to decide what is the truth. In actuality, however, determination of the truth is extraneous to the enjoyment of this film, as it is the fun of the various versions that makes the picture. The stars are very good in all of the roles, with Kelly and Kendall particularly fine. Kendall was one of the most delightful comediennes of British films. She was beginning to have a larger following with American audiences as well by the mid-1950's, but her career was tragically cut short when she died two years after completion of *Les Girls* from leukemia at the age of thirty-three.

While the Cole Porter score is not one of his better ones, as always it is entertaining. There are no "show stopping" numbers in the film, but a few of the specialty numbers such as "Ladies in Waiting" are delightfully staged.

Leslie Donaldson

GO FOR BROKE

Released: 1951
Production: Dore Schary for Metro-Goldwyn-Mayer
Direction: Robert Pirosh
Screenplay: Robert Pirosh
Cinematography: Paul C. Vogel
Editing: James E. Newcom
Running time: 92 minutes

Principal characters:
Lieutenant Michael Grayson	Van Johnson
Sam	Lane Nakano
Frank	Akira Fukunaga
Ohhara	Henry Oyasato
Chick	George Miki
Kaz	Ken K. Okamoto
Masami	Harry Hamada
Tommy	Henry Nakamura

At the outbreak of World War II, Americans of Japanese ancestry were unwelcome in this country. In 1942, Franklin Delano Roosevelt's infamous Executive Order 9066 caused the separation of Japanese Americans from their communities and their relocation into special camps. Approximately 120,000 citizens, guilty only of their Japanese ancestry, were resettled in these "relocation centers." Japanese characters in radio and film series suddenly became Chinese; "Jap" and "nip" villains in Hollywood war films were portrayed by Chinese actors.

Americans of Japanese ancestry were not necessarily disloyal. Many, in fact, fought in the war as members of the 442nd Regimental Combat Team. With the exception of its officers, all of the soldiers in the regiment were Nisei—American-born Japanese. Their extraordinary battle accomplishments are depicted in a sincere, taut, realistic film, *Go for Broke*, released in 1951, six years after the war. The title comes from the 442nd's battle cry, which is Hawaiian dice-shooting slang meaning "shoot the works." The 442nd compiled a record unequaled by any unit during the war. The regiment, composed of three thousand men and six thousand replacements, all volunteers from the continental United States, Alaska, and Hawaii, was honored with more than nine thousand combat citations—more unit and individual awards in proportion to time spent in combat than any other military outfit.

Although Van Johnson appears as Lieutenant Michael Grayson, a young Texas platoon officer in charge of a group of Nisei soldiers, the stars of the film are a small group of men who prepare for and participate in battle. They meet at Camp Shelby, Mississippi, for training. Grayson, who is biased and bigoted, is wary of the Nisei's loyalty and courage and resists his assignment as group commander. He is particularly hard on his men, both during training and after they are shipped overseas to Italy and France. All of the traditional GI "types" are present among Grayson's charges: the smart sergeant, Sam (Lane Nakano); resident clown, Tommy (Henry Nakamura); lazy time-waster, Chick (George Miki); and loud "Irishman", Ohhara (Henry Oyasato). Once the bullets fly, however, they all faithfully defend their flag. A highlight is the team's rescue of the 26th Texas Division, where Grayson has been transferred to act as liaison officer between the companies, from annihilation in the Vosges Mountains, France. Finally, they are decorated in a ceremony at the White House. Grayson finally realizes the true mettle of the men and is proud to have served with them.

Go For Broke is a tightly directed, straightforwardly absorbing and non-romantic presentation of the horrors of war, and a commentary on racial tolerance as well. The soldiers of the 442nd Regimental Combat Team may be of Japanese ancestry, but they are Americans first. Their loyalty to their country is not measured by religion or skin color or ancestry but by the combat record of their regiment.

Although the story line is loose and actually unimportant to the overall impact of the film, the major thrust of the plot concerns the soldiers' attempts to prove that they are good soldiers, and, more importantly, good Americans. The characters are stereotypes of soldiers, perhaps, but not of Japanese. Each man has his own reason for entering the army, but eventually all are unified in their desire to be good combat soldiers. One particularly effective scene near the end of the film illustrates this point. When a startled group of Germans surrender to the 442nd, they ask what kind of soldiers they are—"Chinese?" No, they reply, "Americans."

The film was shot primarily with amateur actors, which was a first for a major Metro-Goldwyn-Mayer production. To the credit of screenwriter/direc-tor Robert Pirosh and producer Dore Schary, Chinese or non-Oriental actors were not hired for *Go for Broke*. The soldiers are portrayed by actual "Heroes of the 442nd Regimental Combat Team" re-creating their combat experiences on the screen. More than six hundred veterans answered the studio's news-paper and radio casting call. No previous acting experience was required, and Pirosh coached the men for a month before shooting began. The film's con-sultant was Mike Masaoka, the first volunteer with the 442nd when it was activated in 1943. Masaoka was one of five brothers who served; four were wounded, and one was killed in action.

In 1949, Pirosh had won a Best Story and Screenplay Academy Award for the Schary-produced *Battleground*, a grim re-creation of the Battle of the Bulge as experienced by the soldiers of an American airborne infantry divi-sion. The goal in *Go for Broke* was similar: to present a gutsy, dramatic, but decidedly unglamorous view of war with flavorful GI talk and realistic battle scenes; and to highlight the accomplishments of the 442nd. The soldiers in both films are not superficially heroic but are men, human beings with fears, hopes, complaints, and senses of humor. The film is sometimes a bit too idealistic. Flowery commentary accompanies marching and landing sequences, and racist Texans far too broadly accept the Nisei. These are minor flaws, however; *Go for Broke* is a generally excellent production. The soldiers are not martyrs, just good and dedicated GI's.

Go for Broke is Pirosh's first film as a director and easily his best effort. He is a successful Hollywood screenwriter; in addition to *Go for Broke* and *Battleground*, he wrote *A Day at the Races* (1937), *I Married a Witch* (1942), *Up in Arms* (1944), and *What's So Bad About Feeling Good?* (1968). Several of the *Go for Broke* actors had limited screen careers. The most prolific was Nakamura, the pint-sized Nisei who plays the outfit's comedian, who is as tough a soldier as any of his comrades. He was featured in *Westward the Women* (1952), *Athena* (1954), *Unchained* (1955), and *Blood Alley* (1955). Nakano, who is particularly fine as the sergeant, also played in *Japanese War Bride* (1952). Akira Fukunaga had a role in *Beachhead* (1954), and Harry Hamada was in *The Frogmen* (1951).

The film received laudatory reviews, with Nakamura's performance singled out. It was a box-office success, and with a gross of $2,500,000, it was ranked a respectable twentieth on *Variety*'s list of 1951's top-earning films. Pirosh received another Best Story and Screenplay Oscar nomination, but, unlike for *Battleground*, he did not win, losing to Alan Jay Lerner for *An American in Paris*.

Rob Edelman

GO TELL THE SPARTANS

Released: 1978
Production: Allan F. Bodoh and Mitchell Cannold for Mar Vista Productions; released by Avco Embassy
Direction: Ted Post
Screenplay: Wendell Mayes; based on the novel *Incident at Muc Wa* by Daniel Ford
Cinematography: Harry Stradling, Jr.
Editing: Millie Moore
Music: Dick Halligan
Running time: 114 minutes

Principal characters:
Major Asa Barker .... Burt Lancaster
Corporal Courcey .... Craig Wasson
Sergeant Oleonowski .... Jonathan Goldsmith
Captain Olivetti .... Marc Singer
Lieutenant Hamilton .... Joe Unger
Cowboy .... Evan Kim
General Harnitz .... Dolph Sweet
One-eyed man .... Tad Horino

Go Tell the Spartans is set in Vietnam, 1964, when the United States had only twelve thousand "military advisers" in the country, and a large issue in the American presidential election campaign was whether Americans were going to be sent to do what the Vietnamese should be doing for themselves. The film tells the story of one mission by a Military Advisory Assistance Group stationed in Penang, but in this specific episode we see the enormity or futility of the entire American involvement in that country. As is usual in war films, the members of the unit represent a wide variety of backgrounds and attitudes, but *Go Tell the Spartans* transcends didactic intent and stereotyped characters. It is a fully realized human tragicomedy firmly rooted in a particular moment of American history.

In command of the Advisory Group is Major Asa Barker (Burt Lancaster), a weary veteran of World War II and the Korean War. His aide is Captain Olivetti (Marc Singer), a gum-chewing young officer with a somewhat cynical view of his duties and the American effort. Olivetti's chief interest is in furthering his military career; he expects to be at least a Brigadier General before he is forty years old.

The film opens with telling details and quickly but artfully establishes its milieu and cast of characters while deceptively introducing the central focus of the plot. After Barker restrains the overzealous, even bloodthirsty, Vietnamese interpreter, Cowboy (Evan Kim), from further torturing a prisoner, he goes to his office where two duties await him: a request for a "complete position paper" on a Vietnamese town of which he has never heard, and a group of new men that he is to receive into the outfit and assign to jobs. He takes care of the position paper first. Because he does not have enough men to investigate the location and because he does not believe in trying to establish and defend static positions, he directs Olivetti to write up and send in a paper stating that the town, Muc Wa, contains only two hundred people and is of no strategic importance.

After supposedly disposing of Muc Wa, Barker meets the new men, one by one. Lieutenant Hamilton (Joe Unger) is patriotic but naïve and expresses his fervent wish to kill Communists for his country. His idealistic statements are greeted with jaded cynicism by Barker and Olivetti. Sergeant Oleonowski (Jonathan Goldsmith) is a battle-weary veteran who has been transferred from the Delta region of Vietnam and who also served under Barker in Korea. Corporal Courcey (Craig Wasson) is the one who most puzzles Barker. He is a college graduate and a draftee who has volunteered for Vietnam even though that increases his period of service by six months. He either cannot or will not give the Major a credible explanation for his decision.

The new men are given whatever jobs Barker can concoct for them since the duties of the Advisory Group are ill-defined and the training and capabilities of the men are ill-suited to those duties that are defined. Hamilton and Courcey, for example, are assigned to the mosquito patrol, which consists of exposing their arms to mosquitos and counting the number of bites. This absurdity is, however, exchanged for another when General Harnitz (Dolph Sweet) arrives by helicopter to tell Barker that he knows his position paper on Muc Wa was faked and that, in fact, Barker's Group has been assigned the task of establishing and defending a garrison at the abandoned outpost. Barker knows that he has neither the men nor the equipment for such a mission and that the garrison will be an inviting target for the Viet Cong, but he must follow the orders.

Hamilton is assigned to command the Muc Wa unit with Oleonowski and Courcey and two other Americans completing the advisory team. Hamilton begins an idealistic speech about defending freedom to the Vietnamese he is to lead, but he stops when the ragged collection of Vietnamese mercenaries, regular soldiers, and farmers bursts into laughter at his words when they are translated by Cowboy, who is also part of the Muc Wa unit.

At Muc Wa they find very little except a French cemetery, the result of another attempt by outsiders to defend the location. At the cemetery gate is a sign that Courcey translates as "Stranger, when you find us lying here, go tell the Spartans we obeyed their orders." It is a quote from fifth century B. C. Greek historian Herodotus about the battle of Thermopylae in 480 B. C. in which three hundred Spartans died defending a pass, and it will prove only too relevant to current events once again.

When a group of Vietnamese appear at the river near the garrison, Cowboy insists that they are Viet Cong, but Hamilton says, "They don't look like Communists to me," and Courcey gives them chocolate and tries to make friends with them. Oleonowski, who has virtually taken over command of the unit because of Hamilton's inexperience and severe attack of dysentery, is infuriated that the people have been brought into the garrison. The audience is given no clue as to whether they are Viet Cong. Indeed, throughout the film the audience is often left wondering whether such characters as Oleonowski are overly cynical or merely realistic. Later Cowboy shoots the group of Vietnamese and claims that they were Viet Cong stealing weapons from the garrison, but the situation is so murky that the audience cannot be absolutely sure that he did not fake the evidence because of his own paranoia or bloodthirstiness.

When a patrol led by Oleonowski is attacked and he returns to Muc Wa leaving a wounded Vietnamese on the other side of the river, Hamilton insists on personally going to get the man. When he reaches him, the man is dead, and Hamilton is killed as he tries to return. This is somehow the last straw for the battle-weary, burnt-out Oleonowski; he exclaims that he is "tired of dinks" and kills himself. (Throughout the film the Vietnamese are referred to as "dinks" or "slopes" and the Viet Cong as "Charlie.")

Barker now has to visit a Vietnamese Colonel (Clyde Kasatsu) to convince him to supply additonal troops and mortar support to Muc Wa. The discussion takes place in the Colonel's ornate and lavishly appointed house. Only by promising the Colonel a large number of extra mortar shells is Barker able to obtain his promise of support. When Muc Wa is attacked and needs air support, however, the air support is refused because there is a rumor of a coup in Saigon, and the South Vietnamese want to save all their military strength for possible use against their own political opponents. Major Barker finally gets the support through a colorful and graphic threat he telegraphs to General Harnitz, but after the battle is over the High Command decides that the garrison should be abandoned, or "exfiltrated," because intelligence shows that the Viet Cong are increasing their pressure on the outpost.

A helicopter, with Barker aboard, arrives to evacuate the "defenders" of Muc Wa. When Courcey sees that only the Americans are going to be allowed on the helicopter, he insists on staying with the Vietnamese. The Americans, he says, cannot simply leave the Vietnamese behind—they brought them to Muc Wa. Barker, inexplicably, stays behind also, and the two have a long discussion as they prepare to leave the camp. Barker says that Courcey is a tourist, out to visit a war. As they leave that night with the Vietnamese, they are ambushed and both Courcey and Barker are wounded. The next morning Courcey awakens to find himself the only survivor. He walks to the cemetery, is almost shot by a strange one-eyed man he had seen there before (Tad Horino), and turns and says, "I'm going home, Charlie."

Go Tell the Spartans is excellent in virtually every aspect. Lancaster gives one of the very best performances of his long career, but he does not overshadow the realistic and often moving acting by the ensemble of relative unknowns. Particularly noteworthy are Goldsmith as the veteran burned out not only by fighting but also by trying to determine an American's place in this Asian war; Singer as the Captain who thinks he can keep a realistic outlook on the war and still use it to advance his military career; and Wasson as Courcey, the Corporal who discovers the difficulty of being a tourist in a war.

Underlying all these human stories, of course, are the larger issues of the war, which the United States was never able to resolve satisfactorily. The American soldiers are unable to understand the war or their place in it. When one Vietnamese brutalizes another, Oleonowski tells the other Americans to ignore the incident. "It's *their* war," he says. A medic who is aiding a wounded Vietnamese remarks that the wounded man could change places with the "slope" who shot him and he would not know the difference. Indeed, the Americans are never able to tell which Vietnamese are on which side until the shooting starts.

In the midst of this confusion, however, the American command decides to establish and defend an outpost at Muc Wa, endangering many Americans and Vietnamese to do so, but the Vietnamese Colonel must be bribed with ammunition to support the effort, and at the crucial time power struggles among Vietnamese on "our" side are more important than the effort against the Vietnamese on the "other" side. Compounding the irony and absurdity is the ultimate decision to abandon Muc Wa.

Ted Post's direction is never pretentious and never pedestrian. He and cinematographer Harry Stradling, Jr., aided by Dick Halligan's effective music, keep the emphasis upon what is happening rather than on landscapes or ostentatious effects. It is, perhaps, this lack of ostentation, the largely unknown cast and director, and the refusal of the filmmakers to sugar-coat uncomfortable issues that kept *Go Tell the Spartans* from achieving the fame of such Vietnam-related films as *Apocalypse Now* (1979) and *Coming Home* (1978), but the virtues of *Go Tell the Spartans* were noticed by many critics, several of whom said it was one of the ten best films of 1978 and two of whom, Stanley Kauffmann and John Simon, said it was the best film they had then seen about the Vietnam war.

Timothy W. Johnson

THE GODDESS

Released: 1958
Production: Milton Perlman for Columbia
Direction: John Cromwell
Screenplay: Paddy Chayefsky
Cinematography: Arthur J. Ornitz
Editing: Carl Lerner
Running time: 104 minutes

> *Principal characters:*
> Rita Shawn .... Kim Stanley
> Dutch Seymour .... Lloyd Bridges
> John Tower .... Steve Hill
> Mrs. Faulkner .... Betty Lou Holland
> Nurse .... Elizabeth Wilson
> Emily Ann Faulkner
> (later Rita Shawn) .... Patty Duke

Being a so-called movie goddess, the idol of millions, hardly points the way to happiness. Paddy Chayefsky's original screenplay *The Goddess* details the life-story of such a star, doomed from childhood to loneliness and discontent. It is told in the realistic style expected of director John Cromwell, who has nevertheless created some haunting moments that are almost sheer poetry in their revelations of a human soul in torment. The story is divided into three parts: Portrait of a Young Girl, Portrait of a Young Woman, and Portrait of a Goddess. Much of the power of the film is generated by Kim Stanley, making her screen debut as the goddess.

The opening scenes set in a small town in the South have a kind of early Tennessee Williams starkness about them. Rita Shawn, as a little girl named Emily Ann Faulkner (Patty Duke), is a fatherless child whose mother, Mrs. Faulkner (Betty Lou Holland), is loquacious and giddy, and works in a five-and-dime store. In school Emily has no close friends; there is something uncommunicative about her that makes other children withdraw in her presence. They do not invite her to participate in their games or to be their companion or friend. Yet there are special days when she needs to communicate. One of these is the day of her graduation from grade school. She tries to tell schoolmates, even strangers, of her accomplishment, but no one will listen. She goes to the store where her mother works, but her mother is busy between sales gossiping with other store attendants, and tells her daughter abruptly to go home; she will see her later. Emily obediently goes to the house where she lives with her mother, and a pet cat commands her attention. Emily pours some milk into a sauce dish and crawls under the kitchen table with the cat. She strokes it fondly, and then whispers in confidence, "Today I graduated."

Emily's life as a teenager (Kim Stanley) is not much different. She is still lonely, and none of the girls her age is a close companion. Her mother now has discovered Jesus, and nightly goes off to sing hymns in praise of the Lord. There is only one change in the even tenor of Emily's days: boys are interested in her. They are drawn to her, because she radiates sexuality to them. She is known as a "hot date" and has no difficulty getting partners at any dance. Although she is not a great beauty, there is something magnetic about her that makes men want to sleep with her. She teases and leads them on, but in the case of one young man, John Tower (Steve Hill), she takes him as a lover and then becomes his wife.

It is not a happy marriage; they have nothing in common, other than the fact that John finds her irresistible sexually, and she does not mind him. John does get her away from the ugly little Southern town, however, and she meets an up-and-coming young prizefighter, Dutch Seymour (Lloyd Bridges). Life with Dutch becomes fun because he moves in a constantly changing social scene. Indifferent to John, she leaves him and marries Dutch. It is inevitable that she meets with theater people, and because of her sensitivity and imagination, she comes alive as an actress. The camera opens a new world to her, and she blossoms while the lenses focus upon her.

Dutch is forgotten and abandoned as his wife climbs to stardom as Rita Shawn. A studio head, signing her to a starring contract, informs her significantly that she will be expected at his house later that evening. Now on a higher echelon is that same existence spelling only further, more acute loneliness for her. She becomes a sex goddess, and her fans worship her. Living on a Hollywood hill in a big modern Hollywood house, she sends for her mother, who predictably is no friend and companion—she never was. She is only a reminder of all that Rita never had as a child. The mother by now has become a religious fanatic and is all too aware of her daughter's sinful ways, but masochistically blames herself.

Rita continues to sleep her way around town, but she also withdraws more and more into another fantasy world, and not even doctors and pills are of any help to her. When her mother dies, she breaks down completely. The only companion she has now is the secretary-nurse (Elizabeth Wilson) paid to stay with her and keep her sedated. On film and to the world, Rita is still a goddess, but it is no longer easy for her to work before the camera. Broken and ill, she is kept alive by sedation and drugs. There is no hope, and it is obvious that the day will soon come when she is no longer a goddess on a pedestal.

The Goddess is one of the better than truer portraits of Hollywood. Actually, there are not many shots taken in Hollywood itself, since the motion picture was filmed largely in the East; but the spirit of a Hollywood that once existed breathes in the film, and Rita Shawn is not unlike some of the past real goddesses of Hollywood, such as Clara Bow and Marilyn Monroe. Some critics named Ava Gardner as the star who had inspired Chayefsky's story, but Gardner was, and is, a beauty, while the point is constantly made that Rita Shawn is not beautiful. She has sexual allure, and her charisma makes her famous. Like all goddesses who epitomize sex, Rita has probably never known a completely happy sexual relationship; men desire her body and use it, but it brings her nothing but a restless lack of fulfillment.

Stanley is in many ways perfectly cast for the part. She is cleverly photographed in the scenes where she is young so that her own personal maturity does not always show, and she does give the illusion of a kind of sexual beauty; in the last half of the picture, when Rita Shawn is mature, she is obviously at home in the part. Ironically, the film might be, in a sense, autobiographical. Stanley starred brilliantly on the Broadway stage, and was regarded by many as the best new actress in the theater. *The Goddess* marked a delayed film debut, and she got stunning notices, but she only played once again in films, in the London-filmed *Séance on a Wet Afternoon*, which won her an Academy Award nomination in 1964 as Best Actress. She flew to London again in 1972 to play with Katharine Hepburn and Paul Scofield in *A Delicate Balance*, but when she had to go before the cameras, she could not do it, and had to be replaced. She had often experienced neurotic spells during her acting career, and after filming *Séance on a Wet Afternoon*, she suffered a complete breakdown. She retired then to New Mexico, her native state, and for a time lived in Taos, eventually getting well enough to teach retarded children. She now lives in Santa Fe and is a full-time drama instructor at the College of Santa Fe. She directs productions for the campus playhouse, known as the Greer Garson Theatre, where one of her most successful productions was William Inge's *Bus Stop*, which in 1955 had won her the New York Drama Critics' Award as Best Actress.

The Goddess has been a much-admired film. Critically, it is still regarded favorably and always draws plaudits in any retrospective devoted to films about Hollywood or the motion pictures of John Cromwell. Cromwell returned to directing with *The Goddess* after a three-year absence from film production. Cromwell was apparently blacklisted by Howard Hughes, for whom he directed *The Racket* in 1958, but he kept busy by going back to the theater, where he never had any difficulty working as director or actor. He had been one of the first top stage directors to come to Hollywood at the beginning of talkies at Paramount in 1929. He worked constantly during the 1930's, 1940's, and into the 1950's, mostly at Paramount, RKO, and Twentieth Century-Fox, and was especially happy working for David O. Selznick, directing such films as *Little Lord Fauntleroy* (1936), the elegant remake starring Ronald Colman of *The Prisoner of Zenda* (1937), *Made for Each Other* (1938), and Selznick's big World War II special about the war at home, *Since You Went Away* (1944). Cromwell, now in his nineties, is still highly respected in the film world, to which he returned as a character actor for Robert Altman's recent *The Wedding* (1979), playing the senile priest who cannot remember the words of the wedding ceremony. He did wonders for Stanley in her film debut in *The Goddess*. An actor himself, he always put actors at ease, and they gave their best for him.

The Goddess has attracted new admirers over the years, and will undoubtedly continue to be one of the most highly regarded of those films about the Hollywood scene. It is one of the truest and the most poignantly tragic.

DeWitt Bodeen

GOLD DIGGERS OF 1933

Released: 1933
Production: Warner Bros.
Direction: Mervyn LeRoy
Screenplay: Erwin Gelsey and James Seymour; based on the play *Gold Diggers* by Avery Hopwood
Cinematography: Sol Polito
Editing: George Amy
Song: Harry Warren and Al Dubin
Music direction: Busby Berkeley
Running time: 94 minutes

Principal characters:
Carol	Joan Blondell
Polly Parker	Ruby Keeler
Trixie Lorraine	Aline MacMahon
Brad Roberts (Robert Treat Bradford)	Dick Powell
Fay	Ginger Rogers
J. Lawrence Bradford	Warren William
Thaniel H. Peabody	Guy Kibbee
Barney Hopkins	Ned Sparks

The year 1933 saw the emergence of an important new talent in the world of the film musical, Busby Berkeley. He produced extravagant musical numbers which were staged for the camera rather than for the theater. His first success was *42nd Street* (1933), and a few months later *Gold Diggers of 1933* arrived to confirm that he was a master of the cinematic musical. In this film, and others like it, the story is not especially important and serves merely as a setting for the true interest, the musical numbers. These numbers, directed by Berkeley, are so dazzling and imaginative that they delight audiences today as much as when the film was first released. The story, directed by Mervyn LeRoy, is simple and unexceptional.

Three out-of-work show girls, Polly, Carol, and Trixie, played respectively by Ruby Keeler, Joan Blondell, and Aline MacMahon, learn that a Broadway producer is casting a new show, a musical about the Depression showing its sad, happy, and cynical sides. When the girls discover that the producer has no money, a young composer and singer they know named Brad (Dick Powell) agrees to put up fifteen thousand dollars to finance the show if Polly has a featured part in it. On opening night Brad is forced to substitute for the leading singer. The next morning the newspapers reveal that he is the son of a wealthy conservative Boston family. Horrified at his connection with show business and his rumored engagement to Polly, the family sends Brad's older brother J. Lawrence Bradford (Warren Williams) and their lawyer (Guy Kibbee) to extricate him from Polly's clutches. Instead, the brother and the lawyer fall in love with Carol and Trixie and give their blessings to Brad and Polly.

Although this slight story provides many opportunities for snappy dialogue and much wisecracking, it is the musical numbers in the show that are the true glory of *Gold Diggers of 1933*. The four big production numbers in the film, "We're in the Money," "Pettin' in the Park," "The Shadow Waltz," and "My Forgotten Man," are representative of Berkeley's best work and show his artistic imagination and innovations. Each of the four begins on an actual stage before taking off into flights of fantasy that could never have been achieved in a real theater. The numbers each begin with the principal performers singing the lyrics to the song: Ginger Rogers in "We're in the Money"; Powell in "Pettin' in the Park" and "The Shadow Waltz"; and Blondell in "My Forgotten Man." After performing their solos they either disappear or merge into the ever-changing, evolving rhythm of the number.

The film opens with a close-up of Fay (Ginger Rogers) singing "We're in the Money," an optimistic, breezy antidote for Depression fears ("We never see a headline about a breadline today"). Fay, the chorus girls, and the stage are decorated with oversized silver dollars. As the number progresses, the camera pulls back to show Fay, seemingly with dozens of arms, rising at the head of a long line of chorus girls, a favorite Berkeley device. She even does a chorus of the song in Pig Latin, a fad of the time.

The next number, "Pettin' in the Park," does not come until the film is more than half over. It displays Berkeley's methods at their best—overhead shots, unexpected but linked images and scenes, transformations, and elaborate sets and costumes. It begins on a stage with Brad singing the lyrics. When the camera leaves him it also leaves behind the pretense that the number is being performed in a theater. As the camera pans across park benches, we see a variety of couples, white, black, Oriental, old, and young. Soon, girls on roller skates appear, followed by roller-skating policemen chasing a roller-skating midget dressed like a baby. At one point the camera shoots between the legs of a long line of policemen as they skate over the midget.

Berkeley then continues variations on the "Pettin' in the Park" theme in winter and summer settings. In a snow scene the chorus girls form changing circles as Berkeley uses his famous overhead shot to record the shifting patterns. Then a bouncing snowball becomes a child's rubber ball in a summer scene. Couples are lying on the grass cuddling. When it begins to rain, the girls run behind a screen, and we see them silhouetted as they change. The midget slyly raises the blind, expecting to see scantily clad girls. Instead, they are wearing metallic costumes with metal tops. The number ends with the midget giving Brad a can opener to open the back of Polly's costume.

"The Shadow Waltz" is another example of Berkeley at his best. It also begins as if it were being performed on an actual stage, with Brad again singing the lyrics. A close-up of Polly holding a flower takes us into the number. That image dissolves into one of many blondes in spiraling white hoop skirts playing white violins on a curving staircase. The violin motif goes through an imaginative progression, including overhead shots of the girls in patterns resembling opening and closing flower petals and ending with an overhead shot of a giant violin formed by many small violins. The violins are outlined with neon tubing for a more spectacular effect against the dark background. The girls are next seen reclining around a circular pool. The camera follows them around the edge of the pool until it comes to Brad and Polly, who drops a flower into the pool. The ripples cause the picture to break up and the number ends as it began, with a flower.

The film ends with "My Forgotten Man." Although it continues the pattern of starting out on an actual stage with one or two of the main performers singing the lyrics, it is unlike Berkeley's other work in several ways. It focuses on a serious social issue of the time, jobless war veterans, something not usually done in a musical. It is also different because there are no such typical Berkeley devices as overhead shots or swaying lines of chorus girls. It does tell a short, dramatic story, however, as Berkeley liked to do.

The number opens with a deserted street corner lit by a single street lamp. Carol, dressed in a tight slit skirt, leans against the street lamp and delivers the lyrics in a dramatic soliloquy. Then the scene shifts to a black woman in a tenement window who sings the lyrics. While she is singing there are vignettes of old, tired, worn, and hopeless women in other tenement windows. Then lines of uniformed men appear, marching to war while crowds cheer, throwing confetti and waving flags. Next, some men are marching in the rain while others are carried in the opposite direction, wounded, After this, the lines of men are not in uniform; they are in breadlines with tired, unshaven faces. In the final sequence, men in uniform are silhouetted at the back of the stage while Carol sings "My Forgotten Man" to men from the breadlines who form a circle, stretching their hands toward her. The total effect is very moving.

In Berkeley one sees a truly artistic imagination at work. Besides the appeal of individual images, he usually links the individual parts together in imaginative ways. Sometimes he tells a story; at other times, he uses a progression, such as the violin sequence, or transformations, such as the snowball becoming a rubber ball. Thus the reaction of the viewer as each new image comes on the screen is first surprise, then comprehension as the connection becomes clear, and then amazement at Berkeley's inventiveness.

One of Berkeley's chief artistic devices is the creation of patterns with his dancers. He uses overhead shots to show geometric or kaleidoscopic patterns that are constantly forming, breaking up, and reforming, into stars, flowers, circles, or abstract figures. He uses dancers as elements in a design or pieces in a jigsaw puzzle rather than as individuals, to create startling effects.

Although some critics of the time felt that a musical should not deal with serious social issues, *Gold Diggers of 1933* was one of the top-grossing films of the year. It remains an entertaining and funny backstage story, with musical numbers created by Berkeley at the peak of his creative powers. Audiences now find it as enjoyable as audiences in the 1930's did.

Julia Johnson

GOLDFINGER

Released: 1964
Production: Harry Saltzman and Albert R. Broccoli for United Artists
Direction: Guy Hamilton
Screenplay: Richard Maibaum and Paul Dehn; based on the novel of the same
name by Ian Fleming
Cinematography: Ted Moore
Editing: Peter Hunt
Music: John Barry
Song: Anthony Newley and Leslie Bricusse
Running time: 108 minutes

Principal characters:
James Bond/007 .... Sean Connery
Goldfinger .... Gert Frobe
Pussy Galore .... Honor Blackman
"M" .... Bernard Lee
Oddjob .... Harold Sakata
Jill Masterson .... Shirley Eaton

Goldfinger was the third in the James Bond series, following *Dr. No* (1962) and *From Russia with Love* (1963). It was the first movie in the series, however, to be extensively concerned with the gadgets which later became a trademark of Bond films, and was a turning point for the series. More attention was paid to supplying Bond with "ultramodern" gimmick machinery than to the number of women he would encounter. Beginning with *Goldfinger*, the Bond/007 emphasis shifted away from his unlimited prowess with women to an increasing fascination with technology, cars, weapons, and other spy equipment. The mastery of all aspects of existence achieved by the superhero spy was more and more a technological, rather than sexual, matter.

Beyond that distinction, however, *Goldfinger* is memorable for other distinguishing characteristics. One is Oddjob (Harold Sakata), the silent Oriental who throws a deadly, razorsharp hat. Sakata repeated his role as Oddjob again in commercials which capitalized on the villain's popularity. Another character who inspired spinoffs was Pussy Galore (Honor Blackman), a judo champ, knockout right-hand-woman to Goldfinger (Gert Frobe). Of course, the movie capitalized with comic-book directness on its gold focus, with the ads and commercial logo of the movie featuring a girl sealed in a skin of gold paint. In the plot, she is the minor character Jill Masterson (Shirley Eaton), killed in an offbeat way by suffocation with the gold paint, but the image expressed the movie's fascination with playful bodies as glamorous objects imperiled by fantastic dangers. Finally, the music of *Goldfinger*, scored by John Barry, is the music most associated with the James Bond pictures starring

Sean Connery. Shirley Bassey powerfully belts out the title song over credits illustrated by writhing golden girls. The expanse of flesh, even though gold-coated, was considered daring for a film at that time, although by contemporary standards the girls seem modest. All in all, the plot of *Goldfinger* may not be easy to recall—it involves robbing Fort Knox and an atom bomb—but chances are that those who cannot recall the plot can nevertheless readily visualize the movie.

The plot is heavy on foreign locations which complement the cool image of James Bond (Sean Connery). M (Bernard Lee) has his ace British spy out hunting Goldfinger, who is criminally tampering with the gold supplies of Britain and the United States. Bond finds his prey in a hotel on Miami Beach playing a crooked game of cards. Bond trails him to a country club outside London for some golf, where he cheats again, but is outwitted by Bond, and then to a gold refinery in the Swiss Alps. Goldfinger then captures Bond and flies him to Fort Knox, Kentucky, to tease him with eyewitness status at the robbery. As it turns out his plan is not to steal the gold, but, as Bond learns, to make it radioactive. By exploding an atom bomb inside Fort Knox, Goldfinger will contaminate the gold and ruin the economy of the Free World. He will also rid the world of Bond by helpfully chaining him near the bomb. A heroic Bond finally frees himself and stops the bomb from detonating—with exactly 0-0-7 seconds to go. The thrill of the movie is clearly not to be found in its intricate plot, which is not complex, but rather, in the compelling interest of seeing James Bond in action.

Goldfinger is an almost camp movie, played for Bond's dry wit and cool command of any situation involving women or danger. Bond's humor involves his ironic distance, maintained at all times, from his superhero image. The use of sex kittens and glamor-girl villains as interests for Bond does not involve any heavy sexual involvement, simply a teasing look of sex play. The women look like so many undressed models in lipstick ads; James Bond is only the slow encroachment of the dry martini pictured on the next page. Bond is made up of expensive tastes; cars, clothes, wine, or smokes all bear witness to his superiority. He belongs to the images of magazine advertisements. His seduction of women hinges upon their well-groomed status as expensive play-things; Bond is the perfect consumer-as-lover, the brand name of danger. A superhero is never in any danger of being tested and found lacking, and so Bond glides through adventures which put his expertise on display like goods in a well-mounted shop window. His cool in dangerous situations results from his close alliance with "billboard" reality, a display of the self-sufficient hero made up of the best of advertising mythology. As is any superhero, Bond is larger than life, and so requires some witty distance from his own actions.

James Bond's women have a habit of dying off fairly early in the film. Lacking a lot of women, his exciting feats of skill become connected to technology. *Goldfinger* provides Bond with a car that is an electronic marvel.

The driver's seat even has an ejection seat; the hubcaps can extend vicious spikes somewhat similar to those on the chariot in *Ben-Hur* (1959). With the villains in close pursuit, Bond's car spits a river of oil into their path at the touch of a button. The car also boasts a radar homing device. All of these car gimmicks pale, however, when compared to later Bond films, each faced with topping all the previous machinery in earlier films.

In the Bond series, *Goldfinger* is also distinguished by being the last to be shot "flat,"—that is, in standard format. Since future Bonds would exploit widescreen formats, *Goldfinger* is the last Bond film which can be shown on television without being extensively cropped to fit television screen size.

The success of *Goldfinger*, in terms of box-office receipts, was phenomenal. It reigned for a number of years well into the top twenty box-office champions of all time, and was only knocked off the list in the late 1970's and early 1980's when ticket prices skyrocketed, along with budgets, and films such as *Star Wars* (1977) and *Superman* (1978) took in more than one hundred million dollars worldwide. So successful was *Goldfinger* that the next Bond film, *Thunderball* (1965), which is not regarded as highly as the former by critics or the public, actually made even more money. One of the secrets of the success of the Bond films was, and continues to be into the 1980's, that the public expects to be entertained based on past exposure, and therefore will pay for tickets without bothering with reviews or even word-of-mouth as an incentive. Although the stories and actors have changed, the so-called "Bond formula," which was firmly established with *Goldfinger*, has been successful for almost twenty years. In terms of tickets sold and profits made, the Bond films have been the most successful series of all time.

Leslie Donaldson

THE GOOD EARTH

Released: 1937
Production: Irving Thalberg for Metro-Goldwyn-Mayer
Direction: Sidney Franklin
Screenplay: Talbot Jennings, Tess Slesinger, and Claudine West; based on the novel of the same name by Pearl S. Buck and the stage play by Owen Davis and Donald Davis
Cinematography: Karl Freund (AA)
Editing: Basil Wrangell
Running time: 130 minutes

Principal characters:

Wang Lung	Paul Muni
O-Lan	Luise Rainer (AA)
Uncle	Walter Connolly
Lotus	Tilly Losch
Old Father	Charley Grapewin
Cuckoo	Jessie Ralph
Aunt	Soo Yong
Elder Son	Keye Luke
Younger Son	Roland Lui

When Pearl S. Buck's novel *The Good Earth* was published in 1931, it won the Pulitzer Prize for Literature and stayed on the best-seller lists for nearly two years. The fifty-year chronicle of the House of Wang familiarized a whole generation of Americans with China, that mysterious and exotic country on the other side of the world. It is not, however, the kind of novel from which great American films are made, or so thought Louis B. Mayer, head of Metro-Goldwyn-Mayer. Irving G. Thalberg, however, Mayer's production chief, regarded it as a viable screen property. Mayer admonished him by exclaiming that if Americans would not buy tickets to films about American farmers why should they pay to see one about Chinese farmers. Thalberg's literary bent prevailed nevertheless, since Mayer had great respect for Thalberg's prestigious track record as a producer: Greta Garbo's *Anna Christie* (1930) and her *Camille* (1936); *Private Lives* (1931); *Strange Interlude* (1932); *Mutiny on the Bounty* (1935); *The Barretts of Wimpole Street* (1934); and *Romeo and Juliet* (1936).

As early as 1934, M-G-M sent talented director George Hill to China to shoot some two million feet of location footage and to bring back actual Chinese props, including two water buffalo and farm implements. Hill had earned a sizable reputation with such films as *Min and Bill* (1930), *The Big House* (1930), and *The Secret Six* (1931), and *The Good Earth* was expected to be his masterpiece. Tragically, he committed suicide in 1934, however, and the directorial assignment was passed on to Victor Fleming. Illness later prevented Fleming from working on the film, and the project was ultimately directed by Sidney Franklin, who had directed *Private Lives* and *The Barretts of Wimpole Street* for Thalberg. M-G-M painstakingly re-created the Chinese locale in the San Fernando Valley, using more than one thousand actors and spending a final budget of $2,816,000, an extraordinary amount of money for any production during those years.

The central theme of Buck's novel is that the earth is the fundamental giver of life, and this philosophy is made manifest through her depiction of the lives of a family of simple farm folk. The film opens almost elegiacally on the morning of the wedding day of Wang Lung (Paul Muni), as we see him prepare to go into town to take as his bride a slave girl named O-Lan (Luise Rainer). He finds O-Lan crouched near a stove in the kitchen of the Great House; she is a simple, awkward, quiet young peasant woman who stoically accepts her fate as the wife of this poor farmer. These opening scenes are utterly convincing and of the utmost importance in creating audience credibility. On the walk back to Wang's farm, O-Lan follows behind her husband-to-be the dutiful number of paces, and when he throws away the pit to a peach he has eaten, she retrieves it. Following the wedding feast, Wang discovers O-Lan planting the seed, for she knows that from the soil it will produce life.

Their life together as husband and wife is one of hard work, loyalty, and respect for each other. Their "good earth" is their strength and salvation, and they must produce sons to help them in the fields. When O-Lan becomes pregnant for the first time, she continues to work in the fields right up until the time she is to give birth. When she faints in the fields, Wang carries her back to their humble home. She refuses to allow him to go for a midwife, and says he must return to the harvest. Alone, with quiet dignity and strength, she gives birth to their first son.

As the family prospers, Wang buys more farm land, including rice fields, and O-Lan bears two more children—another son and, to Wang's great disappointment, a daughter. Their modest prosperity is destroyed by drought, and when starvation sets in, Wang's uncle (Walter Connolly) pleads with his nephew to sell the land. Wang replies, "Before I sell it, I'll feed it to my children." One of the most poignant scenes in the film occurs when O-Lan cooks soil to feed her family. The drought finally forces them to seek refuge in the city like thousands of neighboring farmers. There they are confronted by a political rebellion in which O-Lan is trampled unconscious by a mob fleeing the police. When she awakes she discovers a little purse of jewels. She keeps two pearls for herself and gives the others to Wang, who uses them to buy the Great House and the surrounding land.

Wang prospers as a wealthy landowner but changes from a simple farmer to a socially ambitious man. He becomes enamored of an exotic, lusty tea-house dancer, Lotus (Tilly Losch), whom he takes as his second wife. O-Lan accepts this fate stoically and mutely as she accepts all in life. It is here, as the focus of the film shifts from the land to the passionate entanglement of Wang and Lotus, that the film flounders. When Wang discovers Lotus with his son (Keye Luke), he beats the young man, but is interrupted by the cry that locusts are about to destroy his property.

Once again the "good earth" is of the foremost concern, and the film regains its impetus and believability. In the novel, the locust plague is described in three pages, but in the screenplay it is built into a scene of climactic importance and visually re-created with expert tension and reality. O-Lan joins her husband in the fields to help save their crops from devastation by the swarming insects. The crops are saved, but that evening O-Lan is too ill to attend the wedding feast of her younger son (Roland Lui). Wang comes to her and gives her the two pearls which she had saved. He holds her in his arms and implores her not to die, saying he will do anything, including selling the land, if it will make her well again. She responds, "No, I would not allow that. For I must die sometime, but the land is there after me." The film ends with Wang standing by the tree which grew from the peach seed O-Lan had planted many years before. Realizing that his prosperity has been the result of her steadfast courage, he says, "O-Lan, you are the earth."

Thalberg did not live to see *The Good Earth* completed; he died in 1936 at the age of thirty-seven. During his years as a producer he had never allowed his name to appear on the screen. At Mayer's insistence, *The Good Earth* carries this dedication:

> "To the memory of Irving Grant Thalberg,
> We dedicate this picture,
> His last great achievement."

The Good Earth received almost unanimously glowing reviews, with special commendations for the sepia-toned cinematography of Karl Freund, who received an Academy Award for his work. Freund was a master cinematographer who had worked on such German classics as *The Last Laugh* (1924), *Variety* (1925), and *Metropolis* (1926); much of the visual authenticity in these films was the result of Freund's cinematography.

Rainer's portrayal of O-Lan, which earned an Academy Award for Best Actress, remains one of the cinema's extraordinary performances. As in the novel, O-Lan is a combination of character and symbol, and Rainer's ability to bring her courage and pain and loyalty alive on the screen in a performance consisting almost entirely of pantomime (she had less than two dozen lines of dialogue) is eloquent. It brought Rainer her second Oscar in two years—the first time an actress had won twice in a row (her first Award was for *The Great Ziegfeld*, 1936). *The Good Earth* was not only the third of the nine films Rainer was to make in Hollywood, but was also the high point of one of Hollywood's oddest and shortest careers.

Although the other important acting roles in *The Good Earth* were played by non-Oriental performers, they are for the most part very believable. Muni looks appropriately Chinese, and in the beginning and the end of the film his acting is admirable. In the middle segment, however, which details his life as a prosperous landowner and his love affair with Lotus, his Americanisms detract from his performance. Losch, however, is entirely convincing as the seductress. Overall, *The Good Earth* is exemplary in its depiction of Chinese characters by American performers, unlike the almost laughable *Dragon Seed* (1944), also produced by M-G-M, which unsuccessfully presented Katharine Hepburn, Walter Huston, and other Americans as Chinese farmers. *The Good Earth* is memorable for Rainer's performance and for its attempt to be authentic. It is a fitting epitaph to the career of Irving Grant Thalberg.

After Thalberg's death, the Motion Picture Academy initiated the Irving G. Thalberg Memorial Award for "the most consistent high level of production achievement for an individual producer." This award, different from the more famous Oscar statuette, is given once a year, and only to the very best producers who have sustained their record of excellence over a long period of time.

Ronald Bowers

GOOD NEWS

Released: 1947
Production: Arthur Freed for Metro-Goldwyn-Mayer
Direction: Charles Walters
Screenplay: Betty Comden and Adolph Green; based on the musical comedy by Lawrence Schwab, Lew Brown, Frank Mandel, B. G. De Sylva, and Ray Henderson
Cinematography: Charles Schoenbaum
Editing: Albert Akst
Song: B. G. De Sylva, Lew Brown, Ray Henderson, Betty Comden, Adolph Green, Roger Edens, Hugh Martin, and Ralph Blane
Running time: 83 minutes

Principal characters:
Connie Lane	June Allyson
Tommy Marlowe	Peter Lawford
Pat McClellan	Patricia Marshall
Babe Doolittle	Joan McCracken
Bobby	Ray McDonald
Danny	Mel Torme
Peter Van Dyne III	Robert E. Strickland
Professor Burton Kennyon	Clinton Sundberg
Beef	Loren Tindall

The 1940's and 1950's are often thought of as the Golden Age of the Hollywood musical. It was, in fact, one studio and one production unit within that studio that produced nearly all the landmark films of that era, such as *Meet Me in St. Louis* (1944), *Singin' in the Rain* (1952), *The Band Wagon* (1953), and *Gigi* (1958). That studio was Metro-Goldwyn-Mayer, and the production unit responsible for these films was headed by Arthur Freed. Freed was a lyricist in the early days of the sound film and with Nacio Herb Brown wrote such songs as "Singin' in the Rain," which was used in a number of films before becoming the title song of the 1952 film. As a producer, Freed surrounded himself with such great and famous talents as Fred Astaire, Vincente Minnelli, Michael Kidd, and Gene Kelly to create the musical masterworks of two decades. Another important contribution of the Freed unit was a great number of minor musicals without big stars that aimed for and achieved modest but real virtues and remain entertaining and rewatchable today because of their excellent craftsmanship.

One of these unpretentious but rewarding films is *Good News* (1947), which features Peter Lawford and June Allyson. It was also the directorial debut of Charles Walters, who had previously been a choreographer and would go on to direct such famous films as *Easter Parade* (1948) and *High Society* (1956).

In addition it was the screenwriting debut of Betty Comden and Adolph Green, who later wrote such classics of the genre as *Singin' in the Rain* and *The Band Wagon*.

Except for Allyson, none of the principals was at first enthusiastic about the project. *Good News*, which was first a Broadway play in 1927, had already been filmed in 1930; Comden and Green thought the college football comedy too trivial for them to work on; and Walters was naturally nervous about directing his first film. Lawford did not want to play the lead because he thought his British accent would sound foolish for the role of the all-American football hero. Eventually all these problems and objections were overcome or forgotten, however, and none of them show in the finished film.

The plot does sound trivial, with the two main issues being who the football captain will take to the prom and whether he will be able to play in the big game. It is, however, the easygoing and light-hearted way in which the whole film is presented, the engaging quality of the main performers, and the success of the musical and specialty numbers that make the plot an agreeable confection rather than a ridiculous trifle. It is regarded by many as the definitive college musical.

The setting is a familiar one for a Hollywood musical film: a college in which the main activities are romance, football, and music. Tait College is in fact so much fun, we are informed in the opening song, that no one wants to graduate. After a title that tells us "This story takes you way, way back to another era—1927" and the opening song, we are quickly introduced to Pat McClellan (Patricia Marshall), an egotistical transfer student from a finishing school who continually drops French words into her conversation and is an immediate hit with the male students—"burning up the campus inch by inch," as one of them says. Then, in the football locker room, we meet some of the other main characters: Bobby (Ray McDonald), an inept athlete who is trying out for the team only because girls are attracted to football players; Beef (Loren Tindall), a huge but slow-witted player whose passion for Babe Doolittle (Joan McCracken) interferes with his ability to concentrate on football, and Tommy Marlowe (Peter Lawford), the captain of the team and favorite of all the women. When Bobby asks him if he has seen Pat, he merely responds that he lets the girls come to him. Bobby's request that Tommy explain his technique leads neatly into the next song-and-dance number. The secret, according to the song "Be a Ladies Man," is to walk, talk, and dress "collegiate." It is an energetic number in which Tommy and Bobby are joined by other students, including Danny—played by Mel Torme, the best singer in the film.

The scene then shifts to the sorority house where most of the young women are engaged in frivolous activities, except for Connie Lane (June Allyson), who is under the sink repairing the plumbing. (We will find later that she is also the assistant librarian of the school and an assistant to the French professor.) Pat is also there, but instead of working on the plumbing she is staring at herself in the mirror and saying, "You wonderful creature, why does everyone love you?" The main part of the plot is then set in motion when Pat lets it be known that she is interested in marrying a wealthy man, and the other girls tell her that Peter Van Dyne III (Robert Strickland) is worth twenty-five million dollars. Pat ends the conversation by saying "quel frommage," and Connie has to point out to her that she has just said "what cheese."

At the dance that evening Pat is the focus of attention of all the men and Tommy of all the women except Pat; she is interested only in Peter Van Dyne and his fortune. It is a new experience for Tommy to be rejected by a girl, and he cannot understand it. Pat's attentions to Peter lead into her singing to him "Lucky in Love," which is then continued by various other students at the dance, with some variations. Connie sings that she "never will be lucky in love," and Tommy sings, "Up to *now* I've been so lucky in love."

At the end of the song Pat rebuffs Tommy in French, which inspires him to make his first trip to the library the next day. There he meets Connie, who tells him what the French word means, and when he decides to take a French course to keep up with Pat, Connie tells him the best teacher in the department is Professor Kennyon (Clinton Sundberg), but he is "a tough bird and he hates football players." The discussion between Tommy and Connie leads into a half-spoken, half-sung specialty number, "The French Lesson," written by Comden, Green, and associate producer Roger Edens, in which Connie teaches some French words to Tommy. The ironic aspect of this scene is that Lawford spoke French fluently, while Allyson did not speak the language at all. Before the number, therefore, Lawford had to teach Allyson the words that she would teach him on screen.

Tommy learns a speech in French to say to Pat, but she still spurns him, causing the other students to fear that his being unlucky in love will interfere with his football playing and cost Tait the opening game. Babe therefore tells Pat that Tommy is worth *thirty* million dollars. Meanwhile, however, Tommy has asked Connie to the prom and she is floating on air. "Just think," she says, "I am going out with a football hero." After the game, however, Pat rushes up to Tommy and asks him to take her to the prom. He accepts immediately and does not remember his date with Connie until later; he calls and breaks their date at the last minute. Just before he calls, Connie has put on her prom dress and asked Babe how she looks. Babe gives her what is meant to be the ultimate compliment, "You sure don't look like a librarian."

More complications ensue as Tommy becomes so infatuated with Pat that he neglects his studies and fails his midterm examination in French, thus becoming ineligible for the big game the next Saturday. When he is offered a make-up exam, the other students convince Connie that she must coach him for the good of the school, even though she despises him for what he has done.

The coaching session rekindles their love, but it takes an intentionally failed exam, a change of heart, some manipulation by Professor Kennyon, and a complicated scheme devised by Connie to get Pat out of the way before they are back together in an imaginative love scene that begins with the two shouting at each other. Then Tommy tells Connie that he loves her and will do anything she asks. "Down on your heels," she replies. "Up on your toes." "What's that?" he asks, and the whole student body in the background responds "That's the way you do the Varsity Drag," leading cleverly into the big song-and-dance finale, "The Varsity Drag."

The key to the success of *Good News* is that it is unassuming; it never tries too hard and never pretends to be more than it is. The principal players are not top-flight stars, but they have engaging screen personalities and adequate musical talent. McCracken, in a supporting role, gives an especially good dancing performance in "Pass That Peace Pipe," a musical number performed in the college soda shop.

Clifford Henry

THE GOODBYE GIRL

Released: 1977
Production: Ray Stark for Warner Bros.
Direction: Herbert Ross
Screenplay: Neil Simon
Cinematography: David M. Walsh
Editing: John F. Burnett
Music: Dave Grusin
Running time: 110 minutes

Principal characters:
Elliott Garfield .... Richard Dreyfuss (AA)
Paula McFadden .... Marsha Mason
Lucy McFadden .... Quinn Cummings
Mark .... Paul Benedict
Donna .... Barbara Rhoades
Oliver Fry .... Nicol Williamson

The basic plot of *The Goodbye Girl* is borrowed more or less from a delightful comedy, *The More the Merrier* (1943), which starred Jean Arthur, Joel McCrea, and Charles Coburn and which was remade as *Walk, Don't Run* (1966), starring Cary Grant. Neil Simon "urbanized" the story and changed the characters to the extent of placing them in show business (one is a dancer, one an actor), locating them on New York's Upper West Side, and removing the older man character and replacing him with a child.

By a stratagem that only works in movies and seldom happens in real life, Elliott Garfield (Richard Dreyfuss) arrives from Chicago at the apartment of Paula McFadden (Marsha Mason) the night after her boyfriend has taken off, leaving her with a daughter, Lucy (Quinn Cummings), to support and no money. Lease and key in hand, he asks them to leave, but she has no place to go. After much yelling and bickering they compromise; Paula and Lucy will share Paula's bedroom, Elliott will have Lucy's. While Paula resumes dancing lessons and takes a job pitching in an auto show, Elliott starts rehearsing *Richard III* for the off-Broadway stage. The director, Mark (Paul Benedict), wants him to perform Richard as an outrageous homosexual, an interpretation which causes the show's immediate demise. Elliott then takes a series of jobs, during which time he and Paula stop antagonizing each other and fall in love. Another off-Broadway engagement leads to a movie role, and as Elliott leaves for Hollywood, he proposes to Paula, declaring that he will be back as soon as the film is finished.

Although much of *The Goodbye Girl* is funny and does work, the rapidity of the repartee is wearing. Nobody can deliver comebacks as quickly as these two, and the ping-pong dialogue seems to work against the script's conventions. To compound this problem, Simon has saddled his heroine (and real-life wife) with an equally adroit daughter, the kind of poisonous brat Virginia Weidler played in 1940's comedies such as *The Philadelphia Story* (1940). The audience never gets a rest from the nonstop clashing of egos and the gratuitously hostile repartee which is the couple's defense against feeling.

Fortunately, Dreyfuss and Mason are expert performers, and if the audience frequently wants them to relax and shut up, it is not their fault. Simon substitutes rapid-fire patter for character development, so Elliott and Paula keep bashing away at each other. Both are propelled mostly by bad temper, which makes them something less than attractive to be around for 110 minutes. Their flagrant abrasiveness is initially funny, but often becomes irritating. It is hard to see what they see in each other at first. In fact, they are both such self-involved characters that believing that they could ever pay sufficient attention to anyone else to become emotionally involved is a difficult undertaking.

Simon has sand-bagged Paula with a number of annoying traits. Called upon to deliver a sales pitch at the auto show, she cannot remember her lines for two minutes. Simon also credits her with the worst taste in decorating history. When Elliott and Paula settle down to domestic bliss, she redecorates the apartment, with the result that it looks like a Middle Eastern seraglio; Paula orders Elliott to move heavy furniture around repeatedly while she makes up her mind about its placement.

Simon has the soul of a matchmaker. He wants everybody fixed up and happy by the final reel: Jane Fonda and Robert Redford, Charles Boyer and Mildred Natwick in *Barefoot in the Park* (1967); Walter Matthau and Jack Lemmon in *The Odd Couple* (1968); George Burns and Matthau in *The Sunshine Boys* (1975); and now Dreyfuss and Mason. There have to be reasons for people to get together, however, and in *The Goodbye Girl*, he does not provide enough of them. In place of character Simon gives us jokes, for sentiment he gives us petulant tears, and for warmth we get more jokes— and sex. Simon is nasty about the very things he wants us to believe are lovable; underneath all the screaming are two vulnerable people who just need a little push from fate to become the most adorable couple since Janet Gaynor and Charles Farrell in *Seventh Heaven* (1927).

Director Ross has gotten spirited performances from his stars. Mason, who won a Golden Globe Award as Best Actress for her performance, may be a bit too cuddly-cute for comfort—she was much better, for example, in her brief role in *Blume in Love* (1973) as the woman who was impulsively, sloppily involved with George Segal immediately after his divorce—but she is still enjoyable to watch. Dreyfuss' interpretation of Elliott, however, which won him an Academy Award, is both complex and involving. When he first appears, he is raucous and pushy. We think that we are going to hate him, but then he changes on screen. Forced to mature in order to win Paula, his character gives up the childishness which has been Dreyfuss' forte throughout his acting career in such films as *American Graffiti* (1973), *The Apprenticeship of Duddy Kravitz* (1974), and *Close Encounters of a Third Kind* (1977). Paula is immature enough for both of them, so Elliott *has* to grow up, and he does it with charm and grace. Dreyfuss also provides *The Goodbye Girl* with its one scene of genuine humanity. Publicly embarrassed in his New York debut when *Richard III* flops resoundingly, Elliott gets royally drunk. For once his self-absorption is not exasperating: it is developed out of his character so that the audience can feel his humiliation and sympathize. Dreyfuss' habitual intensity is an organic part of Elliott, and he uses it to round out the man, not as an element applied from outside to add interest to the individual whom he is playing.

Judith M. Kass

GREASE

Released: 1978
Production: Robert Stigwood and Allan Carr for Paramount
Direction: Randal Kleiser
Screenplay: Bronte Woodward; based on Allan Carr's adaptation of the Broadway musical of the same name by Jim Jacobs and Warren Casey
Cinematography: Bill Butler
Editing: John F. Burnett
Running time: 110 minutes

Principal characters:
Danny Zuko .... John Travolta
Sandy .... Olivia Newton-John
Rizzo .... Stockard Channing
Kenickie .... Jeff Conaway
Principal .... Eve Arden
Coach Calhoun .... Sid Caesar
Frenchy .... Didi Conn
Vince Fontaine .... Edd Byrnes
Teen Angel .... Frankie Avalon
Vi .... Joan Blondell
Mrs. Murdock .... Alice Ghostley
Johnny Casino and the Gamblers .... Sha Na Na

Among the popular arts of the 1970's (cinema, television, and pop music), few subjects provided a greater source of inspiration than the rediscovery of the 1950's—1950's fads, foibles, and most of all, 1950's music, rock-and-roll. This rediscovery began to be manifested nationally in 1973, with George Lucas' marvelous *American Graffiti* (set in 1962, but filled with the music and teenage life-style of the previous decade). *American Graffiti* led to television's popular series *Happy Days*, and the rush to nostalgia was on. Before all of these, however, came *Grease*, a musical comedy that was a long-running Broadway hit, making its stage debut in 1972. When the film version was released in 1978, the genre of 1950's-worship reached its apex.

Actually, the play, by Jim Jacobs and Warren Casey, was a natural for the movies, and producers Robert Stigwood (a record company mogul who specialized in coordinating hit films with their wildly successful sound track albums) and flamboyant Allan Carr (who adapted the play for film) were just the men to preside over the transition. They took two hot properties from the 1970's—John Travolta (hard on the heels of his triumph in 1977's *Saturday Night Fever*) and Olivia Newton-John (an Australian-born pop singer in her film debut)—and mixed them with a host of 1950's television and rock stars. The result was a box-office smash: an affectionate, slightly cynical, and highly selective remembrance of things past.

Grease is set in a 1950's never-neverland where all the kids speak with Flatbush accents yet live in California. Most of the action centers around Rydell High (named after Bobby Rydell, a teenage idol of the late 1950's and early 1960's), and the film is a grab bag of 1950's clichés, all seen from the slightly skewed perspective of a later decade. The plot goes something like this: Danny Zuko (John Travolta) meets a girl named Sandy (Olivia Newton-John) on the beach during summer vacation. To Danny's surprise (he is used to thinking of girls as nothing more than sex objects), he develops a genuine affection for Sandy. Their romance is doomed, however; summer is over, and they must go their separate ways, since Sandy is Australian and must return home.

The scene then shifts to Rydell High, where the first day of class is beginning. Danny is reunited with his "gang," the T Birds. The T Birds consist of Danny's pal Kenickie (Jeff Conaway), along with Doody (Barry Pearl), Sonny (Michael Tucci), and Putzie (Kelly Ward), who act like the Three Stooges in motorcycle jackets. The T Birds' big ambition for their senior year is to get a car. The T Birds' female auxiliary is the Pink Ladies, led by the tough-talking Rizzo (Stockard Channing). Rizzo's second bananas are the gorgeous Marty (Dinah Manoff) and Frenchy (Didi Conn), the sweet but dumb girl who drops out of high school to become a beautician. Unbeknownst to Danny, however, the Pink Ladies are about to add a new recruit to their ranks— Sandy, his summer love, who enrolls at Rydell when her parents move from Australia.

In the film's first production number, "Summer Nights," director Randal Kleiser cuts back and forth between the T Birds and the Pink Ladies, as Danny and Sandy tell conflicting versions of their summer romance to their respective cliques. Danny's account is leering and suggestive, as he exaggerates his sexual prowess; Sandy's more demure account is a humorous counterpoint. Travolta and Newton-John are in good voice, and the cast dances (actually, struts and sways) nicely; the whole effect starts the film on a very positive level. Romantic complications arise, however, when Danny and Sandy meet. Unable to transcend the macho image he has built up among the T Birds, Danny treats Sandy very brusquely, and she is rightfully offended. He quickly realizes his mistake, but Sandy is not quick to forgive. Danny spends the rest of the film trying to win her back.

Meanwhile, a number of subplots develop. Sandy has a falling-out with Rizzo, who finds her innocence both naïve and offensive. In "Look at Me, I'm Sandra Dee," Rizzo parodies Sandy's attitudes by equating them with those of the famous virgin queens of 1950's filmdom, such as Sandra Dee and Doris Day, who virtuously fight off their lustful male pursuers in the movies. Later in the film, Rizzo defends her more wanton ways with the song "There Are Worse Things I Could Do," in which she argues that her frank acknowledgement of her sexual appetite is preferable to the hypocrisy that typified that era's approach to such matters. Things end happily for Rizzo, however; after a pregnancy scare, she ends up engaged to the T Birds' Kenickie.

Kenickie acquires a beat-up old jalopy, and the T Birds set out to convert it into a fearsome street machine. With the help of some "borrowed" parts and their auto mechanics teacher at Rydell, Mrs. Murdoch (Alice Ghostley), they do so. Toward the end of the film, Danny wins a hotly contested drag race against a car driven by one of the hated Scorpions, a rival gang.

In an effort to win Sandy back, Danny places himself in the hand of Coach Calhoun (Sid Caesar) of the "Phys Ed" Department. As an athlete, Danny is neither particularly strong nor coordinated; he is, however, aggressive to the point of belligerence. The sequence in which Coach Calhoun attempts to find a sport suited to Danny's particular "talents" is hilarious. When Danny does eventually end up on the track team, his efforts at self-improvement win Sandy back, at least temporarily. She agrees to accompany him to the big dance.

The National Bandstand sequence is the film's longest dance number and its most effective. The whole thing comes about when Vince Fontaine (played by Edd Byrnes, Kookie of television's popular 1950's series *77 Sunset Strip*) decides to bring his national dance contest to Rydell High. Naturally, all of the hot dancers are there, and just as naturally, Danny wins. Unfortunately, his winning partner is not Sandy. As Johnny Casino and the Gamblers (played by the rock group Sha Na Na, 1950's revivalists who function as the spiritual godfathers of the whole film) crank out "Born to Hand Jive," one of Danny's old girl friends, Cha Cha DiGregorio (Annette Charles), cuts in. Sandy leaves the dance floor in a huff as Danny, confused but ultimately too caught up in the beat to care, continues to dance. Couples jockey for favorable camera angles, and when the contest is over, Danny and Cha Cha have won.

Sandy decides that she loves Danny anyway, and finally hits upon a scheme to win him permanently. She enlists the aid of her friend Frenchy, who is back at Rydell High after discovering that beauty school was not all it seemed to be (she took the advice of another 1950's idol, Frankie Avalon, who, as Teen Angel, appeared to her in a vision and urged her to become a "Beauty School Dropout"). Frenchy turns Sandy into the sartorial equivalent of a T Bird. She acquires teased hair, a tight sweater, and black stretch pants and sports a cigarette dangling carelessly from her lips. When she confronts Danny in this guise, he is stunned. He falls to his knees in awe, and begins to belt out "You're the One That I Want" in a duet with Sandy. Thus everything ends happily. The kids get together for a few "bop-sh'bops," and Danny and Sandy drive off into the sunset—literally. Their car has not only been transformed into the wildest looking dragster ever; it has also somehow been given the power of flight.

Obviously plotting is not *Grease*'s strong point; nor is the screenplay by Bronte Woodward anything special. At times, the film seems intent on simply throwing as many 1950's images (everything from hula hoops to an animated toothpaste commercial featuring Bucky the Beaver) as possible into the mix and letting the chips fall where they may. That the film works, despite its occasional excesses, can be credited to the fine cast headed by Travolta and Newton-John as well as to the producers who put the cast together.

Randal Kleiser, whose only previous screen credit was as one of the writers on an atrociously received Italian gangster opus filmed in the United States called *Street People* (1976), keeps the pace of the film fast and furious. Production numbers are well staged and successfully integrated into the flow of the narrative, and Kleiser elicits terrific performances from his entire cast, which consists of a blend of newcomers and well-established character actors.

Travolta's acting prowess was not challenged by the role of Danny Zuko—like the other characters in the film, Danny seems to exist on a level somewhere between a comic strip and a situation comedy—but Travolta gives a terrific performance nevertheless. He is full of exhuberance and wit; his singing voice is pleasant, if unremarkable; and as a dancer, he possesses a feline grace that is beautiful to watch. Newton-John is perfectly cast as the bland/ sweet Sandy; her fresh-faced innocence is ideal for the part. Whether her range is limited to such roles may be a legitimate question, but in *Grease*, her abilities match the role precisely.

There are nearly a dozen important supporting roles in *Grease*, and all of the actors in them do their share to make the film a success. Among the veterans, Arden (who for years played a high-school teacher in television's *Our Miss Brooks*) plays Rydell's cynical principal to the hilt; Caesar is appropriately beleaguered and bemused as the overmatched Coach Calhoun; Blondell is good in a brief role as Vi, a harassed waitress at the T Birds' favorite eatery; Byrnes is fine as the Dick Clark look-alike, Vince Fontaine; and Avalon, as Teen Angel, delivers a knockout "Beauty School Dropout" number.

The younger members of the supporting cast more than match their older colleagues. Channing is hilarious as Rizzo, the bad girl who discovers that she needs love after all; Conn gives an affecting performance as the hapless Frenchy, whose career as a beautician ends after she inadvertly dyes her own hair pink; Charles looks appropriately exotic as Cha Cha, the hot number from St. Bernadette High; and Conaway does well as Kenickie, the hot rodder who yearns for Rizzo.

Despite (or perhaps because of) *Grease*'s huge popularity with the public, the film drew a fair share of disparagement from the critics. Those who disliked *Grease* seemed to base most of their objections on the fact that the film presented a distorted view of the 1950's. As far as it goes, this criticism is entirely valid (producers Stigwood and Carr even hedged their bets on the drawing power of 1950's music, commissioning Barry Gibb of the Bee Gees to write the disco-ish title song); as noted above, the film was written from the perspective of a decade that was (or at least felt itself to be) considerably hipper than the 1950's ever pretended to be. *Grease* laughs at, as well as with, the 1950's. No one would deny that the 1950's were much more complex than *Grease* would indicate.

The counterargument, of course, is that *Grease* does not pretend to be anything but the broadest parody; it is a musical comedy, not a documentary, and it is as a musical comedy that it must be judged. The energetic performances of Travolta, Newton-John, Channing, and the rest of the cast convinced an enormous audience (the film quickly became one of the top money earners of all time) that, as a musical comedy, *Grease* was very good indeed.

Robert Mitchell

THE GREAT FLAMARION

Released: 1945
Production: William Wilder for Republic
Direction: Anthony Mann
Screenplay: Anne Wigton, Heinz Herald, and Richard Weil; based on an original story by Anne Wigton and a character created by Vicki Baum
Cinematography: James Spencer Brown, Jr.
Editing: John F. Fink
Running time: 78 minutes

Principal characters:
Flamarion	Erich Von Stroheim
Connie Wallace	Mary Beth Hughes
Al Wallace	Dan Duryea
Eddie	Stephen Barclay
Tony	Lester Allen
Cleo	Esther Howard
Nightwatchman	Michael Mark
Detective	Joseph Granby
Coroner	John R. Hamilton

Like many a great man of the cinema, Erich Von Stroheim ended his filmmaking days appearing in relatively unimportant productions. From the dizzy heights of directing *Foolish Wives* (1921), *Greed* (1924), *The Merry Widow* (1925), and *The Wedding March* (1928), Von Stroheim fell in the 1930's, 1940's, and 1950's to starring in more than forty films, which ranged from the first-rate, such as *Five Graves to Cairo* (1943), to the mediocre, such as *The Mask of Dijon* (1946).

Somewhere in between came the four films—*The Lady and the Monster* (1944), *Storm over Lisbon* (1944), *The Great Flamarion* (1945), and *Scotland Yard Investigator* (1945)—that Erich Von Stroheim made for Republic, a "B"-picture producer but nevertheless a major force in film production in its day. Of these four Republic features, the most important and the most interesting is *The Great Flamarion*, not only because of the presence of Von Stroheim, but also because it is directed by Anthony Mann, just beginning his directorial career, but showing definite signs of the talent that was to become evident in his productions of the 1950's and 1960's. Mann's choice of shots is sophisticated. His camera angles are carefully thought out, lending credence and sophistication to the cheap Republic sets. Mann even manages to get passable performances from all of his actors, a quite remarkable feat in view of the level of the dialogue with which the performers are expected to work. Of peripheral interest is the producer, William Wilder, the brother of Billy Wilder, who had directed Erich Von Stroheim in *Five Graves to Cairo*.

The Great Flamarion opens in Mexico City in 1936. The camera follows a group of theatergoers into the auditorium of a vaudeville house. While a somewhat second-rate clown is performing, two shots ring out. In the confusion, there are cuts from the audience to the perplexed clown on stage, to the disturbed performers backstage, and to the dressing room where trick cyclist Eddie (Stephen Barclay) has found his wife, Connie, dead. As if rising from the confusion, we see the Great Flamarion (Erich Von Stroheim) climbing a ladder to hide above the stage. From Von Stroheim's overhead perch, we glimpse the police enquiry and the arrest of the protesting Eddie for the murder of his wife. It is a well-conceived opening sequence, demonstrating the ability of the director to handle standard melodrama, and it is, without question, the best sequence in the film.

After the excitement dies down, the clown is alone on the stage when he hears something fall to the floor. We, the audience, see merely a ripple in the curtain and an overhead lamp begin to swing. Behind the curtain, the clown discovers the dying Great Flamarion, whom he recognizes from the time that they had played together on the same bill in Pittsburgh.

The Great Flamarion is a typical Von Stroheim character, a cold and arrogant vaudeville performer uninterested in anyone but himself. Assisting the Great Flamarion in his vaudeville act are Connie and Al Wallace (Mary Beth Hughes and Dan Duryea), a husband-and-wife team who appear in the vaudeville sketch as the Great Flamarion's wife and her would-be lover. In the sketch, the Great Flamarion finds them together and proceeds to demonstrate his prowess with a gun, shooting out light bulbs from around a mirror as Al dodges in front of them, shooting a cigarette from Connie's mouth and a decoration from her garter. The gun as a phallic symbol here is, of course, rather obvious, as is the irony of the situation that soon the Great Flamarion and Al will change roles in a real-life drama.

Al Wallace drinks, so Connie decides to leave him and to offer her affections to the Great Flamarion. She is a cold, calculating woman whose motives are patently obvious to everyone but her victims. She persuades the Great Flamarion to shoot Al accidentally on stage when he is drunk, promising that after a reasonable length of time she will meet him again and they will be married. All goes according to plan. Al is killed in San Francisco, and the coroner brings in a verdict of accidental death. Connie and the Great Flamarion agree to meet in three months' time in a Chicago hotel. In vain the Great Flamarion awaits the arrival of Connie in a hotel suite that bears more than a striking resemblance to a set from Charles Chaplin's *The Great Dictator* (1940). Gradually he realizes that it was all a plot; like others before him he had fallen a victim to Connie's wiles. From a fellow vaudevillian, Cleo (Esther Howard), he learns that while Connie was seducing him she was also having an affair with a trick cyclist, Eddie. The Great Flamarion has only one object in mind: vengeance. He tracks down Connie and Eddie to Mexico City. In her dressing room, he fires at Connie and she shoots him before he finally strangles her. The film closes with the Great Flamarion, a fallen man thanks to a fallen woman, dying in the arms of the clown.

The chief fault of *The Great Flamarion* is the script. It is loaded with clichés; for example, after Connie's murder one of the stagehands pontificates to an actor, "I guess you never know when your exit's coming," and there are also the obligatory references to all the world's being a stage. It is not difficult to tear the script apart—the plot is full of inconsistencies. After the clown discovers the Great Flamarion dying at the back of the stage, the Great Flamarion tells him not to call the police because he will be dead before they arrive. Yet eighty minutes later, he is still alive, and the police *do* arrive despite nobody's having calling them. It is totally inconceivable that any vaudeville act would use live bullets on stage; the danger to the audience and the stagehands would be much too great with all those bullets ricocheting off the scenery. At the start of the film, the show breaks up because the performers and the audience hear *two* gunshots, yet in the retelling of his story, the Great Flamarion fires *four* bullets during his final encounter with Connie. Why did the performers not hear the first two shots?

The other chief problem with *The Great Flamarion* is the acting. Von Stroheim is fine, dominating every moment, even giving himself a scene in which he has his head shaved. There is also a touchingly romantic sequence when, anticipating the arrival of Connie at the hotel, he lightly dances around the suite. Hughes, trying to portray an innocent victim to Von Stroheim while at the same time letting the audience know she is a wicked woman, overacts badly. Duryea is fine as her poor husband; weak-willed and naïve, he immediately gains the audience's sympathy.

Contemporary reviews of *The Great Flamarion* were mixed. Otis L. Guernsey, Jr., in *The New York Herald Tribune* (January 15, 1945), wrote, "In *The Great Flamarion* gun play is right in the act; and with all those bullets and jealousy flying around, you know someone is going to get hurt. What thriller fan can ask for anything more?" *Variety* (April 13, 1945) described the film as "a well-told and suspenseful melodrama." *The New York Times* (January 15, 1945) was particularly scathing: "This melodramatic treatise on death and double dealing among vaudevillians is as labored an excursion as that of a tramp through a quagmire. . . . Great is scarcely descriptive of either Flamarion or this creaking vehicle."

The Great Flamarion was not Von Stroheim's last great American film. In 1950, he costarred in *Sunset Boulevard*. Of the two, *Sunset Boulevard* is the better production, but it is questionable that Von Stroheim's performance in the latter was any better than that in *The Great Flamarion*.

Anthony Slide

THE GREAT GABBO

Released: 1929
Production: James Cruze for Sono Art-World Wide Pictures
Direction: James Cruze
Screenplay: F. Hugh Herbert; based on an original story by Ben Hecht
Cinematography: Ira H. Morgan
Editing: no listing
Running time: 91 minutes

> *Principal characters:*
> Gabbo .... Erich Von Stroheim
> Mary .... Betty Compson
> Frank .... Donald Douglas
> Babe .... Marjorie "Babe" Kane

In recent years, *The Great Gabbo* has become something of a cult favorite with young film enthusiasts, thanks largely to the bravura playing of Erich Von Stroheim and the "camp" nature of the musical numbers. The film should not be regarded merely as a cult curiosity, however, for it contains, after all, Von Stroheim's first appearance in a sound film and was directed by James Cruze, a major force in silent films with such classics as *The Covered Wagon* (1923), *Beggar on Horseback* (1925), *The Pony Express* (1925), and *Old Ironsides* (1926) to his credit.

Cruze's direction is surprisingly good. It only seems second-rate because of the ludicrous nature of the plot and the melodramatics of the dialogue, for which, presumably, blame should be assigned to Ben Hecht, who certainly should have known better. Cruze is particularly brave in the handling of a sound montage sequence—something very unusual for this period—while the Great Gabbo's insanity comes to the surface. The montage does not really work but that is chiefly due to the primitive nature of early sound, and Cruze deserves top marks for attempting such a difficult sequence and for almost pulling it off.

Von Stroheim heads the cast, in the title role of a ventriloquist whose egotism leads to his eventual downfall and madness. The Great Gabbo is a part perfectly suited to the actor/director who, in the silent era, had gained the title of "The Man You Love to Hate," and who was to continue portraying this type of role for the rest of his career. In fact, *The Great Gabbo* is well worth comparing with the later Republic production of *The Great Flamarion* (1945), in which Von Stroheim gives a similar performance. Incidentally, the Great Gabbo's ventriloquist act was based on that of Marshall Montgomery, "America's premiere ventriloquist," who really did eat, drink, and smoke while his dummy, Otto, did the talking. In the film, Von Stroheim did the same trick, but he relied on an unidentified actor to provide the "voice" of

Otto, and at least one critic complained that Von Stroheim's throat displayed not the least sign of movement during the dummy's recitations.

Supporting Von Stroheim in the role of Mary is Betty Compson, in reality Cruze's wife and a busy actress in the early years of sound, continuing a screen career that had started in the late teens. (The role of Mary was originally to have been played by silent star Pauline Starke, but when Compson suddenly became available, Starke was dropped and her film career came to an abrupt end.) Compson is adequate for the part she plays, but the same cannot be said of Donald Douglas as the romantic lead, Frank, who is effetely bland and totally lacking in dramatic ability. Rounding out the cast is Marjorie "Babe" Kane, sister of the popular early talkie star Helen Kane, who sings a few songs in the manner of her sister and delivers a few lines of dialogue with bravado.

The Great Gabbo opens in a small neighborhood theater, where the egocentric ventriloquist is performing, assisted by his partner Mary who serves as little more than "window dressing" for the act, but who constantly tries to please her employer. When Mary accidentally drops a tray on stage during Gabbo's act, she is fired by him.

In time, the Great Gabbo has become one of the stars of the Manhattan Revue, which also features Mary and her new singing and dancing partner, Frank. For effect, the Great Gabbo and his dummy, Otto, eat dinner every evening together in a smart restaurant. To emphasize Gabbo's lofty position, a footman is required to carry Otto from the pair's chauffeur-driven car to their table. When Mary sees the two of them at the restaurant, she comes over and talks to Gabbo through the dummy. The vertriloquist falls in love with her, and his affection for Mary, together with his ego problems, begin to affect his act. When Gabbo overhears Frank and Mary talking outside their dressing rooms and learns that the two are secretly married, he becomes completely insane, and wanders onstage during their final dance number, destroying the performance. He is fired by the management, and the film ends with Gabbo slowly walking away from the theater as workmen remove his billing, "The Great Gabbo," from the marquee. (It should perhaps be noted that throughout the film, the rise and fall of the Great Gabbo is watched by a minor vaudeville husband-and-wife team who had played on the same bill with Gabbo and Mary when they were unknown.)

Although the dramatic sequences are shot in black-and-white, the musical numbers are filmed in color (although no color prints of *The Great Gabbo* appear to have survived). The film features seven such numbers, "The New Step," "I'm in Love with You," "I'm Laughing," "Ickey" (the last two of which were performed by Otto), "Every Now and Then," "The Web of Love," and "The Ga-Ga Bird." The last is seen briefly as part of the montage sequence, but otherwise does not appear in the film as it exists today, and may possibly have been cut prior to the feature's original release. The most ludicrous of the musical numbers is "The Web of Love," which features Mary and Frank (she as a fly and he as a spider) prancing and dancing around on stage while grotesquely garbed chorus girls perform curious gyrations on a large spider's web in the background. The number itself is bad enough, but it is made even more unintentionally funny by having the two principals carry on a stilted conversation as they pause in grotesque positions. The humor is further helped by its being blatantly obvious that doubles are performing for the principals in the long and medium shots of the number, while offstage another performer is singing while Compson mouths the song. Compson's somewhat nasal and common speaking voice was noted for its rich soprano when she sang in early musicals, thanks to the anonymous singers standing just out of camera range and taking care of that chore for the star, in the days before dubbing was invented.

The Great Gabbo received mixed reviews on its initial release. *Variety* (September 18, 1929) wrote, "All the superlatives in a heavy vocabulary can be expanded and yet *The Great Gabbo* will just remain the picture prodigy of the independent ranks and a talker drama, from the standpoints of theme originality and absorbing qualities, above the average show window display of the big companies." Mordaunt Hall in *The New York Times* (September 13, 1929) found the film "highly original," and thought Von Stroheim "punctilious in the earnestness with which he attacks his role." *Photoplay* (December, 1929), however, considered *The Great Gabbo* "a bitter disappointment. . . . Cruze seems to have lost his sense of humor, and the lighting and scenario are terrible."

Today, *The Great Gabbo* stands as both a curiosity and an interesting historical document, a perfect example of a failed early talkie, made with the best intentions and the best of talent.

Anthony Slide

THE GREAT GATSBY

Released: 1949
Production: Richard Maibaum for Paramount
Direction: Elliott Nugent
Screenplay: Cyril Hume and Richard Maibaum; based on the novel of the same name by F. Scott Fitzgerald and the play of the same name by Owen Davis
Cinematography: John F. Seitz
Editing: Ellsworth Hoagland
Running time: 91 minutes

Principal characters:
Jay Gatsby	Alan Ladd
Daisy Buchanan	Betty Field
Nick Carraway	Macdonald Carey
Jordan Baker	Ruth Hussey
Tom Buchanan	Barry Sullivan
Wilson	Howard da Silva
Myrtle Wilson	Shelley Winters
Dan Cody	Henry Hull

The 1949 film of F. Scott Fitzgerald's classic novel *The Great Gatsby* succeeds in being a good film even though it is not entirely successful in conveying many of the essential qualities of Fitzgerald's work. This is not surprising. Cinema and literature are such different forms that it is rare indeed for a masterpiece in cinema to be the result of an adaptation of a masterpiece in literature. The great films are usually made from original screenplays, as was *Citizen Kane* (1941), or from second-rate novels, as was *Gone with the Wind* (1939). Indeed, each of these films is better than any one of the films made from the works of such great writers as Ernest Hemingway, Thomas Hardy, and Gustave Flaubert.

In adapting a masterwork of literature for the more popular medium of cinema, the screenwriter must usually shorten and simplify the original work, since a film containing all the incidents of the average novel would be five to ten hours long. In the process of shortening and simplifying, nuances are lost, and in the process of making a written work into a primarily visual one, distinction and style in language will not survive. Because nuances and verbal style are less important in second-rate books, such books usually withstand the process of adaptation better than do first-rate books.

The film of *The Great Gatsby* is no exception to these precepts. The novel loses a good deal in its translation to film, but enough of the basic elements survive and the quality of the filmmaking is high enough that the film is worthwhile and rewarding if one does not expect it to be as good as the novel.

The film opens in 1948 with Nick Carraway (Macdonald Carey) and his wife Jordan (Ruth Hussey) visiting the grave of Jay Gatsby. Jordan's reminiscences immediately take us back twenty years to the time when young America was "joy-riding on home-made hootch." After a montage of scenes of the lindy hop, bootlegging, and gangsters, we are told by the narrator that Jay Gatsby came out of the 1920's and "built a dark empire for himself because he carried a dream in his heart."

We soon find that Gatsby (Alan Ladd) has bought an old mansion on Long Island that is directly across the channel from the home of the wealthy and prominent Buchanans. He has paid two hundred thousand dollars for the house and plans to spend many thousands more to renovate it, using the same decorator who did the Buchanans' house. After Gatsby gazes across the channel at the Buchanans' residence, there is an abrupt transition to a lively party in progress at Gatsby's now lavishly-redecorated house.

At this party is Nick Carraway, who soon finds that he may be the only person specifically invited. One of the many revelers explains to him that no one is invited to Gatsby's, they just come. It is not long before Nick learns why he has been singled out. First, however, he meets Gatsby and listens to his life story. Actually, Gatsby first tries to tell a false story, but Nick lets him know that he does not believe it, so Gatsby—in a long flashback—explains how he rose from humble origins to ostentatious wealth.

Gatsby began life as plain Jimmy Gatz, but he came to the attention of Dan Cody (Henry Hull), a millionaire who hired the young Gatz to work on his yacht as it went three times around the world. Cody both lived and preached the motto that a person can take anything he wants if he has money. Gatz learned the lesson well. After Cody's death and his own army service, Gatz—who began calling himself Gatsby—amassed a fortune through bootlegging.

Nick then finds out why Gatsby is interested in him. Nick is a second cousin of Daisy Buchanan (Betty Field), and Gatsby wants Nick to arrange a meeting between Daisy and Gatsby by inviting them both to tea some time. Gatsby even offers to assist Nick's business as a bond salesman. He finally becomes quite blunt: "Every man has his price, Mr. Carraway. What's yours?" Nick, however, refuses to agree to arrange the meeting.

We gradually find out, chiefly through two flashbacks, the story of Daisy and Gatsby. They met and fell in love during World War I in Louisville, Kentucky, when Gatsby was a young lieutenant. Daisy wanted to marry Gatsby then, but he insisted on waiting until he had enough money. By the time the war was over, however, Daisy had married the rich, polo-playing Tom Buchanan (Barry Sullivan). Remembering Dan Cody's view that money can buy anything, Gatsby decided to become rich and successful enough to win Daisy back.

Daisy, we find, is not happy. Although she loved Tom when they were married, she now—rightly—suspects him of infidelity. Her two closest friends are Jordan Baker and Nick. We have learned from the opening scene that Jordan will become Nick's wife, but that is still in the future and is not suspected by either one of them. They are, in fact, quite different in outlook and temperament. Nick is principled, but Jordan has tried to cheat in a golf tournament, and when she learns that Gatsby wants to meet Daisy she agrees to arrange it if Gatsby gives her a new Dusenberg roadster.

Gatsby, of course, accepts Jordan's offer, and soon a date for tea at Nick's is set up. They do not tell Nick anything about the plan, and they do not tell Daisy that Gatsby will be there. Nick finds out what is happening when Gatsby arrives one rainy afternoon with five servants and several baskets of food. Then Jordan arrives with Daisy, and she and Gatsby finally meet again (with suitable, if not subtle, music on the sound track).

As always, Gatsby is eager to impress and boasts of keeping his house "full of celebrated people." When he and Nick and Daisy go over to his house, he shows Daisy his closets full of custom-made shirts. Gatsby easily convinces Daisy that she should leave her husband and come back to him. There are delays, but finally there is a confrontation in a hotel in New York; Nick, Jordan, Gatsby, Daisy, and Tom are all there. Daisy tells Tom she is leaving him, but Tom refuses to accept her decision and counters by telling Daisy what he has found out about Gatsby's illegal activities. With the situation still unresolved, the group returns to Long Island, traveling in two identical yellow roadsters—Daisy and Gatsby in one, with Daisy driving, and Tom, Nick, and Jordan in the other.

Tom has been having an affair with Myrtle Wilson (Shelley Winters), the wife of a gasoline station owner. As Daisy and Gatsby drive toward the station on their way back to Long Island, Myrtle—thinking Tom is in the car—rushes out on the road. Daisy hits her but does not stop. When Tom, Nick, and Jordan, drive by a few minutes later and see that there has been an accident, they find that Myrtle is dead. After this horrifying event, everything changes. Gatsby tells Daisy he will say he was driving the car, and when Tom arrives, Daisy tells him what happened and that Gatsby will take the blame. She is hysterical about going to prison and is willing to let him. Nick is disgusted by her reaction and tells Gatsby to forget her.

Later, Myrtle's husband, Wilson (Howard da Silva), comes to Tom's house with a gun looking for the man who took the affection, and then the life, of his wife. Muttering "you and Myrtle," he is about to shoot Tom, but Tom says it was someone else and tells him to look for another yellow roadster— the one with a damaged fender. The climactic scene takes place at Gatsby's swimming pool. Gatsby tells Nick that he has decided to quit trying to be a gentleman. "Look what I've done to myself and everyone else to get where I am," he says. The telephone rings and continues to ring, but Gatsby has dismissed his servants and refuses to answer; he does not know it is Tom,

who has been persuaded by Daisy to call to warn him about Wilson. Soon
Wilson appears and shoots and kills Gatsby. Then, in a final scene, Nick says
he is going to become a writer and Jordan asks to go along and help.

Even though this film of *The Great Gatsby* may have missed some of the
shadings of Fitzgerald's examination of the price of pursuing success regardless
of the cost, it presents its subject quite well for a mainstream Hollywood film.
The acting is neither deep nor brilliant. The characters portrayed are essentially shallow, and when they attempt to show off, they tend to be flashy
rather than radiant. The one exception is Nick Carraway, the observer with
integrity, who is played by Carey in a convincingly understated manner. The
direction, too, is effective if not imaginative.

The Great Gatsby has been popular with adapters. It was presented as a
play staged by George Cukor in 1926, as a silent film in the same year, and
as a sound film in both 1949 and 1974. Perhaps because of the lavish (although
not profitable) 1974 production starring Robert Redford in the title role, the
1949 version of *The Great Gatsby* has been seen by few people in recent years.
The 1974 film was scorned by critics, and, in a sense, this scorn has brought
a greater respect for the earlier film.

Sharon Wiseman

THE GREAT LIE

Released: 1941
Production: Hal B. Wallis and Henry Blanke for Warner Bros.
Direction: Edmund Goulding
Screenplay: Lenore Coffee; based on the novel *January Heights* (*Far Horizons*) by Polan Banks
Cinematography: Tony Gaudio
Editing: Ralph Dawson
Costume design: Orry-Kelly
Music: Max Steiner
Running time: 102 minutes

Principal characters:
Maggie Patterson	Bette Davis
Peter Van Allen	George Brent
Sandra Kovac	Mary Astor (AA)
Aunt Ada	Lucile Watson
Violet	Hattie McDaniel

After her great triumph in a bravura role as a murderess in *The Letter* (1940), Warner Bros. decided to give Bette Davis a sympathetic heroine to portray. She alternated the kinds of ladies she played with a great deal of finesse, always a proof in films of versatility. The vehicle chosen for her was from a Polan Banks novel retitled for the screen *The Great Lie*; it was one of those stories patently manufactured for a female star and appealing to the female members of the audience. In this case, there were really two important female parts—the heroine and the bitch, who turns out to be not such a bitch after all.

Most of the big scenes in the story take place between the two women, as they had in *The Old Maid* (1939), which Bette Davis made with Miriam Hopkins. That was a duel, as everything always was when Hopkins costarred with a member of her own sex; but in *The Great Lie* the two women are played by Davis and Mary Astor. They are enemies in this story, but in real life they admired each other and worked together, sometimes sitting on the sidelines while the lights were being adjusted, reworking their dialogue together.

The story of *The Great Lie* begins when the hero, Peter Van Allen (George Brent), wakes up after ten days of partying to realize that at some time during the drunken celebration he had married Sandra Kovac (Mary Astor), a celebrated concert pianist. Peter deplores his action, because, while Sandra is a handsome woman, he happens really to be very much in love with another girl, Maggie Patterson (Bette Davis). His attorney contacts him, and Peter is startled by another shock: his marriage to Sandra is not legal, because she had not received her final divorce decree from her previous husband.

Peter gets in his private plane and flies directly to Maggie's well-appointed plantation home in Maryland. Maggie is understandably angry; Peter and she have loved each other for years, and now in a rash, drunken moment, he has spoiled her future as well as his. Peter does not tell her about the invalidity of his hasty marriage to Sandra, because he realizes that he has a duty to Sandra to perform first. He goes to Sandra and asks her to marry him on the day her divorce does become effective. Sandra, however, has a concert date in Philadelphia that night, and although Peter suggests that she break it, she goes to Philadelphia. In her dressing-room after the concert, she receives Maggie, who asks her to relinquish Peter because her uncle, who has an important job in Washington, can get him a flying job with the government. Sandra coldly tells Maggie that she intends to hang onto Peter.

When Maggie returns home, Peter is waiting for her, and tells her that his marriage to Sandra is not valid. Maggie is overjoyed, and they are immediately wed at her plantation home. They have only a brief but happy honeymoon, however, which is interrupted when Peter is summoned by the government to fly to South America on a survey flight. Maggie sees him off in Washington and receives a call there from Sandra, who tells her that she is going to have a baby, Peter's child. The worst is yet to come, however; news is flashed that Peter's plane has crashed in a South American jungle and all hope for any survivors has been abandoned.

Sandra now no longer has any interest in bearing Peter's child, but Maggie comes to her with a curious proposal, one that involves the titular "great lie." Her suggestion is that Sandra and she go away together to a lonely ranch she knows about in Arizona, where Maggie will tend and play nurse to Sandra during the period of pregnancy. When the child is born, it will be turned over to Maggie to rear. Nobody will ever know that the baby's mother is really Sandra because Maggie will rear the child as Peter's and hers. Maggie will also pay for everything.

The proposal is too bizarre for Sandra to ignore. She has no use for Maggie, and Maggie dislikes her, but they agree to live together for the months involved, bound in this conspiracy out of their mutual love for one man. They move to the lonely Arizona ranch, and Maggie becomes nurse, companion, and policewoman to Sandra, forcing her to take care of herself, to eat properly, and to exercise regularly. The baby, a healthy boy, is born and is named Peter. Sandra is disinterested in the child and goes off to Australia on a concert tour, while Maggie returns to Maryland with the baby. Then suddenly comes the explosive news: Peter Van Allen has survived the crash and is on his way home, alive and well. There is never any doubt in his mind that Maggie is the mother of his son. She is reluctant to confess the truth, and as the days pass, she is more than ever determined to live out "the great lie."

Sandra returns from her concert tour, but does not yet intend to change events, and for a time she keeps the secret. Then, without warning, she descends upon the Maryland plantation, telling everyone that she has come to see the wonderful baby; but in private she tells Maggie that she intends staying at the Maryland house until Maggie tells Peter the truth. She admits that this is only the first step in her plan; once she has regained custody of the child as her own, she intends to get Peter back as her lawful husband. Maggie bravely tells Peter the truth in front of Sandra, affirming that Sandra now wants her baby, and Peter, stunned, admits that he can understand her feeling; but it must also be understood that he loves Maggie, and he will stay with her. Sandra looks at the two of them and realizes that she has lost the battle. When she tells them that she is leaving, Peter asks what is to be done about the boy. Sandra looks at them both with cynical insolence, saying "I'm leaving him with his mother," and walks out of their lives.

The Great Lie was immediately successful at the box office. The plot is admittedly soap opera, but director Edmund Goulding stages it with style, and the basically artificial, contrived story comes across with great believability. Davis plays with great sincerity, and Astor's performance as Sandra is a personal triumph. She is beautiful and authoritative and offers a stunning portrayal of a temperamental musical artist. It came as no surprise when Academy members voted her the Oscar for Best Supporting Actress. There are several scenes showing her in concert, and Astor plays them so superbly that there was no doubt in many a viewer's mind that it was she herself who had played Tchaikovsky's Piano Concerto so brilliantly. Astor was no stranger to the piano keyboard, so her fingering and gestures while playing are exactly right, but the execution of the concerto itself was dubbed by a professional concert pianist. That year the Tchaikovsky concerto was heard ceaselessly on radio, and numerous recordings of it were sold.

DeWitt Bodeen

THE GREAT ZIEGFELD

Released: 1936
Production: Hunt Stromberg for Metro-Goldwyn-Mayer (AA)
Direction: Robert Z. Leonard
Screenplay: William Anthony McGuire; based on his original screen story
Cinematography: Oliver T. Marsh, George J. Folsey, Karl Freund, Merritt B. Gerstad, and Ray June
Editing: William S. Gray
Art direction: Cedric Gibbons
Costume design: Adrian
Music direction: Arthur Lange
Running time: 180 minutes

Principal characters:
Florenz Ziegfeld, Jr. .... William Powell
Anna Held .... Luise Rainer (AA)
Billie Burke .... Myrna Loy
Billings .... Frank Morgan
Sampston .... Reginald Owen
Sandow .... Nat Pendleton
Audrey Lane .... Virginia Bruce
Fannie Brice .... Herself

The Great Ziegfeld won the Oscar as Best Picture of 1936 over nine other nominated films. Although most of these other films, including *A Tale of Two Cities*, *Dodsworth*, *Anthony Adverse*, and *Mr. Deeds Goes to Town*, have increased their respective standing with film historians over the decades, many critics regard *The Great Ziegfeld* as overblown. At the time of the film's release critical reaction to the film was mixed, with most reviews dwelling on the length and cost of the production. In its era, *The Great Ziegfeld* was a staggeringly extravagant production. Estimated to have cost about two million dollars, it had a larger budget than any other film made by M-G-M up to that time, with the exception of the silent *Ben Hur* (1926). It also boasted a running time of three hours, which was longer than any film previously released in the United States.

The statistics of the film and the twenty-three opulent musical production numbers have made it the butt of much industry criticism, but much of this negative response seems undeserved. The film is too long, and there are too many musical numbers, but *The Great Ziegfeld* does an excellent job of blending a dramatic biographical story line with a musical extravaganza, a successful merging that has rarely been equaled. Robert Z. Leonard, who was nominated for an Oscar for his work, directed the film as two separate works with the musical numbers used to interrupt the drama. This method proved necessary because Florenz Ziegfeld, who had died only a few years before the film was made, had been the impressario of so many stage extravaganzas himself—with his "Ziegfeld Follies" being particularly well known—that to have made the film any other way would have been a mistake. The audience expected to see opulent production numbers in the famous Ziegfeld manner, and any toning down of this aspect of the film would have been a disappointment. Yet, Ziegfeld the man was an interesting figure, and his life story deserved a dramatic retelling. The solution was a drama with many musical numbers rather than a straight musical in which music is a part of the story and advances the plot.

The Great Ziegfeld begins in the mid-1890's when Florenz Ziegfeld, Jr. (William Powell), the son of a music teacher, is a carnival barker promoting a German strong man named Sandow (Nat Pendleton). Sandow is not much of an attraction on the midway until one of his feats causes a woman to faint. Ziegfeld, who is a master at publicity, capitalizes on Sandow's new status. The two tour the United States and earn a great deal of money. Their luck changes, however, when they announce that Sandow will wrestle a tiger, and the animal dies before the match can begin. After this, Ziegfeld decides to go to Europe, and on the voyage he runs into an old friend and carnival rival named Billings (Frank Morgan). The two are always in competition, and Ziegfeld always manages to better his friend. Billings is on his way to Europe to sign a new star to an exclusive American contract, but, not wanting Ziegfeld to ruin things, he refuses to say who the woman is.

After a brief side trip to Monte Carlo, where he loses all of his money, Ziegfeld goes to London, where Billings is also staying. When Ziegfeld asks a doorman who the greatest attraction in London is, he finds out that it is a French singer named Anna Held (Luise Rainer), and it is she whom Billings wants to sign. Ziegfeld is a man of great taste and style, and, as always, he easily charms Anna into signing with him, despite the fact that he has no money with which to pay her. Money never seems to stand in his way, however, and soon Anna Held is the toast of the New York stage. Extravagance and publicity, two of Ziegfeld's specialties, help to promote Anna with the New York carriage trade at the turn of the century. One example of Ziegfeld's flair for publicity, and one which is based on an actual publicity stunt, concerns Anna's milk baths. She became famous throughout America for supposedly taking baths in milk every morning to preserve her well-known beautiful complexion. The film debunks the myth that Anna actually did bathe in the milk by showing that she thinks the baths are silly and does not understand Ziegfeld's craving for publicity. Whether she bathed in milk or not, however, the real Anna Held was an early equivalent of a "super star," with her life and actions followed eagerly by thousands of adoring fans.

Anna marries Ziegfeld, and at first they are very happy both because she is a star and because he is becoming increasingly successful. He never seems to be out of debt, however, as his lavish life-style and craving for bigger and better productions use up his money faster than he can earn it. The main problem between Ziegfeld and Anna, though, is his well-known attraction to beautiful women. Although she suspects infidelity for some time, it is not until she sees him in a compromising position with a drunken showgirl named Audrey Lane (Virginia Bruce) that she leaves him.

The viewer is aware that several years have passed when Ziegfeld is next seen; he is now more subdued and grayer. At a party he meets Broadway star Billie Burke (Myrna Loy), a calm woman who is the antithesis of the emotional Anna. The real Billie Burke is best known today as a twittering, flighty comedienne of such 1930's and 1940's films as *Topper* (1937) and *Girl Trouble* (1942), but in the teens and the 1920's she was a well-known dramatic stage actress. In *The Great Ziegfeld* Billie and Ziegfeld meet when she is escorted to a party by Billings who, as usual, is trying to keep Ziegfeld from hiring her. In actuality, it was British writer W. Somerset Maugham who introduced the pair when he took Billie to a New Year's Eve party in 1913. After Billie and Ziegfeld marry in 1914, they are very happy and live on a large estate with their young daughter, on whom they both dote. Ziegfeld's extravagances now are confined to his family and the stage, and he is no longer the playboy that he was in his younger days.

Ziegfeld's fortunes begin to fail in the mid-1920's, when several of his shows, even the Follies, begin to falter. He does recapture his success temporarily, however, when he has four hit shows running concurrently on Broadway in the 1929 season: *Whoopee!*, *Rio Rita*, *Show Boat*, and *The Three Musketeers*. Predictably, because of the date, Ziegfeld goes broke when he invests his money (for the first time according to the film) in stocks which fail in the market crash of 1929. In the last sequence, Ziegfeld is a sick, broken man who is hoping to make a comeback but does not have the money to finance his dreams. Billings, who is also broke, comes to visit his old rival and promises to finance the new show that Ziegfeld wants, but even Ziegfeld realizes the sham. He dies as he dreams of "higher stairs" for his production numbers.

The dramatic narrative tells the life of Florenz Ziegfeld in a well-presented, well-acted manner. Yet, it is less than half of this very long film. What the film's admirers prefer are the musical production numbers, which are some of the most lavish ever filmed. It is unfortunate that a film which cost so much did not have color to accentuate the beauty of the sets and costumes. With moving sets and dozens of beautiful women wearing magnificent costumes by Adrian, color might have made the numbers even more reflective of the live stage shows which they were supposed to represent. The musical numbers were so lavish, in fact, that many critics felt that even Ziegfeld could not have done as well himself.

In addition to the blockbusters, there are several "small" numbers which are noteworthy in the film. The scene of Anna Held dressed in a long black gown and huge plumed hat singing "It's Delightful to Be Married," as she strolls among eight beautiful chorus singers who have similar costumes in white, is one of these. Anna Held herself was known for considerable charm and sauciness which came through on the stage, and this number captures that charm perfectly. Another delightful number is Fannie Brice's burlesque act. In the film, Ziegfeld goes to Brice's show to see if she might be suitable for his Follies. The real Fannie Brice appears in one of her famous numbers, singing "Mr. Yiddle, on your fiddle, play some ragtime." Later, after a nice comedy scene in which Brice mistakes Ziegfeld for a cut-rate furrier, she auditions for the Follies. This is one of the major disappointments in the film; as Brice begins to sing her theme song, "My Man," wearing a knitted shawl, and with tears running down her cheeks, the scene shifts to Ziegfeld's office, and only the music can be heard in the distance.

Of the major production numbers, the most famous, and one of the most famous numbers ever filmed, is "A Pretty Girl Is Like a Melody." This sequence, which was included in *That's Entertainment* (1974), is often referred to as the "wedding cake" number because of the huge wedding cakelike set used. The number begins when Dennis Morgan (billed as Stanley Morner, and, although an accomplished tenor himself, he lip-syncs the voice of singing star Allen Jones) sings the song in front of a huge curtain. As the curtain opens, a large set appears, revealing dozens of "pretty girls" seated, standing, or dancing along a revolving staircase. The camera follows the movement of the graduated circular staircase so imperceptibly at first that it barely seems to move. Then, as the stairs go higher and the set narrows, it moves faster, sweeping past dancers in a variety of beautiful costumes. At the end, there is only one women sitting on top of the staircase; she is dressed in a full skirted costume which seems to blend into the set. A final sweep of the entire set is made and then the lavish circular curtain closes. Ray June photographed this section of the film (which had several cinematographers for different sections). Interestingly, there is no applause on the sound track or shots of the audience applauding as there are at the end of other numbers in the film. This is fitting, however, as the number is so magnificent that the actual film audience broke into applause, thus replacing what might have been seen and heard on the film. Although they are individually excellent, the large number of musical numbers is the one aspect of the film which tends to make it rather tedious. There are large sections of the film consisting of song after song, which tend to fatigue audiences. This is especially evident in the series of numbers (of which the "A Pretty Girl Is Like a Melody" number is a part) which represents the Follies at its peak.

There is a surprising lack of historical continuity in the film, at least to the extent that the audience does not know what year or even what decade is being represented without a great deal of background knowledge. Actually, "A Pretty Girl Is Like a Melody" was introduced in the 1919 Follies, yet in the film this number precedes Ziegfeld's discovery of Fannie Brice by a few weeks. Brice, however, first appeared in the 1910 Follies. This changing of facts and dates runs throughout the film and tends to be an annoyance to purists, although it does not seem to interfere with the success of the film as a piece of entertainment,

In addition to Brice, several other well-known Follies performers are portrayed in the film, including Will Rogers and Eddie Cantor. Also, Ray Bolger and Harriet Hoctor perform specialty numbers which are enjoyable, if not historically accurate. There are a number of other performers who are mentioned either by their real names or fictitious ones who represent the dozens of well-known personalities who began their careers with Ziegfeld.

The film was nominated for Oscars in several categories but won in only two: Best Picture, and Best Actress for Rainer. Rainer gave a good performance as Anna Held, but it is a curiously small part for a nomination in the Best Actress category, especially considering the length of the film. Rainer had one of the strangest careers in Hollywood. She came to Hollywood after studying under theatrical impresario Max Reinhardt in the mid-1930's and quickly won the Oscar for *The Great Ziegfeld*, followed by another Best Actress Oscar the next year for *The Good Earth*. After these two monumental films, however, her career fell apart and she made only one film after 1938, *Hostages* (1943). She then retired and never acted again. By modern standards her acting seems rather melodramatic. In the scene which was considered her masterpiece, when she calls Ziegfeld on the telephone to congratulate him upon his marriage to Billie Burke, she displays near hysteria, which is almost laughable today. Yet, in 1936, this was very poignant and probably contributed more than anything to her winning the Oscar.

Powell was nominated for an Oscar for his role as the butler in *My Man Godfrey* the year that *The Great Ziegfeld* was released, but he lost to Paul Muni for *The Story of Louis Pasteur*. The role of Ziegfeld was perhaps more challenging than that of Godfrey for Powell, but somehow the light comic touches which he displayed in both films are more effective in *My Man Godfrey*. Also, the film's last scene, which is far too melodramatic, leaves a lingering impression of over-acting which detracts from Powell's overall excellent performance.

The other principal of the film, Loy, gave her standard, underplayed performance. Although she was quite good in the role of Billie Burke, Loy has been criticized because she did not resemble the real Burke in voice or mannerisms. This is an unfair criticism, however, because the real Burke was so well known in the 1930's that any attempt at imitation would have seemed like a caricature, something that would have been inappropriate in a dramatic story such as this. Actually, when one looks at Billie Burke in a film such as *The Wizard of Oz* (1939) where she played Glenda, the Good Witch, Loy's quiet, restrained performance does not seem off the mark. The flighty Burke is the actress who is most frequently remembered, however, and thus many critics find fault with the soft-spoken, gentle Loy.

The rest of the cast, mainly members of M-G-M's stock company, turn in their usual professional performances, especially Morgan who gives his characteristic comic/serious second-banana role sparkle. The other major parts, acted by Owen, Pendleton, and Bruce, also add color to the production's dramatic aspects.

Despite some mixed critical reaction to the film, *The Great Ziegfeld* did well at the box office, ending up in the top five moneymaking films of 1936. It also indirectly gave birth to two later M-G-M films, *Ziegfeld Girl* (1941), about a group of aspiring performers working in the Ziegfeld Follies, and *Ziegfeld Follies* (1946), directed by Vincente Minnelli in which a white-haired Powell has a small part as the spirit of Florenz Ziegfeld. In the latter film, Ziegfeld looks down from heaven on a series of unrelated musical and comedy numbers, showing how the master showman would put on another production if he could. Although Powell's part is the only dramatic aspect of the film, *Ziegfeld Follies* still merits attention for several well-known production numbers, including a famous song-and-dance routine featuring both Fred Astaire and Gene Kelly.

Patricia King Hanson

THE GUARDSMAN

Released: 1931
Production: Metro-Goldwyn-Mayer
Direction: Sidney Franklin
Screenplay: Claudine West and Ernest Vajda; based on the stage play of the same name by Ferenc Molnar
Cinematography: Norbert Brodine
Editing: Conrad A. Nervig
Running time: 83 minutes

Principal characters:

The Actor	Alfred Lunt
The Actress	Lynn Fontanne
The Critic	Roland Young
Liesl, the Maid	Zasu Pitts
Mama	Maude Eburne
A Creditor	Herman Bing
A Fan	Ann Dvorak

Production chief Irving Thalberg had a dream of bringing the best actors from the Broadway theatre to M-G-M in a series of starring film productions that would immortalize their performances and add an extra luminescence to the studio's own stable of contract players. Through his diligent efforts, Helen Hayes became a highly esteemed, Academy Award-winning star for M-G-M. Thalberg also wanted renowned stage star Katharine Cornell at Metro, but she resisted all his offers. Alfred Lunt and Lynn Fontanne, however, the most esteemed acting team in the country, were interested in Thalberg's offer. Each of the Lunts had had some film acting experience in silent films individually, but now that they were married and had become the number-one acting attraction in the Broadway theater, Thalberg wanted them to bring their talents to the cinema. One of their biggest theatrical attractions had been Ferenc Molnar's *The Guardsman*, in which they had costarred for the Theater Guild. When the Lunts signed a contract with Thalberg for a single feature with options for more, it was agreed that this play would be adapted into a film for their talking film debut. So confident was Thalberg that they would be memorable on the screen that he also bought for M-G-M the film rights to Robert E. Sherwood's comedy, *Reunion in Vienna*, in which the Lunts had performed brilliantly onstage, and Thalberg hoped it might be their second vehicle for his studio.

When the Lunts came to Hollywood to film *The Guardsman*, they were given the red carpet treatment, and on release, the film was greatly admired by critics and audiences alike. Although they were both honored with Academy Award nominations for Best Actor and Best Actress, respectively, they did not want to do any more films for M-G-M or for any other film company. The Broadway stage was their home, and they wanted to continue their careers together as stage actors. Their dream of performing for people who would never be able to see them on Broadway was reached by touring their productions nationwide and internationally. Although they were at ease in front of the camera, the theater was their true domain. Thalberg bowed to their decision and turned *Reunion in Vienna* (filmed in 1933) over to two other extraordinarily fine theater stars who had made their mark in films— John Barrymore and Diana Wynyard.

The Guardsman, the only film that the Lunts made, is a prize that still shines. In 1931 it was admired; in 1979, when it was revived at an M-G-M retrospective at the Vagabond Theater in Los Angeles, it left audiences who had never seen it or the Lunts before delighted. It is romantic comedy at its most sparkling, beautifully directed, written, and photographed, and acted with a finesse that only the finest actors have mastered. It was a small production, made with only the two stars and five supporting players. As an exercise in what actors can do when given a good script, it remains unique. It has Continental flavor, sophistication, wit, grace, and sexual energy.

The plot opens in the theater in Budapest, where the reigning favorite actors of the day are concluding a performance of Maxwell Anderson's play *Elizabeth the Queen* (which the Lunts, incidentally, had performed magnificently for the Theater Guild). Thalberg was unsure about asking playwright Maxwell Anderson for the right to buy the final moments of the play, but Anderson had once been under contract to M-G-M and said that he had begun writing the play there in his studio office, while waiting for an assignment, so he willingly let them use his scene free of charge.

Lunt, as Lord Essex, takes his final leave of Queen Elizabeth, played by Fontanne, going to his execution, while she slumps back on her throne, "queen of emptiness." With a roll of drums, the curtain comes down, and then the actors come out together to take their bows to an admiring audience. They retreat behind the curtain into the wings, where Fontanne quickly removes her wig and basic makeup as Elizabeth; they then join hands and go out to bow to an audience that continues to applaud. There is a surprised gasp, and the audience is heard to exclaim upon the actress' true youth and beauty. The Actor and Actress carry on a running conversation under their breath while they smilingly receive the plaudits of their admirers. He tells her to smile at the officers, for he knows she likes men in uniform; she returns his bantering sallies, never losing her smile, even when she is forced to warn him between her teeth, "You're on my dress; you're on my dress."

In the dressing-rooms, their bantering becomes quarrelsome and, on his part, jealously accusative. Alone in his own dressing-room later, the Actor encounters the Critic (Roland Young), and with histrionic despair he confesses that he can sense an unknown rival's approach. His wife now sits in darkened rooms, weeps softly, and plays Chopin. He knows that a new man is coming into her life, or she is at least yearning for one, whom she will welcome with open arms when he puts in an appearance. Driven to desperation, the Actor decides to test the love and fidelity of his wife. He concocts an elaborate scheme whereby he will go off for an overnight trip to a neighboring city which has invited him supposedly to fill in with a performance of Hamlet. He will make all his farewells, leave his wife, and then surreptitiously return to make himself up as a Russian guardsman and woo his own wife, hoping she will resist him, but determined to give his all to entice her to be faithless.

The Critic, who is a delighted voyeur, is privy to the impersonation. The Actress is tempted; she resists, but allows the Guardsman to see her home from the opera. He kisses her passionately, and she hurriedly retires with a gasp of fear into the house, locking the door. The Actor is delighted that, good as his performance has been, she is loyal and has been able to turn him down. Then the window opens above, and she tosses down a key, and with a despairing look at the Critic, the Actor goes in to seduce his own wife.

The final sequence deals with his return the next day from his supposed engagement, his confession of the impersonation, and her defense that she knew all along who he was, that he did not fool her for one moment, and that she simply played the comedy through as he cued her in. In the very final shot of the picture, however, Fontanne is shown as she presses her loving, repentant husband to her breast and looks over to the Critic and smiles enigmatically. Did she really know that it was her husband who seduced her, or did she willingly succumb to the advances of a strange lover for one night of love? The look in her eyes and the smile that curls her lips invites the audience to decide.

The Guardsman is a flawless transcription of a play to cinematic form, and the performances are all exceedingly good. For its day, it was considered extremely racy, but not even the Hays office could object to a husband seducing his own wife, and the audiences, whether of 1931 or 1979, have always been entranced with the film. M-G-M remade the film in 1941 as *The Chocolate Soldier*, a curious combination of the play *The Guardsman* enacted with the music of the Oscar Straus operetta, as sung by Nelson Eddy and Rise Stevens. The result is only a hazy shadow of the skillful 1931 comedy starring the Lunts. Fortunately, since, their version of *The Guardsman* is a wonderful and timeless treasure, the Lunt film survives in very good prints.

DeWitt Bodeen

GUESS WHO'S COMING TO DINNER?

Released: 1967
Production: Stanley Kramer for Columbia
Direction: Stanley Kramer
Screenplay: William Rose (AA)
Cinematography: Sam Leavitt
Editing: Robert C. Jones
Running time: 108 minutes

Principal characters:
Christina Drayton .... Katharine Hepburn (AA)
Matt Drayton .... Spencer Tracy
John Wade Prentice .... Sidney Poitier
Joey Drayton .... Katharine Houghton
Monsignor Ryan .... Cecil Kellaway
Mrs. Prentice .... Beah Richards
Mr. Prentice .... Roy E. Glenn, Sr.
Tillie .... Isabell Sanford
Hilary St. George .... Virginia Christine

Because of producer/director Stanley Kramer's films such as *The Defiant Ones* (1958), *On the Beach* (1959), *Inherit the Wind* (1960), and many others which have dealt with themes of social injustice, his work has often been called "thesis" or "message" cinema. Although not every one of his films has neatly fallen into this category, most of them have, and the body of his work is thus message-oriented. Usually the messages of the films have been presented as highly dramatic statements, often with tragic endings, but his highly successful 1967 film *Guess Who's Coming to Dinner?* is more of a light entertainment with a serious theme as its basis.

The plot concerns the problem of interracial love and marriage, represented by the reactions of one liberal upper-middle-class family to the announcement by their daughter that she is going to marry a black man. In the film, Katharine Hepburn and Spencer Tracy play the parents in their last appearance together. The film also marked Tracy's last motion picture; he died shortly after its completion. Although the film received raves when it was released, did extremely well at the box office, and received many Academy Award nominations, almost fifteen years later, it is the work of Tracy and Hepburn which is the best part of a badly dated film. It has been said by some cinema historians that there is no type of film which becomes more dated than a social message film, and *Guess Who's Coming to Dinner?* proves that axiom.

The main characters are established early in the film. Tracy plays Matt Drayton, a veteran crusading San Francisco newspaper publisher who prides himself on being a champion of justice; Hepburn plays his equally liberal wife, Christina, a gracious woman who owns a fashionable *avant garde* art gallery in downtown San Francisco. When their pretty, blonde, twenty-one-year-old daughter Joey (Katharine Houghton) returns from the University of Hawaii where she has been attending college, she announces that she has brought her fiancé, Professor John Wade Prentice, back with her. She describes the man in such glowing terms that her mother is delighted about the news, but she is shocked at first to learn that the fiancé is not white. When Prentice (Sidney Poitier) enters the room where Christina and Joey are talking, the audience as well as Christina recognize immediately that the family's liberal views will be severely tested. To complicate the problem even further, both Joey and Prentice agree that they will not marry unless they have their parents' permission and approval. If they wanted to defy their parents, the story would be different, but the fact that they want their parents' blessings makes the situation more difficult for everyone, since it forces both sets of parents to face the situation head on.

The story takes place in the space of less than twelve hours because Prentice must leave for an important assignment in New York that evening and Joey wants to go with him. Her decision to go or stay rests with the parents. Most of the action occurs in the Drayton's beautiful French colonial house. During the course of events, all of the major characters come to the house, including Prentice's parents (Beah Richards and Roy E. Glenn, Sr.).

The first one to wholeheartedly accept Joey and Prentice's marriage is Christina, who is soon too swept up in the romance of the whirlwind courtship to wish them anything but good. Matt, however, is something less than enthusiastic throughout most of the film. When he returns from his office in the afternoon, the black maid, Tillie (Isabell Sanford), greets him at the door with "All hell done broken loose." He never actually says no to the marriage, but his struggle eventually to say yes takes up the major portion of the film. This allows the characters to develop in different ways, with each showing his true feelings.

The reactions of various types of people are shown through key characters. Christina's friend Hilary St. George (Virginia Christine) is openly polite and unctuous to Joey and Prentice, but when Christina sees her to her car, Virginia tells her how "heartsick" she is that Christina has to go through such a thing. In one of the better scenes of the film, an equally unctuous Christina tells Hilary, who manages the art gallery, to go to the gallery, write herself a large check, and never come back. Hepburn's smiles and Christine's shocked expression illustrate a classic rebuff to a hypocrite. Another character who visits the Drayton's home is their old friend Monsignor Ryan (Cecil Kellaway), who is totally happy and enthusiastic about the marriage. Naïvely, perhaps, like Christina, he refuses to see any problems for the two which cannot be overcome by love. Prentice's parents seem to parallel the reactions of Joey's parents: his mother is delighted, and his father is merely perplexed and a little disgusted.

There are a number of speeches in the film which delve into the problem of parent-child relationships, as well as the issue of race, but most rely heavily on platitudes. The message which comes through today is that people should understand one another's feelings, rather than the message regarding tolerance which the filmmakers intended. Mr. Prentice and Matt are somehow pitted against their respective families because they are merely being practical, if somewhat cynical, in their views of Joey and Prentice's marriage. Mrs. Prentice accuses her husband and Matt of being dried up old men who cannot understand the passions of youth. "What happens to men when they get old?" Mrs. Prentice asks.

In the large major sequence of the film, Matt delivers a speech which dissects the major issues of the story and slowly analyzes everything that has transpired. He eventually gives his consent to the marriage, but only after he makes everyone think about their own blind reactions to it. He did not "dry up" as Mrs. Prentice says; he still has passion for his wife and love for his daughter. What he wants is for them all to come emotionally back to earth and realistically see the problems which the two will face. If Joey and Prentice still want to get married, then he is in agreement. The film ends as the entire group goes to the airport to see Joey and Prentice off, while on the soundtrack we hear the old song "Glory of Love."

Although the film received a near-record ten Academy Award nominations and won two, one to William Rose for Best Screenplay and one to Hepburn for Best Actress, it is not a particularly outstanding film. There are some beautiful moments of humor and sentimentality in the story, and the acting is excellent, but the script fails to live up to the serious nature of the film's theme. Perhaps the lessening of the social consciousness impact of the film is caused by its typical Hollywood glossy look. Since the white family is well-to-do and the black family middle-class (Mr. Prentice is a retired mailman), some of the problems of racism are skirted. Additionally, Poitier's performance as a "super black" stretches credulity. Prentice is brilliant, handsome, and charming, a physician graduated *cum laude* from Harvard who has written numerous books and scholarly articles, has been a professor at Yale, and now will be the Assistant Director of the World Health Organization. Racial differences aside, it seems difficult to believe that the parents of a naïve, almost frivolous twenty-one-year-old girl would not want him for a son-in-law.

Another problem with the script concerns the differences between Joey and Prentice that do not have anything to do with race. He is forty and a widower, and the problems of the differences in their ages and intellectual development are never discussed. Thus, in some respects the audience's sympathies lie with Matt when he accuses them of not being realistic. To his credit as an actor, Poitier does give a good performance in a characterization which is almost completely preordained by the parameters of the script. He underplays the character's accomplishments instead of stressing them.

Houghton, who is Hepburn's niece in real life, made her acting debut with *Guess Who's Coming to Dinner?* She seems right for the part of the starry-eyed Joey, but she never pursued her acting career and has since retired from films. Others of the cast, including Sanford, who starred in the long-running television comedy series *The Jeffersons*, and veteran actor Kellaway in one of his last roles, give characteristically solid performances. The stars, however, give brilliant performances which make the film. While Hepburn won an Oscar for her performance, it is Tracy, who was ill and close to death during the filming, who gives the best performance. He is the only person who seems to change during the film, evolving from shocked parent to angry curmudgeon to understanding father. As always in his nine films with Hepburn, it is the banter between them which adds sparkle to the script. In the last long speech of the film, however, Tracy, the man of reason, is at his most brilliant. Many of his films displayed long rational, wise speeches, and it was a fitting end to his career that one of his best was included in *Guess Who's Coming to Dinner?* Tracy was posthumously nominated for an Oscar for his performance, but he lost to Rod Steiger for *In the Heat of the Night*. He did, however, win the British equivalent of the Oscar, the "Stella," for his performance.

Janet St. Clair

GUN CRAZY

Released: 1949
Production: Frank King and Maurice King for United Artists
Direction: Joseph H. Lewis
Screenplay: Mackinlay Kantor and Millard Kaufman; based on the short story
  "Gun Crazy" by Mackinlay Kantor
Cinematography: Russell Harlan
Editing: Harry Gerstad
Musical direction: Victor Young
Song: Victor Young and Ned Washington, "Mad About You"
Running time: 87 minutes

Principal characters:
    Annie Laurie Starr .... Peggy Cummins
    Bart Tare .... John Dall
    Packett .... Barry Kroeger
    Judge Willoughby .... Morris Carnovsky
    Bluey-Bluey .... Stanley Praeger
    Dave Allister .... Nedrick Young

Like many "B"-movies, *Gun Crazy* is nourished by an American myth, in
this case one of alienated youth on the run, obsessed by flight, guns, freedom,
and love, and throwing away tomorrow for an incandescent today. The image
of the fugitive couple has created its own subgenre, including Fritz Lang's
You Only Live Once (1937), Edgar Ulmer's *Detour* (1945), Nicholas Ray's
They Live by Night (1949), Jean-Luc Godard's *Breathless* (1959), Arthur
Penn's *Bonnie and Clyde* (1967), Robert Altman's *Thieves Like Us* (1974),
and Terrence Malick's *Badlands* (1974), not to mention variations on the
theme from producers such as Roger Corman.
    The audience knows this story before they enter the theater. In the 1940's
and 1950's they paid to see it performed explicitly, in "B"-movies without
pretensions to high culture. Whatever such films lacked in subtlety they often
made up in speed, energy, and assurance. Producers, after all, knew what
the audience expected. Even in the most formula-ridden of those films there
resided a further possibility. Because the raw materials of the films were so
emotional, so rooted in unconscious fears and desires, it sometimes happened
that moments—even in a lowly "B"-movie—would ignite. In *Gun Crazy* the
whole picture catches fire.
    The film deals with two lovers who have nothing but each other. It suggests
the hunger for oblivion that lurks in their love and the allure that romantic
desolation holds for them. The simple story throws these elements into sharp
relief. A young man, Bart Tare (John Dall), who loves to shoot, meets a
ruthless blonde markswoman, Annie Laurie Starr (Peggy Cummins), who

works in a carnival. Immediately spellbound, he persuades her to go off with him. Their money soon runs out, however, and to hold her, he joins with her in a series of robberies. Eventually the woman kills a bystander and the couple is hunted down by the young man's boyhood friends, who have become lawmen, in a swamp blanketed by fog.

It is less a story than a ritual, in which the world is well lost for love and all taboos exist only to be broken. As in most "B"-movies, the characters seem simpler and larger than life. Cummins gives the definitive portrait of a *film noir* seductress, for whom sex is the deadliest weapon. She is as dangerous as Barbara Stanwyck in *Double Indemnity* (1944), but is portrayed much less realistically. We know nothing of her background or hopes. She exists in bold outline, like a Pop Art figure. Despite a lofty English accent, Cummins is all flash and greedy appetite, with overtones of sadistic dominance. Like the Stanwyck character, she is acutely aware of her limits in a man's world. With a gun in her hand, however, Annie Laurie is as good as any man.

Bart also seems simple at first. Played with weakness and uncertainty, he is torn between love for Annie Laurie and revulsion at his descent into crime. Once he tries to leave the woman, then hurries back. The truth is he cannot leave her, any more than he can dismiss the aggression buried in himself. The lovers' relationship makes sense as one accepts that the woman is the projection of all the boy's own destructive nihilism. Things he cannot even think of on his own are possible while he lives through her.

They meet in a marksmen's duel that sets the style of their romance. These characters are always defined by action; they are what they do. Thus their initial duel becomes a one-scene seduction, climaxing when she puts on a crown of candles, looking like a side-show Athena, and, one-by-one, the fascinated young man shoots out her lights. This electrifying meeting only sets the stage for the delirium to follow. During the robberies, the otherwise doubtful Bart is quick and confident. Especially for him, the robberies are sexual events. The staging and camera movement generate a mad exhilaration. The scenes do not exploit sex and violence; the effect is more subversive and despairing. Sex and violence are fused into a single action, a dance of death for young lovers.

Director Joseph H. Lewis' staging has been justly praised. Perhaps it reaches a peak in the long, single-shot bank robbery. The camera looks forward from the back seat of the couple's car as they drive to the bank. The man goes in to rob it while the woman waits behind the wheel and spends a tortured minute as a bank guard on the street comes over to chat with her. The boy races out and they start their getaway, hurtling down side streets, barely missing other vehicles. For those few minutes the film lives in a heightened "real time." We experience the lovers' claustrophobic tensions and the thrill of their release. We are irresponsible with them; we are seduced.

Lewis counterpoints the swiftness of the film with constant reminders of falling and stumbling. As a boy, Bart reaches for a stolen gun and slips into the grasp of a policeman. Later, Annie Laurie slips during a robbery at a meat packer, stumbles during a dance on a night out, and falls during the swamp scene. Each break in the forward momentum tightens the tension. More tension is produced by a series of contrasting angles, from deep-focus long shots to big, crowded close-ups, often with the driving couple in profile.

The MacKinlay Kantor-Millard Kaufman screenplay is resonant enough to allow a variety of interpretations. Thus we can see Bart as an "artist" with a "talent" forced into an outsider's role by the demands of a materialistic society, personified by Annie Laurie, the bitch-goddess. Every detail in the script counts in several ways. The fog in the last scene is atmospheric, but also ironic. In the impenetrable mist, Bart sees his doom most clearly. Yet for the audience all interpretation comes after the film ends. As it unwinds, one only *feels* it. Nothing interrupts the flow. The sheer velocity of the couple forces us to suspend thought.

As an enterprise, *Gun Crazy* is steeped in poverty, yet it also flaunts that poverty and gains character from it. The King brothers, its producers, were specialists in low-budget films whose previous hit was *Dillinger* (1945). The characters in *Gun Crazy* are poor, and the story springs from the working class, idealizing a couple with nothing to look forward to. The leanness of the narrative is a low-budget necessity. Most of all, however, the film is haunted by the image of its director. Lewis was a major talent, influencing a generation of American and French filmmakers through such works as *Gun Crazy*, *The Big Combo* (1955), and *So Dark the Night* (1946). Yet he was never assigned a major film; all he could do was turn minor ones into gems.

Ted Gershuny

GUNFIGHT AT THE O.K. CORRAL

Released: 1957
Production: Hal B. Wallis for Paramount
Direction: John Sturges
Screenplay: Leon Uris; based on an article by George Scullin
Cinematography: Charles Lang
Editing: Warren Low
Music: Dmitri Tiomkin
Running time: 122 minutes

Principal characters:

Wyatt Earp	Burt Lancaster
Doc Holliday	Kirk Douglas
Laura Denbow	Rhonda Fleming
Kate Fisher	Jo Van Fleet
Johnny Ringo	John Ireland
Billy Clanton	Dennis Hopper
Ike Clanton	Lyle Bettger
Ed Bailey	Lee Van Cleef
Virgil Earp	John Hudson
Morgan Earp	De Forest Kelley
Jimmy Earp	Martin Milner
Betty Earp	Joan Camden

The story of Wyatt Earp and Doc Holliday has attracted filmmakers for decades. *My Darling Clementine* (1946), directed by John Ford, is generally regarded as the best film about the two, and *Doc* (1971), directed by Frank Perry, is probably the least reverent treatment of the story. Falling somewhere between the two in quality and realism is *Gunfight at the O.K. Corral*, directed by John Sturges in 1957. Realism is not, however, necessarily an important criterion in a genre such as the Western, which is usually meant to be closer to myth or legend than to history. What each director and writer chooses to do with the characters and events is much more important than whether they present the known facts with perfect fidelity.

For this treatment of the story of the legendary pair, producer Hal B. Wallis signed Burt Lancaster and Kirk Douglas, even though both had acquired reputations for sometimes being difficult to deal with. To write the script he hired the novelist Leon Uris. The script followed a fairly standard Western formula of building slowly to a final showdown at the end, just as the film's title promised. Within that framework, and ultimately of more interest than the victory of the good guys at the end, are Doc Holliday's ambivalent relationships with both Wyatt Earp and Kate Fisher.

The film is divided into three sections, each in a different location and each beginning with a shot of the boot hill, or cemetery, of the town in which that section takes place. The first section is set in Fort Griffin, Texas, where we are introduced to Doc Holliday (Kirk Douglas), who is alternately throwing knives in a door and drinking whiskey. A gambler who used to be a dentist, he is now afflicted with a tubercular cough and is involved in an almost sadomasochistic relationship with Kate Fisher (Jo Van Fleet). He expects her to be loyal to him and to be with him when he needs her, but otherwise he largely ignores her and her needs. Douglas had researched the character of Doc, finding that he was "a meticulous dresser," but actually, no ladies' man. "He slept until noon . . . and consumed oceans of whiskey." These characteristics are used by Douglas in his portrayal of the man even though the script, as has been noted, made no attempt at historical accuracy.

At the first meeting of Doc and Wyatt Earp (Burt Lancaster), neither admires the other. Earp is a Dodge City lawman trying to track down Johnny Ringo (John Ireland) and Ike Clanton (Lyle Bettger), and he goes to see Doc only for information on their whereabouts. Doc refuses to tell him anything, but he does receive some valuable information from Wyatt. Ed Bailey (Lee Van Cleef), a man who is waiting for Doc at the saloon to avenge the death of his brother, carries a small pistol in his boot. When Doc goes to the saloon, that information saves his life. He kills Bailey with a knife when he sees him draw the pistol from his boot. Although Doc is in the right according to the frontier code, it soon becomes evident that he is in danger of being lynched as a result of popular opinion. Kate appeals to Wyatt for help, but he responds, "I don't want any part of him; I don't even like him." When Wyatt sees that the probability of Doc's being lynched is real, however, he helps him escape with Kate. It is nothing personal, Wyatt explains; he just does not like lynchings. Doc then says he will go to Dodge City to express his thanks properly, but Wyatt tells him that he can best express his thanks by staying out of Dodge City. Nevertheless, a bond has now been established between the two men that will find them standing side by side at the O.K. Corral by the end of the film.

The scene then shifts to Dodge City, Kansas, some time later. Wyatt receives the news that Doc and Kate have just arrived. He goes to tell Doc that he must leave immediately, but Doc says that he has just been run out of Abilene and has no money. Finally Wyatt agrees to let Doc stay if he will promise "no knives, no guns, no killings." Not long after, Wyatt accepts Doc's offer to help him chase some bank robbers, and Doc saves Wyatt's life. At this same time, Wyatt has begun a romance with Laura Denbow (Rhonda Fleming), a woman gambler who arrived in Dodge City on the same day that Doc did. The romance is presented in an unconvincing fashion, but it does give Wyatt another reason for his plan to give up being a lawman and move to California. Meanwhile, Kate has grown tired of Doc's callousness toward her and has taken up with Ringo, who "blew into town" while Doc was out after the bank robbers. Doc goes to Ringo's room and confronts her, but he refuses to fight Ringo because of his promise to Wyatt. He even lets Ringo throw a drink in his face without reaching for a gun.

Wyatt's plans of retiring to a life of peace are disrupted when he learns that his brother Virgil (John Hudson), a lawman in Tombstone, Arizona, is in trouble. He tells an upset and disappointed Laura that he must help his brother, and, as he rides off to Tombstone, Doc joins him. When the scene shifts to Tombstone, we find that all the Earp brothers—Morgan (De Forest Kelley) and Jimmy (Martin Milner), as well as Wyatt and Virgil—have assembled to combat the Clanton gang, which is trying to run stolen cattle through Tombstone. After the Clantons try bribery and every other means that they can think of, they decide that the only way to overcome the Earp brothers is to provoke them into a shootout. They plan to shoot Wyatt one night, but when his brother Jimmy goes on the rounds that night instead, the Clanton gang shoots him down in cold blood. Wyatt has been the voice of reason throughout the film and has frequently been taunted about his "holy" attitude, but finding Jimmy lying in the street is too much: it is now a personal battle between the Earps and the Clantons. A gunfight at sunup at the O.K. Corral is arranged.

The confrontation is to be between the three Earp brothers and six of the Clanton gang, including the youngest Clanton, Billy (Dennis Hopper). Earlier Wyatt had tried to talk Billy out of being a gunfighter, telling him no gunfighter lives to see his thirty-fifth birthday and all are lonely; "they live in fear and die without a dime or a woman or a friend." He thought he had convinced the young man, but he finds that he had not. Wyatt goes to Doc for help, but he finds him unconscious and being looked after by Kate, who tells him that Doc is dying. Virgil's wife Betty (Joan Camden) also tries to talk the brothers out of the showdown by pointing out that as lawmen, "Your duty is to people, not to your own pride."

Nothing, however, can keep the Earp brothers from their vengeance. They head for the confrontation walking tall, as have countless Western movie heroes. Along with the three Earp brothers is Doc Holliday, who has gotten up from what seemed to be his deathbed because, as he tells Kate, he wants to die with the only friend he ever had. Although the actual shootout apparently took only a few seconds, it is extended on the screen to several minutes. The Earp brothers and Doc kill all of the Clanton gang except young Billy, with Doc finally getting his own revenge by shooting Ringo. Billy, who is wounded, makes his way to a nearby building, followed by Wyatt. Although Wyatt gets a chance to shoot Billy then and there, he waits, apparently hoping that Billy will remember what he has told him and throw down his gun. Instead, Billy painfully raises his gun to aim at Wyatt. At just that moment Doc looks in the window, sees what is happening, and kills Billy with one shot. A disappointed Wyatt drops his gun and badge by Billy's body and walks out.

There remains only one last sequence in which Wyatt and Doc meet in the saloon. We learn that Wyatt's brothers, although wounded, will be all right and that Wyatt plans to leave for California immediately. He tells Doc that he should go to the hospital in Denver, but Doc only responds, "So long, preacher." Then he joins the card game in progress at the saloon and Wyatt rides off across the desert landscape, accompanied by a song sung by Frankie Laine that has punctuated the major sections of the film throughout.

Gunfight at the O.K. Corral fits the classic formula of the Western in that it presents a conflict between civilization and anarchy in which there is some ambivalence in the heroes. Wyatt Earp is particularly ambivalent. He wants three conflicting things: to get married and settle down, to uphold the law, and to avenge his brother's death. Although Wyatt's feelings are mixed, he spends most of the film being so righteous that other characters sarcastically call him "preacher," and his romance with Laura is neither directed nor written well. As a result, Doc Holliday is a more complex and interesting character than Wyatt. Doc's character also has many facets: his upper-class family background, his past career as a dentist, his need for Kate along with his inability to give her anything, his ability to win fights even though he never provokes them, and his strange affection for the upright lawman, Wyatt Earp. Douglas conveys all this well. The other notable performance is by Van Fleet as Kate. She makes us see the hurt that Doc inflicts as well as the reasons that she cannot leave him permanently.

The music by Dmitri Tiomkin often goes overboard in underscoring and emphasizing emotions and events, but that was the style of music for "big" films in the 1950's. In addition, the ballad sung by Laine during various interludes in the film might seem better had the device not been used more effectively in *High Noon* (1952). Despite some weaknesses in the script and the less than imaginative direction by John Sturges, the performances of Douglas, Van Fleet, and Lancaster as well as the superb color cinematography by Charles Lang, make *Gunfight at the O.K. Corral* a solid, entertaining Western that was quite popular at the box office.

Marilynn Wilson

THE GUNFIGHTER

Released: 1950
Production: Nunnally Johnson for Twentieth Century-Fox
Direction: Henry King
Screenplay: William Bowers and William Sellers; based on an original story
   by William Bowers and Andre de Toth
Cinematography: Arthur Miller
Editing: Barbara McLean
Running time: 84 minutes

Principal characters:
Jimmie Ringo	Gregory Peck
Peggy Walsh	Helen Westcott
Sheriff Mark Strett	Millard Mitchell
Molly	Jean Parker
Mac	Karl Malden
Hunt Bromley	Skip Homeier
Charlie	Anthony Ross
Mrs. Pennyfeather	Verna Felton
Mrs. Devlin	Ellen Corby
Eddie	Richard Jaeckel

The Western has been called America's most enduring contribution to the cinema. No other genre has better captured the American spirit or provided more insight into American mythology. For the purpose of definition, the Western period is generally limited to the years from 1860 to 1890—thirty years in which the great American frontier was settled. Even if the period of the California gold rush and the first wagon trains to Oregon were included, the entire Western era lasted less than fifty years. Nevertheless, this short period has provided the world with endless tales and adventures, many of which have become part of American mythology.

The Gunfighter is about only one of those myths. Unlike the dozens of other films which have chosen to focus on the gunman, however, this film is different. It is an adult Western, dealing with adult concerns. This is in itself very unusual, as Westerns often rely on a more simplistic formula, in which complex themes and motivations are reduced to a child's level of comprehension. As a result, the Western has often been ignored by critics and film historians. *The Gunfighter*, however, is neither simplistic nor traditional. It explores the psyche of a man who has lived by the gun and is now tired of that life. *The Gunfighter* is in fact the first psychological Western.

As the film begins, Jimmie Ringo (Gregory Peck), a professional gunman, has returned to the town of Cayenne after many years' absence. He is weary of killing and wants no more of it. Instead, he has come to pick up his long-estranged wife Peggy (Helen Westcott) and his son and take them to a place where they can live quietly and peacefully. His wife, however, has long ago learned to live without him, free from notoriety. Nevertheless, Ringo waits in a saloon hoping that she will arrive before the train comes and takes him away forever.

As word of Ringo's presence in town gets around, he is visited by Sheriff Mark Strett (Millard Mitchell) a friend and former gunman himself, who warns him to get out of town before there is trouble. Ringo is tired of running but promises to leave as soon as his train arrives. In the meantime, he agrees to stay out of sight inside the saloon. Children begin to gather at the windows to catch a glimpse of the famous gunman. Among them is his own son, who is unaware that this man is his father. Inside, Ringo's only companion is the bartender Mac (Karl Malden), who confides that he is very excited about meeting the famous Jimmie Ringo.

Not everyone, however, is content with merely looking at him or talking to him. As he has experienced time and time before, there is always one man who wants to challenge the gunman's reputation. In this case, it is Hunt Bromley (Skip Homeier), a brash young punk. Eager to avoid a confrontation with yet another young gun looking for a reputation, Ringo tries to ignore him; but Hunt is determined to prove himself by goading Ringo into action. Taunting him with remarks such as "He don't look so tough to me," he finally forces Ringo to defend himself, and the young man is left dead.

Outside the saloon, the presence of Ringo has become the subject of everyone's conversation. Women lament the state of their town when a known killer is allowed to remain within its boundaries. Nevertheless, the excitement far outweighs the concern. There are those who want Ringo dead. One man is waiting at a window with a rifle, ready to shoot him down the moment he steps out into the street. It seems that this man believes that Ringo is responsible for the death of his son and wants to take revenge, all of which leads to a very tense atmosphere.

Finally, Ringo's wife goes to the saloon to talk with him. She acknowledges the change in her husband but knows he is doomed to live out his life as a gunman, unable to shake off the label of "fastest gun alive." When Ringo leaves, he is shot from behind by yet another young man eager to be known as a "fast gun." His arm shattered by the bullet, Ringo knows he is helpless and doomed. Before leaving, however, he pronounces what amounts to a sentence of death on the young man, warning him to be prepared for others eager to prove themselves against the man who shot Ringo.

Unlike other Westerns, which never questioned the thoughts and feelings of gunfighters, *The Gunfighter* provides insights and stimulates speculation. As Ringo, Peck brings intensity and seriousness to the role. His low-key performance is perfect for a man tired of the notoriety his trade has brought him. Director Henry King wisely focuses the action primarily within the spatial confines of the saloon. He knows that the action must center on this one man, as it has throughout his entire career.

In addition to its deserved reputation as one of the first psychological Westerns, the film is also noteworthy for the sociological implications of its release time. The year 1950 was a time of turmoil for both the country and the film industry. Senator Joseph McCarthy was attacking the film industry for harboring Communists, and the war in Korea was just beginning. For many who had fought in World War II and had enjoyed five years of peace, the desire of Ringo to rest and settle down was one with which they could identify. Few were eager to rush back into war.

As a result of this film, many other psychological or adult Westerns, such as *High Noon* (1952) and *Shane* (1953), were produced; but there were those who deplored a trend which seemed to be destroying many of the traditional aspects of the genre. As Robert Warshow pointed out in his famous essay "The Westerner," published in 1954: ". . . The spectator derives his pleasure from the appreciation of minor variations within the working out of a pre-determined order. One does not want much novelty."

The Gunfighter inspired new interpretations of traditional Western myths. Ringo was allowed to think and act according to a code other than the long-accepted one of the Western hero. Audiences were allowed to see what happened to all those men after they had ridden into the sunset. The Western never fully returned to the simple stories and attitudes of the pre-1950's. Furthermore, filmmakers learned that it was often easier to deal with con-troversial themes within a genre such as the Western than in straight dramatic stories. Directors and writers were beginning to explore more complex themes, and Westerns offered them a vehicle in which to present them. America had outgrown the simple Western.

James J. Desmarais

GUNGA DIN

Released: 1939
Production: George Stevens for RKO/Radio
Direction: George Stevens
Screenplay: Joel Sayre and Fred Guiol; based on Ben Hecht and Charles MacArthur's adaptation of the poem of the same name by Rudyard Kipling
Cinematography: Joseph H. August
Editing: Henry Berman and John Lockert
Art direction: Van Nest Polglase
Music: Alfred Newman
Running time: 117 minutes

Principal characters:
Archibald Cutter	Cary Grant
MacChesney	Victor McLaglen
Ballantine	Douglas Fairbanks, Jr.
Gunga Din	Sam Jaffe
Guru	Edward Ciannelli
Emmy	Joan Fontaine
Higginbotham	Robert Coote
Colonel	Montagu Love

Gunga Din, George Stevens' cinematic adaptation of Rudyard Kipling's famous poem, is one of the greatest pure adventure films of all time. If there is, as it happens, little of Kipling in the end product, the film suffers not at all as a result. Writers Ben Hecht and Charles MacArthur took the title, the setting, and the last few lines from Kipling's Barrack Room Ballad, and turned them into a full-fledged epic.

The setting is mysterious India; the time, late in the nineteenth century. The sun has yet to set on the British Empire, and, as *Gunga Din* opens, we meet the film's heroes ("protagonists" is a much too intellectual word to describe them) Sergeants Cutter (Cary Grant), MacChesney (Victor McLaglen), and Ballantine (Douglas Fairbanks, Jr.) of the Imperial Lancers. Stevens introduces the three men with a bang: they are the instigators of a knockdown-dragout brawl with some of the locals over a map to an emerald mine. Bodies fly out windows, plummet from rooftops, and tumble down stairs as the three comrades, grinning all the while, singlehandedly subdue what seems like half the population of the teeming subcontinent. The scene would have done quite nicely as the climax for a lesser adventure film, but Stevens is just getting started.

Stevens and his writers quickly introduce the conflicts which propel the film forward. First, and most importantly, the three friends are in danger of breaking up. Sergeant Cutter is forever pursuing the chimera of lost treasure, and

Sergeant Ballantine is on the verge of an even worse sin: he intends to get married and leave the service altogether. Sergeant MacChesney is determined to keep his friends together by whatever means. Gunga Din (Sam Jaffe), the lowly Indian water boy (who plays a less important role in the film than its title would seem to indicate), desperately wants to join the British Army. To top everything off, the natives are restless. The Thuggees, members of a dreaded murder cult, have resumed their depredations in the hills.

The Thugs are led by their Guru (Edward Ciannelli), a hooded figure with a piercing gaze that reveals a perpetually crazed glint in his eye. They worship the many-armed goddess Kaili (a note at the end of the credits explains that this is historical fact) and practice murder as a religious sacrament, digging graves for their intended victims before carrying out the murder. Inactive for years, the Thugs have risen once more, swearing to rid their country of the colonial British. Their first target is the village of Tantrapur, which they overrun with ease.

Cutter, MacChesney, and Ballantine lead a detachment of Lancers to retake the village. When they reach Tantrapur, they find it to all appearances deserted, but it does not stay that way for long. Screaming their defiance, the Thugs attack. Once again, Stevens stages a long battle scene, replete with hand-to-hand combat and the usual acrobatic derring-do on the part of the heroes. Cutter is particularly nonchalant amidst the carnage that rages around him.

The good guys win, of course, and head for home to report. Gunga Din tags along like a puppy at their heels, never missing an opportunity to express his wish to be a soldier. The sergeants are amused by his presumption—the idea of a native water boy in the lordly Lancers is preposterous—and urge him to content himself with his lot. Cutter does permit Din to keep a bugle that he has found. "Very regimental, Din," he says, patting the diminutive Indian on the head approvingly.

Cutter and MacChesney are more concerned about Ballantine, who is apparently serious about marrying his girl friend Emmy (Joan Fontaine) and going into the tea business. His potential loss is made all the more unbearable when their Colonel (Montagu Love) replaces Ballantine with Sergeant Higginbotham (Robert Coote), a humorless prig whom Cutter and MacChesney loathe. They contrive to make Higginbotham unbattle-worthy by spiking the punch at Ballantine's pre-wedding ball with elephant medicine; and the Colonel is forced to reassign Ballantine to the regiment for the brief duration of his enlistment.

Meanwhile, Archibald Cutter is interested in treasure again. Rumors of a golden temple have reached the fort, and Cutter is anxious to investigate. Annoyed when MacChesney forbids the treasure hunt, he picks a fight with his powerfully built friend. The quarrel ends quickly. MacChesney decks Cutter with a single punch, and Cutter wakes up in the brig. Undeterred, he persuades Gunga Din to help him escape. Annie, MacChesney's pet elephant, is the vehicle of Cutter's deliverance; guided by Din, she knocks over the whole stockade. Cutter hops aboard, and he and Din head off in search of the golden temple.

They find the temple, but unfortunately, it turns out to be the Thug head-quarters. Din's eyes pop as the Thug rituals unfold ("Kill, kill, kill," the cultists chant), but Cutter keeps his head. "The Colonel's got to know," he says, and sends Din for help. Cutter distracts the Thugs by walking into their midst singing a merry tune. "You're all under arrest," he announces calmly to the hundreds of killers. "Her Majesty's very touchy about having her subjects strangled." Despite this show of bravado, Cutter is quickly over-powered and imprisoned by the Thugs.

Meanwhile, Gunga Din has apprised the Lancers of Cutter's predicament. MacChesney prepares to set off alone; when Ballantine insists on coming, MacChesney scowls "I ain't takin' any bloody civilians with me." Grinning wolfishly, he insists that the only way Ballantine can join the rescue mission is to reenlist. The stratagem works; as the once-again Sergeant Ballantine explains to his furious bride-to-be, "I hate the blasted army, but friendship, well that's something else." With that, he, MacChesney, and Gunga Din ride off to save Cutter.

They reach the temple and immediately are captured by the Thugs. "Where's the troop?" demands Cutter. "Another fine mess you've gotten us into," replies MacChesney; but the Lancers are not dead yet. When the Guru himself arrives to interrogate Cutter ("I want to know about your army." "Why don't you enlist?"), the sergeants quite improbably manage to capture him and lock his followers outside the temple. The situation seems stalemated. The Lancers will not release the Guru, and the Guru will not call off his men. He reveals that he is using the three sergeants as bait to ensnare their entire regiment. "Two come to rescue one, then the others follow," he reasons, until he has rid the entire country of the British.

As he had hoped, the sound of bagpipes signals the approach of the British Army. The Guru, his plan nearing fruition, breaks the impasse by leaping to his death from the top of the temple, but the Thugs storm in after the Lancers. Gunga Din grabs a bayonet and makes short work of one attacker. "Good work, soldier," cries Cutter approvingly, and Din glows with pride. Their triumph is short-lived, however; MacChesney and Ballantine are captured, and Cutter and Din are stabbed and left for dead.

The sergeants watch helplessly as the British march towards certain death. Suddenly, Gunga Din appears on the screen once more. Although seriously wounded, he still has the strength to bring his beloved bugle to his lips and blow a warning. A Thug bullet cuts him down, but the water boy has saved the regiment. The British form ranks and slowly but surely fight off their attackers. In the meantime, Cutter, who was not dead after all, rescues MacChesney and Ballantine.

The last scene strikes the only false note in the film—false because it ends a marvelous lark with a note of almost sanctimonious solemnity. Gathered round the campfire after the battle, the Colonel makes Gunga Din a posthumous corporal. Then, with the sound track swelling portentously, the Colonel recites Kipling's famous lines: "Though I've belted you and flayed you/ By the living God that made you/You're a better man than I am, Gunga Din." The sound track then leads into "Auld Lang Syne," and an image of Gunga Din is superimposed on the screen. Wearing a clean white British uniform, he snaps off a crisp salute, grinning wildly.

It would not do to overanalyze *Gunga Din*; the film is, after all, entertainment. It is great entertainment, however, and credit must go where it is due. The film's success must be attributed to its writers, its fine cast, and to Stevens, its director. Hecht and MacArthur fashioned a terrific adventure story out of a few lines of poetry. It is full of a lot of nonsense, of course, but fantasy allows such license. The script by Joel Sayre and Fred Guiol is full of excitement, loyalty, and heroism—everything but romance. Emmy, Ballantine's unfortunate intended, is given a very small part by the writers; evidently women have no place in this particular fantasyland.

The male characters, however, are interesting, even if they are substantially broader than they are deep. Grant as the witty, impetuous Cutter and McLaglen as the gruff and burly MacChesney ham it up ferociously. Fortunately, Fairbanks, as Ballantine and Jaffe as Gunga Din, underplay their roles—the screen would not have been big enough to hold them otherwise. Mention must also be made of Ciannelli who plays the Guru of the Thugs. He radiates an evil fanaticism that must be seen to be believed.

Stevens weaves these fine performances into some of the most furious action sequences ever filmed. RKO spent the then-incredible sum of two million dollars to produce *Gunga Din*, and Stevens used their money well. The sets are lavish and exotic, under the artistic direction of Van Nest Polglase, and the traditional "cast of thousands" look is exploited effectively. Indeed, the first two fight scenes, wherein the three sergeants subdue hordes of their enemies with an incredible nonchalance, are expertly staged and are as witty in their own way as anything the dialogue has to offer.

Gunga Din was remade twice (Tay Garnett's *Soldiers Three* in 1951 and John Sturges' *Sergeants 3*, with Frank Sinatra, Peter Lawford, Dean Martin, and Sammy Davis, Jr., in 1962); and generous portions of the film's substance and spirit have shown up in such unlikely quarters as Richard Lester's 1965 Beatles epic, *Help!* This far-reaching influence is testimony enough, if testimony is needed, to the durability and greatness of Stevens' *Gunga Din*.

Robert Mitchell

HAIL THE CONQUERING HERO

Released: 1944
Production: Preston Sturges for Paramount
Direction: Preston Sturges
Screenplay: Preston Sturges
Cinematography: John F. Seitz
Editing: Stuart Gilmore
Running time: 101 minutes

Principal characters:
Woodrow Truesmith .... Eddie Bracken
Libby .... Ella Raines
Mr. Noble .... Raymond Walburn
Sergeant .... William Demarest
Mrs. Truesmith .... Georgia Caine
Libby's Aunt .... Elizabeth Patterson
Committee Chairman ....Franklin Pangborn
Bugsy .... Freddie Steele
Doc Bissell .... Harry Hayden

By 1944, Preston Sturges had written and directed five films for Paramount, spoofing everything from politics to motherhood. Nothing was safe from his satirical eye. Described by other studio employees as "eccentric" or "screwball," Sturges nevertheless had the respect of the front office, who had seen his gamble on *The Great McGinty* (1940) turn into a box-office smash and who acceded to his demands because his films were proven moneymakers. Sturges once described his credo for making good films to one of the Hollywood trade papers, and it bears repeating as representative of his sense of humor:

1. A pretty girl is better than an ugly one. 2. A leg is better than an arm. 3. A bedroom is better than a living room. 4. An arrival is better than a departure. 5. A birth is better than a death. 6. A chase is better than a chat. 7. A dog is better than a landscape. 8. A kitten is better than a dog. 9. A baby is better than a kitten. 10. A kiss is better than a baby. 11. A pratfall is better than anything.

Hail the Conquering Hero, considered by many to be Sturges' finest film, certainly contains all of the elements that his fans had come to expect: the usual cast of lovable bumblers and stuffed shirts, and an equal blend of sly wit with raucous slapstick.

In this film, Woodrow Lafayette Pershing Truesmith (Eddie Bracken) is the son of a World War I hero who joins the Marine Corps at the start of World War II, only to be washed out shortly thereafter because of his chronic hay fever. Ashamed to go home to face the family and friends who expected great things of him, Woodrow takes a job in a shipyard. He perpetrates a hoax by having departing Marines send letters to his mother (Georgia Caine) from the South Pacific. In one of these letters he writes to his girl friend Libby (Ella Raines) that he has found someone else. The dejected Woodrow plans to stay away from his hometown.

One day, while having a few drinks in a bar, Woodrow meets a group of Marines back from the Pacific theater and tells them of his deception. Bugsy (Freddie Steele), one of the men, has a deep and profound respect for mothers, and Woodrow's plight nearly brings him to tears, so he decides to make Woodrow a hero for his mother's sake. He makes a phone call to Woodrow's mother, telling her that her hero son will be returning home for a visit. The Marine Sergeant (William Demarest) convinces Woodrow that they can put him in uniform temporarily, sneak him into his home town, and give his mother the joy of seeing her son a true hero. Woodrow is uneasy about the whole idea, but the Marines put him in uniform and whisk him aboard a train before he can change his mind.

News spreads fast, and when Woodrow and his "honor guard" step off the train at Oakridge, they find the entire town at the station to greet the returned warrior. Blustery Mayor Noble (Raymond Walburn) leads the ceremony, which includes brass bands and political hoopla. The embarrassed Woodrow attempts to explain the hoax, but the crowd mistakes his words for modesty, and Truesmith fever sweeps the entire community. The mortgage of his mother's home is burned as a gallant gesture to her son's heroics, others propose that monuments be erected in his honor, and some begin promoting Woodrow for mayor. Woodrow later tries to sneak away, mortified at the results that his little hoax has wrought, but Bugsy and the others foil his attempts to escape, using his mother's pride as the means of keeping him home.

Finally, Mayor Noble learns of the deception, and, furious, attempts to expose the youth; but the heartsick Woodrow beats him to it, making a public confession before the townspeople at a special meeting. He denounces himself as a liar and a coward and then leaves in shame. At that point the Sarge takes command, telling the assembled townspeople that it was the group of Marines who plotted the hoax; Woodrow was an unwilling participant from the start, and his public confession is itself a heroic act that took as much courage as any victory on the battlefield. Woodrow, meanwhile, makes his way dejectedly to the train station, where he plans to return to the shipyard. The crowd marches to the station, however, and catches up to him just as his train arrives. Old Doc Bissell (Harry Hayden) comforts him by telling him that acting out a little lie to save one mother from humiliation is a fault of which any man could be proud. The townspeople are impressed by Woodrow's honesty, and they ask him to stay and run for mayor.

Hail the Conquering Hero certainly shows Sturges at his best, combining the best elements of comedy and pathos in a delightful film. Bracken (a Sturges favorite who had also performed well in *The Miracle of Morgan's Creek* for the director that same year) gives one of his finest performances as the harried Woodrow Truesmith, bringing to the role his own special brand of goofiness. Lovely Raines does not have much to do but makes the most of her screen time as a beautiful companion for Woodrow. The Sturges stock company of character actors (Walburn, Demarest, Franklin Pangborn, and others) are shown to good advantage as well, and the scene in which Woodrow returns home to find a mob waiting for him is memorable for Walburn's flustered attempts to deliver a speech while master of ceremonies Pangborn fails to hold the bands in check, creating total pandemonium for the returning Woodrow. The group of Marines, headed by Demarest, lends much to the manic atmosphere of the film as they whirl a reluctant Woodrow from event to event. Steele as Bugsy, the shell-shocked Marine whose devotion to mothers borders on the obsessive, is particularly good.

The most notable aspect of the film, however, is the dexterity with which Sturges moves the story along, combining slapstick with sentiment. Scenes that could easily have been maudlin are saved by honest, straightforward delivery, and they are made to seem more poignant by contrast to the wilder comedic scenes.

After his contract with Paramount ran out in the middle 1940's, Sturges left the studio system for the pleasures of independent filmmaking, but his subsequent efforts were far inferior to the seven films that he directed for Paramount. He died in 1959 at the age of sixty, before the new critical acclaim for his motion pictures reached the filmgoing community. He was thus robbed of the satisfaction that the rediscovery of his work would have afforded him.

Ed Hulse

HAIR

Released: 1979
Production: Lester Persky and Michael Butler for United Artists
Direction: Miloš Forman
Screenplay: Michael Weller; based on the play of the same name by Gerome Ragni, James Rado, and Galt MacDermot
Cinematography: Miroslav Ondricek
Editing: Stanley Harnow and Alan Heim
Choreography: Twyla Tharp
Music: Galt MacDermot, Gerome Ragni, and James Rado
Running time: 118 minutes

Principal characters:
Claude	John Savage
Berger	Treat Williams
Sheila	Beverly D'Angelo
Jeannie	Annie Golden
Hud	Dorsey Wright
Woof	Don Dacus
Hud's fiancée	Cheryl Barnes
Fenton	Richard Bright
The General	Nicholas Ray

Hair, a "tribal love rock musical," is based upon the stage play which was produced by Joseph Papp at the off-Broadway New York Public Theater in 1967 and on Broadway in 1968. Shocking to many because of its antiwar, and free-love sentiments, drug orientation, and nudity, the relatively plotless musical contained such eyebrow-raising numbers as "Sodomy" and "Colored Spade." More than ten years after its Broadway run, in which such future stars as Diane Keaton and Keith Carradine had small parts, director Milos Forman translated the musical from stage to screen. Although the play created a sensation with its anti-establishment antics, the film version is rated a mild P. G. for its one brief nude swimming scene. Considerably less defiant than the play, the movie presents a nostalgic, idealized, glossed-over view of the 1960's.

The expanded plot, with its more realistic narrative, takes place in 1968 and concerns a naïve, short-haired, clean-cut Oklahoma Kid named Claude, winningly played by John Savage, who stops in New York City for a three-day fling before his induction into the army. In Central Park, he meets a romping group of hippies, including the frizzy-haired leader, Berger (Treat Williams), long-haired blonde Woof (Don Dacus), the arrogant black Hud (Dorsey Wright), and the pregnant, childlike waif Jeannie (Annie Golden), who does not know if Woof or Hud is the father of her child. The troupe attempts to show Claude the free-living-and-loving side of life.

When the shy Claude is smitten by a beautiful debutante named Sheila (Beverly D'Angelo), Berger takes him to the girl's family's estate in Short Hills, New Jersey. Claude and Sheila fall in love and the ingenue is coaxed into joining the group. After Claude leaves for his basic training at the Nevada desert boot camp at which veteran film director Nicholas Ray plays the general, the tribe decides to follow him. Joining them on the cross-country trip is Hud's "straight" girl friend (Cheryl Barnes) and their small son, whom Hud had temporarily abandoned after "dropping out." Upon their arrival in Nevada, Sheila seduces a sergeant out of his uniform; Berger then dons the outfit, sneaks into the military camp, and changes places with Claude, who leaves base for a reunion with Sheila. In the film's final, bittersweet moments, Claude does not return to the camp in time and Berger is accidentally shipped off to Vietnam in his place. We soon learn that Berger subsequently was killed in the war. The dream of the flower children, unfortunately, does not last.

A rock fantasy musical like other films of the late 1970's such as *The Wiz* (1979), *Sgt. Pepper's Lonely Hearts Club Band* (1979), and *Grease* (1978) this high-energy production makes use of realistic locations such as the "be-in" in Central Park and the protest at the Lincoln Memorial in Washington, D. C., for example. These open-air locales add to the film's fresh, breezy spontaneity and charm. The exuberant cast of newcomers, the outrageous costumes, the dazzling staging, and the innovative choreography by Twyla Tharp, who appears with her ensemble and several members of the American Ballet Theater, create an exhilarating and euphoric picture. Even the horses canter in step to the music.

The now-classic twenty-seven songs, which are fluidly integrated into the plot, include the title song, "Age of Aquarius," as well as "Good Morning Starshine," and "Let the Sunshine In." At Sheila's formal and staid "coming-out" party, Berger goes berserk, dances on the table, and belts out "I Got Life." Barnes, as Hud's fiancée, performs a touching, riveting, and magnificent Aretha Franklin-like rendition of "Easy to be Hard." There is also the rousing antiwar song "3-5-00," led by two cast members from the original stage production, Melba Moore and Ronnie Dyson. Another number, "Black Boys, White Boys" is shot and edited so that a group of male military personnel, creating homosexual overtones, and a group of wildly dressed girls are both shown singing the song.

Written by Michael Weller, author of the play *Moonchildren*, also about youth in the 1960's, *Hair* is the seventh film directed by Forman, the 1975 Academy Award-winning director of *One Flew over the Cuckoo's Nest*. After seeing the play *Hair* on off-Broadway in 1967, Forman tried unsuccessfully to produce it in his native Czechoslovakia. Interestingly, the East-European expatriate, now an American citizen, does indeed capture the atmosphere of

1960's Americana, its flower children, protest marchers, and peaceniks.

Forman's direction is very effective, as is the cinematography of Miroslav Ondricek, also a native of Czechoslovakia. The camera is whimsical in its careening movement and innovative angles. The film's lyrical, visual splendor is particularly evident in the "Hare Krishna" production number, a surrealistic LSD sequence in which the characters float in the air at an imaginary wedding ceremony that juxtaposes Eastern and Western religions.

There are some who feel that the twelve-million-dollar film, which took two years to make, is outdated and was made ten years too late. There are also those who feel that the irresponsible, hedonistic characters are not commendable. Indeed, they take money from tourists and commandeer a car from Sheila's uptight, conservative ex-boyfriend. Others feel that the politics in the film is mindless and shallow, and that the film does not really examine the era or represent any ideological statement. Without becoming sentimental or platitudinous, however, *Hair* does indeed contain social observation about the 1960's and at times creates an affecting drama. Most importantly, the film is a celebration of discovery and friendship. Full of vitality and bouyancy, *Hair* is a refreshing tribute to the flower-power era and to the love and peace generation of the not-so-long-ago 1960's.

Leslie Taubman

HALLOWEEN

Released: 1978
Production: Debra Hill for Compass International
Direction: John Carpenter
Screenplay: John Carpenter and Debra Hill
Cinematography: Dean Cundey
Editing: Tommy Wallace and Charles Bornstein
Music: John Carpenter
Running time: 93 minutes

Principal characters:
Doctor Loomis	Donald Pleasence
Laurie	Jamie Lee Curtis
Michael Myers (younger)	Will Sandin
Michael Myers (older)	Nick Castle
Annie	Nancy Loomis
Linda	P. J. Soles
Tommy	Brian Andrews
Lindsay	Kyle Richards

Despite the fact that *Halloween* is credited with initiating a disturbing trend toward graphic screen violence, it stands as a hallmark within the horror genre. With its relentless, visceral delivery resulting in effective shock appeal, *Halloween* joins a select group of low-budget films, including George A. Romero's *Night of the Living Dead* (1968) and Tobe Hooper's *Texas Chainsaw Massacre* (1973), that extended the boundaries of the horror film. (Although *The Exorcist*, 1973, had a similar effect, it achieved its fame largely through a big budget and a name cast.)

In terms of manipulative screen horrors, *Halloween* redefined audience expectations. In years to come, however, it is probable that the film will be best known as a showcase for John Carpenter's terse and invigorating directorial style. *Halloween* served as Carpenter's springboard to recognition among audiences and throughout the industry. Its manipulative, grisly nature aside, *Halloween* is also extremely well made, and although many critics have been contemptuous of the onslaught of bloody successors triggered by the film and of the (mostly) nihilist views of Carpenter's films, there is unanimity that the director is an excellent craftsman.

Filmed during twenty days for a scant $320,000, *Halloween* had grossed in excess of sixty million dollars by 1981. The most successful independent film ever made to date, it remains a perennial favorite at the box office and on television. Released in 1978 with phenomenal success, it spawned near-record numbers of imitators during the late 1970's and into the 1980's. Sporting such uneasy titles as *He Knows You're Alone* (1980), *Don't Go in the House* (1980),

When a Stranger Calls (1979); and a penchant for holidays, as evidenced by *Prom Night* (1980), *Graduation Day* (1981), and *Happy Birthday to Me* (1981); and killers brandishing sharp-edged weapons such as knives, hatchets, razors, and chainsaws, these films evoked a kind of mad scientist syndrome, with the filmmakers wielding the scalpels. *Halloween* popularized the notion that a successful horror film can be a young filmmaker's ticket into the industry. It is notable that of the many who attempted to cash in on the bloody screen trend, however, none have shown Carpenter's skill at creating critically admired, commercially viable products.

In *Halloween*, Carpenter offers an inventive treatment of the familiar plot about an escaped maniac who terrorizes and murders teenage girls. A skilled trickster, he utilizes his mastery of the fluid camera to convince audiences that every space and every shadow is threatening. Moreover, through the use of a subjective camera which records events from the killer's point of view, each character seems a potential victim. These unnerving qualities serve to underline Carpenter's belief that "film is a feeling medium."

A graduate of the cinema school at the University of Southern California (where he did music, editing, cowriting, and some codirecting on the 1970 Academy Award-winning short film, *The Resurrection of Bronco Billy*), Carpenter garnered initial industry attention with his 1974 feature film, *Dark Star*. A space saga parody about "spaced-out" astronauts, the film did not succeed at the box office at the time of its release, but has since become a popular cult film on the midnight circuit. Carpenter's collaborator on the film and also its star was Dan O'Bannon, who went on to coauthor the story and screenplay for the blockbuster *Alien* (1979).

Carpenter made *Assault on Precinct 13* in 1976. One of his most wrenching works, the film is a grim depiction of a crime spree in a Los Angeles ghetto; after taking a blood oath, gang members launch a kamikaze attack on a nearly deserted police precinct. Independently made on a $200,000 budget, the film bears several now-familiar Carpenter trademarks. Liberally doused with blood, the film presents violence with an ironic, doomed edge; in fact, the violence is unleashed with the shocking death of an eight-year-old child who is shot at point blank range while ordering an ice cream cone. Once the warfare begins, there are additional sardonic inferences, including the fact that two of the film's "good guys," those defending the precinct, are Death Row prisoners. Known for paying homage to veteran directors he admires, Carpenter gives innumerable Hawksian traits to *Assault on Precinct 13*, a film which essentially transplants Howard Hawks's *Rio Bravo* (1959) to the ghetto. Carpenter himself has labeled this film an "urban Western," and he edited the film under the name of John T. Chance, the name of John Wayne's character in *Rio Bravo*.

Although *Assault on Precinct 13* is today recognized as a shattering foray into the crime genre, reaction was lukewarm at the time of its release. It was not until 1977, when the film emerged as the surprise hit of the London Film Festival, that *Assault on Precinct 13* and Carpenter were "discovered." As a result, producer Irwin Yablans, whose company had distributed the film, approached Carpenter about directing the first motion picture from his newly formed Compass International. Yablans had a concept called "The Babysitter Murders," which ultimately evolved into *Halloween.*

Mirroring familiar low-budget genre traits, *Halloween* abounds in ominous shadows, nubile teenaged girls, and illicit sex. The film opens with a brutal murder, and the story then jumps ahead fifteen years (this time-shift ploy was much imitated by succeeding "knife" films), when the lunatic has returned to continue his terror spree. While the basic format is certainly predictable, *Halloween* is not without distinctive strains. In the character of the murderous Michael Myers there are mythical qualities suggesting he is not human, but rather, the embodiment of evil. Dr. Loomis (Donald Pleasence), the psychiatrist who observed Michael for fifteen years, alludes to the theory throughout the film. "This isn't a man," he tells an investigator, describing a "blank, pale, emotionless face and the blackest eyes" that stand for "purely and simply evil." To the ire of many reviewers, *Halloween*'s murders appear to be precipitated by illicit sex or the intention of illicit sex. Indeed, the film's heroine is a virgin who survives because her repressed sexuality gives her the strength to fight back against the relentless killer.

To a lesser degree, *Halloween* also examines the role fate plays in lives. This intriguing nuance surfaces when Laurie (Jamie Lee Curtis) helps her real estate agent father by dropping off a key at the notorious Myers house, the scene of the brutal knifing fifteen years earlier. Unknown to Laurie, Michael (Nick Castle) is hiding inside the house watching her as she makes her brief stop. Later that day, during a classroom discussion about fate ("fate caught up with several lives here," drones the teacher), Laurie finds herself inexplicably uneasy. Staring out the classroom window, she briefly glimpses a figure in the distance watching her. Now, fate will catch up with her life.

Set in the seemingly quaint town of Haddonfield, Illinois, *Halloween* opens on Halloween night, 1963, with a suspenseful sequence that speaks for the film's suspenseful pulse. Watching through the windows of a wood frame house, we are voyeurs as a teenage girl and her boyfriend engage in petting; their passions lead them upstairs to the bedroom. Later, after the boyfriend has left the house (with an obligatory "I'll call you soon"), the audience realizes that the voyeurism is actually the killer's point of view. As the camera moves indoors one sees through his eyes, around corners and through doorways. In the kitchen a menacing knife is pulled from a drawer; then the camera climbs the stairs to the bedroom. Once inside, vision is somewhat impaired, for like the killer, the audience is seeing through the eyes of a confining Halloween mask, which is similar to a view through binoculars. A quick survey of the bedroom reveals soiled bedsheets and a teenaged girl, partially nude, brushing her hair at a vanity table. Turning in surprise, she recognizes her assailant: it is her brother Michael (Will Sandin), and she is unable to fend off his furious stabbing. Afterward, the killer descends the stairs and wanders out the front door. As the sequence comes to a close, a shocked couple arrives home to discover their young son clutching a bloodied knife and standing motionless in his Halloween clown costume.

The story line then shifts to Smith's Grove, Illinois, on October 30, 1978. Dr. Loomis, who has deemed it necessary to keep Michael institutionalized, is distraught when Michael manages to escape in the institution's car. Again the setting shifts, back to Haddonfield. It is now Halloween day, and Michael has returned home.

Throughout the day Loomis attempts to retrieve his patient, convinced that he will return to Haddonfield, and he vainly tries to make local officials understand the imminent danger. Meanwhile, Laurie begins to sense that she is being stalked. Her nervousness grows when she sights a person watching her; he wears a plain face mask which lends an eerie, dreamlike quality as viewed from a distance. Tommy (Brian Andrews), the youngster she frequently babysits, endures the torment of classmates that day who insist that "the bogeyman" is going to come after him. Later that night, when Laurie babysits Tommy, both will realize their nightmares.

Laurie's friend Annie (Nancy Loomis) also has a babysitting job, across the street from Tommy's house. Unlike Laurie, however, Annie is rather negligent of her young ward, Lindsay (Kyle Richards), and plans a sexual tryst with her boyfriend. Another girl, Linda (P. J. Soles), and her boyfriend also have a sexual encounter at the house where Annie is sitting; "Everyone's having a good time tonight," Laurie says glumly, peering through venetian blinds at the house across the street which is the site of the planned romances. Of course, it is Laurie (and Tommy and Lindsay) who will have the best times that night, for they will manage to survive the relentless attack.

Annie, Linda, and Linda's boyfriend are gruesomely murdered. Although Laurie is wounded, stabbed in the shoulder, and dazed by the events, she fights back. Ultimately, it is she who drives the knife through Michael; but still he comes at her, with the attack ending only when Loomis arrives in the nick of time and coolly shoots the murderer. Stabbed and shot, Michael's body tumbles from the bedroom window onto the ground below. Turning to her rescuer in a state of near shock, a bloodied Laurie asks, "That's the bogeyman?" "As a matter of fact," says Loomis, "that was." The supernatural thread becomes joltingly real when the camera returns for a final glimpse of Michael, only to reveal that his body is gone.

In addition to directing and cowriting *Halloween* (along with his partner, writer-producer Debra Hill), Carpenter scored the film's erratic music, a simple but effective piano melody that repeats constantly, signifying pending suspense. (In films such as *The Fog*, 1980, and *Escape from New York*, 1981,

Carpenter's scores are heavily synthesized.) Applauded by audiences for its edge-of-the-seat suspense but condemned by some critics for its violence, *Halloween* is a taut thriller that serves as Carpenter's industry calling card. It also stands as a memorable introduction for Jamie Lee Curtis, the daughter of Tony Curtis and Janet Leigh, who makes her film debut in *Halloween*. This casting ploy garnered press because, in a sense, she was following her actress mother's footsteps, since Leigh played the famed victim of the shower assault in Alfred Hitchcock's *Psycho* (1960). Curtis has since gone on to "scream queen" status, with roles in horror vehicles such as *Prom Night, Terror Train* (1980), and *Road Games* (1979). Within the genre she is known for her gutsy characterizations (always the heroine, she never "dies") and commendable work.

Carpenter's credits since *Halloween* have included the inventive ghost film, *The Fog*, about a band of bloodthirsty leper pirates, and *Escape from New York*, a commercially popular film which looks at the future through a grim, clouded crystal ball (among other things, Manhattan Island is a maximum security prison in the year 1997). Carpenter is equally skilled working within the framework of television. In 1978, he made the television film *Someone Is Watching Me* (released theatrically in Europe as *High Rise*), a thriller inspired by Hitchcock's *Rear Window* (1954) which starred Lauren Hutton. In 1979, Carpenter's longtime interest in rock and roll and the legendary Elvis Presley culminated with his three-hour television film *Elvis*. A ratings blockbuster (toppling much-publicized competition from network showings of *One Flew Over the Cuckoo's Nest* and *Gone with the Wind*), *Elvis* starred one-time Disney studio star Kurt Russell in the title role. Russell's performance was one of the television season's biggest surprises, and his role as the surly antihero Snake Plissken in *Escape from New York* was one of the most widely lauded of 1981. Russell is presently at work on a third Carpenter project, a remake of the Howard Hawks film *The Thing* (1951).

Carpenter, who served as executive producer for the sequel *Halloween II* (1980), tends to work with a familiar ensemble. Producer Hill often teams with him; Curtis has starred for him twice, the second time in *The Fog*; Castle, who plays *Halloween*'s deadly Michael Myers (the credits label the character "The Shape"), coauthored the script for *Escape from New York* with Carpenter. Carpenter's wife, Adrienne Barbeau, noted for her success in television, including the long-running series *Maude* as well as for her voluptuous figure, also appears regularly in his films.

Prior to achieving his status as a versatile, inventive filmmaker, Carpenter authored the screenplay "Eyes," which, after some dozen rewrites, became the 1978 film *Eyes of Laura Mars*. This film, which departs widely from Carpenter's original script, is not at all in keeping with his since-evolved style. "I like to be as simple as possible. I don't like to show off," says Carpenter; thus, his films have concise story lines and economical technical sleekness.

As a result, many critics argue that his work lacks defined characters with whom the audience can sympathize or relate. To date, however, the Carpenter flair for fast-paced, high-action storytelling—sometimes at the expense of characterizations—is a signature of an industry original. If this director's "great" film is yet to come, his track record is an exciting one.

Pat H. Broeske